Second

LITERACY for CHILDREN in an INFORMATION AGE

Teaching Reading, Writing, and Thinking

Vicki L. Cohen

Farleigh Dickinson University

John Edwin Cowen

Farleigh Dickinson University

WADSWORTH
CENGAGE Learning™

Australia • Brazil • Japan • Korea • Mexico • Singapore • Spain • United Kingdom • United States

Literacy for Children in an information Age: Teaching Reading, Writing, and Thinking, 2e
Cohen, Cowen

Acquisitions Editor: Linda Schreiber-Ganster

Freelance Development Editor: Melissa Kelleher

Assistant Editor: Rebecca Dashiell

Editorial Assistant: Linda Stewart

Associate Media Editor : Ashley Cronin

Marketing Manager: Kara Kindstrom

Marketing Communications Manager: Martha Pfeiffer

Project Manager, Editorial Production: Pre-Press PMG

Art Director: Maria Epes

Print Buyer: Linda Hsu

Permissions Editor: Roberta Broyer

Production Service: Pre-Press PMG

Text Designer: Marsha Cohen

Photo Researcher: Pre-Press PMG

Cover Designer: Marsha Cohen

Cover Image: © Ariel Skelley/Corbis

Compositor: Pre-Press PMG

For product information and technology assistance, contact us at
Cengage Learning Customer & Sales Support, 1-800-354-9706

For permission to use material from this text or product, submit all requests online at **cengage.com/permissions**
Further permissions questions can be emailed to
permissionrequest@cengage.com

Library of Congress Control Number: 2009940459

ISBN-13: 978-0-495-80953-1

ISBN-10: 0-495-80953-5

Wadsworth
20 Davis Drive
Belmont, CA 94002
USA

Cengage Learning is a leading provider of customized learning solutions with office locations around the globe, including Singapore, the United Kingdom, Australia, Mexico, Brazil, and Japan. Locate your local office at:
international.cengage.com/region

Cengage Learning products are represented in Canada by Nelson Education, Ltd.

For your course and learning solutions, visit **academic.cengage.com**

Purchase any of our products at your local college store or at our preferred online store **www.ichapters.com**

Notice to the Reader
Publisher does not warrant or guarantee any of the products described herein or perform any independent analysis in connection with any of the product information contained herein. Publisher does not assume, and expressly disclaims, any obligation to obtain and include information other than that provided to it by the manufacturer. The reader is expressly warned to consider and adopt all safety precautions that might be indicated by the activities described herein and to avoid all potential hazards. By following the instructions contained herein, the reader willingly assumes all risks in connection with such instructions. The publisher makes no representations or warranties of any kind, including but not limited to, the warranties of fitness for particular purpose or merchantability, nor are any such representations implied with respect to the material set forth herein, and the publisher takes no responsibility with respect to such material. The publisher shall not be liable for any special, consequential, or exemplary damages resulting, in whole or part, from the readers' use of, or reliance upon, this material.

Printed in the United States of America
1 2 3 4 5 6 7 13 12 11 10 09

FOR JOHN AND JAY,
WHO HELPED US THROUGH
THIS LONG BUT REWARDING PROCESS.

BRIEF CONTENTS

CONTENTS

CHAPTER 3
A Balanced Literacy Approach   72

CHAPTER 4
Emergent Literacy in the Classroom   102

CHAPTER 5
The Study of Words   152

CHAPTER 6
Strategies to Promote Vocabulary Development 210

CHAPTER 7
Reading Comprehension: An Interactive Process 260

CHAPTER 8
The Process of Writing, Listening, and Speaking   318

CHAPTER 9
Assessment in the Literacy Classroom

382

CHAPTER 10
Approaches and Strategies that Promote Literacy

432

CHAPTER 11
Using Literature to Promote Literacy

480

CHAPTER 14
Managing and Organizing a Literacy Program   624

In classrooms across the country, today's teachers are facing many new demands: the need to address state and professional standards within the curriculum, the pressure of raising students' scores on state-mandated assessments, the need to teach an increasingly diverse population of children, and the proliferation of new technologies that are currently changing the notion of what "literacy" means. *Literacy for Children in an Information Age: Teaching Reading, Writing, and Thinking* is designed to help prospective and current teachers form a deeper understanding of the meaning of literacy in today's technological and diverse world, and to inform teachers about research-based best practices in literacy. The intent is to develop effective teachers within our classrooms who will raise achievement for all children in our multicultural and technological society. This means that prospective and current teachers need to know how to integrate technology into the curriculum, how to tailor instruction to meet the needs of all children, how to effectively design and assess instruction, how to be culturally responsive and sensitive to students from diverse backgrounds, and how to stay current in the field of literacy.

Literacy for Children in an Information Age: Teaching Reading, Writing, and Thinking emphasizes the importance of integrating technology into the literacy curriculum. With the increase of smart cell phones, text messaging, social networking, twittering, blogging, and Internet searches, today's world is a very different place than it was 10 years ago. New technological applications are changing the way that people around the world communicate, socialize, and access information. The challenge for teachers is to help students learn how to use technology to promote higher order thinking and to solve problems in language arts, science, math, and social studies. Tasks such as using online tools to promote writing, creating visual representations using multimedia formats, constructing charts and graphs, searching and researching using the Internet, and communicating using online tools all help students develop higher-level thinking and prepare them for the skills they will need in a global world.

Literacy for Children in an Information Age: Teaching Reading, Writing, and Thinking also emphasizes the need for a balanced approach in teaching literacy, and examines how to develop a comprehensive reading program based on best practices stemming from current knowledge and research on how children learn to read. Its focus is to examine what "literacy" means in our new information-driven society and how to teach literacy to our increasingly diverse population of children. Effective practice is grounded in solid knowledge of language and literacy, whereby children read and write quality texts and engage in rich, enjoyable literacy experiences. In a balanced literacy classroom, teachers use many different approaches to address the diverse literacy needs of their students.

Purpose

Literacy for Children in an Information Age: Teaching Reading, Writing, and Thinking is designed to be used in an introductory reading course for both preservice and inservice teachers. Its primary purpose is to prepare teachers to make reading a joyful and meaningful experience for diverse children while also helping them meet state and professional standards in literacy so that they are qualified, competent, and caring professionals who reflect excellence in literacy practices. This book will emphasize that literacy is not just an "end product" of reading and writing, but a continuous and developmental process that is constantly changing in our information-driven society. Teachers need to integrate a balanced literacy approach into every subject area and to increase the proficiency of their students' writing skills. This book will examine how the new technologies are affecting literacy instruction and will expand on the notion of "literacy" to include information literacy and visual literacy.

A major goal of this book is to help teachers put into practice what has been proven to work through a balanced literacy approach. Ultimately, we believe we can help our children learn how to read more successfully than ever before, particularly by taking advantage of evidence from research about the effectiveness of specific strategies which support reading instruction. *Literacy for Children in an Information Age: Teaching Reading, Writing, and Thinking* will elaborate on these research-based strategies that teachers can use in their classrooms to ensure success for all children.

Overview of the Chapters

The organization of *Literacy for Children in an Information Age: Teaching Reading, Writing, and Thinking Second Edition* has been reorganized to emphasize the need for incorporating technology into a balanced literacy curriculum, and parallels the way that topics are commonly introduced in a beginning reading methods course. It starts out with an overview of literacy instruction and an explanation of a balanced approach to literacy. **Chapter 1, Literacy: A New Definition**, explores the definition of literacy, expanding it to include a new emphasis on technological literacies and emphasizing the need for incorporating state and professional standards into the literacy curriculum. It introduces the concept of a balanced reading approach. **Chapter 2, Literacy and Communication: From E-Mail to the Internet**, explores how technology can be incorporated into the literacy classroom. It discusses electronic forms of communication, such as blogging and the Internet. It describes five ways that technology can be integrated into the literacy program and discusses how students can use the Internet to conduct research. **Chapter 3, A Balanced Literary Approach**, focuses on a "balanced" approach to literacy. It presents essential principles of a balanced approach that will help teachers see the "big picture" in teaching reading. **Chapter 4, Emergent Literacy in the Classroom**, focuses on the concept of emergent literacy in young children and the importance of viewing literacy as a long-term developmental process. Children's development in early reading and writing from birth to kindergarten is discussed. The next three very important chapters—**Chapter 5, The Study of Words; Chapter 6, Strategies to Promote Vocabulary Development;** and **Chapter 7, Reading Comprehension: An Interactive Process**—focus on the basic processes and skills needed to teach reading in today's classroom. The emphasis in these chapters is on balancing direct, systematic instruction in phonics and word study, vocabulary development, and comprehension strategies with the reading of rich, quality literature. Practical examples are given to help teachers incorporate research-based best practices into their classroom instruction and include technological resources, including recommended Internet sites and teacher-made websites. **Chapter 8, The Process of Writing, Listening, and Speaking,** explores writing as a process and looks at how speaking and listening should be taught as part of the literacy classroom. **Chapter 9, Assessment in the Literacy Classroom**, focuses on the need to use assessment data in the classroom to help children develop literacy processes. **Chapter 10, Approaches and Strategies That Promote Literacy**, reviews different approaches teachers can use to teach literacy, such as visual tools/graphic organizers, and explores different types of texts teachers can use to support children reading. **Chapter 11, Using Literature to Promote Literacy**, explores how quality literature can be used in the classroom to promote literacy and engage children in enjoyable literacy activities. **Chapter 12, Informational Text to Improve Content-Area Comprehension**, focuses on how teachers can use informational texts in the classroom to motivate children to read and write while promoting research and comprehension. **Chapter 13, Developing Effective Units of Study in Literacy**, describes how to create lesson plans and units of study in literacy based upon state and national standards.

It presents different instructional models that teachers can use to create effective instruction and incorporate technology into the lesson. **Chapter 14, Managing and Organizing a Literacy Program**, explores how a teacher can create an effective environment for literacy development through literacy learning centers. It describes and gives specific examples of classroom management strategies, including working with children in guided reading groups and working with a whole class.

Special Features

Literacy for Children in an Information Age: Teaching Reading, Writing, and Thinking has the following special features incorporated into the chapters:

- **Technology applications** are included throughout the book and are emphasized as an integral part of literacy instruction.
- **Strategies for teaching English language learners** are presented throughout the book. Most chapters have special sections highlighting ideas that teachers can use to teach English language learners; strategies are also integrated into the main text.
- **Strategies for teaching students with learning disabilities** are offered throughout the book. Most chapters have special sections summarizing practical tips for teaching students with learning disabilities; tips are also included in the main text.
- The beginning of each chapter lists the **International Reading Association Professional Standards** that are addressed in that chapter. Teachers will become familiar with the professional standards that define the field of reading for professionals.
- Each chapter of the book includes **descriptions of exemplary websites and software products for literacy education**. Hotlinks to these websites are built into the book's companion website. The website is frequently monitored for broken links and updated to reflect the latest developments in the field.
- **Teachers' Voices** allow practicing teachers to talk about their experiences in the classroom and offer helpful insights and hints.
- **Vignettes** introduce the content of each chapter, providing an example of research-based best practices.
- **Strategy Boxes** at the end of each chapter help teachers focus on important practical strategies they can use in the classroom. These boxes "revisit" the classrooms depicted in the chapter-opening vignettes.
- **Focus Questions** help teachers identify important concepts covered in each chapter.
- **Application: Exploration of Concepts** contains activities that teachers can use to apply content and concepts introduced in each chapter.
- The **Chapter Overview** outlines the section headings and concepts taught in each chapter.
- **Final Thoughts** sum up the main ideas of each chapter that teachers should carry away with them.
- **State and professional standards** are referenced throughout the book and help teachers become knowledgeable about professional expectations in the field of literacy.
- **Grade-level sections** are provided in Chapter 4 (The Study of Words) so that teachers can become familiar with research-based best practices for each grade level, commensurate with how state and professional standards are presented.
- **Five Ways Technology Can Be Incorporated into the Classroom** is provided in Chapter 2, Literacy and Communication: From E-Mail to the Internet. This chapter explores the use of technology in the classroom and offers specific ways in which teachers can integrate technology into the literacy classroom.
- **Video Cases** with accompanying video footage of actual teachers implementing model lessons are available on the premium website.

New Features to the Second Edition

The following new features have been incorporated into *Literacy for Children in an Information Age: Teaching Reading, Writing, and Thinking, Second Edition:*

◆ The **Home–School Connection** is a special section at the end of each chapter which provides practical ways in which teachers can connect with parents, guardians, and family members regarding the development of literacy in all children.

Chapter introductions feature streamlined vignettes about practicing teachers implementing best practice strategies in their classrooms.

◆ **Updated weblinks** are provided in every chapter.

◆ **A section on Response to Intervention** has been added to Chapter 10.

Supplemental Materials Accompanying This Textbook

These supplemental materials are available to assist the instructor in providing quality instruction:

◆ The Instructor's Manual and Test Bank are available electronically. The *Instructor's Manual* contains chapter summaries, chapter outlines, essential questions, introductory activities, focus questions, and additional activities and discussion topics. The Test Bank contains multiple choice, short answer, and essay questions.

◆ The instructor area on the premium website includes the following resources:

  ◆ Instructor's Manual
  ◆ PowerPoint slides

Access the premium website at www.cengage.com/login.

◆ The PowerLecture DVD is a one-stop digital library and presentation tool containing:

  ◆ The Instructor's Manual and Test Bank
  ◆ Preassembled Microsoft® PowerPoint® lecture slides
  ◆ ExamView testing software with all of the test items in electronic format, enabling the instructor to create customized tests
  ◆ The videos referenced in the text
  ◆ An image library with graphics from the text

◆ WebTutor™ Toolbox for WebCT™ or Blackboard® provides the instructor with customizable, rich, text-specific content within these course management wystems.

◆ For students, useful study tools and resources available on the premium website include:

  ◆ Visual tools and graphic organizers from selected chapters can be printed out and used with students; an icon next to a visual tool in the chapter means that it can be found online
  ◆ Links to related sites for each chapter of the text
  ◆ Online glossary flashcards
  ◆ Access to the Video Cases, including exercises

Visit www.cengage.com/login to register using an access code. If the text has not come with an access code, go to www.ichapters.com to obtain one.

About the Authors

Vicki Cohen is a professor at Fairleigh Dickinson University and director of the School of Education. She received her doctorate from Teachers College, Columbia University. She taught special education and reading in public schools for many years. She is an expert in the field of literacy and technology and has published many articles and presented numerous papers on literacy and technology at national and international conferences. Dr. Cohen serves on the editorial board of *Journal of Computers in Schools* and is an active member of the International Reading Association. She has taught language development and literacy, the beginning graduate literacy class, for over 19 years and is very proud of her many students who go on to become effective literacy teachers.

John Edwin Cowen is a professor of literacy and education at Fairleigh Dickinson University, where he coordinates and teaches in the Literacy/Reading Certification Program. He earned his doctorate at Teachers College, Columbia University, and has taught reading/language arts and special education in the public schools for 20 years. He has written numerous articles and published seven books, including a major research book in reading for the International Reading Association (IRA), *A Balanced Approach to Beginning Reading Instruction: A Synthesis of Six Major U.S. Research Studies* (2003). He is past president of the New Jersey Reading Association and served on the editorial advisory board for the IRA *Journal of Reading*. Dr. Cowen is also the *Parnassus Literary Journal*'s first prize award–winning poet in international competition, and editor of the 2008 Penguin Classic book, *Doveglion: Collected Poems* by José Garcia Villa.

Acknowledgments

We would like to especially acknowledge Melissa Kelleher, our developmental editor, who patiently helped us through the comprehensive process of developing a second edition textbook. We would also like to acknowledge and thank our respective spouses, John Cohen and Jay Cowen, who endlessly encouraged us and allowed us to cover our offices with piles of books, papers, and manuscripts, and who granted us time away from family chores so we could write this important edition for guiding future classroom teachers in effective literacy strategies.

LITERACY for CHILDREN in an INFORMATION AGE

Teaching Reading, Writing, and Thinking

LITERACY: A NEW DEFINITION

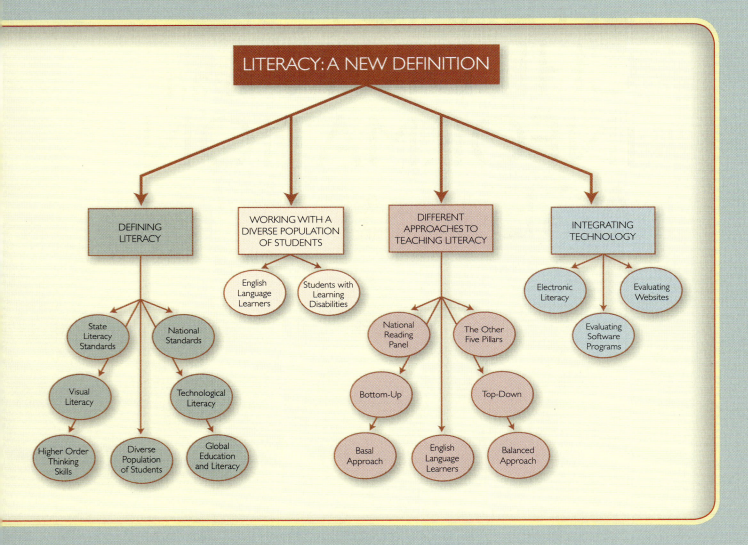

Key Terms

hypertext
hypermedia
state standards
national standards
visual literacy
higher order thinking skills
technological literacy
global education
dyslexia
balanced approach
bottom-up approach
decoding
top-down approach
basal series
comprehensive literacy program
electronic literacy
electronically supported reading
electronically supported writing
electronic communication
electronic literacy assessment
speech-to-text technology
social networking

Focus Questions

1. What is the new definition of literacy and what is included in this definition? How have state and national standards affected our definition of "literacy?" What is visual literacy and how can it be taught in the classroom? What is technological literacy?

2. Why is it increasingly important to address the needs of diverse learners? What strategies can be used in the classroom to promote literacy for English language learners? For students with learning disabilities?

3. What are the key areas of reading instruction that all classrooms should include in their instruction? What is the difference between the bottom-up and top-down approach to literacy? What are the components of a balanced reading approach?

4. What are different ways that technology can be integrated into a literacy classroom? Why is it important to evaluate Internet websites and literacy software?

Welcome to Miss Wilcox's Third Grade: Helping Students Achieve Literacy

Miss Wilcox looked at the class of third grade students sitting expectantly in front of her. It was the first day of school and she did not yet know what their strengths and weaknesses were, nor was she familiar with their learning styles and individual preferences. She did know that of the 20 students in her class, 7 were English language learners (ELLs), or students whose native language was not English. She also knew that five children were classified as students with learning disabilities. She would be working closely with specialists in the school to design individual programs for these diverse students with special needs.

With the district's strong emphasis on literacy development, Miss Wilcox was prepared to meet both the state standards and International Reading Association (IRA) Standards. She had accumulated a wide variety of books for her class library, which included many different genres and represented many different cultures throughout the world. During Internet Workshop, the students in her class will communicate with other classrooms around the world and be taught strategies to comprehend electronic text.

Miss Wilcox had set up her classroom with a comfortable chair, easel, and rug in one corner for her shared Reading Time, and she had different centers with interesting activities spaced throughout the room. In the back of the classroom, she had set up a classroom library so that children could choose their own books. She had placed a table facing the learning centers where small guided reading groups will meet. Colorful posters were hung on the walls displaying different phonic rules and games for word study. Miss Wilcox had participated in a district staff development program to help her implement a balanced literacy approach with her third grade class, and she was eager to use many of the different strategies that had been introduced. She felt confident that by collecting data on each of her student's progress throughout the year and using that data to make informed instructional decisions, each of her students would achieve and continue their literacy development in her classroom.

Defining Literacy

This book will tell you a story as you read through its chapters: It is the story of what literacy means in the twenty-first century and how educators can teach literacy in their classrooms. As a current or future teacher who instructs our children in the classroom, your knowledge of literacy and how to teach it to our students is an essential and ongoing process. If children are not literate, they cannot succeed in school or in our society, or participate in our democracy as effective citizens. Literacy is the key to personal, professional, and global growth in our world, and because it is so important, this may be the most important book you will read as you go through your professional career. This book will give you the foundation for teaching our children how to be literate based on current research in the field, recommended best practices, and an understanding of what children need to succeed in the twenty-first century.

But what is literacy? Is literacy static, or is it an ever-changing process reflecting new ideas and growth in our society? Is literacy composed of reading and writing, or does it include a broader conception? Do teachers teach literacy skills using the same methods today as when you went to school? Do children learn to read the same way as they did 100 years ago? If not, what does the research recommend as the best way to teach reading and literacy?

For centuries, long before the development of the printing press, our writing system has been linear—that is, a line of symbols written sequentially across the page, from one side to the other, from top to bottom. Writing has really been in one dimension—from beginning to end scanning from left to right, right to left, up and down. However, with the advent of electronic digital media, linear text is being replaced with **hypertext**—that is, text that is no longer linear but interactive and dynamic. The "user" can apply any sequence to access information using embedded electronic links that enable users to easily explore relevant materials as they choose. Hypertext is, in effect, three-dimensional, and it is difficult to define its boundaries—just where does the text begin and end? **Hypermedia** approaches go even beyond hypertext in that they combine on-screen text with pictures, animation and graphics, and increasingly sound and video, while also having the organizational features of hypertext. Thus, hypermedia offers much more interactivity than regular books, and it provides many alternative paths to follow (Eagleton, 2002; Leu, Kinzer, Coiro, & Cammack, 2004; Topping, 1997). How does this new way of interacting with text affect our definition of literacy?

Has the population of students that are in our classrooms changed in the past 20 years, thereby impacting how literacy should be taught? Current surveys show that the amount of time children spend on the Internet exceeds the number of hours they spend watching television.

93 percent of teens use the Internet and 75 percent of teens have a cell phone (Raine, 2009). 85 percent of teens ages 12–17 engage at least occasionally in some form of electronic personal communication, which includes text messaging, sending e-mail or instant messages, or posting comments on social networking sites. The Pew Internet & American Life Project (Lenhart, Arafeh, Smith, & Macgill, 2008) has found that 64 percent of online teens ages 12–17 have participated in one or more of the following activities:

◆ 39 percent share their own artistic creations—such as artwork, photos, stories, or videos—online.

◆ 33 percent create or work on web pages or blogs for others, including those for groups they belong to, friends, or school assignments.

◆ 28 percent have created their own online journal or blog.

◆ 27 percent maintain their own personal web page.

55 percent of online teens ages 12–17 have created a profile on a social networking site such as Facebook or MySpace; 47 percent have uploaded photos where others can see them, although many restrict access to the photos in some way; and 14 percent have posted videos online (Lenhart, Arafeh, Smith, & Macgill, 2008).

These students evidently have a high comfort level with technology and do not even consider computers to be part of "technology." This population of students never knew a time when there were no computers. What's more, they find the use of technology in schools to be disappointing. They indicate that the way they see technology used in classrooms is uninspiring, and they consider themselves more Internet-savvy than many of their teachers (Oblinger, 2003).

In addition to the changes that have occurred in the way our teenagers use technology, the population of our country is also radically changing, affecting the way that literacy will be taught in the classroom. ELLs are becoming a greater proportion of the student population in our schools. According to the National Center for Education Statistics, in 2000, 17 percent of all public school students were Hispanic, and by 2025, nearly one in four school-age children will speak Spanish as their primary language (National Center for Education Statistics, 2003). In many school districts, a large percentage of the population will speak many different languages and come from many different locations from around the globe. As our students live in an increasingly diverse, digital world, it is important that they learn the literacy, social, and interpersonal skills

Learning to read in today's technological world involves using computers and books in a classroom setting.

necessary to succeed in a global world. Teachers must meet the needs of all children and help them become literate so that all students have equitable access to the competencies required to succeed.

As the story of how literacy can be taught in the classroom unfolds in the upcoming chapters, our emphasis will be to provide you with the latest national research studies in the field of literacy and to give you practical strategies for implementing the best practices. Your definition of literacy will grow as you progress through this book to include many different factors that comprise this ever-evolving term. In an increasingly global and technological world, this book takes the stance that the literacy classroom must integrate technology and its applications as part of the literacy process. Teachers must also know the latest research that informs best practices in literacy instruction, so that all children from all backgrounds will develop the literacy skills necessary to succeed.

State Literacy Standards

People often define the term *literacy* as the ability to read, write, and understand what is read and written. However, literacy is more than this. It is a complex, multifaceted process that requires a wide variety of instructional approaches. This chapter expands the traditional definition of literacy to include a more comprehensive overview that reflects current developments in our world. Literacy today means more than basic reading, writing, and computing skills. It means knowing how to use knowledge and skills in the context of modern life. Schools need to increase their emphasis on the new literacies that students will need for the twenty-first century, using the tools that are essential to everyday life, communication, and workplace productivity (Partnership for 21st Century Skills, 2004).

One of the factors that has influenced our definition of literacy has been the development of state and professional standards. **State standards** usually describe what students should know and be able to do on completion of a 13-year public education. Revised periodically, state standards provide local school districts with clear and specific benchmarks for student achievement in different content areas, such as reading, math, social studies, and science. State standards are usually developed by panels of teachers, administrators, parents, students, and representatives from higher education, business, and the community; they are impacted by **national standards,** research-based practice, and student need.

Standards articulate the concepts and skills students should be taught and should learn; they tell us what to assess. Performance standards are often developed as well;

these describe more concretely and specifically what students should demonstrate to show proficiency. Standards are meant to help teachers develop a broad view of literacy and to specify specific teaching strategies that are recommended practices in literacy development. At the state level, teachers are required to follow these standards; while at the national level, standards are more general suggestions for classroom practices. Literacy instruction has been more difficult to "define" through these standards because it involves strategies and skills, as opposed to a more content-oriented field such as science or social studies. Literacy is a tool that must be used in every content area, and therefore transcends any specific content or subject: it must be taught throughout each subject area and throughout the day. It should be the guiding focus of all instruction in the classroom. As such, standards help delineate what literacy is, but they do not go far enough in allowing teachers to see that literacy instruction is not just the teaching of skills and strategies, it is a basic philosophical approach to instruction.

In many states, the Language Arts Literacy Standards focus on four broad areas: reading, writing, speaking, and listening. For example, New York divides the English Language Arts Standards for elementary grades into four areas: "Students will read, write, listen and speak for literary response and expression" (New York State Department of Education, 2005). California divides the English Language Arts Content Standards for first grade into the following areas: Reading, Writing, Written and Oral English Language Conventions, and Listening and Speaking (California State Department of Education, 2007). Indiana's Academic Standards divide English/Language Arts into Reading: Word Recognition, Fluency and Vocabulary Development; Reading: Comprehension and Analysis of Nonfiction and Informational Text; Reading: Comprehension and Analysis of Literary Text; Writing: Processes and Features; Writing: Applications; Writing: English Language Conventions; and Listening and Speaking: Skills, Strategies and Applications (Indiana State Department of Education, 2007).

Teachers' VOICES   Using Standards in the Classroom

When creating my weekly lesson plans for Language Arts, I follow the state standards, as well as my district's Outcome Goals. I try to create universal lesson plans applying Gardner's multiple intelligences (Gardner, 1993) and Bloom's taxonomy (Bloom, 1956), while using a structured literacy text. The standards are the basis of my foundation for my lessons. The text we use in my district consists of a thematic unit that contains a different story every week.

The state standards are used every day in class. My students write daily to improve their writing skills, which is one of the state standards for language arts. We spend a two-week period creating a writing assignment on a specified theme. Students then practice reading their assignments aloud and complete the two-week period by presenting their writing assignments to the class. One of the Language Arts standards, listening, is key for reading, speaking, and writing. If students do not listen to me or to each other, they cannot follow what is occurring in the classroom.

—*Jennifer Hendershot, Sixth Grade Teacher*

Some states define their literacy standards a bit broader to also include a fifth and sometimes sixth area, which usually includes **visual literacy** and sometimes media or technological literacy. For example, New Jersey divides its Core Curriculum Content Standards in Language Arts Literacy into five areas: Reading, Writing, Speaking, Listening, and Viewing and Media Literacy (New Jersey Department of Education, 2004). Florida divides its Language Arts content standards into Reading; Writing; Listening, Viewing, and Speaking; Language; and Literature (Florida State Department of Education, 2004). Wisconsin Model Academic Standards for English Language Arts divides the standards into six areas: Reading/Literature, Writing, Oral Language, Language, Media and Technology, and Research and Inquiry (Wisconsin Department of Education, 2004). Those states that are moving toward the integration of visual, media, and technological literacies into their content standards are establishing a new, twenty-first century definition of "literacy." The more indicators that are satisfied by a state and its local education agencies in their implementation of educational technologies, the more complete and aligned the state's policies are in ensuring effective usage to improve student learning and standards-based reform (Dede, 2004).

When analyzing the English Language Arts standards of different states, literacy is not seen as any one of the components in isolation, but rather as a combination of all of the indicators working in balance. Literacy can be viewed as a language process that involves all of the language skills listed earlier, including a student's ability to effectively manipulate information and communicate using new technologies. The standards emphasize a student's ability to construct meaning with text, with others in social engagement, and with information. If children develop their literacy skills individually and with others, they will discover personal and shared meaning throughout their lives. If they develop literacy that includes an emphasis on effective use of educational technologies, they will be prepared to participate in an increasingly sophisticated and global workplace and society. It is highly recommended that all teachers review the Language Arts standards for the state they will be teaching in and note the extent to which technology is incorporated into them.

A direct link to every state's English language arts content standards is provided on the *Literacy for Children in an Information Age* premium website **(http://www.cengage.com/login)**.

National Standards

At the national level, National Council for Teachers of English (NCTE) and IRA have developed a set of standards that give teachers a framework from which to operate. They are not as specific as state-level standards, but they provide a general foundation on which curriculum should be developed. They are based on the notion that all students must have the opportunities and resources to develop the language skills they need to participate fully as informed, productive members of society. These standards assume that literacy growth begins before children enter school and is therefore a developmental process of learning how to read, write, and associate spoken words with their graphic representations. The Standards for English Language Arts sponsored by NCTE and IRA are as follows (National Council for Teachers of English, 1996):

1. Students read a wide range of print and nonprint texts to build an understanding of texts, of themselves, and of the cultures of the United States and the world; to acquire new information; to respond to the needs and demands of society and the workplace; and for personal fulfillment. Among these texts are fiction and nonfiction, classic and contemporary works.

2. Students read a wide range of literature from many periods in many genres to build an understanding of the many dimensions (e.g., philosophical, ethical, aesthetic) of human experience.

3. Students apply a wide range of strategies to comprehend, interpret, evaluate, and appreciate texts. They draw on their prior experience, their interactions with other readers and writers, their knowledge of word meaning and of other texts, their word identification strategies, and their understanding of textual features (e.g., sound–letter correspondence, sentence structure, context, graphics).

4. Students adjust their use of spoken, written, and visual language (e.g., conventions, style, vocabulary) to communicate effectively with a variety of audiences and for different purposes.

5. Students employ a wide range of strategies as they write and use different writing process elements appropriately to communicate with different audiences for a variety of purposes.

6. Students apply knowledge of language structure, language conventions (e.g., spelling and punctuation), media techniques, figurative language, and genre to create, critique, and discuss print and nonprint texts.

7. Students conduct research on issues and interests by generating ideas and questions, and by posing problems. They gather, evaluate, and synthesize data from a variety of sources (e.g., print and nonprint texts, artifacts, people) to communicate their discoveries in ways that suit their purpose and audience.

8. Students use a variety of technological and information resources (e.g., libraries, databases, computer networks, video) to gather and synthesize information and to create and communicate knowledge.

9. Students develop an understanding of and respect for diversity in language use, patterns, and dialects across cultures, ethnic groups, geographic regions, and social roles.

10. Students whose first language is not English make use of their first language to develop competency in the English language arts and to develop understanding of content across the curriculum.

11. Students participate as knowledgeable, reflective, creative, and critical members of a variety of literacy communities.

12. Students use spoken, written, and visual language to accomplish their own purposes (e.g., for learning, enjoyment, persuasion, and the exchange of information).

Teachers' VOICES   Literacy Standards

The state literacy standards help me include elements of reading, writing, listening, speaking, and viewing into all academic areas of my curriculum. It is easy for teachers to get caught up in the idea of "just teaching students to read," that is, decoding strategies. Teachers also need to remember that literacy is more than just decoding words on the page. Literacy standards can be incorporated into all subject areas.

—*Zaneta Shannon, Special Education Teacher*

NCTE/IRA standards are designed to encourage the development of curriculum and instruction that make productive use of the emerging literacy abilities that children bring to school. Furthermore, they are not meant to be prescriptions for particular curriculum or instruction, but to provide opportunities for teachers to be creative and innovative in their literacy instruction. They differ quite radically from state standards in that they do allow for so much latitude and flexibility. State standards are often quite prescriptive and phrased as performance assessments, because states use their standards as measures by which to assess students in their state. Notably, in Standard 8, educational technology as an essential tool to communicate and access information is stressed as part of the literacy process.

In addition to standards that have been developed for students, IRA has developed *Standards for Reading Professionals* (2004), which are being revised and expected to be released in 2010. A draft of new IRA standards can be found at http://www.reading.org/resources/issues/reports/professional_standards.html. At the beginning of each chapter in this textbook, there is a list of IRA standards addressed in that chapter. For a copy of IRA *Standards for Reading Professionals*, go to http://www.reading.org. These standards specify the performances that reading professionals entering the field should demonstrate to meet the reading instructional needs of all students. The five standards are:

1. Candidates have knowledge of the foundations of reading and writing processes and instruction.

2. Candidates use a wide range of instructional practices, approaches, methods, and curriculum materials to support reading and writing instruction.

3. Candidates use a variety of assessment tools and practices to plan and evaluate effective reading instruction.

4. Candidates create a literate environment that fosters reading and writing by integrating foundational knowledge, use of instructional practices, approaches and methods, curriculum materials, and the appropriate use of assessments.

5. Candidates view professional development as a career-long effort and responsibility (IRA, 2004).

As you go through this book, you should keep these standards in mind and use them as benchmarks for performances that all teacher candidates and teachers should meet.

Visual Literacy

Visual literacy, which is a component of different states' English Language Arts standards, is the ability to interpret graphical information, to understand the visual message, and to use that information effectively to solve problems. It is also the ability to present information graphically so that others can use it effectively. In essence, there are two sides to visual literacy: (1) the ability to view and interpret visual information, and (2) the ability to design and create visual representations of information. In the first instance, the student reads and comprehends what is being presented visually and graphically. In the second instance, the student must actively create visual representations that then can be used for several purposes: to help the student retain and comprehend the material to be learned, to present information to others in a graphical way, or to help other students effectively comprehend and retain what is to be learned.

Teachers' VOICES   Using Standards in the Classroom

The literacy standards are important as a reference to how I structure my reading lessons. I have second and third graders in my class who are reading on various levels, from beginning first grade to the middle of the third grade. Access to the standards provides me with a frame of reference to develop objectives that meet each child's reading level and not their expected grade level. Although some children may be in the third grade, they may not have developed appropriate reading skills in the first or second grade. These same students may have a wonderful comprehension of stories and a wide vocabulary that allow me to create challenging literacy experiences on their grade level through read-alouds and discussions in various genres. It is important to recognize the difference between children's reading abilities and their comprehension levels. The two may not always go hand in hand. The standards provide me with a reference to develop literacy benchmarks across grade levels and in the area of literacy.

—*Stephanie Lawlor, Special Education Teacher*

Visual literacy facilitates the development of a child's understanding of language, but is often overlooked as an essential component of cognitive development: children need to learn how to interpret symbol systems and understand relationships and patterns of symbols. Visual literacy is a language of icons, signs, pictures, and art that is "read" as any other symbol system with specific rules, common uses, and meanings (Campbell, 2007). Visual images help learners make connections between linear thinking and a more holistic, nonlinear thinking that encourages students to see thematic interrelationships (Campbell, 2007; Hyerle, 1996). Visual tools, such as concept mapping or webbing, provide a strong link between teaching content and developing thinking processes by encouraging students to graphically represent thoughts and ideas in a holistic fashion. Visual tools allow students to represent their thoughts graphically, and thereby attend to new alternatives and perspectives. Visual representations of information contribute to students' becoming more visually attuned and literate, so that when they access information, they are aware of high-quality images that promote learning, as well as low-quality images that confuse and confound them.

Higher Order Thinking Skills

An important aspect of literacy for children in an information age is the ability to apply what is read, to use **higher order thinking skills** to solve problems, to synthesize information into new creations, and to effectively make decisions that are based on solid understanding of surrounding conditions. This definition of literacy goes far beyond the traditional definition.

Higher order thinking means that students use literacy as a tool to solve real-life problems that are interdisciplinary in approach, and that teachers develop an atmosphere whereby a community of learners uses literacy to explore understandings. It means that teachers encourage risk-taking and diverse thinking, rather than valuing "right" answers and one way of seeing the world. Students puzzle over the complexities of learning and realize that not every problem can be solved or answered fully, and the teacher becomes a part of the learning community, helping students pose and research questions. Higher order thinking means we invent ways and processes to solve problems and share these with each other. In classrooms that promote higher order thinking, students reflect on their experiences in writing, talking, and thinking—and they get new chances.

You might see the following situations in a classroom that encourages higher order thinking:

◆ Literacy discussion groups about all kinds of books that children have read
◆ A diverse range of literature and informational content-area books that children can choose to read
◆ Writing about a wide range of topics
◆ Rich and exciting discussions about meanings of texts
◆ Collaborative groups working on problems, such as how to make the local park cleaner or how to have healthier lunches in the cafeteria
◆ Individual students pursuing their own interests
◆ Continuous assessment through a variety of means, such as portfolios, performance assessments, and running records
◆ Acceptance of others' opinions and ideas as being valuable and worthwhile
◆ Use of reading, writing, speaking, listening, visual literacy, and technological literacy for research

You will *not* see the following situations in a classroom that encourages higher order thinking:

◆ Emphasis on skill sheets, workbook pages, and multiple-choice questions
◆ Reading groups based on ability level (the sharks, the tigers, and the turtles) that are set for the year and not flexible in grouping the students
◆ Children asked to answer five questions after reading a story with no discussion
◆ One textbook or reader for the whole class as the primary focus of the literacy program
◆ Heavy emphasis on skills and not on enjoyment of literature
◆ Exclusive use of a textbook
◆ Testing that is one-dimensional, short-answer tests and the exclusive method of assessment
◆ A classroom that stifles questions, discussions, and collaboration between students

Figure 1–1 is a checklist provided for teachers to assess whether a lesson plan is promoting higher order thinking skills. The checklist stresses the need to develop lessons that are not narrow in focus, but rather relate to ideas and concepts that students can use outside the classroom. It also stresses the need to engage children in the lesson and have them solve problems that they may encounter in the real world. It stresses the need to teach skills not as an end in itself, but within the broader context of meaningful literature and meaningful activities.

FIGURE 1-1   **Checklist to Assess Higher Order Thinking in a Lesson**

LITERACY CHECKLIST:
DOES MY LESSON PROMOTE HIGHER ORDER THINKING?

Name: _____   Lesson: _____

Date: _____

Use this checklist to assess whether your lesson promotes higher order thinking. Give yourself 1 point for each item you check off below. See how many points you accumulate after analyzing your lesson.

_____ 1. Does my lesson/activity represent a big idea having enduring value beyond the classroom?

_____ 2. Does this lesson/activity involve "doing" the subject matter, rather than studying about the subject?

_____ 3. Does this lesson/activity uncover abstract or often misunderstood ideas?

_____ 4. Does this lesson/activity engage students?

_____ 5. Does this lesson/activity help students to explore essential questions, link key ideas, or rethink initial ideas?

_____ 6. Does this lesson/activity involve students problem solving?

_____ 7. Does this lesson/activity relate to real-world activities/problems?

_____ 8. Does this lesson involve one of the main components of literacy (reading, writing, speaking, listening, visual literacy, computer literacy, research)?

_____ 9. Is this lesson/activity assessed authentically, i.e., through a performance assessment, a portfolio, or a product?

_____ 10. Is this a lesson/activity I, myself, would enjoy doing for an extended period of time?

_____ Total points

Comments about the lesson:

Technological Literacy

Technology is and will continue to be a driving force in communities, personal lives, and workforce productivity in the twenty-first century. The need for technology-literate citizens is ever-increasing in our society; it is imperative that our schools teach our students how to use technology tools to solve problems, communicate, access information, and foster life-long learning (Partnership for 21st Century Skills, 2004). Today, reading, writing, and communicating have changed our preconceived notions of literacy and literacy instruction. Technological literacy requires students to become proficient in technologies such as gaming software, video technologies, search engines, web pages, social networking, text messaging, and many more new applications yet to emerge (Coiro, Knobel, Lankshear, & Leu, 2008).

Technological literacy is the mastery of learning skills by using twenty-first century tools, and it needs to be integrated into all the core subject areas (Coiro, Knobel, Lankshear, & Leu, 2008; Educational Testing Service, 2002). Learning skills comprise three broad categories:

(1) Information and communication skills, which include communication, information processing, and research tools such as word processing, e-mail, groupware, presentation tools such as PowerPoint, web development, and Internet search tools;

(2) Thinking and problem-solving skills, which include tools such as spreadsheets, decision support software, and design tools;

(3) Interpersonal and self-direction skills, which include personal development and productivity such as e-learning, time management/calendar tools, and collaboration tools.

The International Society for Technology in Education (ISTE) has developed national standards in technology for both students and teachers. ISTE is a nonprofit professional organization with a worldwide membership of educators who are interested in promoting educational technology in our schools. The National Educational Technology Standards (NETS) for Students is designed to provide teachers, technology planners, teacher preparation institutions, and educational decision makers with frameworks and standards to guide them in establishing enriched learning environments supported by technology for our K–12 students. These standards have become the national guidelines for the integration of technology into the classroom. ISTE also developed NETS for Teachers, which have become the national standards that teachers should meet to be technologically literate. These standards define the fundamental concepts, knowledge, skills, and attitudes for applying technology in educational settings. All candidates seeking certification or endorsements in teacher preparation should meet these educational technology standards. The Internet link to the ISTE NETS for students and teachers can be found on the *Literacy for Children in an Information Age* premium website for this chapter (http://www.cengage.com/login).

Using computers is one way children become technologically literate. Children use computers and other classroom technology to communicate, problem-solve, and collaborate.

The NETS Educational Technology Standards for Students include:

1. Creativity and Innovation
2. Communication and Collaboration
3. Research and Information Fluency
4. Critical Thinking, Problem Solving, and Decision Making
5. Digital citizenship
6. Technology Operations and Concepts (ISTE, 2007)

The NETS Educational Technology Standards for Teachers include:

1. Student Learning and Creativity
2. Digital-Age Learning Experiences and Assessments
3. Digital-Age Work and Learning
4. Digital Citizenship and Responsibility
5. Professional Growth and Leadership (ISTE, 2008)

By expanding our definition of literacy to include technological literacy, we are preparing students to live in an increasingly complex, digital society. We are closing the gap between how students currently live at home and how they learn in school. Students are increasingly using instant messaging, text messaging on their cell phones, blogging, downloading music, watching films on laptops, joining social networking sites such as Facebook, and accessing data from the Internet as part of their daily lives. When they arrive at school, they revert to a different world, where time has virtually stood still and information is transmitted through chalk and overhead projectors.

Global Education and Literacy

In this rapidly changing world, there was an accelerated growth of global interdependence based on new economic, political, ecological, technological, and environmental realities that occurred as the Berlin Wall fell and a wave of democracy swept Eastern Europe in the 1990s. Global interdependence can be seen in the expansion of networks that connect different people, cultures, civilizations, and regions. When the Berlin Wall collapsed, the Cold War disintegrated, and a new world order emerged based on global trading and accelerated by the new electronic forms of communication that made the world a much smaller place to live in (Anderson, 1990). Globalization has become the dominant paradigm that influences us today and, while shrinking the world, has expanded our horizons beyond just the borders of our classroom, village, town, city, state, or country. With globalization have come benefits, as well as severe opposition to many of its perceived effects. Many people enjoy the economic and cultural benefits of a more open trading system; for example, watching televisions made in Korea, driving cars made in Japan, using computers made in Malaysia, wearing less expensive clothing made in Mexico, and sipping wines from all over the world. There are also those who debate the benefits of this open trading system, citing as disadvantages human rights issues, genetically altered foods, loss of jobs, loss of national pride, protectionism, and Americanization and homogenization throughout the world through institutions such as McDonald's or Disneyland.

Global education involves learning about those problems and issues that cut across national boundaries and about the interconnectedness of systems—ecological, cultural, economic, political, and technological (Sloan, W., 2009; Smith & Czarra, 2003; Tye, 1990). Global education involves the perspective of taking or seeing things through the eyes of others; we are all part of a global community that must work together to solve common problems and act as responsible citizens to maintain the health and well-being of our world. It means promoting changes in attitudes, knowledge, and skills. Global education aims to facilitate critical thinking and problem solving such that students can effectively access, evaluate, and use the vast amount of information that is currently available through traditional and nontraditional means. Students will need to work constructively with others, use intercultural communications skills, and develop empathy and new perspectives based on the people around them. Students will need to evaluate ethical and moral dilemmas and apply solutions to these problems.

What does this have to do with literacy? With this new worldview, teachers must realize that there is not just one type of literacy—the ability to read, write, speak, listen, and view. Throughout this book, you will learn that students need to become competent in technological, information, and global literacies. Students need to use their basic literacy skills as a tool that they can apply effectively to solve problems, think critically, evaluate moral dilemmas, research a problem, evaluate web pages, and use and create information. Literacy teachers need to provide their students with a "worldview" on the use of literacy; that is, although students may be able to read, write, listen, speak, and view competently enough to pass standardized examinations, they need to use these skills as tools to effectively live in a global world and act responsibly as global citizens. Teachers need to teach literacy skills using global content, and they must allocate significant time and energy to staying current so that content and skills are taught within a global and international context that addresses significant issues and concerns, such as global warming, preserving the world's limited resources, and combatting world poverty. Students must be able to think globally and understand the forces that are shaping our increasingly, sometimes dangerously, interconnected world. As educators, we have a responsibility to prepare our youth to meet these new global challenges in an interdependent world (Sloan, 2009; Smith & Czarra, 2003).

In our increasingly global world, where traditional national and international boundaries are breaking down, the balanced literacy classroom needs to effectively use the Internet as a new form of communication to develop information literacy and technological literacy. Leu (2001) claims that in our global economy there are four skills everyone will need to master: (1) identifying important problems within one's own area of work, (2) gathering relevant information and critically evaluating it, (3) using the appropriate information to solve the identified problems, and (4) clearly communicating the solution to others. It is time that we, as literacy teachers, incorporate these Internet technologies into our classroom and teach the appropriate strategies to help develop this new literacy in all children growing up in an information age.

As a current or future teacher, your knowledge of the different approaches to teaching literacy to students is essential. There are many different views about what is the most effective approach to teaching literacy in the classroom; however, a literacy teacher must use many different approaches in the classroom to meet all students' needs. These different approaches are explained in detail in upcoming chapters. There is also a brief explanation in the following section so that you may start thinking about the definition of literacy within the broader context of varying philosophical frameworks as you go through this book.

Working with a Diverse Population of Students

English Language Learners

Students learning English as a new language is the fastest growing segment within our public schools today. These students come from a multitude of different countries and represent many different cultural backgrounds. They speak many different languages and experience great cognitive demands as they try to assimilate into a new culture, learn a new language, and keep up with the curriculum of their new schools (Vardell, Hadaway, & Young, 2006). Their level of reading ability varies from not being able to read English at all to reading English at a fairly proficient level.

This book uses the term *English language learners (ELLs)* to refer to those students whose native language is not English and who are in the process of learning English. Other terms commonly used to describe ELL students are *English as a second language* (ESL) *students* and *second-language learners.* However, these terms may not be accurate because English may not be the second language the students are learning. In fact, it may be their third or fourth.

According to the United States Census Bureau, by 2030, students who speak a language other than English at home will constitute 40 percent of the school-age population. In 2001, 4.6 million ELLs were enrolled in the nation's public schools—a full 10 percent of the total enrollment in grades preK–12. Of these students, 78 percent spoke Spanish, and 15 percent used a language represented by less than 1 percent of the ELL population. Between 1990 and 2000, ELL enrollment in public schools doubled, while the overall school population increased by only 12 percent (Girard, 2005).

These statistics demonstrate that the number of ELLs in our schools is increasing at an unprecedented rate, and this is creating new challenges for teachers, administrators, and communities. With dwindling budgets, overcrowded classrooms, and strict performance standards for students, teachers need to be better prepared to accommodate all students in the classroom. A recent report on language-minority children and youth (August & Shanahan, 2006) states that language-minority students are not faring well in U.S. schools. For the 41 states reporting, only 18.7 percent of ELLs scored above the state-established norm for reading comprehension. While 10 percent of students who spoke English at home failed to complete high school, the percentage was three times greater (31 percent) for language-minority students who spoke English and five times greater (51 percent) for language-minority students who spoke English with difficulty (National Center for Education Statistics, 2004). The report also states that language-minority students who cannot read and write proficiently in English will not be able to participate fully in U.S. schools, workplaces, or society, and they face limited job opportunities and earning power. The report claims that one of the most pressing problems our schools are facing today is ensuring that ELLs are developing reading and writing proficiency in English and will become productive members of our society.

Teachers' VOICES   Supporting ELLs in the Classroom

When I was in elementary school, my teacher stayed after school twice a week until about 6:00 P.M. and we would go through the vocabulary that the class learned that day. This was an excellent reinforcement strategy because it helped me with my writing and reading comprehension. She also went through some writing skills and reviewed what the opening, middle, and conclusion of an essay were. She helped me write a paragraph both in Spanish and English, and she reviewed grammar in both Spanish and English. She used the word wall to review many of the words. She was a great teacher—very patient and I did not feel uncomfortable with her at all. I felt she knew exactly where I was coming from—an English language learner who needed assistance. By staying late and tutoring me, she challenged me by raising the standards of what was expected of me in school. Tutoring was essential for me and really helped me in my schooling. It is an excellent strategy for ELL students and for students with learning disabilities, because they have to work twice as hard to keep up with the other students in the classroom. My teacher was always positive with me and gave me great comments, such as "You're doing a great job!" and "You're a great student. I know you can do this." I hope to be a teacher just like her one day and use similar strategies. She is my hero.

—*Fina Espinal, Teacher*

Students with Learning Disabilities

In a similar fashion, there has been a phenomenal growth in the number of students (ages 3–21) receiving special education since the inception of PL 94-142 (now IDEA) in 1975; PL 94-142 was landmark legislation that ensured a free and appropriate public education for all children with disabilities. Each year, states report a continuously increasing number of students enrolled in special education programs. Since this landmark legislation in 1975, the number of pupils being provided with special education has increased by more than 80 percent (Gargiulo, 2006). The population of students identified as learning disabled has grown dramatically and accounts for 50 percent of all students enrolled in special education. With the passage of PL 99-457 in 1986, services for infants, toddlers, and preschoolers with special needs have also significantly increased. During the 2000–2001 school year, almost 600,000 preschoolers with special needs were receiving services due to this legislation (Gargiulo, 2006).

Since the mid-1990s, there has been a trend toward more inclusive classrooms, whereby children with special needs stay in the regular classroom and receive instruction from their regular classroom teacher, rather than going to a resource room and receiving instruction from a special educator. During the 1999–2000 school year, almost 45 percent of all students with learning disabilities received services in the regular classroom. This means that about 8 of every 10 students with learning disabilities spent some, most, or all of their school day in a regular classroom (Gargiulo, 2006).

Most educators agree that the primary characteristic of students with learning disabilities is a deficit in academic performance. Well over half of all students identified as learning disabled have problems with reading and are *dyslexic*. **Dyslexia** is a type of reading disorder in which the student fails to recognize, process, and comprehend written words. These students often exhibit deficits in written language, including spelling, handwriting, and composition. Students with learning disabilities often need intensive literacy instruction and much support within the classroom to develop proficiency in reading and writing.

With the changing composition of students in our classroom today, many traditional assumptions about literacy must be reexamined and reconceptualized. Classroom teachers today must know many different types of approaches to teaching reading and writing, and they must view literacy as a long-term developmental process that is unique for each student. Teachers need to feel comfortable with many different cultural backgrounds, they need to address many different styles of learning, and they must embrace a diverse population of students. Most importantly, we need to develop instruction that is sensitive to the needs of all children and will help them achieve.

STRATEGIES FOR TEACHING DIVERSE LEARNERS

Promoting Literacy Achievement for English Language Learners

1. English language learners (ELLs), as well as all children learning how to read and write, should be instructed in the key components of literacy. These components include but are not limited to instruction in phonemic awareness, phonics, fluency, vocabulary, and text comprehension.

2. Oral proficiency in English is a critical factor in teaching ELLs to read and write proficiently in English. Well-developed oral proficiency in English is associated with English reading comprehension. Extensive oral English development must be incorporated into successful literacy instruction. It is best to provide instructional support of oral language development in English, together with high-quality instruction in literacy strategies. Tutoring and individual support are beneficial.

3. It is helpful to use ELL's native language to facilitate literacy development in English. It is beneficial when ELLs can develop proficiency in their first language; however, although this is valuable, it is not absolutely necessary for language-minority students to become strong readers in their native language if they receive the necessary support and instruction in beginning reading to help them learn English.

4. English literacy development is a dynamic process, and the teacher must account for individual differences in language proficiency, age, English oral proficiency, previous background, cognitive abilities, and the similarities and differences between the first language and English. The teacher needs to account for individual differences and base instruction on each student's needs and developmental level.

5. It is important to constantly assess each child's strengths and weaknesses.

6. The teacher should try to establish a home–school connection and involve the family in the student's education. This will increase motivation and participation in classroom instruction. See this chapter's Home–School Connection box.

7. ELLs should continue to read and use material that is in the language they know best. They should also read culturally meaningful and familiar material that will facilitate comprehension.

Based on the findings of the National Literacy Panel on Language-Minority Children and Youth (August & Shanahan, 2006).

Different Approaches to Teaching Literacy

In examining the different state English Language Arts standards, we can determine the various components of literacy: reading, writing, speaking, listening, visual literacy, and technological literacy. However, how a literacy curriculum is implemented depends significantly on the approach that a teacher takes to teaching literacy skills.

Children benefit from working collaboratively with students from different cultural and linguistic backgrounds.

Often, a school district will adopt a specific approach, then mandate that all teachers follow the guidelines of that approach in teaching reading. This is happening with greater frequency as federal mandates from No Child Left Behind are being implemented with its emphasis on standardized testing every year that a child is in school. With pressure for all children to attain passing scores on these high-stake tests, critics argue that teachers are given less and less freedom to adopt the approaches they believe are best.

Key Areas of Reading Instruction: National Reading Panel

The National Reading Panel (NRP) issued a report in 2000 (National Institute of Child Health and Human Development [NICHD], 2000) that responded to a Congressional mandate to help parents, teachers, and policymakers identify key skills and methods that would promote reading achievement. The NRP was charged with reviewing research in the field of reading instruction and identifying methods that successfully promoted reading achievement in kindergarten through third grade. Panel members reviewed more than 100,000 studies and tried to define "what works" based on scientific evidence. The NRP identified five key areas of reading instruction that it claims must occur in the literacy classroom:

1. Phonemic awareness
2. Phonics
3. Vocabulary
4. Fluency
5. Text comprehension

Key Areas of Reading Instruction: The Other Five Pillars

Many educators believe the findings of the NRP do not adequately represent all aspects of instruction that need to be addressed. Richard Allington (2005) listed "The Other Five Pillars" that contribute to literacy achievement in the classroom:

1. Classroom organization
2. Matching pupils and texts so that all children are reading the appropriate level of text

3. Giving children access to interesting texts, allowing them to choose their own texts, and having children collaborate on literacy activities

4. Writing and reading throughout the curriculum throughout the day

5. Expert tutoring by qualified and knowledgeable tutors

In the upcoming chapters, all the above areas, as well as other important aspects of literacy instruction, are explored in detail as key features of a balanced literacy classroom.

STRATEGIES FOR TEACHING DIVERSE LEARNERS

Promoting Literacy Achievement for Students with Learning Disabilities

1. Multisensory teaching is recommended for students with learning disabilities. This refers to any learning activity that includes the use of two or more sensory modalities simultaneously to take in or express information. This frequently involves a "hand-kinesthetic" component in literacy instruction, such as teaching alphabet letters by having the student feel and name three-dimensional forms or using Tinker toys to model the shape of letters (Birsh, 1999; Shaywitz, 2003).

2. In an inclusive classroom, the teacher creates a learning environment that is enabling and supportive of all students' needs. Lesson plans and instructional practices must meet the needs of all children.

3. The teacher should consult with the school specialist who has the appropriate state licenses and training to support students with learning disabilities so that they can successfully achieve in the classroom.

4. A wide range of accommodations and modifications are necessary for the student with learning disabilities to achieve success in the classroom. This might mean giving some children additional time for testing, creating a quiet area where they can complete their work, or providing additional support and practice so they can learn the task/strategy.

5. Teachers need to work with parents and families to develop and implement an individualized education program for the student with learning disabilities.

6. The teacher should capitalize on the student's strengths and provide opportunities for success by developing lessons that are within each student's ability to achieve.

7. Students with learning disabilities need high structure and clear expectations. They also need frequent, positive feedback about appropriate social and academic skills at home and at school.

8. Teachers should use technology to support students with learning disabilities, such as software to support reading and writing, laptops or keyboards to facilitate note taking, tape recorders to help remember lectures, and word processing to assist poor handwriting ability.

Based on Gargiulo (2006).

Key Areas of Reading Instruction: English Language Learners

Any method that is used in a literacy classroom needs to ensure that children's reading achievement is the primary goal of the classroom. With increasing numbers of ELLs arriving at school each year, and with inclusion of children with learning disabilities into regular classrooms, it is challenging for teachers to know what approach works best for different children. Therefore, it is important for teachers to know many different approaches to teaching literacy skills. No one approach succeeds with all children, and a teacher needs to be flexible, adaptable, and willing to learn many different ways to teach and reteach skills.

All children must be treated respectfully and offered equal educational opportunities that honor basic educational principles. According to IRA's *Second-Language Literacy Instruction; A Position Statement* (2001b), teachers should:

◆ Facilitate learning through collaborative and engaging activities that children will enjoy

◆ Develop literacy skills throughout all instructional activities and across the curriculum, including mathematics, science, and social studies

◆ Teach literacy skills and content through the experiences and cultural background of the children in the class

◆ Challenge students to develop higher order thinking skills and cognitive complexity

◆ Engage all students through dialogue, especially during instruction which involves discussing, interacting, and using language extensively to answer questions

Throughout the years there have been discussions and conflicts regarding which approach works best for teaching reading. In education, it appears as if the pendulum swings radically from one side to the other, with each year bringing new sets of recommendations. This book takes the position that a **balanced approach** that includes practices from different methods is the best one to adopt in the classroom. Chapter 3 describes the balanced approach in detail. As stated earlier, no matter to which side the pendulum is swinging, the five key literacy recommendations from the NRP and Allington's "Five Pillars" (2005) should be incorporated into all classrooms.

Bottom-Up Approach

One approach to teaching reading has been used in the classroom for years; the emphasis starts on having students work on the smallest unit in our English language, the letter, and its associated sound or phoneme. By associating the letter with its sound (that is, the letter *c* is pronounced $/k/$), a child learns to quickly put sounds together to blend them into words. Thus, a child who sees *c-a-t* and knows the associated sound for each of the three letters can decode that word by blending the three sounds into *c-a-t* for *cat*. The **bottom-up approach,** therefore, starts with **decoding** as its first step, because children must learn individual sounds and words before they can successfully read text. After children learn how to sound out individual words, they start to learn the referent meaning behind the word. For example, now that a child can read the word *cat*, the teacher would emphasize the meaning of the word *cat*.

Therefore, the next step in the bottom-up approach is to emphasize the vocabulary meaning behind a word, once it has been decoded. Then, the next step is to combine words into sentences so that now a child might be able to read *The cat is small* and comprehend its meaning.

Meaning is emphasized as a child's ability to decode words and associate meaning to the words increases, leading to sentence comprehension. The next step is to have the child work on paragraph comprehension and, finally, text comprehension as the child's ability to decode sentences and assign meaning to the text increases.

In the bottom-up approach, recognizing the individual word starts first and text comprehension comes last. The rationale for this is that children cannot read until they can identify individual words on the page. As you probably inferred, this approach is also known as the phonics approach to teaching reading (Figure 1–2).

Top-Down Approach

The **top-down approach** starts with the top of the sequence of steps—text comprehension. This approach assumes that children learn how to read by reading and understanding enjoyable text. It starts with the assumption that by reading simple, predictable, patterned text in an enjoyable, comfortable shared environment, children will learn what reading is all about first—comprehending text and enjoying reading. When

FIGURE 1-2

Phonic Approach

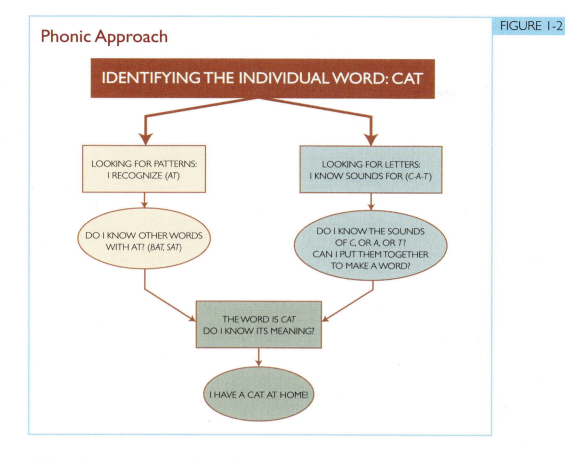

children sit next to a parent, older sibling, or caretaker and read a story together, they learn about books, print, and language, and they also learn that reading is enjoyable, easy, and fun. In the same way, when a teacher sits on a chair in the reading corner and reads a fun book aloud to a class of children sitting on a rug, a shared literacy experience occurs, and the children learn to read for meaning and learn that reading is fun. Predictable books such as *Brown Bear, Brown Bear, What Do You See?* or *The Three Billy Goats Gruff* allow children to chime in when they know what is coming next, giving them an opportunity to "read" books and understand what they mean without having to decode every word in the text.

In the top-down approach, after children discuss text and what it means, the teacher then concentrates on individual paragraphs and what clues might be located in those paragraphs to help children construct the meaning of the whole text. Teachers also point out individual sentences and talk about what sentences mean and how they can give clues to unlocking the meaning of the whole text. They might point out how sentences begin with capital letters and end with periods (or questions marks or exclamation points). They might note how commas mean we pause when we read out loud, and how quotation marks mean someone is going to speak. They demonstrate how sentences convey meaning within the context of the whole story. Teachers then point out keywords in the sentence and discuss the meaning of those words. Those words might be introduced as a prereading activity, but vocabulary words are taught within the context of the whole text and how each word fits into the meaning of the story. Lastly, if necessary, the teacher focuses on individual words and helps students decode words by providing clues and prompts to unlock pronunciation and meaning. Word study is within the context of meaningful text and contributes toward comprehension of the book they are reading. The lesson is not broken down into discrete skills, but rather concentrates on building meaning by examining the text that is being read, through decoding and phonics, through vocabulary development of individual words, and through sentence and paragraph comprehension.

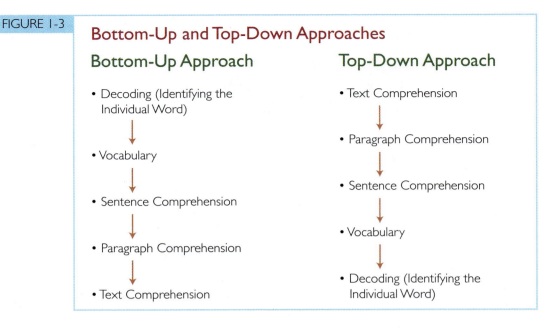

FIGURE 1-3

Bottom-Up and Top-Down Approaches

Bottom-Up Approach

- Decoding (Identifying the Individual Word)
  ↓
- Vocabulary
  ↓
- Sentence Comprehension
  ↓
- Paragraph Comprehension
  ↓
- Text Comprehension

Top-Down Approach

- Text Comprehension
  ↓
- Paragraph Comprehension
  ↓
- Sentence Comprehension
  ↓
- Vocabulary
  ↓
- Decoding (Identifying the Individual Word)

The top-down approach clearly is different from the bottom-up approach, although many of the same strategies are used (Figure 1–3). Usually the top-down approach does not emphasize skills and is a child-centered approach to learning. The whole language approach, which was much in favor in literacy instruction across the country in the mid-1980s and early 1990s, used many of these strategies to teach literacy. In the bottom-up approach, phonic skills are emphasized, and often these skills are taught in isolation; that is, the skills are not tied to any book, but are taught out of context of meaningful text as separate skills to be mastered.

The top-down approach has been criticized for not explicitly teaching phonics and incorporating skills directly into the literacy curriculum. Research studies such as the NRP (NICHD, 2000) claim that phonics needs to be directly and explicitly taught in the classroom for reading achievement of all children. Because of this criticism, the whole language approach has fallen out of favor in many school districts across the country, although it has brought to literacy instruction a new emphasis on the importance of comprehension and the benefits of using a child-centered approach that focuses on quality literature as a means to teach reading. Many of the techniques of whole language have been integrated into the balanced approach, which primary education classrooms have adapted and are currently using across the country. These different approaches to teaching literacy are discussed in more detail in Chapter 10.

Basal Series

School districts often adopt a basal series to teach reading, and then require all teachers to use this approach. A **basal series** is a comprehensive reading program produced by a publishing company that contains texts for all grade levels from kindergarten through eighth grade. The series usually comes with one or two books per grade level, and it is usually an anthology of stories, poems, and essays that have been "graded" for reading difficulty so that a third grade teacher knows this reader is written on a third grade level. The series also contains a teacher's guide that outlines a lesson plan for every day of the week and specifies which skills, strategies, worksheets, vocabulary, reading comprehension questions, and activities should be administered on a specific day of the week.

The basal series approach to literacy is highly structured and does not allow much creativity for teachers, but it ensures that skills will be integrated into the literacy curriculum. It contains workbooks, posters, skill pads, overhead transparencies, and other supplemental material to support the teacher. It also contains assessments that allow the teacher to evaluate the students on a daily and monthly basis. Because of its comprehensive approach and emphasis on skills, school districts are confident that children will learn how to read with this series in place; thus, this has become one of the most popular and pervasive approaches to teaching reading across the country. Nevertheless, research has shown that most basal reading series lack balance and are not as effective as other approaches (Cowen, 2003a).

Balanced or Comprehensive Approach

The term *balanced approach* has come to mean so many different things to different educators and researchers that some educators have argued that balanced literacy should be called a **comprehensive literacy program** (Snow, Burns, & Griffin, 1998). Being that the balanced approach continues to predominate in classroom practice today, it is important to carefully define the term. Traditionally, a balanced approach meant that teachers make thoughtful decisions each day about the best way to help each child become a better reader and writer, by balancing a top-down approach with a bottom-up approach based on the child's needs. Literacy would be balanced between a child-centered approach emphasizing comprehension of quality literature and an approach that focused on explicit instruction in phonic skills and word study. In fact, the concept of a balanced approach has expanded to mean that all aspects of literacy are taught within the classroom including reading, writing, speaking, listening, and viewing. This instruction centers on the needs of our students and includes effective practices based on research findings.

The balanced approach to literacy instruction is a commitment to ensuring that reading, writing, listening, viewing, and speaking receive appropriate emphasis within a literacy program. In a balanced approach, teachers start by working with the students to learn what their needs are, basing instruction on what they see, hear, and observe in the classroom. In a balanced approach, teachers respond quickly to new issues in literacy, while also maintaining what research has already shown to be effective. It is an approach that requires and frees a teacher to be a reflective decision maker and to fine-tune and modify what he or she is doing each day to meet the needs of each child (Hibbert & Iannacci, 2005).

A balanced approach can look different at different grade levels and is based on the needs of diverse learners. Balance in this perspective does not mean "one size fits all," but rather that teachers must carefully take into account their students and school culture when developing, implementing, and revising their literacy programs. The 2007 California Reading Language Arts Framework (available online at http://www.cde.ca.gov/CI/rl/cf/) adopted a balanced approach whereby all skills and standards are not emphasized equally; students' needs determine what skills and standards should be

Courtesy of Guilherme Cunha

Teachers demonstrate a balanced approach to literacy by emphasizing speaking and writing, as well as reading, viewing, and listening.

TEACHSOURCE VIDEO CASE

A Talk with Ms. Abrew, principal of Lowell School

Ms. Abrew feels very strongly that new teachers need to know the culture of a school and work closely with the district literacy coordinator and technology coordinator when first setting up a literacy classroom. Ms. Abrew is the principal of Lowell Elementary School in Teaneck, New Jersey. Lowell School is a first through fourth grade school that has approximately 375 students: 46 percent are African American, 24 percent are Hispanic, 16 percent are white, and 14 percent are made up of students from Asia and other countries. She believes strongly that teachers should practice a balanced literacy approach and that they need to know many different strategies that work in the classroom. The most important thing is to achieve success and improve student learning.

Ms. Abrew says that when she walks into a classroom, one of the first things that she does is go over to the book shelves and look at what literature the children are being exposed to. She wants her students to read quality fiction and nonfiction books and be provided with opportunities to explore literature in many different ways. Children learn best when they are engaged in meaningful activities by teachers employing best practice approaches to literacy.

Ms. Abrew talks about the need for principals to keep their teachers

current by exposing them to the most recent research in the field of literacy. One way to do this is by having the teachers help develop the literacy curriculum themselves.

Ms. Abrew also feels that principals need to provide teachers the opportunity to examine assessment data from state tests. These tests should help drive instruction and inform the teacher as to what the students' needs are. Student assessment should always be about student learning. Teachers need a good grasp of the state and national standards to determine how the curriculum is aligned with the standards. This will help ensure that

the students are meeting these standards and that the assessment tests are being used wisely and fairly. When teachers have the opportunity to collaborate and work together on lesson planning, curriculum development, and assessment practices, student learning will certainly improve.

Some of the strategies Ms. Abrew suggests for teachers include the following:

◆ Become familiar with the culture of the school.

◆ Know your state and national standards and make sure your curriculum addresses the standards.

◆ Make student achievement the main goal of your classroom. All children can achieve by using different instructional approaches and applying best practices in literacy.

Questions:

1. What role does an educational leader like Ms. Abrew play in promoting student achievement in the school?

2. How can Ms. Abrew promote a balanced literacy program in her school?

Go to www.cengage.com/ login to register your access code for the premium website for *Literacy for Children in an Information Age,* where you can watch an in-depth video exploration of Ms. Abrew's conversation.

emphasized in the classroom. Fitzgerald (1999) added to this understanding through her view of balance that includes local, global, and effective knowledge about literacy.

Balanced literacy uses a whole-part-whole approach; that is, instruction begins with the use of whole texts focusing on the whole child. It then deconstructs textual features into its component parts for students to learn, such as focusing instruction on phonic elements or word study or specific comprehension strategies during the process of reading the whole text. It then synthesizes this instruction back into a new whole based on application and transfer of learning into authentic reading and writing experiences (Hibbert & Iannacci, 2005). Therefore, balance is about knowing our students and balancing what they need with best practices in literacy instruction. Our ability as teachers to do this well is contingent on ongoing professional development and knowledge of current literacy research (Hibbert & Iannacci, 2005; Weaver, 1998).

This book uses the term *balanced approach*, although it is often called a comprehensive approach in the literature. For us, a balanced approach is based on listening to our children in the classroom and implementing best practices based on their needs. It is an approach that draws on 30 years of research in the field of education and literacy and emphasizes literacy achievement for all children (Cowen, 2003a). It applies the best practices from different approaches and combines them together into effective classroom practice. Chapter 3 describes in detail what a balanced approach to literacy is and how a teacher can implement this approach in the classroom. You can watch a principal, Ms. Abrew, discuss a balanced literacy approach in TeachSource Video Case 1.

Integrating Technology into a Literacy Classroom

Electronic Literacy

In this information age, children are spending increasing numbers of hours reading digital text, using technology to write text, communicating via electronic devices, and listening to digital music. Many of these literacy activities involve using electronic media. **Electronic literacy** refers to literacy activities that are delivered, supported, accessed, or assessed through computers or other electronic means rather than on paper. This term should not be confused with "technological literacy" or "computer literacy," which is applied to knowledge and competencies in using technology and computers, such as searching the Internet, or using the Windows environment, among others (Topping, 1997).

There are a number of categories that can be considered part of electronic literacy:

◆ *Electronically supported reading:* Many of today's computer programs can scaffold and prompt successful reading. Electronic "talking books" are a good example of this feature. Students can choose to hear digitized pronunciations of individual words, or they can choose to hear the whole text read to them. Talking books have self-selected digitized speech, second language versions, the option of playing instructional games, and various other special effects such as clicking on an object and watching it become animated. Examples of talking books include Wiggleworks, CAST eReader, the Talking Computer Project, and Living Books. Many of these products have been specially developed to support children with reading disabilities, and they use digitized speech and a structured phonics-based approach to improve reading skills.

◆ *Electronically supported writing:* Many writing programs also scaffold and prompt the writing process. When the student is unsure of what to write next, the program prompts with alternatives. The computer remembers the words that the child used and the prompting becomes more personalized. These programs are excellent resources for children with learning disabilities and help support their writing skills. Examples of current supportive writing programs include Co-Writer, Write Away, and Creative Writer 2. Many of these programs also prompt the students via digitized speech, rather than on the screen, and are therefore known as "talking word processors."

◆ *Electronic communication:* Students are increasingly using the Internet to communicate with others via e-mail, instant messaging, discussion boards, and blogs. Students write to e-mail pals on the other side of the world, participate in discussion forums, or publish articles online. Classes participate in online Internet projects and share information with other classes in a different geographic location.

◆ *Electronic literacy assessment:* Many computer programs assess reading comprehension and reading skills. Students can conduct self-tests on books read at home and school, including those read by the teacher. In addition to providing analysis and reports for the teacher, such programs also generate take-home reports to promote parental involvement. Standardized tests are also being offered via the computer, with the latest technology promoting adaptive testing whereby the student receives test questions based on previous responses.

◆ *Speech-to-text technology:* Many struggling writers have trouble expressing themselves on paper. With speech-to-text technology, children with learning disabilities can dictate their ideas and have the computer convert them into text. Spoken words are converted directly into text in a word processor. This technology is becoming more powerful and accessible with each passing year. Excellent resources are Dragon Naturally Speaking and Philips Speech Processing.

◆ *Social networking:* Students engage in social networking programs such as Facebook, MySpace, Friendster, and Twitter. A social network service builds web-based, online communities of people who share interests and/or activities. They provide new ways for students to interact and communicate. Many schools are using these networks for educational purposes. English classes use wikis and blogs to encourage students to write.

Electronic literacy is when a teacher develops and implements literacy activities that use electronic media to support instruction. There are many different resources that can be used in the classroom to support diverse learners in the development of literacy competencies in reading and writing. These resources provide scaffolding for children with learning disabilities, ELLs, and children at risk.

Evaluating Internet Websites

The Internet is a valuable resource for teachers and students alike, providing a wealth of lesson plans, interactive activities, research articles, recommendations for best practices in the classroom, and Internet projects. Websites and on-line resources can be integrated into a literacy classroom in a multitude of ways (each of the upcoming chapters in this book outlines various ways). Each chapter lists many different websites that you can explore; other sites appear as hotlinks on the companion website. The selected literacy websites provide teachers with interactive resources for each topic covered in the upcoming chapters; however, they may not be suitable for every class or lesson, so teachers need to evaluate and analyze them carefully before using them.

The process of evaluating websites is a valuable activity for teachers and students alike. It is important that as teachers visit websites, they evaluate each one according to certain criteria to determine whether the site is appropriate for the lesson, for the students, and for the skill/process being taught. Figure 1–4 presents a literacy website evaluation form that uses the following criteria to assess the quality of the site:

◆ *Does the site promote literacy?* Does the site promote literacy in one or more of the following categories: writing, phonics, word study, vocabulary, research skills, and comprehension? The website should support the state content standards in

English/Language Arts and promote an aspect of literacy that is being taught in the classroom.

◆ *Is the site age appropriate?* Is the site appropriate for the grade level of the children who will use it? Does it have appropriate graphics, text size, and page layout? This is an important consideration because many children will try to use websites that are designed for adults or older students, and thus may not comprehend what they are reading or feel comfortable navigating the site.

◆ *Does the site reflect current research in literacy?* Does the site promote methods that support current research in literacy? Is the site current and up to date? Is the URL (address) one that can be trusted? Sites ending in *edu* (education), *gov* (government), or *org* (organization) are usually more trustworthy than those ending in *com* (commercial), although there are many excellent sites ending in *com* or *net*. It is also important to determine whether the web page is dated, because many sites can be posted on the Internet and never change for years. If the page reports on research or current methods in literacy, it is important to make sure that, in fact, it is current. Look at the bottom of the page to see whether the author noted the last time it was updated.

◆ *Are there additional literacy resources available?* Are there additional resources for the student to explore? Are there additional resources for the parent/other teacher to use? Is this a site that provides rich resources to explore in literacy? Additional links provide the user with alternative information and allow for a deeper exploration of topics, skills, and research.

◆ *Is the site easy to use?* Does the site load quickly? Is it easy to navigate? Is it "user friendly" and easy to find different resources/pages? There is nothing more frustrating than waiting for a page to load, and then finding it difficult to use. The page should be designed to allow the user to find important information quickly.

◆ *How is the visual layout?* Is the site easy to read? Can you access the information you need quickly? Is it pleasing to look at? Are the images pleasing? Is the text laid out so it is easy to find information, or is it overloaded with text and images? Many pages are so crowded with graphics and information that the user does not know where to begin. This can be overwhelming for children, and cause them to be distracted. Another common problem with websites is the color scheme that is used to display background and text—it is difficult to read text on a dark or very busy background. This can also interfere with comprehension and be distracting.

◆ *What is the readability level?* Is the site written at a reading level that is appropriate for the audience who will use it? Is the site easy to read and comprehend? Is the vocabulary appropriate for the audience? This is an extremely important consideration for teachers. Too often children are trying to read web pages that are too advanced for their reading level; teachers would never assign a book or article to students that is too difficult for them to read, yet many teachers allow children to read websites beyond their reading level. This could lead to plagiarism because children who do not fully comprehend the text will be tempted to cut and paste it right into a document, rather than paraphrase the material.

◆ *Is the site accurate?* Are there spelling and grammar errors? Does the site appear to be well constructed and well written? Is the information accurate? A teacher needs to consider whether the information provided on a website reflects current practice in the field of literacy. The site should be written well and free of errors.

◆ *How are the links on the site?* Are the links valuable? Do they all work? Do they link to sites that are worthwhile? Keeping links current and working is difficult on the Internet because so many sites change their address frequently or are "shut down." Therefore, it is important to check the last time that the page was updated. If many of the links no longer work, it can be frustrating for the user, whether he or she is a student, teacher, or parent. It is also important to check all the links on a page before a student uses the site because many links change addresses and the teacher wants to be assured that the link takes the student to a safe, secure site.

◆ *Is the site biased?* Does the site display any bias toward a specific political or philosophical viewpoint? Is the site trying to "sell" something—an idea, a product, viewpoint, or political argument? Many sites have an ulterior motive and are biased, trying to sell something to the user. Children should not be exposed to sites that are trying to sell them something or convince them of a point of view. A good example

Literacy Website Evaluation Form

Name: _____   Date: _____

Website: _____   URL: _____

	5 Highly Recommend	4 Somewhat Recommend	3 Recommend	2 Barely Recommend	1 Not Recommend
1. Is literacy being promoted? Does the site promote literacy in one or more of the following: writing, phonics, word study, vocabulary, research skills, comprehension?					
2. Is the site age appropriate? Is the site appropriate for the grade level of the children who will use it?					
3. Does the site reflect current research in literacy? Does the site promote methods that support current research in literacy? Is the site current and up to date?					
4. Are there additional literacy resources available? Are there additional resources for the student to explore? Are there additional resources for the parent/other teacher to utilize? Does this site provide rich resources to explore in literacy?					
5. Ease of use: Does the site load easily? Is it easy to navigate? Does it load quickly?					

FIGURE 1-4A

continued

Literacy Website Evaluation Form—cont'd

	5 Highly Recommend	4 Somewhat Recommend	3 Recommend	2 Barely Recommend	I Not Recommend
6. Visual layout: Is the site easy to read, and can you access the information you need quickly? Is it pleasing to look at? Does it contain pleasing images?					
7. Readability level: Is the site written at a reading level that is appropriate for students who will use it? Is the site easy to read and comprehend?					
8. Accuracy: Are there spelling errors, grammar errors? Does the site seem well constructed and well written?					
9. Links: Are the links valuable? Do they all work? Do they link to sites that are worthwhile?					
10. Bias: Does the site display any bias toward a specific political or philosophical viewpoint? Is the site trying to "sell" you something—an idea, a product, a viewpoint?					
11. Worthwhile: Is this a site you would bookmark? Is it a site you believe is valuable and would come back to again? Would you use this site in your classroom to promote literacy?					

Comments about the site:

FIGURE 1-4B

of this occurred in a sixth grade classroom when a student was researching racism in the South as an introductory activity to *Roll of Thunder, Hear My Cry,* by Mildred Taylor. The student did a search on the Ku Klux Klan and excitedly went to the teacher after spending some time on the computer. "I found a great site, Mr. T!" she said to him. "Come and look." He went over to examine the site and found she had gone to the official site of the Ku Klux Klan. He quickly told her what that site was about and helped her with her search, also directing her to other books in the class.

Teachers need to teach students about bias in sites so they are aware of this. Many publishers have excellent sites to support teachers that provide extensive student and teacher resources; however, the teacher needs to be careful that these sites do not sell products and thus interfere with the literacy lesson. Teachers also need to be careful that the site they are visiting for research or professional development is not biased and does not promote political or philosophical ideology. The Internet is a wonderful, expansive repository of information, but the user must take care to be a selective consumer of that information.

◆ *Is the site worthwhile to use?* Would you come back to this site again? Would you use this site in your classroom to promote literacy? This is probably one of the most important criteria to consider, because if you consider the site worthwhile, you will bookmark it and want to go back and visit it again.

Evaluating Literacy Software Programs

Many of the same criteria that apply to evaluating literacy websites also apply to evaluating educational software that you can purchase from a company. It is important that before a teacher buys software, he or she has the opportunity to carefully evaluate it. Many of the reading and writing software packages are basic, providing a "drill and practice" or gaming format. It is important that the classroom computer has the correct specifications to run the software because many programs require a specific hardware configuration, a certain amount of memory, and often contain additional features such as a microphone that will need to be installed. A teacher must also be aware that many of the descriptions of programs in catalogues promise many different things but are really quite limited in scope. Therefore, a teacher must be a wise consumer of software products.

It is important that teachers evaluate websites and software programs themselves using the criteria listed earlier, or go to reliable sites that have already evaluated software programs and websites. Many school districts have lists of software products

STRATEGY BOX

Helping Students Achieve in Literacy

Miss Wilcox is very motivated to help her students achieve in their literacy skills. The following strategies will help her support all her students in their literacy development:

1. She uses the state standards and NCTE/IRA standards to develop instruction that is based on the emerging literacy abilities that her students bring to school.

2. She is creative and innovative in her literacy instruction, building on her students' strengths and areas of need.

3. She stresses reading, writing, speaking, listening, and visual literacy in her classroom throughout the year and across the curriculum.

4. She encourages higher order thinking so her students are challenged to use literacy to solve authentic problems.

5. She is sensitive to all children in her classroom and supports those who are just beginning to learn English, as well as those who have special learning needs.

6. She has developed a balanced approach to teaching literacy that includes shared reading of quality literature, class discussions, hands-on projects, and enjoying time spent together.

and websites that the district has already evaluated and approved. Different states and organizations also provide software evaluation reviews that may be helpful to the teacher. Critical analysis and evaluation of software and websites are mandatory steps that the teacher must conduct before any program is used in a lesson.

Final Thoughts

As you proceed through this textbook, it is important to keep in mind this new definition of literacy, which takes into account the changing demographics of our school-age children and the impact of an increasingly technological and global world on literacy. This definition should help guide your inquiries into what literacy means and how it should be taught in the classroom. In addition, the latest research in the field of literacy will inform best practices in the classroom and help you determine how literacy should be taught.

It is also important to keep in mind standards and how they are affecting literacy instruction across the country. Each state has its own conception of how literacy should be taught and assessed, based on scientifically based research and the impact of national standards set up by professional organizations such as IRA and NCTE. Technological literacy standards developed by the ISTE for students and teachers also impact the definition of literacy. These technology standards stress the importance of integrating technology into the content areas and incorporating them into literacy lessons.

Therefore, our definition of literacy includes reading, writing, speaking, listening, visual literacy, and technological literacy. It is important to stress higher order thinking skills in the classroom by incorporating challenging activities that require children to use literacy as a tool to solve problems, think critically, and evaluate ideas. It is also important to place literacy within the context of global issues and concerns so that our children become world citizens prepared to meet the challenges of an interdependent and multifaceted society. Our children need to be competent in the new literacies that the twenty-first century requires.

Chapter 2 expands on our new definition of literacy by exploring how a teacher can integrate technology into the literacy classroom. It discusses electronic forms of communication, such as e-mail, instant messaging, and the Internet, and how these tools are altering the ways we communicate with others. Chapter 3 explores a balanced approach to literacy and describes recommended strategies to teaching literacy in the classroom. Once a balanced literacy classroom is conceptualized, this book describes the various components that comprise a balanced approach: phonological and phonemic awareness, phonics instruction, comprehension strategies, vocabulary instruction, writing instruction, and incorporating literature into the classroom.

EXPLORATION   Application of Concepts

Activities

1. Go to the *Literacy for Children in an Information Age* premium website for this chapter (http://www.cengage.com/login) and look up your state's English/Language Arts standards. Compare your state's standards to the national NCTE/IRA standards. Then compare your state's standards with three other states' standards and determine how those states define literacy. Also become familiar with the ISTE NETS for students and teachers, and discuss how this affects your definition of literacy. Additional teacher resources on electronic literacy can be found on the companion website.

2. In groups, write down how you think today's population of children is different from students who attended elementary school 20 years ago. Write a list of characteristics of today's children that are different from 20 years ago. Determine how that might change the way literacy is taught in the classroom.

3. Visit this chapter of the *Literacy for Children in an Information Age* premium website at http://www.cengage.com/login. Explore different types of electronic literacy software products listed, including Talking Books, electronically supported reading, electronically supported writing, and electronic speech-to-text conversion. Write a brief description of each product you review and explain how it can be used to support literacy in the classroom.

4. Develop a semantic map of your "new" definition of literacy. Discuss your definition in groups, and then share it with the class. Have the class develop its own definition of literacy, and then relate it to the state English/Language Arts standards. This should be a good introductory overview of the course and guide future discussions throughout the course.

HOME–SCHOOL CONNECTION   Parents are Teachers, Too!

A home–school connection is pivotal to a child's academic success in school. Parents and guardians need to be informed of the instruction and techniques that are being taught and used with their children in school. If informed, they can use similar strategies with their child to reinforce material and skills learned through the academic school day.

Here are five ways to stay connected with each student's home life:

1. Send a packet home each time a new unit or skill is being introduced. For example, when starting a unit on teaching a phonic skill, send home a letter written in English and Spanish (or other native language) to explain tips that might help a child practice the new phonic skill at home at night.

2. At Back to School Night, introduce parents and guardians to the class or school website. When parents and guardians navigate the site either at home or at the library, it is helpful if they find activities and additional information that correspond to current and past skills. It is also worthwhile to send home a newsletter that contains similar literacy games that children can play at home.

3. Keep parents and guardians informed of the state and national standards that the teacher is addressing in day-to-day instruction. It may be helpful to send home a copy of the standards or to provide a link on the class website.

4. Share with parents and guardians any game or activity that the students may be doing at school that helped them master a skill. This demonstrates to students that what they do at school is valued and important because it can be shared at home with family members.

5. Communicate frequently with parents and guardians and give them feedback on how their children are achieving in the classroom. Keep a record of this in a "parent–teacher communication" book. Suggest skills to work on at home and encourage parents and guardians to write back with any concerns, feedback, and successes that they have had with their child.

The home–school connection is a critical component of a child's academic success, because children learn that their teachers and families are working together for their educational benefit.

Based upon writings of Jennifer Tack—Resource Room Teacher

2 NEW LITERACIES: FROM E-MAIL TO THE INTERNET

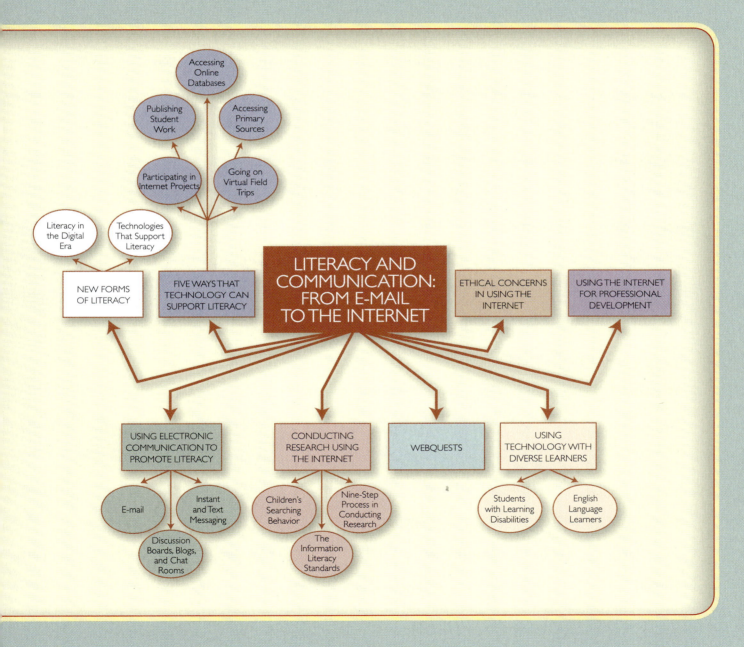

Key Terms

new literacies
Internet projects
virtual field trips
primary sources
online databases
online libraries
instant messaging
asynchronous
synchronous
e-mail
discussion boards
community of learners
chat rooms
search engine
plagiarism
searching strategies
keyword
WebQuests
assistive technology
Acceptable Use Policy

Focus Questions

1. How are new electronic forms of communication changing the way we define the term *literacy*? What new "literacies" should children be developing in response to new technological tools of communication?

2. What are five different ways that technology can be integrated into the literacy classroom?

3. How can e-mail promote literacy in the classroom?

4. Why is it so important that children be taught appropriate strategies for using the Internet for research?

5. What are WebQuests and how do they promote higher order thinking skills?

6. What ethical concerns do teachers need to consider when using the Internet?

7. How can the Internet promote professional development for teachers?

Welcome to Mr. Mancuso's Fifth Grade Classroom: Using Technology in the Literacy Program

Tim Pannell/Flirt/CORBIS

Mr. Mancuso is working with his fifth grade class on a unit entitled "Economics and the Environment." His school is located in a city predominately composed of recent immigrants from the Dominican Republic and Colombia, and the majority of his students are English language learners. He has three computers located in the back of the room and is implementing a problem-based WebQuest that he has developed. The students will work in teams to solve a real-life problem that was originally written up in the *New York Times*. The problem is whether the Mexican government should develop a salt mine in a pristine lagoon, thereby providing needed jobs to the local economy, or maintain this lagoon as a preserve for whales that travel thousands of miles from Alaska to mate there. The students will go through various steps to solve this problem, including conducting research on the Internet, e-mailing a pen pal in Mexico, going on a virtual fieldtrip to Mexico, calculating and charting the migration path of the whales using online documents and primary sources, and reading literature about whales and Mexico. Each team must present its solution to the teacher at the end of the unit. After these presentations, the teacher will read the follow-up article in the *New York Times* that explains what the Mexican government finally decided to do—maintain this lagoon as a preserve. Mr. Mancuso has chosen this WebQuest because he believes that many of the students can relate to the cultural background, he wants them to use their native language to communicate with students in Mexico, and he wants them to learn more about South America.

Before beginning this WebQuest, Mr. Mancuso instructs the class on how to search for material on the Internet, how to evaluate whether the information is reliable and appropriate, and how to use the information so they are not just copying and pasting directly from the original source. He has made up a series of lessons with accompanying visual tools and charts to fill in as they progress through the unit. The teams are required to create a product for each lesson, which will be handed in and graded. Some of the products are multimedia presentations using PowerPoint software, some are research summaries from work on the Internet, and some are maps and charts that needed to be filled in.

Mr. Mancuso has divided his class into six teams of four students, trying to group those who are more proficient in English with those who are more proficient in Spanish. He believes both languages will help the group in their activities and research. For the first lesson, which involves learning about Mexico—its geography, major cities, and location in relation to the United States—three teams work on the computer to obtain information about Mexico, and the other three teams work on different activities as a group using other resources, such as maps, books, magazines, travel brochures, podcasts, a digital camera, and videotapes. Each group has structured activities to complete. As the groups work, Mr. Mancuso moves around the classroom, offering help and guidance to different groups. He monitors all groups closely and makes sure that the teams on the computers are visiting sites that they can read and comprehend, and that contain relevant information. He also gives the students strategies to help them comprehend text on the Internet and shows them how to find and access information. He makes sure that the English language learners are contributing and given opportunities to discuss and share ideas in English.

After 30 minutes, he asks the teams to switch: the three teams working on the computers continue at their desks, while the other groups get a chance to use the computers. All three computers are set up with Write: OutLoud software (Don Johnston, Inc.), which is a "talking word processor" that provides support for struggling readers and writers. If the teams choose to write up their research, this software will help.

The class continues working on this WebQuest for approximately two weeks. At the conclusion of the unit, Mr. Mancuso asks parents, the principal, other teachers, and community members to become part of the "United Nations Environmental Council." On a designated day, each team presents its multimedia PowerPoint presentation outlining its research and recommendations to the "United Nations Environmental Council."

This scenario shows how a teacher can promote new literacies by integrating technology into a problem-based unit plan that incorporates literacy, social studies, math, and science. By using a "real problem" from current events, students learn how to use literacy to solve problems and think critically. They learn how to use technology as a tool to research information, write reports, and make professional presentations that are engaging and fun. The following sections will provide an in-depth look at how teachers can integrate technology into a literacy program, even with only a few computers available in the classroom.

New Forms of Literacy

Literacy in the Digital Era

Electronic forms of communication, such as e-mail, text messaging, social networking and blogs, are drastically altering our concept of literacy and how we communicate with others. It is the Internet, however, that has brought unprecedented changes to the way in which people spend their time and access information. No previous technology has been adopted so quickly and by so many people in such a short period of time. No previous technology has impacted the way people read and process text by connecting us to the greatest repository of information in the history of civilization (Coiro, Knobel, Lankshear, & Leu, 2008; Leu, O'Bryne, Zawilinski, McVerry, and Everett-Cacopardo, 2009). This rapid expansion of the Internet has contributed to the notion that the way people read, communicate, and process information will change rapidly as the technology changes, and that literacies will continuously be new, multiple, and rapidly disseminated (Coiro, et al., 2008). The term **new literacies** implies that new technologies are continuously emerging that will require students to read text and comprehend meaning in different ways, using different processes.

Technology always affects the way we communicate and disseminate information, and in turn, it affects the task of reading and writing and how we define the term *literacy* (Reinking, 1997). As Leu (2001) argues, what it means to be literate is continuously changing as new technologies of literacy rapidly appear in our global society. This creates new opportunities, as well as new challenges, for literacy educators. Our primary question should not be, "How do we teach our children to be literate?" but rather, "How do we help children be literate in the new literacies that are emerging?" With globalization drastically changing the way we work and view the world, everyone must be literate in identifying important information, gathering and evaluating information, using the information to solve problems, and clearly communicating the solution (Leu, 2001).

Literacy educators cannot expect others to teach these new literacies in a different classroom or computer laboratory. Educators must reflect about how technology affects reading and writing, which, in turn, will affect our concept of literacy and how it should be taught. Often, the concept of literacy is confined to print-based materials, and literacy teachers believe that technology detracts from their prime mission—to encourage children to read books, magazines, and newspapers and to develop a lifelong love for reading. In fact, today, 93 percent of teens use the Internet and 70 percent of online teens use some sort of social networking site (Jones & Fox, 2009). Children, teens, and adults read more on the Internet today than they do print materials, whether it be through instant messages, e-mails, text messages, or web pages. What guidelines should we teach students to follow in composing and reading e-mail messages? Is proofreading for accurate spelling as critical when using a computer (Reinking, 1997)? How do we teach children to carefully evaluate the vast amount of information they find on the Internet? How do children effectively navigate through web pages to find the information they want? These are all key questions that should help determine how literacy is being taught in our classrooms.

Technologies That Support Literacy

Some of the different technologies that support literacy in the classroom are as follows:

◆ *Electronic books:* Electronic books, also known as *e-books,* have become increasingly popular in recent years, especially with the new devices that have been designed to read electronic text, such as the Kindle (from Amazon.com). There are over 24,000 e-books for sale on Amazon.com alone. Titles can be read on a special device, on some smart cellphones, and on a personal computer. Google is in the process of digitizing millions of books so they will be available to read electronically. The Internet provides a wide variety of full-text material online, including books, plays, short stories, magazines, and reference materials (see Chapter 10 for a more detailed discussion of e-books).

◆ *Podcasts:* Podcasts are an excellent way to supplement instruction in any content area and to provide struggling readers with the audio component of a text. Mobile learning is changing the way that content is delivered. Many students have mobile access, not just with iPod players, but also with smart phone devices and portable computers. There are sites on the Internet that provide podcasts for educators to use or instruction on how to create your own podcast:

    ◆ The Education Podcast Network: http://epnweb.org/

    ◆ Education Podcast: http://education.podcast.com/

    ◆ Poducateme: http://poducateme.com/

Students develop effective literacy skills by using technology.

Courtesy of Guilherme Cunha

◆ *Electronic Talking Books:* Electronic Talking Books, also known as CD-ROM storybooks, are electronic texts that provide embedded speech and interactive features on the screen. Many children's books have been converted to Electronic Talking Books in which digitized speech reads the selection aloud and different objects on the screen provide interactive activities. According to some research, the use of talking books has shown positive results in improving comprehension of texts and decoding skills (Holum & Gahala, 2003). They also are motivating for young readers who enjoy interacting with their favorite characters on the screen. (See Chapter 11 for a more detailed discussion of Electronic Talking Books).

Teachers' VOICES   Using Technology in the Classroom

I use technology to keep my classroom organized and well managed. The majority of our assessments are created on my computer. My grade book is on Microsoft Excel, and I interact with my students outside of the classroom for homework help via the Internet.

It is apparent that a goal for many districts is to have computers in every classroom, and as a teacher, I cannot wait for this to occur in my district.

—*Jennifer Hendershot, Sixth Grade Teacher*

◆ *Word processing:* Word processing has probably had the greatest effect on literacy instruction than any other technological device. It has drastically changed the way we write and conceptualize the writing process. Although it requires basic keyboarding skills, word processing has made it easier for writers to compose and revise their work. Such tools as spelling checkers and grammar checkers are useful devices that help improve student writing. Research has shown that students who use word processors write longer papers, spend more time writing and revising, and show improved mechanics and word choice (Holum & Gahala, 2003). Research also shows that using a word processor does not replace the need for effective writing instruction on the part of the teacher. Students need to be guided carefully and provided with constant feedback throughout the process (see Chapter 8 for an in-depth discussion of technology's impact on the writing process).

◆ *Multimedia composing:* Many software programs allow students to combine text, graphics, digital photographs, animation, video, and music in one composition. A popular program is HyperStudio, and schools are using PowerPoint to accomplish this as well. The final multimedia product can be combined into an interactive program or a slide show. Students find these programs highly motivating. Multimedia composing programs allow students to use many different forms of expression while supporting reading and writing skills.

◆ *Software programs to reinforce reading/writing skills:* There are many different software programs that reinforce reading and writing skills through drill and practice, gaming, and instruction. Many of these programs are motivating to students and are excellent ways to provide reinforcement of skills, strategies, and processes taught in the classroom.

◆ *Digital photography and video production:* With the advent of inexpensive digital cameras and cell phones, students can easily take pictures and then incorporate them into their own writing, whether they are researching a report for the teacher to read or creating a web page to share on a social networking site. Digital images have become ubiquitous and easy to create. Cell phones have become an easy way to take digital pictures, which are quickly sent electronically for others to view and use. With the use of editing software, such as Adobe Photoshop, students can take digital photographs, edit them, and insert them into a multimedia production, a written essay, or a creative story. They can create a poster, a montage, a travel brochure, a book jacket, or an illustrated story. Digital video cameras also have become quite popular and allow students to express themselves through different learning styles other than traditional text-based activities. Students can create documentaries, advertisements, stories, cooking shows, research reports, and interviews using video cameras and editing software. These productions then can be viewed separately or incorporated into web pages.

◆ *Blogs and wikis:* A blog is an interactive web page where individuals post entries, articles, links, and pictures, and ask others to join in conversations. Some students and teachers use them as vehicles to develop critical thinking, reading, and writing skills. Wikis are collaborative tools that allow users to create and edit online content. Teachers can develop wikis that collaborative groups can use to share their research and ideas as the project progresses. (See Chapter 8 for more information on blogs and wikis.)

◆ *SmartBoard:* A SmartBoard system consists of a touch-sensitive white board connected to a projector and computer. Teachers can run any computer application to appear on the Smartboard and can interact with that application using just a finger. Teachers can use many different applications in all content areas, including literacy. (See Chapter 14 for a more in-depth discussion on how to use a SmartBoard in the classroom.)

◆ *Streaming video:* Sites such as YouTube (http://www.youtube.com) have become a wonderful depository of streaming video clips that can be used in the classroom. Teachers can access educational video clips from many different sites, such as The Discovery Channel (http://streaming.discoveryeducation.com/) and the Learning Tube (http://mylearningtube.com/). These videos can be used to develop prior knowledge, enhance comprehension of a topic, and reinforce content that the students previously learned in class.

◆ *Internet-based activities:* The Internet has grown into a vast resource that provides almost unlimited access to information from all over the world, and there are many different ways that literacy teachers can use this tool. From conducting online searches using search engines to communicating via e-mail, students use literacy skills to conduct authentic, real-world activities. Perhaps of all of the technologies, the Internet has the greatest potential to impact the classroom and change the way we conceptualize literacy instruction. Today, educators and students can access global curriculum-based materials at any time of the day, engage in class discussion with other students across the world, share real-time data on volcano eruptions or earthquakes, partake in pen pal activities using e-mail, collaborate on class projects with other classes, and publish student work online. All these activities are becoming more and more commonplace and need to be incorporated into our literacy classrooms. The following section describes five different ways that Internet technology can be incorporated into the literacy classroom.

Literacy instruction, activities, and projects that utilize technology— like student video production— enhance children's visual literacy.

Teachers' VOICES Using Technology to Teach Literacy

I have been using a great deal of technology to teach literacy in my classroom. I use a commercial reading program that had an enormous technological component. The students read and record passages into the computer; have passages read to them through headphones on the computer; take various assessments in reading, vocabulary, and spelling on the computer; and listen to background information clips before reading stories. I also use books on tape, word processing on the computer for writing, and the Internet to look up pictures of unknown nouns while the class was reading a story. I will continue to use these techniques in my classroom for both motivational and academic reasons. If I am teaching the lower grades, perhaps I can incorporate phonics using technology programs as well.

—*Heather Bruno, Seventh Grade Teacher*

Ways in Which Technology Can Promote Literacy

Because of the vast potential of the Internet to impact literacy instruction and change the way that teaching and learning occurs in our society, it is important to examine how it can be integrated into literacy instruction. Both teachers and students are affected by these new online literacies (Hagood, 2003) that are having such a dramatic effect on our students' lives outside of the classroom. Literacy teachers can use the following five activities to help integrate technology into literacy instruction:

1. Participate in Internet projects
2. Go on virtual field trips
3. Publish student work
4. Access primary sources
5. Access online libraries and databases

Internet Projects

Internet projects engage children in classrooms at different locations in collaborative work to solve a common problem or explore a common topic (Leu, 2001). Classrooms across the country and world share information and collaborate in completing the project. These collaborative projects are "hosted" by a particular teacher or school and are designed for classrooms as young as kindergarten. Internet projects allow children to collaborate on a common problem or theme and share their work with classrooms at different locations. They learn to problem solve, gather information, and communicate electronically, which are all activities they will need experience with when they enter the world of work.

Leu (2001) claims there are at least two different types of Internet projects: permanent and temporary website projects. Permanent projects are coordinated by an individual or group through a website and continue over the course of years. Classes can continue to participate and share student work that has accumulated over the years. Temporary Internet projects involve those projects that are developed by individual teachers to address a specific curriculum need. The teacher will try to find collaborating classrooms to participate in the project, and usually these classrooms complete the project together and share their work.

An example of a collaborative project was the "Cinderella Project," where participating classes read multicultural versions of Cinderella. After reading the story, students engaged in language arts, social studies, math, or science activities that were showcased on a website. Each year different Internet projects are hosted by teachers throughout the country and world. Teachers can use the Internet projects listed in the following to engage students in motivating literacy activities. Many additional teacher resources on Internet

Additional teacher resources can be found on the *Literacy for Children in an Information Age* Book premium website for this chapter (http://www.cengage.com/login).

projects are found on the *Literacy for Children in an Information Age* Book premium website for this chapter (http://www.cengage.com/login). Other Internet projects include:

Flat Stanley

http://www.flatstanley.com/how.html

The Flat Stanley project is based on the book *Flat Stanley* by Jeff Brown (1996, Harper-Collins). In this book, Stanley Lambchop is flattened by a falling bulletin board. He then finds many adventures ahead of him when his parents mail him to California in an envelope. In this project, small groups of children make a Flat Stanley on paper, contribute several entries to a journal, and then mail their work to a collaborating class. The recipient class responds to the journal entries and sends it back to the first classroom or can send it to other classrooms, thereby creating a chain. Many of the journal entries are done via e-mail.

My Hero Project

http://myhero.com/home.asp

The My Hero project allows classrooms to share whom they consider heroes and heroines. Students can read about the heroes and heroines that other classes have posted, and then they can write about their own personal hero or heroine.

Mrs. McGowan's Site

http://www.mrsmcgowan.com/projects/index.html

Mrs. McGowan's website hosts many different current Internet projects for elementary classrooms. A current list of projects and projects from previous years are listed and can be explored.

Virtual Field Trips

Students take a **virtual field trip** by visiting sites that record a series of events as they are happening or provide the student with an experience of being in a new setting. A class can visit a website that has a camera hooked up to a computer so the students can watch birds being hatched. Students can partake on a journey with someone who is recording data as part of a field expedition or trip. An example of this is a site hosted by a university; each year a professor visits a rainforest and records his or her stay there with pictures and allows students to correspond with him or her via e-mail. Students can take a journey into the rainforest together with this professor who is recording his or her adventures. Virtual field trips are excellent activities to supplement reading informational text (see Chapter 12 for a description of informational text). They provide a concrete way to extend and enrich informational text that children are reading as part of the literacy curriculum or in math, science, and social studies.

Virtual field trips have three main focuses. First, the virtual field trip may be created before the actual trip the students will take. Teachers can prepare students for the adventure they will have and help them focus on particular points of interest that they should key in on. The teacher can send the students to the "field trip" site and have them explore various concepts and points of interest. This will build up background knowledge and better prepare the students for the upcoming actual trip. It will also help the students become motivated about the trip, especially if the virtual field trip has an accompanying written guide to foster questions and structure the experience for the students. Second, a virtual field trip can also be created after the actual trip. This type of web experience reinforces the concepts taught and also serves as a type of "online scrapbook" for the trip. Third, the last type of virtual field trip is just that, virtual. The students do not actually go on a trip, but visit a destination via the Internet. These pages make the students feel that they are actually visiting the location. Videos, graphics, sounds, and photographs are often used on these pages to help create the effect of visiting the location. This is an excellent way of bringing locations that the students are unable to visit right into the classroom. In all cases, it is recommended that the "field trip" be structured and guided so that the students learn specific objectives from their visit.

The sites listed in the following can be used in a classroom and incorporated into literacy activities. Students can write up a summary of what they saw, develop a travel brochure, critique the site, and develop a webliography of links that lists further resources available on the Internet to learn more about the topic or location visited.

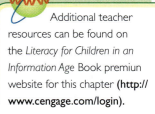

Virtual Field Trips Hosted by Utah Educational Network

http://www.uen.org/utahlink/tours

Easter Island Tour by *NOVA* and PBS

http://www.pbs.org/wgbh/nova/easter/textindex.html

Visit the White House

http://www.whitehouse.gov/kids/tour

Visit the Kremlin

http://www.kremlin.museum.ru/main_en.asp

Visit a Virtual Cave

http://www.goodearthgraphics.com/virtcave

Visit Graceland, Elvis Presley's home

http://www.photo.net/summer94/graceland.html

Visit a Virtual Volcano

http://volcano.oregonstate.edu/kids/adventure/index.html

http://www.field-guides.com/tours/sci/volcano/_tourlaunch1.htm

An example of how a teacher can take students on a virtual field trip after reading a book is by having a group of students who are interested in art read the award-winning book *Seurat and La Grande Jatte: Connecting the Dots* by Robert Burleigh. After they finish reading the book, the students can join their literature circle to discuss the book and their interpretations, feelings, and impressions. The students then can take a virtual field trip to the Louvre Museum in Paris, France (http://www.louvre.fr/llv/commun/home.jsp), which has a collection of Seurat paintings and drawings. It can be quite exciting and motivating to many students to see a famous museum's collection. Another example is after children finish reading the book *Secrets of the Sphinx*, written by James Cross Giblin and illustrated by Bagram Ibatoulline, they can go on a virtual field trip to the Tomb of Tutankhamen (http://ngm.nationalgeographic.com/ngm/tut/mysteries/index.html); this site is hosted by National Geographic.

Many different sites offer links to virtual field trips, and a search using a search engine such as Google (http://www.google.com) will yield many different "field trips"; a class can use the specific location as the keyword or search under the keyword phrase "virtual field trip."

Publishing Student Work

Many sites allow students to publish their work online. This can be a great incentive for students to become authors and experience what it is like to publish written material. Teachers can use this as part of the publishing phase of the writing process. Not all children will feel comfortable with submitting their work to be published online, and the teacher should carefully select and work with those children who choose to do so. It is helpful for the teacher to initially introduce the websites as part of a literacy lesson, so that children can first read other students' published work and the class can start to feel comfortable with the layout and navigation of the website.

Examples of how a teacher could incorporate publishing student work into the classroom are as follows:

- After students complete a writing assignment, the teacher might suggest that they publish their work at the sites listed in the following section. The teacher should have the students go to the sites first and read the articles that have been submitted by other students. There should be a match between the magazine and the type of article that the students have written. Many of these magazines are excellent resources for reading and increasing literacy skills, even if the students choose not to submit their own work.

- Individual students who show particular interest in writing should be encouraged to pursue publishing their work online.

- Students should be encouraged to review books that others in the class might be interested in reading. These reviews can be submitted to various online magazines and published.

Teachers use the websites listed in the following section to share stories and poems online. Many additional teacher resources on publishing student work can be found on the *Literacy for Children in an Information Age* Book premium website for this chapter (http://www.cengage.com/login). See Chapter 8 for more information and other websites on publishing student work.

recommended websites for children to share stories and poems online

Kids Can Publish University

http://www.fivestarpublications.com/kidscanpublish/

This website is designed to promote student authors. Students can submit their best writing entry, photograph, illustration, or cartoon strip to the site's monthly contests.

Weekly Reader

http://www.weeklyreader.com

Weekly Reader promotes reading and writing literacy for students in all grades. The site has interesting and fun writing activities where students can submit their work, and if chosen, have published online.

Topics Online Magazine for Learners of English

http://www.topics-mag.com

This site is an online magazine where English language learners can express their ideas and opinions on topics of interest to them. Readers can explore an international world. This is a great site for ELLs to read what other students who are learning English have to say and also to publish their own pieces on various topics of interest.

The Poetry Forge

http://www.poetryforge.org

This site provides many tools for both teachers and students to create poetry and share it with others. There are poetry generators and open forums where students can share their ideas and poems.

Primary Sources

A great advantage to the Internet is the access it provides to original documents that have been digitized and are now available to the public free of charge. This is a wonderful opportunity for students to read actual letters by authors, view original documents, and get a glimpse of history in the making. What are primary sources and how can they be used in a literacy classroom? **Primary sources** are literally billions of items that are evidence of our daily lives; but most of these items are lost, destroyed, or never documented. Fortunately, many clues about the past—primary sources—do survive, and we use them to learn about bygone times. Primary sources can include newspapers, maps, documents, photographs, music clips, film clips, advertisements, journals, diaries, cartoons, and artifacts. Many online sites have archived collections of primary source materials. Many of these items are quite exciting and can be used in an elementary classroom. They include wonderful photographs, video images, sound clips, and text documents of which children can take advantage. Some suggestions for using primary sources in the literacy classroom are:

◆ Have students select a historical image or film footage of a street scene. Have the students give written or oral description of the sights, sounds, and smells that surround the scene, presenting evidence from the photograph itself and other sources about the time period. Examine the image to find clues about the economics and commerce of the time. This can be adapted to meet the needs of any age group.

◆ Have students choose a sample of a primary source cookbook from a different time period. Have them research a recipe for a common food (for example, bread, cake) in the cookbook, and then report on differences in the vocabulary of the cookbooks over time. How have terms for measurement, ingredients, portion size, and accompaniments changed? Prepare the food from recipes from two of the time periods. Hold a taste test of the end results.

◆ Have students choose a sample of a primary source advertisement from a different time period. Examine the fashion trends, household articles, and lifestyles of a particular period. Use other sources of information to reconstruct a picture of family life at that time.

◆ Have students research a historical figure and look up primary source material that can accompany the report, such as photographs of the person, photographs of the time period, film clips, audio footage of speeches, and textual documents.

◆ Have students research firsthand accounts of journals, letters, and diaries written by children or young people (for example, *Diary of Anne Frank*). Have students begin keeping their own journals with an emphasis on including current events topics in their entries.

www Additional teacher resources can be found on the *Literacy for Children in an Information Age* Book premium website for this chapter (**http://www.cengage.com/login**).

websites of primary sources that elementary and middle school children will find enjoyable

American Memory

http://memory.loc.gov/ammem/index.html

American Memory is hosted by the Library of Congress and is an online archive of more than 100 collections of rare and unique items important to America's heritage. The collections contain more than 7 million primary source documents, photographs, films, and recordings that reflect the collective American memory. They contain unique personal items from another period in time—old records, letters with exquisite penmanship and arcane language, clothing, keepsakes, or faded photographs. These collections are "snapshots" providing a glimpse into America's past.

The Learning Page

http://memory.loc.gov/ammem/ndlpedu/index.html

The learning page is designed especially to help teachers use and integrate American Memory into the classroom. It contains lesson plans, features, and themes that teachers can easily incorporate into curriculum units.

U.S. National Archives and Records Administration

http://www.archives.gov/index.html

The National Archives and Records Administration (NARA) is an independent federal agency that preserves U.S. history and oversees the management of all federal records. The cornerstone documents of our government can be accessed at this site: the Declaration of Independence, the Constitution of the United States, and the Bill of Rights. NARA is a public trust on which our democracy depends and enables people to inspect for themselves the records of our government.

Primary Sources at Yale

http://www.yale.edu/collections_collaborative/primarysources/

This site provides primary sources within all of Yale's 22 libraries as well as at the Peabody Museum of Natural History, the Yale Center for British Art, and the Yale Art Gallery.

New York Public Library Digital Library Collection

http://digital.nypl.org

The New York Public Library has developed a searchable database of visual materials documenting culture studies and social history internationally from the ancient world to the present. It contains over 600,000 images from the arts, humanities, performing arts, and sciences, including artwork, maps, photographs, prints, manuscripts, illustrated books, and printed ephemera. The collection contains digital podcasts that can be downloaded, streaming video, animated talking picture books, video storybooks, and many e-books that are being digitized by Google. Picture Collection Online (http://digital.nypl.org/mmpco) contains 30,000 digitized images from books, magazines, and newspapers, as well as original photographs, prints, and postcards, mostly created before 1923. A search for the word "hats" brought up approximately 20 images of old cartoons, photographs, and advertisements about hats. This is a very exciting and rewarding site to explore.

When accessing primary source material, it may be important that children learn where the author got the documents. The best sites clearly state the source of the original material and verify that the source is an authentic primary source. Figure 2–1 lists some ways that students can determine the origins of primary sources.

The Internet is an excellent repository of primary source material that students will find motivating and interesting. These original documents provide students with real-world artifacts that address national and local standards.

Online Libraries and Databases

The age of the card catalog is long past and students need to know how to use **online databases** and catalogs to access materials and books. Whether they are accessing a local library's online holdings or visiting the Library of Congress webite, students need to know what is available to them, how to access the material, and how to retrieve it.

Some suggestions for how teachers can incorporate **online libraries** and databases into the literacy classroom include:

◆ Conduct "author studies" and have children research books by a particular author. The students then choose a particular book that they would like to read.

Determining the Origin of a Primary Source

If you have accessed a primary source online, it may be important to determine where the author got the documents. The best sites clearly state the source of the original material. Different factors need to be considered based on the format of the document and type of site:

- **Scanned image of a document**

  The image of scanned documents usually illustrates what the original documents look like. The origin of the documents at a website may be determined by the creator of the website. For example, the Library of Congress website generally supplies documents from its own manuscript collections, but providing in-house documents is not always possible. Sometimes, websites will present texts from other document collections, or may provide links to documents at other websites.

- **Transcribed document**

  Transcribed documents do not illustrate the original image of the document but only provide the content in plain text format. It is important to discover the original source of transcribed documents to determine whether the transcription is complete and accurate. The source, which may be the original documents or published editions, should be cited.

- **Links to external documents**

  "Metasites" that link to external documents require you to track down the original website for the documents for evaluation purposes. A reliable website may link to a document in another not so reliable site and vice versa.

(Written by the Instruction & Research Services Committee of the Reference and User Service Association History Section in the American Library Association. Available at:http://www.lib.washington.edu/sub ject/History/RUSA)

FIGURE 2-1

- Have children use the online libraries to research books on a specific topic that different cultures may cover. For example, many different books cover the Cinderella or the Little Red Riding Hood theme. Another example is that many cultures have different myths and folktales that students can explore. The teacher might also choose the theme of "cooking" and explore how different cultures cover this in their literature. Children can use the online databases to find books that address the theme.

- Assign a variety of books, ask the students to find reviews of these books online, and then choose one book that sounds interesting. Many of the sites listed in the following section have book reviews.

- Research all the authors of children's literature that live in one particular geographic area. Correlate this to the social studies curriculum if the students are studying a particular area in the United States, or explore authors who live in the same state as the students.

- During a research project, assign students to visit the online reference desk listed in the following section as one of the first steps in finding resources; the students can explore the resources listed there as part of their research.

- Encourage students to go to their local town, county, or state online catalog of books that teaches them how to locate books and take books out from home. Most libraries have many different online services that will facilitate finding books and ensure that the books are available or in local libraries.

online libraries and databases that teachers can use in the literacy classroom

The Internet Public Library (IPL)

http://www.ipl.org/

The IPL is an internet-based public library founded at the University of Michigan School of Information and hosted by Drexel University. It offers a wealth of resources for all content areas and has a Kidspace and Teenspace.

Librarians' Internet Index (IIL)

http://www.lii.org/

Librarians' Internet Index (LII) is a publicly funded website and weekly newsletter serving California, the nation, and the world. Every Thursday morning the site sends out a free newsletter, *New This Week*, which features dozens of high-quality websites carefully selected, described, and organized by a team of librarians. Topics include current events and issues, holidays and seasons, helpful tools for information users, human interest, and more.

International Children's Digital Library

http://www.icdlbooks.org

The International Children's Digital Library offers children many books from different countries. Children can search for books using a keyword, author, or title and can read the books online. This collection specializes in books from all over the world, including places such as Croatia, Egypt, Japan, New Zealand, the United States, and more.

Bookhive: Your Guide to Children's Literature and Books

http://www.plcmc.org/bookhive/

Bookhive is a website designed for children that contains hundreds of book reviews written on a variety of reading levels and addressing many different interest areas. The reviews are written by the staff of the Public Library of Charlotte-Mecklenburg County and submitted to a team of children's librarians for editing and posting. The titles reviewed are staff recommendations from books already in the library's collection. At least 12 new reviews appear each month in the various categories. This is a great site for children to pick out books that interest them because there are comments written by children about each book.

The Project Gutenberg

http://www.gutenberg.org/wiki/Main_Page

Project Gutenberg is the first and largest single collection of free electronic books, or e-books. The collection was produced by thousands of volunteers. There are over 27,000 free e-books in the Project Gutenberg Online Book Catalog, and over 100,000 titles available at Project Gutenberg Partners, Affiliates, and Resources.

Refdesk.com

http://www.refdesk.com

Refdesk is a website that indexes Internet sites and provides a wide variety of information in many different subject areas. This site is hosted by a private individual who lists the criteria for choosing his sites: They are free, the author's credentials are available and valid, the information is objective and does not contain any biases, and the links are updated regularly. This is a good site for teachers or children to use when they are beginning to research various topics, searching for additional primary sources, or needing more information in one area.

   These five different ways to integrate technology in the literacy classroom—participating in Internet projects, going on virtual field trips, publishing student work, accessing primary sources, and accessing online libraries—are all excellent ways to connect reading and writing to different technologies that support authentic reading, writing, collaboration, student-centered learning, and interdisciplinary approaches to learning. These strategies will help teachers use these new tools as part of the literacy curriculum so that children are taught how to use technology effectively. Teachers will help children become literate in identifying important information, gathering and evaluating information, using information to solve problems, and communicating solutions. The literacy curriculum will promote new forms of literacy that are integral to our new global society.

Using Electronic Communication to Promote Literacy

The Internet is having a major impact on how people interact and communicate with each other. Electronic means of communication from e-mail, text messaging, chat rooms, to **instant messaging (IM)** are drastically changing the way that communication functions in society. Within this new paradigm of learning, educators are increasingly emphasizing the importance of electronic communication within the classroom to promote digital literacy practices (Cohen, 2003). Electronic communication is quite beneficial in education in that it is not restricted to time and place and is primarily visual and textual, rather than aural. This allows for the following results: (1) increased accessibility to information and the ongoing dialogue about the information; (2) more pedagogically sound interaction with the information by students; (3) more thoughtful discussion by students about the information; (4) more equal participation in the ongoing discussion by all students; (5) enhanced student interaction outside of class; (6) unique classroom assessment techniques; (7) archival and retrieval of students' work; and (8) access to diverse sources of information via the World Wide Web (Cohen, 2003). This type of communication is called **asynchronous** because it does not take place in real time; rather, users can send e-mail or post a message on a discussion board and read and respond at a later time. This is in contrast with **synchronous** communication, which occurs in real time like a true conversation; all parties are present, and their interaction and response is immediate.

E-mail in the Literacy Classroom

E-mail is one of the most popular form of electronic communication, especially among adults. A study conducted in 2008 shows that the worldwide installed base of active mailboxes will increase from 2 billion in 2008 to over 2.7 billion in 2012. This represents an average annual growth rate of 8 percent over the next four years. (Radicati Group, 2008). More than 90 percent of Internet users between 18 and 72 said they send and receive e-mail, making it the top online activity (just ahead of search engines), according to Pew Internet & American Life Project (Jones & Fox, 2009). The average e-mail user in the United States has two or three e-mail accounts and spends about an hour every day reading, sending, and replying to messages. It is getting to the point that one must have e-mail to stay "connected" in this global world.

It is easy to see why e-mail has become so popular. It is cheaper, faster, and easier than writing a letter, and often more convenient than a phone call. You can send an e-mail message anywhere in the world that has an online computer at any time of the day or night. It is easy and convenient to attach photos, documents, video, or even voice messages, and it allows much flexibility in schedule—you can choose when to send and read e-mail.

E-mail can be a useful tool in today's literacy classroom. One great way to promote literacy using e-mail is with pen pals. These pen pals could be in the same class, same school, same state, or in a different country. There are many websites that offer educators a chance to incorporate this wonderful activity into the curriculum. Just assigning a "buddy" to each student so that they can e-mail each other is an excellent way of incorporating it into a literacy class. In addition, e-mailing other teachers within the same school or in other schools is a helpful device for professional development. Many sites on the Internet provide free services to connect classrooms around the world with pen pals. One site is ePALS (http://www.epals.com). A classroom that was studying Mexico contacted this site to set up pen pals with students from the United States.

The Mexican students were learning English in school and were eager to make contact with English-speaking classrooms. A unique relationship was established to enhance this unit and promote literacy in an exciting way.

When e-mail is used in the classroom, it is important that rules for writing are clearly established. Every message should be a reflection of a teacher's literacy standards in the classroom. The first rule is not to perpetuate the "sloppy" language that now permeates e-mail, and to teach students etiquette that they will hopefully apply to all of their communications.

Some rules all e-mailers should follow include:

1. E-mail is an electronic form of communication; therefore, there is no security or true privacy. What is written can be traced back to whoever sent the message and can be read by others. Therefore, emphasize that messages should not contain any questionable language or content. Students should always double-check who will receive the message before sending it.

2. Students should keep messages short and to the point, because readers do not want to read a long e-mail message. This is an excellent way to teach students how to edit and summarize important points in writing.

3. The "subject" line should be filled in with a word or brief phrase describing what the message is about. This is an excellent way to teach identifying the main idea and topic of a written passage.

4. The student should use capital and lowercase letters in the message, because all capital letters signifies "shouting." Appropriate punctuation should always be used, in complete, grammatically correct sentences.

5. All messages must be signed with the writer's name because many user names are so cryptic that no one could guess who wrote the letter.

6. Finally, for the older students, it is helpful to teach them how to send attachments. When sending an attachment, the student must be sure that the receiver has the same application program on his or her computer (usually Word or Appleworks for word processing); otherwise, the attachment should be sent in RTF (rich text format), which most word processors can display. Another helpful hint is to advise students not to send attachments that are too large, because they may take quite a while to download and "clog" up the person's e-mail program. Sending attachments to a "buddy" is an excellent way to promote collaborative writing between two students or even within a group. One student can write the initial draft, send it as an attachment to another student, and the second student could revise it and add to the content. This attachment could be sent back and forth between team members until the final version was ready to be "handed in" to the teacher via e-mail.

Instant Messaging and Text Messaging in the Literacy Classroom

E-mail has lost much of its popularity among teens as texting, instant messaging, and social networking sites facilitate more frequent contact with friends (Lenhart, Madden, Macgill, & Smith, 2008). As cell phones proliferate, students are using text messaging and instant messaging (IM) as their primary means of communication. Lewis and Fabos (2005) have investigated IM as a means of promoting literacy in a digitally mediated age. What they discovered is that to be a proficient IM user, one must shift voices moment to moment for many different audiences at once, writing fluently and reading textual material in a hybrid language to communicate with many users simultaneously. They find that there is a visual and aural element of IM: visual in the purposeful use of icons, letters, colors, and font types to convey meaning, and aural in the way that text closely represents speech. Although this type of reading and writing is different from the standard, traditional way that reading and writing is taught in schools, Lewis and Fabos (2005) argue that we need to reconceptualize literacy in digitally mediated times. This type of reading and writing need not replace or negate more analytic or linear forms of literacy, but it is complex, can promote higher order thinking, and can foster an evolved style of writing that is useful in the world of work or global communication.

IM and text messaging can be useful in the classroom as a form of instant pen pals for students, to collaborate with other classes on projects, or to get instant help from other teachers in your school. Teachers in the same school can use IM to convey messages back and forth concerning curricular, logistical, or instructional matters without leaving their classrooms.

Using technology as a means of communication is a wonderful strategy to promote literacy in a classroom. Students run home to go online so they can communicate with friends and do research over the web. By using this powerful literacy tool within the classroom, we teach students effective strategies, appropriate rules, and organized ways to communicate and promote literacy.

Electronic Discussion Boards, Blogs, and Chat Rooms

Discussion boards (also known as Internet forums or web forums) allow a group of users to hold discussions without e-mail by posting messages onto a "bulletin board" to which other users can respond. A group of users can "chat" and share ideas about a particular topic, but not in real time. That is, a user can read a message, post a response to it, and at a later date come back to the discussion to read responses and post new messages. Discussion boards are an integral part of online distance learning classes that are offered over the Internet and are becoming widely used in education, especially in high school and higher education where online courses are proliferating quickly.

Blogs are interactive web pages where individuals can post entries, articles, links, and pictures, and ask others to join in conversations. Blogs have become very popular, especially with high school students, and are quickly being adapted as useful tools within the classroom to promote writing. Blogs are described further in Chapter 8.

Many classrooms use discussion boards and blogs to promote writing and to expand class discussions. These applications allow students to exchange ideas online, to work together in small groups on projects at home, and to critique and discuss online magazines, newspapers, and student-posted work.

Discussion boards and blogs used in the classroom can promote a collaborative, interactive environment. The cooperative efforts of the participants contribute to what is called a "community of learners." A **community of learners** is a group of students who share a common interest in a topic, share a particular way of giving out information about the topic, and together build collaborative knowledge with a set of common collective tasks (Cohen, 2003). Various activities for promoting such a community include: having each student post a short biography sketch for the class to read, forming collaborative learning teams among students who will work on a specific task online, assigning specific discussion questions for teams to respond to, using a problem-solving/case study approach for a group of students, and having students present projects or reports online for the class to read and respond to (Cohen, 2003).

Chat rooms involve synchronous or real-time communication among users who are logged on at the same time to a specific "chat room" on the Internet and are able to discuss topics and ask questions of each other. Students can access experts in different fields and collaborate with students from other parts of the world. One elementary school teacher (Grigsby, 2001) used chat rooms with her first grade students. The students were given strict rules that they could not use any bad language or be rude, and that there could not be any talking out loud during this period in the chat room. She used the chat rooms to communicate with other classes, preferably from other states. The children sent a photograph of each class to the other teacher so students would have a visual image of their partner classroom. She then turned this into a classroom project by having students create stories or slide shows about what they learned from their partner classroom. This teacher also used chat rooms with second, third, and fourth grade students, who thoroughly enjoyed collaborating on projects with students in other towns. She had the older students share their "expertise" with younger students and found that the activity increased literacy development in her students.

A Visit to Ms. Civitello's Classroom: Integrating Technology into the Literacy Classroom

Ms. Civitello is sitting on a chair in the corner with her second grade children gathered around her on the floor. She is currently using a technology lab with 15 different computer stations set up. Using whole-class instruction, she is reviewing their ongoing investigation into different types of whales. She emphasizes the need to know what a **keyword** is and why keywords are important when searching for information. She reminds the students that keywords are important words that help them remember something. They can use keywords to write sentences about their topic. She also reviews the importance of collecting data, which can be words as well as numbers, and the need to record and organize the data onto a graphic organizer. She hands out a graphic organizer that the students will be using. In one column she has listed all the attributes that the students will be finding information on. In the other column she tells them to write down key words about each attribute. She goes over each attribute that they will need to investigate about whales, such as *size, color, fins,* and *blowhole.* She models for them how the attribute *size* might have keywords such as *feet, inches,* or *millimeters.*

Ms. Civitello then reviews how the children can access the website they will be using for this lesson. She reviews how to open a folder, find a file, and open the specific webpage that has been placed in the folder. She divides the class into pairs, gives each pair one

A Visit to Ms. Civitello's Classroom: Integrating Technology into the Literacy Classroom

type of whale to investigate, and has each pair go to a computer station to start locating information related to the attributes listed on the organizer.

The children quickly open the webpage and start working together to fill in the graphic organizer. Ms. Civitello walks around the room monitoring their progress. The children work on the website, investigating the assigned whale and using the graphic organizer to record and organize their data.

After approximately 20 minutes, Ms. Civitello tells the children to finish their work and come to the corner of the classroom with their graphic organizers. She then tells them that they did an excellent job and that as part of their investigation she would like them to compare and contrast two different whales. She talks about using the Venn diagram as a useful tool to help them compare and contrast two different

whales, such as the sperm whale and the grey whale. She then introduces a website from the ReadWriteThink website (http://readwritethink.org) produced by the International Reading Association (IRA) and the National Council of Teachers of English (NCTE). This website uses an interactive Venn diagram whereby the students can input two different whales, placing their attributes into the outer circles if they are different, or in the inner circle if they are the same. She models how to use the interactive Venn diagram and then divides the class into pairs of students, each of whom have investigated a different whale, so that they could compare and contrast the information they found.

The students work actively at the computer using their graphic organizers to compare and contrast different attributes of whales. The students are successfully using the interactive Venn diagram to complete their work. After approximately 15 minutes, Ms. Civitello calls the class over to the corner again. She assures them that if they did not finish their work on the Venn diagram, they can continue their work tomorrow. She then summarizes what they learned today and the processes they used to conduct an investigation. She asks them, "Why is it important to use keywords to conduct an investigation? What tools did you use to learn about whales? Why is it important to organize your data? What did you learn about whales?"

In reviewing this lesson, Ms. Civitello integrated technology into a lesson on conducting investigations. She used the computer as a tool to help her students locate and organize information about whales. Some of the strategies she used were:

- Activating prior knowledge by having students review what they knew about whales and the process of investigating using keywords
- Using whole-class instruction to review concepts from previous lessons, teach new concepts, and introduce an activity
- Pairing the students for collaborative learning using the computer
- Ensuring her students knew how to access a webpage that was appropriate for this lesson and their reading abilities
- Monitoring students as they worked on the computer
- Using a graphic organizer to help them record and organize their data
- Reviewing as a whole class what they had accomplished before starting the next activity
- Locating an excellent literacy resource on the Internet
- Being extremely well prepared by being familiar with all resources that the students were using
- Discussing the content and processes they had learned

Questions:

1. What are the best strategies that teachers should use when young children conduct a search on the Internet? When children in the upper grade levels conduct a search on the Internet?

2. How can you help students locate and comprehend information on the Internet?

3. How can graphic organizers and visual tools promote comprehension when conducting a search on the Internet?

Go to www.cengage.com/login to register your access code for the premium website for *Literacy for Children in an Information Age*. Then watch an in-depth video exploration of Ms. Civitello's classroom and to see how she used valuable strategies.

In the second stage, *interpreting the information gathered*, the student must make sense of the material and evaluate whether it is helpful. At this stage, students can begin to prepare an outline, listing the major areas that the report will cover. This stage will overlap with the first stage, and the student might find that he or she needs to gather more information in certain areas and to conduct further searches based on a more refined phrase or a subtopic of the report. Organizing the material into a coherent and meaningful outline is an important step because it helps the student interpret and focus on how the material should be presented.

In the third stage, *creating a research report*, the student will create a first draft and then a final report. This total process is described in the following section in a nine-step process that teachers can follow when conducting research.

A Nine-Step Process in Conducting Research

Research should be based on solving a problem, not just investigating a topic. The following nine steps outline the recommended procedure for conducting research based on solving a problem.

1. *Define the problem.* What are your students trying to prove, predict, evaluate, critique, compare, or recommend? Teachers should provide a variety of motivating problems to help start the process for the students. It is important that the teacher guides the students toward "generative" topics or problems; that is, those topics that generate a multitude of ideas and solutions, rather than closed, single-answer reports. For example, a report on whales may be interesting, but it is a single focus and a closed topic. A more generative topic would be on a current event article: Should a refuge be created for whales in Australia that would prevent hundreds

of jobs from being created and not allow people to enjoy beautiful beaches, or should this area remain accessible to people and development? In choosing topics for research, *try to phrase them as problem-based*, rather than as topic-based. This will be more exciting for students and encourage them to use higher order thinking skills.

2. *Brainstorm the problem.* Your students should write many words, phrases, and ideas that relate to the major problem/topic that requires research. Have them review their list and sort and sift for the best-connected words and phrases that represent key ideas and concepts. The software package Inspiration will help students map out their initial and refined brainstorming ideas. These "idea maps" will allow teachers and students to see the interconnected core of ideas, keywords, and concepts that will form the basis for the information search process. Concept maps also facilitate cooperative research activities because these ideas can be divided into clusters, which can then be assigned to individual team members to research. If there is more than one topic to choose, the students should choose the topic(s) they would like to research.

3. *Determine the best possible sources to acquire information/data.* What resources are available to students? Do they have access to books, magazines, CD-ROMs, the Internet, online databases, journals, interviews, and primary sources? Some resources such as certain journals are not available online and students will have to go to the library to access them. Students should be required to have a mix of both electronic and printed sources. Have your students determine and then list what resources are available.

4. *Phrase the search request effectively.* Teach your students the search language and how to pinpoint keywords or phrases from their brainstorming. A few keywords and phrases should be developed. Students will need to know that if their keyword is too broad, they will get too many "hits," and if their keyword is too narrow, they will not get enough information. They should also be aware that if they are using two words in their search request, such as "gray" and "whale," some search engines require that it be typed in as "gray&whale" or else the search will look for everything that includes the words "gray" and "whale." Students need practice in determining what a keyword is and how to make it broader in focus, narrower in focus, and to derive other phrases that may give them more information.

5. *Conduct the search and limit it to significant information only.* The teacher can instruct the class on how to determine whether a source of material will be helpful. As the students do their search, they will come up with too many sources to read and too many sources that are irrelevant. Students must learn to use different search engines and evaluate the sources of information from the results of their search. This is probably the most time-consuming and important step in the whole research process (as opposed to what most students think, which is that writing up the report takes the most time). Searches can be overwhelming, and students can spend fruitless hours going nowhere if they are not properly directed at this point.

There are many different search engines that students can use to conduct their search. The most popular is Google (www.google.com), which provides an overall search of websites and information on the Internet.

search engines that children can use

Google

http://www.google.com

The general search engine Google is a good place to start, but may yield too many sites and be overwhelming for some children. Also, some of the sites may be inappropriate for children, so a teacher or parent needs to carefully monitor use of this search engine.

Yahoo! Kids

http://kids.yahoo.com/

The Yahoo! Kids search engine is designed for web surfers ages 7 to 12. The sites are selected and monitored by the YAHOO! Inc. staff, so this may be a more appropriate search engine to use in the classroom.

Ask Kids

http://www.askkids.com/

In this search engine, a student types in a question. The search engine finds sites that will help answer it, first searching a database of selected sites.

KidsClick!

http://www.kidsclick.org/

KidsClick! is a good search engine for children that searches a database of more than 6,400 sites compiled by librarians.

Kids Search Tools

http://www.rcls.org/ksearch.htm

This site lists many different search tools that children can use for specialized purposes, such as looking up words in a dictionary or searching for a topic in an encyclopedia.

Another important point is that as students go to sites, they need to evaluate those sites for their quality and source of information. Figure 2–3 provides a website evaluation form that students and teachers can use to assess how reliable the information is at a website. A search may yield what the student thinks are excellent resources, but are those sources of information valid? Do they contain information that is based on research and objective criteria? The student needs to consider who is hosting the site. A university or government agency is usually a more reliable source of quality, research-based information. A personal web page compiled by an unknown person may be interesting, but not provide reliable information. By analyzing the URL, a student can determine where this information is coming from. Another way to evaluate validity of information is by trying to determine whether the information is fact or opinion. Certain keywords or key phrases, such as "believe" or "feel" or "posit," may signify opinion. Again, students need to be aware of this.

Students need to know that as they visit sites that they might use in their report, they must write down the URL or address of the site, or keep track of it in a "favorites" or "bookmark" file. Many teachers are starting to require that students print out and hand in all websites that they have used in their research to assure that they haven't plagiarized material. The teacher can then also assess the quality of the websites that the student is visiting and give recommendations for future searches.

1. *Save the significant information and list the sources.* Without technology, this step is time-consuming and often overlooked by the students. With computers, students can browse, copy and paste the document to an open document, type in the URL and source, and save to a disk or print it out. They can also compose a series of "bookmarks" using a browser that can then be printed out. They should also make sure that their references are valid sources of information and reflect solid, research-based websites. If they find a site that is being hosted by a "questionable" source but would still like to use it, a notation should be included questioning the validity of the information.

General Website Evaluation Form

Name:_____   Date:_____

Website:_____   URL:_____

	5 Highly Recommend	4 Somewhat Recommend	3 Recommend	2 Barely Recommend	1 Not Recommend
1. **Quality Information:** Does the author seem to be an authority on this subject? Is there a biography? e-mail?					
2. **Reliability of Information:** What does the URL end in? Does the site seem to be reliable (education, school, government, library, museum)? Is the information from reliable sources?					
3. **Bias:** Does the site seem biased? Are there words which signify an opinion? Did you link from a site you trust? Are there links to sponsors?					
4. **Currency:** Is the information up to date? Do all the links work? Is there a date when it was created?					
5. **Pertinent:** Does this site contain information that is central to the question being researched? Does this site answer the question?					
6. **Ease of Use:** Does the site load easily? Is it easy to navigate? Does it load quickly?					
7. **Visual Layout:** Is the site easy to read and access the information you need quickly? Is it pleasing to look at? Does it contain pleasing images?					
8. **Readability Level:** Is the site written at a reading level that is appropriate for who will use it? Is the site easy to read and comprehend?					
9. **Accuracy:** Are there spelling errors, grammar errors? Does the site seem well constructed, well written?					
10. **Links:** Are the links valuable? Do they all work? Do they link to sites that are worthwhile?					
11. **Worthwhile:** Is this a site you would bookmark? Is it a site you feel is valuable and would come back to again?					

Comments about the site:

FIGURE 2-3

2. *Prepare an outline.* Students need to know how to make a logical sequence of the information that they gathered. Many students do not use outlines and do not know how to construct them. They must create a strong, logical outline before they start writing. For younger grades, a semantic map using either Inspiration or a printed form may be substituted for the outline. In intermediate grades, students should learn how to convert their mapped ideas into an outline (Inspiration does this very well), and both should be required. For older students, an outline should be required with a map being optional.

3. *Create the first draft.* Using their outlines, students should select significant information and write the first draft of their report. Students should photocopy or print out copies of their sources of information and attach these printouts to the report. This will provide citations of significant content and reduce the possibility of plagiarism. The teacher should go over the first draft carefully with each student and help him or her edit and revise the paper for its organization, logical development of ideas, mechanics, style, grammar, spelling, and punctuation.

4. *Prepare the final draft.* Although a written report is traditional, students can express themselves through oral reports, multimedia presentations, debates, and web pages. A key question is: Should each step be graded, or only the final draft? What about the student who hands in an excellent final paper but did not do well with the outline? What about the student who handed in an excellent outline but did not hand in a well-written final paper? Should all steps be worth equal points? Whatever the teacher decides, a rubric should be developed for the research project, specifying how many points each step is worth.

Information Literacy Standards

Information literacy standards were developed by the American Association of School Librarians and the Association of Educational Communications Technology (see Figure 2–4). These standards define the information-literate person as one who can recognize when information is needed and can locate, evaluate, and use information effectively. Educators should incorporate these standards into their literacy curriculum and teach children how to conduct research, locate information, evaluate information, and use information effectively and ethically. Information literacy forms the basis for lifelong learning and is common to all disciplines, learning environments, and levels of education. It enables learners to master content and extend their investigations, become more self-directed, and assume greater control over their own learning. Information literacy requires learners to develop advanced research methodology and have the ability to discriminate between high- and low-quality information. This ability is dependent on being computer literate, but it goes beyond just being able to use technology effectively. It requires higher order thinking skills and critical problem-solving skills to effectively search, locate, evaluate, and use information to solve problems. These are skills that every adult must master to be "fluent" in our society (American Library Association, 2005).

WebQuests

WebQuests are a wonderful way to incorporate technology into a literacy classroom while promoting higher order thinking skills. WebQuests are an inquiry-oriented activity in which some or all of the information that students interact with comes from resources on the Internet. WebQuests are computer-based activities that are designed to take students on a quest or journey to different sites on the Internet, where they will be directed to find certain information to solve a problem or answer a question.

WebQuests revolve around a central question that is posed by the teacher. This question or problem should be a "real" one that students may confront in their actual lives; thus, the WebQuest is "authentic" and requires students to apply problem-solving strategies. This technique increases student motivation because they are given real tasks and authentic resources with which to work. With the web, students can directly access individual experts, searchable databases, and current reporting and articles written on the topic for insight. Usually a WebQuest is done in a cooperative group, where members of the group develop expertise on a particular aspect or perspective of the problem they are trying to solve.

The Nine Information Literacy Standards for Student Learning

Information Literacy

1. The student who is information literate accesses information efficiently and effectively.

2. The student who is information literate evaluates information critically and competently.

3. The student who is information literate uses information accurately and creatively.

These standards express the importance of students' ability to find and use information resources accurately. Once the resources are accessed in the most effective and efficient manner possible, a student must evaluate the information to determine whether the information represents quality information or if it is biased, inaccurate, or irrelevant for the task at hand. Lastly, the student must figure out the best way to use the resources to enhance the outcome of the intended search. This means that the student must be familiar with different search engines on the Internet and how to properly conduct a search. The student must be able to critically assess websites, and the student must know the correct way to incorporate this information into his or her research project.

Independent Learning

4. The student who is an independent learner is information literate and pursues information related to personal interests.

5. The student who is an independent learner is information literate and appreciates literature and other creative expressions of information.

6. The student who is an independent learner is information literate and strives for excellence in information seeking and knowledge generation.

These standards show the need for students to become independent learners and for educators to provide the framework and knowledge necessary for students to continue their pursuit of information beyond the classroom walls. Students need to continue to appreciate literature and continue to seek creative ways of expressing themselves. Students need to use their knowledge acquisition skills to obtain information about things they are interested in and enjoy.

Social Responsibility

7. The student who contributes positively to the learning community and to society is information literate and recognizes the importance of information to a democratic society.

8. The student who contributes positively to the learning community and to society is information literate and practices ethical behavior in regard to information and information technology.

9. The student who contributes positively to the learning community and to society is information literate and participates effectively in groups to pursue and generate information.

These standards stress the need for students to recognize the moral and ethical implications in using information accessed and used. With the Internet, information is freely available for all to preview and use. Students must have ethical responsibility when using others' information: They must reference all material that is not their own and not use others' material freely within their own writings; they must use information that is appropriate and respectful of others; and they must recognize when information is biased, inaccurate, and stating an opinion from a particular perspective when using that information. In addition, students must recognize the moral imperatives about not passing along inflammatory comments electronically, about not visiting sites that are inappropriate, and not using the Internet in a way that is subversive or questionable. Lastly, students need to work collaboratively in groups to pursue and create new ideas concerning information that they obtained.

FIGURE 2-4

There are two types of WebQuests. The first is short term and designed to be completed in two to three class periods. This WebQuest is for knowledge acquisition and integration. Its purpose is to introduce students to a significant amount of new knowledge and to make sense of it. The second type of WebQuest is long term and designed to be completed in a week to a month. The purpose is to extend and refine knowledge: The students will analyze information, work with it deeply to understand the concepts, and apply the information to create something new (Dodge, 1997).

The critical components of a WebQuest are as follows:

1. The *introduction* should orient the learner as to what the WebQuest will be about and motivate the student to undertake this activity. This step presents the question or problem to be solved to the student.

2. The *task* gives an overview of what the student will need to do to complete the WebQuest. It further describes the problem and what needs to be done to solve it. This step outlines what the final product or expectations will be on completion of the WebQuest.

3. The *process* outlines in sequence exactly what steps the student needs to take in this WebQuest.

4. *Information resources* provide the student with the online links and websites he or she needs to visit to solve the problem. This step should also include off-line resources that the student can use. It is helpful to have the resources organized by topics so students can locate specific information.

5. The *evaluation* provides rubrics to assess performance and to prepare the students so they know exactly what to expect.

6. The *conclusion* summarizes key points and helps the students bring closure to what they have learned. It is helpful to make connections to other disciplines or topics that relate to the activity.

Some other attributes of a WebQuest are:

1. WebQuests are most likely to be group activities.

2. WebQuests often motivate students by giving them a role to play (for example, investigator, scientist, member of a committee) and a scenario to frame the problem they will solve (for example, "You've been asked by the Secretary General of the U.N. to submit a report on whether the San Ignacio Lagoon in Mexico, a breeding ground for whales, should be developed into a salt mine").

3. WebQuests can be designed within a single discipline or they can be interdisciplinary (Dodge, 1997).

Teachers' VOICES   Using Technology in the Classroom

I use technology quite a bit, but there are a few ways I would like to include or do more of it in my classroom. I definitely want to have the students do WebQuests. I feel that WebQuests offer students a lot of opportunities to explore and find information about a topic they are studying. They get a lot of practice using the computer to find information. This activity allows students to develop their research and word processing skills. I also want them to be able to create PowerPoint shows on projects they are doing. I already use the digital projector a lot, but I want to use it more in centers and have students work on it to create words and poems. I also use listening centers so students can listen and record their reading. I want to do more recording of students reading so they can listen to themselves and to their classmates reading on tape. This will help with fluency and give them practice in decoding and self-monitoring skills as they try to read the book as well as possible after practicing for the recording.

—*Ellen Treadway, Third Grade Teacher*

The WebQuest page (http://webquest.sdsu.edu) and techtrekers.com (http://www.techtrekers.com/webquests/) provide many examples of WebQuests for every grade level and subject area. WebQuests are a wonderful way to integrate technology into the literacy classroom using an interdisciplinary approach.

Using Technology with Diverse Learners

Students with Learning Disabilities and Technology Use

For students with learning disabilities, **assistive technology** in the classroom has great potential. Assistive technology is any device that is used to increase, maintain, or improve the capabilities of individual with disabilities [IDEA 2004, Part A, Sec. 602(1)]. Assistive technology serves two purposes: (1) to support an individual's strengths, thereby counterbalancing the effects of the disability; and (2) to provide an alternate way of performing a task (Quenneville, 2001). When students with learning disabilities use assistive technology, it allows them to compensate for their disability, and even circumvent it entirely. For example, word processors help students with poor mechanical handwriting skills and provide a way of facilitating motor coordination and producing a document that is neat and legible. Assistive technology can help students with learning disabilities with their written expression, reading, mathematics, spelling, and organization, in addition to promoting social acceptance and building self-esteem.

The following technological applications have great potential for yielding benefits in the classroom for students with learning disabilities:

◆ *Speech synthesis (text-to-speech) programs or talking word processors:* Speech synthesis programs work by translating text that appears on the computer screen into computerized speech. This allows students to hear what they have written and provides auditory feedback to reinforce the writing process. Several studies have shown that the use of this software in the classroom is not only assistive but provides remedial benefits (Forgrave, 2002).

◆ *Word prediction:* Word prediction software enables the student to make choices, find words, and complete sentences. The software displays words, usually at the bottom of the screen, based on frequency of use, grammatically correct usage of words, and most recently used words. The student types a letter, and as each letter is typed, the software predicts what the word will be by displaying a word. If the intended word is not predicted, the user continues typing letters until the next prediction occurs. At times, the student must type the whole word. The built-in dictionary will then remember this word and predict it the next time it is used. Users can also add words to the dictionary based on specific content needs. This tool helps support spelling, grammar, and vocabulary.

◆ *Portable note-taking devices:* These tools enable students with learning disabilities to record ideas and take notes in a classroom without having mechanical difficulties in handwriting impede progress. AlphaSmart is a portable keyboard that contains a simple operating system and allows the user to connect to a computer and printer. Laptops and netbooks are also becoming more popular in the classroom for all students to use for note-taking and writing purposes.

◆ *Prewriting organizers:* Software programs that allow students to develop graphic organizers and webs are helpful. Inspiration is an excellent program to help students with learning disabilities generate ideas, content, and outlines.

◆ *Voice recognition software (speech-to-text):* Voice recognition software can help students with learning disabilities bypass the need to write down or type their ideas. Students wear a headset and operate the computer by voice commands. This allows students to get their ideas down quickly before they are forgotten because of slow typing speed. This technology is beneficial in improving writing skills, as well as bypassing typing difficulties across a range of age and ability levels (Forgrave, 2002).

◆ *Prewriting prompts:* Many multimedia programs allow students to draw pictures and then write a story about it. This type of software program can help students with learning disabilities by providing the necessary visual prompts and graphic scenes to motivate them to write their stories.

Courtesy of Guilherme Cunha

The use of technology improves the literacy curriculum for all students.

It is important that the classroom teacher seek assistance from the school's learning disabilities specialist when planning for assistive technology. The specialist can evaluate the students' technological needs in collaboration with the classroom teacher, related services staff, parents, and students. The team then determines an appropriate match among devices, setting up specific goals and meeting with the classroom teacher and parents to provide assistance and guidance.

Assistive technology can help students with learning disabilities compensate for many of the difficulties they encounter, especially in the area of writing. The technology can ease frustration, increase motivation, foster self-esteem, and improve self-confidence and productivity in the classroom and at home. Students with learning disabilities find technology exciting and will benefit from many of the applications described in this chapter such as WebQuests, field trips, and collaborative Internet projects.

English Language Learners and Technology Use

The use of technology in the classroom can greatly benefit English language learners. Research in second language acquisition underscores the need for learning to take place in collaborative situations where students interact with each other and partake in authentic learning activities (Krashen & Terrell, 1983). Technology provides many opportunities for students to interact with classmates or other students located in a different location. It allows students to engage in authentic, real-world learning tasks where they can work collaboratively to solve problems. English language learners benefit from one another's knowledge, and practice their listening comprehension and verbal skills by listening and responding to their partners.

Anxiety and lack of motivation can impede second language learning by acting as filters to block comprehension (Krashen & Terrell, 1983). Technology assists the teacher in creating a supportive, student-centered environment that will motivate English language learners. Technology allows students to gain confidence and builds self-esteem through the nonjudgmental nature of the computer, which can correct errors without embarrassment or anxiety.

Technology can be used to provide assistance in learning a new language in reading, spelling, writing, and vocabulary development. It can strengthen English language learners' home–school connection and allow them to make connections to their native culture and with other students from similar backgrounds. Technology can be used with students in the following ways (Heinze, 2005; Dukes, 2005):

◆ *Image galleries:* The Internet has a wealth of images that can be downloaded for free with no copyright protection limiting their use. These images provide English language learners with concrete images to support the text that they are reading. These images will provide contextual clues and help students with reading comprehension. Google's image searches (http://images.google.com) allow the user to search via keywords for photographs and illustrations, which can then be downloaded and printed. Enchanted Learning (http://enchantedlearning.com) has printable picture dictionaries that are available in English-French, English-Spanish, and English-Italian.

◆ *Creating multilingual books:* When English language learners read books in their native language, it helps them transfer their reading skills to English. Students can publish their own multilingual books using Microsoft Word, PowerPoint, and other graphics programs available in the classroom. Students can write the books in both English and their native language, and then either print them out and add them to the classroom library or put them on a CD-ROM for other students to view and read. This type of technology integration can be seen at the Dual Language Showcase of the Thornwood Public School in Toronto, Canada (http://thornwood. peelschools.org/Dual).

◆ *Multimedia projects:* Many programs allow students to develop stories and projects using text, graphics, animation, photographs, video, and audio resources. These projects use multiple modalities that help students with different learning styles and allow them to broaden their repertoire of cognitive strategies. This also helps English language learners study content areas in greater depth and learn more complex vocabulary and content-related concepts in a fun and motivating way.

◆ *Using the Internet to connect with other cultures:* English language learners can listen to sound bites of authentic conversations on varying topics, watch video clips of current news headlines, and listen to popular music online. The Internet is a motivating and enriching resource, especially when it connects to students' native cultures or teaches them about another culture. An example of such a website is Voice of America, which documents the news in English and many other languages (http:// www.voanews.com/english/index.cfm). Teachers can also visit other classrooms around the world through Internet projects, chats, or e-mail pen pals. Two excellent sites that will connect classrooms around the United States or the world are Global SchoolNet (http://www.globalschoolnet.org/index.cfm) and iEARN (International Education and Resource Network) (http://iearn.org/).

◆ *Publishing online:* English language learners can increase their writing proficiency by publishing their work online. They can publish their experiences on a blog (short for "web log"), so that anyone on the Internet can read their journal. The online

STRATEGIES FOR TEACHING DIVERSE STUDENTS

Using Technology

1. Use assistive technology with students with learning disabilities and English language learners, especially when teaching writing. Be sure to consult the school's learning disabilities specialist or English as a second language specialist to create a program that meets the needs of each student.

2. Have students create multimedia projects as an alternative to writing reports. Multimedia allows diverse learners to use multiple modalities and helps students with different learning styles.

3. Use authentic learning activities that promote problem solving and involve technology such as Internet projects, researching a topic of interest, and WebQuests. Provide support and guidance to diverse learners through constant feedback, and help them with their reading and writing skills when necessary.

4. Allow collaborative teams to work together using the computer to solve a problem. This provides support for diverse learners, encourages English language learners to use English in natural contexts, and builds self-confidence. It allows diverse learners to interact and contribute to a team effort.

5. Provide opportunities for diverse learners to connect with other students in other classrooms through chat rooms, e-mail, and Internet projects.

6. Allow diverse learners to use digital cameras and video to enhance their learning and decrease the linguistic demands placed on them through writing and reading. Provide alternative ways for them to meet the requirements of tasks using technology.

7. Use digital images downloaded from the Internet to help provide contextual clues and support for reading.

8. Provide reinforcement of basic skills through software programs that use gaming and story-like approaches to learning. These drill-and-practice programs should not be the only application of technology in the classroom, but they can provide support to students in learning basic skills.

magazine Topics Online Magazine for Learners of English (http://www.topics mags.com) targets English language learners (for a description, see the Publishing Student Work section in this chapter).

◆ *Writing programs:* Similar to students with learning disabilities, English language learners find assistive writing programs on the computer beneficial. These programs can help them with their writing skills and vocabulary development. Computer-generated writing prompts, outlines, and other graphic organizer programs such as Inspiration are all recommended.

◆ *Drill and practice programs:* Although there is much criticism regarding drill-and-practice programs, they can be valuable in reinforcing practice of specific skills. Pronunciation programs allow English language learners to visually compare the voice patterns of their speech with that of a native speaker. Students can practice grammar, phonics, and vocabulary development through self-paced instruction that is often presented in a gaming or story-like approach. Many of these programs have record-keeping features that help the teacher keep track of the students' progress and plan for future instruction.

Technology can enhance the curriculum for all students and can help the teacher meet the needs of students from diverse backgrounds. It is recommended that the classroom teacher work with a team of professionals within the school to set up a program that effectively uses technology in the curriculum to support diverse learners. Such resources as the technology teacher/coordinator, the English as a second language specialist, other experienced teachers, and parents can all be involved in helping create a program for English language learners.

Ethical Concerns in Using the Internet

It is important that teachers discuss ethics in using technology and accessing information. Most districts have an **Acceptable Use Policy** in place for both teachers and students. This is a written contract or guideline that helps monitor technology use throughout the school system. It covers student conduct, rules, and regulations regarding equipment and material, Internet use, and consequences for violations. It may also require parents, students, and teachers to sign this contract.

Plagiarism, search strategies, and the correct use of or access to Internet sites, together with general ethical behavior while using e-mail or web pages, must be discussed in the classroom and closely monitored. Teachers must be responsible for maintaining a code of ethics in their classrooms and be carefully tuned in to what their students are doing and producing when using technology.

One growing problem with the use of the Internet for accessing information is plagiarism. A teacher cannot assume that a student knows how to conduct an ethical search using the Internet. Students must be taught how to determine what an appropriate search consists of. They can do this by asking questions such as:

◆ Is the site biased or promote one perspective or point of view?

◆ Is this site useful? Is it relevant to the topic?

◆ Does this site contain accurate information that can be used in a report?

◆ How does a student incorporate the information into a paper? What is plagiarism?

◆ What ethical questions must a student ask about using information from a site?

◆ How does one cite and reference work from the Internet?

This complex and sensitive subject is relatively new to education, and teachers need to be aware that it is increasingly important that these issues be discussed and reinforced throughout the school year. Teachers should collaborate with the library media specialists to teach students how to conduct proper searches and what constitutes ethical behavior in this process. This whole area of ethical responsibility reinforces the need for the information literacy standards.

Using the Internet for Professional Development

The Internet is a wonderful way for teachers to stay current in the field of literacy and education. The Internet provides many wonderful sites where teachers can explore different topics and read journals written by both experts and teachers. Many free research reports are available on the Internet that are invaluable tools for keeping up to date with the latest developments in the area of literacy. The websites listed in the following are excellent resources that all reading teachers should use:

International Reading Association (IRA)

http://www.reading.org

The IRA website should be the first stop for any educator who is interested in literacy. It provides a wealth of resources in the area of literacy. The IRA's online journal (http://www.readingonline.org) is also an excellent resource for current research in the field of literacy and technology.

ReadWriteThink

http://readwritethink.org

ReadWriteThink is a partnership between the International Reading Association (IRA), the National Council of Teachers of English (NCTE), and the Verizon Foundation.

It offers an amazing array of resources for the teacher, including lesson plans, resources, standards, and student materials. This is one of the first places a literacy teacher should go to find quality information on the web.

Center for the Improvement of Early Reading Improvement (CIERA)

http://www.ciera.org

Center on English Learning and Achievement (CELA)

http://www.albany.edu/cela/index.html

CELA is a national center dedicated to improving the teaching and learning of English and language arts. CELA's research seeks to learn what elements of curriculum, instruction, and assessment are essential to developing high literacy and how schools can best help students achieve success. It is a great site to explore literacy.

Clearinghouse on Reading, English, and Communication

http://reading.indiana.edu/

This is an excellent site to explore research papers on literacy.

National Assessment of Educational Progress (NAEP)

http://nces.ed.gov/nationsreportcard

The NAEP conducts national assessment in reading. Teachers can assess how our students are faring in reading.

Learning First Alliance

http://www.learningfirst.org

The Learning First Alliance is a partnership of 12 leading educational associations that collaborate to improve student learning in U.S. public elementary and secondary schools.

Pew Internet & American Life Project

http://www.pewinternet.org/

The Pew Internet Project studies the social impact of the Internet. All reports, presentations, and data sets dating back to the year 2000 are available for free. The mission of the Pew Internet Project is to make it easy for people to find—and share—its research.

National Writing Project

http://www.nwp.org/

The National Writing Project site promotes writing as a procee and encourages teachers to share experiences with each other. It has been a successful model of encouraging writing in the curriculum.

The Internet is a rich source of professional development for teachers and can contribute to lifelong learning. Teachers can form study groups within their schools to discuss articles and research reports obtained online or through reading books and journals. This type of sharing helps promote a community of learners, which is an essential part of teacher satisfaction within schools and a significant factor that impacts student achievement (Langer, 2000). Literacy support groups, curriculum development groups, and teacher study groups are excellent ways in which teachers learn new teaching strategies, share ideas, and keep current with the latest research in the field of literacy. These groups help sustain and support teaching efforts and practices. The Internet can be a vital component in maintaining this community of learners by providing teachers with information on new state licensing codes and helping them communicate with each other via e-mail and online bulletin boards.

STRATEGY BOX

Using Technology in the Literacy Program

Mr. Mancuso has implemented a problem-based WebQuest in his class that incorporates technology applications. Because he has only three computers and 24 students, he needs to develop print-based materials that all the students can read. He divides the class into six groups of four students, and then provides authentic and motivating activities that allow three teams to work on the computer while the other three teams work at their desks. He chooses a problem that he believes will motivate his students, providing them with activities that allow them to use their native language, Spanish, while also promoting literacy development in English. The activities have been designed for many different learning styles and include searching on the Internet for information, reading both narrative and informational texts, filling out visual tools, using print-based and multimedia resources, sharing ideas and information among team members, watching videos, and creating a multimedia presentation.

Mr. Mancuso integrates technology into his classroom as part of an overall goal to promote new literacy skills. Technology is an integral part of the unit; it is not an "add-on" or used for reinforcement or supplemental learning. Students need to use technology as a higher order tool to successfully solve a problem. Mr. Mancuso uses the following strategies in his classroom:

1. He supports students in the acquisition of critical thinking skills through problem-based learning and the use of technology.

2. He teaches students how to assess the relevance and reliability of web-based information as they search for information related to their research.

3. He supports students in acquiring search strategies.

4. He teaches reading strategies for comprehending text on the Internet.

5. He uses an inquiry-oriented curriculum, in which assignments include searching for information on the web and using the information to solve a problem.

6. He uses assistive technology to support struggling readers and writers.

7. He manages the classroom effectively by dividing the class into teams that take turns using the classroom's three computers.

8. He uses an authentic problem from a newspaper to develop a meaningful problem-based unit that integrates technology into every lesson.

9. He develops activities that are designed for many different learning styles and multiple intelligences.

10. He emphasizes visual literacy through the use of visual tools and the incorporation of digital photography and video.

11. He selects a topic that is meaningful to his students and that uses his students' native language to help them do research.

12. He encourages and supports English language learners to use their native language, as well as to develop competencies in English.

13. He includes school personnel, community members, and parents in the process of learning and allows students to showcase their multimedia presentations and new knowledge to this group.

Final Thoughts

This chapter explores electronic forms of communication, such as e-mail, instant messaging, and the Internet, and how these tools are drastically altering our concept of literacy and how we communicate with others. Technology is greatly affecting the way we read and write in our society, which thereby impacts the definition of literacy. Educators need to make an effort to connect literacy instruction in the classroom to different technologies that support authentic reading and writing. Our classrooms must be a place where our students learn about the new literacies to become knowledgeable citizens in this global world.

EXPLORATION   Application of Concepts

Activities

1. *Explore different Internet projects that are available on the Internet.* Using the links provided earlier in this chapter or those listed on this chapter's website, pick out an Internet project that you would like to participate in. Develop a lesson plan based on the Internet project that emphasizes specific literacy skills and present it to the class.

   1. *Develop a lesson plan based on a virtual field trip.* Using the links provided earlier or on the website for this chapter, present a field trip and lesson to the class and explain how it promotes literacy in the classroom.

   2. *Evaluate three different sites that publish K–12 students' work and determine which site you would recommend to teachers.* Share the site with the class and explain what criteria was used to

choose this site as an exemplar of candidate work.

3. *Find one site that contains primary sources and develop a lesson plan based on that site.* Present your lesson plan to the class or to a group and discuss how the lesson promotes literacy.

4. *Use two different online libraries or databases to locate material for a lesson plan.* Explain which database was used and how easy or difficult it was to locate material.

5. *Go to the WebQuest site (http://webquest.sdsu. edu) and evaluate three different WebQuests.* Present to the class the WebQuest you liked the best and explain why. Discuss what literacy strategies are being promoted in the WebQuest.

HOME–SCHOOL CONNECTION Staying Connected

Technology is a wonderful way for teachers to stay connected to families, and for families to find out what is going on in their child's classroom. Often schools and teachers maintain their own webpages. These webpages are designed for students and parents to stay involved with the classroom. The webpage often has links that allow parents and guardians to see spelling lists, homework, classroom policies, topics in the curriculum, and examples of student work. The websites are also a great way for students to stay in touch with their teacher, especially if they are absent and need to make up work. It is worthwhile to find out if the school and/or classroom hosts a website that families can access. A good example of such a website is Mrs. Dingman's Third Grade (http://mrsdingman.homestead.com/home.html).

Another wonderful way to stay connected is through e-mail. Most teachers now have school-based webmail accounts and use these to contact parents and guardians. E-mail is an easy and effective way for a parent and/or guardian to find out how a student is doing in the classroom and to ask the teacher specific questions about a child's progress.

As social networking, blogs, and videoconferencing develop and become more secure, these technologies will offer much potential for busy parents and guardians to stay connected. Technology offers many opportunities for families and students to keep in touch with the teacher and classroom activities.

Leu, D.J., O'Byrne, I., Zawilinski, L. McVerry, J.G., and Everett-Cacopardo, H. (May 2009). Expanding the new literacies conversation. *Educational Researcher*, 38(4), 264–269.

3 A BALANCED LITERACY APPROACH

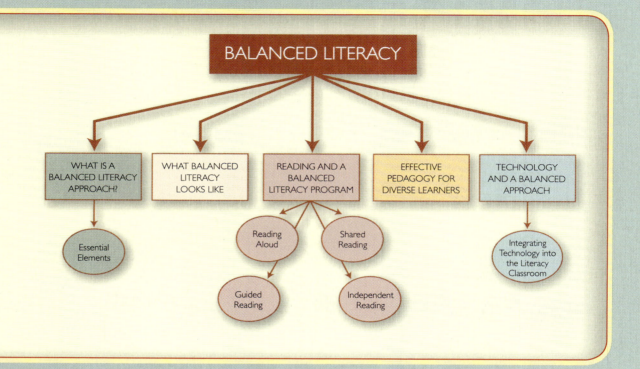

International Reading Association Professional Standards Addressed in this Chapter:

IRA STANDARD 1: FOUNDATIONAL KNOWLEDGE

Candidates have knowledge of the foundations of reading and writing processes and instruction. Candidates:

1.2 Demonstrate knowledge of reading research and histories of reading.

IRA STANDARD 2: INSTRUCTIONAL STRATEGIES AND CURRICULUM MATERIALS

Candidates use a wide range of instructional practices, approaches, methods, and curriculum materials to support reading and writing instruction. Candidates:

2.1 Use instructional grouping options (individual, small-group, whole-class, and computer-based) as appropriate for accomplishing given purposes.

2.2. Use a wide range of instructional practices, approaches, and methods, including technology-based practices, for learners at differing stages of development and from differing cultural and linguistic backgrounds.

IRA STANDARD 4: CREATING A LITERATE ENVIRONMENT

Candidates create a literate environment that fosters reading and writing by integrating foundational knowledge, use of instructional practices, approaches and methods, curriculum materials, and the appropriate use of assessments. Candidates:

4.1 Use students' interests, reading abilities, and backgrounds as foundations for the reading and writing program.

4.2 Use a large supply of books, technology-based information, and nonprint materials representing multiple levels, broad interests, and cultural and linguistic backgrounds.

Key Terms

Big Books
leveled books
trade books
Little Books
graphophonic cues
semantic cues
syntactic cues
grouping for instruction
homogeneous groups
heterogeneous groups
differentiated instruction
reading aloud
shared reading
shared writing
guided reading
independent reading

Focus Questions

1. What is a balanced approach to literacy? What does "balance" imply? How does a balanced literacy approach help a teacher become more effective in promoting literacy achievement in the classroom?

2. What does a balanced literacy classroom look like? What are the four different types of reading that should take place in a balanced literacy classroom? Describe what occurs during each type of reading.

3. What is effective pedagogy for diverse learners? What strategies can be implemented in a balanced literacy classroom for English language learners? For students with learning disabilities?

4. What are five different ways that technology can be integrated into a literacy classroom?

Welcome to Mrs. Batista's First Grade Classroom: Implementing a Balanced Literacy Approach

Paul Conklin/PhotoEdit

On Mondays and Tuesdays, Mrs. Batista and her first grade class read a Big Book together in the reading corner at the back of the room. While Mrs. Batista sits in a rocking chair next to an easel which holds the book, she previews the book and has the children do a "book walk" of the pictures, having the students predict what they think this book might be about. On Mondays, she will read aloud to the group and have them discuss what the book is about and how it relates to their own lives. On Tuesdays, the class will do a shared reading, reading the same book again together at certain points in the text. The class actively participates in reading the book and discussing new insights and meanings they gather.

On the other days, Mrs. Batista does guided reading with groups of students while the other students work at centers or complete work at their seats. She writes instructions in "picture format" on the Work Centers Board, and then verbally instructs the students on the directions they are to follow. Students are divided into groups on these days: each group is assigned to work at a different center in a different order to prevent congestion at any one center. Every student has a "contract" that must be completed independently. Each guided reading group takes about 30 minutes to complete. Mrs. Batista created

the groups after assessing each child at the beginning of the year. The groups are made up of students on the same ability level, but they shift rapidly from one group to another depending on their monthly assessment.

Mrs. Batista sits facing the class to monitor the activity. One student is an English language learner and one student has been diagnosed as having a learning disability. Mrs. Batista has been working with the specialists in her school to ensure that she is meeting their individual needs. She hands out small, "little" books with big pictures and a few words on each page to each child in the group. They review the front cover and discuss what an author and an illustrator do when writing a story. They predict what the story will be about and then each student takes a turn reading out loud while the other students follow along. When a student is having difficulty with the word "that," Mrs. Batista takes out a phonic card with the word and picture of "hat" on it. The card also has the word "hat" written in Spanish to assist the English language learners in her class whose native language in Spanish. The teacher instructs the students to say the word "hat," and then reviews the "th" sound and has the student blend that sound to the "at" part of the word. Mrs. Batista has found that pictures and visual images help all the children, especially those whose native language is not English and the struggling readers. At the end of the book, Mrs. Batista asks several questions about what was read and what rhymes with certain words. After 30 minutes, Mrs. Batista tells the groups to stop their contract work and go to an assigned center, and she calls another group to the back of the room for a guided reading session.

All students knew the rules of the classroom, including "Ask three, then me": when students have a question, they must ask at least three other students before asking the teacher. Mrs. Batista believes strongly that a comprehensive approach—that includes an emphasis on teaching strategic knowledge to help children understand what they read, an emphasis on having students use phonics to help them read, practicing culturally responsive teaching to support a diverse population of students in her class, and developing a love of reading for all students—is the best way to teach literacy to her class.

As you read through this chapter, try to figure out what strategies Mrs. Batista is using to implement a balanced literacy program. Try to think about how you would set up your classroom to promote literacy for all children.

What Is a Balanced Literacy Approach?

Throughout the years there have been many disagreements about which approach to teaching reading works best—a skills-based phonics approach that emphasizes breaking down the individual word into its component sounds, or a more child-centered approach that emphasizes reading texts and obtaining meaning through enjoyable shared readings with the class. In a balanced reading approach, reading, writing, listening, viewing, and speaking receive appropriate emphasis within a literacy program. This approach is not based on any one philosophical stance; rather, teachers start with what students need and base instruction on what they see, hear, and observe in the classroom. It combines elements of all approaches into a comprehensive, language-rich literacy program consistent with the best practices of literacy instruction. This approach looks at literacy as a continual lifelong process, which takes into account that students have different learning styles and come from different cultural and linguistic backgrounds and, therefore, will benefit from different approaches to literacy instruction. In addition, a balanced approach is based on research about how children learn. When teachers adopt a balanced approach to literacy, they are basically saying that they are open to many different instructional methods, that they believe all children can learn how to read, and that rich literature is essential to the literacy program, as well as learning how to sound out words and use them in meaningful contexts. By using a balanced approach, teachers are saying that they implement best practices based on research that promote literacy within the classroom, that the literacy classroom is child-centered and supports all children in literacy development, and that students are assessed using specific techniques that are research-based, ongoing, and supportive of continuous literacy growth. In a balanced literacy classroom teachers use technology to promote the new literacies of comprehending electronic text, communicating on-line and and using on-line tools for research, analysis, and synthesis. Twenty-first century skills are emphasized and incorporated into the literacy curriculum.

Strong research findings support the use of a balanced approach (Cunningham & Hall, 1998; Fitzgerald, 1999; Fountas & Pinnell, 1996; NICHD, 2000; Pressley, 1998). Reading research must help future teachers make decisions about what to teach and how to teach in the classroom. According to Fitzgerald (1999), a balanced reading program includes three broad categories of knowledge that children need to know to be able to read: (1) local knowledge about reading such as how to use phonics and knowledge of sound–symbol relationships to read words and guess at their meanings; (2) global knowledge about reading such as understanding, interpreting, and responding to what is read and applying specific strategies to help children understand text; and (3) affective knowledge or love of reading that includes positive feelings, a positive attitude, and the desire to read. Teachers need to address these multiple types of knowledge in their classroom and consider them *equally* important and interconnected; that is, all three types of knowledge should be taught together as part of the total reading process, not as isolated entities. Reading research emphasizes the importance of such a comprehensive approach to literacy that includes both direct instruction of skills such as phonics and a more child-centered, literature-rich environment that encourages the use of strategies to comprehend text. This chapter introduces the basic concepts and components of a balanced literacy approach; subsequent chapters in this book expand and elaborate on these concepts.

Essential Elements of Balanced Literacy

Teachers who practice the balanced approach to literacy adopt the following 13 principles:

1. *The primary goal of a balanced literacy program is to teach reading, not as a skill broken into isolated steps, but as a lifelong learning process that promotes higher order thinking, problem solving, and reasoning.*

Reading is an extremely complex process that is developmental in nature. A child does not just suddenly become a "reader" in the third or fourth grade; rather, reading is a long-term developmental process that continues to change and grow as a person matures. A college student reading a textbook requires different and more complex processing of material than a high school student reading a novel or a textbook.

Teachers' VOICES A Balanced Approach

A balanced approach to reading should be comprehensive and support students and their individual learning styles. It is important for teachers to remember that teaching reading through a "balanced" approach means more than just incorporating whole-language instruction and phonics. A balanced approach should expose students to "active" learning experiences in meaningful contexts. Instructions within a balanced approach to reading should be direct and explicit and should include opportunities for modeling of effective skills and strategies. As teachers, we should always keep in mind the effective strategies that good readers use and ask ourselves if our students apply these strategies. If not, we must determine why. I believe that a balanced approach to reading instruction should include self-monitoring activities that encourage problem solving; systematic instruction in phonics and phonemic awareness; exposure to several literacy genres; and immersion in reading, writing, listening, speaking, and viewing experiences that will increase understanding.

—*Zaneta Shannon, Special Education Teacher*

Our society normally refers to "literacy" as including reading, writing, speaking, and listening, which could be termed "basic literacy" skills. A balanced approach to literacy looks at literacy as a process that is used in everyday life to solve problems, reason, and evaluate material. Too often, school reading programs teach reading as an end unto itself. Rather, reading should be viewed as a tool to help children function effectively in society and help them engage in activities that will promote lifelong learning. Thus, children need to see the purpose of literacy activities by using their literacy skills in solving problems, applying higher order reasoning, and evaluating ideas and materials. In our increasingly global, technologically advanced, information society, it is not enough that children learn how to read and write. They must learn how to interpret written material and apply what they have read. The ultimate goal of any literacy program must be to foster higher order thinking and what Langer (2001) terms "higher literacy."

Langer (2001) claims that higher literacy means that students use literacy as a tool to solve real-life problems. Teachers develop an atmosphere in which a community of learners uses literacy to explore understandings. Teachers encourage risk taking and diverse thinking, rather than valuing "right" answers and one way of viewing the world. It means that classes puzzle over the complexities of learning and realize that not every problem can be solved or answered fully and that the teacher does not know the answer for every question. *Higher literacy* is reflected in a student's ability to engage in thoughtful reading, writing, and discussion about content being taught, to use his or

Courtesy of Guilherme Cunha

In a balanced classroom, reading comprehension is an active process.

her knowledge and skills in new situations, and to perform well on reading and writing assessments, including high-stakes tests (Langer, 2001).

A balanced approach to literacy must start with an emphasis on promoting higher literacy. Literacy must be seen as a vital process that can be used to help understand the complexities of problems, as a means to communicate vital information to others in real-world tasks, and as an important component of effective citizenship in this information age.

2. *The classroom or reading area is a print-rich environment with many varied sources of readings and a comfortable atmosphere that promotes reading. The primary reading material is quality literature and authentic materials from the real world, such as letters, newspapers, menus, and posters.*

A balanced literacy classroom is filled with a variety of print resources, which are used in many different ways throughout the day. Following is a general list of resources that Fountas and Pinnell (1996) recommend:

◆ **Big books** in a range of genres: Big Books are large copies of a book that can be placed on an easel so the whole class can view and share the book together

◆ **Leveled books** for guided reading: leveled books are books found in the classroom that have been evaluated according to reading difficulty and placed into a specific category or level based on specific criteria the teacher has set up

◆ Hardcover or paperback books for independent reading: Picture books for beginners and chapter books for older students; also known as **trade books**

◆ **"Little" Books:** Little Books are books for beginning readers that are short in length and presented in a series of levels; they are commonly used in guided reading sessions

◆ Quality children's literature for the teacher to read aloud to the class

◆ Quality children's informational books that cover many different content areas

◆ Multicultural literature and books to which English language learners can relate

◆ Quality children's software programs that promote literacy

◆ Charts of poems and songs

◆ Dictionaries

◆ Stories and written text produced by the children in the class

◆ Poetry books

- ◆ Menus
- ◆ Magazines on various topics of interest
- ◆ Newspapers
- ◆ Brochures advertising various activities
- ◆ Letters written by the class and received by the class
- ◆ Directions to games, hobbies, activities
- ◆ Posters on the wall including other children's work
- ◆ Word walls: Words that are frequently used by children are placed up on a wall and organized alphabetically; a word wall is created by the teacher and children throughout the year
- ◆ A classroom library: An inviting place to read with many different types of books on display for children to enjoy in a comfortable setting

A wide variety of reading materials is essential for a balanced literacy program. Independent reading is fostered in such an environment, where children can browse materials during free time. Comfortable corners set aside for reading signal to children that print is valued in this classroom and that reading and writing are enjoyable, lifelong activities.

3. *The primary focus of children is to understand what they read and to enjoy and relate to what they read. The overall purpose of reading is comprehension and requires both a top-down and a bottom-up approach.*

A classroom organized to promote literacy is created so that it invites children to explore print in purposeful ways. The environment is one that is print rich and fosters social interaction and discussion about print. The learners develop confidence, take risks, learn to work independently, and develop social skills. The students learn that reading is a process to solve problems and obtain skills necessary to survive in our society. They are exposed to material that is part of their everyday life, and they focus on strategies and skills that will help them understand what they read. They learn that the goal of reading is for understanding. Effective reading instruction depends not only on what one does to obtain meaning, but also on the depth and quality of the understandings by which it is guided (Adams, 1990). Teachers must understand that effective instruction should include both activities that teach children how to recognize words and activities and strategies that help children derive meaning from text. During the reading process, good readers process every single letter using efficient eye movements, while also actively constructing hypotheses and generating inferences about what the text means based on prior knowledge (Pressley, 1998). Clearly, bottom-up and top-down processing interact as part of the whole process in skilled reading.

The top-down approach advocates that children should be reading literature in a comfortable, shared literacy experience where the emphasis is on understanding of text in an enjoyable context. Children exposed to rich, repetitive, and predictable text will learn about reading and writing in a natural and enjoyable setting. Skills are taught only when an apparent need arises, and reading is seen as one aspect of a holistic process that also includes writing, speaking, listening, and language development.

A bottom-up approach to reading stresses the need to teach phonics and word study through explicit instruction and a systematic approach. This approach advocates that children cannot learn how to read until they can decode the smallest unit of meaning, the word; to do this, children need to be able to identify the smallest unit of sound, the phoneme. For many children, such as English language learners and struggling readers, a major impediment in their learning how to read is that they do not have a large number of sight words in their memory and, therefore, they need phonics to help them break the code. In a balanced approach, rich experiences with print will foster children's appreciation of reading as an enjoyable and rewarding activity. Children learn that comprehension is an ongoing process beginning with the first introduction of the text and continuing through their active reading of the text and their response and interpretation of what the text means. Reading must ultimately result in comprehension and interpretation of written text.

4. *Phonemic awareness, phonics instruction, and word study are all taught as part of a broader emphasis on comprehension and enjoyment of reading. Balanced classrooms integrate authentic reading and writing with purposeful word study.*

A balanced approach to literacy is a decision-making process through which a teacher makes thoughtful decisions each day about the best way to help each individual child become a better reader and writer (Spiegel, 1999). There is no one correct way to teach reading; some methods of teaching reading work better for some children than other methods. Each child has a unique learning style; one child may be a visual learner, while another child may learn best through an auditory or kinesthetic approach. In a balanced approach, the teacher will assess each child's strengths and weaknesses, and then develop an instructional program based on that child's learning style and needs.

Strickland (1998b) maintains that skills and meaning should never be separated, and that intensive skills instruction should be based on identified needs of the child. In the early years of instruction, this means that teachers need to pay attention to basic skills, as well as expose children to rich literature in the classroom. In the earliest grades, such as preK and kindergarten, children need to learn the letters of the alphabet and identify and manipulate the sounds within spoken words, commonly known as phonemic awareness. Explicit instruction and practice with sound structures that lead to familiarity with spelling–sound conventions and their use in identifying printed words should be stressed within the context of meaningful and enjoyable literature. In upper primary grades, children need to develop a real joy of reading and read a wide variety of materials, including expository (nonfiction) and narrative (fiction) texts. Instruction should concentrate on providing quality literature appropriate to each child's current reading level, teaching of comprehension strategies, and teaching specific words that appear in students' readings, and writing. Again, skills-based instruction in grammar, word study, and spelling should be balanced and integrated with enjoyable and engaging reading and writing assignments that reflect "real-world" or authentic activities. Such activities may be writing a persuasive letter to the principal about an area of concern, writing invitations to parents and members of the community to a class event, reading a travel brochure and developing an itinerary for a vacation, or reading an award-winning novel and partaking in a book discussion with a group of students. Within all of these activities, skills should be taught and emphasized, not as isolated worksheets and drills, but as part of an interesting, engaging, and meaningful task.

5. *Comprehension involves active processing of the ideas in the text, with prior knowledge allowing the reader to make ongoing hypotheses and inferences. Comprehension strategies are taught as conscious, active processing of text or as metacognitive skills whereby children become aware of how they read and what strategies best promote comprehension at a given point in the reading process.*

During the reading process, there are certain reading strategies that each reader must actively and continuously apply and use to effectively comprehend the meaning of the text. There is evidence that some readers are more active than others, but excellent readers are consciously active throughout the whole reading process, beginning before reading, continuing during reading, and persisting after the reading is completed (Pressley, 1998). Before reading, excellent readers start predicting what the text will be about, using prior knowledge to develop a hypothesis. They will know their purpose for reading, preview the text, and develop a "reading plan" to facilitate their efficient reading of the text for maximum comprehension. This might mean skimming certain parts they deem unimportant and taking notes on other sections. During reading, excellent readers will consciously continue to make predictions and determine whether their predictions were on target. They will make inferences about word usage or about the author's intent. They will jot down notes about what they are reading, or they will make a mental note of what they consider important. They will consciously sequence material to make sense of it, and they will self-monitor by asking questions to make sure that active comprehension is occurring. They will continuously interpret the text, which will help them to draw conclusions as they go along. Once the reading is completed, excellent readers will continue to actively and consciously apply strategies to understand the text. They will construct a summary, confirm their predictions, and draw conclusions and self-monitor,

FIGURE 3-1

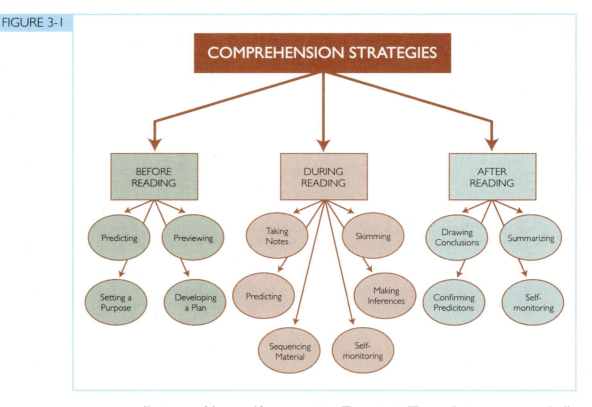

rereading parts of the text, if necessary (see Figure 3–1). The teacher must systematically teach these strategies as active and conscious processes that are involved in reading. These strategies need to be taught as part of a balanced literacy program so that readers become aware of when and how to use these strategies to comprehend text.

6. *Literacy instruction needs to balance the emphasis of children using three cueing systems: (1) semantic (meaning) cues, (2) syntactic (grammar/sentence structure) cues, and (3) graphophonic (letters, letter clusters, and corresponding sounds) cues.*

When children read, they need to identify words and comprehend written messages to determine what the passage means. To do this, they apply strategies that make use of various "cues" or prompts, which signal that a particular strategy will be needed to decode or unlock the meaning in the text. For example, when a beginning reader sees the word *cat*, picture cues may be used to aid in word identification in conjunction with using knowledge of letters and corresponding sounds to sound out the word *c-a-t*. This use of phonics to decode a word depends on alphabetic knowledge of letters, letter clusters, and corresponding sounds and is known as **graphophonic cues.**

Decoding is also dependent on a reader's background knowledge, which is an essential component of unlocking meaning from text. A reader's previous experience with cats and animals will help him or her relate the concept "cat" to prior knowledge, feelings, and impressions. If the reader has never seen a cat before, the concept is abstract, dense, and undecodable. Prior knowledge allows the reader to bring meaning to what is being read and prompts the reader to use a second cuing system, **semantic cues.** Semantic cues are derived from the context of the sentence, which provides the reader with essential information to unlock unknown words. Clay (1991) provides the following example of a semantic cue:

TEXT: Fish swim in the sea.

CHILD: *Fish swim in the water.*

No. That's not water. It doesn't begin with "w." It begins with "s" (sounds it out) . . . sea (self-correction achieved). (He rereads it.) Fish swim in the sea. (p. 000)

Here the child is using meaning to determine the unknown word (*water* for *sea*), sees a visual mismatch between the "s" and the "w," and then using letter sound while holding the meaning in his mind, figures out the correct word. Both the semantic and the graphophonic cuing systems are in evidence in the above example.

The third cuing system, **syntactic cues,** allows the reader to decode words from the grammar or sentence structure. For example, if the sentence is "I love the ocean," the reader will realize that "I love the open" is not appropriate because it does not make sense grammatically. Because of their interrelated nature, semantic, syntactic, and graphophonic cues are known as the three cuing systems of reading (Strickland, 1998b). Marie Clay (1991) claims that the learning task that beginning readers need to focus on is developing new ways of discovering cues in the text and increasing accurate responses. The teacher cannot teach the child the thousands of possible cues in print. The teacher's lessons must orient the children to the types of features they can use and then let children use self-discovery to decode text. The key in a balanced literacy program is that all three cueing systems are actively being taught and practiced as reading strategies.

7. *Children can and should be on different levels within the classroom, and this is accounted for instructionally. Flexible groupings are used constantly throughout the day.*

Grouping for instruction is a key component within a balanced literacy program. A balanced literacy teacher is aware that, throughout the day, the class can be grouped into different configurations based on the objective of the lesson and not teach to the entire class throughout the day. See Figure 3–2 for a summary of the different configurations. One ineffective approach is to use "ability grouping," in which a group of students who are reading at the same level are put in one group, placed into one level reader, and kept in this group for the total year. This has led to the advent of group names such as "The Sharks" or "The Turtles," which has led to feelings of low self-esteem and poor achievement by those who were placed in the slower groupings.

In a balanced classroom, a teacher will use flexible groupings in teaching literacy. Each grouping will depend on the overall purpose of the lesson. Flexible grouping is used in guided reading when a small group of children who need to work on the same skills and processes work together on specific reading strategies and skills. Guided reading groups are flexible in that children will not be in the same group for extended periods of time, but will be placed in different groups depending on the strategy to be taught; these groups are known as **homogeneous groups.** The purpose of these small groups is to have the teacher select appropriate reading material and support children in their literacy skills at the appropriate level.

Another type of flexible grouping that teachers use is during cooperative learning when a small group of children with mixed abilities work together on a task to attain a common goal; these groups are known as **heterogeneous groups.** The teacher usually selects the members of the group and then assigns specific tasks and assignments for the group to complete. Such activities as literature circles, readers' or writers' workshop, and hands-on science or social studies projects are excellent activities for this type of grouping.

English language learners and students with learning disabilities benefit from working in both small homogeneous and heterogeneous groups. Small, flexible homogeneous groups give diverse learners the opportunity of working at their appropriate level with other students who need similar instruction. Often, students can feel overwhelmed and left behind when they are not working at their appropriate level or reading material they do not comprehend. Small, flexible groups allow the teacher to focus on specific literacy skills from which the individual students can benefit. It also allows the teacher to choose material that is culturally relevant and written at the correct developmental level. Small heterogeneous groups also benefit English language learners and students with learning disabilities by allowing them to work with others to process text, discuss ideas, and complete a task that might be overwhelming if done alone. English language learners get a chance to practice English in a supportive and informal environment and to make contributions to the group, which contribute to self-esteem and self-confidence. Students with learning disabilities are often quite articulate and have much to contribute in a group where reading and writing are shared activities. Peer interaction is an excellent way to support diverse learners in a variety of prereading and during-reading activities during which they can discuss new vocabulary words, present examples that can help diverse students make connections, read passages to one another, and set a framework for comprehension of text.

Teachers' VOICES   Classroom Observations of a Second Grade Classroom

After observing the lesson, I had the opportunity to speak with Mrs. W. about her school, her class, and teaching in general. She told me that the school and class use trade books almost exclusively. These books are leveled, and the students engage in something called B.E.A.R. (Be Excited About Reading). Students often will be assigned miniature book reports or character analyses to confirm that they are reading and comprehending their books. They also engage in shared reading among peers. Mrs. W. told me that groups are used extensively and are often homogenously assembled by ability level. The struggling readers typically will participate in picture walks, word family exercises, and other activities within their groups that help strengthen their fundamental skills. Students in the school are also given developmental reading assessments at various times throughout the year to initially determine their strengths and

weaknesses, and subsequently to ensure that proper progress is being made, while also assisting with tailoring lessons to student needs. Mrs. W. informed me that one of her students leaves her class at times for special instruction because she is an English language learner. She also said that the students with special needs remain in the classroom; one way in which she is able to address their needs is by pairing them with a stronger student using a "buddy system." She explained that the students enjoy helping each other, and she can still provide any additional help on an as-needed basis. Typically, Mrs. W. will try to meet with the reading groups at least three times per week, and all students read and write on a daily basis. She emphasized that this was a critical aspect of the balanced literacy program that the school uses.

—*Christopher Markowski, Future Teacher*

In **differentiated instruction,** the teacher will plan lessons for students to complete independently or in groups, based on the students' specific needs. Activities such as independent reading and independent writing provide an opportunity for independent application of reading and writing strategies with the teacher's constant guidance. Differentiated instruction focuses on the processes and procedures that ensure effective learning will take place for every student in the class. A teacher is attuned to each student's varied learning needs and will make modifications in how students obtain access to important ideas and skills (Tomlinson & McTighe, 2006). Differentiated instruction is responsive teaching—that is, attending to students' backgrounds and needs, their learning profiles, developmental readiness, and personal interests. This is especially important when dealing with a diverse population of students such as English language learners and students with learning disabilities who come from many different cultural backgrounds, who display many different learning styles, who have many different interests, and who are on many different developmental levels with regard to literacy development. Differentiation does not mean that a totally different program must be developed for each student in the class, but rather that teachers support each student in achieving success in ways that work for that particular student. This support involves having clear educational goals in mind and continuously assessing how the student is progressing toward those goals (Tomlinson & McTighe, 2006).

Teachers should also use whole-class instruction during part of the school day to introduce new topics, model new skills and strategies, provide class discussion on a topic of interest, and wrap up and summarize a lesson. One type of literacy experience well suited for the whole class is **reading aloud,** where the teacher reads a book or text aloud to the whole class. Another experience is **shared reading,** where using an enlarged text or a Big Book that all children can see, the teacher involves children in reading together following a pointer. Children actively engage in reading along and in responding to the text, usually by sitting on a rug in a reading corner. Another whole-class literacy experience is **shared writing,** where the teacher and children work together to compose messages and stories. During these writing sessions, the teacher can engage in *interactive writing,* whereby the teacher and children compose messages and stories that are written using a "shared" pen technique, a child will come up to the easel and actually write part of the text with the teacher's guidance. All of these experiences are excellent uses of whole-class lessons that support rich literacy experiences. Figure 3–2 summarizes different types of groupings that a teacher can use flexibly throughout the day.

Teachers should use flexible groupings for instruction in a balanced classroom to support learning objectives. Children must be in an environment that supports their developmental needs. By varying the grouping in a classroom, a teacher is ensuring that a student's learning style is being met and that literacy is viewed as an enjoyable activity in which the student can receive support from many different sources including peers. Students enjoy the chance to work within different contexts and interact with different students.

8. *Visual literacy is balanced with reading, writing, speaking, and listening in the literacy classroom. Visual literacy is emphasized with the use of technology. Visual and nontextual graphic organizers such as semantic maps, Venn diagrams, and story maps are used to construct meaning from texts.*

A balanced literacy program not only emphasizes balance in using a top-down with a bottom-up approach, but also balances the various components of literacy. Literacy comprises reading, writing, speaking, and listening, as well as visual literacy. Visual literacy is the ability to interpret visual symbols and graphical information and effectively construct meaning from these visual representations. It is also the ability to present information graphically so that others can use it effectively. In essence, there are two sides to visual literacy: (1) the ability to view and interpret visual information, and (2) the ability to design and create visual representations of information. In the first experience, the student reads and comprehends what is being presented visually and graphically. In the second instance, the student must actively create visual representations. These representations can be used for several purposes: to help the student retain and comprehend the material to be learned, to present information to others in a graphical way, or to help other students effectively comprehend and retain what is to be learned.

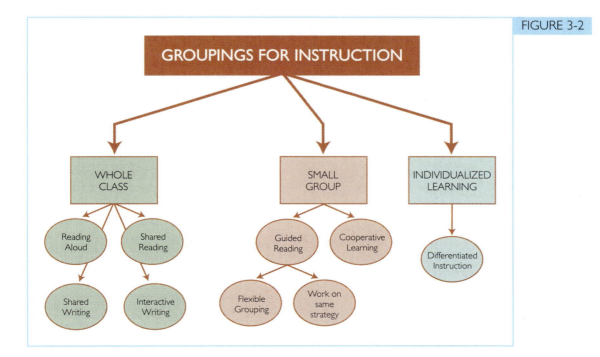

FIGURE 3-2

GROUPINGS FOR INSTRUCTION

WHOLE CLASS — Reading Aloud, Shared Reading, Shared Writing, Interactive Writing

SMALL GROUP — Guided Reading, Cooperative Learning, Flexible Grouping, Work on same strategy

INDIVIDUALIZED LEARNING — Differentiated Instruction

Visual images provide the connections between the abstract theory and the practical, graphical representation of that theory. These images help learners make connections between linear thinking and a more holistic, nonlinear thinking that encourages students to see thematic interrelationships. Visual tools, such as concept mapping or webbing, provide a strong link between teaching content and developing thinking processes by encouraging students to graphically represent thoughts and ideas in a holistic fashion (Hyerle, 1996). Students can use visual tools to represent their thoughts graphically, thereby attending to new alternatives and perspectives. Visual representations of information contribute to students becoming more visually attuned and literate, so that when they access information they are aware of high-quality images that promote learning, as well as low-quality images that confuse and confound them.

Visual tools such as concept mapping or webbing are excellent tools to support students with learning disabilities in comprehension of text. The visual tools graphically display the key ideas of text and help students to identify the main points of what they just read, to make connections between various concepts being presented, and thereby to process it more efficiently. Visual tools are also beneficial to English language learners, who are often struggling readers and need support in key reading and writing processes. By representing the text visually and supplying keywords in their native language, visual tools help English language learners to overcome language deficits and to make connections to their background knowledge.

A "visual" shift in classrooms has occurred (Hyerle, 1996). First, learning theory supports the use of visual representations of concepts to support learning. The old adage "A picture is worth a thousand words" holds true. Students learn material faster and easier when they have a visual representation of it to store in their memories. In addition, technology is having a major impact on the way in which information is presented and organized. Students are exposed to visual displays of information using computer technology, the Internet, and television. They are inundated with new visual images of information, and are required to process it. More and more information is presented graphically than ever before. In our highly technological world, it is essential that students learn how to effectively process visual information, as well as to express themselves through graphical representations. Students need to use their literacy skills as a tool that they can apply effectively to solve problems, think critically, research a problem, evaluate web pages, and use and create information. In a balanced literacy program, all aspects of literacy are promoted, including visual literacy.

9. *In a balanced literacy classroom, children respond to what they read in varied ways. Their response to text is a valued part of the comprehension process. Teachers balance the way that children respond to what they read.*

Readers need to articulate and formulate responses about what they read and how they interpret text; through this process of responding, students learn to share and organize their thoughts about the text, and thereby clarify within their own minds what the text means. In a response-based curriculum, teachers view readers as active meaning-makers whose personal experiences affect their interpretations of text. Therefore, there is no one "correct" interpretation of the text, but each reader might have a very different, very valid interpretation of the same story. Such activities as literature discussion circles, class discussion, drama, art projects, and shared writing all contribute to each individual's interpretation of what is read. The curriculum should not be centered on delivering content, but rather on responding to what the students have read about the content and developing critical thinking skills through social and personal examination of the text.

10. *Reading and writing are seen as complementary processes that are taught together across the curriculum. Students write daily and engage in peer editing and publishing activities.*

Reading and writing are complementary processes that support each other; what is learned in one area relates directly to what is applied in the other area (Fountas & Pinnell, 1996). When children read text, they are interpreting what an author has to say. When children are writing text, they are conveying a message that readers will try to understand. Reading and writing are reciprocal and interrelated. Children need an abundant amount of time to write in the classroom. Preschools and primary classrooms should have writing centers that contain a wide variety of materials to encourage the development of writing. Through individual conferencing, mini-lessons (short lessons that are about 10 to 15 minutes in length), and whole-class writing activities, teachers can help children develop as authors. Writing and reading should also be taught in every subject area. Writing materials can be available in the science center for students to take notes and keep records and in the social studies center to record feelings and label graphs and pictures. Every subject area uses reading and writing, and a teacher incorporates literacy activities throughout the curriculum.

11. *Diversity is valued and encouraged within the classroom and throughout the curriculum, particularly through multicultural literature and a multiple perspectives approach to comprehension.*

Schools are a microcosm of our global world, and diversity is very much a valued part of our society. Every classroom has students who reflect different racial, ethnic, linguistic, socioeconomic, gender, religious, and learning differences. Each child brings special needs into the classroom that must be addressed. The teacher must encourage the students to appreciate their own uniqueness, and thereby value the diversity of others (Bieger, 1996). This can be accomplished through using multicultural literature in the classroom that promotes recognition, understanding, and acceptance of cultural diversity and individual uniqueness. By promoting diversity, children become sensitized to the experiences of others and learn to empathize through the stories that are told. They briefly share in the lives and feelings of characters rather than learn about facts and dates (Bieger, 1996). In addition, it is important that children learn that all stories can be told through different perspectives. Children should read about historical incidents presented from the point of view of the people involved and concerned. Children often read about their culture from one point of view only; thus, they develop feelings of low self-esteem and do not feel they are valued members of society. A wonderful way to introduce multiple perspectives is through the retelling of *The Three Little Pigs*. In a humorous book, *The True Story of the 3 Little Pigs* by Jon Scieszka, the wolf gives his retake on the classic story, and children learn that there may be many ways to view a story. Another example is through reading parallel versions of the same fairy tale from different cultures. Children can read *Cinderella* and compare it with *Mufaro's Beautiful Daughters* by John Steptoe, an African version of the same tale. Teachers in a balanced literacy classroom emphasize multicultural education, value diversity, and incorporate a wide range of multicultural literature and activities into their classrooms.

12. *Authentic assessment is used to assess the child's reading and writing. Running records, individual reading inventories, checklists, and portfolios are all used on a continuing basis. Frequent and continuous feedback and encouragement are given to each child.*

Ongoing assessment is a key component of a balanced literacy program. Assessment has many different purposes in the classroom: to assess a child's strengths and weaknesses; to help a teacher make instructional decisions regarding each child; to document progress for parents and students; to summarize achievement over a period of time; and to report to administrators, school board members, and state department officials the level of achievement of a group of students. As it relates to reading and other literacy areas, assessment enables a teacher to gather meaningful information or data concerning or impacting the child's reading of school-related textual materials, as well as recreational materials (Flippo, 2003). The primary purpose of assessment is to gather data from multiple sources to inform instruction; therefore, assessment must help the teacher in making appropriate literacy improvements for all children within the classroom. Assessment needs to focus on the individual student and be *diagnostic* in nature; that is, it must focus on what that child's specific strengths and weaknesses are. It needs to be continual and multidimensional so that it is not just a "snapshot" like a photograph that captures a particular instant in time, but might not accurately reflect the total picture or profile. Assessment should yield a *prescription* or a blueprint

Courtesy of Bill Lisenby

Regular assessment of student learning by teachers helps to inform literacy instruction.

for instruction that builds on the student's strengths and helps overcome specific weaknesses. Some form of assessment should occur every day, whether it is a formal observation, a running record of a student reading out loud to the teacher, or a writing sample. Assessment should be collected in a portfolio that represents the student's achievement in different areas of literacy, and assessment should reflect multiple ways of collecting data in the same area. Therefore, the portfolio can document reading progress by containing running records, observations, anecdotal notes that the teacher keeps in a systematic way, tapes of the student reading out loud, and informal reading inventories that determine the reading level of the student. The portfolio can also document more formal evaluation by containing records of standardized reading tests, state required tests, and district-mandated tests. Assessment should also involve children and parents in the process. Students should receive constant feedback with regard to progress and have the opportunity to reflect on their growth. Parent involvement is crucial, and parents can participate in helping their children progress toward specified goals by working with them at home.

13. *A balanced literacy program promotes ongoing family involvement in the literacy development of the children.*

Families must be involved with the development of the children's literacy growth. The foundation for reading success is formed long before a child comes to school. Parents, care providers, and other community members all contribute to giving children a strong base of cognitive skills related to print, background knowledge, and love of books. What the child learns about language at home is the foundation for literacy learning in the classroom. Early experiences with written language may occur during the first year of life, such as listening to stories read from books, playing with blocks, scribbling with crayons, listening to songs and rhymes, and just interacting with other significant members of the family and community. One of the more significant factors associated with success in reading is being read to at home. Such connections must continue through children's progression through school. Families must stay involved and support literacy learning at home. Reading and writing must be valued at home so that children view literacy as an important part of their world. Teachers must involve parents in their children's education by sending home letters regarding children's progress, involving the family in collaborative literacy projects, involving the family, and educating families to become more knowledgeable about the current research underlying the school's approach to teaching literacy.

What a Balanced Literacy Classroom Looks Like

A balanced literacy classroom is an active place where children are engaged in *doing* literacy; they are reading, solving problems, writing, creating, discussing, listening, viewing, and working independently. Therefore, the space and furniture needs to be organized so that children can work effectively and independently on their tasks. When children are busy discussing a book, they should not disturb those students who are quietly writing. When working with a small guided reading group, the teacher needs to manage the other students, as well as work with the small group. Literacy-rich classrooms should have the following areas set up (Fountas & Pinnell, 1996):

◆ *Large-group area* where demonstrations and meetings will take place. Many teachers use a large rug as the central point of this area.

◆ *Small-group areas* where children can work at a table together, work in pairs, or work independently on projects. Groups of desks can form a work table, and there should be enough space so that children do not feel crowded or frustrated.

◆ *Independent work areas* where children can work independently without distraction. Small study carrels or individual desks can be used in a quiet section of the room.

◆ *Guided reading area* where the teacher can work with a small group of students while also keeping watch on the rest of the class. The teacher can sit with the children in a semicircle in a part of the classroom where the teacher can face the rest of the class.

◆ *Centers* where children can work in groups or independently on the specified activities that are part of the center. There may be some permanent centers, such as writing, listening, word study, or technology centers, as well as centers that periodically change; for example, a rain forest center could be created to correspond to a unit the students are studying. Each center is located in a designated area or at a separate table and has appropriate materials that enable children to explore a specific topic or task. Centers are task-oriented with clear expectations, but open-ended enough to foster inquiry and higher order thinking. Centers have an ongoing routine set up where children know exactly what is expected of them and how long to work at a center before moving on to the next one. The teacher provides clear rules and guidelines in advance so that children work responsibly and are on task. Learning centers are discussed in more detail in Chapter 14.

◆ *A classroom library* where many different types of books are on display for children to enjoy in a comfortable setting. Some teachers have couches or comfortable chairs available for children to enjoy while reading. Books are on display and are varied throughout the year to stimulate interest and correspond with units being taught. The library should contain a variety of genres including fiction and nonfiction books.

◆ *Storage area* for maintaining and storing records of students' progress. Folders, portfolios, plastic crates, cardboard boxes, and plastic containers are all good resources to have available for organizing and storing records. It is helpful to have these records located in one location in the classroom for easy access and organization.

As outlined above, the balanced literacy classroom should be a comfortable, enjoyable, and organized environment that supports literacy development in a student-centered and caring atmosphere. Many different types of print resources should be available, and furniture should be arranged so that the teacher can manage classroom instruction easily and effectively.

Reading and a Balanced Literacy Program

In a balanced approach to literacy, children engage in many different forms of reading throughout the day and week. Each type of reading has its own specific purpose and allows children to engage in a variety of literacy experiences. Teachers should carefully observe children reading in each type of experience listed below and assess each student's progress in the different situations. The chart on page 88 (adapted from Fountas & Pinnell, 1996) summarizes the different types of reading that should occur in the classroom.

Each type of reading described in the chart should be implemented in a balanced literacy classroom and used throughout the day.

Reading Aloud

During reading aloud, it is the teacher who reads the text, not the students. Research and current practice support the use of teacher read-alouds as a significant component of instruction across grade levels (Fisher, Flood, Lapp, & Frey, 2004). Read-alouds model expressive, enthusiastic reading while transmitting the pleasure of reading and inviting listeners to become part of the literacy process. When reading aloud, the teacher should read with expression, maintain a slow reading pace, and engage the students in the text by looking up from the book frequently to maintain eye contact. Reading aloud is one of the most common and easiest means of sharing books in a pleasurable experience. It helps older children become better readers (Galda & Cullinan, 2002). Reading aloud adds pleasure to the day for all ages of students, primary to high school.

Teachers' VOICES   A Balanced Approach

In my third grade class, I stress the importance of reading for meaning through building on prior knowledge, making predictions, learning new vocabulary, and using higher order thinking skills to develop a deeper understanding. A balanced reading approach includes opportunities for whole-group learning, as well as individualized instruction to address particular needs and build on strengths. When instruction is done effectively, students should become active learners and develop self-monitoring strategies.

—*Stephanie Lawlor, Special Education Teacher*

There are many reasons to read aloud throughout the year: It enriches students' general knowledge, it demonstrates different writing styles and forms of written language, it stimulates interest in different subjects, it introduces different genres that children may not be inclined to read, it exposes children to new words and sounds, and it introduces children to different authors. Pinnell and Jaggar (2003) demonstrate the importance of read-alouds in the growth of oral language for both first- and second-language speakers. Read-alouds can lead to an improvement in language expression throughout all curriculum subjects and help children understand the components, structure, and function of narrative storytelling (Fisher et al., 2004).

Fisher et al. (2004) recommend seven components of an interactive read-aloud:

1. *Select the text carefully.* Teachers should select high-quality texts based on the interests and needs of the students in the class. Often, award-winning books that have received notice are recommended.

2. *Preview and practice the text before reading.* Teachers should practice the text out loud before attempting to conduct a read-aloud. This greatly increases the effectiveness of the reading.

3. *Establish a clear purpose for the reading.* Teachers should establish a clear purpose as to why this book is being read and tie the book into the lesson's theme and objectives. The teacher should also tie the book into the students' background knowledge about the topic.

4. *Model fluent reading.* By practicing the read-aloud ahead of time, the teacher can provide a model of fluent oral reading and keep errors to a minimum.

5. *Read with animation and expression.* It is important that the teacher exhibits animation and expression by changing voice levels to denote different characters' emotions and moods. Using hand gestures, facial expressions, and props also provides motivation for children to become engaged with the reading.

6. *Discuss the text with the students.* Teachers should discuss the book with the students before, during, and after the read-aloud. Using sticky notes placed on the pages of the book with questions on them is a helpful device. Teachers should pause to ask

Type of Reading	Description	Purpose(s)	Types of Text
READING ALOUD	The teacher reads aloud to the whole group. In the primary grades, this usually takes place on a rug or in a comfortable group area. Quality children's literature is used representing many different genres.	◆ Provides a model of phrased, fluent reading ◆ Promotes oral language development ◆ Develops concepts of print ◆ Allows children to enjoy books that are too difficult to read themselves ◆ Involves children in an enjoyable reading experience	◆ Quality literature ◆ Books with bright and colorful illustrations ◆ Multicultural themes ◆ Humorous books ◆ Books with dialogue ◆ Books with action that hold children's interest ◆ Books that fit into the class theme or topics being studied
SHARED READING	The class engages in reading a book together, usually an enlarged big book for the primary grades.	◆ Allows the class to engage in an enjoyable shared literacy experience ◆ Allows teacher to model specific reading strategies ◆ Increases children's knowledge of print	◆ Predictable and rhyming text ◆ Books that follow a pattern so children can fill in the words ◆ Humorous books ◆ Books with illustrations that the class can enjoy and share ◆ Poetry ◆ Word walls
GUIDED READING	The teacher works with a small group of students who are on approximately the same level of reading and have similar needs. The group works with books that have been selected by the teacher to match the group's reading level. The group reads the book out loud and the teacher works with each member to support basic reading strategies. Specific skills and strategies are taught in a supportive session.	◆ Provides the opportunity for students to receive help on specific needs and to read books on their specific level ◆ Provides the opportunity for students to receive "scaffolding" or support on reading strategies ◆ Allows teacher to individualize instruction for each group and to work with each student based on data collected during continuous assessment	◆ Books that are on the student's level of reading ◆ At first, books that are easy and short; later, some longer texts and chapter books ◆ Books that reflect a wide range of content, topics, and genres ◆ Information-rich texts; that is, those in which meaning is signaled in multiple ways—the illustrations, the syntax, the context, the print
INDEPENDENT READING	Children read books independently that have been chosen by the teacher, or that they have chosen from a range of material on their own level. The teacher carefully selects a range of books that the students can read based on current reading level.	◆ Allows students to practice reading independently ◆ Provides an opportunity for children to practice reading strategies on their own ◆ Promotes reading at home when children see independent reading being modeled by everyone in the classroom ◆ Allows children to choose their own books and read them in a comfortable and enjoyable setting	◆ A variety of picture books, trade books, chapter books ◆ Many genres including nonfiction should be provided ◆ Books that have been "leveled" or graded according to certain criteria so that they match the students' reading ability ◆ Manuals, reference materials such as dictionaries, menus or recipes, charts, diagrams, and maps

questions and allow students to share their thoughts, reactions, predictions, and concerns about the book; this is an important part of the read-aloud.

7. *Connect the read-aloud to independent reading or writing.* Teachers can provide students with journal writing time immediately after the read-aloud or select books for independent reading that are related in some way to the read-aloud. For younger students, hands-on projects and illustrating the story are also effective follow-up strategies.

During the read-aloud, teachers have different opinions about showing the students the illustrations. Some teachers believe that the illustrations are an important aspect of the literacy experience and should be shared as the book is being read. Others believe that the pictures should be shown after the read-aloud to help children develop visual representation of the story. Still other teachers show only the pictures first to help students predict what the story will be about. The method you use depends on your objective for reading the book. If you want to teach prediction skills or identifying clues from the illustrations, then do a "book walk" showing only the pictures in the first run through the book. If you want to teach how to mentally visualize material as text is being read, then show the pictures only at the end of the reading. If the objective is to enjoy a book and model reading strategies, then the pictures and the text should be enjoyed together. Whichever method a teacher chooses, reading aloud should be a daily activity in the classroom, continuing through middle school and even into high school.

It is *not* recommended that students read aloud a passage from the text in round-robin fashion, because it often places students in an embarrassing situation when they are not fluent with the material. This activity should be reserved for guided reading sessions in small groups, when the teacher can support the reader and provide necessary guidance to promote fluency and comprehension.

Shared Reading

During shared reading, the teacher or other student guides the children through the reading using a pointer of some sort to point to each word as it is being read. This technique was originally developed in New Zealand (Holdaway, 1979) as a means of engaging children in the reading process and concentrating on print at the same time. Texts are usually enlarged so that the whole class can see the print clearly and they can participate in group reading. Either big books, which many publishers currently provide, or projector can be used. Usually, the big book is placed on an easel next to a low chair that the teacher sits in while the class sits on a carpet or pillow surrounding the teacher and easel. Shared reading should begin early in kindergarten before children read many words and should continue through the primary grades. It helps students develop concepts about print: letters, words, phrasings of sentences, tracking of eyes from left to right, story lines, and rhyming. During shared reading, the teacher reads the text first, pointing to each word as it is being read. The book is reread several times so that children become familiar with the text. They can even read small versions of the book with a buddy or in a small group. After the initial reading, different children can be called on to point to the individual words and to assist the teacher. The book selected should be one that the children enjoy and request reading again. Usually, books that are predictable and repeat a similar pattern from page to page are good choices because they help students memorize the words and predict the story line.

Guided Reading

Guided reading usually begins in kindergarten when children are starting to read and are introduced to a more formal reading session. Usually, there is a smooth transition from shared reading to guided reading, because many of the activities will carry over into a small group setting. In first grade, guided reading should become the foundation of the literacy program (Fountas & Pinnell, 1996) and continue through third grade. Guided reading sessions can continue with upper primary children as well to support comprehension strategies, especially as the curriculum shifts from narrative texts (stories) to expository texts (informational text). Children should participate in a guided reading session three to five days a week. At first, children will start with short books that can be completed in one session and can be read independently. The teacher provides skills and strategy support to each child. The teacher will want to see continuous progression in the children's literacy skills and ability to read fluently by working intensely with students at their own level. As children progress in reading ability, longer books can be read, until one chapter per session can be covered. The focus of each session should be targeted on the specific strategy/skill that the teacher believes needs support. This focus will change from session to session, and as children improve their literacy skills, they should be moved to a different group. Flexible grouping is ongoing and is based on assessed needs of the child. In the upper grades, the sessions can concentrate on more advanced strategies, such as analyzing texts according to theme, development of characterization, and identifying different types of writing styles. Groups do not have to read the same book, because there should be a wide selection of leveled books from which to choose. The teacher or child chooses specific books according to interest and reading level.

TEACHSOURCE VIDEO CASE

A Visit to Mr. Bryan's Classroom: Text-to-Text and Text-to-Self Connections

Mr. Bryan's classroom is very cheerful, with many literacy-rich decorations for the children to observe, including a large amount of multicultural books in a very accessible classroom library. The children eagerly join Mr. Bryan at the front of the room to sit in a semicircle. Mr. Bryan greets the children once they are settled and tells them that they will be starting their "Readers Workshop." During the Workshop, he will introduce a new reading strategy to the class in a "mini-lesson," he will conduct a shared reading session with the class, and then while students are reading independently, he will meet with one guided reading group.

Mr. Bryan introduces the Readers Workshop by asking the children, "What is it that you love most about reading?" One student remembers that he learned about making text-to-text connections so that he can compare one text to another, both of which

have similar elements, such as settings, problems, or characters.

Mr. Bryan starts the "mini-lesson" by introducing his objective: "Today we are going to learn about making another kind of connection about a book—one that reminds us of

something from our own lives. When we read a book we make connections about our own personal experiences that are similar to the kinds of experiences in the stories we have just read. Today we will learn about making text-to-self connections." Mr. Bryan then picks up a book entitled *Could Be Worse*, by James Stevenson. It is about a grandfather telling his grandchildren that something might be difficult or bad, but that it "Could be worse!" Mr. Bryan then goes on to read the book to the class in a shared reading session, with the children joining in the refrain, "*It could be worse!*"

When he is midway through the book, Mr. Bryan goes to the easel, which has a graphic organizer with two columns. He labels one column, *The Author Said*, and he labels the other column, *That Reminds Me Of?* He then models for the children how to make a text-to-self connection.

(continues)

STRATEGIES FOR TEACHING DIVERSE LEARNERS

The Balanced Literacy Classroom and English Language Learners

- Practice responsive teaching in the classroom by building on the diversity among students. Learn about your culturally diverse students and become familiar with their language, interactional style, learning styles, and values.

- Differentiate instruction to meet the needs of all students in the class.

- Carefully choose reading materials to which English language learners can relate. Allow them to choose their own books to read independently in class and at home.

- Focus on high-level thinking and problem solving. Often, literacy instruction focuses on low-level mechanics or pronunciation at the literal or word level, with little attention given to comprehension of meaningful texts.

- Build on the strengths of the students in a child-centered classroom. Poor achievement scores, cultural differences, a dual-language background, and limited familiarity with academic language skills in English do *not* mean that these children lack the ability to perform higher level cognitive tasks. All children have linguistic and cognitive strengths regardless of their first language or the income level of their homes (Strickland, 1998c).

- Encourage authentic talk and communication in the classroom so that English language learners interact with other students and with the teacher to discuss ideas, share perspectives, relay facts, and enjoy conversations. Communication allows English language learners to build social relationships, model good oral and written discourse strategies, expand background knowledge, and help each other elaborate on ideas (Barnitz, 1998).

- Use multicultural material in read-alouds and in shared reading.

- Provide software programs to reinforce reading strategies and help with writing. Provide electronic talking books in students' native language, if possible.

STRATEGIES FOR TEACHING DIVERSE LEARNERS

The Balanced Literacy Classroom and Students with Learning Disabilities

- Provide direct instruction in phonics and be sure to reinforce these skills continuously throughout the year. Many students with learning disabilities have deficiencies in phonological processing of sounds and need intense instruction in this essential reading skill.

- During read-alouds and shared reading, place students with learning disabilities in the front of the class, next to the teacher, to ensure that they can adequately see the book, hear the teacher, and attend to directions.

- Closely monitor students with learning disabilities during cooperative learning experiences to make sure that they are receiving the support they need and are interacting in a positive manner with the other members of the group.

- Work closely with the families of students with learning disabilities and suggest that read-alouds and shared reading of familiar books be conducted at home. It is especially helpful if the children can take home the books read in class to practice reading at home.

- Provide guided reading instruction to students with learning disabilities as often as possible. The small, intensive group instruction in basic reading skills is beneficial.

- Provide hands-on projects and many different ways for students with learning disabilities to respond to what they read. Use a multisensory approach to instruction.

A balanced literacy classroom includes a reading center and a guided reading group, shown here, as well as a computer center, storage areas, and a classroom library.

Technology and a Balanced Literacy Approach

This chapter discusses literacy as reading, writing, listening, speaking, and visual literacy. However, this definition is not broad enough. In this new multimedia world, we need to expand our definition even further. If we expect students to deal effectively with new technologies, they must be able to find meaning in many different information contexts. Technology delivers the information, but students must know what to do with this raw material and become "information literate." Technology requires students to process information in new ways. It is a highly visual medium; therefore, visual literacy becomes an essential part of processing information. Computer technology such as the Internet is not a linear medium, and a person easily can be distracted from his or her initial goal and wind up reading and searching for something totally different than that which was initially intended. This can be beneficial to those who feel comfortable exploring topics freely, but many students need goal-directed activities that must be completed in a specified period of time. In addition, text is difficult to read on the screen. Unlike a book, the screen requires different skills to process information; layout must be more graphical and carefully designed. Therefore, specific strategies for supporting guided searches, reading from the screen, and processing information are needed in the balanced literacy classroom.

STRATEGY BOX

Implementing a Balanced Literacy Approach

Mrs. Batista uses various strategies to implement a balanced approach in her classroom. She uses the following strategies to help her support all her students:

1. She uses read-alouds to model fluent reading of text and to introduce high-quality literature to the students.

2. She connects the read-alouds to independent reading and writing by encouraging students to explore related themes and topics in their choice of books and in journal writing.

3. Children engage in shared reading, rereading the text numerous times. Each time they read, she allows them to take on more responsibility for reading the text. Rereading of text increases fluency.

4. She creates small, flexible groupings for guided reading and provides direct instruction of reading strategies and skills during these sessions. She focuses on the individual student's needs and continuously assesses the students. As they progress and their needs change, she moves them to another group. She keeps changing the groups according to students' needs.

5. She uses leveled books in the classroom and in guided reading groups. She makes sure students are reading books on their correct reading level.

6. She creates a print-rich environment with a variety of reading material for all students to read independently. Multicultural books and reading material are available for a diverse population of students; these books address her students' native cultures and deal with topics to which they can relate.

7. She weaves technology into the curriculum and uses many different activities to promote literacy such as Internet projects, virtual field trips, and accessing online databases. She directly teaches students how to comprehend electronic text and how to find information from a CD-ROM or website.

8. She engages students in conversation and dialogue. This is especially helpful for English language learners.

Following is a list of ways that technology can be used to promote literacy in a balanced literacy classroom:

◆ E-mail
◆ Word processing programs
◆ Internet searches
◆ Research using the Internet
◆ Writing programs, such as The Amazing Writing Machine
◆ Reading programs that emphasize reading skills, such as Reader Rabbit and Word Munchers
◆ Electronic Talking Books, such as "Just Grandma and Me" or the "Arthur Treacher" series, which present a story and read it to the child
◆ Large assessment programs, such as Accelerated Reader, which allow a student to be tested on material from books that are read
◆ Visual tools programs, such as "Inspiration" or "Kidspiration," which allow the user to create webs or maps
◆ Hand-held devices to assist in delivery of instruction and assessment
◆ MP3 players or iPods for pod-casts
◆ The use of wikis and blogs to promote writing and social interaction
◆ Assessment programs to assess a child's reading ability
◆ Visual tools programs, such as Inspiration, that allow the user to create webs or maps
◆ Handheld devices to assist in delivery of instruction and assessment
◆ This list is just a beginning in exploring how technology promotes literacy in a balanced classroom. Can you think of other ways? Children must be taught technology literacy skills in purposeful and meaningful ways. Classrooms need to adopt these new tools as part of their literacy program so that children are taught how to use them properly.

There are many important issues that need to be considered when teaching technology and literacy. Many of them have positive or questionable effects on our students. The one thing we know is that technology is not going away—it will only increase in its effect on our lives and on how children learn. Therefore, it is essential that teachers carefully study and learn about technology and its implications within the balanced literacy classroom in this information age.

Technology Connections

Integrating Technology into the Literacy Classroom

The Internet is perhaps the most powerful technological advancement that has brought unprecedented changes to our world. It has impacted our perspective of literacy, forcing us to confront the issue of what skills are required of our children to succeed in this global world. The Internet has been adopted across the world in such a short period of time, and its effects have been profound. It provides access to so much useful information and provides a new means of communication—from wikis, to blogging, to twittering, to social networking, to texting, to sending videos instantaneously around the world. A new model of literacy has developed, and is in the process of developing as we read this chapter (Coiro, Knobel, Lankshear, & Leu, 2008).

Integration of technology into the curriculum is an integral part of the balanced literacy classroom. Many state literacy/language arts standards include visual and media literacy as an integral component of literacy development. Some powerful ways this can be done are:

1. *Collaborating online with other schools:* Classrooms across the country and world can share information and work together. This can be done through Internet Projects, which is described in Chapter 2. Projects are "hosted" by a particular teacher or school and are designed for classrooms from kindergarten through high school. An example of a collaborative project is "Holidays Around the World," where students from different cultures and faith traditions share their favorite holidays. Students participate in this project by researching their favorite holiday and writing a brief essay about it. They also will share photos or pictures they've drawn and scanned of their families celebrating the holiday. Students will paste their essays and photos, along with a picture of their nation's flag. Another example of collaborating with other classrooms is through blogging. Some teachers are using blogs to link with outside resources, where students read a book and then have a chance to discuss the book with students in other classrooms, and other schools.

2. *Researching deep and relevant topics of interest:* Research is perhaps the main reason to use the Internet in the classroom. Students have a wealth of information available for them to access. School and public libraries often have a limited number of resources available and the Internet has become the first and foremost resource that students turn to first when conducting research. Teachers need to ensure that students have the appropriate skills to search, comprehend, evaluate, and use the information available to them. They also need to know how to provide appropriate attribution to their source by providing adequate citation. This will be covered in more depth in Chapter 12.

3. *Using technological tools which will promote creativity and problem solving:* Software programs such as *Inspiration* and *Kidspiration* allow students and teachers to present concepts and ideas in graphical representations through maps and visual tools. Students can combine text, sounds, graphics, animation, audio, and/or video together to increase literacy skills and promote creative problem solving. The Internet has many different free resources available for students to use in their multimedia productions. They need to learn how to access these resources, evaluate how appropriate they are to the topic, and combine them into focused presentations that communicate what they intend. Students also need to learn copyright issues regarding the media that they access and want to use on the Internet.

www

A direct link to different ways technology can be integrated into the literacy classroom is provided on the *Literacy for Children in an Information Age* Book premium website (http://www.cengage. com/login).

You will be exploring how to integrate technology into a balanced literacy classroom in the upcoming chapters. Each upcoming chapter demonstrates different ways that teachers and students can develop the new literacies through technolgy applications.

Final Thoughts

The balanced approach to literacy combines a child-centered emphasis on reading and comprehending good literature with the integration of instruction in explicit and systematic phonics. As Jill, a first grade teacher, says, "I believe in a combination of whole language and phonics, but I need to stress phonics to help my students read. I find that a number of students have trouble identifying letters and sounds and need the phonics instruction." The balanced approach allows teachers to literally take advantage of both the top-down and bottom-up approaches to meet the needs of all students. As Mrs. Kantrowitz says, "My approach includes shared reading, independent reading, reading with a partner, reading aloud, and guided reading. I favor shared reading because it provides the class with the opportunity to feel successful in a low-pressure learning environment. The big books are my favorite reading material because they allow everyone to get involved and all the students feel successful."

As authors, we offer the following definition of balanced reading that synthesizes the essence of this chapter and will help you place the following chapters in the appropriate context: "A balanced reading approach is research-based, assessment-based, comprehensive, integrated, and dynamic, in that it empowers teachers and specialists to respond to the individual assessed literacy needs of children as they relate to their appropriate instructional and developmental levels of decoding, vocabulary, fluency, reading comprehension, motivation, and sociocultural acquisition, with the purpose of learning to read for meaning, understanding, and joy" (Cowen, 2003a, p. 10).

It is important that you, as a future or practicing teacher, learn about the balanced approach to literacy right at the beginning of this book. The balanced approach serves as a model of how effective reading instruction should be taught. It is important that as you go through this book, you visualize what an effective classroom looks like. As theory and practice are explained, you need to see the big picture of a literacy classroom in motion and then place these descriptions into the framework of a balanced reading approach. This approach is not only a philosophy but also a blueprint for effective literacy instruction that you will put into place piece by piece as you go through the following pages.

In the next chapter, we examine how literacy develops in young children and the factors that affect literacy development. Emergent literacy (or the preschool years from birth to age 4) is an important area to examine because it sets the stage for a child's future success or failure in school. During this time, more learning will occur than in any other period of life, and the experiences that a child has will influence his or her life forever. Chapter 4 describes theories and educational applications for preschool children.

EXPLORATION   Application of Concepts

Activities

1. Visit the weblinks for this chapter (http://www. cengage.com/education/cohen) and investigate the five ways in which technology can be integrated into the balanced literacy classroom.

2. Visit a teacher's website to see how classrooms are integrating the Internet into their curriculum.

Choose a grade level below and see if you think a balanced literacy curriculum is being used. Discuss how parents might use these sites for a home–school connection. Visit these classrooms:

• Mrs. Dingman's Third Grade:

http://mrsdingman.homestead.com/home.html

- Mrs. DeCosa's School Web Page

  http://oswego.org/staff/jdecosa/web/

- Ms. Ross's First Grade Class

  http://www.msrossbec.com/index.shtml

- Mr. Fontanella's Kindergarten Class

  http://www.jsd.k12.ak.us/hbv2/classrooms/
  Fontanella/fontanejhbvHome.html

3. Visit a real classroom, and using the balanced literary approach form, assess whether you think a balanced curriculum is being implemented.

Is a Balanced Literacy Approach Being Used In This Classroom?

Student Name: _____   Classroom or URL: _____

Checks off all items that you think apply to this classroom. If you haven't observed it or cannot make an assessment of the item, write NS (not seen) in the space.

_____ 1. Comprehension of material is being stressed in this classroom.

_____ 2. A variety of print sources are being used to promote literacy.

_____ 3. Both a top-down and bottom-up approach are being used.

_____ 4. Word study, phonics instruction, and phonemic awareness are being taught as part of literacy instruction. They are taught within the context of reading literature, not in isolation.

_____ 5. Comprehension strategies are being taught such as prediction, inferencing, and drawing conclusions.

_____ 6. Flexible groupings are used in the classroom.

_____ 7. Guided reading groups are used.

_____ 8. Centers are part of the classroom.

_____ 9. Writing as a process is used throughout the day.

_____ 10. Literature is read throughout the year.

_____ 11. The class partakes in shared reading experiences.

_____ 12. Technology is infused in the classroom.

_____ 13. Diversity is valued and children engaged in multicultural literature and activities.

_____ 14. Children are assessed through portfolios, running records, and rubrics.

_____ 15. The class is a child-centered, enjoyable, and print-rich environment.

_____ TOTAL NUMBER OF POINTS

Comments:

4. Using the semantic map provided, in a group fill in the bubbles with what each aspect of a balanced approach means to you. Give specific examples.

5. Divide your paper into four columns with these headings: Read Aloud, Shared Reading, Guided Reading, and Independent Reading. Now brainstorm all the ideas you have for each heading, including methods, types of books, materials needed, and purpose. In a group, have each member role-play the teacher for each type of literary experience.

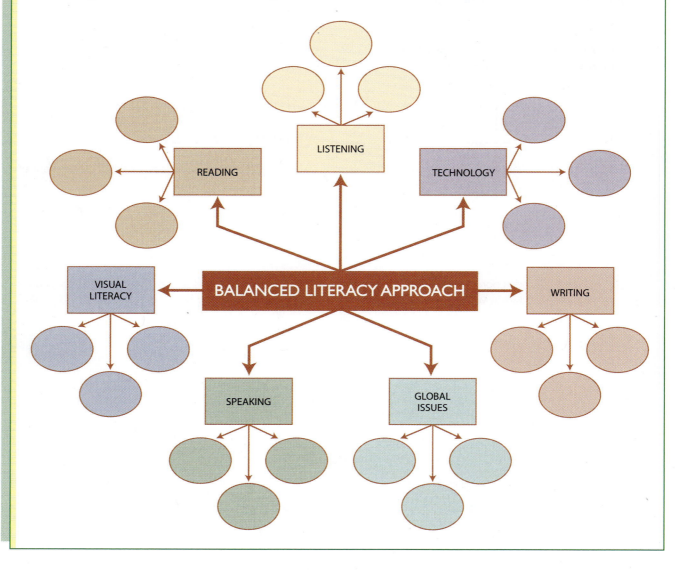

HOME–SCHOOL CONNECTION The Wired Classroom

When parents and/or guardians are involved in their children's education, students demonstrate improved grades, have higher test scores, display a more positive attitude toward school, have a higher rate of homework completion, and show improvement in self-esteem. One way to communicate with parents and guardians is through developing a website for your classroom. The website can be a "window" through which parents and guardians can view what is happening in the classroom and feel connected to their child's education. The teacher can post an update each month, called "Monthly Happenings." This will allow parents and guardians to become familiar with the curriculum and know how to reinforce it at home. The website can also have links to other resources that will provide more information on completing assignments, researching reports, and preparing for tests. Students' work and current projects in the classroom can be posted. Spelling lists, study guides, rubrics and instructions for assignments can be uploaded regularly for parents to review and print out if they wish. This is an excellent way for parents and guardians to stay current and knowledgeable about their child's education. Communication with parents and guardians is vital in helping them stay involved with their children's education and to have them become partners in the educational process. As educators, we need to ensure that there is a consistent and open home–school connection.

Based upon the writings of Jessica DePiano, Elementary Teacher

4 EMERGENT LITERACY IN THE CLASSROOM

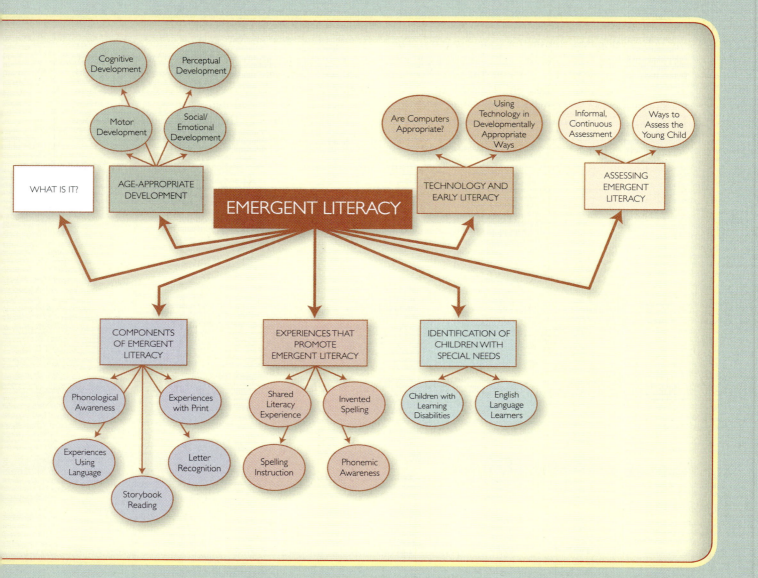

International Reading Association Professional Standards Addressed in this Chapter:

IRA STANDARD 1: FOUNDATIONAL KNOWLEDGE

Candidates have knowledge of the foundations of reading and writing processes and instruction. Candidates:

1.1 Demonstrate knowledge of psychological, sociological, and linguistic foundations of reading and writing processes and instruction.

1.2 Demonstrate knowledge of reading research and histories of reading.

1.3 Demonstrate knowledge of language development and reading acquisition and the variations related to cultural and linguistic diversity.

1.4 Demonstrate knowledge of the major components of reading (phonemic awareness, word identification and phonics, vocabulary and background knowledge, fluency, comprehension strategies, and motivation) and how they are integrated in fluent reading.

IRA STANDARD 2: INSTRUCTIONAL STRATEGIES AND CURRICULUM MATERIAL

Candidates use a wide range of instructional practices, approaches, methods, and curriculum materials to support reading and writing instruction. Candidates:

2.2. Use a wide range of instructional practices, approaches, and methods, including technology-based practices, for learners at differing stages of development and from differing cultural and linguistic backgrounds.

IRA STANDARD 3: ASSESSMENT, DIAGNOSIS, AND EVALUATION

Candidates use a variety of assessment tools and practices to plan and evaluate effective reading instruction. Candidates:

3.1 Use a wide range of assessment tools and practices that range from individual and group standardized tests to individual and group informal classroom assessment strategies, including technology-based assessment tools.

3.2 Place students along a developmental continuum and identify students' proficiencies and difficulties.

IRA STANDARD 4: CREATING A LITERATE ENVIRONMENT

Candidates create a literate environment that fosters reading and writing by integrating foundational knowledge, use of instructional practices, approaches and methods, curriculum materials, and the appropriate use of assessments. Candidates:

4.1 Use students' interests, reading abilities, and backgrounds as foundations for the reading and writing program.

4.2 Use a large supply of books, technology-based information, and nonprint materials representing multiple levels, broad interests, and cultural and linguistic backgrounds.

4.3 Model reading and writing enthusiastically as valued life-long activities.

Key Terms

alphabetic principle
phonological awareness
reading readiness
cognitive development
concept development
language development
English language learners
listening skills

Focus Questions

1. What does the concept of emergent literacy mean? How does "emergent literacy" differ from "reading readiness"?

classification

quantitative skills

perception

auditory perception

auditory discrimination

auditory memory

auditory sequencing

auditory blending

visual perception

visual discrimination

visual memory

perceptual development

motor development

social and emotional
   development

shared literacy experience

social mediation

zone of proximal
   development

invented spelling

graphemes

phonemic awareness

children with learning
   disabilities

Individualized Educational
   Plan (IEP)

Focus Questions (continued)

2. For the following areas, what activities at home and in a classroom would promote age-appropriate development in the preschool years?

   • Cognitive development

   • Perceptual development

   • Motor development

   • Social and emotional development

3. What five components are an important part of early childhood literacy development and substantially affect the ease with which children learn to read, write, and spell?

4. What is invented spelling? Why is it recommended during emergent literacy? What are some objections that parents might have to invented spelling?

5. What is phonemic awareness, and why is it so important for children to master at the emergent literacy stage? What are some ways it can be taught in the classroom?

6. Why is shared literacy experience so important to literacy development in young children? How did Vygotsky's theories influence literacy instruction? What are the key concepts that children learn in shared literacy experiences?

7. Why is it important to identify those children who have special needs? What are some of the characteristics that children with learning disabilities may exhibit at a very young age? What are some activities a teacher can do to promote literacy on the part of children who are culturally and linguistically diverse?

8. What role should technology play in the emergent literacy classroom? What is the appropriate use of technology with young children?

9. What does the research recommend for assessing emergent literacy? Name some methods that can be used in a preschool classroom.

Welcome to Mr. Abrams' PreK Classroom: Promoting Emergent Literacy in Children

Jupiterimages/Goodshoot/Jupiter Images

The walls of Mr. Abrams' preK classroom are brightly decorated with children's artwork. There are tables set up throughout the room, and primary colors appear to dominate. Shelving on the side of the room holds a multitude of games, puzzles, and interactive manipulative toys, including blocks, Legos, and colored shapes that can be arranged in different patterns. An easel with paints is off to one side of the room and newspaper is spread out underneath it to catch the paint drippings. The room appears to be chaotic, but as the observer settles into watching the class, she modifies her first impression to be "orderly chaos." Children are actively involved in doing something throughout the whole room while Mr. Abrams is engaged in working with a few children on an art project. Some children are working with puzzles, others are playing with blocks, others are pretending to cook a meal in the "kitchen," others are looking at books, and still others are drawing and coloring. One child is at the easel painting, and two children are at the computer working with an aide on a software program that teaches letter recognition.

After a short while, Mr. Abrams calls the children over to a corner; while the children sit on the floor around him, he reads a story out loud to them. They are quiet while the story is being read, and they are all quite enthusiastic to share personal stories that relate to the book afterward. He has to remind them constantly that they must raise their hand. The children love to tell long stories, some of them not quite relating to the book. Mr. Abrams is patient, always encouraging the children to use language to express themselves. When the reading is over, he has the children draw a picture about the story and try to write "words" describing what their picture is all about. He accepts any "spelling" that the children use, and when a child asks how to spell a word, he quietly tries to help him or her figure out what sounds are in the word and what letter is associated with that sound. Mr. Abrams has the children share these pictures and "writing" with the class when they are finished. A few of the children do not speak English, but he gently encourages them to use English words when talking and writing.

In the following sections you will be learning about emergent literacy and how to promote literacy in young children. Mr. Abrams uses strategies described in the following sections that are aligned with early literacy standards and benchmarks based on current national and state standards and that reflect research on early literacy development at the preK and kindergarten levels.

What Is Emergent Literacy?

Although many of the children in the above scenario appear to be involved in random activities that are fun and engaging, in fact, all of the activities described promote literacy in young children. From puzzles to manipulative blocks to pretend play to painting on an easel, children are learning the precursor skills needed for literacy development. Throughout the early years of a child's life, a rich array of hands-on and manipulative activities promote language use, encourage psychomotor development, and help children be creative and inquisitive about the world around them. This is the age for exploration in an environment that allows risk taking and encourages cognitive growth. This is not the time for children to sit at desks or to passively absorb information. This period of phenomenal growth before children start attending "formal" schooling is known as the emergent literacy stage.

What is emergent literacy? Researchers agree that emergent literacy begins during the period before children receive formal reading instruction; encompasses learning about reading, writing, and print before schooling; it is acquired through informal activities, as well as adult-directed home and school activities; and it facilitates acquisition of specific knowledge of reading (Gunn, Simmons, & Kameenui, 2004). Emergent literacy involves the range of settings and experiences that support literacy development, including how the child constructs his or her meaning of the world, as well as the diverse experiences and background that the child has during these formative years.

Children come to the classroom with diverse background experiences that will affect their literacy development and with differing knowledge about what literacy is all about. Teachers need to be aware that a child's background directly affects literacy achievement; family characteristics such as academic guidance, attitude toward education, parental aspirations for the child, conversations in the home, reading materials in the home, and cultural activities have a major impact on child development. Therefore, teachers of young children must design and deliver literacy instruction that not only builds on what the individual child already knows but also accommodates the varied literacy backgrounds that all the children in the classroom bring with them. It is important that teachers design their programs so that the following areas are covered (Gunn, Simmons, & Kameenui, 2004):

◆ Experiences with print (through reading and writing), which help preschool children develop an understanding of the conventions, purpose, and functions of print

◆ Experiences with using language so that children can learn the conventions of formal language and interact with others who model effective language use

◆ Letter recognition, whereby children learn that the English language consists of symbols (the **alphabetic principle**)

◆ **Phonological awareness,** whereby children learn to associate each letter with a specified sound

◆ Storybook reading, which directly affects children's knowledge about, strategies for, and attitudes toward reading

The most important factor to remember with all children is the strong relationship between language development and literacy skills. Teachers of young children must encourage them to use language throughout the day, to listen to models who speak English fluently and effectively, and to practice language learning in reading and writing.

Reading as a Long-Term Developmental Process

The concept of emergent literacy is based on the notion that children learn about literacy from the moment they are born and this process continues throughout the early years of a child's life. Literacy is a continuous, developmental process that is greatly affected by the home and community environments. Children start to learn about language naturally from their experiences and activities during the first year of life. Playing with alphabet blocks, listening to stories read from books, playing with cardboard or cloth books, listening to music, and babbling sounds repetitively all contribute to effective literacy development. Children progress through developmental stages in oral language, from babbling to mature speech, and in written language, from scribbling to legible writing, in a natural, connected way that extends over a considerable period of time. What the child learns at home is the foundation for all literacy development. The adults at home, particularly family members, model the use of literacy through activities that involve reading and writing. Children will scribble a message, which has meaning to them, and then try "reading" it back to someone. In doing this, children are acquiring basic knowledge about print and language at an early age. Thus, emergent literacy is seen as an ongoing, natural process that evolves and develops over time. It also points out the importance of the child being nurtured in a literacy-rich environment with adults who spend time modeling literacy activities.

Children who enter school with limited background and knowledge of reading-related skills are at high risk for failing in school and being referred for special education services; there is a strong relationship between the skills with which children enter school and their later academic performance (Whitehurst & Lonigan, 2001). Children from low-income families are at particular risk for reading difficulties and are more likely to be slow in developing oral language skills, letter knowledge, and phonologic awareness. These children often are not prepared for the reading instruction they will receive as they enter kindergarten and first grade, and this will have a significant impact on their later success in school. Learning to read is the primary milestone for success in school and in a literate society (Whitehurst & Lonigan, 2001). Those children with poor reading skills will continue to fall further and further behind their classmates.

Therefore, the emergent literacy stage of life is an especially important time when children develop the foundational skills needed to succeed in life. Intervention programs benefit children and help prevent reading difficulties because they are designed to increase exposure to the essential skills and background knowledge that all children need to succeed. Children learn a great deal about reading and writing before they begin their formal reading instruction, and these building blocks emerge during the emergent literacy stage.

How Does Emergent Literacy Differ from "Readiness"?

The concept of **emergent literacy** is relatively new. It grew out of Bond and Dykstra's (1967) first grade studies conducted from 1964 to 1967, and continued with Marie Clay's studies with 5-year-old children in New Zealand (Clay, 1966). Previous to these studies, educators believed that children must reach a certain level of physical, mental, and emotional maturity before they start formal reading instruction. This notion of **reading readiness** implied that there is a best time to begin reading instruction and that there are a series of prerequisite skills that children must master before instruction begins. For many years, educators used something called "mental age"—an age based on a child's chronological age plus a score on an intelligence test—to determine reading readiness. From the 1930s through the 1960s, a 6.5 mental age became the benchmark for deciding when reading instruction should begin. This correlated with the first grade curriculum. If children were not ready to read, they were given a series of activities to prepare them for formal instruction.

According to Clay (1991), by the time children come to school they already know a great deal about print from cereal boxes, television, advertisements, and signs that they see every day. They have already learned to associate printed symbols with specific meanings and will point to a sign such as "McDonald's" and demand lunch. Today, the concept of literacy has been broadened to include cultural and social aspects of language learning. Literacy is seen to be emerging naturally as the child develops starting from birth, not just beginning at a specific point in time. However, the ability to read and write does not develop naturally without careful planning and instruction.

A central goal during the preschool years is to enhance children's exposure to and concepts about print (Adams, 1990; Clay, 1979, 1991; Holdaway, 1979). Children need regular and systematic interactions with print, both in oral and written form. Children should have planned instructional experiences that motivate them to use print as a tool (International Reading Association and National Association for the Education of Young Children, 1998). They should have shared literacy experiences, both at home and at school, which give them a chance to practice what they have learned and to share literacy experiences with others.

Courtesy of Becky Stovall

Emergent literacy is an important time for children to learn essential foundational skills.

Age-Appropriate Development in the Preschool Years

From the moment of birth, there is an indispensable relationship between an infant's social interactions and emotional relations with caretakers and the infant's development of cognitive processes, which continues throughout the child's life. Vygotsky (1978) posed that social interactions with others are a major factor in developing children's thinking abilities. Children acquire speech intuitively: it is a continuous, natural process in which they imitate speech sounds and model what they hear in their environment. However, language development is more than just imitation, because social interactions and emotional bonds provide the motivation for speaking; the child is immersed in an environment that provides the rich language exchanges that enable the child to take risks and try out different types of communications with others. The child is reinforced every time a babble or sound emerges, and this communication is slowly shaped into recognizable sounds and words.

Comprehension of words emerges somewhat before the ability to produce words, at approximately the time of a child's first birthday. During the second year of life, there is a sharp increase in the number of words that a child understands (Snow, Burns, & Griffin, 1998). Vocabulary growth is rapid during the emergent literacy years, and it is quite variable among individual children. One study found vocabulary acquisition to be dependent on socioeconomic status, with first graders from higher income backgrounds having twice the vocabulary than first graders from lower income backgrounds (Snow, Burns, & Griffin, 1998). Vocabulary size continues to increase with schooling, and it is estimated that students acquire about 7 new words per day or almost 3,000 words per year during elementary school and continuing through high school (Snow, Burns, & Griffin, 1998). By the time they get to kindergarten, children have amassed a vocabulary of approximately 8,000 words and know almost all of the basic grammatical forms of their language (Gleason, 2001).

Research on grammatical development in young children suggests rapid acquisition of the basic syntactic (or grammatical) structures (Snow, Burns, & Griffin, 1998). Soon after reaching 2 years of age, children are able to comprehend simple sentences and to combine words that display some grammatical order and structure. During the preschool period, children's ability to form longer and more complex sentences using three to four or more words grows at a rapid rate. By the time most children enter school, they are able to produce and comprehend fairly complex grammatical sentences, although this ability will continue to grow throughout their schooling and into adulthood.

As children grow more sophisticated in their ability to use language, they also become more capable of using verbal communication to engage in more complex social exchanges with adults and other children. During shared reading with an adult, a child will go from focusing on an object in an illustration to questioning what the actual story is about. The child grows increasingly capable of thinking and discussing more abstract ideas, such as "What might have happened if. . . ?" or "What does it mean when she is happy?" (Snow, Burns, & Griffin, 1998).

As children become increasingly proficient in producing language, they gain "metalinguistic" skills; that is, the ability not only to use language to convey meaning but to think about what language is, to play with it, talk about it, analyze it, and evaluate whether it is being used correctly. Metalinguistic skills appear to emerge in some children as young as 3 years, although a considerable degree of metalinguistic insight about the nature of words, sentences, speech sounds, and meanings is seen in children 4 to 5 years old. Through discussions of shared literacy experiences, children get a chance to explore their metalinguistic understandings and to develop them further.

The development of language is intricately tied to a child's ability to think, communicate, and understand concepts, or what is commonly known as **cognitive development.** Cognition involves the psychological events and processes that comprise what we call "thinking," "perceiving," "remembering," and other "higher mental processes" (Flavell, 1977). Cognitive growth, at every level, depends on a child's ability to use language as a means of conveying information, as a means of expressing oneself, and as a means of thinking about the world abstractly. Thinking and expression are intricately woven together into a tapestry of cognition and language development. Educators must be aware of the relationship between language and cognition; by providing activities that encourage the use of language, they are fostering significant cognitive growth as well.

Cognition and language development occur throughout the lifetime of a person, starting from the moment of birth. Learning does not just suddenly start when a child

Courtesy of Becky Stovall

Children develop their cognitive skills through active listening and responding.

reaches 5 or 6 years old and enters school. During the preschool years, children are involved in learning many varied processes and skills that contribute to their ability to learn how to read. During those years, children absorb much knowledge, information, and skills from their environment. However, many of these skills can be taught directly and reinforced in structured ways. When you walk into a good preschool classroom, the environment looks inviting, engaging, and often chaotic, but it should also be carefully designed to help develop those skills that are essential for literacy development.

Children who become successful readers tend to exhibit age-appropriate development in cognitive, sensory, perceptual, motor, and social and emotional skills as they progress through the preschool years. Many factors can affect development in these areas, ranging from the mother's mental and physical health to conditions of housing, temperament, nutrition, and stress (Snow, Burns, & Griffin, 1998). These factors bear a direct relationship to a child's ability to mature. However, by focusing on different activities that foster growth in cognitive development, perceptual development, motor development, and social and emotional development, caregivers and teachers can help increase the chances that children will succeed in later academic challenges. Teachers can directly incorporate activities into a child's day that will positively affect future reading and literacy development. The following sections examine each of these areas and discuss different activities that can promote literacy development.

Cognitive Development

Teachers can nurture cognitive development in young children by developing instructional activities in five areas: concept development, language development, listening skills, classification, and quantitative skills. These areas will build the appropriate foundation for literacy growth in the young child.

Concept development is a major factor in cognitive development and a child's ability to understand abstract terms. During the emergent literacy years, it is important that children develop knowledge about basic concepts, such as *up/down, in/out, near/ far, here/there*. These concepts can be reinforced in a structured environment through fun activities such as arts and crafts, singing and dancing, and poems. Television programs such as *Sesame Street* have been a model in teaching such concepts directly to preschoolers through the use of characters, such as Grover, who demonstrate in a funny way what different concepts like *near* and *far* signify to a child.

Activities that promote the use of **language development** will foster cognitive development in all children. Such activities are also excellent for **English language learners** (ELLs), because they encourage them to use English in a supportive and enjoyable environment. Show-and-tell is a favorite activity that is not used enough in the upper grades. All children, young and old, love to bring objects into school and share their experiences and feelings about them. Story hour in which children discuss the story is another excellent way to promote language. Sitting in a circle on the floor and talking about difficult issues and events is another excellent way to develop language, as well as teach character development and morals. Cooperative learning and project-based learning promote language use between children and motivate them to share ideas. General whole-class discussions are also recommended ways to have children use language, as long as the focus remains on the topic at hand and is not haphazard and random. In all these activities, it is important that the teacher stay focused on the main objective of the discussion and encourage children to address the topic being discussed using their language and not stray too far from the main idea.

Listening skills are an important part of cognitive development and language learning during the emergent literacy years. Listening is an often neglected element of language learning, and children are expected to acquire the ability to listen critically by the time they enter formal schooling, without receiving any special instruction in this area. More than half the people referred to hearing specialists for suspected deafness have no defect at all in hearing acuity and no organic pathology that would cause their seeming hearing impairment (Lerner, 2003). Listening is a basic skill that can be improved through practice and direct instructional activities. There is a distinct difference between *hearing* and *listening;* hearing is a physiological process that does not involve interpretation, while listening demands that one select and interpret ideas presented and then organize them into a meaningful message (Lerner, 2003). Listening is the foundation of all language growth, and a child with a deficit in this area will have a disability in all the communication skills.

The following listening skills can be developed through systematic instruction and instructional activities:

◆ *Auditory awareness of language sounds:* Children need to be able to perceive and recognize the sounds of our language. Children must be able to hear the individual phoneme sounds of the language and be aware that words are composed of sounds.

◆ *Understanding words and concepts and building a listening vocabulary:* Listening requires that children build up a listening vocabulary of words that they understand. They must know names of objects, actions, qualities, and more abstract concepts. This can be built into the preschool experience by emphasizing the names of objects and continuously repeating abstract concepts out loud as they are being demonstrated.

◆ *Understanding sentences:* Students need structured practice in understanding complete sentences and sentences that are strung together to make up a meaningful message. This can be done by providing students with practice in following directions and listening to riddles, such as "I am thinking of a word for a machine that you use to get to school in the morning."

◆ *Listening comprehension:* The listening comprehension skill is similar to what is called reading comprehension, but with this skill the information is received by hearing rather than by reading. Listening comprehension can be developed through storytelling time, having children listen for details of a story, instructing children to listen for the sequence of events, and requiring children to determine the main idea of the story they just heard.

◆ *Critical listening:* Children not only need to comprehend what they have heard but also evaluate the information and make judgments about its value. This can be done through telling stories that have silly phrases or information in them and then asking what is wrong with the story. Another good activity is instructing students to listen to advertisements and then determine what the advertiser is trying to sell and if the information seems correct.

Classification is another area that is important to develop during the emergent literacy years and that contributes to cognitive development. Classification is a strategy for grouping objects, ideas, or concepts into groups based on some common characteristic or set of common features that determine the groups, and then assigning a name to the group composed of the individual objects or events (Haywood, Brooks, & Burns, 1992). For example, a child can classify a group of play animals into different classes based on their biological features (birds, dogs, horses, reptiles), or where they live (barn, house, pen), or their color (brown, black, gray); then the child must also assign a name to the group based on what feature was used to group the animals. Classification is a higher order thinking skill that helps us clarify relationships between two concepts (animals and where they live, or animals and color) and allows us to see the more comprehensive category that a group might fit into based on similar attributes (all animals with feathers and two legs and beaks are "birds"). It is an important process in developing cognitive and language learning (Haywood, Brooks, & Burns, 1992). Sorting is a lower order version of this skill where the categories are already named and the child will take a group of objects and sort them into the appropriate category. Classification works best as a strategy that promotes higher level thinking when students must devise their own categories after being given a group of objects, words, or concepts, and then think of the larger, organizing features that make some of these objects fit into one category, while others fit into a different category. This strategy is effective throughout the school years for teaching in many different content areas. For example, in vocabulary instruction, the teacher might give students a list of words from a biology chapter, and ask them to classify the words into different categories and explain why each group was chosen and what attributes similar words shared. This helps students gain a much deeper understanding of not only the word, but also the relationships that exist between this word and other concepts. In the emergent literacy years, it is important that children have a wide range of opportunities to classify objects in many different ways so that they start to see that objects share certain features in some instances (for example, a horse lives in a barn and can be grouped with a white cow; a horse also is brown and can be grouped with a brown dog or bird).

Quantitative skills are also important areas to develop for cognitive development. In the preschool years, children need to learn the concepts *more than* and *less than*. They need to be able to recite their numbers and then learn how to count by assigning one number to one object. They start to understand the concept of *adding* and *taking away*, especially when it deals directly with the amount of toys or candy they have. Numbering, sequencing, and learning the amount of something are all important cognitive concepts that will contribute directly to language learning and literacy development.

Perceptual Development

Reading is a perceptual process that involves both auditory and visual processes. Both visual perception and auditory perception play a significant role in school learning, especially reading. **Perception** is the process of recognizing and interpreting sensory information. It is the ability to give meaning to sensory input. For example, when a square is seen, it must be viewed as a whole configuration, not as four separate lines. Perception is a learned skill and can be taught; it is reinforced from an infant's first discrimination of a face through the preschool years (Lerner, 2003). Recent research on the brain using new brain imaging technologies show that different perceptual systems are located in different areas within the brain. This helps explain why some children may have different strengths and weaknesses in different learning tasks and learn how to read in very different ways. For example, a child who displays great difficulty with auditory perception of the sounds in words is likely to have difficulty learning phonics. This child may need additional practice in recognizing sounds in words, as well as additional practice in dictation. The teacher needs to recognize each child's strengths and weaknesses and use alternate styles and strategies to teach children (Lerner, 2003).

Auditory perception is the ability to recognize or interpret what is heard. It is an important process for children to develop throughout the emergent literacy years. Accumulating research shows that many poor readers have auditory, linguistic, and phonological difficulties (Lerner, 2003). These children do not have problems hearing, but they have difficulty recognizing, processing, or interpreting what is heard. Many teachers assume that by the time children come to school these processes have developed. The auditory perception skills children need to develop to read effectively are phonological awareness, auditory discrimination, auditory memory, auditory sequencing, and auditory blending.

As mentioned earlier, phonological awareness is the ability to recognize that words are made up of individual sounds. For example, for the word *cat*, a child who has developed phonemic awareness can isolate the three sounds (or phonemes) that comprise the word: /c/a/t/. Children who lack this skill are totally unaware of how words are put together, cannot isolate sounds in words, cannot "play" with those individual sounds; these children usually have difficulty rhyming words (cat, fat, mat). This skill has been recognized as a major precursor to learning how to read and needs to be taught throughout the emergent literacy years. The term *phonological awareness* refers to the general appreciation of the sounds of speech as distinct from their meaning. When children grasp that words can be divided into a sequence of phonemes, or sounds, this subset is termed *phonemic awareness* (see a detailed discussion of this later in the chapter) (Snow, Burns, & Griffin, 1998).

Auditory discrimination is the ability to discriminate between different sounds. For example, if a child hears "thing" instead of the pronounced "think," the child is not discriminating between the "ng" and "nk" sounds. This might indicate a problem with auditory discrimination; a teacher could help develop auditory discrimination by providing exercises such as dictation, sorting, and games that help the child discriminate troublesome sounds. Auditory discrimination is a key task that children must use when reading, writing, and spelling. They must be able to hear the sounds being voiced, discriminate which sounds they just heard, and then associate those sounds with the correct letter, letters, or words. This process is then translated into either spelling a word out loud or writing it down.

Auditory memory is the ability to remember what is heard. This is a mandatory skill that children need to succeed in school and in literacy development. Auditory memory allows a child to listen to and follow directions. If children cannot remember what they were told, they will be disorganized, lack follow-through, and behave in ways that are frustrating to others. Auditory memory will affect whether a child can comprehend what was read aloud and respond appropriately to questioning.

Auditory sequencing is the ability to remember the order of items in a sequential list that is given verbally. This will affect a child's ability to remember the alphabet, number sequencing, days of the week, and months of the year. It is an integral part of learning how to read and remembering patterns that form language.

Auditory blending is the ability to hear individual sounds as a whole. The child who has a deficit in auditory blending is unable to blend individual sounds into a word. He or she may know the individual phonemes but cannot combine them together. For example, the child may know the sounds of the letters b-a-n-k but then read it as "back."

Visual perception is the ability to interpret what is seen. Visual perception plays a significant role in school learning, particularly in literacy development. It is imperative that children receive support and instruction during their emergent literacy years that helps develop their visual perception and prepares them for literacy instruction. Children who have problems in this area cannot remember what they see, cannot tell the difference between similar-looking letters, cannot identify many of the differences between two objects, and become confused with focusing their attention on a page to identify main ideas. These children do not have trouble seeing, but they do have difficulty interpreting what they see.

Visual discrimination is the ability to differentiate one object from another. For example, a child might be asked in a preschool assessment to identify the rabbit with one ear in a row of rabbits with two ears; or, a child might be asked how many humps the letters m and n have to see whether they can discriminate between these two letters. Visual discrimination involves recognizing the differences between objects by color, shape, pattern, size, or brightness (Lerner, 2003). This skill is essential in learning how to read, and those children who can recognize letters when they are in preschool perform better in reading. As an infant, one important aspect of his or her emotional bond with a caretaker is the development of the infant's ability to make visual discriminations. The infant must be able to discriminate visually between different faces and recognize one in particular for any social–emotional bonds to take place. The same argument can be made for the infant's ability to discriminate between voices, thereby developing auditory discrimination (Flavell, 1977). Both visual and auditory discrimination are skills that begin the moment a child is able to distinguish a caretaker and they develop throughout a child's life, helping promote reading and literacy during school-age years.

Visual memory is the ability to remember what is seen. This allows children to distinguish the different letters of the alphabet and associate them with the correct name and sound. It allows children to remember commonly seen words that become part of their sight vocabulary. Visual memory affects children's ability to process the meaning behind the illustrations of a book and thereby comprehend the material.

In summary, **perceptual development** is an important part of the emergent literacy stage, and teachers need to be aware that there are many activities that can encourage and reinforce perceptual development. However, perceptual learning does not necessarily transfer directly to higher reading achievement. These skills are important developmentally and may help students succeed as they are being taught specific literacy skills.

Motor Development

Educators have long been aware of the close relationship between **motor development** and learning. Early childhood educators view motor growth as a cornerstone of child development (Lerner, 2003). Activities designed to develop motor growth are typically included in the regular curriculum for preschool children. The emergent literacy years are not only a time of great cognitive growth for children but also when they are developing sensorimotor learning, which contributes to their success in school. Many areas of academic and cognitive performance are based on successful motor experiences that involve gross- and fine-motor coordination.

Gross-motor skills involve the large muscles of the neck, trunk, arms, and legs. Activities that develop gross-motor coordination are walking, running, catching, and jumping. It is important that children learn gross-motor skills and practice them in a fun, safe environment; these skills are the foundations on which fine-motor coordination develops.

Fine-motor skills involve the small muscles. Activities that develop fine-motor coordination are drawing, coloring, picking up small objects such as beads or chunks of food, cutting with scissors, using a fork and spoon, buttoning, and playing with blocks and small toys.

Play is an important way for children to practice motor skills. The playground provides many different opportunities for children to run, stretch, skip, ride a bicycle, and use their large muscles. In the classroom, arts and crafts activities and structured games help develop fine-motor coordination. Painting pictures, playing with clay, cutting and pasting, building with Legos, doing puzzles, and playing with blocks help children learn how to use their small muscles. All these activities contribute to a child's self-confidence and their future ability to write letters, discriminate letters, and sound out increasingly complex sounds.

Social and Emotional Development

The **social and emotional development** of emergent readers is of utmost importance because children must be able to interact with other children, as well as adults, in the learning environment to make developmental strides toward their reading development. Despite the National Research Council's (NRC's) study *Eager to Learn: Educating Our Preschoolers*, which shows that children aged 2 to 5 are much more capable of learning than previously believed, children cannot be moved too quickly into an academic start without also providing for their emotional needs (Allen, 2001). A balanced approach to an early start toward literacy should also stress the need to nurture a child's emotional and social needs.

Allen (2001) reports a major study that shows that children entering kindergarten develop faster academically only when they have built strong relationships within the home. Children who lack appropriate nurturing by parents and other caretakers will more likely have a poor beginning in kindergarten and will not develop a positive self-concept. Such children also will have difficulty succeeding in their early attempts at literacy. The study cites one survey of teachers who report that many entering kindergartners had problems following directions and lacked the basic social skills needed to communicate within a group setting, a prerequisite for being successful students in school.

Teachers must be aware of the emotional needs of all children, including those with special needs, and be diligent in providing the support and mediation that will help make the transition to school a happy and successful one for each child. Children will still need time to learn how to socialize and how to learn these skills through play. Early beginnings of literacy, therefore, must not be exclusively academic, and early childhood teachers must find a suitable balance that combines the social aspects of learning with the new early childhood cognitive standards. Cooperative grouping, peer sharing, and learning through play provide children with fun ways to learn while simultaneously teaching them about the process of give-and-take in a nonthreatening, cooperative

Skill		Description	Activity
COGNITIVE DEVELOPMENT	Concept Development	Ability to understand abstract terms such as *here/there, near/far*	◆ Play games such as Simon Says ◆ Perform demonstrations of abstract terms ◆ Use board games that reinforce the concepts ◆ Ask children to demonstrate the concept to you
	Language Development	Ability to understand and use language in increasingly complex ways	◆ Show-and-tell ◆ Class discussions ◆ Cooperative learning ◆ Projects with hands-on activities that involve discussion
	Listening Skills	Ability to listen and understand what one hears	◆ Read out loud to the class and discuss the story ◆ Have children practice following increasingly complex directions ◆ Give children oral riddles to solve ◆ Have children practice listening comprehension by focusing on main idea or one character after the story is read aloud
COGNITIVE DEVELOPMENT	Classification	Ability to group objects into a class according to specific attributes	◆ Instruct children to classify animals into their categories ◆ Instruct children to classify common objects found in the classroom into categories ◆ Instruct children to classify their toys into categories that will help the class organize the room for playtime
	Quantitative Skills	Ability to develop mathematical and numerical concepts	◆ Play game "Which Has More? Which Has Less?" ◆ Have children count objects found in the classroom ◆ Sing songs and play games that help children learn to count ◆ Have children learn how to sequence a series of events using the words *first, second, next, last*
PERCEPTUAL DEVELOPMENT	Phonological Awareness	General ability to attend to sounds of language as distinct from meaning (Snow, Burns, & Griffin, 1998)	◆ Play with words (pancake, canpake, cancake) ◆ Rhyming ◆ Alliteration (boy, butterfly, boat, bat) ◆ Count syllables ◆ Count words
	Auditory Discrimination	Ability to discriminate between different sounds that one hears	◆ Ask if two words are the same or different ◆ Play with words that are minimal pairs; that is, they differ by one phoneme or sound (mitt-mat, big-pig) ◆ Ask children to listen for one word in a sequence and instruct them to raise their hands
	Auditory Memory	Ability to remember what is heard	◆ Ask a child to do three activities in sequence (put away book, open door, take out crayon) ◆ Read a short story and ask questions about what happened ◆ Recite a short poem and have children repeat it back to you

(continued)

	Skill	Description	Activity
	Auditory Sequencing	Ability to remember the order of items in a sequential list that is given verbally	◆ Give children a list of items to remember in order ◆ Play games where students must remember the names of classmates in order ◆ Teach songs and poems that help children remember the sequence of things
	Auditory Blending	Ability to hear individual sounds as a whole word	◆ Dictate individual phonemes and have children blend them into a word ◆ Sing songs that play with sounds, emphasizing blending the sounds into words
PERCEPTUAL DEVELOPMENT	Visual Discrimination	Ability to differentiate one object from another	◆ Play the game "Which Picture Is Different from the Others?" ◆ Play the game "Hidden Objects," in which specific objects are "hidden" in a large picture and children must find them ◆ Put puzzles together ◆ Play with shape boxes, in which children must place cubes, balls, and spheres into the correct shape to fit into the box ◆ Have children work with geometric shapes to make predrawn pictures ◆ Ask children to find a specific object in an illustration
	Visual Memory	Ability to remember what one sees	◆ Play the game "What's Wrong with This Picture?" ◆ Ask children to remember what they saw in an illustration ◆ Ask children to tell you or draw what they just heard and saw during story time
MOTOR DEVELOPMENT	Gross-Motor Coordination	Ability to use large muscles to accomplish tasks	◆ Dance ◆ Skip ◆ Play in the gym or playground ◆ Ride bicycles
	Fine-Motor Coordination	Ability to use small muscles to accomplish tasks	◆ Draw and color ◆ Cut and paste ◆ String beads ◆ Button and zip ◆ Play with Legos ◆ Build with wood blocks
SOCIAL/ EMOTIONAL DEVELOPMENT	Social/Emotional Development	Ability to develop the appropriate social and emotional behaviors to succeed in a classroom	◆ Cooperative grouping ◆ Peer sharing ◆ Learn and share through play ◆ Develop a safe and supportive environment ◆ Create class rules together ◆ Appreciate linguistic and cultural differences

environment. Being part of an audience during sing-a-long time or part of a read-aloud group, a shared reading group, or a small, guided group helps create a community of learners in which even the most neglected child soon learns to feel comfortable and wanted. Including students in the establishment of classroom rules that are consistently carried out also helps children take ownership and build commitment to becoming good classroom citizens.

Being aware of emerging readers' linguistic, cultural, and learning differences and celebrating these differences in diverse classrooms are also important for building a positive environment. Establishing preschool and kindergarten multicultural libraries and sharing picture books that depict diverse characters as positive role models also can influence children's tolerance and appreciation of differences. Teachers who value their children's native language backgrounds and provide literacy opportunities for them through the use of their own language, multilingual texts, and other instructional support approaches help improve ELLs' self-esteem and overall literacy achievement (Snow, Burns, & Griffin, 1998).

The chart on pages 115–116 provides a description of activities that promote age-appropriate development in cognitive, perceptual, motor, and social and emotional skills for all children as they progress through the preschool years.

Components of Emergent Literacy Instruction

The research in emergent literacy specifies certain components that are an important part of early childhood literacy development and substantially affect the ease with which children learn to read, write, and spell (Gunn, Simmons, & Kameenui, 2004; Hiebert, 1988; National Early Literacy Panel, 2008; Weir, 1989; Whitehurst & Lonigan, 2001). Each of these areas develops concurrently, is interrelated, and continues to develop across the preschool and kindergarten periods. The five areas discussed in the following sections (phonological awareness, experiences with print, experiences with using language, letter recognition, and storybook reading) are significant components of emergent literacy and need to be addressed in all preK and kindergarten classes. Figure 4–1 provides definitions for key beginning literacy terms that are used throughout this chapter and may be useful as we proceed through the following sections.

Phonological Awareness

Phonological awareness refers to the child's ability to perceive spoken words as a sequence of sounds, and it is of crucial importance to reading ability (Gunn, Simmons, & Kameenui, 2004; Whitehurst & Lonigan, 2001). Phonological awareness includes the ability to detect and manipulate the sounds of oral language, including identifying words that rhyme, blending syllables or phonemes together to form words, deleting syllables from spoken words, and counting the number of sounds in a spoken word (Whitehurst & Lonigan, 2001). Phonological awareness has long been tied to research and practice in the teaching of phonics and other decoding skills, but it has been neglected in emergent literacy because of the tendency to view phonological awareness as traditional and bottom-up in theory. Many researchers have argued that young children must be helped to notice that words encode sounds as well as meaning (Gunn, Simmons, & Kameenui, 2004; Hiebert, 1988; Weir, 1989; Whitehurst & Lonigan, 2001).

Phonological awareness abilities typically develop in a set sequence. Skills such as rhyming and alliteration (repeating the same first letter over and over again) usually emerge in informal contexts before children start schooling and are seen in young children who can neither read nor spell. Other phonological awareness abilities typically begin when children display the ability to divide sentences into semantically meaningful word groups. The ability to divide sentences into individual words emerges next, followed by the ability to segment words into syllables. The most complex of these skills is the ability to segment words into phonemes or sounds. This general

FIGURE 4-1

Definitions of Beginning Literacy

PHONOLOGICAL AWARENESS:
> a broad term that refers to the study of spoken language and includes phonemes, rhymes, syllables, onsets and rimes, and words

PHONEMIC AWARENESS:
> the ability to hear, to identify, and to manipulate sounds in spoken language

PHONICS:
> the understanding that phonemes (sounds) in spoken language are related to graphemes (letters) in written language that can be used to sound out words for reading and writing

PHONEME:
> the smallest part of spoken language that makes a difference in the meaning of words, i.e., h/a/t (3 phonemes for "hat"); ch/e/k/s (4 phonemes for "checks")

GRAPHEME:
> the smallest part of written language, or letters representing phonemes used to spell a word

SYLLABLE:
> the part of a word that contains a vowel

ONSET AND RIME:
> parts of spoken words, where the onset is the initial consonant(s) of a syllable, and the rime begins the syllable with a vowel and all that follows it, i.e., globe = "gl" (onset)–"obe"(rime)

order to emergence has been supported by research in phonological awareness (Gunn, Simmons, & Kameenui, 2004).

Research supports that training children in phonological awareness positively affects their early reading skills (Gunn, Simmons, & Kameenui, 2004; Hiebert, 1988; Weir, 1989; Whitehurst & Lonigan, 2001). Individual differences in preschool and kindergarten students' phonological awareness are directly related to early reading acquisition; therefore, activities that promote phonological awareness should be stressed in any formal schooling program for young children.

Children from culturally diverse backgrounds may have particular difficulties with phonological awareness. Exposure to language at home, exposure to reading at an early age, and dialect all affect the ability of children to understand the phonological distinctions on which the English language is built. Teachers must be sensitive to all children's backgrounds and use a variety of techniques to help children learn these skills when standard English is not spoken at home (Lyon, 1994).

Experiences with Print

Experiences with print through reading and writing allow preschool children to learn about language and that language can be represented through written symbols. These experiences give children an understanding of the conventions, purpose, and function of print—understandings that have been shown to play an integral part in learning to read (Gunn, Simmons, & Kameenui, 2004). Children learn the conventions of print through storytelling; that is, that print tells a story and that the stories have a structure—a beginning, middle, and end. They learn that English print begins at the top of the page, moves from left to right, from top to bottom, and continues on each page thereafter until the story ends. They learn that pictures accompany text, and that the pictures can give clues as to what the story is all about. Children also learn the conventions of print through writing; they learn to mimic the conventions of print before they can even form letters by progressing from scribbles to letter-like forms to characters that look like letters, especially the letters from the child's name (Hiebert, 1988).

Teachers' VOICES   Phonemic Awareness

In my class, I absolutely drench the kids in print. From day one, phonemic awareness begins with their names written on tag board. The 3-year-old children sit on my lap and learn to identify their names, proceeding at their own rates. (This is all done one-on-one in the early morning.) Then they begin learning the first letter of their name. After they have mastered their own name (naming all letters of their first and last name, and identifying each consonant sound or digraph in their name), they choose a friend's name. By midyear, my 3-year-olds can read the name chart and can read their classmates' names in many contexts. Names are read on line-up charts, name plates used at the writing table, job charts, and sign-in lists for learning centers where they must circle their name.

—*Julie Williams, PreK Teacher*

Print has many purposes—from writing a shopping list, to composing a letter to a friend, to telling a story, to conveying information. Children learn the purpose of print when they understand that words convey a message and that their oral language can be represented in written symbols. Children who have had a wide range of print experiences have bridged the gap between oral and written language and understand how the two are intimately related. They also usually have acquired a vocabulary to talk about print; they can describe a book, a page, point out letters, talk about what story they like, and even describe their favorite title and author.

Experiences with Using Language

There is a strong link between oral language skills and reading, with vocabulary acquisition being critically important in reading instruction (National Institute of Child Health and Human Development [NICHD], 2000). The NRC concluded that the majority of reading problems could be prevented by, among other things, increasing children's oral language skills (Snow, Burns, & Griffin, 1998; Whitehurst & Lonigan, 2001). Research on emergent literacy has shown that there is a direct relationship between vocabulary size and phonological awareness. Children with larger vocabularies have more developed phonological awareness, and this relationship begins early in the preschool period (Whitehurst & Lonigan, 2001). Teachers need to encourage the use and development of oral language in all children, especially during the preschool years, when oral proficiency is such a strong indicator of future reading achievement.

Children from low-income families are at particular risk for reading problems and are more likely to be slow in developing oral language skills, letter knowledge, and phonological processing skills before coming to school (Whitehurst & Lonigan, 2001). Reading is the process of translating visual symbols into meaningful language and understanding that oral language can be represented by a series of visual symbols. Different aspects of the home literacy environment directly affect early literacy development and oral language skills of young children. Such factors as shared reading, print exposure, active listening, asking questions, and quality interactions with young children have been attributed to increasing oral language development and emergent literacy (Whitehurst & Lonigan, 2001).

Children growing up in a home where English is not the native language are being exposed to at least two languages. If young children are to learn that reading is about constructing meaning from oral language, then learning to read in a new language they are not comfortable with yet is not feasible (Tabors & Snow, 2001). It is recommended that children first become proficient in their native language and learn to practice literacy skills successfully within the language they can use effectively. In this way, they will learn how to construct meaning in pleasurable contexts. It is important that teachers establish a home–school connection so they can find out about the language and literacy background of the ELLs in their classroom. Asking some simple questions about home literacy experiences and the language associated with them can be helpful in establishing the child's emergent literacy skills. It would also be beneficial to encourage parents to maintain their first language at home and use it (if they are comfortable doing so) to participate in literacy activities with the child. The critical factor is the quality of the social engagement and interactions with the child, not the language in which it occurs (Tabors & Snow, 2001). The crucial point is that young ELLs *do* have literacy skills that they bring with them to the classroom, even if their oral language development is not in English. Teachers need to know what those skills are and how to take advantage of them, so that the process of literacy development can be optimized for all young children.

Letter Recognition

Letter recognition and knowledge of the alphabet (the *alphabetic principle*) in kindergarten children is one of the best predictors of eventual reading achievement (Adams, 1990; Gunn, Simmons, & Kameenui, 2004; Whitehurst & Lonigan, 2001). Letter recognition helps children develop strong word-recognition strategies; a beginning reader who cannot recognize and distinguish the individual letters of the alphabet will have difficulty learning the sounds those letters represent and decoding words. Letter knowledge can be acquired through formal instruction in preschools or incidentally through informal experiences at home or play. Research has found that children's exposure to letter names and sounds during the preschool years was positively associated with linguistically precocious performance on selected literacy measures (Gunn, Simmons, & Kameenui, 2004).

Teachers' VOICES   Alphabetic Principle

One of my favorite original ideas is my letter basket. Choosing a letter of the alphabet within the context of our thematic unit (I do not believe in letter of the week), I make a letter basket. I use a big basket and write the highlighted letter on the side (P, for example). I then ransack my house and the classroom for articles the children will be able to identify by name and put them in the P basket. I put items such as pigs, pants, pictures, penguins, pears, and pajamas in the basket. The kids love to hold *real* objects. During circle time, each child gets to choose any one of the P items from the rug and put it in the P basket. They must say its name. For 2 to 3 weeks, we sing P songs and recite P mother goose rhymes. We give P compliments such as "pretty" or "perfect." By the end of our P segment, we have a scavenger hunt. The P items are hidden and the children run around and find them and put them in the basket. We'll enjoy a final activity by preparing and eating P foods such as pancakes or pumpkin pie.

—*Julie Williams, Preschool Teacher*

Despite the strong correlation between letter knowledge and later reading, programs that teach children letter names alone do not appear to be effective (Adams, 1990). It seems best that children learn letter knowledge through engaging in literacy activities in which they learn about print, books, and phonological awareness all at the same time. Isolating the skill of identifying letters can be boring, repetitive, and not meaningful to young children whose attention span is short and precarious at best. Activities such as a shared literacy experience (discussed later in this chapter) are recommended approaches to teaching letter recognition.

Storybook Reading

Reading stories to children is a primary factor in promoting early literacy acquisition (Hiebert, 1988). Children who read storybooks aloud by parents, guardians or other adults learn phonological awareness, concepts of print, and letter recognition. Research suggests that most successful early readers are children who have had contact at home with written materials. Children who became poorer readers had less experience with books and reading than children who became better readers (Hiebert, 1988).

During storybook reading, children learn a routine that creates a predictable format. The reading usually starts with a discussion of the title and examination of the pictures on the cover, and then progresses to a beginning, middle, and end, at which time a discussion about the book usually occurs even if it is only about whether the child liked the book. This pattern helps children learn how to participate in and gradually take more responsibility for storybook reading activities. These routines, including the language and social interactions that occur during discussions of the book, appear to explain what makes storybook reading such a powerful influence in literacy development (Gunn, Simmons, & Kameenui, 2004).

Findings from the National Early Literacy Panel

In 1997, the U.S. Congress asked a panel of reading experts to conduct a review of research to determine best practices in reading and writing achievement based upon scientifically based research studies. The *Report of the National Reading Panel: Teaching Children to Read* (NICHD, 2000) has influenced many of the instructional practices being implemented in classrooms across the United States today. However, that report did not address the instructional practices used with children from birth through age 5. To address this gap in the knowledge base, the National Early Literacy Panel (NELP) was convened. This panel was asked to review the research to determine best instructional practices for young children so that parents and teachers could better support their emerging literacy skills.

Developing Early Literacy: Report of the National Early Literacy Panel (NELP, 2008) found that six variables representing early literacy skills had a significant and predictive relationship with later measures of literacy development. These six variables include:

◆ Alphabet knowledge: knowledge of the names and sounds associated with printed letters
◆ Phonological awareness: the ability to detect, manipulate, or analyze the auditory aspects of spoken language (including the ability to distinguish or segment words, syllables, or phonemes), independent of meaning
◆ Rapid automatic naming of letters or digits: the ability to rapidly name a sequence of random letters or digits
◆ Rapid automatic naming of objects or colors: the ability to rapidly name a sequence of repeating random sets of pictures of objects (e.g., "car," "tree," "house," "man") or colors
◆ Writing or writing one's own name: the ability to write letters in isolation on request or to write one's own name
◆ Phonological memory: the ability to remember spoken information for a short period of time.

reading is a developmental process that is influenced by a child's previous background knowledge, or schema.

Why Is Shared Literacy Developmentally Important to A Child? It is widely accepted by literacy researchers that the environment a preschool child experiences before coming to school is a critical factor in determining that child's ability to read and write (Adams, 1990; Clay, 1991; Pressley, 1998). Many researchers are now investigating how interpersonal relationships contribute to the development of literacy. One researcher, Lev Vygotsky, has been very influential in this area. Vygotsky lived during the first part of the twentieth century in the former Soviet Union, and his theories have had a major impact on literacy. In his book *Mind in Society* (1978), Vygotsky posits that social interactions with others are a major factor in developing children's thinking abilities. He believed that learning is a social matter and that interaction between child and adult and between child and child are essential for a student to internalize concepts, and thereby work independently. Vygotsky believed that *learning is* **socially mediated** and that interaction and shared social activities form the basis of instruction. Vygotsky's theory is a radical change from traditional classroom practice in which children sit independently at desks and work alone silently. His theory suggests that classrooms should be centers of discussion, collaboration, and shared literacy experiences, with the adult acting as the mentor and facilitator.

One of Vygotsky's most influential theories is the **zone of proximal development.** He describes the zone of proximal development as being that zone encompassing the gap between a child's level of *actual development* and his or her level of *potential development*. Children can demonstrate their zone of proximal development through problem-solving activities that they can do either independently or with support provided by an adult through collaboration and feedback. Vygotsky believed that children should receive instruction in their zone of proximal development, and thereby be engaged in an activity that is just a bit too difficult to perform independently. This instruction should continue until the child is able to function independently at that level; then instruction moves to a new zone of proximal development, which would again be a bit too difficult for the child to perform independently. An adult or capable peer should provide the needed "scaffolding" so that children can accomplish tasks "just beyond their reach" and continue to push their zone of proximal development outward to further levels (Dixon-Krauss, 1996b) (Figure 4–2). Vygotsky's theories suggest that children learn from socially mediated experiences, which form the basis of their learning.

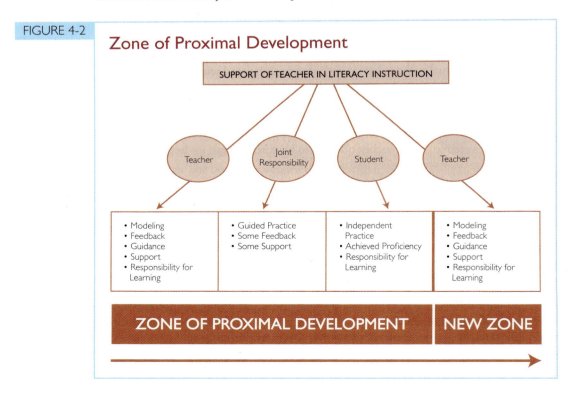

FIGURE 4-2

Zone of Proximal Development

An example of Vygotsky's concept of the zone of proximal development within the emergent literacy stage can be seen during the shared literacy experience, when the teacher is reading a storybook to a group of children. During reading, the teacher tailors the social interaction and the reading activity to help guide the children's participation and comprehension of the story. As the storybook reading progresses, the teacher relinquishes more of the responsibility for creating the social interaction and supporting the comprehension of the text to match the children's increasing capabilities. After repeated readings, the children may be capable of reading the text independently and creating the social interaction to support comprehension. At this time, the teacher moves on to another story, perhaps a bit more complex and requiring different comprehension strategies (Dixon-Drauss, 1996b).

The role of the teacher becomes essential with Vygotsky's theories. The teacher must mediate or support the children's ability to perform various learning tasks through social interaction and cooperative guidance. The teacher's role as mediator must be flexible, depending on the feedback received from children while they are engaged in learning. If children indicate the need for more support, then similar to an adult at home, the teacher should provide it. If children indicate the need for more independence, then the teacher must retreat and provide less mediation. The teacher's support can range from modeling the activity and giving explicit directives while sitting with the individual child to providing only clues or prompts and letting the child work independently.

Mediated instruction becomes an important part of literacy instruction. Literacy is very much a shared social experience between readers. During the emergent literacy stage, just as in any other stage of development, young children need to work in their zone of proximal development and teachers need to provide the support, scaffolding, and guidance required of mediated learning. Shared literacy experiences and mediated learning have become the cornerstones of the balanced literacy classroom.

Invented Spelling

What Is Invented Spelling? When left to their own devices, children are naturally imitative and inventive, especially in play. From their rather studious and perceptive observations of parents and siblings writing notes, lists, and longer written communications, emergent readers soon begin to imitate their elders by inventing spelling words and by writing their own made-up versions. **Invented spelling** (sometimes referred to as "temporary" spelling) begins long before children receive formal instruction; first by scribbling, then by creating letter-like formations, and later by approximating conventional

Courtesy of Becky Stovall

According to Vygotsky, learning is a social activity.

spellings—especially once they know that letters of the alphabet are used to write words. Gradually, these invented spelling attempts progress to closer approximations, using initial consonants, final consonants, and eventually medial vowel approximations so that these invented spellings of words start to resemble conventional spellings.

Until recently, formal reading, writing, and spelling instruction have been postponed until children entered first grade. Historically, a commonly held belief was that young children were too immature and were incapable of learning how to read, spell, and write until they could cope with abstract symbols, including manipulating letters with sounds, which is prerequisite to reading. Spelling was even postponed until after the child learned how to read and write. This practice changed as the movement for integrated language arts developed during the late 1970s and early 1980s.

Recent cognitive and brain research has expanded our knowledge about the capacity of emerging learners' knowledge, providing new evidence that young children are able to learn more at a younger age (Allen, 2001). More children are being exposed to preschool programs, and more homes, particularly in higher socioeconomic communities, are providing rich, early literacy experiences for their children. Harvard professor Jerome Bruner (1960), a disciple of Piaget, writes that regardless of age, children can be taught any concept that is developmentally appropriate if it is done so within the child's instructional ability range. Hence, geometry can be taught to early learners by introducing circles, squares, and triangles so that even kindergartners or first graders are able to grasp these symbols at their developmental levels. Nevertheless, most educators continue to believe that children would be "hurried along" before they were capable of learning how to read, write, or spell in a formal setting. Such thinking, however, is now being questioned due to the pioneering research and observations of reading experts such as Clay (1993) and Snow, Burns, and Griffin (1998).

A first grader uses invented spelling to compose a story about Dr. Seuss.

Courtesy of Becky Stovall

Invented spelling is one of the many advances made with regard to emergent literacy that philosophically has supplanted the concept of reading readiness. Once children have begun to master the alphabetic principle, the basis of our English language, they can begin using their knowledge of letters and sound correspondences to compose words and sentences.

Five Stages of Spelling Instruction Figure 4–3 shows developmental stages of spelling that children exhibit as they progress from writing random marks and representational drawings to representing sounds in words with vowels and consonants (Gentry & Gillet, 1993). In the first stage, the *precommunicative stage,* children use random marks, wavy lines, and letter-like writing with little awareness of the alphabetic principle. Spelling in this stage progresses from writing random marks with no direction, to going from

Stages of Spelling

Stage	Description	Writing Sample	Translation	Age
PRECOMMUNICA-TIVE	Spelling cannot be read by others; characterized by random strings of symbols, shapes, and mock letters.	EOiiVE OJiiTN	Story of a boy with a dog outside a house.	3 years–6 years
SEMIPHONETIC	Alphabetic principle is demonstrated; words represented by one or two letters; often consonants used to spell words.	ALD MN SKL BAK	Allowed Mine School Back	5 years–9 years
PHONETIC	Stage that represents invented spelling: spelling a word the way it sounds. Spelling is close enough that others can read it.	MI MUME S FNE ND NIS I FOWND A LITL DG TUDA.	My mommy is funny and nice. I found a little dog today.	6 years–12 years
TRANSITIONAL	Writers use vowel sounds in every syllable; words look like "real" words. Common patterns start to appear and sight words are spelled correctly.	We went to the stor and bote a littel kitten. It is cut and luves to clime things.	We went to the store and bought a little kitten. It is cute and loves to climb things.	7 years–12 years
CONVENTIONAL	The writer is spelling 90% of the words in a written piece correctly. Formal instruction in spelling can begin.	When I woke up this morning I saw two birds in the back yard whitch were very pretty.		8 years to adult

(Adapted from Gentry, R. J., & Gillet, J. W. (1993). *Teaching kids to spell.* Portsmouth, NH: Heinemann.)

FIGURE 4-3

left to right but with no distinct letters seen, to letter-like writing going across the page. In this stage, children are just beginning to develop phonological awareness and recognize that symbols can represent language through letters. Children usually display this type of behavior from approximately 3 years of age through first grade, and it is associated with emergent literacy in reading and writing.

In the second stage, the *semiphonetic stage*, children progress to exhibiting the alphabetic principle by being able to associate individual sounds with the corresponding letter; they also exhibit some phonological awareness by associating initial and final sounds of a word to the correct letter. Often in this stage, children omit the middle vowel and concentrate on the initial and final consonants spelling a word; for example, the word *mine* might be spelled as "m" or "mn." Some children at this stage are also able to identify vowel sounds and could spell "mine" as "min." This stage is usually from kindergarten through the end of first grade.

Teachers' VOICES   Invented Spelling

Invented spelling just comes naturally. I prompt my students to start by opening the journals they use for writing or drawing. I might ask them, "What are you drawing?" They respond, "mommy," for instance. I invite them to write "mommy." If they do not want to, I back off. The idea is for teacher and student to have a little conversation in print if the child wants. If they want to "pen pal" with me, I will say the word *mommy* and stretch it out sound by sound. They will begin with the *m* and usually end with an *e*. The pen pal idea really works. Some children are ready to extend this activity and write letters to friends, parents, or the teacher. Children like to explain their drawings to me and then try to write a phrase to express a thought, for example, "Wlz r bg" (Whales are big.).

—*Julie Williams, Preschool Teacher*

In the third stage, the *phonetic stage*, children can identify long and short vowel sounds and patterns in words, which they may or may not spell correctly. In this stage, they are associating initial and final sounds of words, as well as the more complex vowel patterns of the English language. This stage occurs from first grade to mid-third grade.

In the fourth stage, the *transitional stage*, the speller realizes that he or she must write not only what English sounds like but also what English looks like. The speller moves from relying almost exclusively on sound to figure out how a word should be spelled to greater reliance on visual and orthographic representations. The speller realizes there are basic conventions of English that must be followed, although he or she may not yet recognize that the word "looks right." This stage can start for some children as early as second grade.

In the last stage, the *conventional stage*, the speller is ready for more direct spelling instruction; that is, the student needs multiple opportunities to study words in depth and to start recognizing the visual and orthographic patterns that make up different words. At this stage, formal spelling instruction can begin with word lists that include emphasis on spelling and vocabulary development. Some children begin this stage in mid-second to third grade.

Invented spelling can help teachers assess what stage of spelling their students are in by noting the way that they spell words when writing. If a teacher notices that a child is spelling words by ignoring the middle vowel sound, then specific word study activities can be used to help develop the child's ability to recognize words and develop phonemic awareness. If a child is using vowels regularly in spelling, then the teacher can start working with word families and vowel patterns (Gentry & Gillet, 1993).

During the emergent literacy stage, teachers can determine what stage each student is in and provide encouragement and support for continuing literacy development. Teachers can talk and read to children to help them associate the sounds and meanings of language;

they can play alphabet games to help develop letter recognition and letter naming; they can have children sort objects into different categories to develop vocabulary; and they can sort pictures by beginning consonants to promote phonemic awareness. Most importantly, teachers should be aware that spelling and writing are developmental processes, and that students in the same classroom will be in many different stages of development.

Why Is Invented Spelling Important? Research evidence (Bear, Invernizzi, Templeton, & Johnston, 2000; Gentry & Gillet, 1993) shows that children who begin matching spoken sounds to letter names of the alphabet have developed the two most fundamental language insights necessary for becoming successful readers and writers: (1) understanding of the alphabetic principle (that is, spoken words are represented by written spellings known as **graphemes**), and (2) understanding of **phonemic awareness** (that is, spoken words are made up of sounds that can be manipulated). Therefore, through invented spelling, these emergent learners are demonstrating their knowledge of the alphabetic principle and phonemic awareness; that is, that spoken words are made up of a sequence of letters or phonemes that can be used to form written words to communicate information and ideas (Adams, 1990; NICHD, 2000; Snow, Burns, & Griffin, 1998). Eventually, kindergartners begin to write anything they can say and are able to read their own writing. Some experts suggest that learning to write is easier than learning to read for most children, and writing is viewed as a reciprocal learning process. By writing, children are moving from the known to the unknown; whereas when reading, they must decipher language from the unknown before they can know or understand the given text (Sipe, 2001). Thus, many preschool children learn to read by writing and, in turn, learn to write by reading. Preschool and kindergarten teachers also capitalize on this write first, read later approach, which research supports as a means of having children teach themselves phonemic awareness, phonics generalizations, and even develop an awareness that words and writing convey meaning that can be written down and understood by other children and adults (Adams, 1990).

Adams (1990) goes so far as to say that, through invented spelling, children not only develop the ability to express themselves in writing, but that in the process they are actually learning to discover the phonemic structure of the English language, resulting in more rapid development in phonics knowledge compared with their peers. In fact, research indicates, "Emphasis on writing activities is repeatedly shown to result in special gains in early reading achievement" (Adams, 1990, p. 95). Furthermore, Adams states, "The process of inventing spellings is essentially a process of phonics. . . In addition, there is evidence that invented spelling activity simultaneously develops phonemic awareness and promotes understanding of the alphabetic principle" (Adams, p. 95). These facts alone are extremely encouraging, because the two greatest predictors of young children's ability to learn how to read are their understanding of the alphabetic principle and phonemic awareness (Adams, 1990; Snow, Burns, & Griffin, 1998).

Nevertheless, parents and many teachers express concern that invented spelling, even though it is regarded to be *temporary*, may confuse children in the long run, causing them not to recognize conventional spellings when reading, or that invented spellers will continue to write in this unconventional way throughout elementary school or beyond. In fact, several spelling studies have shown that this is not true. Research indicates that children's invented spelling is truly a temporary process that begins to develop gradually, reflecting an increasing knowledge of conventional spellings of frequently used words, and helps children learn how to spell overall. Research also appears to indicate that children using invented spelling have a definite advantage over those taught through more traditional spelling methods (Adams, 1990).

Bear et al. (2000) point out that learning the alphabetic principle is a major hurdle for children; that is, it can be difficult for children to realize that letters of the alphabet can be matched from left to right to form words, either singly or in pairs, such as in one-to-one correspondence shown in writing "c-a-t" or in using "ch" in "ch-i-n." At the early emergent stage of writing and spelling, invented spellings or use of sound-to-letter correspondences by the child are approximate and temporary until they learn or are taught conventional spelling patterns.

Teaching Invented Spelling The two questions frequently asked by teachers about helping children make the transition from invented spelling to conventional spelling are: (1) Do I just let children use invented spelling without teaching them anything about conventions? (2) If not, when do I begin to intervene, and where do I start?

Some teachers believe that a hands-off or laissez-faire approach to invented spelling should be practiced. However, according to Clay (1991), teachers need to take an active role in student writing and spelling, or children may continue writing "nonsense." Sipe (2001) exhorts balanced reading teachers to take an active role, stating that the "anything goes" approach to invented spelling is misguided. He calls instead for a co-constructivist approach that provides interactions between the student and an "expert other" who will help the child move from the known to the new. Other experts recommend a more active role for the teacher in teaching those children who need explicit instruction in spelling, but caution against interfering with their independence or self-worth (Calkins, 1986; Delpit, 1988; Ladson-Billings, 1994; Routman, 1994). Donald Graves (1994), often referred to as the "Father of the Writing Process," wrote, "When first-grade children learn to spell, they need much more teaching than I've demonstrated in the past" (Graves, 1994, p. xvi). It appears from this statement that Graves is advocating a more balanced approach to literacy.

Some examples of helpful teacher interventions that enable children to make the transition to more conventional forms of spelling include helping children hear sounds in words using Elkonin boxes. Some children with learning disabilities may have difficulty hearing sounds in words; therefore, certain phrases or statements are not useful, such as, "Write it like it sounds and I'll be able to read it" (Sipe, 2001). Therefore, for many children, use of the Elkonin boxes (Figure 4–4) activity can be helpful in two ways: (1) It scaffolds the process to enable children to hear the sounds of a word more distinctly and clearly, and (2) it helps children write down words using conventional spelling under the guidance of their teacher. In this activity, first designed by the Russian educator D. B. Elkonin, a teacher draws a rectangle and draws partitions or boxes in it to correspond to the number of sounds in the word study. Markers or coins are placed below each box, and the child is encouraged to "stretch out" the word to hear each distinct sound and to move the marker into the box once the initial sound is identified. This activity is used aurally with young emergent readers who are not yet ready to use letters, but it is also an excellent activity to use with ELLs and with children who are reading and writing with letters. Usually, the child begins with the initial consonant, goes to the final consonant, and then listens to hear for the medial vowel sound. If the word is *hat*, for instance, the child tries to sound out *hat* by stretching the word to hear each phoneme, and then to identify its corresponding alphabetic letters: *h-a-t*. As the child tells the teacher what sound is heard, the child moves the marker up into that corresponding box. For example, once the /h/ sound is identified, the marker is moved up to indicate that the child has identified its sound. Then the marker is removed and the letter *h* is written

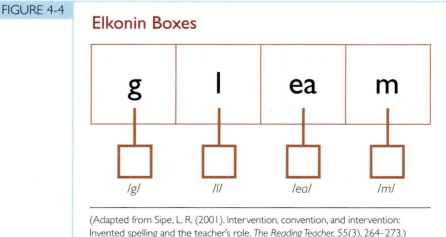

FIGURE 4-4

Elkonin Boxes

g	l	ea	m

/g/   /l/   /ea/   /m/

(Adapted from Sipe, L. R. (2001). Intervention, convention, and intervention: Invented spelling and the teacher's role. *The Reading Teacher, 55*(3), 264–273.)

in that box. The final consonant /t/ sound is identified next, and the corresponding marker is moved into the third box; the child replaces the marker with the letter *t*, which is written in this box. Finally, the child stretches out the word to hear the medial vowel sound and repeats the steps above (Sipe, 2001). As the child progresses to the point that he or she is beginning to spell more words conventionally, the boxes corresponding to the number of letters—rather than the sounds in the word— that are used to help the child identify what looks right, as well as what sounds right; therefore, rather than constructing four boxes for the word *g-l-ea-m*, five boxes are used (Sipe, 2001).

Bolton and Snowball (1993) introduced the four-column "Have-a-Go Chart" (Figure 4–5) that helps children correct misspellings once they are willing and capable of learning conventional spellings when working with a text. In short, the student writes spelling words identified as incorrect by writing them in the far left column *(Word from Text)*. In the second column *(Have-a-Go)*, with the help of a peer or teacher, the child tries to spell the word correctly. The teacher or peer can help the speller, using scaffolding techniques such as clapping syllables or stretching out the word (see earlier). The child writes a spelling revision of the word in the third column *(Correct Spelling)*. If still incorrect, the teacher writes the word or refers the child to the dictionary or the thesaurus. In the last column *(Copied Spelling)*, the child writes the words correctly, then studies the words to commit their correct spelling to memory (Sipe, 2001).

Phonemic Awareness

What Is Phonemic Awareness? Phonemic awareness refers to an awareness that words are made up of individual sounds, called phonemes. Often, phonological awareness and phonemic awareness are used interchangeably, and both terms are used widely throughout the literature. However, phonological awareness refers to the broader notion that words consist of syllables, "onsets and rimes" (where the beginning consonant *b* in a word such as *boat* is the onset and *oat* is the rime), and phonemes. Phonemic awareness refers to sound units smaller than the syllable and is therefore much more specific. The literature on emergent literacy is also specific with regard to phonemic awareness activities that young children should practice to improve reading achievement.

Long before children attend kindergarten or begin learning how to read, they have learned to produce and hear phonemes, the stream of sounds that make up words and are used for speaking and reading (Yopp & Yopp, 2000). At this emergent stage, children use words only to convey meaning and do not consider how these words are constructed. However, we cannot expect emergent readers to have acquired phonemic awareness—the knowledge that spoken and written words are made up of smaller units of separable sounds—on their own (Adams, 1990).

Until recently, it was not readily understood how important phonemic awareness could be as an aid to helping children learn how to read. In fact, researchers discovered that low-achieving readers have great difficulty making the shift from spoken language to reading because they lack the ability to conceptualize that a stream of sounds or letters in printed form make up words. According to Adams's (1990) research, "phonemic awareness is the ability to think consciously about the sound structure of words and to see words separable and capable of manipulating sounds in words" (p. 40). Yet, most children learn how to speak fluently and, therefore, have this ability to use phonemes that "are the smaller-than-syllable sounds that correspond roughly to individual letters" (Adams, p. 40).

FIGURE 4-5

Have-a-Go Chart

Word from text	Have-a-Go	Correct spelling	Copied spelling
grils	girls		girls
bars	bers	bears	bears

Yopp and Yopp (2000) point out that children who are phonemically aware can recognize that spoken language is made up of a sequence of small sounds. When asked to clap out each sound they hear in the word *fish*, children who are phonemically aware will clap three times as they identify three separate sounds (that is, /f/-/i/-sh). When the teacher sounds out the word *hop* in three separate phonemes or sounds (/h/-/o/ -/p/), phonemically aware children are able to blend these segmented phonemes together to form and say the word *hop*. In short, children who are phonemically aware know that words are formed by small chunks of sounds, and they are able to identify and manipulate them at will. This awareness that each new word encountered is made up of small units of sounds that can be manipulated or sounded out in a variety of ways is a conscious act that does not usually develop without intervention or direct, explicit teaching. Children make dramatic strides in a balanced reading program that includes explicit instruction in phonemic awareness.

The balanced reading teacher of children entering preschool, kindergarten, and in some cases, first grade should teach phonemic awareness as a "priority goal." Some general guidelines (Yopp & Yopp, 2000) that teachers should consider as they are planning their interventions are that phonemic awareness instruction should have the following characteristics:

◆ Engage children in playful and engaging activities

◆ Have social interaction as a key component

◆ Stimulate curiosity and experimentation with language

◆ Ensure that instruction focuses on specific objectives

◆ Teach as part of regular daily instruction in reading and writing

◆ View as only one part of a much broader literacy program

◆ Teach as one part of a comprehensive literacy program

Phonemic awareness tasks that are most widely used to assess and to improve children's phonemic awareness through instruction and practice include but are not limited to the following tasks (Ehri, Nunes, Willows, Schuster, Yaghoub-Zadeh, & Shanahan, 2001):

1. Phoneme isolation, which requires recognition of individual sounds in words; for example, "Tell me the first sound in paste." (/p/)

2. Phoneme identity, which requires recognition of the common sound in different words; for example, "Tell me the sound that is the same in *blue, boy,* and *bell.*" (/b/)

3. Phoneme categorization, which requires recognition of the word with the odd sound in a sequence of three or four words; for example, "Which word does not belong: *bus, bun,* or *rug*?" (rug)

4. Phoneme blending, which requires listening to a sequence of separately pronounced sounds and combining them to form a recognizable word; for example, "What word is /s/ /k/ /u/ /l/?" (school)

5. Phoneme segmentation, which requires breaking a word into its sounds by tapping out or counting the sounds or by pronouncing and positioning a marker for each sound; for example, "How many phonemes in *ship*?" (three: /sh/ /i/ /p/)

6. Phoneme deletion, which requires recognition of what word remains when a specified phoneme is removed; for example, "What is *smile* without the /s/?" (mile)

Yopp and Yopp (2000) suggest that children appear to be better able to capture and gain control over larger units of sound before they learn to control smaller units of sound. Therefore, a teacher's general plan should be to move from larger to smaller units of sound with younger preschool and kindergarten children, or when teaching older students who are not aware of or sensitive to sound structure in words. These sound sequences are as follows (Yopp & Yopp, 2000, p. 133):

◆ Rhyming activities
  "What rhymes with *cow*?" (now)

- Syllable unit activities [or, syllable splitting]

  "Clap twice for Mary's name." (*Mar* (clap) – *y* (clap))

- Onset and rime [segmentation task]

  "Say the first part of *brown*." (br)

- Phonemes activities [blending task]

  "Let's put these sounds together: /ch/ - /a/ - /n/." (chain)

Teachers' VOICES   Teaching Tip on Phonemic Awareness

NAME THAT SOUND

Begin with two paper or plastic cups. One cup should be labeled with a "B" for beginning sound and the other cup with an "E" for ending sound. You also will need some sort of snack or little "chips" to play the game. You will ask the students a series of questions to determine whether the child can distinguish between beginning and ending sounds in a given word. For example, you will ask the students, "Where is the /t/ sound in the word *hot*? or "Where is the /b/ sound in the word *bed*?" For each correct response, a snack or "chip" is placed into the corresponding cup. When each student has completed a set of words, they may eat the snack inside each cup or count their "chips" to see how many they earned. This game can be modified or adapted to various grade levels and can be used for assessing other phonic skills. You may want to use this game with consonant blends and digraphs (taught in Chapter 5) or long/short vowel sounds (label the cups "L" and "S"). I found that students enjoy participating, it holds their interest, and they cannot wait to devour their prize!

—*Heather Di Serio, Third Grade Teacher*

The Yopp–Singer Test of Phonemic Segmentation can be used to help assess a child's phonemic awareness (Figure 4–6). There are also other phoneme awareness tools that teachers can use to informally assess a student's ability to identify beginning sounds and to match different phonemes (Figure 4–7).

Teachers' VOICES   Teaching Tip on Phonemic Awareness

FINGER SPELLING: THROW AND CATCH

Finger spelling is a systematic, multisensory approach to think through the sound–symbol relationship. This approach is used to help students hear the sounds in words while they write. When a student asks me to spell a word, I play the throw-and-catch game. This approach is good to use during interactive writing, guided writing, shared writing, independent writing, and conferencing.

STEPS FOR FINGER SPELLING

1. The teacher says a word (*bat*).
2. The student repeats the word.
3. The teacher puts the word in a sentence (*The bat is flying around*).
4. The teacher says the word again, "throwing" it to the student.
5. The student catches the word (*bat*) in his or her nondominant hand/fist. In this way, the student can write with the other hand while sounding out the word.
6. The teacher says, "Clench your fist tightly. Do not let the word out of your fist."
7. The teacher says, "Starting with the thumb, let the word out a sound at a time." The teacher models showing how the thumb comes out with the /b/ sound, the first finger comes out with the /a/ sound, and the second finger with the /t/ sound.
8. The student picks up pencil and records the symbols as each sound is vocalized with each finger.

—*Kim Miranda, Reading Teacher K–4*

Yopp–Singer Test of Phonemic Segmentation
Directions for Administering

1. Have one test sheet for each child in the class.

2. Assess children individually in a quiet place.

3. Keep the assessment playful and game-like.

4. Explain the game to the child exactly as the directions specify.

5. Model for the child what he or she needs to do with each of the practice words. Have them break apart each word with you.

Children are given the following directions upon administration of the test:

> Today we're going to play a word game. I'm going to say a word and I want you to break the word apart. You are going to say the word slowly, and then tell me each sound in the word in order. For example, if I say "old," you should say "oooo-llll-d" (The teacher says the sound, not the letters.) Let's try a few words together.

The practice items are *ride, go,* and *man.* The teacher should help the child with each sample item—segmenting the item for the child if necessary and encouraging the child to repeat the segmented words. Then the child is given the 22-item test. If the child responds correctly, the teacher says, "That's right." If the child gives an incorrect response, he or she is corrected. The teacher provides the appropriate response. The teacher circles the numbers of all correct answers.

If the child breaks a word apart incorrectly, the teacher gives the correct answer:

	Child Says	You say
Uses onset and rime	/d/ - /og/	/d-/o-/g/
Repeats word	dog	/d-/o-/g/
Stretches word out	d - o - g	/d-/o-/g/
Spells letters in word	"d" - "o" - "g"	/d-/o-/g/
Says first and last sounds	/d/ - /g/	/d-/o-/g/
Says another word	bark	/d-/o-/g/
Says a sentence	I don't know	/d-/o-/g/

The child's score is the number of items correctly segmented into all constituent phonemes. No partial credit is given. For instance, if a child says "/c/-/at/" instead of "/c/-/a/-/t/," the response may be noted on the blank line following the items but is considered incorrect for purposes of scoring. Correct responses are only those that involve articulation of each phoneme in the target word.

A blend contains two or three phonemes in each of these and each should be articulated separately. Hence, item 7 on the test, *grew,* has three phonemes /g/-/r/-/ew/. Digraphs such as /sh/ in item 5, *she,* and the /th/ in item 15, *three,* are single phonemes. Item 5, therefore has two phonemes and item 15 has three phonemes. If a child responds with letter names instead of sounds, the response is coded as incorrect, and the type of error is noted on the test.

Students who obtain high scores (segmenting all or nearly all of the items correctly) may be considered phonemically aware. Students who correctly segment some items are displaying emerging phonemic awareness. Students who are able to segment only a few items or none at all lack appropriate levels of phonemic awareness. Without intervention, those students scoring very low on the test are likely to experience difficulty with reading and spelling.

FIGURE 4-6A

Student Test Sheet
Yopp–Singer Test of Phoneme Segmentation

Student's name _____   Date _____

Score (number correct) _____

Directions: Today we're going to play a word game. I'm going to say a word and I want you to break the word apart. You are going to tell me each sound in the word in order. For example, if I say "old," you should say "/o/-/l/-/d/." (Administrator: Be sure to say the sounds, not the letters, in the word.) Let's try a few together.

Practice items: (Assist the child in segmenting these items as necessary.)

                ride   **go**   **man**

Test items: (Circle those items that the student correctly segments; incorrect responses may be recorded on the blank line following the item.)

1.	dog	_____	12.	lay	_____
2.	keep	_____	13.	race	_____
3.	fine	_____	14.	zoo	_____
4.	no	_____	15.	three	_____
5.	she	_____	16.	job	_____
6.	wave	_____	17.	in	_____
7.	grew	_____	18.	ice	_____
8.	that	_____	19.	at	_____
9.	red	_____	20.	top	_____
10.	me	_____	21.	by	_____
11.	sat	_____	22.	do	_____

(From Yopp, H. K. (1998). The validity and reliability of phonemic awareness tests. *Reading Research Quarterly, 23*(2), 159–177.)

FIGURE 4-6B

Identification of Preschool Children with Special Needs

Children with Learning Disabilities

Many children who display deficits and developmental problems in cognitive, perceptual, motor, or social and emotional development may have a **learning disability.** The term *learning disabilities* refers to a neurobiological disorder that affects how one's brain works. This disability may influence a person's ability to speak, listen, read, write, spell, organize information, or do mathematics. If provided with the appropriate support and intervention, children with learning disabilities can succeed in school and have

FIGURE 4-7

Phoneme Awareness Test

Phoneme Isolating

Directions: I will say some words. Listen to the beginning sound of each word. Tell me the first sound of the word you hear. Let's do one together.

Model: Listen to this word: *dog*
I hear a */d/* sound at the beginning of the *dog*.

Guided Practice:
Let us say the word together: *help*
What is the sound at the beginning of *help*?
I hear a */h/* at the beginning of *help*.

Assess: Say each word after me and tell me the beginning sound:

moose
find
table
boy
girl

Phoneme Matching

Directions: I will say some words. Listen to the beginning sound of each word. Tell me which two words begin with the same sound. Let's do one together.

Model: Listen to these words: *kite, king, run.*
Two of the words begin with the same sound; *kite* begins with the same sound as *king*.

Guided Practice: Let us say the words together. Two of the words begin with the same sound. Can you tell me which two begin with the same sound? Listen: *pig, frog, pick.*

Assess: Listen to each group of words and tell me which two have the same beginning sound.

moose	*pet*	*mouse*
tooth	*tail*	*help*
girl	*run*	*goat*
find	*fast*	*sing*
boy	*cat*	*bat*

successful careers later on in life (Lerner, 2003). Some major points about the definition of learning disabilities are:

1. Individuals with learning disabilities exhibit many types of behaviors and characteristics.

2. Learning disabilities are due to factors within the person rather than to external factors, such as the environment or the educational system.

3. The problem is presumed to be related to a central nervous system dysfunction.

4. Individuals with learning disabilities can have several problems at the same time, such as learning disabilities and emotional disorders (Lerner, 2003).

Figure 4–8 provides a more in-depth examination of the definition of learning disabilities.

FIGURE 4-8

Definition of Learning Disabilities

There are many different definitions for the term *learning disabilities,* but the most widely accepted definition is set forth in the Individual with Disabilities Education Act (PL 101-746) commonly called IDEA, and is incorporated, with few word changes, in the 1997 reauthorization of IDEA, PL 105-17.

"Specific learning disability means a disorder in one or more of the basic psychological processes involved in understanding or in using language, spoken or written, which disorder may manifest itself in an imperfect ability to listen, think, speak, read, write, spell, or do mathematical calculations. Such term includes such conditions as perceptual disabilities, brain dysfunction, dyslexia, and developmental aphasia. Such term does not include a learning problem that is primarily the result of visual, learning, or motor disabilities, of mental retardation, of emotional disturbance, or of environmental, cultural or economic disadvantage" (IDEA, 1997, SEC.602.26).

The key elements of most definitions that are currently in use are:
• Intellectual functioning within normal range
• Inference that learning disabilities are not primarily caused by other disabilities or extrinsic factors
• Difficulty in learning in one or more academic areas
• Presumption of central nervous system dysfunction

(From Gargiulo, R. M. (2006). *Special education in contemporary society,* Belmont, CA: Thomson Higher Education.)

Because of the great developmental difference that occurs in the emergent literacy years, educators are reluctant to label young children (younger than 6 years) as having a learning disability. Rather, the term *developmental delay* often is used to identify those young children who may exhibit some characteristics of having a learning problem. Some of the characteristics that learning disabled children may exhibit at a very young age are:

◆ Inadequate motor development, in which the child displays "clumsy" and awkward behavior for gross-motor tasks and inability to accomplish many fine-motor tasks

◆ Language delays, in which the child exhibits delayed speech development and is slow in forming complete sentences; the child can also exhibit trouble in listening, paying attention, and following directions

◆ Speech disorders, in which the child is not pronouncing words correctly at the appropriate developmental stage

◆ Poor cognitive and concept development, in which the child does not understand basic concepts and displays an inability to understand stories or to communicate properly at an appropriate developmental level

Common examples of children who might display symptoms of developmental delay at the preschool level are:

◆ The 3-year-old who cannot catch a ball, hop, jump, or play with manipulative toys because of poor motor development

◆ The 4-year-old who does not use language to communicate, has a limited vocabulary, and cannot be understood when talking

◆ The 5-year-old who cannot count to 10, name colors, or work with puzzles

◆ Children with learning disabilities may also exhibit hyperactivity and a poor attention span.

Once a child has been formally diagnosed as having a learning disability and is enrolled in a school, the law requires that an **Individualized Educational Plan (IEP)** be developed for that student. The IEP is developed by a team—the child's parents, teachers, other school staff, and often the student—to examine closely the student's unique needs. The IEP guides the delivery of special education support services for the student with a disability. It outlines a specific educational plan that the child must receive in school and the services that will be provided. Figure 4–9 provides a more detailed examination of an IEP and what needs to be included.

Researchers have shown that children who are particularly likely to have difficulty with learning to read in primary grades are those who begin school with less knowledge and skill in cognitive, linguistic, and perceptual development. They lack verbal abilities, phonological knowledge, print knowledge, and letter knowledge. Children from poor neighborhoods, children with limited proficiency in English, children with hearing impairments, children who exhibit delays in language or cognitive growth and may have a learning disability, and children whose parents had difficulty learning to read are particularly at risk for failure and falling behind from the outset of schooling (Snow, Burns, & Griffin, 1998). Systematic and widespread education of parents and other caregivers, as well as the public, should occur. Parents need to know the importance of reading books at home with their children and providing opportunities for children to build language and literacy growth through everyday activities in their home and surrounding environment.

Experience and research show that intervention for young children is effective and educational efforts have a high payoff (Lerner, 2003). It is therefore extremely important that children with learning disabilities and those who are at high risk for failure due to environmental factors, such as poverty and crime, are placed in early intervention programs. Early intervention programs are designed to positively influence the course of language and literacy development in children from infancy to 8 years old. Research evidence indicates that a pattern of school failure starts early and persists throughout a child's school career (Strickland, 2002). Longitudinal studies show that there is an almost 90 percent chance that a child who is a poor reader at the end of grade 1 will be a poor reader at grade 4 (Strickland, 2002). This shows that children grow to dislike reading because they cannot do it properly and, therefore, read considerably less than good readers. This is important because it has been reported that time spent reading is highly correlated with achievement; that is, children who read more have better results in school.

Early intervention programs—such as Head Start, the most famous of these programs—are beneficial for children with learning disabilities and those children who are disadvantaged. Early intervention programs offer a substantial financial savings for the community by reducing the number of children who will need special education services in the future (Lerner, 2003). Research also shows that these programs enhance intelligence, promote substantial gains in all developmental areas, reduce family stress, and save the nation and society substantial health-care and education costs. Early intervention programs accelerate cognitive and social development and reduce behavioral problems. Many disorders can be overcome to a large extent, and other problems can be successfully managed so that the child can succeed in an academic environment.

Emergent Literacy and English Language Learners

The latest research in emergent literacy and ELLs indicates that ELL children and native speakers of English develop prereading skills in a similar way. Phonological awareness, or the awareness of speech sounds, plays a significant role in learning how to read. Researchers have found that awareness of individual speech sounds in one's native language correlates with the awareness of individual speech sounds in learning English. For example, phonological awareness in Spanish helps children become aware of individual sounds in the English language, which is a predictor of success in reading and spelling in both languages. Therefore, most research suggests that, when possible, it is best to have young ELL children develop literacy skills in their native language first,

Individualized Education Plan

What Is an IEP?

Each public school child who receives special education and related services must have an Individualized Education Program (IEP). Each IEP must be designed for one student and must be a truly *individualized* document. The IEP creates an opportunity for teachers, parents, school administrators, related services personnel, and students (when appropriate) to work together to improve educational results for children with disabilities. The IEP is the cornerstone of a quality education for each child with a disability.

To create an effective IEP, parents, teachers, other school staff—and often the student—must come together to look closely at the student's unique needs. These individuals pool knowledge, experience, and commitment to design an educational program that will help the student be involved in, and progress in, the general curriculum. The IEP guides the delivery of special education supports and services for the student with a disability. Without a doubt, writing—and implementing—an effective IEP requires teamwork.

What Needs to be Included in an IEP?

By law, the IEP must include certain information about the child and the educational program designed to meet his or her unique needs. In a nutshell, this information is:

- **Current performance.** The IEP must state how the child is currently doing in school (known as present levels of educational performance). This information usually comes from the evaluation results such as classroom tests and assignments, individual tests given to decide eligibility for services or during reevaluation, and observations made by parents, teachers, related service providers, and other school staff. The statement about "current performance" includes how the child's disability affects his or her involvement and progress in the general curriculum.
- **Annual goals.** These are goals that the child can reasonably accomplish in a year. The goals are broken down into short-term objectives or benchmarks. Goals may be academic, address social or behavioral needs, relate to physical needs, or address other educational needs. The goals must be measurable, meaning that it must be possible to measure whether the student has achieved the goals.
- **Special education and related services.** The IEP must list the special education and related services to be provided to the child or on behalf of the child. This includes supplementary aids and services that the child needs. It also includes modifications (changes) to the program or supports for school personnel, such as training or professional development, that will be provided to assist the child.
- **Participation with nondisabled children.** The IEP must explain the extent (if any) to which the child will not participate with nondisabled children in the regular class and other school activities.
- **Participation in state- and district-wide tests.** Most states and districts give achievement tests to children in certain grades or age groups. The IEP must state what modifications in the administration of these tests the child will need. If a test is not appropriate for the child, the IEP must state why the test is not appropriate and how the child will be tested instead.
- **Dates and places.** The IEP must state when services will begin, how often they will be provided, where they will be provided, and how long they will last.
- **Transition service needs.** Beginning when the child is age 14 (or younger, if appropriate), the IEP must address (within the applicable parts of the IEP) the courses he or she needs to take to reach his or her post-school goals. A statement of transition services needs must also be included in each of the child's subsequent IEPs.
- **Needed transition services.** Beginning when the child is age 16 (or younger, if appropriate), the IEP must state what transition services are needed to help the child prepare for leaving school.
- **Age of majority.** Beginning at least one year before the child reaches the age of majority, the IEP must include a statement that the student has been told of any rights that will transfer to him or her at the age of majority. (This statement would be needed only in states that transfer rights at the age of majority.)
- **Measuring progress.** The IEP must state how the child's progress will be measured and how parents will be informed of that progress.

(From U.S. Department of Education. *A Guide to the Individualized Education Plan*, Washington, DC: Office of Special Education and Rehabilitative Services.)

FIGURE 4-9

because the acquisition of basic literacy skills in English will develop at a more rapid pace when they are proficient in their native language (Gersten & Geva, 2003; International Reading Association, 2001b; Slavin & Cheung, 2003). For ELLs, learning to read in a language in which children are not yet proficient is an additional risk factor for reading difficulties. However, with a strong understanding of ELL children and a carefully designed emergent literacy program that monitors student progress and provides additional support for children identified as at risk for reading difficulties, classrooms can teach the acquisition of English literacy skills and language proficiency at the same time to ELL children (Lesaux, 2003).

STRATEGIES FOR TEACHING DIVERSE LEARNERS

Working with Students with Learning Disabilities: Emergent Literacy

It is important to remember that deficient phoneme awareness is one of the primary traits of children with learning disabilities who are at risk in the classroom. It is therefore important to concentrate on developing phonological awareness through early intervention programs and to start working with the young child as early as possible.

1. The initial goal is to draw the child's attention to the sounds of language. Children with learning disabilities will vary in their progress; some children will need to go through each step very slowly, while others will progress at a more rapid rate. The end point is for a child to develop phonemic awareness, the foundation of all subsequent reading and spelling instruction (Shaywitz, 2003).

2. Try emphasizing phonemic awareness activities for about 15 minutes each day, starting as early as preschool with 3-year-olds and continuing onward into kindergarten (Shaywitz, 2003).

3. Work on rhyming. Read stories and poems aloud that joyfully play with the sounds of language and teach the child that words rhyme.

4. Have children separate words into syllables by clapping out each syllable. Starting with the child's

own name is a good place to start; for example, *Sa-man-tha* has three claps.

5. Have children try to separate each syllable or small phonetic word into its individual phonemes. Have them clap for each sound they hear; for example, *spring* has six claps.

6. Work on the child's gross-motor coordination first such as catching a ball, skipping, jumping, and throwing. Also work on fine-motor coordination with puzzles, coloring, tracing, painting, cutting, beading, and sorting.

7. Work on the child's visual discrimination by sorting shapes into shape boxes, putting puzzles together, working with large Legos and blocks, and playing games.

8. Work on the child's auditory discrimination with songs, poems, music, and read-alouds.

9. Partake in enjoyable writing and drawing activities that involve coloring, tracing, and copying patterns. If children are ready, have them write stories using invented spelling.

Research also has shown that there is a strong positive correlation between literacy and proficiency in the native language and learning English, and that the degree of children's native language proficiency is a strong predictor of their English language development (Antunez, 2004; Snow, Burns, & Griffin, 1998). Oral language proficiency in a child's native language establishes the knowledge, concept, and skill base that transfers from the native language to reading in a second language. Hiebert and her colleagues at the Center for the Improvement of Early Reading Achievement (CIERA) synthesized reading research and recommended that ELLs learn to read initially in their first language (Hiebert, Pearson, Taylor, Richardson, & Paris, 1998). In its report *Preventing Reading Difficulties in Young Children*, the NRC recommends that ELLs learn to speak English before being taught how to read English. Oral language development provides the foundation for phonological awareness and provides the support for learning about print. The NRC made a two-part recommendation concerning ELLs (Snow, Burns, & Griffin, 1998):

◆ If language-minority children arrive at school with no proficiency in English but speaking a language for which there are instructional guides, learning materials, and locally available proficient teachers, these children should be taught how to read in their native language while acquiring oral proficiency in English and subsequently taught to extend their skills to reading in English.

◆ If language-minority children arrive at school with no proficiency in English but speak a language for which the above conditions cannot be met and for which there are insufficient numbers of children to justify the development of the local capacity to meet such conditions, the initial instructional priority should be developing the children's oral proficiency in English. Although print materials may be used to support the development of English phonology, vocabulary, and syntax, the postponement of formal reading instruction is appropriate until an adequate level of oral proficiency in English has been achieved. (p. 324)

Research suggests that the age of the ELL is an important factor to consider in acquiring a new language. Perhaps contrary to what most people believe, older children acquire a second language at a more rapid rate than younger children. Research comparing children and adults learning a new language does not support the notion that younger children are more efficient at learning a second language. However, this is based on the degree of children's native language proficiency, which is a strong predictor of their English language development. Another important point is that evidence from preschool programs suggests that proficiency in a native language does not impede the acquisition of English. Children are quite capable of learning two languages at once (DiCerbo, 2000). In fact, research supports that children experience important cognitive gains through bilingualism, but these gains are experienced only when both languages develop to a point of proficiency where the child can transfer knowledge from one language to the other (Lenters, 2004). In an ideal world, children would receive instruction in their native language to the point where they were proficient in all aspects of it, and then transition to English language learning. The transition would typically occur at about the age of 7. At that time, reading instruction builds on the child's knowledge of the native language and what he or she already knows about reading and print. However, this type of dual instruction takes place in few schools, and most districts do not have the resources to embrace such a practice nor are the teachers adept enough in the many different languages required to institute such a program (Lenters, 2004).

One of the implications from this research is that teachers should not expect miraculous results from young children who are ELLs, and they must be supportive and patient in developing their oral proficiency in both languages, if possible. Teachers need to create an environment where oral language is modeled, encouraged, and accepted through a variety of rich and engaging literacy activities. Often, pairing a child who is learning English with one who is already proficient is beneficial for both children and helps promote language development.

Our classrooms today must accommodate children from many different cultural, ethnic, and linguistic backgrounds, whether they are fluent in English or just learning it. This mixture of backgrounds makes learning in such a classroom a rich and rewarding experience when children have the opportunity to learn about each other's customs, beliefs, and language. It also makes teaching in such a classroom challenging because many of the children's values and customs are different from those of the school. Teachers must react positively to children's linguistic and cultural diversity, rather than viewing student differences as a deficit. Limited expectations are damaging to children whose abilities within their own cultural context may be well developed. We should never use a child's dialect, language, or culture as a basis for making judgments about the child's intellect or capability (International Reading Association and National

Association for the Education of Young Children, 1998). The classroom needs to be supportive of a child's native language and not make the child feel ostracized, ashamed, and inferior because of linguistic differences.

A teacher can do many things to promote literacy on the part of children who are culturally and linguistically diverse. The teacher should encourage all students to use language as much as possible, and help those who are just learning English contribute to the discussion, even if it is with only one word in English. The teacher can use diversity as a positive and enriching learning experience by teaching simple words of the child's language to the class and comparing it with English. Children can learn to count in the many different languages that are represented in one class and learn the different customs and beliefs that classmates may share. The teacher can pair children together as "buddies," with one helping the other whose English is just emerging. Cooperative groups and hands-on projects encourage children to discuss, share, and communicate with each other and are excellent strategies to help children use English to communicate ideas (International Reading Association, 2001b). It is most important during the emergent literacy stage that the teacher accepts and supports both the child's native language and the emerging English, and that the teacher makes the child feel special and part of a warm and caring environment.

STRATEGIES FOR TEACHING DIVERSE LEARNERS

Emergent Literacy and English Language Learners

1. When possible, have young English language learners (ELLs) develop literacy skills in their native language first, because the acquisition of basic literacy skills in English will develop at a more rapid pace when they are proficient in their native language.

2. Stress oral language development in the classroom and have young children develop oral proficiency in English before asking them to read. Oral language development provides the foundation for phonological awareness and provides the support for learning about print.

3. Pair a child who is learning English with one who is already proficient; this is beneficial for both children and helps promote language development.

4. Use multicultural literature from the children's native culture within the class and for read-alouds.

5. Encourage the children to contribute to the classroom literacy program by teaching the class to speak simple words or count in their native language.

6. Have children write books and illustrate books together with the ELLs, contributing words and sentences from their culture.

7. Create a safe, nurturing, and accepting environment where the children feel that they are valued and that their background, culture, and knowledge are accepted.

8. Encourage children to talk and discuss as part of the everyday classroom routine. Encourage children to use English as much as possible.

9. Use cooperative groups and buddies as much as possible to support the young child.

Technology and Early Literacy

Are Computers Appropriate for This Age?

It is not uncommon to see a 3-year-old sit at a computer and act totally computer literate, moving the mouse with ease, navigating from frame to frame, and typing in the correct responses. Preschool children are one of the fastest growing groups to be online. Only 6 percent of children aged 2 to 5 used the Internet from any location in 2000

(Corporation for Public Broadcasting, 2002). Today, market researchers have identified that the largest software growth has been in new titles and companies serving the early childhood educational market (NAEYC, 1996). Software programs targeted for this age group are proliferating at a rapid rate and are one of the "hottest" selling programs on the market.

Technology for young children can include the use of online resources on the Internet, software programs on the computer, DVDs, digital cameras, cell phones, hand-held devices, e-mail, and electronic communication using social networking programs. Even many children's toys could be called "technology," for they include sophisticated chips and advanced technological applications. For this discussion, we will refer to technology as being the use of the computers, including access to the Internet.

Electronic media such as the Internet, software programs for the computer, CD-ROMs, digital cameras, and handheld devices all use multimedia technologies to present information, whether it be video clips, music, gaming, or animated graphics. Multimedia can affect how our students learn and access information. The way in which information is presented and accessed using electronic media can be considered a new means of representing ideas, concepts, and information. Much as language and mathematics are different forms of representation—one using letters and words to convey information and the other using numbers and equations—multimedia presents information through visual, graphical, and multisensory representations. The way in which multimedia presents information influences the meanings one arrives at, the cognitive skills that are called for, and the perceptions one derives of the world (Salomon, 1997). Children who access information via multimedia formats must call on different mental processes than those who use a book or watch a DVD. Researchers have shown that different symbolic forms of representation are processed by different sets of mental skills and capacities (Eisner, 1997; Greeno & Hall, 1997; Salomon, 1997). This has powerful implications for teachers who must understand the positive and negative implications of this new media, especially when dealing with young children.

Research suggests that technology can enhance social, language, and cognitive skills in young children (Clements, 1994; NAEYC, 1996; Seng, 1998; Scoter, Ellis and Railsback, 2001). Studies highlight the opportunities that computers provide for language use, social interaction and increased motivation. Computers also allow children to engage in experiences and "field trips" that they might not be able to experience in the real world, providing increased exposure and understanding of important concepts and issues. Electronic mail and telecommunications allow children to share different cultural and social interactions with other classes and children, previously limited by physical location (NAEYC, 1996).

Research also indicates that computers should supplement, not replace, highly valued early childhood activities and physical materials, such as blocks, sand, water, books, crayons, and art materials. Computers can be used in developmentally appropriate ways as well as misused; technology cannot take the place of reading a book with an adult or sharing in conversation. The supportive context of the family and a rich social environment in which adults engage with children are key factors in early childhood development. However, a number of features of technology can support early learning when used appropriately. Interactive technologies can make it easier to create environments in which students are learning by doing with hands-on projects. Technology can also help children visualize difficult-to-understand concepts and bring to life abstract and remote experiences (Scoter, Ellis, & Railsback, 2001).

Many researchers claim that technology can enhance an early childhood classroom and is a powerful learning tool that can complement the rhythms of classroom life; technology can help meet the literacy needs of young children (Labbo & Sprague, 2002; Leu, 2002; Turbill, 2002). These researchers are pointing to the success of integrating technology into many different classrooms through the use of Internet projects such as Frosty Readers (http://kids-learn.org/kidspired2007), in which classrooms across the world read the same book, engage in the same activities, and then share their results by posting to a website. This type of technology integration has been successful in preK and kindergarten classes, as well as through the elementary, middle, and high school years. Children get a chance to read books and create drawings or hands-on projects, which are then posted online (usually using a digital camera) so that children can see their own work "published." Students are also exposed to other children's work from all over the world and share in a global, intercultural curriculum. These Internet projects are promoting cross-cultural understanding through new forms of literacy, while reinforcing basic reading and writing processes.

Teachers' VOICES   Technology in the Preschool Classroom

Without a doubt, technology promotes literacy in the classroom. We start with the children reading the computer chart, which tells the kids which pair of students will have the first turn on the computer during choice time. The children read their names and the day of the week, using semantic and phonemic cues. So, they are reading before they even start up the computer. Within the programs available to the children, they practice all five strands of literacy: reading, writing, speaking, listening, and visual literacy. They must listen to the directions spoken by the characters on the program; speak and confer with their partner about what steps to take next; read the letters, numbers, and high-frequency words on the screen so that they can complete the task; and "write" whenever the program instructs them to enter their names or other information using the keyboard. Visual literacy is used throughout because children's software is highly visual and requires the children to literally draw connections with the mouse and sort items into columns (such as colors or shapes, among others). The children also *love* it, and it gives this teacher great pleasure to see the kids tying together all the literacy strands to complete the tasks presented on the software. I see technology being detrimental only if used for the teacher's convenience. I have witnessed preschool classrooms in which the computer was put on a table, the volume raised high, and tuned to a program in which cute characters dance and sing. The children sit passively, transfixed as they would while watching a video.

—*Adrienne Kosmoski, Preschool Teacher*

Leu (2002) believes that with the Internet technologies becoming such a force in our lives, new literacies have emerged that need to be taught to our children. These new literacies include the skills, strategies, and insights necessary to successfully use the information and communication technologies that are increasingly part of our global world (Leu, 2002). It is no longer enough to consider literacy as addressing print-based materials alone. Literacy includes reading, writing, and interpreting electronic forms of information, as well. Children are being exposed to this requirement in their everyday life, and it is the teacher's responsibility to teach students to be thoughtful, reflective, and competent in this new literacy.

Preschool children can use technology in the following ways:

- Software programs designed for young children to learn preschool concepts through problem solving and gaming
- Software programs that help children "write" and compose their own stories using clip art and draw programs to illustrate them
- Interactive storybooks that read the text of a book out loud to the student and allow him or her to explore a page that is interactive; that is, if a student presses an owl, it might fly out of a tree and hoot
- Basic skills programs that teach the alphabet and numbers
- Draw/paint programs that allow a child to draw pictures, import clip art, and create slide shows
- Access to Internet sites developed for young children such as those by Disney, Sesame Street, and Scholastic
- Virtual field trips where children visit another country, school, or site

◆ Internet projects as described earlier in this chapter; many of these projects are appropriate to use with preK and kindergarten classes

A direct link to Internet projects is provided on the *Literacy for Children in an Information Age* Book premium website: http://www.cengage.com/login

Using Technology in Developmentally Appropriate Ways

Appropriate use of technology for young children can be integrated into the classroom in the following ways.

◆ Teachers need to evaluate and carefully choose software, keeping in mind the development and learning styles of the students. Teachers should also carefully observe and monitor individual children using software to identify the way in which the software should be used and to make appropriate adaptations.

◆ Parents and teachers should both participate with children while they are using technology. They should encourage children to interact and share with their peers as well as encourage the children to use computers independently.

◆ If children are using computers independently, an adult should closely monitor the use and be available for support and guidance. Children should not sit at the computer for a prolonged period of time on their own, nor should the computer function as a "baby sitter" or "time filler" while an adult is busy elsewhere.

◆ A classroom can be set up to encourage interaction by having two seats in front of one computer and placing computers close to each other to facilitate sharing ideas. The computers can be located in a central spot to invite class participation and social interaction.

◆ Computer activities should be built into the curriculum to enrich it, extend concepts across subject matter, and provide a deeper understanding of the concepts. For example, after a shared reading experience, children could read an interactive e-book in which they press icons to see objects move and explore different interactive pages to gather a deeper understanding. They could also partake in an Internet project online focusing on the same theme, in which they share their ideas with another class in a different part of the state or country.

◆ Teachers should promote equitable access to technology for all children and their families (NAEYC, 1996). Special care needs to be given to ensure equity in technology access for gender, race, and social class. Girls need equal amount of time on computers as boys, and teachers should ensure that girls' interests are reflected in the chosen educational software and Internet sites used in the class. In addition, research has shown that children who are economically disadvantaged have less access to computers at home, and this is related to their technological competence and confidence. These children might need to be provided more in-school computer access, which must be meaningful and move beyond drill and practice. Families should also be involved and encouraged to learn how to use technology as a meaningful tool.

◆ Children with special needs should have technology to assist and accommodate their needs when this is helpful. There are many assistive technology products available to assist young children with disabilities, such as speech-to-text software products, and products that read the text to the user. Assistive technology allows children with disabilities to be included in many activities and gives them the independence and support to be included in classes with their peers.

◆ Teachers should match the appropriate software and activity to the child's interest and ability level. The teacher should make sure the program is not too difficult for the child and that the child is interested in the content. The software programs or Internet sites should emphasize problem solving and reasoning, rather than drill and practice.

◆ Teachers should provide information to parents on the benefits and uses of appropriate software and Internet sites. Parents can become involved in helping choose software that can be used at home, as well as learning about excellent Internet sites which support a child's developmental level.

In summary, technology can be a valuable and enriching learning experience for young children. It should not replace rich social interaction with adults and peers, nor take the place of playing in sand, working with Play-Doh, building with blocks, and cutting out pictures. Technology should be an enriching supplemental resource that helps develop cognitive and linguistic growth.

Assessing Emergent Literacy

The Importance of Informal, Continuous Assessment

With the recent trend in administering standardized assessment tests to children in schools, it is highly recommended to use informal, functional assessment measures for preschool children that are more authentic and allow an educator to observe the children in a natural environment (Lerner, 2003). Formal standardized assessment tests are not appropriate measurements for young children. One of the purposes of any informal assessment is to identify those children who may display developmental delays and may need special services. It also allows a school to determine whether the child is ready to progress on to kindergarten and then to first grade.

At school entry, which is usually into kindergarten, schools use a combination of informal measures of development, which would include observational data, as well as a checklist. These measures would assess:

◆ Cognitive Development
  ◆ Identifying colors
  ◆ Naming parts of the body
  ◆ Rote counting (up to 10 or 15)
  ◆ Demonstrating an understanding of one-to-one correspondence (for example, "Show me four blocks.")
  ◆ Demonstrating understanding of concepts such as on, under, between, middle
  ◆ Identifying letters
  ◆ Sorting chips by color, size, and shape
◆ Motor Development
  ◆ Catching a ball, jumping, hopping, skipping
  ◆ Building a four-block design
  ◆ Matching and copying shapes
  ◆ Writing one's own name
  ◆ Drawing a picture of oneself
◆ Communication Development
  ◆ Speaking clearly in sentences
  ◆ Understanding directions or a story told to the child
  ◆ Verbal memory for stories and sentences
  ◆ Naming of vocabulary
◆ Social and Emotional Development
  ◆ Observing how well the child relates to other children
  ◆ Observing how well the child relates to adults

- Observing the child's self-concept, which can be assessed through the child's drawing of a person and seeing how well developed the figure is (does the figure include a head, neck, body, arms coming off the body, legs in the proper place, and so forth)
    - Observing a child's self-help skills, such as toileting skills, dressing skills, eating skills, and ability to separate from parents
- Letter Knowledge Assessment
    - Assessing whether children can identify the letter names of the alphabet
- Concepts About Print
    - Can a child locate the front and back of a book?
    - Does a child know that print contains meaning?
    - Does a child know that print moves from left to right?
    - Can a child follow with a finger word by word?
    - Can a child follow a book from left page to right?
    - Does a child know about punctuation marks: capital letter, period, comma, question mark, and quotation mark?
    - Does a child know first and last letter of word?

Ways to Assess the Young Child

Teachers have many different ways to assess children in the emergent literacy stage, including:

- *Portfolio assessment:* Teachers can use the portfolio to determine how well a child is responding to in-class activities by collecting samples of the student's work that reflect progress toward a specified objective. Such samples could be pictures, projects, photographs, computer files, and records of observations taken by the teacher.

- *Checklists:* Teachers often develop their own checklists and keep an account of how each child is progressing by recording information in anecdotal notebooks or logs. These checklists are important guideposts that aid and serve as reminders to classroom teachers that their children are meeting specific goals or objectives. A "Checklist for Assessing Student's Concepts About Print" is shown in Figure 4–10.

- *Anecdotal records:* Teachers also keep anecdotal records while they observe and interact with their students to learn more about their reading and writing attitudes and behaviors. Children's attitudes and behaviors toward reading and writing are important to assess, because motivation to read and to eventually become a lifetime reader is particularly valuable information for classroom teachers to know.

- *Published assessment and evaluation tests:* Although it is not recommended that standardized tests be used on children in the emergent literacy stage, there are many published resources that provide information about early language and literacy observation and assessment tools for preschoolers. These resources include:

- *Bader Reading and Language Inventory* (6th edition), developed by Lois A. Bader and Daniel L. Pearce (2009) and published by Prentice Hall

- *Early Language and Literacy Classroom Observation (ELLCO) Toolkit,* developed by Marion W. Smith and David K. Dickerson in collaboration with Angela Sangeorge and Louisa Anastasopoulos Smith (2007) and published by Brooke Publishing

- *A Framework for Early Literacy Instruction: Aligning Standards to Developmental Accomplishments and Student Behaviors,* developed by Mid-continent Research for Education and Learning (MCREL 2000), and available on their website as a pdf file at http://www.mcrel.org/topics/Literacy/products/7/

- *Phonological Awareness Literacy Screening (PALS PreK),* Curry School, University of Virginia, available at http://pals.virginia.edu

Checklist for Assessing Student's Concepts about Print

	Behavior	Directions	Correct?
1.	Does the student know the concept of front of the book?	Hand book to the student in a vertical position, spine toward the child. Say, "Show me the front of the book." Check the box if answer is correct.	
2.	Does the student know the concept of print?	Open to the first page of text. There should be a picture on this page. Say, "I will read this book to you. Show me where to read." Check the box if the student points to the first word on top of the page.	
3.	Does the student know which way to read?	Turn to the second page of the book. Say, "Point to where I start reading." Check the box if the student points to print somewhere on the first page.	
4.	Does the student know that print is read from left to right?	Say, "Which way do I read this page? Which way do I go?" Check the box if the student moves finger from left to right.	
5.	Does the student know at the end of the line to return to the next line?	Say, "Where do I go after the first line?" Check the box if the student "return sweeps" to the left.	
6.	Does the student have the concept of a word (one-to-one match with voice to print)?	Check the box if the student matches your voice to the print as you read.	
7.	Does the student understand the concept of first and last?	Turn to a new page. Say, "Show me the first part of this story." Say, "Show me the last part of this story." Check the box if the student points to any of the following combinations: -the first and last words on a line -the first and last words in a sentence -the first and last words on a page -the first and last words in the book	
8.	Does the student know that the left page is read before the right page?	Turn the page so that there is a left and right page to read. Say, "Where do I start reading?" Check the box if the student points to the left page.	
9.	Does the student know the meaning of a question mark?	Point to a question mark in the text. Say, "What is this for?" Check the box if the student says "question mark" or "when you ask something."	
10.	Does the student know the meaning of a period?	Point to a period in the text. Say, "What is this for?" Check the box if the student says "period" or "the end of the sentence."	

(Adapted from Klein, A. Assessing Student's Concepts about Print, Los Angeles County Office of Education. Retrieved May 2006, from http://teams.lacoe.edu/reading/assessments/print/concepts.html)

FIGURE 4-10

◆ *Systematic observation of emergent readers:* Observing emergent readers reading from authentic, leveled texts or examining children's early writing attempts allows the teacher to behave like a scientist or a researcher. The emergent literacy teacher gradually learns how to systematically observe the child's behavioral patterns, referred to by Marie Clay (1993) as "kid watching." Daily observations and ongoing assessment help the teacher develop instructional plans.

In summary, assessment is an important component of the emergent literacy classroom. It helps a teacher determine children's progress toward specified goals and objectives and how to plan instruction accordingly. Classroom teachers are moving toward more informal, continuous, and ongoing assessments, rather than using formal standardized testing formats. The types of assessments mentioned above, such as portfolios, checklists, observations, and anecdotal records, are the recommended formats for assessing young children.

STRATEGY BOX

Promoting Emergent Literacy In Children

When we go back to our opening description of Mr. Abrams' preK classroom, the following strategies will help teachers promote emergent literacy in their students:

1. Read, read, and read to the children. Do read-alouds through shared literacy experiences. Do shared reading and model expressive, fluent reading.

2. Write, write, and write with the children. Encourage them to express themselves in writing through pictures and invented spelling.

3. Encourage the children to use language to express themselves. Provide opportunities in structured discussions, in class presentations such as show-and-tell, in cooperative learning, and in informal play sessions.

4. Get the parents involved in promoting literacy. Have the parents participate in literacy activities at home and in the classroom whenever possible. Encourage parents, siblings, and/or caretakers to read books to the children at home.

5. Surround the classroom with printed materials of all kinds: picture books of stories, content-area books, magazines, menus, comic books, and posters.

6. Involve children in constructive play involving pretend activities and manipulatives such as blocks, Legos, and puzzles.

7. Always have an adult sit with the child when using the computer to monitor and interact with the child. Provide quality software programs for the child to use.

8. Limit the amount of time young children spend on the computer and watching television at home and at school.

Final Thoughts

This chapter has explored one of the more important stages in a person's life—the period before formal schooling begins when there is a phenomenal spurt of growth over a short period of time. Language development and cognition are intricately tied to the social and emotional environment that surrounds the child. Rich language experiences, nurturing interactions, and supportive and loving family members all contribute to a child's ability to develop emergent literacy skills. The significance of the child's home environment cannot be underestimated when talking about emergent literacy and the child's future growth and progress in school.

In the next chapter, you will learn about the next stage in a child's life, when he or she moves from emergent literacy to beginning literacy. In Chapter 5, you will learn about how children begin to identify and read words and sentences, and how they can attain fluency in reading. However, the success of every child is based on the solid foundation that he or she gains in the emergent literacy stage of life. Therefore, as you go through the succeeding chapters, remember that reading is a long-term, developmental process, and the skills and processes effective readers use are based on the appropriate cognitive, perceptual, motor, and social and emotional development garnered during the preschool years.

EXPLORATION   Application of Concepts

Activities

1. Explore how preschool and kindergarten classes are using technology in their classrooms by visiting the *Literacy for Children in an Information Age* Book premium website for this chapter at http://www. cengage.com/login. Explore the links and visit the different classrooms. Make notes on how these sites are promoting the home–school connection and communicating with parents. Present to the class or a group which two sites you like best.

2. Visit a preschool or kindergarten classroom. Make a list of all the activities and instructional materials being used in the classroom. Next to each one, write down the area(s) that this activity is promoting; for example, visual discrimination, auditory memory, fine-motor coordination, and cognitive development, among others.

3. As a class, develop a preschool curriculum by designing different learning centers. Divide the class into four or five groups. Assign each group a different learning center, for which they are to develop activities: Reading Center, Art Center, Computer Center, Kitchen Center, Water/Sand Table Center, and any other center that the class elects to develop. After they develop activities for each center, have each group specify what specific skills and processes are being taught at that center. Have each group present its learning center to the class.

4. Develop phonemic awareness activities to teach to a prekindergarten class. Present your activities to your classmates for feedback and discussion.

5. In a small group, model a read-aloud and shared reading or writing approach. Conduct a mini-lesson modeling a think-aloud. Have your classmates give feedback on how you read the book aloud (was your voice loud enough, did you show the pictures to the class, did you read slowly and with expression?) and how you conducted the shared reading/writing activity.

HOME–SCHOOL CONNECTION   Increasing Awareness About Print

Parents and guardians can help children increase their awareness about print and the importance of reading by:

1. Reading aloud to children, which is the single most important activity parents and/or guardians can do to help their children become skillful readers.

2. Writing and sharing grocery lists with their children and encouraging them to add to the lists using emergent writing, even if they just scribble.

3. Pointing out how to read labels on boxes and cans that they purchase together at the supermarket.

4. Reading traffic signs together, starting with the familiar red stop sign and identifying others such as curve, railroad crossing, school—slow down.

5. Having children match a familiar icon with its name, such as matching *McDonald's* with its golden arches, or reading the brand names of favorite products, such as *Fruit Loops, GE, SONY,* or *Apple.*

6. Writing and sharing messages, directions, and letters, which teaches children how important writing is in everyday life.

7. Encouraging children to write their own messages, which is empowering and motivational.

8. Teaching the ABC's and nursery rhymes, which helps children learn how to read words.

9. Introducing children to the library and letting them choose their own books.

Families and teachers should work together to increase awareness of print in young children. This will ultimately increase literacy achievement in all children as they progress through school.

(Adapted from: Ortega, A. and Ramirez, J. (May, 2002). Parent literacy workshops: One school's parent program integrated with the school day. *The Reading Teacher,* (55)8, 726–729.)

5 THE STUDY OF WORDS

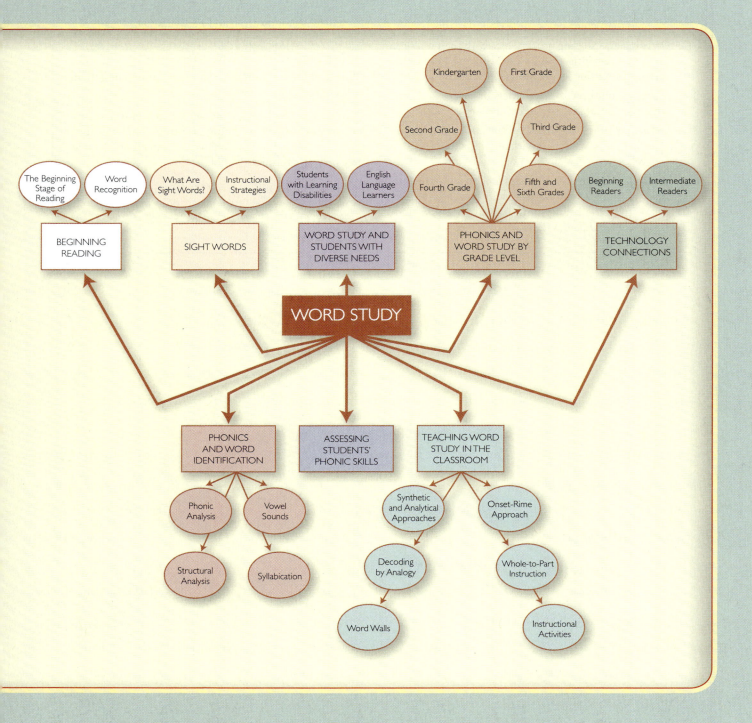

International Reading Association Professional Standards Addressed in this Chapter:

IRA STANDARD 1:   FOUNDATIONAL KNOWLEDGE

Candidates have knowledge of the foundations of reading and writing processes and instruction. Candidates:

1.1 Demonstrate knowledge of psychological, sociological, and linguistic foundations of reading and writing processes and instruction.

1.2 Demonstrate knowledge of reading research and histories of reading.

1.3 Demonstrate knowledge of language development and reading acquisition and the variations related to cultural and linguistic diversity.

1.4 Demonstrate knowledge of the major components of reading (phonemic awareness, word identification and phonics, vocabulary and background knowledge, fluency, comprehension strategies, and motivation) and how they are integrated in fluent reading.

IRA STANDARD 2:   INSTRUCTIONAL STRATEGIES AND CURRICULUM MATERIAL

Candidates use a wide range of instructional practices, approaches, methods, and curriculum materials to support reading and writing instruction. Candidates:

2.2 Use a wide range of instructional practices, approaches, and methods, including technology-based practices, for learners at differing stages of development and from differing cultural and linguistic backgrounds.

2.3 Use a wide range of curriculum materials in effective reading instruction for learners at different stages of reading and writing development and from different cultural and linguistic backgrounds.

IRA STANDARD 3:   ASSESSMENT, DIAGNOSIS, AND EVALUATION

Candidates use a variety of assessment tools and practices to plan and evaluate effective reading instruction. Candidates:

3.2 Place students along a developmental continuum and identify students' proficiencies and difficulties.

IRA STANDARD 4:   CREATING A LITERATE ENVIRONMENT

Candidates create a literate environment that fosters reading and writing by integrating foundational knowledge, use of instructional practices, approaches and methods, curriculum materials, and the appropriate use of assessments. Candidates:

4.1 Use students' interests, reading abilities, and backgrounds as foundations for the reading and writing program.

4.2 Use a large supply of books, technology-based information, and nonprint materials representing multiple levels, broad interests, and cultural and linguistic backgrounds.

Key Terms

automaticity
fluency
word identification
decode
grapheme–phoneme connection
sight words
high-frequency words
phonic patterns
structural patterns

Focus Questions

1. Why is word identification so important in the reading process?

2. How do sight words help in the process of reading? What are some strategies a teacher can use to teach children sight words?

syllabic patterns

phonic analysis

consonant sounds

long vowel sounds

short vowel sounds

consonant blends

digraphs

CVC words

CVCe words

decoding by analogy

diphthongs

structural analysis

prefixes

suffixes

roots

syllabication

synthetic approach

analytic approach

onset-rime approach

word families or phonograms

whole-to-parts instruction

word walls

cloze activity

word sorts

Focus Questions *(continued)*

3. What are three types of patterns used in word identification recognition?

4. What are different approaches to teaching phonics in the classroom? Give examples of how you would use each approach in teaching word identification.

5. What word identification strategies can you use to teach students with learning disabilities? English language learners?

6. What are some methods for assessing students' ability to recognize words?

7. What are the literacy skills that each grade level should know? What are the different instructional strategies teachers should use in the class-room to teach literacy skills?

8. How can technology be integrated into the literacy classroom to teach word identification? What precautions should a teacher take before using the Internet in a literacy lesson?

Welcome to Ms. Rosen's Second Grade: Teaching Word Study in the Classroom

Radius Images/Jupiter Images

Ms. Rosen, a second grade teacher, has placed five struggling readers in a guided reading group. Two of the students are English language learners (ELLs) and need the individualized instruction that guided reading groups provide. Ms. Rosen has identified that the ELLs do not have a basic sight vocabulary to instantly recognize many of the common words in the English language, and that they are having trouble with basic phonic skills, such as identifying beginning consonant sounds and recognizing familiar phonic patterns that occur in the English language. She has spoken to their parents and knows that both students can read and write in Spanish, their native language, and she has encouraged the parents to continue reading to them at home in Spanish so they will continue to develop their literacy skills.

For the guided reading session, Ms. Rosen has chosen easy books for the students to read, which have predictable and patterned text and illustrations that provide clues to the content to help support their reading. Each page contains a large illustration and one or two simple sentences that emphasize a phonic pattern. She reads the first page to them, and then asks them to read along with her, repeating the same page. She then has one student read aloud the same page. She has each of the students read aloud the same page and when the student is struggling with a word, Ms. Rosen writes it down for the student's word bank so these words can be reinforced at a later time. For the two ELLs, she writes the Spanish word (looking it up in a Spanish–English dictionary, if necessary) on the back of each card. After the reading, Ms. Rosen provides a short mini-lesson on one particular phonic pattern that all students need to know: how to recognize words that fall into the CVC (consonant-vowel-consonant) pattern such as *fat*, *pit*, *bed*, and *sun*. The students then write stories using the words from the book and illustrate their pictures, sharing them with the group. They are then instructed to read the book out loud to their buddy. The guided reading session with this group takes no more than a half-hour.

As you read through this chapter, try to figure out what strategies Ms. Rosen is using to teach her students word identification skills and to become more fluent readers. Think about how you might use these strategies that are based on state and national standards and reflect current research in literacy to improve students' literacy development.

Beginning Reading

Beginning Stage of Reading

The beginning reading stage refers to the period when students are just beginning to learn how to read the first words presented in the classroom reading program (Carnine, Silbert, Kame'enui, & Tarver, 2004). Some students who come to school are able to read many words, while others have little ability to read. Those children who lack the literacy background in their preschool years will take longer to "catch up" before moving on to more fluent and advanced reading. During this stage, children will "read" from books that have been frequently read to them by modeling the behavior they see, increasingly using the word patterns, intonations, and phrasing that they have heard. They will look carefully at the pictures and will start to recognize some letters and even words. The children may practice "silent" reading whereby they sit alone and "read" to themselves, modeling the behavior of silent reading.

Word identification is an important component of the beginning reading stage and must be seen philosophically and theoretically as part of the balanced reading program. When we see children struggling to learn how to read in the classroom, we need to ask what these children know about print and whether they have been frequently read to in their preschool years. For those children who lack a strong literacy background, we need to start reading to them as frequently as possible and expose them to a print-rich environment. We need to provide them with meaningful and pleasurable experiences with print so that they will be better able to start identifying words within the text and acquire letter–sound knowledge (Moustafa, 1998). They need to start using language to express themselves and start seeing the connection between their spoken words and printed words. As Moustafa states, "Powerful reading instruction builds children's knowledge of language and the world, *and* builds *on* their knowledge of language and the world" (Moustafa, 1998, p. 154).

Research has provided information about how words are understood: Word meanings and sometimes their pronunciations are dependent on the context of the sentence. Context is important in interpreting the meaning of a word, and skilled readers interpret meaning much better than do novice readers (Snow, Burns, & Griffin, 1998). Therefore, it is important that readers encounter words within meaningful text so that they have a context within which to base the meaning and pronunciation of the word. An example of this is encountering the word *bank*. *Bank* can refer to the place you keep your money or can have a totally different meaning; for example, "The girl stood at the bank of the stream to see the fish." Another example is the word *read*. Based on the context of the sentence, the pronunciation would be different; for example, "I will read the book now" versus "She read the book to him yesterday." Therefore, teaching words within the context of meaningful text is a significant factor that all teachers should consider when teaching word recognition.

Another important component of the beginning reading stage is the child's development in building **automaticity,** the ability to recognize words quickly and automatically. Automaticity is developed over time and is dependent on the amount of reading the child does. The more exposure children have to words in meaningful contexts, the more likely they will learn those words instantaneously so that they are committed to memory and recognized automatically.

Word Recognition

According to the National Reading Panel (NRP), **fluency** is the ability to read text quickly, accurately, and with proper expression (National Institute of Child Health and Human Development [NICHD], 2000). The most critical factor leading to fluency in reading is the ability to recognize letters, spelling patterns, and whole words effortlessly, automatically, and visually. The basic goal of all reading instruction—comprehension—depends totally on this ability (Adams, 1990). Fluent readers recognize words and comprehend at the same time, making connections among the ideas in the text and between the text and their background knowledge (NICHD, 2000). The identification of a printed word is necessary for fluency, from novice readers to adult

Word knowledge is essential for skilled reading.

Courtesy of Guilherme Cunha

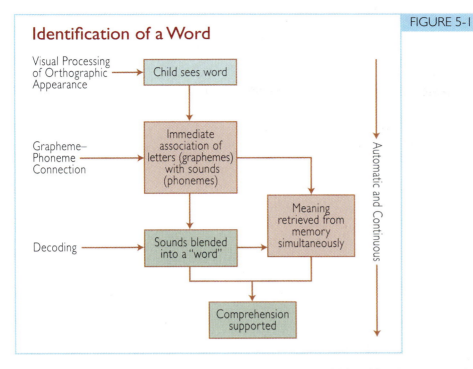

FIGURE 5-1

Identification of a Word

readers, and is crucial for comprehension. The term **word identification** means that the reader can pronounce a word but does not necessarily understand what the word means (Snow, Burns, & Griffin, 1998, p. 65).

For the skilled reader, the identification of a word begins with the visual processing of its orthographic appearance, or how the word is structured letter by letter (Figure 5–1). This visual processing initiates the immediate association of the orthographic structure of the word to the phonological **decoding** processes, or the sounds of the small units within the word. Research on reading has developed an important consensus that phonological decoding is a routine part of skilled word identification (Adams, 1990; Snow, Burns, & Griffin, 1998). That is, when a child sees a word in print, an automatic association must occur between recognized visual patterns of letters (graphemes) and their associated sound(s) (phonemes), called the **grapheme–phoneme connection.** These sounds are instantaneously blended together into a "word." This process is automatic and continuous. Research also supports that once the grapheme–phoneme association has been made and retrieved from memory, meaning is also retrieved simultaneously. Therefore, word identification supports comprehension for recently read text (Snow, Burns, & Griffin, 1998).

Skilled readers differ from unskilled readers in their ability to recognize words, attach meaning to the words instantaneously, and apply specific strategies to help them construct meaning about what they read (Snow, Burns, & Griffin, 1998). Word knowledge is essential for skilled reading of text and is an essential (but not sufficient) factor for comprehension. Although most beginning reading programs focus on word identification, it is an important component of adult reading as well.

Teachers' VOICES   Teaching Tip on Decoding

A teaching strategy that I use for decoding, as well as other reading techniques, is the "helping hand." The helping hand is something in our district's language arts curriculum that is used to help students become readers. It is a hand that has five different points about reading.

The first finger says to listen to what makes sense when reading words in a book. If you are reading a word in a sentence and it does not sound like the appropriate word, then most likely it is not the correct word. The second finger says to check the pictures. This strategy helps the students look at the pictures to determine whether the words they are reading make sense. The third finger says to go back and reread. Sometimes if you go back and reread, you will realize the word does not make sense and you will be able to correct yourself. The fourth finger says to get your mouth ready. This step helps students who are having a hard time pronouncing a word. And the last finger says to look for chunks in a word. If you look for chunks, it will be easier to read the word instead of sounding it out letter by letter.

I begin using the helping hand in the middle of the year when I am placing the children into guided reading groups and when they are reading on their own. This is a fun and easy way to remember this strategy, and when I ask the students to make sure when they are reading that they are using their helping hand, they understand what I am talking about and they are cautious while reading.

—*Jennifer Pietropaolo, First Grade Teacher*

As you go through this chapter, you will be introduced to many different ways that children in the beginning stages of reading can learn how to identify words. One way is through recognition of sight words. Another way is applying generalizations to unlock the pronunciation of words through phonic analysis. You will also learn that there are many different approaches a teacher can use to teach word recognition. As you read this chapter, it is important to keep in mind that children's knowledge of print words is only one of many factors that influence their ability to figure out unfamiliar words. According to Moustafa (1998), perhaps the most important factor is the extent to which children have been exposed to experiences with print.

Sight Words

What Are Sight Words?

When children enter kindergarten, they often can recognize several words, usually their name and several other words to which they have been exposed consistently. Through shared literacy experiences, many children have learned that language is represented by symbols, and that words represent spoken language. Many children have developed concepts about print and knowledge of books. As described in Chapter 4, they have developed a degree of phonemic awareness, have learned some letter names and sounds, and are expressing themselves through invented spelling. In general, most children's "reading" at this stage consists of **sight words,** those words they have memorized and are able to recognize automatically. At this early stage of literacy development, a child may know 1 to 2 percent of the words in a given text exclusively as sight words; the rest of the words in a given text need to be decoded through some form of word identification strategies. By the time we become adults, 99 percent of the words that we read are sight words and all other words need to be identified by decoding. That 1 percent of words usually consists of names, foreign words, or technical terms that we rarely encounter. Thus, the process of reading goes from knowing a small number of sight words and needing tools to identify the other words, to knowing a large amount of sight words and needing tools to decode only the few infrequently used words that may appear in text.

How should we decide which words to teach as sight words? What is the best way to teach sight words? The following section presents instructional strategies teachers can use to teach children sight words.

Instructional Strategies for Teaching Sight Words

High-frequency words are the most common words in our language, and all children should have these commonly used words committed to memory so that they instantaneously recognize them. The 100 most common words actually make up about 50 percent of the material we read (Figure 5–2)! The 25 most common words make up

High-Frequency Word List

These are the most common words in English, ranked in frequency order. The first 25 make up about a third of all printed material. The first 100 make up about half of all written material. Is it any wonder that all students must learn to recognize these words instantly and to spell them correctly also?

THE INSTANT WORDS FIRST HUNDRED

Words 1–25	Words 26–50	Words 51–75	Words 76–100
the	or	will	number
of	one	up	no
and	had	other	way
a	by	about	could
to	word	out	people
in	but	many	my
is	not	then	than
you	what	them	first
that	all	these	water
it	were	so	been
he	we	some	call
was	when	her	who
for	your	would	oil
on	can	make	its
are	said	like	now
as	there	him	find
with	use	into	long
his	an	time	down
they	each	has	day
I	which	look	did
at	she	two	get
be	do	more	come
this	how	write	made
have	their	go	may
from	if	see	part

(From Fry, E. B., & Kress, J. E. (2006). *The Reading Teacher's Book of Lists*, 5th Edition. New York: Jossey-Bass, with permission.)

FIGURE 5-2

about one-third of written material (Fry, Kress, & Fountoukidis, 2000). Children need to learn to recognize and automatically spell these high-frequency words to help them process meaning. Constantly stopping to figure out a new word or pausing to spell a word while writing severely hampers fluency in reading and writing and interferes with processing of meaning. Another reason for learning these words is that many of them are not pronounced or spelled in logical ways. For example, if *the* was pronounced like other words, it would rhyme with *he*, *be*, and *me*; *said* would rhyme with *maid* and *paid*; and *have* would rhyme with *cave* and *wave* (Cunningham, 2000). Many struggling readers have a great deal of trouble with these high-frequency words because they do not follow traditional patterns in the English language, because many of them share the same letters (*the, they, there, them, their, then*), and because many of the words have no concrete meaning (*of, where, with, from, for*).

The following strategies will teach children to recognize sight words automatically and thereby increase fluency and comprehension of text. Emphasis should be on high-frequency words that children will need as "glue" to process meaning, as these words make up about half of all written material.

◆ *Labeling* everything in the classroom is one of the most common ways to increase the number of sight words a child recognizes. The labels will help children recognize the words associated with common objects, as well as high-frequency words. For example, a label could read "a box *of* chalk" or "flowers *from* home." This helps to ensure that the child is exposed to the same words day in and day out and will start to recognize the patterns of many words.

◆ *Visual configuration* of the word or words often is used in conjunction with labeling. In this technique, a teacher will trace out the word or words so that the child will learn to discriminate visually between words that may appear structurally similar. Visual configuration is especially helpful with children with learning disabilities who may need the visual cues to discriminate between two similar words such as "better" and "potter." This method also works well with phrases that have similar words in them, for example, "a box of cookies" or "a box from home."

Labeling with Visual Configuration

Note: Visual configuration is presenting a word with added visual attributes that help the reader identify the word. So, for the above example, the word "look" has eyes.

◆ *Shared literacy experiences* are another way to increase a child's sight word vocabulary. When children read the same story multiple times in many different ways, they are exposed to the same words over and over again. The teacher may read the book to the class first, then have the students read the book together with her a few times, and then do a pair-share where two students read the book to each other. Through reading repetitive and predictable text multiple times, children often learn to recognize many words and commit them to memory.

◆ *Games* are a motivating way to teach sight words. Games such as Bingo and card games with sight words on them can be used. Games reinforce the use of these words in a fun way.

◆ The *context of the story* is another strategy for teaching sight words. This is when the reader identifies what an unknown word is through clues in the text. Pictures can provide invaluable clues about an unknown word. For example, if the story is about a boy and his guitar and the child does not know the word *guitar,* the picture should be able to provide the necessary information to help unlock that word. Teachers need to teach students how to use the illustrations in books to help unlock the meaning of the story and to give them clues to figuring out unknown words. In a similar fashion, other words in the sentence can help the student figure out an unknown word. If the child knows a few words in the sentence, these words might provide the clues to unlocking the unknown word. These unknown words should go into the child's word bank and be studied. A child must study each word that is not familiar and become aware of the pattern of letters that the word consists of and have practice using that word in reading, writing, spelling, and speaking. Each time an unknown word is ignored, an important opportunity is lost to expand the sight vocabulary of that child.

◆ *Daily routines* that occur each morning or afternoon are another excellent way to teach sight vocabulary words. Many classrooms have a routine of discussing the morning weather and looking at the calendar. By reviewing the days of the week and the months of the year each morning, children quickly learn to recognize these words. They also quickly learn about capitalizing certain words and how to sequence according to days and months; mathematical concepts are reinforced as well.

Phonics and Word Identification

When children come across a word they do not know during reading, they must have tools to unlock the pronunciation and meaning of this word. Word identification strategies provide children with those tools to help them decode words. Word identification strategies are based on certain assumptions:

1. Word identification strategies are used only with unfamiliar words.
2. Word identification makes use of language patterns.
3. Not all words follow the pattern or rule that is being applied; therefore, word identification will not unlock 100 percent of words 100 percent of the time.

Word identification allows children to apply helpful tools to identification of unknown words and to focus on common patterns that occur in the English language that may or may not help in unlocking those unknown words.

The philosophy in teaching word identification is that each reader needs to become an "investigator" and discover units with which he or she is familiar, recognize patterns of letters that frequently are seen together in the English language, and unlock unfamiliar words by gathering clues as to the word's pronunciation. The better a child is at discovering clues, the better a reader the child will become. The reader should study each unknown word carefully and use the tools to uncover its possible pronunciation. By studying a word, the child becomes familiar with its structural configuration and starts to instantly recognize the patterns that occur frequently in the English written language.

Three types of patterns are used in word identification: (1) phonic, (2) structural, and (3) syllabic patterns. **Phonic patterns** are the language sounds represented by written letters or graphemes. **Structural patterns** are affixes (prefixes and suffixes) added to root words to change their meaning. **Syllabic patterns** are the groupings of vowels and consonants that indicate syllabication. Notably, students do not need to know the terminology listed below or be able to recite the generalization. However, teachers should become familiar with the specific terms and generalizations, so that they are able to understand when reading about word identification and discuss this with other reading professionals. *Teachers should avoid teaching these generalizations as rules to be memorized, but rather as examples of language patterns that children may put to strategic use for reading and spelling.*

Phonic Analysis

In **phonic analysis,** the sound used to represent a letter or letters in a known word can be used to unlock the pronunciation of unknown words in which these particular letters occur. It involves identifying individual sounds or phonemes in words and blending them together to form a word. This means that beginning readers need to be able to identify the many phonemes associated with the consonants and vowels of the English language. For example, a student would need to blend the following sounds together to identify the word: *p-a-n*. It also means that the student needs to be able to recognize familiar patterns that frequently occur in the English language and use those patterns to unlock unknown words. For example, if a student is trying to unlock the pronunciation of the word *stand* and knows that his name begins with *st* as in *Steven*, and he already knows the word *and*, he should be able to unlock this unfamiliar word using his knowledge of patterns from familiar words. Phonics requires a reader to discriminate between patterns (*st* and *sp* or *sh*), remember previous patterns and their associated sounds (*st* and *and*), and blend these two patterns together to form a new word (*st + and = stand*).

Children should be introduced to phonic analysis in kindergarten, and many of the generalizations listed below should be included in first, second, and even third grade teachings. For struggling readers, phonic analysis is an essential tool that will provide them with the support they need to learn how to read and identify words. The generalizations listed below should not be memorized by children but provide the teacher with phonic patterns that many English words follow. It is helpful to teach these patterns as "word families" and decoding by analogy (both approaches are described later in the chapter) and to have children become familiar with words that follow these generalizations.

Phonic generalizations are as follows:

- *Letters of the Alphabet:* Research shows (Adams, 1990) that there is a high correlation between being able to identify every letter of the alphabet as an automatic response and future success in reading. It is, therefore, extremely important that every child knows the letters of the alphabet as an instantaneous and automatic response.

- *Consonant Sounds of the Alphabet:* Children need to know the sounds of each consonant of the alphabet so that it is an automatic response.

- *Long Vowel Sounds:* The long vowel sounds are an easy step to master because they just say their own name. Other vowel sounds are a bit more difficult to master.

- *Short Vowel Sounds:* Short vowel sounds can be difficult to master. A good strategy in teaching and remembering the short vowel sounds is to associate each sound with a visual image: *a – apple, e – elephant, i – insect, o – octopus, u – umbrella*. These images can help trigger the necessary recall of the sound when needed. Routman (1994) claims that short vowels should be taught later in the reading process because they are so difficult to master, and that these vowel sounds are better addressed after the child's reading has improved.

- *Consonant Blends in both Initial and Final Positions:* Blends are two phonemes or sounds represented by two letters or graphemes that are blended together. Blends such as *sm*, *sl*, *br*, *sp*, *tr*, and *pr* are all used in initial positions of words. Blends such as *ng*, *nt*, *nd*, and *lt* are all blends used in the final positions of words. You can also have triple blends such as *spr*, *str*, and *spl*.

- *Consonant Digraphs:* **Digraphs** are two letters or graphemes that form one sound or phoneme, almost as if we ran out of letters to represent sounds in the English language. Digraphs are *ch*, *sh*, *th*, *ph*, and *wh* in initial and final position of words. Thus, if you pronounce the word *this*, you will notice there are three phonemes, or sounds—*th*, *short i*, and *s*—although there are four graphemes, or letters.

- *CVC (consonant-vowel-consonant) Words:* These words are simple, phonetically regular words that make up the basis of the English language. The vowel is always short in CVC words; *cat, dog, pin, get, but, hit, fig*, and *cap all* make up

CVC words. Consonant blends and digraphs can also exist in initial and final positions in CVC words, for example, *this*, *step*, *chin*, *bring*, *bent*, and *spring*. All words follow the same rule: The vowel is short.

◆ ***CVCe (consonant-vowel-consonant-e) Words:*** These words are also simple, phonetically regular words that make up a large part of the English language. The vowel in the middle is always long and the *e* at the end of the word is always silent, for example, *cake*, *pine*, *rude*, *hate*, and *like*. Consonant blends and digraphs can also exist in initial positions in CVCe words, for example, *plate*, *shine*, *shame*, and *white*. Teachers can teach CVC and CVCe words together and help children distinguish between these two phonic elements.

These generalizations describe basic phonic patterns that occur with regularity in the English language, and they can help children identify unknown words. However, for phonic generalizations such as CVC and CVCe, there are exceptions to these rules. That is why it is most useful for young readers to find patterns of these generalizations in known words that can then be applied to unknown words.

Vowel Sounds

Teaching vowels is perhaps one of the more difficult tasks in the English language. Vowels have many variable sounds depending on the word they are used in, and they are unpredictable. For example, look at the letter *e* in the following words: *end*, *feet*, *made*, *eat*, and *fern*. *End* has a short *e* sound, *feet* has the long *e* sound, *made* has a silent *e*, *eat* is combined with *a* for a long *e* sound, and the *e* in *fern* is *r*-controlled. Some other vowel sounds, such as *a*, may be even more complicated (Cunningham, 2000).

When we look at fluent readers, we could be amazed at how they recognize so many words with so many variant vowel sounds! Poorer readers struggle with the vowel sounds and often rely on the consonants to give them clues as to the correct pronunciation of words. Yet, there are consistent vowel patterns that can help readers generalize to pronounce unknown words. If you look at these nonsense words, you will probably be able to pronounce all of them fairly quickly and accurately: *dalk*, *sait*, *quare*, *clape*, *jouse*, and *befuse*. That is because you are using familiar patterns from words you know and applying them to unknown words.

Research supports that readers decode words using spelling patterns from words they already know (Adams, 1990; Cunningham, 2000). When readers see an unfamiliar word such as *dalk*, they relate the word to other familiar words they know, such as *talk*, and apply the spelling pattern and pronunciation that has been successful before. Using words you know to decode unknown words is called **decoding by analogy** (Cunningham, 2000). This is an excellent way to teach vowel sounds, but spelling patterns are often unreliable and will not work with all words. An example of this is the high-frequency word list (see Figure 5–2); these words often are not pronounced or spelled like other words, which is why they need to be taught as sight words and committed to memory. *To* and *do* should rhyme with *go*, and *said* should be spelled like *red*; *what* should rhyme with *hat*, and *you* should be spelled as *blue* or *to*.

Therefore, it is recommended that children use multiple strategies in trying to identify a word. The vowel pattern box in Figure 5–3 lists the most frequently used spelling patterns and generalizations that apply to the English language. A teacher should not try to have students memorize these rules, but should introduce some of these patterns and have children become familiar with some of the words that follow these generalizations.

Structural Analysis

Structural analysis is used to decode words by analyzing the **prefixes, suffixes,** and **roots** of words to determine their pronunciation and meaning. Most of the common prefixes, suffixes, and roots are derived from Latin. Prefixes and suffixes are added to

Vowel Patterns Box

1. Long vowel sounds

a. The final "e" at the end of a word, makes the preceding vowel long.

        Example: fate, game, nose, tame

b. In the vowel digraphs *oa, ea, ee, ai,* and *ay,* the first vowel is usually long and the second is silent. (When two vowels go walking, the first does the talking.)

        Example: coat, reap, bead, wait, play

c. A single vowel that concludes a word or syllable usually has the long sound.

        Example: me/ter, be, ti/ger, lo/co/mo/tive

2. Short vowel sounds

a. A single vowel followed by a consonant in a word or syllable usually has the short vowel sound (CVC rule).

        Example: bit, tin, top, get, lip, fat, thin

3. Vowel digraphs have one vowel sound or phoneme but two letters or graphemes (sometimes *y* functions as a vowel).

ay – day, pay, say	ey – key, monkey
ai – bait, raid, paid	ie – tie, lie
au – haul, laurel	oa – boat, float, moat
ee – feet, seed, sheet	oo – look, foot,
ea – beak, beat, please	food, moon

4. Vowel **diphthongs** (vowel blends) have two-vowel sounds or phonemes, both of which contribute to the speech sound.

        oi – foil

        oy –boy

        ou – our, loud, house

        ow – cow, growl

5. Single vowel sounds followed by "r" usually result in a blended sound. They are also known as "Bossy" r sound.

bar	fern	horn
car	bird	worm
hard	firm	burn
farm	torn	turn
guard	born	

6. The letter *y* at the end of words containing no other vowel has the letter sound of long "i."

        my, try, sky, shy

The letter *y* at the end of words containing two syllables or more has the letter sound of long "e."

        country, happy, sorry, merrily

FIGURE 5-3

the root of a word to change the meaning of the root; the meaning of the root is not altered, but rather modified. For example, if you add *re-* to *trace,* you get *retrace,* or "to trace again"; if you add *im-* to *possible,* you get *impossible,* or "not possible." In addition, many suffixes indicate the function the word plays in a sentence or its "part of speech." For example, *govern* is a verb and denotes an action, but *government* is a noun and is "the means or instrument of governing." Words ending in *-ment* are usually nouns, those ending in *-ly* are adverbs, and those ending in *-able* are adjectives.

Starting in second grade with the teaching of contractions and inflectional endings, students should start becoming familiar with many of the structural analysis generalizations listed below. By the time the student is in fourth grade and reading textbooks, it is essential that the teacher spend considerable time emphasizing structural analysis of words to support the student's comprehension of content-area vocabulary words that are based heavily on prefixes, suffixes, and roots.

1. Inflectional endings are added to nouns to change number, case, or sex; added to verbs to change tense or person; and added to adjectives to change degree. The words that result are called *variants*.

   a. Regular plurals:
      ◆ Add *s* to nouns

      boy – *boys*; book – *books*

      ◆ With *ch*, *sh*, *x*, *s*, add *es*

      church – *churches*; dish – *dishes*; glass – *glasses*; box – *boxes*

      ◆ Change *f* to *v*

      half – *halves*; knife – *knives*

      ◆ Change *y* to *ies*

      cry – *cries*; baby – *babies*

      ◆ Irregular plurals:

      sheep, feet, children, men

   b. Possessive forms:

      man – *man's*; children – *children's*

   c. When a word is CVC, you double the final consonant when adding *ed* or *ing*

      bat – *batting*; hit – *hitting*; hop – *hopping*

   d. When a word is CVCe, you drop the final *e* and add *ed* or *ing*.

      hope – *hoping*; tape – *taping*; write – *writing*

   e. Comparative forms:

      fast, faster, fastest

      long, longer, longest

2. Notice the structure of compound words and recognize the smaller words within the larger word.

   cowboy, firehouse, sometime, nowhere

3. Prefixes and suffixes are sequences of letters that are added to root words to change their meanings or parts of speech, or both. Following is a brief list of common prefixes and suffixes:

Common Prefixes

un-	not
in-	not
bi-	two
dis-	not
multi-	many
non-	not
pre-	before
pro-	before
post-	after, behind
re-	back
semi-	half
sub-	under

Common Suffixes

-ful	full of
-less	lacking
-ment	result of
-ship	state of being
-ous	full of
-ward	in the direction of
-tion	act of
-sion	act of
-able	capable of being
-ness	condition

4. In contractions, the apostrophe indicates that one or more letters have been left out when two words were combined into one word. Children need to be able to recognize the original words from which the contractions were formed. Following is a list of common contractions:

can't – cannot	I'll – I will
couldn't – could not	I'm – I am
don't – do not	I've – I have
hadn't – had not	won't – will not
hasn't – has not	wouldn't – would not
he'll – he will	you'll – you will
he's – he is	isn't – is not
I'd – I would	let's – let us
they'd – they would	she'd – she would or she had
they'll – they will	we've – we have
they're – they are	they've – they have

Syllabication

A syllable is a word part that includes a vowel sound. When we pronounce a word, some syllables are stressed and some are unstressed. Awareness of syllables is an important part of reading, writing, and spelling. It helps children see that words are made up of smaller parts, and that these smaller parts can be pronounced while reading or sounded out while spelling (Pinnell & Fountas, 1998). **Syllabication** helps children identify larger words they may be afraid to try to pronounce without knowing how to break the word up into its smaller units. It also allows children to become familiar with repetitive patterns in the English language that comprise syllables, for example, prefixes and suffixes such as *sion*, *able*, and *pre*.

Syllabication is also important in spelling because it allows students to break down words into manageable components so they can spell the recognizable pattern. Often, those students who read well but have few phonic skills are whole-word readers, and although they are able to read well, their lack of phonic analysis is evident in their spelling ability.

The generalizations listed below should be taught from kindergarten on and emphasized in third and fourth grade as students move toward fluency in reading and writing.

1. Words contain as many syllables as they have vowel sounds.

   Examples: *enclose* (has two sounded vowels because the final *e* is silent, and thus has two syllables), *break* (has one sounded vowel sound, and thus one syllable), *defeat* (has two sounded vowels and has two syllables).

2. A multisyllable word usually is divided between the two consonants that are single and identical (VC/CV).

   hap/pen   nar/row   lad/der   but/ter

3. A multisyllable word usually is divided between two consonants that are single and not identical (VC/CV).

   Pen/cil   har/poon   cac/tus   tim/ber

4. When a consonant is in the middle of two vowels, the consonant usually goes with the next syllable, and the preceding vowel is long (V/CV). A vowel at the end of a syllable is known as an open syllable and is usually long.

   Fa/tal   to/tal   pa/per   de/lay   o/ver   po/lite

5. When a consonant is in the middle of two vowels, sometimes the consonant goes with the first syllable and the first vowel is short (VC/V). A vowel in the middle of a syllable is known as a closed syllable and is usually short.

   shiv/er   tax/i   ped/al   trav/el   rock/er   mim/ic

   Note: With the VCV syllable pattern, it is important that children learn to play with the syllables when unlocking the pronunciation of a word, and try out the long and short vowel sound to see which sounds correct. For example, the word would not be fat/al or tot/al or shi/ver or pe/dal. It is important that children learn to be flexible in sounding out syllables and use strategies that allow them to unlock the pronunciation of the word.

6. Divide a word between the compound words. Find the smaller words in the compound word.

   Any/one   some/where   cow/boy   tooth/brush

7. Always divide a word between its root and its prefix and suffix.

   Go/ing   pre/fer   in/ac/tive   ex/pect   trans/por/ta/tion

8. The suffix -ed sometimes forms a separate syllable.
   ◆ When the word ends in t or d, you add a syllable.

   want/ed   paint/ed   need/ed   land/ed

   ◆ When a word does not end in t or d, it is not a separate syllable.

   played   helped   wished   jumped

9. When a word ends in le, the consonant immediately preceding the le usually begins the last syllable (V/Cle).

   pur/ple   an/kle   ta/ble   jun/gle   sim/ple

10. Consonant blends and digraphs are always considered one consonant and are not divided.

    chil/dren   an/chor   en/close   pump/kin   ath/lete

Students should start learning about syllables as soon as they are learning how to read, beginning even in kindergarten. Children can clap out the number of syllables in their names and learn that words are made up of separate yet combined speech sounds. As children learn how to read, syllabication becomes an important part of sounding out words and allows children to break down long, perhaps intimidating words into accessible parts.

Teaching Word Study in the Classroom

Perhaps one of the most important things that teachers should remember when considering how to teach word study is that effective instruction depends on applying principles of learning theory that relate to all effective instruction. Children must be engaged in the learning process, children must clearly understand what they are learning and why they are learning it, and instruction must address the multiple needs of the students and be multifaceted (Cunningham & Cunningham, 2002). When children are engaged in literacy activities, you see an active and involved classroom that is often noisy and hums with excitement. You see eager faces and motivated children, and you feel that the classroom is an exciting place to be. This means that children are reading quality literature they are excited about, the teacher is involved in mentoring and facilitating literacy development, and the class is involved in interesting hands-on projects and activities.

Students should also clearly understand what they are learning and be clear as to why the task is an important one. This is called *cognitive clarity* (Cunningham & Cunningham, 2002), and it is an important component of literacy development.

Too often, phonics is taught as an isolated skill and children do not see the importance or reason for mastering the skill. Teachers often take for granted that children understand what the end product will be and assume that they should just follow directions, without having a full understanding of what it is that they are working toward. Children need to see why phonics and word study are important and understand what the end result will be.

Lastly, instruction should be based on each child's needs and be multifaceted. Each child has his or her own learning style and preferred way of doing things. Howard Gardner introduced seven multiple intelligences in 1993 (Gardner, 1993), whereby he pointed out that there are many different intelligences that people can have, and that teachers need to be sure that all different intelligences are accommodated in the classroom. His original seven intelligences were: linguistic intelligence, logical-mathematical intelligence, musical intelligence, bodily-kinesthetic intelligence, spatial intelligence, interpersonal intelligence, and intrapersonal intelligence. Gardner added naturalistic type of intelligence in 1997 (Gardner, 1999). Teachers need to be aware of each student's learning style and design instruction that meets all children's needs.

Many approaches to teaching phonics exist from which a teacher can choose. This section reviews the following approaches: synthetic approach, analytic approach, onset-rime approach, decoding by analogy, and whole-to-part approach. Many of these approaches can be combined into an effective balanced literacy classroom. What is important to remember is that the NRP reviewed the experimental findings on teaching reading and determined that *systematic and explicit phonic instruction is more effective than nonsystematic phonic approaches* and is particularly more effective than reading programs that do not teach phonics at all (NICHD, 2000).

Synthetic and Analytic Approaches to Phonic Instruction

Phonics is a term that is frequently misinterpreted to mean that there is only one strategy or approach to word identification; but, in fact, there are two major approaches: synthetic and analytic. In the **synthetic approach,** the teacher instructs children in memorizing individual speech sounds that are associated with each letter, whereby each individual phoneme is sounded out in isolation, and then blended back together to form a word. The teacher usually holds up a card or points to an individual letter on the wall and instructs the class to pronounce in unison the individual sound that is associated with that letter. The goal is to have the children rapidly pronounce each sound so it becomes automatic, and then to gradually introduce blending of the sounds into a word. Blending is the key factor in the success of this approach; however, often it is not emphasized enough during instruction. Many commercial programs use this approach. This approach works well with certain phonetically regular words that fit clear phonic patterns, such as *smile, frog,* and *bat.*

Following is an example of synthetic phonic instruction:

Say to the children, "Look at this word: *bat.*"

Say to the children, "*b, b.* This is *b,*" while pointing to the *b.*

Say to the children, "Everyone say *b.* Again, *b, b, b.*"

This sequence would continue with the letter *a* and then the letter *t.*

Later sound blending would be introduced where children are taught to slide slowly from one sound to another while the teacher uses an arrow or pointer from left to right under the letters as a directional clue. For example:

Say to the children, "Let's follow the arrow and say the sounds. Listen to me first: *b-a-tt, b-a-tt, b-a-tt.*" Each time the teacher would go faster until the word *bat* is pronounced.

Next, the children would follow along and say the same thing going faster each time and always following the arrow or pointer. Say to the children, "*Bat. Bat. Bat.* I'm very happy you did such a great job!"

Some researchers (Cunningham, 2000; Moustafa, 1998) recommend using the **analytic approach,** in which sounds are taught as part of words that the child has learned previously. Sounds are not taught in isolation and drilled as individual units, but are taught within the context of words that are known and part of a child's sight vocabulary. A good example of the analytic approach is an activity that Cunningham (2000) calls "Using Words You Know." In this activity children are given four words that they know, such as *bike, car, van,* and *train.* The spelling pattern of each word is introduced and underlined in each word: *ike, ar, an,* and *ain.* The teacher then asks the class for rhyming words for each word, emphasizing that the rhyme usually has the same spelling pattern. The teacher will then give the students a list of 10 new words that fit the spelling patterns of the 4 words the students know, such as *hike, jar, pan,* and *pain.* The teacher then asks the children to write each new word under the word they know that has the same spelling pattern. Different students will go to the board or easel and write the words under the correct column as everyone is writing them on their papers. After all words are written on the board in the correct column, the children will pronounce the words aloud, with the teacher emphasizing how they rhyme and how the spelling patterns are the same. This activity is an excellent example of how analytic phonics works in a classroom. Children work with familiar words to identify word patterns and sounds in unfamiliar words.

It is possible that a synthetic approach of blending individual phonemes and an analytic approach of using word patterns are used in combination to decode words, such as *special* (spe-cial) or *nation* (na-tion). According to Moustafa and Maldonado-Colon (1998), children who are ELLs, especially those whose native language is Spanish, may benefit more by listening to the text of a nursery rhyme or a poem and by learning to recite the text before actually learning to decode it. These types of learners benefit from using an analytic approach of identifying word patterns within words. Using phonemes to break down words is more difficult for some ELLs, particularly if their native vocabulary is formed more naturally by word patterns and phonogram clusters than by individual phonemes.

The NRP (2000) investigated whether some types of phonic instruction are more effective than others. In examining both synthetic and analytic phonic programs, they found that specific systematic phonic programs are all significantly more effective than nonphonic programs and these programs do not appear to differ significantly from each other in their effectiveness in the classroom, although more research needs to be done to verify these findings.

Onset-Rime Phonic Approach

One approach to teaching analytic phonics that is highly recommended by many educators (Cunningham, 2000; Fountas & Pinnell, 1996; Moustafa, 1998) is the **onset-rime approach.** With this approach, words of one syllable may be broken into an opening part—usually consisting of a consonant, consonant blend, or consonant digraph—and an ending part. The opening part (the consonant) is called the *onset,* and the ending part that contains the vowel(s) is called the *rime* (Pinnell & Fountas, 1998). For example, in the word *bat, b* is the onset and *at* is the rime. The rime (the ending part of the word) is also called a word family or phonogram. **Word families or phonograms** share the same significant spelling and sound patterns; for example, *bill, fill, pill, will,* and *hill* are all part of the *ill* word family or phonogram (see Figure 5–4 for a list of frequently used phonograms and rimes).

Wylie and Durrell's (1970) widely used list, "37 High-Frequency Spelling/Word Patterns," can be used to help children read and spell more than 500 words derived from these 37 patterns.

Onset and Rimes

A phonogram, or rime, is a cluster of letters, a word part, or a spelling pattern. A rime is usually a vowel sound plus a consonant sound in a single syllable. The rime units listed below appear in three or more fairly common single-syllable words.

Rime	Words	Rime	Words	Rime	Words	Rime	Words	Rime	Words
-ake	cake, make, take	-ate	plate, ate, late	-at	cat, that, sat	-eat	seat, eat, treat	-eal	seal, meal, deal
-ab	cab, tab, crab	-all	ball, all, fall	-aw	saw, draw, straw	-ean	bean, mean, clean	-ell	bell, well, tell
-ack	tack, back, sack	-ale	whale, tale, sale	-ay	hay, may, stay, play	-ear	ear, near, tear	-en	ten, then, when
-ad	had, bad, mad	-am	ham, am, jam		day, say, way	-ed	bed, red, sled	-end	send, bend, lend
-ade	made, shade, trade	-ame	name, came, same	-alk	chalk, walk, talk	-ee	bee, see, tree	-ent	tent, went, sent
-ag	bag, wag, tag	-an	can, an, ran, man	-ast	fast, last, past	-eed	seed, weed, speed	-et	net, get, let, pet
-age	page, stage, cage	-and	hand, and, grand	-ar	car, jar, far	-eel	wheel, feel, peel	-ew	new, blew, crew
-ail	tail, pail, fail	-ank	bank, thank, drank	-e	me, he, she, be, we	-een	green, seen, queen	-est	best, rest, test
-ain	train, rain, pain	-ait	wait, bait			-eep	jeep, keep, sleep	-eet	feet, beet, street
-id	lid, did, kid	-ip	ship, trip, slip	-od	rod, God, nod	-ool	school, stool, fool	-ut	nut, but, cut
-ide	ride, side, wide	-ice	mice, nice, rice	-ock	clock, lock, shock	-oy	boy, toy, joy	-us	bus, us, Gus
-ie	pie, lie, tie	-ish	fish, wish, dish	-og	dog, fog, log	-oom	broom, room, zoom	-up	cup, up, pup
-ig	pig, big, wig	-it	sit, it, bit	-oil	boil, soil, spoil	-oon	moon, soon, spoon	-ust	just, must, crust
-ight	night, might, right, bright	-ite	kite, white, bite, write	-oke	smoke, broke, joke, choke	-op	mop, hop, stop, shop	-ue	blue, glue, true, Sue
-ike	bike, like, Mike	-ive	hive, five, drive	-old	gold, old, told	-ope	rope, slope, hope	-un	sun, run, fun
-ill	hill, will, still	-ive	give, live	-ole	mole, hole, pole	-ound	round, found, ground	-y	very, funny, daddy
-im	him, Jim, rim	-ind	find, kind, blind	-one	bone, phone, stone	-out	out, shout, scout	-y	my, why, fly
-ime	time, slime, crime	-ile	smile, while, pile	-ow	cow, now, how	-ub	sub, rub, tub		
-in	pin, in, win	-o	no, go, so	-own	clown, down, brown	-uck	duck, truck, luck		
-ine	nine, fine, mine	-oad	toad, road, load	-ong	song, long, wrong	-ug	rug, bug, mug		
-ing	ring, thing, king	-oat	boat, goat, coat	-ook	book, look, took	-um	gum, sum, drum		
-ink	pink, think, stink	-ob	Bob, rob, job	-ot	pot, not, got, lot				

(From Allen, L. P. (November 1998). An integrated strategies approach: Make Word Identification instruction work for beginning readers. *The Reading Teacher, 52*(3), 254–268. Used with permission of the International Reading Association.)

FIGURE 5-4

37 High-Frequency Spelling Patterns

ack (back)	ail (mail)	ain (pain)	ake (fake)	ale (sale)
ame (name)	an (fan)	ank (tank)	ap (lap)	ash (rash)
at (sat)	ate (late)	aw (paw)	ay (lay)	eat (treat)
ell (fell)	est (rest)	ice (nice)	ide (side)	ick (lick)
ight (fight)	ill (fill)	in (pin)	ine (line)	ing (bring)
ink (sink)	ip (rip)	it (fit)	ock (lock)	oke (poke)
op (top)	ore (more)	ot (not)	uck (luck)	ug (rug)
ump (lump)	unk (junk)			

About five of these spelling/word patterns should be displayed in the classroom and introduced to children each week to help them read, write, and spell the common rhyming patterns shown above.

Learning these 37 patterns helps children spell and decode more than 500 of the most commonly used words found in beginning children's literature suitable for first grade reading. Furthermore, if a spelling pattern such as *ack* is used to make up multisyllabic and compound word forms such as *backpacking* or *knapsacks*, older or advanced young readers can derive more than 50 words from just this one phonogram, learning more than 1,000 multisyllabic words from these same 37 phonograms.

Teachers' VOICES   Teaching Tip on Decoding

In the younger grades, I teach word families to assist in the students' knowledge of decoding. One of my favorite activities is making word wheels. The only materials you really need are paper, fasteners, and crayons. Many teacher resource books have already made word wheels that require only making copies, cutting, and fastening. I enjoy using word wheels with my class to help students practice decoding. In the beginning of the year, the word wheels are already set up for the students with multiple onsets and a rime. In the early stages, I like the students to become comfortable with the mechanics of the word wheel. They need to understand the different parts of the word wheel: the onset, the rime, and the picture. They also need to be comfortable looking in the window to help them sound out the word or as

a reassurance that they read the word correctly. As the students become familiar with the idea and concept of the word wheels, I begin to modify the wheels. In the beginning, I delete some of the onsets and keep the pictures. The students use the picture to identify the word they are making, and then record the letter sounds. I also like to remove the pictures and allow the students to illustrate the wheel appropriately. This modification is great for my student artists! One of the last modifications that I make is to remove the rime on the wheel. The students then have to identify the word family of the words they are making. This modification is last because it tends to be the most difficult for the students.

—*Susan Myshkoff, Special Education Teacher*

It is also recommended that vowel sounds are taught as part of "word families" or rimes, and that these word families be used in many different activities and games that are fun for the children. Children can see consistent patterns within the word family and generalize to other words with similar vowel sounds and pronunciations. Using word families will help children remember the different sounds vowels make within certain patterns.

The major point about word walls is that they become an integral part of the literacy classroom and are used each day to teach and reinforce word study. Teachers should incorporate word walls into their daily activities by having children write these words in their journals, use these words in their writing, and include these words in class readings.

In conjunction with word walls, many teachers also use *word banks;* that is, sets of words written on note cards that are stored in the students' desk or cubby and specifically chosen based on the individual's need. One child might be having difficulty with a word from his or her reading, and this can be written down quickly and put into the word bank for future reinforcement and study. This bank can be used as the source of writing assignments, spelling lists, sorting activities, homework assignments, and other activities. Teachers can choose a few words to send home with the child so that parents can work with the child. As these words become part of a child's sight vocabulary, they can be removed into an inactive word bank and brought out periodically for review. It is not recommended that more than 20 words be in an active word bank at once.

Instructional Activities to Teach Word Study

Many word identification activities exist that a teacher can use in the classroom to reinforce word identification strategies. Arts and crafts activities using phonic, structural, or syllabic generalizations are always helpful. Young children can color various objects that represent different sounds or letters of the alphabet, or cut-and-paste a dictionary of pictures. Older children can create game boards, compose charts based on prefixes and suffixes, and create illustrated stories using multisyllabic words and/or words with prefixes and suffixes. Sorting activities is an excellent reinforcement for children of all ages. They can take words and sort them into categories based on their word family, their prefixes or suffixes, their syllabic pattern, or any number of phonic generalizations. Tape recording children reading aloud is an important and helpful activity to increase fluency. Children enjoy listening to themselves on tape, and through repeated readings, children learn how to apply word identification strategies in a consistent manner to familiar words.

Writing – Writing should be a primary way that children learn word identification strategies. Writing is an important reinforcement of word study and helps children apply the generalizations they are learning about in their own spelling. With young children, this might translate into invented spelling, where they are learning to associate the grapheme with the phoneme. Older children can compose stories using word families or words from a word bank. Children of all ages can also compose poetry and learn about word families through the rhyme and rhythm of poetic structure. Shared writing, where the teacher and the class compose a story together on an easel or board, is a wonderful way for teachers to emphasize word identification strategies. Teachers can make purposeful errors during shared writing, and then ask the class to identify the error and correct it, using the correct generalization as a rationale for the word correction. After the story is composed, the teacher can also point out specific generalizations, such as which word has the VCCV syllabic pattern (*butter, happen,* and so on), and then ask the students to identify other words in the story that have the same structure. Small mini-lessons in word pattern generalizations can result from shared writing experiences that help reinforce lessons learned during reading. Reading and writing are reciprocal processes that complement each other; therefore, any lesson learned during reading and spelling needs to be reinforced through the writing process.

Literature – Literature is a wonderful way to teach word identification strategies. As children read stories that are rich in syntactic structure and semantic meaning, they learn that reading is an enjoyable activity that requires the use of word identification strategies. Word identification should not be taught in isolation, but through the context of reading text. Words should be taken from books that children read and used as their word banks and word walls. In addition, there are many books that emphasize a specific phonic rule or vowel sound. There are a number of books that reinforce the long and short vowel sounds: the short *a* sound in *The Cat in the Hat* (Seuss, 1957), the long and short *a* sound in *Caps for Sale* (Slobodkina, 1940), the short *e* sound in *First the Egg* (Seeger, 2006) and *Zen Shorts* (Muth, 2005), the long *e* sound in *Ten Sleepy Sheep* (Keller, 1983), the short *i* sound in *Whistle for Willie* (Keats, 1964), the long *i* sound in *Let It Shine* (Bryan, 2007), the short *o* sound in *Fox in Socks* (Seuss, 1965) and *Olivia* (Falconer, 2000), the long *o* sound in *The Giant's Toe* (Cole, 1986), the short *u* sound in *Thump and Plunk* (Udry, 1981), and the long *u* sound in *Music, Music Everyone* (Williams, 1988). Many other books are available to teachers that purposefully or inadvertently reinforce a phonic rule and are excellent resources to teach word identification within the context of good literature.

Cloze Activity – The **cloze activity** is one of the most widely researched in literacy and it is used to develop comprehension, vocabulary development, and high-frequency sight word usage. The cloze technique can also be used as an assessment tool to evaluate a student's literacy abilities in each of these three areas. The cloze technique can be used to develop vocabulary and comprehension effectively by:

◆ Selecting a passage, and with a black marker, crossing out every ___th word (excluding proper names, dates, and numbers)
◆ Directing the student to choose a word that best fits the meaning of the missing word and counting only exact words (not synonyms) in scoring the activity

A score of 67 percent or better is considered satisfactory, and a score less than 67 percent is considered unsatisfactory. This activity is most effective when using material that is at or slightly above the student's independent level; once the student appears not to be challenged any longer when using the cloze strategy, the teacher should increase the reading difficulty slightly to match the student's instructional level. It is necessary to monitor that the student does not score below satisfactory (below 67 percent) or at the level of frustration. Figure 5–5 provides directions for building a cloze exercise.

Games – Games are a wonderful way to reinforce word identification strategies and engage children in fun activities that encourage word study. Many software programs have reading and word identification games included in them. However, there are many different simple games that a teacher or the class can make and use in a learning center. The games described in the following sections can be played either as a whole class, in small groups, or individually.

Baseball. In baseball, two teams are chosen. The teacher "pitches" (flashes) a word card. If the first batter knows it, she scores a hit and moves to first base. If the next batter knows the next word shown, she moves to first base and the child already on first moves to second base, and so on. If a batter does not give a correct answer, it is an "out." The teams change after three outs. The team with the most "runs" wins. (You may want to mark the bases with beanbags.) Use words from word families or word walls.

Old Maid. For old maid, a card deck with about 20 cards with the same word on two cards is needed, so that the deck is made up of 10 pairs of words. The words should be those that emphasize a word family, phonic rule, or sight word that the teacher is trying to reinforce. In addition, there needs to be one card for the old maid. All of the cards are dealt to the players. Beginning with the player at the dealer's left, turns should be taken drawing cards, each player drawing from the player at his right. As the pairs of cards are formed, the words are pronounced and the pairs are placed on the table. This process is continued until all the cards are matched and one person is left with the old maid card. This player has lost the game and is called the old maid.

Dominoes. Dominoes is similar to the regular domino game except that words are used instead of dots on the dominoes. This is an excellent game to reinforce blends, digraphs, or word families. Examples of words that could be used to emphasize digraphs are:

| that | then | there |
| what | when | where |

Directions for Building a Cloze Exercise

1. Select a passage of suitable length, format, and readability. Make sure that there are enough cues to make closure possible.

2. Decide on the instructional purpose: vocabulary development, use of syntax, precise use of synonyms, etc.

3. Determine a deletion pattern that fits your objective:

   Example:

   a. Delete only nouns, verbs, adjectives that are spaced between six and twelve words apart.

   b. Delete only prepositions and conjunctions.

   c. Delete only every _____th word.

   d. Delete only words that have several synonyms with slight shadings of differences.

   (Deletions in entry-level activities should occur at intervals no closer than every tenth to twelfth word. In more difficult exercises, the space between deletions may be reduced to as narrow a span as every fifth or sixth word.)

4. Keep first and last sentences intact as major cues.

5. Determine the pattern of response to be made:

   • Free choice by student

   • Choice from two or more options that are all grammatically plausible

   • Choice from two or more options that are all semantically plausible

6. Avoid deletion of number words, color words, keywords, or proper names unless passage gives explicit cues that control appropriate choices.

7. Identify the instructional purpose clearly for students and include precise directions for completion.

FIGURE 5-5

You can write the words you wish to use in the game on the ends of rectangular 1" × 2" cards. Each word should appear six times, as a double (same word on each end) and in a combination with each of the other words. Each player takes seven dominoes and the remaining dominoes are placed face down in the remaining pile. The first player must play a double domino; the second player must play a domino with the same word on one end. He or she must name the word in the exposed end. The third player tries to match the exposed ends and, in turn, names the word the next player must match. If a player cannot play on either end, he must draw from the bone pile until he draws a domino that he can play. The first player to play all of his dominoes wins the game. Variation: The player must match just the initial digraph or word family (for example, *that* and *there*, or *bike* and *mike*), instead of the exact same word.

Initial Consonant Bingo. To play initial consonant bingo, have the children make up game cards from magazine pictures or workbooks, using pictures of words that are from a word wall or word family. Paste or draw a picture in each square. Be sure that the name of the picture begins with a single consonant. Do not mix blends and consonants. Also make up a set of key cards using words to be called out during the game. These words should begin with the same initial consonant as the keywords on the card but be different words. Use the same 24 pictures that are used on each card but placed in a different order in the squares. Play the game by having the teacher call out the word for the players. Players cover the picture on the cards that has the same beginning sound as the key picture. Cover only one picture at a time even though there may be more than one with the same sound on the card. The first child to completely cover the row or column is the next caller. Variation: (1) Use pictures to represent keywords from a word family (such as *car* for *ar*) and have children cover words that belong to the same word family; or (2) use words on the cards and when the same word is called out, children cover that word.

Word Race. For word race, prepare a game board using a basic game board design (a series of spaces on a board that the player can move to with a marker). Print words to reinforce (either sight words or words that reinforce a word family or phonic rule) in each space. If desired, the board can be laminated or covered with adhesive plastic, and the words can be written in with ink that can be erased. Use dice or one die and cut out squares of cardboard for markers. Each player rolls the die and moves the number of spaces indicated. The player will pronounce each word on the space that the marker lands on. If a player is unable to call the word out, he or she must move back one space. The first to reach the end wins.

Name Puzzles or Word Puzzles. Name or word puzzles (Pinnell & Fountas, 1998) are especially helpful to those children who have low letter knowledge. The child's name is written on a strip of paper and then cut up, letter by letter. The letters should be large enough to see clearly and manipulate (about two inches tall). The letter pieces are placed in an envelope. The child's name is written clearly in black letters across the top of this envelope in about the same size as the puzzle pieces. The envelope is then used as a model by which the child can configure the name or word. Used every day in a kindergarten class, children quickly learn the letters in their names.

Teachers' VOICES   Spelling Approaches

PYRAMID SPELLING

One of the best strategies I have used with my students is having them break down each spelling word using a spelling pyramid. This enables a student to visually break down each word to recognize how the letters in a given word can be broken down and put back together. The child begins with one word such as *giraffe*. At the top of the pyramid goes the letter *g*, on the line below that *gi*, then *gir*, continuing with *gira*, *giraf*, *giraff*, and finally, on the last line *giraffe*. To complete the pyramid, the word must be spelled correctly and each letter accounted for. This strategy/technique has really worked for my students with difficult vocabulary/spelling words.

EXAMPLE:

```
              g
            g  i
          g  i  r
        g  i  r  a
      g  i  r  a  f
    g  i  r  a  f  f
  g  i  r  a  f  f  e
```

TRACEABLE LETTERS

Another strategy I use to teach my students spelling or vocabulary words is called "traceable letters." Tracing letters allows students to visualize a word by what size and shape the letters take in its formation. After the student copies down one of the spelling words, he or she must carefully trace around the letters, focusing on the height of each letter. My students like this activity, especially with those words that prove to be the most challenging each week.

EXAMPLE:

FLIP BOOKS/LETTER CARDS

For my students to learn common spelling patterns, we created several flip books that contain numerous rimes, clusters, and word families. Vowel combinations and multisyllabic words, which prove difficult for many students, improve by using the book. Phonograms such as *-aint, -aise, -ealth, -eat, -ield, -oad, -our*, and *-ouse* have been used to recognize and solve difficult word patterns. Letter cards are used for similar purposes, with one exception. All the consonant letters are printed in one color (blue) and the vowels are printed in another color (yellow). By distinguishing between consonant letters and the vowels in a given word, the students are able to see certain letter combinations and recognize patterns of previously spelled words.

PHONICS/SPELLING CENTER

I have many learning centers in my classroom that are used to enhance and enrich our third grade curriculum.

Items such as pyramid spelling, letter cards, flip books, and various games can be found in this center. This is a place where "buddies" get together to make and check new vocabulary while reviewing previously spelled words. Children can work in pairs or groups to complete some of the activities collaboratively while practicing the skills they have acquired.

—*Heather DiSerio, Third Grade Teacher*

Word Study and Students with Diverse Needs

Working with Students with Learning Disabilities

For many children with learning disabilities, the typical reading lesson in the regular classroom may not provide enough support for them to adequately learn how to read (Simmons, Fuchs, & Fuchs, 1991). Words are not repeated frequently enough, there is not enough explicit instruction in phonics, and many of the high-frequency words cause problems because they do not follow any regular pattern. As a result, many students with learning disabilities may have a difficult time in the classroom in the beginning reading stage.

Students with learning disabilities who have trouble reading may be diagnosed as having *dyslexia* (Figure 5–6). Dyslexia affects at least 80 percent of the learning disability populations and thereby constitutes the most prevalent type of learning disability. Students with dyslexia most often have phonologically based reading disabilities or difficulty in recognizing that words can be broken into phonemes and that letters have sounds. These students have difficulty in decoding words and in reading fluently. Dyslexia is neurobiological in origin; that is, there is disruption of neural systems in the left hemisphere of the brain.

Usually, synthetic phonic instruction is recommended for children with learning disabilities because it explicitly teaches the letter–sound correspondence and sound-blending skills necessary to "unlock" the code. Students with learning disabilities need repetition and explicit teaching of phonics; they also need training in phonemic awareness at an early age and an emphasis on learning the alphabetic principle.

Multisensory strategies are commonly used to teach reading to students with learning disabilities. A multisensory strategy is one that combines the use of two or more sensory areas simultaneously. This technique involves visual, auditory, tactile-kinesthetic, and/or articulatory-motor components in the carefully sequenced teaching of language structure. For example, students learn alphabet letters by feeling, naming, and matching three-dimensional forms or tracing on rough surfaces. Students learn the identity of phonemes by feeling and seeing the position of the mouth, lips, and tongue (Moats & Farrell, 2005). The more senses students use, the more likely they will learn and remember the task and skill. A multisensory, synthetic phonic program that is often used to teach children with disabilities is the Orton–Gillingham approach. This approach emphasizes the necessity for explicit language teaching to be systematic, cumulative, direct, and sequential (Moats & Farrell, 2005). The Orton–Gillingham approach has become quite popular and is being used by teachers in the regular classroom for instruction in explicit phonics.

Definition Of Dyslexia

Dyslexia is a specific learning disability that is neurobiological in origin. It is characterized by difficulties with accurate and/or fluent word recognition and by poor spelling and decoding abilities. These difficulties typically result from a deficit in the phonological component of language that is often unexpected in relation to other cognitive abilities and the provision of effective classroom instruction. Secondary consequences may include problems in reading comprehension and reduced reading experience that can impede growth of vocabulary and background knowledge.

The key elements of this definition are:

1. *Dyslexia is a specific learning disability*—This identifies dyslexia as a specific learning problem in contrast to the more general term *learning disabilities*. Dyslexia affects at least 80% of the learning disability populations and thereby constitutes the most prevalent type of learning disability.

2. *It is neurobiological in origin*—This phrase recognizes the neural basis for dyslexia with recent research in functional imaging of the brain during performance of a cognitive task. Investigations from scientists around the world have shown that there is disruption of neural systems in the left hemisphere of the brain when dyslexic students are reading.

3. *It is characterized by difficulties with accurate and/or fluent word recognition and by poor spelling and decoding abilities*—This phrase recognizes one of the most important attributes of a dyslexic reader: the inability to read fluently. Dyslexic readers can improve in reading words more accurately as they mature, but continue to lack fluency in the reading.

4. *... the provision of effective classroom instruction*—It is important to consider a struggling reader's instructional history and schooling. Many children who are at risk for reading failure come from disadvantaged backgrounds where quality early childhood education and preschool experiences were not provided. These children's reading failures predominantly lie with a disadvantaged background. In contrast, many children who exhibit reading problems come from effective instructional programs and were provided with adequate preschool experiences. It is therefore important to consider the role of the reader's instructional history when defining dyslexia.

5. *Secondary consequences may include problems in reading comprehension...*—Phonological difficulties lead to problems in accuracy and fluency, which in turn lead to problems in vocabulary development and background knowledge. These factors impact comprehension and reading for understanding.

(Adapted from Lyon, G. R., Shaywitz, S. E., & Shaywitz, B. A. (2003). Defining dyslexia, comorbidity, teachers' knowledge of language and reading. *Annals of Dyslexia,73*, 1–14.)

FIGURE 5-6

Developing Word Recognition for English Language Learners

Currently, our assumptions about effective reading instruction for ELLs are based on what is known about interventions with native English speakers (Vaughn, Mathes, Linan-Thompson, & Francis, 2005). In general, research supports that there are many persisting advantages for young ELLs who are given early structured phonics teaching (Quiroga, Lemos-Britton, Mostafapour, Abbott, & Berninger, 2002; Stuart, 2004; Vaughn et al., 2005). Early structured phonics teaching, which includes phonemic awareness (segmentation and blending training), as well as learning of grapheme–phoneme correspondences, can have long-lasting effects on ELLs' literacy skills.

STRATEGIES FOR TEACHING DIVERSE LEARNERS

Tips for Working with Students with Learning Disabilities: Word Study

1. Work on the alphabetic principle. Be sure the students know every letter in the alphabet and can identify every consonant sound and long vowel sound. Often, students with learning disabilities have trouble remembering the sounds to all the letters.

2. Be sure to provide much repetition and practice on identifying words for students with learning disabilities.

3. Use as many multisensory techniques as possible. Have students trace letters with their fingers; write

letters in sand; and pronounce, hear, and read the words as many times as possible.

4. Use visual configuration to help children visually discriminate between words that have a similar orthographic configuration but different visual configuration (for example, *pan* and *ban*).

5. Provide the students with word banks of high-frequency words. Start off with only a small number of words in their banks and have students read them to the teacher at least once a day. Have students sort these words by category or beginning sound, draw pictures of them, and use them in oral sentences.

6. Be sure to teach explicit and direct phonics to de-code words. Point out phonetic patterns in words and have students start to recognize words that follow the same patterns.

7. Use prompts and provide clues to scaffold the reader's attempt to decode the word. If a reader is having trouble decoding a word, point out a picture which may help, or provide the beginning consonant (onset) or ending (rime) to scaffold the reader's effort.

8. Help the student find clues that will help identify the unknown word. These could be pointing out the picture, showing a word family on a word wall, or using the context of the sentence.

9. Be patient and provide repetition and practice. Maintain words already mastered.

Quiroga et al. (2002) have found that phonological awareness training with explicit instruction in the alphabetic principle (in English) and repeated reading of engaging English text with comprehension monitoring (in English) increased the literacy development of Spanish-speaking ELLs in first grade.

Many of the same strategies recommended for native English speakers are also recommended for ELLs. These include a structured, systematic approach to teaching explicit phonics, as well as reading engaging and quality literature. Multicultural texts are recommended because children need to relate to what they read so they have a context within which to recognize unknown words. In addition, word walls are beneficial to reinforce word recognition, and children can develop word banks of new words they are learning. For ELLs, the word could be written in English on one side of an index card and in the child's native language on the other side. Reading and rereading of text is highly recommended to help children become fluent and recognize new words. Children could be paired with native English speakers and do shared reading together, hearing fluent models of the text being read. Books on tape are beneficial as well as many software programs, which provide text-to-speech capability and can read the text aloud as the child is reading along. Vaughn et al. (2005) recommend teaching ELLs to be "flexible decoders." In their research, children were taught that "sometimes parts of words did not sound out quite right," but that sounding out a word usually produced a pronunciation that was close enough to figure out what the word really was. Children were taught that they should sound out any word they did not know automatically, but if the resulting word was not a "real word," they had to be flexible.

STRATEGIES FOR TEACHING DIVERSE LEARNERS

Ideas to Develop Word Recognition for English Language Learners

1. Have English language learners (ELLs) work with text material that they can relate to and have some background knowledge in so that they can use this knowledge to help them recognize unknown words. Avoid texts that require much background knowledge the students may lack (Jesness, 2004).

2. Have ELLs recite a poem or a nursery rhyme first to become familiar with the text before asking them to read it and decode the words. This will help build up the background knowledge required to decode the words.

3. Use word walls organized into word families to prompt ELLs to recognize a word. Many ELLs will learn how to decode words better using word families, rather than trying to pronounce individual phonemes.

4. Develop a word wall or poster with the English words placed next to the ELLs' primary language. This will help them associate the word with its translation. Use these words in a word bank and have a buddy help the student sort the English words by beginning sound, by phonic pattern, or by any other category.

5. Teach word study within the context of meaningful text so that the ELLs have some reference within which to learn the unknown words. It is highly recommended that the students read books about their own cultures, if at all possible.

6. Have the students play games to learn the words. Such games as Bingo, Old Maid, and board games can be adapted to reinforce recognition of words.

Assessing Students' Ability to Identify Words

When a student is having trouble reading, it is important that the teacher conducts an assessment to determine the student's strengths and weaknesses. The teacher must know what the specific problems are with regard to comprehension, as well as word identification strategies. If a student does not comprehend text, there is a possibility that the reason is caused by poor word identification strategies and that the student needs instruction in this area. If the student is unable to identify keywords in the text, the student cannot attain fluency and will be unable to comprehend the passage.

Many different ways exist to assess the child's ability to identify words during the reading process. The process of assessment should be a continuous part of the literacy curriculum in which the teacher uses many different methods to collect data. Some of these methods are listed below.

◆ *Miscue analysis:* The teacher should be listening to the student read aloud either individually or in guided reading groups making note of all errors in pronunciation made as the student reads recording this as part of the daily record-keeping. This process is known as a miscue analysis (see Chapter 9 for a detailed discussion of miscue analysis). By carefully examining these errors, or miscues, the teacher should look for patterns that might exist in types of errors. Does the student consistently mispronounce a specific vowel combination? Specific blends? A specific word family? What words does the student have the most trouble with? Does the student need help with recognizing the most familiar words in English (sight words)?

◆ *Assessment of writing samples:* The teacher should also be examining the student's writing to determine whether any patterns in spelling errors exist. The writing should reflect the student's ability to decode words and make connections between the phoneme (sound) and the grapheme (letter). Although excellent readers are not always excellent spellers, the writing sample should give the teacher some indication as to problems a student may be having in working with the orthographic structure of the English language. If common words are frequently misspelled, the student needs to practice these common words, both in spelling and in identification.

◆ *Informal assessment on daily activities:* The teacher should be examining any worksheets, games, activities, and projects the student is working on to determine whether there are any problems in word identification strategies. These activities are an excellent way for the teacher to informally assess the student and give feedback in a nonstressful environment. Patterns should be noted and recorded in a daily record-keeping log.

◆ *Administer informal inventories:* The teacher can also give informal assessments to determine whether there are any word identification problems. Figures 5–7 and 5–8

Identifying Capital and Lower Case Letters

Identifying Capital Letters Named

Directions

Say, "Today we are going to play a game. I am going to say some letters and you are going to find them on your paper and put a circle around them. First we are going to look for the capital letters that I name." (Hold up a copy of the test—be sure the children are working on the correct column.) Say, "Put your pencils under this first line, like this." (Demonstrate.) "I am going to say one of the letters in this first row. See if you can find the letter I say. E—put your finger on it. That's right. Now draw a circle around it. Now move your pencil under line 2 and find C." Continue this way.

Key letters are:

1—E	6—L	11—U	16—B	21—F
2—C	7—O	12—W	17—N	22—K
3—Z	8—S	13—P	18—X	23—G
4—H	9—Y	14—T	19—V	24—I
5—A	10—R	15—D	20—M	25—J
				26—Q

Identifying Lowercase Letter Names

Directions

Follow the same pattern as in administering "Identifying Capital Letters Named" above. The key letters are:

1—s	6—l	11—n	16—p	21—t
2—c	7—z	12—i	17—g	22—j
3—x	8—k	13—v	18—m	23—d
4—y	9—e	14—q	19—o	24—u
5—f	10—r	15—b	20—h	25—a
				26—w

FIGURE 5-7　　　　　　　　　　　　　　　　　　　　　　　　　　　　　　　　*continued*

provide examples of two informal inventories a classroom teacher can easily give to a whole class of students at the same time. Figure 5–7 is a tool to help teachers determine whether a student can identify capital and lowercase letters of the alphabet. This is extremely important to know because one of the greatest indicators of future success in reading is whether a student can instantaneously and automatically identify all 26 letters of the alphabet. This is a particularly important area to assess when a student is having trouble reading. Many students with learning disabilities and second language learners may not know every single letter of the alphabet, and that alone could be interfering with their ability to decode words. It is essentially the first skill that needs to be assessed when there are reading problems. Figure 5–8 is a Group Phonics Inventory that allows the teacher to determine a student's ability to identify initial sounds, final sounds, blends, and vowels. If a student does not earn 100 percent correct in each of the columns, the teacher needs to instruct the student in his or her areas of weakness. Both of these inventories are excellent ways to determine whether a student needs more instruction in specific areas of phonics, and the information helps the teacher place students into guided reading sessions or mini-lesson groups.

Identifying Capital and Lower Case Letters–cont'd

Identifying Capital Letters Named

1.	E	F	A	Y	L		14.	D	C	G	T	B
2.	H	C	D	O	T		15.	O	D	C	T	G
3.	F	J	K	R	Z		16.	B	L	H	V	L
4.	I	H	E	L	F		17.	N	O	M	K	E
5.	B	E	R	F	A		18.	U	P	J	X	L
6.	N	I	Z	B	L		19.	A	Y	C	T	V
7.	U	B	O	F	P		20.	L	W	F	N	M
8.	E	N	S	O	C		21.	M	T	W	E	F
9.	F	I	J	Y	L		22.	B	L	D	V	K
10.	B	R	X	E	P		23.	Z	G	N	K	F
11.	U	S	O	Z	C		24.	Y	K	I	L	V
12.	W	P	F	V	T		25.	J	M	U	G	N
13.	B	P	S	C	D		26.	T	X	C	Q	T

NAME: _____   SCORE: _____

FIGURE 5-7

continued

Phonics and Word Study by Grade Level

The following sections describe how word study instruction should be implemented in each of the grade levels from kindergarten through sixth grade. The recommended skills and processes that every K–6 student should know are provided as a basic, minimal requirement, which are not intended to be a complete listing of structural elements for any grade level. In fact, these skills and processes represent a broad-based recommended skills array commonly used by exemplary teachers who use a balanced approach to reading instruction. Every preservice and in-service teacher should be knowledgeable about these basic skills and processes that are included in most successful balanced literacy programs.

In addition, state departments of education across the United States have begun to move in the direction of developing grade-specific standards to provide more clarity and specificity with regard to phonics instruction and related word study skills. Many revised standards for language arts literacy include a grade-by-grade listing of word study and related literacy skills with attention given in the primary grades to the teaching of phonics. Some of the states that include benchmarks by grade levels similar to those

Identifying Capital and Lower Case Letters—cont'd

Identifying Lowercase Letters Named

1.	o	s	y	b	m	14.	d	b	g	p	q
2.	r	a	f	m	c	15.	g	b	d	q	p
3.	s	m	o	x	z	16.	b	d	p	q	g
4.	g	p	q	h	y	17.	q	p	d	g	b
5.	k	t	f	l	h	18.	r	m	n	u	o
6.	k	l	h	f	t	19.	o	a	u	g	c
7.	m	f	s	z	c	20.	h	f	l	t	k
8.	l	t	b	k	h	21.	t	e	j	l	i
9.	o	a	e	c	g	22.	g	q	y	j	i
10.	a	r	e	o	c	23.	m	n	u	d	b
11.	n	u	w	r	m	24.	u	n	v	w	m
12.	k	i	g	t	y	25.	c	d	a	e	o
13.	m	v	u	c	h	26.	w	y	v	n	u

NAME: _____   SCORE: _____

FIGURE 5-7

presented in the following section include: Connecticut, California, Indiana, Maryland, Massachusetts, New Jersey, Pennsylvania, and Texas. For example, first grade expectations for phonological awareness in Connecticut include: identifying initial, medial and final sounds in words; distinguishing long and short vowel sounds in spoken one syllable words; and deleting, adding, and substituting letter sounds in initial position to make different words (*Connecticut PK-8 English Language Art Curriculum Standards*; 2008).

Priscilla Vail's (1991) book, *Common Ground; Whole Language and Phonics Working Together,* offers specific literacy strategies for each of the primary grade levels. Vail claims that this grade-level sequence of strategies allows teachers to know where their students should be headed and provides them with a framework to "see the holes that need to be plugged and how to consolidate" (p.7). This word study section follows Vail's recommendations in that it is organized by grade level beginning with kindergarten through grade 4, and then it combines grades 5 and 6.

Kindergarten

Developmental Background – Kindergarten children are learning to use language in new and powerful ways. Instead of using actions to display their happiness, frustration, and anger, they are learning to use language to control their behavior (Vail, 1991). Kindergartners often can recognize as many as 35 words by pointing to them on posters,

Group Phonics Inventory

For this inventory, have the children fold a paper into columns (4). Number the columns 1, 2, 3, 4. In each column, place numbers from 1 to 20. Give one test at a time and teach whatever is unknown.

Column 1. Say: "Listen to the first sound in the word I shall say. Then think of the letter that stands for the first sound. The word is MUSIC. Yes, *m*." (Write "1. m" on the board). "Now I am going to say some more words and you are to write just the first letter after the number. One, MUSIC. Two, RADIO." (Continue until the list is finished.)

Column 2. "Listen to the word I shall say and tell me the *last* sound you hear. FLOCK. Yes, *k* is the letter for the last sound. In Column 2 you are to write the last letter of each word I say. One, FLOCK. Two, BAN." (Continue until the list is finished.)

Column 3. "The words in Column 3 are a little harder because you are going to write two letters this time. These words have double sounds at the beginning. Who can tell me what the two letters are at the beginning of DRESS? Yes, *dr*. Now you are going to write the first two letters of each word I shall say. One, DRESS. Two, CHIME." (Continue until the list is finished.)

Column 4. "Listen to this word and tell me which vowel you hear at the *beginning* of the word. The word is APRON. Yes, *a*. In Column 4 you are to write the vowel you hear at the beginning of the word. One, APRON. Two, ELDER. For diagnosis, separate the long and short vowels. (Continue until the list is finished.)

1 Initial Sounds	2 Final Sounds	3 Double Sounds	4 Vowels
1. music	1. flock	1. dress	1. apron
2. radio	2. ban	2. chime	2. elder
3. lemonade	3. nail	3. plant	3. umpire
4. furniture	4. weed	4. swing	4. idle
5. witness	5. hug	5. thumb	5. igloo
6. camera	6. shock	6. stamp	6. actor
7. mustard	7. purr	7. price	7. oval
8. sandwich	8. chap	8. blink	8. union
9. dynamite	9. muff	9. shape	9. olive
10. pebble	10. ram	10. group	10. eager
11. vacation	11. less	11. scant	11. anvil
12. husband	12. shoot	12. flick	12. iris
13. nephew	13. buzz	13. spine	13. unit
14. gallop	14. heat	14. twist	14. opera
15. tumble	15. mill	15. queer	15. enter
16. jungle	16. fed	16. snack	16. illness
17. zebra	17. grab	17. clip	17. ancient
18. ketchup	18. rig	18. bridge	18. utter
19. yesterday	19. stain	19. smear	19. easel
20. building	20. glass	20. those	20. ogre

FIGURE 5-8

in books, and on food containers (Glazer & Burke, 1994). Their language is becoming more sophisticated and so is their ability to complete tasks to solve problems. They love to read books about naughty children or ill-behaved creatures such as *Where the Wild Things Are* by Maurice Sendak or *Curious George* by H. A. Rey (Vail, 1991).

Kindergarten children are also learning about language patterns and the structure of their language. Children at this age love to play with language and sounds. They love to play games having to do with rhymes and silly words, and they love to sing simple songs. Sometimes it appears as if kindergartners will never get tired of reading their favorite story one more time. In this way, children are learning that the structure of a story has a beginning, middle, and end; they are learning how to recognize clues to predict what happens next, and they are learning about words and how words represent meaning.

At this stage, children love to read simple Dr. Seuss books that play with words in predictable ways such as *The Cat in the Hat*. They love to read stories with predictable plots, story lines, and structures, so that they can actively participate in the reading. They are learning about words and learning to play with words. They are also starting to make the grapheme–phoneme connection: that letters are represented by sounds.

Skills/Processes Kindergartners Should Know – Following is a list of skills and processes that kindergartners should know:

- The conventions and structures of spoken language
- Development of new words and concepts to their speaking vocabularies
- How to identify the separate words in a sentence; that words are "isolated" patterns that have meaning
- Identification of letters of the alphabet
- Phonemic awareness
- Segmentation (breaking a word down into its component syllables or parts, for example, *monkey, mon-key*) and blending (taking individual sounds and blending them into a word, for example, *c-a-t, cat* and *h-o-r-s, horse*)
- Concepts about print: text is read left to right and top to bottom; print conveys meaning; language is represented by print
- Reading is a fun and pleasurable activity and an activity worth pursuing independently

Instructional Strategies for the Teacher

Reading Aloud. The teacher selects and reads a book or other text while the class listens quietly, usually sitting around the teacher on the floor. Teachers should choose texts that are rich in meaning and language structures so that children are exposed to books that model effective use of print and language. They should read favorite texts over and over again so that children will learn to assimilate the concepts and language structure so they can eventually produce it themselves. Reading aloud should begin on the first day of kindergarten and continue throughout the children's school life in years ahead. Even high school students love to have books read to them. Rich literature allows the teacher to make connections to events and feelings that might otherwise go unexplored (Fountas & Pinnell, 1996).

Shared Reading. The teacher introduces and reads a Big Book or a small text, of which each child has a copy. At certain times in the reading, children will chime in, reading in unison. This occurs usually during refrains, repetitive passages, and predictable points in the text as the teacher follows along with a pointer, pointing to each word as it is read. The shared response will occur more frequently as the text is read over and over again, until at certain times, the children can read the whole text together with the teacher. Children can also do shared reading on their own with their own small versions of the book. Books selected for shared reading are different in text structure than those used for reading aloud. In shared reading, leveled texts that are generally predictable and repetitive are used, usually with only a few lines of print on each page. In kindergarten, with children beginning to engage with text, one line of text per page, with clearly marked spaces between words, is best. In reading aloud, the teacher can choose text that is a bit more difficult to read and understand because the children will be listening to the story, not interacting with the print (Fountas & Pinnell, 1996).

Shared Writing. During shared writing, the children are able to convey their ideas to the teacher, who acts as a scribe and records their story on an easel, demonstrating the writing process. The children get a chance to see their ideas transformed into words, which reinforces the grapheme–phoneme connection.

Interactive Writing. During interactive writing, the children actually interact with the teacher in writing the story by coming up to the easel and sharing the pen with the teacher for certain words. This helps in word identification and involves more intensive attention to hearing the sounds in words and to spelling patterns (Fountas & Pinnell, 1996). This type of writing helps the child connect reading a word to writing a word, and it provides necessary support to make the transition to independent writing.

Play Centers. Creative play facilitates language development and can be fostered through the use of centers that focus on real-world contexts that are familiar to the student. In kindergarten, children need to express themselves through play, which helps develop cooperative, collaborative, and cognitive skills. Children will learn to attend to tasks, take turns, solve problems, and express ideas (Rog, 2001). Vygotsky (1978) believes that play enables children to develop symbolic, abstract thought, a precursor to literacy development. In addition, he emphasizes the need for a "more literate other," or one who will oversee the cognitive development of the child and guide the child along the way. A kitchen, a post office, a restaurant, or a physician's office are often favorite play centers for kindergartners. It is important that the teacher build in literacy experiences for the children at each center.

Literacy Center. A literacy center is commonly the central point of a kindergarten classroom, providing a space for quiet reading and writing and a gathering spot for reading aloud and shared reading. In this inviting space, there should be a Reading Corner with comfortable chairs for reading and often small pieces of carpet for children to sit on. A classroom library should be available with age-appropriate literature that is easily manageable by kindergarten hands. There is also a "writing spot" with a table and an assortment of paper and writing materials that change frequently. An "author's chair" can be placed here, so that children who complete a piece of writing may present it to the class to become part of the classroom library. This is where an easel is placed to hold a Big Book and large sheets of paper for group writing activities (Rog, 2001).

Labeling. By labeling many different items in the classroom, kindergarten children will soon commit many words to memory and increase their sight word vocabulary. Labeling the items in play centers is especially helpful and provides necessary literacy connections during play.

Letter of the Week. The letter-of-the-week strategy, or many variations of it, is frequently used in kindergarten classrooms. One letter of the alphabet is introduced each week. During that week, the children bring in items from home that begin with that letter, use that letter in shared or interactive writing, eat foods beginning with that letter, participate in art projects that involve the shape of that letter, and build word walls using words that begin with that letter. Teachers must continuously reinforce all the letters previously learned as the class moves onward in the alphabet. A helpful hint is to keep confusing look-alike letters well separated in time.

Sound/Symbol Cards. The sound/symbol cards activity (Vail, 1991) is a variation on the letter-of-the-week activity. As a class together, the children make individual collections of cards that are attached to a ring. Each card has a letter on it with a clue material or word to help the child remember what sound the letter makes. One example would be pasting cotton balls in the shape of a *c* for the *c* card. For the *a* card, they can draw or cut out a picture of an apple, the *d* card could be stick-on dots, the *l* could be lollipop sticks in the shape of an *l*, and the *y* could be yellow yarn. Once these cards are attached to rings, the teacher can play many games, such as "Who can think of a sound that begins with *g*?" A similar strategy can be used to make a letter scrapbook for each child.

Keeping a Calendar. Children will learn about time and how to recognize the months and days of weeks by keeping an individual or class calendar. This is also an excellent way to reinforce the letter of the week by using words to describe a particular day. "It is a rainy but rather nice day to read a rhyme about rats."

Rhyming and Linguistic Play. Rhyming is a wonderful way to teach phonemic awareness skills. Some children at this age find rhyming easy, while others have more difficulty.

By reading rhymes and creating poems, children get a chance to hear words and play with sounds in a playful and enjoyable activity. Kindergartners love silly rhymes and nonsensical words. There are a great many books that include wonderful poetry and rhymes for children of this age, including nursery rhymes. Teachers can read a rhyme to the class and then try to write one together using the same structure and format. This allows children to actively work on rhyming skills, including blending, segmentation, and isolation of sounds.

First Grade

Developmental Background – Children enter first grade with more literacy and reading knowledge than most teachers realize, which will vary greatly based on the children's literacy experiences in the home. Literacy learning in kindergarten should have benefited each child so that this group of children enters first grade with a rich background of oral language that teachers can use to help each child learn how to read. Word study is based on the child's knowledge of how oral language works (Strickland, 1998b).

Learning about what makes the first grader "tick" will also help teachers better understand the universality and the developmental nature of children at this age level, including their diverse backgrounds, cultures, and linguistic differences. Teachers benefit greatly by knowing their students' sociocultural and psychological makeup, their loves and fears, their learning styles, and their multiple intelligences, all of which help teachers make many important process decisions about reading, such as selecting children's literature, word study activities, cooperative learning groups, higher-order thinking skills, field trips, and interesting topics for inquiry or discussion purposes.

First graders are unique because they are so eager to learn new things; they are like a team of energetic explorers in search of a new world. Teachers need to consider these important characteristics of first graders when making decisions about what their students should listen to, speak about, read and write about, and visually explore:

- Making sense of their new social world that is becoming more real and less dependent on fantasy
- Enjoying their newfound logic, yet enjoying moving back and forth from fantasy to reality
- Wanting fairness and equality—especially to see small people, creatures, or things triumphant over big people, creatures, or things
- Being obsessive about tattling on their peers, judging right from wrong about everything, including changing "best friends" on a daily basis because of hurt feelings (for example, "My friend did something wrong!")
- Beginning to work cooperatively; children's playful experiences are important now as they grow socially and academically
- Exhibiting their egocentricity; they want to share personal stories and are proud of any accomplishment or "tangible product," no matter how tiny or seemingly insignificant as they work toward building their own confidence
- Asking many questions and anxiously awaiting any opportunity to respond, regardless of whether they really can answer the question posed

First graders just seem to grow up overnight; they go from being very dependent on their teachers to becoming more and more independent by the end of the school year.

Skills/Processes First Graders Should Know – Research on beginning reading indicates that there is no exact, *best* sequence and pace to teach reading because they are dependent on the individual learner (Fountas & Pinnell, 1996). Nevertheless, there are skills and processes that must be taught directly and explicitly (either through analytic or synthetic phonics or through a combination of these two approaches). The following sequence is a more general approach that is typical of the recommended skills found in literacy curriculum documents and state departments of education's Literacy/ Language Arts Standards.

- ◆ Being aware of sound–symbol relationships in spoken language known as phonological or phonemic awareness
- ◆ Knowing how to blend and segment phonemes in one syllable words
- ◆ Being able to identify the number of syllables in given words
- ◆ Being able to add, delete, and change spoken sounds in words
- ◆ Identifying and sounding out beginning consonants and beginning sounds to decode unfamiliar words in reading and writing (phonics)
- ◆ Identifying and sounding out beginning consonant blends *(bl, st, tr, dr)*
- ◆ Identifying and sounding out ending consonant blends *(-nt, -nd, -ed, -nk)*
- ◆ Learning about digraphs *(th, wh, ch, sh)*
- ◆ Rhyming words and identifying short vowels in word families
- ◆ Being aware of short vowels as CVC patterns *(fat, sit, not)*
- ◆ Learning to apply the "magic e rule" (CVCe) (mat – *mate*; pin – *pine*)
- ◆ Recognizing most frequently used phonograms in word or spelling patterns
- ◆ *(-ack, -ent, -ick, -ong, -ump)*
- ◆ Being knowledgeable about integrated word study, including word recognition, alphabet study, phonics, vocabulary, and spelling

Notably, some of the skills and procedures listed above for the first grade level were introduced previously to kindergarten students. These skills and procedures will continue to be developed within monosyllabic words and will continue to be expanded later as children are exposed to authentic reading and writing opportunities and begin to learn multisyllabic words that contain more sophisticated and complex spelling patterns.

Instructional Strategies for the Teacher

Writing: A Link to Phonics. Children who can write words and short phrases or sentences have already made a link to phonics. If they can spell words by writing phonetically, they can begin to use this same knowledge to decode new words when reading. The teacher might ask some more able students to write a sentence or a brief story to determine what they know about the structure of writing. Some may know only a little; others might be able to write down what they can say, even though their writing lacks structure or form. The child who is writing is already using phonics as a tool and soon will be able to make the next leap to reading for understanding. Some children will have much more difficulty writing words and lack the ability to write. These children will need much more individual attention before they can link writing and spelling to phonics. Often, they will need to be exposed to a great deal of oral language and print before they actually begin reading or writing at the preprimer or prekindergarten level. In a nurturing, print-rich classroom environment, these eager-to-learn first graders will begin to thrive and soon will be reading and writing.

Spelling: A Link to Phonics. The first grade teacher must continue to encourage children to use invented spelling as they write freely, without inhibitions. How each child uses invented spelling to write informs the teacher and helps determine how much literacy and background knowledge a given child has attained. Literacy experts believe that analyzing children's invented spelling reveals much about their knowledge about print and is a link to understanding phonics (Bear, Invernizzi, Templeton, & Johnston, 2000). Analyzing children's spelling will indicate whether they know sound–symbol relationships based on the alphabetic principle. Ongoing assessment of a child's invented spelling and attempts at conventional spelling will serve as a guidepost for teaching children phonic skills, as well as conventional spelling skills. It is highly recommended that teachers use the children's spelling errors to plan word study.

Word Study: Letter Name/Alphabetic Stage. Usually, first grade children will begin the school year knowing most of the letter names of the consonants and their corresponding sounds. Some may even know the letter sounds of the alphabet, or will know how to name the long vowel sound. Word study instruction for these children should begin with emphasis on teaching the alphabetic principle. This is an important stage in beginning to read. Knowing the alphabet and the corresponding sounds of each letter of the alphabet teaches children that sounding out words depends on their ability to sound out each consonant and vowel that makes up each word. Therefore, the letter name or alphabetic stage includes many of the identified skills and procedures for first grade word study.

Identifying and Using Patterns. As the classroom teacher begins to create opportunities to help children identify initial consonants, consonant blends, digraphs, and short vowels, they must also teach these skills in context, to help the children practice by continuing to read texts that are selected at their independent (easy-to-read) level. Children in first grade should be given practice in identifying and using simple word patterns found in words, such as *at (bat, fat, cat)*, *un (fun, sun, bun)*, and *ate (rate, skate, gate)*. This practice will help first graders develop confidence and fluency as they learn to identify more sight words and to sound out words automatically.

Alphabet Strategies: Learning Consonants and Consonant Blends. All children should learn the "Alphabet Song," and it should be sung daily until the children can recite the alphabet without having to sing it as a memory prompt. Some programs use more contemporary melodies and rhythms that children can use for variety, if not for motivational purposes, including reggae, salsa, hip-hop, calypso, and other contemporary musical styles (Snow, Burns, & Griffin, 1998). Teachers often use the letters from classmates' names as a springboard to other words that are meaningful to the children. For example, the teacher asks Walt, "What letter does your name begin with, Walt?" "W," answers Walt. The teacher asks, "Didn't we read a *word* in the story today that also begins with *that* same sound?" Walt grins, and says, "*Wash!*" The teacher continues in this way, and asks, "Did anyone else find a word in the story that begins with the same letter as your name?" Other songs and chants can be used to help children learn the alphabet, as well as blends and digraphs. The familiar tune "Old MacDonald Had a Farm" can be used to insert consonants, blends, vowels, and endings.

Published ABC Books. Every K–1 classroom should have several versions of illustrated alphabet books, counting books, and patterned or predictable books in their library (Figure 5–9). A word of caution, however, is that in selecting these books, it is important that the artwork and illustrations be simple and clear, not gaudy, elaborate, or overly decorative. Alphabet books should be stimulating and esthetically pleasing to the eye, but not so much so that the child gets bombarded visually with imagery that becomes superfluous, confusing, or negates the purpose of helping the child learn the letters of the alphabet and their sound correlations.

Children-Made Alphabet Books. Children should create their own alphabet books. They should have the choice of working alone, working in pairs, or working in small collaborative groups. By working collaboratively, children can share in the joy of creating illustrations or in finding and choosing photographs and illustrations as a representative sound clue and a resonating visual clue. These clues will always trigger the right response for this particular letter when it suddenly presents itself in a novel word or sentence embedded in the shapes of sounds from a brand-new book.

The Letter(s) of the Week. As in kindergarten, some first grade teachers will want to use the letter-of-the-week activity to introduce one letter of the alphabet each week. During that week, the students bring in items from home that begin with that letter, use that letter in shared or interactive writing, eat foods beginning with that letter, and engage in art projects that involve the shape of that letter.

List of ABC Books and Rhyming, Predictable Books

ABC and Counting Books

Anno, Mitumasa, *Anno's Alphabet*

Aylesworth, Jim, *The folks in the Valley: A Pennsylvania Dutch ABC*, illustrated by Stefano Vitale

_____, *Old Black Fly*, illustrated by Stephen Gammell

Bowen, Betsy, *Antler, Bear, Canoe: A Northwoods Alphabet Year*

DeVicq de Cumptich, Roberto, *Bembo's Zoo: An Animal ABC Book*

Ehlert, Lois, *Eating the Alphabet*

Fisher, Leonard Everett, *The ABC Exhibit*

Giganti, Paul, Jr., *How Many Snails? A Counting Book*, illustrated by Donald Crews

Girnis, Meg, *ABC for You and Me*, photos by Shirley Leamon Green

Grossman, Virginia, *Ten Little Rabbits*, illustrated by Sylvia Long

Hayes, Sarah, *Nine Ducks Nine*

Hughes, Shirley, *Lucy & Tom's 1 2 3*

Isadora, Rachel, *Listen to the City*

_____, *1 2 3 Pop!*

Johnson, Stephen T., *Alphabet City*

Katz, Michael Jay, *Ten Potatoes in a Pot & Other Counting Rhymes*, illustrated by June Otani

Kellogg, Steven, *Aster Aardvark's Alphabet Adventures*

Kitamura, Satoshi, *From Acorn to Zoo: And Everything in Between in Alphabetical Order*

Lester, Mike, *A is for Salad*

Lobel, Anita, *Alison's Zinnia*

_____, *One Lighthouse, One Moon*

Lobel, Arnold, *On Market Street*

MacCarthy, Patricia, *Ocean Parade: A Counting Book*

MacDonald, Suse, *Alphabatics*

_____, *Puzzlers*, illustrated by Bill Oakes

Martin, Bill, Jr., and John Archambault, *Chicka Chicka Boom Boom*, illustrated by Lois Ehlert

McKenzie, Ellen Kindt, *The Perfectly Orderly House*, illustrated by Megan Lloyd

McMillan, Bruce, *Beach Ball—Left, Right*

Merriam, Eve, *Halloween A B C*, illustrated by Lane Smith

Owens, Mary Beth, *A Caribou Alphabet*

Paul, Ann Whitford, *Eight Hands Round: A Patchwork Alphabet*, illustrated by Jeannette Winter

Rankin, Laura, *The Handmade Alphabet*

Rockwell, Anne, *Bear Child's Book of Hours*

Ryden, Hope, *Wild Animals of Africa A B C*

Scott, Ann Herbert, *One Good Horse: A Cowpuncher's Counting Book*, illustrated by Lynn Sweat

Shannon, George, *Tomorrow's Alphabet*, illustrated by Donald Crews

Sis, Peter, *Waving: A Counting Book*

Sloat, Teri, *From Letter to Letter*

Tudor, Tasha, *1 Is One*

Walsh, Ellen Stoll, *Mouse Count*

Wormell, Christopher, *An Alphabet of Animals*

Ziefert, Harriet, *Big to Little, Little to Big*, illustrated by Susan Baum

_____, *Clothes On, Clothes Off*, illustrated by Susan Baum

_____, *Count Up, Count Down*, illustrated by Susan Baum

_____, *Empty to Full, Full to Empty*, illustrated by Susan Baum

Pattern/Predictable Books

Carlstrom, Nancy White, *Jesse Bear, What Will You Wear?* illustrated by Bruce Degen

Cummings, Pat, *Angel Baby*

Ehlert, Lois, *Feathers for Lunch*

Fleming, Denise, *In the Tall, Tall Grass*

Fox, Mem, *Hattie and the Fox*, illustrated by Patricia Mullins

Gammell, Stephen, *Once upon MacDonald's Farm*

Guarino, Deborah, *Is Your Mama a Llama?* illustrated by Steven Kellogg

Hennessy, B. G., *Jake Baked the Cake*, illustrated by Mary Morgan

Hort, Lenny, *The Seals on the Bus*, illustrated by G. Brian Karas

Hutchins, Pat, *What Game Shall We Play?*

Katz, Michael Jay, *Ten Potatoes in a Pot: And Other Counting Rhymes*, illustrated by June Otani

Kovalski, Maryann, *The Wheels on the Bus*

MacDonald, Amy, *Rachel Fister's Blister*, illustrated by Marjorie Priceman

Martin, Bill, Jr., *Brown Bear, Brown Bear, What Do You See?* illustrated by Eric Carle

_____, *Polar Bear, Polar Bear, What Do You Hear?* illustrated by Eric Carle

Martin, Bill, Jr., and John Archambault, *Chicka Chicka Boom Boom*, illustrated by Lois Ehlert

Marzollo, Jean, *Pretend You're a Cat*, illustrated by Jerry Pinkney

Neitzel, Shirley, *The Jacket I Wear in the Snow*, illustrated by Nancy Winslow Parker

_____, *The Bag I'm Taking to Grandma's*, illustrated by Nancy Winslow Parker

Peters, Lisa Westberg, *Cold Little Duck, Duck, Duck*, illustrated by Sam Williams

Robart, Rose, *The Cake That Mack Ate*, illustrated by Maryann Kovalski

Rosen, Michael, *We're Going on a Bear Hunt*

Schaefer, Lola M., *This Is the Sunflower*

Shaw, Nancy, *Sheep in a Shop*, illustrated by Margot Apple

Stojic, Manya, *Rain*

Stow, Jenny, *The House That Jack Built*

Suteyev, Vladimir, *Chick and the Duckling*, translated by Mirra Ginsburg, illustrated by Jose Aruego and Ariane Dewey

Swope, Sam, *Gotta Go! Gotta Go!* illustrated by Sue Riddle

Waber, Bernard, *Do You See a Mouse?*

Walsh, Ellen Stoll, *Mouse Count*

_____, *Mouse Paint*

Walsh, Melanie, *Do Donkeys Dance?*

_____, *Do Monkeys Tweet?*

_____, *Do Pigs Have Stripes?*

Zelinsky, Paul, *The Wheels on the Bus*

(From Galda, L., & Cullinan, B. E. (2002). *Literature and the Child*. Belmont, CA: Wadsworth/Thomson Learning, by permission.)

FIGURE 5-9

Sound/Symbol Cards. The use of sound/symbol cards is a good activity to continue with first graders. In this literacy activity, each child is given 26 blank file cards on which to illustrate each letter of the alphabet.

Word Sorts. Word sort activities can help students search for specific features or patterns in words for the purpose of learning the alphabetic principle. The teacher decides in advance and then tells the students the features or patterns to search for, and the children repeat these activities until they have learned the phonic skills that become more apparent to them through these enjoyable, competitive, gamelike activities (Bear et al., 2000). Specific phonic patterns that students can search for in a stack of cards with words written on them include:

- A beginning consonant: *b – bat; c – cat; d – dim*
- An ending consonant: *-s – bats; -t – last; -k – back*
- A beginning consonant blend: *bl – blow; cl – clap; st – stop*
- An ending consonant blend: *-nk – bank; -st – fist; -sk – risk*
- Words that end in the letter *y: cry, why, fry*
- Words that have two vowels: *teach, meet, coat*
- Words that have short vowels: *mat, bed, fin, hot, bud*

Word Walls. A word wall (see earlier) is useful in helping first grade children identify and learn noncontent or frequently used "glue words" that do not normally follow a particular spelling pattern (for example, *the, of, from, to*). A word wall is also used to help children learn phonics by recognizing familiar phonogram patterns.

Second Grade

Developmental Background – Second graders are growing up in a comparative world of childhood and babyhood. They can no longer be considered the "babies," as they were so often called in kindergarten. Second graders love to explore different cultures and learn facts about people from all over the world. Second graders are like anthropologists and behavioral scientists who want to know all about the history, customs, and habitats of a certain culture or people. Nevertheless, these fertile-minded individuals suddenly appear to be more insecure and fearful of being "left alone."

Teachers' VOICES **First Graders**

Many children in kindergarten and first grade have low attention spans or display hyperactivity, often because they are being asked to focus more or to sit longer. So it's essential that manipulatives, word sorts, and word hunts are used for teaching reading skills, such as phonemic awareness and beginning phonic skills, and time is given for cooperative learning, language centers, art, drama, and play.

—*Jill Morrison, First Grade Teacher*

Learning is best when my children are actively involved and receive positive feedback. My students strive to build relationships by opening their minds to new information by relating it to their own personal lives in order to make meaning from it.

—*Kristin Crisafi, Reading Recovery Teacher*

My first graders like to follow my instructions eagerly and to a fault. If I say write two sentences in their journals, they will never write more than two sentences!

—*Laura Heitman, First Grade Teacher*

Second graders are able to see the cause and effect in humor. They can be real jokesters, stand-up comedians, and love the humorous books or the humor portrayed by the outrageous images and juxtaposing words found in Shel Silverstein's and Jack Prelutsky's poetry (Vail, 1991). Teachers find that they can take advantage of the second graders' shifting moods, love of facts, history, humor, wordplay, and longer, complex words to engage them in a new genre of reading materials. This variety of nonfiction information includes a wide range of topics and interests that are available to read about in books on science, social studies, and related multicultural and ethnic issues.

Skills/Processes Second Graders Should Know – Following is a list of skills and processes that second graders should know:

◆ Phonological awareness and phonemic awareness strategies for segmenting and blending spoken sounds that are prerequisites for developing phonic skills

◆ Deleting and changing middle sounds to manipulate words: *c-at* to *c-ut*

◆ Continued mapping of sounds-to-print and print-to-sounds (grapheme–phoneme connection) to sound out words

◆ Distinguishing and sounding out various vowel digraphs and diphthongs: *ai, ay, ea, ou, ow, au, aw, oi, oy*

◆ Developing word identification strategies, such as *navigating the word*, in order to:
  ▶ Identify the whole word and its rime
  ▶ Spell parts of words as directed, by visually configuring it on paper
  ▶ Sound out parts of a word as directed, by auditorily interpreting the word through speech sounds
  ▶ Spell whole words and sound out whole words, as directed
  ▶ Sound out *r*-controlled vowel sounds: *c-ar, h-er, b-ird, p-ort, f-ur*

◆ Decoding of words with one or more syllables

◆ Decoding multisyllabic words

◆ Continuing to identify rimes to decode new words: *s-ong, r-ang, st-ick, p-ack, r-ope, l-ink*

◆ Identifying suffixes through structural analysis: jump-*ing*, songs, joy-*ful*, end-*ed*

Instructional Strategies for the Teacher – Most children entering second grade should have developed phonemic awareness skills in first grade and should have been learning how to apply the alphabetic principle by developing phonic strategies. Therefore, for the most part, these children enter second grade knowing most of the letter names and consonant sounds—which form the basis for learning phonogram and spelling patterns—so that they can continue to learn to decode and spell new and bigger words. It is also important that second graders learn to decode new words with greater facility and automaticity, so that their reading comprehension also improves. Fluency strategies must be stressed at this stage of development because research informs us that children's reading comprehension skills improve dramatically as they learn to read with greater ease and speed (NICHD, 2000).

Continuous Assessment of Word Identification Strategies. There is a great deal of overlapping of the skills, instructional strategies, and approaches introduced to first grade students that must be taken into account and repeated with most second grade students. Once again, teacher observation and continuous assessment of student progress will inform the second grade teacher which skills introduced in first grade need to be retaught and reinforced. Naturally, continuous assessment of individual students' progress is essential for the second grade teacher to determine how ready each of his or her students is to use this knowledge to learn new patterns for improving his or her phonic skills.

Once the second grade teacher has reviewed incoming students' first grade reading records and assessed their strengths and weaknesses, he or she should establish a similar instructional routine described for first grade, including read-alouds, shared reading, guided reading and writing, and interactive writing activities. During guided reading lessons, the teacher works closely with each child in a small group to reteach and introduce new instructional skills.

Word Families and Spelling Pattern Walls. It is important that once children have learned the alphabetic principle and know the beginning sounds to words, they must also learn how to use rhyming patterns to help them sound out chunks of words and learn how to use these patterns to spell. The onset-rime approach to teaching words is an important instructional strategy that second graders must master. Word walls should be used to display these word families for children to view and learn.

Navigating the Word. Children can begin navigating the word as early as first grade. By second grade, children need to learn how to sound out words using a combination of approaches, for example, by using phonemes (individual letters and small units) and phonograms (chunks, spelling patterns). As the child encounters more and more multisyllabic words, navigating the word becomes a most useful strategy that children easily learn following teacher modeling. Usually, children can sound out the initial consonant(s) or onsets without too much difficulty. However, teachers have observed that children usually skip medial vowel sounds and have trouble decoding multisyllabic words. Therefore, it is important that children learn how to "navigate" the word.

g	p	n
st	s	ai
d	t	l

Vowel Digraph Squares. Vowel digraph squares is a "game" that first and second graders like to play that uses different vowel digraphs. Letters are scrambled in a square containing three vertical and horizontal rows of nine individual little squares within one large square. Each little square contains a letter (mostly consonants), and in one of the squares is a vowel digraph. Students make their own squares to trade with a partner. The partner has to find all the words within the nine little squares and record them on a "score card" listing the number of words found and the total points earned. For example, a student might make the words *sail* and *pain* from the box. A sample of the digraph square is shown at left.

Making Word Families with Dice. Using removable blank stickers, the teacher writes word families on the stickers that are placed on the sides of the dice. One set serves as the beginning letter or cluster. The other set can be used to make word families. Three sets of dice can be used to change the vowel in the middle of the word and to add endings to the word. For example, one die can be used to practice the short *a* word families (-at, -ad, -am, -an, -ag). The other die contains the beginning consonant sounds (m, h, s, c, b, r). The children must put the consonant and the short *a* sound together to form a word (mat, mad, had, ham, can, ran, bag).

Glue Words as Sentence Completers. Noncontent words are sometimes referred to as "glue words" because they are the little "high-utility" words that are most frequently used, but that often cause struggling readers great difficulty. Context or the use of predictable language is highly recommended to help such readers; for example:

> John can go to the store _____ his mother. *(with)*
> "I will go back _____ the store _____ milk," said John. *(to) (for)*

Daily practice using glue words as *sentence completers* can help children learn these nonphonetic, noncontent words. This activity can also be used effectively with students who are ELLs because it reinforces the use of these noncontent words that often cause confusion with ELLs.

Visualizing Activities. Children who struggle with reading for meaning and with word identification often have difficulty visualizing what is being stated by the author. Having these students do a "picture walk" is one way to help them visualize what a story is about. If the story is *Jack and the Beanstalk,* for example, have the children visualize what the "beans" looked like before they were planted. Children should illustrate a handful of beans or show what the beans might have looked like inside the bag. The students should be asked to visualize how the first stalk broke through the ground and should be asked to describe and draw that first growth. Finally, the children should return to the book to compare how much the beanstalk had grown since the day it began to grow.

Teachers' VOICES Second Graders

My second-graders are constantly seeking my attention, approval, and reinforcement while they are trying to become more independent by completing tasks, class work, projects, or by just being helpful in the classroom.

—Stephanie Lawlor, Special Education Teacher

My students love jokes and spend a great deal of time solving riddles. They can laugh at wordplay, use onomatopoetic sounds of chickens clucking, sheep baaing, or bees buzzing. They love learning BIG multisyllabic words and have little difficulty learning the biggest of words, including the most popular and the longest word in the English dictionary—supercalifragilisticexpialidocious.

—Rachel Manzo, Second Grade Teacher

My students respond well to simple, step-by-step directions before being asked to perform a task.

—Juliet Cowen, Second Grade Teacher

Fluency Strategy/Choral Reading. Choral reading is something of a lost art that teachers are only recently returning to as a regular activity for teaching reading fluency. Poems, chants, stories, and theater scripts can be read in unison by the whole class. Children should be reading from a script so that they are all developing the skill of reading fluently at the same time. Sometimes the scripts can be adapted from published texts, or they can be read as originally intended. Students can write their own scripts or poems to be performed in chorus. Some books are written expressly for choral reading, such as *Joyful Noise: Poems for Two Voices* by Paul Fleischman (2004) , which is an excellent way to have children read books dramatically with fluency.

Third Grade

Developmental Background – As children enter third grade, they have already had three years of formal schooling, including kindergarten, and a great deal of attention and focus has been given to each child's literacy development. Most third graders should have developed a linguistic background to draw on and to serve them in their quest for new challenges, especially as they are introduced to a more comprehensive curriculum with demands that include reading in content areas such as social studies, science, mathematics, and health education. During three brief years, third graders have spent much time learning how to decode a new symbolic system known as reading, and now more than ever before, they are expected to put this knowledge to practical use and to read to learn and interpret information about the world's ecology, its history, and its daily events. In fact, it is noteworthy that the *No Child Left Behind Act* mandates that every child will be able to read by the end of third grade.

Third graders appear to be more developmentally ready and able to learn about organizational skills. They are interested in the future and are more in tune with learning about the past as they become more in tune with themselves in relation to time and space. They have also begun to make use of their wide repertoire of vocabulary and language development to reason, debate, and even to engage in negotiating what is fair. Their discovery of more mythic and linguistic constructs enables them to explore other genres such as poetry, mythology, and folklore. The *Harry Potter* series appears to have captured the attention of this eager age group that seems to be more interested in learning about differences, whether it be in the supernatural world of wizards and kings or in the origins of the world. It appears that overnight these youngsters have become verbal enough to explore new places and are ready to explore more vicarious experiences that are both real and unreal. Some of the favorite authors of third graders include D'Aulaire, Sendak, L'Engle, Cleary, Prelutsky, and Silverstein (Vail, 1991), all of whom write about fanciful worlds of make-believe and characters who are engaged in new and unusual adventures. This is a time when third graders must go beyond learning to read and develop fluency so that they can read to learn; they need to read independently and have opportunities to discuss their reading with other peers during reading circles or reading workshops. Teachers can help develop reading fluency with all children by encouraging choral reading with such rhyming texts as classic poems, contemporary poems of Shel Silverstein and Jack Prelutsky, Joanna Cole's *Anna Banana: 101 Jump Rope Rhymes,* and choral readings from Ruth Dowell's *Move Over, Mother Goose!* (Cunningham, 2000).

Skills/Processes Third Graders Should Know — By third grade, most children should be able to manipulate spoken language by segmenting and blending individual phonemes to sound out words. By third grade, the children should have been introduced to a combination of phonic approaches discussed throughout this chapter. Third grade reading is becoming more and more challenging because the vocabulary is richer, longer, and more multisyllabic. Developing automaticity is necessary because reading for meaning in a variety of content areas requires new strategies for encoding or comprehending text, as well as decoding text. Third grade instruction in word identification strategies makes use of all of the approaches introduced at each of the previous levels including kindergarten through second grade.

The skills/processes third graders should know include:

- Continued reinforcement of the grapheme–phoneme connection: the sophisticated development of sound–symbol relationships using blends, digraphs, and diphthongs
- Continued development of decoding/word recognition and overall phonics ability
- Solid knowledge of different vowels and vowel combinations; they should be familiar with *r*-controlled vowels or "Bossy"-*r* words (single vowel sounds followed by *r* usually result in a blended sound such as *bird, fur, firm*); these *r*-controlled words are excellent words for spelling lists, as well as for word walls and word sorts (Sort the following words that have the same vowel sound into different groups based on their orthographic spelling: *firm, fern, burn, worm.*)
- Introduction of structural analysis including simple prefixes (such as *pre-, re-, ex-*), simple suffixes (such as *-ing, -ed, -tion, -sion, -able*), and roots (*reac*-tion)
- Knowledge of inflectional endings and how these endings affect the meaning of the base word and affect pronunciation (boy – *boys*; church – *churches*; half – *halves*)
- Correct use of homonyms in writing; that is, words with identical sounds but different spellings and meanings (to/two/too, their/there/they're, pane/pain, vain/vein, main/mane)
- Use of contextual clues to read homographs; that is, multiple meaning words with the same spellings (for example, piggy *bank* and river *bank*)
- Introduction to beginning rules of syllabication to help readers identify multisyllabic words. Third graders should be familiar with how to divide words between like consonants *(let-ter)* and how to divide compound words *(snow-ball)*. They should also begin to know about closed syllables (a vowel in the middle of a syllable is known as a closed syllable and is usually short; for example, shiv/er, tax/i, ped/al, trav/el, rock/er, mim/ic) and open syllables (a vowel at the end of a syllable is known as an open syllable and is usually long; for example, fa/tal, to/tal, pa/per, de/lay, o/ver, po/lite). They should also know that when a word ends in *le,*

the consonant immediately preceding the *le* usually begins the last syllable (for example, pur/ple, an/kle, ta/ble, jun/gle, sim/ple).

Instructional Strategies for the Teacher – The strategies described in the following sections are recommended for building the children's repertoire of skills and for increasing their speed and fluency along the way.

Making Little Words from Big Words. Children like to play games and enjoy being challenged to make as many words as they can from one big word. For example, from the word *dinosaur* the children work in teams to make as many words as they are able to say and to spell, reusing letters as often as needed (a dictionary can be used to check spellings as well), such as *roar, din, sin, rind, sad, sour, soar.*

Word Sorting. Words can be sorted in a variety of ways; for example, by word family, by beginning consonant, by vowel sound, or by concept.

Alliteration Awareness ("Lobsters licking lemon lollipops"). Students read an alliterative story like *Marti and the Mango*. After defining what alliteration is, they begin hunting for alliterative phrases. After reading the story, the students go back through the text identifying all the alliteration, and they record the phrases in their notebooks. They then discuss that all the phrases had the same beginning sound, such as a "kangaroo collecting kiwis." They brainstorm a list of animals, verbs, adjectives, and nouns that helps them think of their own alliterative phrase. Finally, the students create sentences, which they illustrate colorfully.

Vocab-Automat-Activity. A major cause of students' difficulty with comprehension skills stems from their limited knowledge of unfamiliar sight words or vocabulary knowledge. The student usually lacks the ability to recognize the new word with automaticity (Bukovec, 1979). In the following activity the teacher instructs the students to:

◆ Select two words each day from his or her independent reading or skill materials that are either difficult to pronounce or the definition of which is unknown to him or her.

◆ Record these words on the individual vocabulary slips found in his or her portfolio pocket (Figure 5–10).

◆ Review these words with a partner to figure out the pronunciation and meaning (check the dictionary or thesaurus) if having difficulty.

◆ Check with the teacher for pronunciation and meaning during guided reading time.

◆ Study new words before meeting in guided reading in anticipation of a teacher review. Student must be prepared to know the pronunciation, meaning, and spelling of the new word (and should be able to say or write it in a meaningful complete sentence).

Teachers' VOICES   Third Graders

My students enjoy learning and using new and interesting words in their writing. They typically enjoy a lot of freedom when they write, especially choosing their own topics.

—*Donna Friedrich, Third Grade Teacher*

Third graders are more discriminating between fact and fiction. They still enjoy picture books, particularly at the beginning of the school year, but they are interested in reading longer chapter books as the year progresses. They want to be heard! They are very concerned with fair and unfair, right and wrong. They also like reading clubs, literature circles, guided reading, and reciprocal teaching.

—Katie Kanning, Stephanie McKee,
and Or-el McNamee, Third Grade Teachers

I have developed a *word study procedure:*.

Monday: The students are given 15 to 20 words and are asked to see whether they can decide how they should sort out the words into groups. The children cut out the word cards and find different ways to sort the words. The class goes through each word, one at a time, pronouncing it and discussing its meaning.

Tuesday: I ask the students to sort their words using the CVC and CVCe patterns or another pattern. Students needing extra help meet with me in a small group to practice the pattern again. The others paste their words onto a two-column chart that is labeled with the patterns on top to practice for homework.

Wednesday: Students complete the word hunt with a buddy. They look for the patterned words they have been studying and include other words that also fit the patterns found in their reading.

Thursday: The children are placed into groups of three or four to create a "word ladder." On a big piece of paper, divided into two columns, the children label the top of the paper with the new spelling patterns. Then as a group, they see how many more words they can come up with that fit the spelling patterns and that can be added to the chart paper.

Friday: The students are tested on the words. I dictate sentences using these words. They will have to spell the words correctly and use these spelling pattern words in sentences showing that they also know their meaning.

—Alexis Dubrowski, Third Grade Teacher

Once the student shows mastery on three days during the week in each area (pronunciation, meaning, and spelling, and has written a sentence demonstrating the ability to use the word correctly), the student is considered to have mastered the vocabulary word. Mastered vocabulary words are recorded on a Vocabulary/Spelling Mastery Form (Figure 5–10).

Decode-a-Word Bank. Students are instructed at the beginning of the third grade to gather words that they cannot sound out (decode) and to put these words in their word bank. Before placing a word in their bank (a decorated empty tissue box), students must underline the part or parts of the word that they are having difficulty pronouncing.

◆ First, they must decide whether there are any *peel-away prefixes* or *suffixes* (Cunningham, 2000). If there are, they must peel them away before trying to sound out the root word or look for any spelling patterns or word families that they can identify.

◆ Second, they should consult their decoding buddy to see whether, together, they can figure out how to sound out the word.

◆ Finally, they should consult their teacher during guided reading to go over the difficult words in their decode-a-word banks.

Fourth Grade

Developmental Background – By fourth grade, children have become more independent learners who are social, self-conscious, and interested in what others think about them. They are interested in learning new and interesting words, word origins, synonyms, and opposites. It is a great time to introduce spelling rules and spelling exceptions (spelling demons). Fourth graders are beginning to enjoy longer books, including novels, and are exploring different genres to see what piques their interest. Fourth graders also enjoy reading more emotional stories and can identify with characters more readily now because they are capable of empathizing and are excessively compassionate about the plight of others (Vail, 1991). Reading multicultural fables such as *Mufaro's Daughters*, chapter books and novels such as *Sounder*, and historical books such as *Martin Luther King* and *Lincoln: A Photobiography* can be highly motivational to this age group. Fourth graders are usually assigned to write book reports and are often required to respond critically or analytically to longer fictional works, including chapter books and novels.

Vocab-Automat-Activity

FIGURE 5-10

Teacher, aide, or student checks to see if the student being reviewed:
1. Pronounces the new vocabulary word correctly (P)
2. Knows the meaning of the new word (M)
3. Writes it in a sentence correctly (S)

A checkmark will be placed in each box each time the student correctly performs these three tasks. The word continues to be reviewed until checkmarks are awarded in each of the three areas for three different dates reviewed. For example, if a child is studying the word *goat,* the child will need to pronounce the word (P row), state the meaning of the word (M row), and write the word in a sentence (S row). The child will need to do this on three different dates, and then the word is placed on a Master List (below).

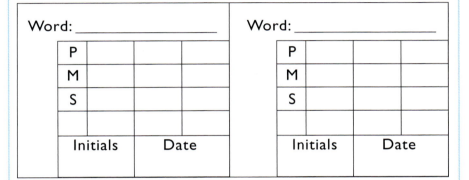

Vocabulary/Spelling
MASTER LIST REVIEW

NAME _____

01 _____	11 _____	21 _____	31 _____
02 _____	12 _____	22 _____	32 _____
03 _____	13 _____	23 _____	33 _____
04 _____	14 _____	24 _____	34 _____
05 _____	15 _____	25 _____	35 _____
06 _____	16 _____	26 _____	36 _____
07 _____	17 _____	27 _____	37 _____
08 _____	18 _____	28 _____	38 _____
09 _____	19 _____	29 _____	39 _____
10 _____	20 _____	30 _____	40 _____

(From Cowen, J. E. (1979). *Human Reading Strategies that Work.* Trenton, NJ: New Jersey Department of Education, by permission.)

Fourth grade is also a time when children must read more widely in nonfictional content areas across the curriculum. It is extremely important that fourth graders exhibit fluency of reading by the time they enter fourth grade because they are now assigned many textbooks and are expected to comprehend them. Formal reading instruction with phonics and comprehension instruction is no longer a part of the curriculum, and teachers assume fourth grade readers can "keep up." Many school districts across the country, including the New York City public schools, have experimented with holding third graders back if they cannot pass the formalized reading tests.

Statewide language arts and literacy standards are usually assessed at the fourth grade level. Most fourth grade teachers are aware that the term "fourth-grade slump" is often used to describe a frequently observed phenomenon at this grade level: a sudden drop in standardized test scores (Snow, Burns, & Griffin, 1998, p. 78). High-stakes testing at this grade level also assesses the children's ability to write more complex, multi-paragraph compositions and to use grammar, mechanics, and descriptive vocabulary in more sophisticated ways. Although this can be a stressful time for both student and teacher, it is also a challenging and rewarding experience because these fourth grade children are taught how to meet such high expectations.

Skills/Processes Fourth Graders Should Know – Following is a list of skills and processes that fourth graders should know:

◆ Continued development of a sophisticated understanding of sound–symbol relationships of blends, digraphs, and diphthongs

◆ How to sound out multisyllabic words with greater automaticity using structural analysis; fourth graders should have greater sophistication in recognizing many prefixes, suffixes, and roots

◆ How to sound out multisyllabic words with greater automaticity using syllabication; fourth graders should be using more sophisticated syllabication rules to unlock multisyllable words

◆ Reinforcement of common word families for decoding multisyllabic words and for learning compound words, contractions, and abbreviations

◆ How to use word derivations to unlock meaning of words across the various content areas, for example, social science, science, and mathematics

Instructional Strategies for the Teacher – Teachers in fourth grade should concentrate on building fluency in reading longer and more difficult materials, such as novels and textbooks. The emphasis should be on strategies that promote comprehension of text such as vocabulary development and study skills. It is important that fourth graders learn how to identify multisyllable words and understand their meaning within the context of meaningful text.

Rapid Recognition of Target Decoding Words. Research has proved that training children to thoroughly recognize a group of high-frequency target words automatically— that is, to decode or read each targeted word without hesitation to the point of rapid recognition—improves reading comprehension (Pressley, 1998). Students can be taught to decode words automatically by identifying the onset and rimes in words through direct teaching. Pair-share approaches such as peer-study-review, a process similar to studying for a spelling or vocabulary test, can be used. In this situation, the teacher places greater emphasis on training students to identify spelling patterns (phonograms or families). The teacher also provides brief training so students learn the meaning of the targeted words, while stressing the students' ability to decode words rapidly. Once comfortable with reading the words, the student is required to read the words without hesitation to the teacher with few mistakes. Only those words that are read without hesitation and mistakes are recorded as mastered. Otherwise, errant words are retaught and retested at a later time. The number of target words should depend on how many individuals or small groups of students can learn rapidly during a one-week time frame. It is recommended that teachers start with 10 words per week and work up to 20 or more per week, for a total of about 100 words per month.

Rapid Recognition of Targeted Vocabulary Words. Vocabulary words can be taught directly using similar techniques, including peer review, as explained earlier. The key to improving reading comprehension through direct teaching of new vocabulary words to fourth grade students within a five-month period is to engage them in multiple approaches in which they can encounter new words in a variety of novel contexts so they can form vocabulary-definition linkages over an extended period (Pressley, 1998). Vocabulary instruction is addressed in detail in Chapter 6.

Teacher–Student Conferencing. "Kid watching" or student observation/assessment is important for two reasons: (1) It informs the teacher about how individual children learn how to decode and/or read for meaning; and (2) it informs the teacher as to the optimum instructional skill level at which the child learns best, or in Vygotsky's terminology, determines the child's *zone of proximal development.* Reading conferences are opportunities for teachers to meet with individual or small groups of children in guided reading instruction (Fountas & Pinnell, 1996).

Decoding by Analogy: "If I know . . . then I know . . . and I know . . . " As explained earlier, if a student encounters a new, difficult multisyllable word, the student uses smaller words or patterns that he or she already knows to decode the unknown word. This is an important strategy that fourth grade students should be using to identify unknown multisyllable words.

Echo Reading. Echo reading is where the teacher reads a sentence or passage from the text and the student copies or echoes what the teacher has just read. It is suggested that the teacher begin modeling echo reading by using a few words at a time so that the student can mimic or echo the phrasing, inflections, rhythm, or cadence in the exact way modeled by the teacher. As the student's proficiency develops, longer sentences and even paragraphs can be used to practice echoing. This helps students to become fluent readers. This is an excellent strategy to use with ELLs and students with learning disabilities.

Neurological Impress Reading. Struggling readers for whom the echo reading approach and other fluency activities do not appear to be effective might benefit by using a one-on-one approach known as *neurological impress reading.* With this approach, the teacher sits closely behind the student so that the teacher can track the line of print for the student, reading slightly faster than the student, who tries to keep up with the speed and cadence of reading. The teacher does not stop when the student stumbles or misses a word but continues reading at the normally set pace, and the student picks up and continues along. Eventually, the student will take over the tracking, as well as taking on more responsibility while reading, and will start reading for speed and fluency.

Teachers' VOICES Fourth Graders

My fourth grade students' interests are much more varied, and through mini-lessons they are able to understand the different components that make their own writing more interesting, such as using dialogue and describing character traits.

—*Judith Hanratty, Fourth Grade Teacher*

My fourth graders especially enjoy long-term collaborative projects; they are at a stage when they can begin writing more critically about what they are reading and they can write longer paragraphs with main ideas, using compound sentences followed by descriptive details. I have developed a technique for helping one of my students who has great difficulty reading with fluency. He reads slowly and laboriously and when we met in a reading conference about this problem, he was willing to give my plan a try. First, he prereads a reading assignment for homework. Then in class, he reads a 10- to 12-sentence paragraph to me. I read the passage back to him, modeling fluency. He reads the same passage again, but this time with a big improvement in both cadence and fluency. He is beginning to read the punctuation better. He now reads in thought groups and, as a result, is reading with better comprehension.

—*Loraine Johnson, Fourth Grade Teacher*

Fifth and Sixth Grades

Developmental Background – Academically, fifth graders have begun to develop an increasing ability to deal with abstract thinking and to analyze fictional characters that are more multidimensional. Fifth graders are also able to concentrate for longer periods, to discuss books with greater analysis in reading circles, and to write more sophisticated essays and book reports.

Sixth graders are much more concerned about their appearance and like to be noticed in a positive way. As they enter this period of puberty, sixth graders appear to be in a constant state of disequilibrium and have a problem remaining on task. They appear to enjoy working in cooperative groups, perhaps because they enjoy interacting and socializing with each other; this can be a positive factor, but it can also be a major distraction to learning. However, when they are "on task," they are able to write long paragraphs with a topic sentence and detailed sentences, and they are capable of writing a strong introduction and conclusion. Sixth grade teachers report that their students are reading more complex, sophisticated chapter books such as *Holes* by Louis Sachar, *Number the Stars* by Lois Lowry, and *View from Saturday* by E. L. Konigsburg.

Fifth and sixth graders are also able to predict, infer, summarize, and find cause-and-effect relationships in their reading and writing for meaning. They appear to learn best when they can relate the content to their own lives. They prefer shared guided reading, brainstorming ideas, and mini-lesson projects, which they can record and present to the whole class. Many new middle school teachers hear the horror stories about discipline and unruly student behavior, but more experienced teachers express that middle school can be a terrific, fun place because the students are still children, excited about learning new things, yet they are sophisticated enough to think critically and be involved in problem-based learning. Fifth and sixth graders want to be challenged and are eager to learn new ideas, theories, and complex concepts.

Skills/Processes Fifth and Sixth Graders Should Know – Following is a list of skills and processes that fifth and sixth graders should know:

- Continued ability to identify and comprehend multisyllable words through structural analysis: identifying roots, prefixes, and suffixes
- Continued ability to read and spell multisyllable words through use of syllabication
- Ability to use grammatical conventions and rules in writing
- Ability to read fluently with speed and accuracy, reading at or above average speed when reading orally or silently
- Ability to understand and use in writing vocabulary words from content areas of science, mathematics, and social studies
- Ability to learn and comprehend multisyllable words through word derivations and the use of word sorts

Instructional Strategies for the Teacher

Quick Word Write. The "quick word write" activity can be used with individuals or with small and large groups of students. Simply instruct the students to write down as many words as they can within a given time frame (usually 5–10 minutes). It is beneficial to tie this activity to a content area or theme being studied. Students compete (with peers or themselves) during a given time frame, and the student with the highest percentage points and rate of accuracy is deemed the winner. In case there are ties, a runoff can be used, and the student who writes down the most accurate number of words within one minute wins. The quick word write can be used for practicing prefixes, suffixes, multisyllabic words, and compound words.

50-Word Automaticity Drills. The teacher can use a computer to generate a form that makes 5 boxes (columns) across the top of the page, and 10 boxes (rows) down the page for a total of 50 boxes. In these boxes, the teacher determines what word identification or spelling skill(s) to practice (for example, the open and closed vowel in multisyllable words can be practiced following the V/CV or VC/V pattern with words such as *o/pen* and *shiv/er*). Words following the rule can be placed randomly in the boxes for students to practice automatic retrieval or use with a buddy for practice. This can be made into a game to determine who read the most words correctly.

25 Prefix/Meaning Chunk Words. Students pair up to quiz each other's memory of 25 chunk words. These chunk words, selected by Cunningham (2000), are the 25 most widely used prefixes that are found in 97 percent of all prefixed words.

  By knowing the meaning of the chunk words, the student also knows the meaning of the 25 prefixes that make up hundreds of words. By peeling back the prefix and suffix of each new prefixed word, the student is in a better position to figure out the base or root word and better able to figure out the meaning of the word in question because of prior knowledge and familiarity with the meaning of the 25 prefix/meaning chunk words. This same activity can be done with suffixes and roots.

re-placement (back)	*sub*-marine (under)	*re*-arrange (again)	*mid*-night (middle)	*de*-odorize (take away)
in-dependent (not)	*semi*-final (half)	*im*-possible (not)	*trans*-portation (across)	*mis*-understand (wrong)
il-legal (not)	*under*-weight (below)	*ir*-responsible (not)	*un*-friendly (not)	*fore*-head (front of)
dis-honest (not)	*anti*-freeze (against)	*in*-vasion (in)	*im*-pression (in)	*inter*-national (between)
en-courage (in)	*super*-markets (really big)	*non*-living (not)	*pre*-historic (before)	*over*-power (too much)

Word Sorts for Older Students. Lists of words taken from fifth and sixth grade textbooks in science, social studies, and mathematics can be used in word sorts. The student working alone, with a buddy, or in a group sorts the words into different categories: those words that have prefixes, those words that have suffixes, and compound words. In addition, the words can be sorted according to subject matter, or similarity of meaning.

  For example, the following words are from sixth grade textbooks in science and social studies. Have the students sort these words into different categories based on suffixes and parts of speech.

archaeologist	generator	fluoroscope
astronomer	irrigation	magnetic
chemist	independently	measurement
condensation	celebration	meteorologist
erosion	constitution	senator

Summary

Word identification is an important part of a balanced approach to reading instruction, but it is not an end unto itself. In fact, phonemic awareness and phonic instruction cannot stand alone, but must be seen as part of an integrated, comprehensive approach to literacy that is seamlessly woven into the fabric of reading and writing as a whole. Learning the code, therefore, is dependent on the child's emerging literacy development of reading, writing, listening, speaking, and visualizing different forms of communication. This chapter has shown that literacy is a complex process, and that its ultimate goal is to teach children to read for meaning and enjoyment. This chapter shows the importance of phonics and skill development and their relationship within the whole-part-whole approach to learning how to read and think effectively. Indeed, it is through the balance of reading instruction that teachers can best help children access language efficiently and effectively to become successful readers.

Teachers' VOICES Fifth and Sixth Graders

When fourth graders were the oldest students in the elementary school, they tended to be bossy and overly confident. Now it appears to be the exact opposite as they are lowly fifth graders in the new grades 5 to 8 middle school.

—*Ms. Bucci, Fifth Grade Teacher*

My typical sixth grader is on the verge of puberty, or having already reached it, which causes many "ups and downs" in a sixth grader's life. My students also enjoy the opportunity to be a part of the lesson planning process where they can offer suggestions.

—*Dennise Ramsey and Diane Macritchie, Sixth Grade Teachers*

Technology Connections for Word Study

Technology Connection for Beginning Readers

Technology can offer pre-K, kindergarten, and first grade teachers an excellent resource for reinforcing many of the word recognition strategies and skills taught in the classroom. As mentioned in Chapter 4, some educators question whether the use of computers is appropriate for very young children. They emphasize that children younger than 6 years should be playing with manipulatives such as blocks, Legos, and dolls at this stage in development and should be engaging in imaginative play activities. However, technology can be integrated into a beginning reading classroom with careful thought, planning, and strict rules. Children should not be left in front of the computer alone, but should always have an adult available to guide them. Software programs should encourage more interactive and thoughtful engagement and not just be a drill-and-practice activity. Any use of technology should be integrated carefully into the curriculum so that the time spent on the computer is worthwhile, meaningful, and reinforces important concepts, skills, and strategies that were taught in the classroom.

The computer can be used in at least three different ways: (1) as a resource for the teacher to learn valuable information about current research and practices on how to teach reading; (2) as a resource for the student who can use the computer to engage in interactive activities on reading; and (3) as a class Internet project in which the whole class participates in a project that is found on the Internet and shares their activities with classes across the world. All three approaches are valuable contributions to the literacy classroom.

The sites that you will explore can be divided into four basic categories: (1) commercial sites that have been developed by publishers and organizations to support a book, television show, or to provide a service to teachers; (2) noncommercial sites that have been developed by schools, nonprofit organizations, universities, and government agencies to provide a resource; (3) author's Web sites in which an author or illustrator has developed a Web site to supplement and enhance books that he or she has published; and (4) teacher-made Web sites in which individual teachers around the world have published their own Web page or Web site as a resource to the students, parents, community, and world at large. This last group can be one of the most exciting developments in promoting literacy in the classroom because we are allowed to "peek" into another teacher's classroom and view published student work, daily routines, favorite resources, and even pictures of the children themselves.

The Internet has become an exciting place for teachers to learn about literacy and obtain valuable resources. There is a wealth of information available for teachers, and the list below should help you focus on a few recommended sites for beginning readers that emphasize word recognition, the alphabetic principle, and phonics instruction. These sites are only a few of the many sites available on the Internet for this age group. *When using any site, it is important that the teacher previews the site first before integrating it into the classroom.* Many sites change addresses quickly and may not be current; or there may be technical difficulty at a site and the server may not be working.

Additional teacher resources can be found on the *Literacy for Children in an Information Age* premium Web site for this chapter (**http://www. cengage.com/login**).

Starfall

http://www.starfall.com

Starfall is an online program designed to help students learn how to read. It is based on a methodology that includes phonemic awareness and phonics instruction. It has printable materials to accompany the program. This site is worthwhile for children in kindergarten through grade 4, or for those who need reading skill reinforcement.

Sesame Street Central

http://www.sesamestreet.org

http://pbskids.org/sesame/

Both of these sites have games, stories, and activities to reinforce reading that feature characters children will recognize.

ABC Teach

http://www.abcteach.com

ABC Teach is a great site for both children and teachers. It offers many different basic games and activities to reinforce beginning reading skills.

Seussville

http://www.seussville.com/

The Seussville site can be used after reading a Dr. Seuss book. Go to "Playground" for simple games and activities for young children.

Scholastic Kids: The Stacks

http://www.scholastic.com/kids/stacks/

This site reinforces basic skills and has interesting activities for kids of all ages.

Technology Connection for Intermediate Readers

Students who have mastered the basics of reading can visit many sites that reinforce word identification strategies. Many of these sites have games and activities that enable students to practice skills taught in the classroom. As explained earlier, some of these are commercial sites hosted by companies such as Scholastic; some have been created by nonprofit agencies, such as school districts or universities; some are the work of authors who wish to supplement their books with materials and services to their reader; and some have been created by teachers to use in their classroom. As always, it is important to evaluate any site before using it in a classroom to ensure that it meets the goals and objectives of the lesson plan to be implemented.

The sites below are designed for those students who have mastered the basics of reading and are on the road to fluency. These activities require more complex word identification strategies.

recommended general sites for kindergarten through sixth grade students. each provides a wide range of activities for all grade levels.

Mrs. Jacoby's Second Grade Site

http://www.geocities.com/ljacoby_2000/window.html

Ms. Jacoby's class Web site contains many different literacy activities for students to become engaged in.

Phonics Link

http://www.sdcoe.k12.ca.us/score/Phonics_Link/phonics.html

Phonics Link was developed by the California Department of Education to support the California Literacy Standards. This is a great resource for teachers on how to teach phonics, offering activities and lesson plans from pre-K through grade 6.

National Film Board of Canada

http://www3.nfb.ca/sections/thematique.php?id=122

The National Film Board of Canada has created an excellent site for kids of all ages with interesting literacy games and activities.

STRATEGY BOX

Teaching word Study in the Classroom

In the Introduction's opening scenario, Ms. Rosen was using specific strategies to teach word study to her students in their guided reading sessions. She uses the following strategies to promote literacy and to help her students become fluent readers:

1. She continuously assesses her students' progress and knows what their strengths and weaknesses are. She knows exactly what lessons she needs to teach, what skills to reinforce, and what strengths she can build on for each child in the class.

2. She groups her students according to their strengths and weaknesses and will move them into different groups continuously throughout the year based on the objectives of her lesson.

3. She explicitly teaches specific word identification strategies and phonics skills that her students need to become fluent readers.

4. She varies the reading material based on the students' abilities. She does not ask students to read material that is too difficult or too easy for them.

5. Struggling readers are given reading material that allows them to use many cuing systems to identify words: They can use the pictures to help identify words; the text is predictable and patterned to help them predict which words come next; and many of the words follow phonic patterns so that students can use orthographic cues to identify the words.

6. Students develop their own word banks that they use to reinforce word identification.

7. She uses short mini-lessons to focus on one particular phonics pattern. She pulls words from books that the class is reading and tries to keep the words and phonics lessons within the context of reading material they are using in the classroom.

8. She uses technology to reinforce word study skills taught in the classroom, which her students find highly motivating. She has a computer center set up where students can reinforce their word identification skills by using carefully selected software programs and visiting carefully chosen Web sites.

9. She involves parents in her students' literacy development. She tries to speak regularly with families of her ELLs and encourages them to read, write, and converse with their children in their native language so that the students will continue developing literacy skills.

10. She reinforces word identification for ELLs by pairing the English word with the word in their native language, whenever possible.

11. She recognizes that all her students have literacy skills that need to be developed and that some students are at different stages than others. She tries to be sensitive to the cultural and linguistic differences of her students and support all her students to become fluent readers.

12. She makes reading fun and reads books and poems that motivate the students. She tries to make her students laugh, and they enjoy reading quality literature from many different genres.

Final Thoughts

This chapter introduces the topic of word identification and why it is so important in learning how to read. The most critical skill for fluent word reading is the ability to recognize letters, spelling patterns, and whole words effortlessly, automatically, and visually. The basic goal of all reading instruction—comprehension—depends totally on this ability. A teacher should keep in mind that reading enjoyable text and responding to the text is the most important factor in developing literacy in beginning readers.

EXPLORATION   Application of Concepts

Activities

1. Observe a teacher teaching beginning reading in kindergarten or grade 1. Try to observe an exemplary master teacher who has been recommended. Determine how the teacher teaches word identification strategies such as phonics and reading comprehension skills. Indicate what techniques and approaches were successful and explain why. Discuss these approaches within a cooperative group or with another classmate, raising issues related to balanced reading instruction practice.

2. Reading has been compared with playing a piano, the engine of a car, and a symphony orchestra. With one or more members from your cooperative group, try to create your own analogy or metaphor related to the reading process. Illustrate your analogy, for example, using an art form, a graphic organizer, or poetry.

3. Divide into different groups. Each group should develop at least one lesson plan using different word identification strategies: phonics, syllabication, and structural analysis.

4. In a group, develop a word wall using word families demonstrating how onsets-rimes can be developed.

5. Explore the teacher resources available on the *Literacy for Children in an Information Age* premium Web site: http://www.cengage.com/login. Choose two of your favorite Web sites and share them with the class or small group. Be prepared to discuss how the sites promote word study in the classroom.

HOME–SCHOOL CONNECTION   Sounding Out Unfamiliar Words

Parents and guardians frequently ask, "How can I help my child sound out unfamiliar words?" First, it is always a good idea to meet with the teacher to make sure that anything being done at home is not conflicting with the classroom approach. Parents and guardians can reinforce teaching "word families" that share the same spelling pattern, or *rimes*. This approach, known as *onset-rime*, refers to the *onset*—the initial consonant (such as *b*, *c*, *l*) or blend(s) (such as bl, cr), and the *rime*—the spelling pattern that follows the consonant (*ack*, *all*, *it*, *ent*). For example, in the word *black*, *bl* is the onset and *ack* is the rime or word family.

When the child can't sound out a word like *black*, the parent or guardian simply tells the child that the word is pronounced *black*, and that the rime is pronounced *ack*. (The child repeats/echoes the parent and/or guardian.) The parent or guardian then asks, "What other words belong in the *ack* family? Some examples might be: *rack, crack, lack,* or *stack*. If the child can only give one word, the parent or guardian supplies others. A word card or slip should help the child learn the *ack* rime and other examples of words that belong to the same word family. This chapter has an extensive list of onsets and rimes that the teacher can send home. The teacher can work closely with the parents or guardian to help reinforce word study skills that are being taught in the classroom.

6 STRATEGIES TO PROMOTE VOCABULARY DEVELOPMENT

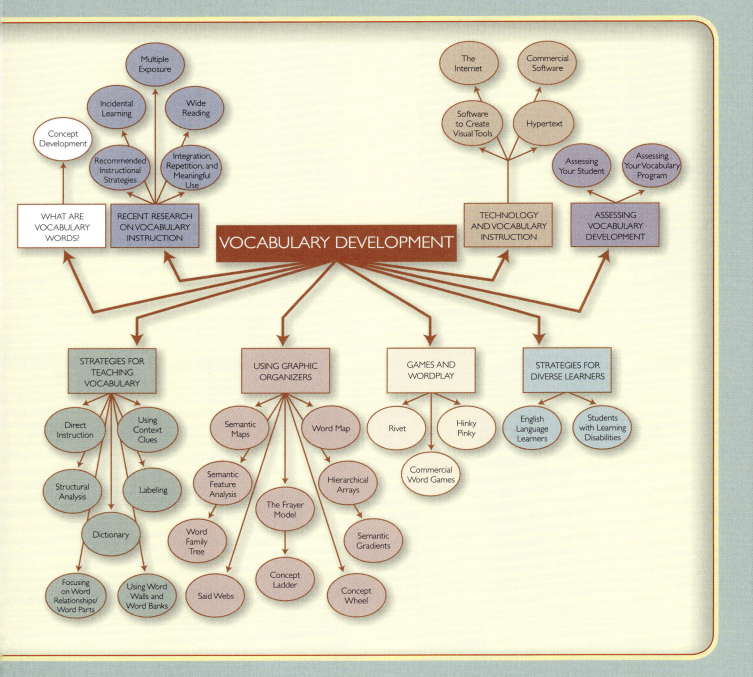

International Reading Association Professional Standards Addressed in this Chapter:

IRA STANDARD 1: FOUNDATIONAL KNOWLEDGE

Candidates have knowledge of the foundations of reading and writing processes and instruction. Candidates:

1.1 Demonstrate knowledge of psychological, sociological, and linguistic foundations of reading and writing processes and instruction.

1.2 Demonstrate knowledge of reading research and histories of reading.

1.3 Demonstrate knowledge of language development and reading acquisition and the variations related to cultural and linguistic diversity.

1.4 Demonstrate knowledge of the major components of reading (phonemic awareness, word identification and phonics, vocabulary and background knowledge, fluency, comprehension strategies, and motivation) and how they are integrated in fluent reading.

IRA STANDARD 2: INSTRUCTIONAL STRATEGIES AND CURRICULUM MATERIALS

Candidates use a wide range of instructional practices, approaches, methods, and curriculum materials to support reading and writing instruction. Candidates:

2.2. Use a wide range of instructional practices, approaches, and methods, including technology-based practices, for learners at differing stages of development and from differing cultural and linguistic backgrounds.

2.3 Use a wide range of curriculum materials in effective reading instruction for learners at different stages of reading and writing development and from different cultural and linguistic backgrounds.

IRA STANDARD 3: ASSESSMENT, DIAGNOSIS, AND EVALUATION

Candidates use a variety of assessment tools and practices to plan and evaluate effective reading instruction. Candidates:

3.1 Use a wide range of assessment tools and practices that range from individual and group standardized tests to individual and group informal classroom assessment strategies, including technology-based assessment tools.

3.2 Place students along a developmental continuum and identify students' proficiencies and difficulties.

3.3 Use assessment information to plan, evaluate, and revise effective instruction that meets the needs of all students, including those at different developmental stages and those from different cultural and linguistic backgrounds.

IRA STANDARD 4: CREATING A LITERATE ENVIRONMENT

Candidates create a literate environment that fosters reading and writing by integrating foundational knowledge, use of instructional practices, approaches and methods, curriculum materials, and the appropriate use of assessments. Candidates:

4.1 Use students' interests, reading abilities, and backgrounds as foundations for the reading and writing program.

4.2 Use a large supply of books, technology-based information, and nonprint materials representing multiple levels, broad interests, and cultural and linguistic backgrounds.

4.3 Model reading and writing enthusiastically as valued lifelong activities.

4.4 Motivate learners to be lifelong readers.

Key Terms

sight vocabulary words

reading vocabulary words

concept

attributes

integration

repetition

meaningful use

repeated readings

sustained silent reading (SSR)

direct instruction

indirect instruction

mini-lesson

structural clues

phonic clues

semantic clues

syntactical clues

context clues

structural analysis

affixes

labeling

classifying

word banks

denotation

connotation

graphic organizers

semantic maps

semantic feature analysis

hierarchical arrays

word family tree

semantic gradients

said webs

concept wheel

concept ladder

Frayer model

sheltered language approach

incidental learning

cognates

structured talk

content-area vocabulary

concrete aids

content-specific words

general-utility words

homonyms

homophones

homographs

idiomatic language

hypertext

receptive vocabulary

expressive vocabulary

Focus Questions

1. What are vocabulary words, and why is it so important to teach vocabulary instruction to children?

2. What does the research say about the best way to teach vocabulary?

3. Discuss how each strategy can be used in the classroom to promote vocabulary development: giving direct instruction, using context clues, focusing on word relationships, using word walls and word banks, using the dictionary, using graphic organizers, and playing word games.

4. What are some recommended strategies for vocabulary instruction to use with English language learners? With students with learning disabilities?

5. What are some ways that technology can be integrated into vocabulary instruction?

6. What are some recommended ways of assessing students' vocabulary acquisition?

Welcome to Mr. Crow's Third Grade Classroom: Helping Children Acquire Vocabulary Words

Michael Newman/PhotoEdit

The most enjoyable part of Mr. Crow's day "is helping my third grade students learn about words by reading interesting books." He believes that a rich vocabulary develops most effectively when new words and phrases are taught just *before, during,* and *after* children read. Today, he is going to introduce Madonna's children's book *The English Roses* (2003) to his third graders.

First, he asks if anyone knows Madonna—the *singer.* Several of the children respond by raising their hands and calling out some of Madonna's songs. Then, Mr. Crow asks the children if they know Madonna—the *author.* Mr. Crow announces that the book he will share and read with the class today is *The English Roses* by Madonna.

Before Mr. Crow begins to read the book aloud, he first highlights keywords by defining and illustrating them, either by reading them in a sentence or by discussing them further. For example, to explain the idiom ". . . . practically glued at the hip," he points out to the class that the four Rose sisters are always together. He asks the children, "What do you think this phrase could mean?" One child

answers, "*glued* means that the sisters are all 'stuck' together." Another says, "*Glued at the hip* means that they never leave one another's hip or side." Mr. Crow gives positive feedback to the students and then clarifies students' understanding by asking, "Do you think they are all gooey or sticky?" When the children understand the meaning of this phrase, Mr. Crow says, "These words can paint a picture for us so that we can imagine and understand things more clearly."

After predictions have been made about what the book is about, he reads it aloud to them, using shared reading techniques. During the reading, he points out key words and explains their meanings. After he finishes reading, he discusses the book with them, asking them if their predictions were correct, and having the students retell the story using their new vocabulary words As a follow-up, he places the children in several small groups and asks them to use their copies of *The English Roses* to identify any new words. They use different-colored markers to write these new words and phrases on long strips of paper that can be placed on the word wall or in a pocket chart. As the children work in their small groups, Mr. Crow provides direction and assists children who appear to be struggling with the assigned activity. He has the children use semantic maps and also plans to use the computer center to reinforce many of the words introduced today.

This scenario shows how Mr. Crow effectively teaches vocabulary to his third grade students using research-based strategies to support their reading comprehension. Mr. Crow teaches the vocabulary words within the context of an enjoyable story and helps the children visualize the words and "make them their own." As you go through this chapter, note specific strategies that you can use to teach vocabulary words to your students and thereby increase their comprehension of text.

What Are Vocabulary Words?

Despite that there is a body of formidable vocabulary research that indicates how critical word meaning development is in promoting reading comprehension, it continues to be overlooked as an integral classroom instructional strategy (Beck, Perfetti, & McKeown, 1982; Blachowicz, 1986; Blachowicz & Fisher, 2002; Johnson, 2001; National Institute of Child Health and Human Development [NICHD], 2000; Rupley, Logan, & Nichols, 1998/1999; Schwartz & Raphael, 1985; Stahl, 1986; Tennyson & Cocchiarella, 1986.) The consensus of literacy experts is that vocabulary has not been a hot topic for the past several years. Nevertheless, to become successful readers, students need to be engaged in the essential components of a balanced reading program that include various opportunities for teaching vocabulary, including direct instruction; active and deep processing of word meanings; multiple contextual situations; and practice applying these newly learned vocabulary words through reading and writing activities. A balanced vocabulary approach to reading demonstrates that "vocabulary is the glue that holds stories, ideas and content together and that it facilitates making comprehension accessible for children" (Rupley, Logan, & Nichols, 1998/1999). Until recently, the way to teach vocabulary has been debated; that is, should vocabulary be taught indirectly or directly? Or can word meanings be taught effectively using both approaches? Using literature to teach vocabulary, as shown in the scenario above, continues to gain much support and remains a viable and an important approach.

When we speak of vocabulary words, we really need to differentiate between two different ways the term *vocabulary* is used in literacy classrooms. There are sight vocabulary words and reading vocabulary words. **Sight vocabulary words** are those words that a reader can recognize automatically and instantaneously during the process of reading. The assumption with sight vocabulary words is that the reader can pronounce them correctly. This does not mean that the reader understands the referent meaning behind the word, and thereby comprehends the passage. In **reading vocabulary words,** the student may not be able to automatically recognize the word in print, but does know the referent meaning behind the word.

When a child says, "I don't know that word," the teacher needs to find out what that exactly means. Does it mean that the child cannot pronounce the word (it is not a sight vocabulary word), but the child knows the meaning of the word? Does it mean that the child can read the word, but does not know the meaning of it? Does it mean that the child cannot pronounce the word and also does not know the meaning? An effective teacher needs to find out the answers to these questions.

Armbruster, Lehr, and Osborn (2001) claim that there are four types of vocabulary words: (1) *listening vocabulary,* or words we hear and understand; (2) *speaking vocabulary,* or words we can use fluently in our speech; (3) *reading vocabulary,* or words we must comprehend when reading; and (4) *writing vocabulary,* or words we must use correctly when writing. It is therefore helpful to define what we mean by vocabulary word.

In this chapter, the phrase *vocabulary word* refers to those words that the reader does not know the referent meaning behind the visual configuration of the word. That would refer to any word that is not understood by the student whether it be in listening, speaking, reading, or writing. Therefore, if a child says, "I don't know that word," for the purpose of this chapter, we are assuming they do not know the meaning of that word.

Concept Development

The basis for understanding vocabulary words are concepts. A **concept** is an object or abstract idea that has specific characteristics or attributes that differ from other similar or different objects and ideas (Gagne, Wager, Golas, & Keller, 2005). There are two types of concepts: concrete and defined. A *concrete* concept is one that can be seen and, therefore, can be touched, smelled, or heard. A table is a concrete concept just as a chair, bed, and television are. Each can be defined by identifying their physical

100 Words You Need to Know

a	has	my	these
about	have	no	they
after	he	not	this
all	her	now	time
an	him	of	to
and	his	on	two
are	how	one	up
as	I	only	use
at	if	or	very
be	in	other	was
been	into	out	water
but	is	over	way
by	it	people	we
called	its	said	were
can	just	see	what
could	know	she	when
did	like	so	where
do	little	some	which
down	long	than	who
each	made	that	will
find	make	the	with
first	many	their	words
for	may	them	would
from	more	then	you
had	most	there	your

Courtesy of Guilherme Cunha

Displaying a list of essential sight vocabulary words in the classroom helps to ensure that students learn and use them.

attributes, such as a table has four legs and a hard surface, and is flat on top. A *defined* concept is one that is abstract and cannot be defined by physical attributes but by its abstract definition. Examples of defined concepts are love, democracy, happiness, and conservation.

When looking at concepts, it is important to point out that many concepts share the same attributes, and therefore can cause confusion to children, especially English language learners (ELLs). Figure 6–1 shows how two concepts, *chair* and *bed*, can share many of the same attributes and be easily confused if not properly defined. The key attributes that distinguish these two concepts is how they are used, or their function. It is therefore important that a teacher carefully map out the attributes of concepts, including those that make the concept distinct from other similar concepts and might confuse students.

FIGURE 6-1

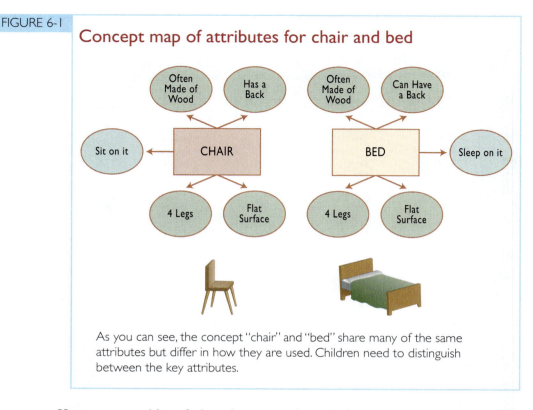

Concept map of attributes for chair and bed

As you can see, the concept "chair" and "bed" share many of the same attributes but differ in how they are used. Children need to distinguish between the key attributes.

How can we avoid confusion when we teach vocabulary words and their underlying concepts? The following steps are recommended for concept development:

1. Offer as concrete an experience as possible. Bring in a picture that illustrates the meaning of the vocabulary word. If it is a defined concept, try to provide concrete examples.

2. Discuss the attributes of the concept. Use a webbing technique to map out all of the attributes of the concept. Discuss each attribute separately.

3. Give examples and nonexamples of the concept, pointing out attributes that distinguish examples from nonexamples. For example, if the teacher is defining *chair,* he or she might bring in various pictures of different types of chairs, pointing out how the relevant attributes stay the same for each example. The teacher could then bring in examples of nonexamples, especially those nonexamples that share many of the same attributes, such as a table, a desk, and a bed. The teacher should then point out the attributes that distinguish one concept from the other.

4. Have students try to identify other examples and nonexamples. At this time, the students identify examples of the concept and also identify nonexamples explaining why they are not instances of the concept.

5. Have students practice applying the concept in various situations for reinforcement and retention. It is important to remember that true understanding of the concept goes beyond just being able to recite the definition and requires the student to apply the concept in varied situations with the teacher providing guidance and feedback.

Concept development is the foundation for vocabulary growth and reading comprehension. It is essential to teach the basic concepts behind the meaning of a word; otherwise, confusion can arise quickly. An example of this happened in a college classroom where preservice teachers were learning how to teach a science lesson by demonstrating a hands-on lesson to the class. There also happened to be a few children in the class who could give feedback to the future teachers. The lesson was about the property of different substances such as liquids, gases, and solids, and was designed for fourth or fifth grade students. The preservice teachers introduced the lesson by preteaching the vocabulary words, which were located on a poster. One teacher got up in front of the class and read each word and its definition to the class. One of the words was *property*, which was the key concept that this lesson was based on. Without any reinforcement of the key vocabulary words, the lesson progressed. After the lesson was over, the instructor asked one of the children, "So what does *property* mean?" The child answered, "That's what my mom and dad own . . . like my house." Evidently, the child had missed the key concept of the lesson. At the beginning of the lesson, the concept of *property* should have been mapped out to identify its attributes, and examples and nonexamples should have been shown. In addition, the teacher should have carefully pointed out that this word is a homograph (a word that is spelled the same but has different meanings) and reviewed the attributes of each meaning. By carefully focusing on concept development of key vocabulary words, the lesson would have been much more effective: the children would not have concluded erroneous misconceptions, and the teachers would have built a solid foundation for developing more concepts related to the lesson.

Recent Research on Vocabulary Instruction

Recommended Instructional Strategies to Use in the Classroom

According to research findings, the knowledge of a wide range of vocabulary words and their meanings is one of the major predictors of a child's reading comprehension ability (Beck, Perfetti, & McKeown, 1982; Nagy, 1988). Children develop their understanding of words in a variety of ways that accrue through indirect listening and reading contextual experiences. *Research supports that direct and explicit instruction of vocabulary is an effective and necessary approach in the classroom* (NICHD, 2000; Snow, Burns, & Griffin, 1998).

Preteaching of new vocabulary before reading in the content areas has shown to be particularly effective when direct instructional approaches are used (Johnson, 2001; Nagy, 1988). In fact, long-term vocabulary instruction that is taught directly, explicitly, and over time to motivated readers is especially effective when specific new words are introduced just before the actual reading of meaningful text (Adams, 1990); this is illustrated by the opening scenario that describes Mr. Crow's lesson in teaching new word meanings. Nagy (1988) concludes that when teachers reinforce instruction by modeling these new words through the use of definitions, discussions, and illustrations, significant reading comprehension improvement can result.

Children use their knowledge of learning words by applying these new labels to develop a greater understanding of known content and newly introduced concepts. Children can learn new words through context, word derivations, dictionary study, semantic mapping, technology/computer software, and games or wordplay. Word learning flourishes best when the preteaching of vocabulary is related to the texts students are about to read and to which they have been motivated to read. According to Nagy (1988), the primary purpose of effective vocabulary instruction is to have a knowledgeable teacher choose research-based strategies and vocabulary learning activities proved to maximize the students' reading comprehension. Children can also be taught to select unknown words from a text they are reading, which becomes a reliable source for maximizing the effectiveness of vocabulary and reading comprehension learning. Otherwise, time spent on vocabulary instruction that is unrelated to the text is usually unproductive, unless the instruction is about *learning how to learn* and the purpose is metacognitive by design.

Marilyn Jager Adams (1990) has researched studies and methods to determine what kinds of vocabulary instruction are most effective. She concludes that "Across studies, methods in which children were given both information about the words' definitions and examples of the words' usages in contexts resulted in the largest gains in both vocabulary and comprehension measures" (p. 147). Therefore, it is important that teachers explicitly teach the definitions of vocabulary words, and then provide examples of how each word is used in different types of text.

The National Reading Panel's (NICHD, 2000) findings echo many of the research conclusions described throughout this chapter, including that "reading vocabulary is crucial to the comprehension processes of a skilled reader" (p. 43). As a result of this important research conclusion, there are several implications for instructional practice:

- Direct instruction of vocabulary is required for specific text.
- Repetition and multiple exposures to vocabulary in context are important.
- Vocabulary learned in specific content areas can be used in many contexts and facilitate comprehension in different content areas.
- Computer vocabulary instruction shows positive learning gains over traditional methods; therefore, it should be used advantageously.
- Preinstruction of vocabulary words before reading can facilitate both vocabulary acquisition and comprehension.
- Richness of context for vocabulary learning is important.
- Active student participation with multiple exposures and approaches to learning new word meanings results in optimal learning.
- Vocabulary assessment and evaluation procedures can result in improved instruction.
- Combining the teaching of definitions with context, meaning, and usage can have effective results that lead to improved comprehension.
- More reading is needed to help children understand difficult words embedded within complex sentences.

Integration, Repetition, and Meaningful Use of Vocabulary Words

Nagy (1988) introduces three principles of vocabulary instruction that lead to improved comprehension: integration, repetition, and meaningful use. **Integration** involves showing the relationship of new information to what we know by connecting new words with familiar concepts and experiences. Approaches to accomplishing integration include activating background knowledge and assessing student background knowledge as a basis for reading and writing. Other proven effective ways of integrating unknown words to children's background knowledge include:

1. Semantic mapping
2. Categorizing words
3. Relating new words to familiar words or concepts
4. Brainstorming, mapping, and prereading activities

TEACHSOURCE VIDEO CASE

A Visit to Ms. Rosenblatt's Classroom: Using Word Sorts and a Question Generating Strategy to Develop Vocabulary

When we enter Ms. Rosenblatt's third grade classroom, we sense that this is a very organized, orderly, and secure place for children to feel comfortable about reading to learn. The walls are cheerfully decorated with student work, word walls, word charts, visual tools, and graphic organizers.

The children are busy working independently at their desks, clustered in groups of four, and are called to the reading area by Ms. Rosenblatt in their respective cluster groups. They are told that they will learn many new words and a new strategy called "I wonder." Using a "think aloud," Ms. Rosenblatt begins modeling the "I wonder" strategy using word sorts to form an "I wonder" question. She shows the children how to sort the words in categories based upon content, meaning, or any other attribute they wish to use. Once the words are sorted into a category, she models how to generate a question starting with the phrase, "I wonder. . . ."

The students are divided into pairs by Ms. Rosenblatt and given their own sets of words to sort. The children work with their partners to sort the words and generate their own "I wonder" questions. They write these questions down on sticky notes so that they will be able to share them with their classmates.

Once the children indicate that they are ready, they are called up to the chart that Ms. Rosenblatt has prepared in advance, which is placed in front of the room. Pairs of students are called to the front of the class to post their questions on the chart labeled "parking lot" and to read their questions to the class. Some of the questions that the students ask are: "I wonder if this text is about animals in their habitat?" and "I wonder who was exploring animals in Africa?" After all the pairs had a chance to share their questions, Ms. Rosenblatt reads a portion of a book about Jane Goodall to the class and gives the children time to re-sort their words, using the context of the story to make further connections. The students now use two or three words to create their own sentences related to the passage and also to create illustrations to accompany their sentences.

Ms. Rosenblatt ends the lesson by summarizing and asking the children to think about how the word sort

activity and the "I Wonder" strategy helped them with their reading comprehension. The children are quick to give many reflective responses before Ms. Rosenblatt tells the children that previewing the text and the words in context will give them the foundation needed to read the biography of Jane Goodall successfully.

The word sort and question-generating strategy that Ms. Rosenblatt used shows that preinstruction of vocabulary words before reading can facilitate both vocabulary acquisition and comprehension. It also shows that when she read the passage from the book about Jane Goodall, the students' questions became more meaningful and they used the words in more thoughtful, appropriate sentences.

In reviewing Ms. Rosenblatt's lesson, she used the following strategies:

- Using a Think Aloud to model a key reading comprehension strategy
- Using direct instruction of vocabulary to increase reading comprehension
- Using repetition and multiple exposures to vocabulary words in context
- Teaching vocabulary words from the content area of science that would be useful to her students in many different contexts
- Preteaching vocabulary words before reading, which facilitates both vocabulary acquisition and comprehension
- Having students try to predict the word meanings from word sorts and context
- Having her students generate questions using the words
- Having the students reflect on what they learned and how this strategy will help them become better readers

Questions:

1. How could Ms. Rosenblatt incorporate technology into her vocabulary lesson? What are excellent websites to reinforce vocabulary development?
2. What other strategies could Ms. Rosenblatt use to promote vocabulary development before the students read their book about Jane Goodall?

Go to www.cengage.com/ login to register your access code for the premium website for *Literacy for Children in an Information Age*, where you can watch an in-depth video exploration of Ms. Rosenblatt's classroom and to see how she used these valuable strategies.

Repetition helps develop automatic knowledge of word meanings that is important to reading comprehension. A limited knowledge of vocabulary meaning could interfere with reading comprehension. This negative effect on reading comprehension is sometimes referred to as "verbal efficiency hypothesis" or "bottleneck hypothesis" and is used to illustrate the reader's inability to know keywords that are necessary for understanding the text. One solution is to provide several opportunities to read the text (repeated readings), or to see words several times in context so that these multiple encounters with the new vocabulary help the reader figure out the meaning of the essential words that are masking the reader's understanding of the passage.

Meaningful use is an important research discovery, indicating that vocabulary learning is most beneficial when many opportunities for active participation in *deep processing* of word meaning occurs, rather than simply learning its definition. Many children learn rote definitions based on the simple task of having to "look up words" in the dictionary. However, these same children might have a much more difficult time when asked to use the same words in a complete sentence or to use them properly when speaking. Therefore, it is important that children learn to process words meaningfully, and until they do, they will not have meaningful use of these newly introduced words.

Incidental Learning

Research (NICHD, 2000) shows that children can learn a great number of words incidentally through context by engaging in oral conversations, listening to teachers, having adults read to them, and reading independently in school and at home. Children build most of their vocabulary understanding through context—perhaps as much as 85 percent or more—compared with learning words through direct vocabulary instruction. Therefore, it is important that teachers provide opportunities for children to continue their development of oral language.

Social interaction provides opportunities for children to learn vocabulary through spoken language. As they speak and listen to others speak, they continue to learn new words as a result of this form of communication. Rosenblatt (1978) has studied the effects of social communication, or transactional dialogue among children, and indicates that children in such environments improve their vocabulary, speech, and comprehension. Johnson (2001) indicates similar results in studies that engaged children in developing their use of oral language. Johnson cites the following five major benefits:

1. Increasing student talk and reducing teacher talk enables students' vocabularies to grow significantly.

2. Important progress in oral language development occurs when students have opportunities to talk and to learn via storytelling, word games, improvisation, creative dramatics, and role-playing.

3. Increasing oral communication opportunities enables students to construct knowledge and to learn content using oral language as the medium for learning.

4. Facilitating student opportunities to lead discussions and projects in the classroom is central to oral language development.

5. Learning to display their knowledge through oral language, students develop opportunities for improving vocabulary, as well as their confidence in communicating their competence.

Researchers identify several dominant social functions that teachers need to consider in planning instructional opportunities for improving students' language and vocabulary through context. Research shows how oral language skills can flourish in language-rich environments where students are encouraged to practice their verbal communication skills in collaborative groups and in other social functions by conversing and discussing, seeking information, informing, persuading, and imagining and telling stories (Johnson, 2001).

Multiple Exposure to Vocabulary Words

The use of **repeated readings** and multiple exposures to vocabulary materials, including fiction and nonfiction texts, have shown that significant vocabulary gains result with younger children, as early as prekindergarten, kindergarten, and first grade (NICHD, 2000). Similarly, results from scientific research studies conducted by Kameenui, Carnine, and Freschi (1982) show that providing repeated information on difficult vocabulary with immediate feedback also helps improve vocabulary and reading comprehension with students in grades 4 through 6. As children start using the computer to read more and more information, this should also create more opportunities for incidental learning for a new, growing audience of readers who are not prone to reading from the more conventional or linear-style text formats.

Adams (1990) also finds that repeated reading of text can produce marked improvement in word recognition, fluency, and comprehension. Repeated readings may increase the reader's appreciation of the syntax of passages, or the grammatical structure of the passage. Active readers, who frequently read books for pleasure, often comment that the author "is an excellent writer." Basically, what this comment refers to is the way the author constructs a sentence syntactically and how this grammatical structure adds to the total pleasurable experience of reading. This appreciation can also affect how the reader constructs sentences in writing, inducing the writer to take risks and construct syntactically interesting sentences.

Adams also points out that when children come to an unknown word, they must process the spelling—the orthographic structure–of the unknown word; when they skip unknown words, no learning can occur. After working over a new word, the child should return to the beginning of the phrase and then the sentence, rereading the whole passage. Rereading will thereby improve comprehension and fluency. Improvements in phrasing will also occur when children are asked to reread the passage along with an expressive model.

Teachers' VOICES Vocabulary Strategies

One of the objectives for my students in vocabulary development is that they will increase their vocabulary by finding unfamiliar words in reading passages and by completing the "detective" strategies.

1. Students will find an unfamiliar word in their reading and mark it using a sticky note or highlighter tape.

2. The student must first try to "guess" what the word means using "context clues."

3. Next, the student can complete one or more of these activities in their language arts notebook:

a. Write the definition of this word.

b. Use this word in a sentence.

c. Find a synonym and antonym for this word.

d. Draw a picture showing that he or she understands what this word means.

e. Teach the new word to a friend.

f. Was the first guess at this word a good one? Why or why not?

—*Marybeth Kopacz, Third Grade Teacher*

Wide Reading and Vocabulary Development

Studies demonstrate that individuals learn new words at a rate of about 3,500 each year until age 30; it stands to reason that most of these words are learned incidentally through the context of recreational reading (Johnson, 2001). Therefore, it is important to engage students in a great deal of reading, particularly at their independent level. Despite recent findings by the National Reading Panel (NICHD, 2000), which conclude that no appreciable improvement in reading comprehension resulted from independent classroom reading practices (that is, **sustained silent reading [SSR]**), further studies are required to investigate this widely used practice, which is favored by many teachers and students. As such, one important way to help children develop vocabulary is to encourage them to read extensively both at home and in the classroom. In so doing, these children will encounter new words repeatedly through independent reading. The opportunity to read in the classroom is extremely useful with regard to struggling readers, including students with learning disabilities and ELLs, who are less likely to read for recreational purposes when at home. These children require extensive vocabulary reinforcing opportunities that can be derived through extensive reading. Block and Mangieri (2002) believe there are many reasons to maintain recreational reading such as SSR:

> Students who spent more time in recreational reading activities (a) scored higher on comprehension tests in grades 2, 4, 8, and 12; (b) had significantly higher grade point averages; and (c) developed more sophisticated writing styles than peers who did not engage in recreational reading. (pp. 572–573)

After reading, children should be paired or grouped to form reading circles, enabling them to raise questions, discuss their common reading experiences, and/or write personal reactions about their readings in their journals. Meanwhile, from their readings, they should have been encouraged to list new vocabulary words, which they should explore with their peers and teacher, much as Adams (1990) suggests. Furthermore, Johnson (2001) recommends instruction that includes independent word identification strategies that allow students to learn words independently, automatically, and at an accelerated rate.

In summary, from a comprehensive analysis of vocabulary research, it is safe to add that there is no one vocabulary approach that works the best, but rather, to be effective, vocabulary instruction must use a variety of approaches, including direct and indirect methods. Classroom programs must emphasize the value of children reading a wide variety of rich fiction and nonfiction literature from which words are learned. Instruction should emphasize the importance of technology and provide strategies for learning new words such as analyzing prefixes and suffixes or figuring out the meaning of a word from clues in the passage. The more active the learner, the more exposure the student will have to words in rich contexts, ensuring better word retention, fostering a deeper appreciation of learning new words, and ultimately promoting better reading comprehension.

Reading a wide variety of fiction and nonfiction literature increases children's vocabulary development.

Courtesy of Guilherme Cunha

Strategies for Teaching Vocabulary

It is essential that vocabulary instruction be an everyday part of literacy instruction in the classroom. Vocabulary knowledge directly impacts reading comprehension and overall school achievement in all content areas, but it is a vastly underemphasized area in the curriculum. Research informs that the best way to increase vocabulary development in children is through reading rich and varied types of text that engage the reader. Preteaching of vocabulary before reading is also recommended as part of the prereading activities, as well as teaching students how to infer meanings of unknown words through the context of the sentences as a during-reading activity. Postreading activities should stress vocabulary development and reinforce new conceptual learning.

Although vocabulary is critical to reading at all stages of development, vocabulary demands increase substantially in about the fourth grade because of the use of textbooks and emphasis on content areas such as social studies and science. Students with poor vocabulary development are especially vulnerable to difficulties in reading comprehension from the middle elementary grades onward. Furthermore, lack of vocabulary may affect school achievement in written expression, mathematics, social studies, and science (Spear-Swerling, 2006).

Teachers need to use many different instructional strategies to teach vocabulary development because there is no one vocabulary approach that works the best. Vocabulary instruction must include both direct and indirect instruction. **Direct instruction** involves the teacher explicitly teaching vocabulary as part of the curriculum through preteaching activities, an emphasis on strategies that the student can use to improve word retention, and understanding and reinforcement of vocabulary in postreading activities. **Indirect instruction** occurs when the teacher establishes a literacy-rich classroom that emphasizes rich literature, wordplay, read-alouds of different types of books, and a supportive environment that encourages social interaction and use of language. By using both direct and indirect instruction in vocabulary, the teacher should be emphasizing the value of rich literature, the importance of technology, and the use of engaging activities in which children can make words "their own." The more active the learner, the more motivated the student will be to read text, ensuring better word retention and better reading comprehension. The strategies described in this section should all be part of a literacy classroom's emphasis on vocabulary development.

Direct Instruction of New Words

Although a large proportion of a child's total vocabulary is learned through reading, conversation, and listening (indirect instruction), it is important that students learn new words through various teacher-directed instructional strategies as well. A consistent and recognizable approach to teaching new words will benefit the students, who can then model the same approach when they come to a new word. This is especially helpful for students with learning disabilities and ELLs who need a systematic approach to learning new words. The following strategy can be taught in a **mini-lesson,** a short teacher-directed lesson (approximately 10 minutes or shorter) that involves the whole class or a small group of students. The following steps can be adapted and expanded to suit individual classrooms and to meet individual student's needs:

Teachers' VOICES Teaching Tip on Vocabulary

Read-alouds play a critical role in the development of vocabulary and concepts. The books provide background knowledge that some children may not have experienced. The children enjoy listening to stories about weather, seasons, planting seeds, different animals, different lands, and much more. Through these read-alouds, the children develop basic vocabulary and information necessary to comprehend written texts.

I read the book *Butterfly* by Susan Canizares to my students in the spring. This book has colorful photos of butterflies, caterpillars, eggs, and chrysalis that fascinate the children. It also shows the insect body parts, feelers, wings, shell, and more to illustrate the information and to reinforce new vocabulary words. The children get excited and are like sponges absorbing all the new information. I list the new words on chart paper as the children identify them while rereading the story. I type the new words in a sentence that also helps to define the word. The sentences are displayed on the wall together with the students' life cycles of the butterfly. I also add the new vocabulary words to the word wall.

A word sort can be made by using pictures from the Internet or cut out from magazines and pasted onto 4" X 4" colored paper. The vocabulary word should be pasted onto the back of the paper for self-checking. On another sheet of 4" X 4" colored paper, the student can paste the vocabulary word. The children can work individually or in groups to match the words with the correct pictures and to group them in order.

The students enjoy playing Hangman using the new vocabulary words. Hints are given using meanings of the vocabulary words. I found a great website (http://superkids.com) that allows the children to make word scramble puzzles, word searches, and many other vocabulary challenges. I use these activities with the new vocabulary words and my first graders love them.

—*Patricia L. Hook, First Grade Teacher*

1. *Pronounce the word:* The first step in teaching new words is to have the students correctly pronounce the word. This will also support learners in decoding the word while supporting auditory and visual memory (Shaywitz, 2003). Have all students say the word out loud together two or three times. If it is a long and/or unusual term, it is beneficial to have the students pronounce each syllable. For older children, this can be done quickly, emphasizing each syllable instead of pausing. For example, "A new word we are going to learn today is *transportation*. Please say the word with me now: 'Transportation.' Good! Now let's pronounce each syllable: 'trans-por-ta-tion.' Excellent! Let's say the word again: 'transportation.' Great!"

2. *Explain the word:* The teacher should provide a clear explanation of the meaning of the word, using language that is familiar and understood by the students. It usually is not helpful to read directly from the dictionary because, as stated earlier, definitions alone will not be a meaningful learning experience for students. If possible, provide a synonym or known phrase to help the student understand the meaning of the word. For example, "The word *transportation* means the act of carrying something from one place to another. When we go on our field trip next week, you will be provided transportation to the zoo by going on the bus."

3. *Provide examples of the word:* Provide concrete examples of the word, preferably drawn from a variety of different contexts, not only referring to the text but to the students' own experiences. It is helpful for the teacher to provide the first example and then have students generate their own examples using the new word in a complete sentence. This allows the students to "make the word their own" and allows them to become more comfortable in using the word. For example:

   TEACHER: The United States has built a system of transportation that helps us carry goods from one state to another.

   STUDENT #1: Transportation of wheat is shipped by trains traveling across the country.

   STUDENT #2: Trains, cars, and airplanes provide transportation for people.

4. *Elaborate on the word:* Have the children elaborate on the word by drawing pictures, developing graphic organizers, and generating their own additional examples. Have

students write sentences and stories using the words and develop word games using the new word. Have them study the words to figure out if there are any prefixes, suffixes, and root words. For example, "Draw a picture of something that provides transportation and explain what it is transporting," or "Write the word *transportation* in the middle circle of this web and write down five different things that provide transportation in your town."

5. *Assess the word:* It is important to incorporate continuous informal assessment into the regular classroom routine. Quick informal checks for understanding of vocabulary words can occur during guided reading sessions or individual conferencing with each child. More formal quizzes and tests also can be used, but it is helpful to stay away from simple memorization or matching tasks and require students to demonstrate an understanding of the word by asking for students to write original sentences and to evaluate whether the words are used correctly in sentences.

The above strategy is a foundational starting point for teaching vocabulary words explicitly in the classroom through direct instruction. Students will not learn a new word the first time they encounter it and must be exposed to it multiple times in multiple contexts. Therefore, a variety of instructional techniques must be used that actively engage the student in activities that will foster the students' word consciousness and increase their understanding of words in speaking, reading and writing, and listening.

Using Context Clues

One of the most important ways that children learn new words is incidentally through the context of recreational reading. Therefore, it is important to engage students in plenty of reading, particularly within their comfort zone or independent level. Children learn these new words by searching for clues within the sentence or paragraph that would give them an indication of what the unknown word might be. By using the context or surrounding passages to unlock meaning, children become word detectives and learn that they can comprehend sentences when they do not know every single word in the passage.

To unlock the meaning of unknown words, children can use four types of clues:

◆ **Structural clues** where they analyze the prefixes, suffixes, and roots to unlock the meaning

◆ **Phonic clues** where they use phonic patterns to determine how to pronounce the word

◆ **Semantic clues** where they search for synonyms or other phrases that would indicate the meaning of the unknown word

◆ **Syntactical clues** where the student will try to determine what part of speech the unknown word is, and then determine whether that helps unlock the meaning of the word.

It is important that teachers model how to use **context clues** to discover the meaning of new or difficult words. First, the teacher needs to choose *context-rich sentences* with which to model the activity. These are sentences that provide rich clues to help students uncover difficult words. For example, the following sentence does not really tell us much about what the word *malicious* means: "The boy is being malicious." We know it is an adjective and describes the boy, but that is about the only clue we can gather. This would not be a good sentence to use to model this strategy. However, the following sentence gives many more clues about the definition of the unknown word: "The boy was malicious because he was being mean to the young children in the school yard by teasing them and calling them names." In this sentence, there is a synonym for malicious: "being mean." In addition, the sentence provides clues as to how the child was being malicious: "teasing them and calling them names." The second sentence would be a much better sentence to model how to use semantic clues to unlock the meaning of words. In addition, this word *malicious* can be unlocked using structural analysis by looking at its prefix *mal-*, which means bad or evil. This prefix also follows the CVC (consonant-vowel-consonant) pattern with a short vowel sound. The suffix *-cious* is a common suffix that connotes an adjective or describing word (such as delicious) and is always pronounced as *shus*. Thus, in this one sentence, we can use structural, phonic, semantic, and syntactical clues to help unlock an unknown word in a context-rich sentence.

The teacher should model this strategy with many different sentences. He or she can gather context-rich sentences with challenging words from literature or textbooks that the students are reading and model the strategy with the first sentence (Figure 6–2). The teacher can then have groups or buddies work together to try to figure out the unknown words using the four types of clues. When the groups are finished, they should share how they uncovered the meaning of the words and what specific clues helped them to be a detective.

The following steps will help children use context clues to unlock unknown words. A word detective should:

◆ Look for immediate words in the same sentence (before or after the unknown word).

◆ Look for words in sentences that immediately precede or follow the unknown word.

◆ Gather the clues to figure out the unknown word.

◆ Predict the meaning of the unknown word.

FIGURE 6-2

Context-rich sentences

Context-Rich Sentences from Children's Literature

1. Nothing pleased her more than to overhear the **vagabond** players tell of their adventures in this town and that along the road. (*Mirette on the Highwire* by Emily Arnold McCully)

2. Then they heard a **hideous** roaring that filled the air with terror and seemed to shake the ground. (*Saint George and the Dragon* by Margaret Hodges)

3. He was greeted by a **frenzied** barking of dogs. They burst through the stockade and rushed toward him, halting only a few feet away, **menacing** him so furiously that he dared not take another step. (*Sign of the Beaver* by Elizabeth George Speare)

4. Panic and **pandemonium** broke out among the travelers, and James Henry Trotter, glancing up quickly, saw the faces of a thousand furious Cloud-Men peering down at him over the edge of the cloud. The faces had almost no shape at all because of the long white hairs that covered them. There were no noses, no mouths, no ears, no chins--only the eyes were visible in each face, two small black eyes glinting **malevolently** through the hairs. (*James and the Giant Peach* by Roald Dahl)

5. Omri had never arrived at school with more **apprehension** in his heart, not even on spelling-test days. And yet he was excited too. (*Indian in the Cupboard* by Lynne Reid Banks)

- Reread the sentence to see whether the predicted meaning of the word seems correct.
- Check later with the dictionary, the teacher, or a classmate for verification.

Focusing on Word Relationships/Word Parts

Teachers and literacy experts recently reported that the vocabulary strategy they found most successful in the classroom was working with word relationships and word parts (Berne & Blachowicz, 2008/2009). Teachers help students learn about words by showing them how word parts and word relationships can help them comprehend text when they encounter an unknown word.

Synonyms and Antonyms: Synonyms are words that have the same or similar meanings. For example, a few synonyms for *smart* are *intelligent, brilliant, clever,* or *genius.* Synonyms can help a student's writing become more powerful and bring words to life. Brainstorming different meanings of a vocabulary word is an excellent strategy for generating synonyms.

An antonym is a word with the opposite meaning of another word. For example, a few antonyms for *bored* are *excited, thrilled, energized,* and *engaged.* Some words have only one antonym, such as black and white, while other words have many antonyms. Brainstorming is an excellent strategy for generating antonyms. Reading rich quality children's literature also develops readers' appreciation for different words and their relationships to each other.

Homonyms (Homophones): Homonyms (also called homophones) are words that sound the same but have different meanings and usually different spellings. Students often find homophones interesting and it can be fun teaching them! They can be taught as they come up in everyday spelling and reading, or they can be taught through direct instruction. Students find these type of sentences enjoyable to read and to compose:

The wind *blew* my *blue* shirt into the bushes.

Keesha *rode* next to us as we *rowed* the boat to the nearby road.

We have never *seen* such a wonderful *scene.*

Dad wanted a *site* for our new house that will be out of *sight.*

See Figure 6–3 for a list of 50 common homonyms.

Homographs: Homographs are words that are spelled the same and have different meanings and different origins. Some homographs are also heteronyms, which mean that they are spelled the same but have a different pronunciation, such as "I read the book yesterday" and "I will read the book today." Again, students often find working with homographs interesting and can compose their own sentences using homographs, such as those listed below.

He walked along the river *bank* so he could deposit his money in the *bank.*

After Tina *left* the show, she turned *left* at the next corner to go home.

My mother measured five *yards* so she could build a doghouse in our back *yard.*

If the judges are *fair,* our horse will win a ribbon at the *fair.*

See Figure 6–4 for a list of 40 common homographs.

Idiomatic Expressions (Idioms): Idiomatic expressions cannot be understood from the literal meanings of their words. Idiomatic expressions are often used within conversations to describe a situation. They are usually not acceptable in formal writing unless they are part of dialogue or used on purpose for emphasis. Some children might have trouble understanding these phrases, especially English language learners. Sentences with idiomatic phrases are:

It cost me *an arm and a leg* to buy that television.

It is *raining cats and dogs* outside.

Fifty Common Homonyms

Homonyms (also called homophones) are usually words that sound the same but have different meanings and usually different spellings.

ad (advertisement)	for (in favor of)	one (number)	son (male offspring)
add (addition)	fore (front part)	won (triumphed)	sun (star)
	four (number)		
allowed (permitted)		pail (bucket)	stake (post)
aloud (audible)	knew (did know)	pale (white)	steak (meat)
	new (opposite of old)		
ant (insect)		pain (discomfort)	steal (rob)
aunt (relative)	hair (on head)	pane (window glass)	steel (metal)
	hare (rabbit)		
ate (did eat)		pair (two of a kind)	tail (animal's appendage)
eight (number)	hear (listen)	pare (peel)	tale (story)
	here (this place)	pear (fruit)	
bare (nude)			their (possessive pronoun)
bear (animal)	heard (listened)	plain (simple)	there (at the place)
	herd (group of animals)	plane (flat surface)	they're (they are)
be (exist)			
bee (insect)	hoarse (husky voice)	right (correct)	threw (tossed)
	horse (animal)	rite (ceremony)	through (finished)
brake (stop)		write (inscribe)	
break (smash)	hole (opening)		to (toward)
	whole (complete)	road (street)	too (also)
buy (purchase)		rode (transported)	two (number)
by (near)	in (opposite of out)	rowed (used oars)	
bye (farewell)	inn (hotel)		wait (linger)
		sail (travel by boat)	weight (heaviness)
cell (prison room)	know (familiar with)	sale (bargain)	
sell (exchange for money)	no (negative)		ware (pottery)
		scene (setting)	wear (have on)
deer (animal)	made (manufactured)	seen (viewed)	where (what place)
dear (greeting; loved one)	maid (servant)		
		sea (ocean)	weak (not strong)
fair (honest; bazaar)	mail (send by post)	see (visualize)	week (seven days)
fare (cost of transportation)	male (masculine)		
		sew (mend)	weather (climate)
feat (accomplishment)	meat (beef)	so (in order that)	whether (if)
feet (plural of foot)	meet (greet)	sow (plant)	
	mete (measure)		which (what one)
find (discover)		some (portion)	witch (sorceress)
fined (penalty of money)	oar (of a boat)	sum (total)	
	or (conjunction)		
	ore (mineral deposit)		

(Adapted from Fry, E. B., & Kress, J. E. (2006). The Reading Teacher's Book of Lists, 5th edition. New York: Jossey-Bass.)

FIGURE 6-3

When he stayed home from school due to a cold, it was *a blessing in disguise.*

That test we took in biology was *a piece of cake!*

See Figure 6–5 for a list of idiomatic phrases.

Structural Analysis

One of the most important strategies to help students develop vocabulary is through **structural analysis,** or studying parts of words. Using meaningful parts of words includes identifying and learning the meanings of prefixes, suffixes, roots, base words, compound words, and even abbreviations. It is highly recommended that teachers have several resources in their classrooms that will help students learn word derivations and structural analysis, including age-appropriate dictionaries, thesauruses, and word history/etymological dictionaries and root/base word texts.

Common **affixes,** the term commonly used to refer to both prefixes and suffixes, are parts of words added on to the base word or root word. Affixes are important to study

Forty Common Homographs

Homographs are words that are spelled the same and have different meanings and different origins. Some homographs are also heteronyms, which mean that they have a different pronunciation; these are marked with an asterisk (*).

arms (body parts)	fair (beautiful; lovely)	miss (fail to hit)	spell (say the letters of a word)
arms (weapons)	fair (just; honest)	miss (unmarried woman	spell (magic influence)
	fair (bazaar)	or girl)	
ball (round object)			
ball (formal dance)	file (drawer; folder)	pine (type of evergreen)	tap (strike lightly)
	file (steel tool to smooth	pine (yearn or long for)	tap (faucet)
bank (place of financial business)	material)		
bank (row of things)		pitcher (container for	*tear (drop of liquid from
bank (land along a river)	fine (high quality)	pouring liquid)	the eye)
	fine (money paid as punishment)	pitcher (baseball player)	tear (pull apart)
bark (tree covering)			
bark (sound a dog makes)	firm (solid; hard)	pool (tank with water)	toast (browned bread slices)
	firm (business; company)	pool (game played with balls on	toast (wish for good luck)
bat (club)		a table)	
bat (flying animal)	fly (insect)		top (highest point)
	fly (move through the air	pupil (student)	top (toy that spins)
bear (large animal)	with wings)	pupil (part of the eye)	
bear (support; carry)			will (is going to)
	hide (conceal; keep out of sight)	rare (unusual)	will (deliberate intention
blow (hard hit)	hide (animal skin)	rare (not cooked much)	or wish)
blow (send forth a stream			
of air)	*lead (show the way)	rest (sleep)	yard (enclosed space around
	lead (metallic element)	rest (what is left)	a house)
can (able to)			yard (36 inches)
can (metal container)	lean (stand slanting)	ring (circle)	
	lean (not fat)	ring (bell sound)	
*close (shut)			
close (near)	left (direction)	root (underground part of	
	left (did leave)	a plant)	
down (from a higher to a lower		root (cheer for someone)	
place)	mine (belonging to me)		
down (soft feathers)	mine (hole in the earth to	saw (did see)	
	get ores)	saw (tool for cutting)	
duck (large wild bird)			
duck (lower suddenly)	*minute (sixty seconds)	sock (covering for foot)	
	minute (very small)	sock (hit hard)	

(Adapted from Fry, E. B., & Kress, J. E. (2006). The Reading Teacher's Book of Lists, 5th edition. New York: Jossey-Bass.)

FIGURE 6-4

because they help children learn the meanings of unknown words. Bear, Invernizzi, Templeton, and Johnston (2000) suggest modeling how words grow from base and root words. Students practice by working in small groups with word-tree graphic organizers to complete different word forms on individual branches (Figure 6–6).

Children can learn to unravel the meanings of words by using prefixes. Nearly two-thirds of all vocabulary words contain the prefixes *un, re, in,* and *dis;* and 18 other prefixes—*en/em, non, in/im, over, mis, sub, pre, inter, fore, de, trans, super, semi, anti, mid,* and *under*—account for 97 percent of all prefixed words (Cunningham, 2000). Prefixes are basically stable and easily learned and remembered by children because they are seen frequently in their reading materials and because their meanings are rather straightforward, appearing at the beginning of the word and maintaining the same spellings; for example, *real, unreal* (not); *do, redo* (again); *direct, indirect* (not); *appear, disappear* (opposite).

Suffixes are also few in number: *s/es, ed,* and *ing* account for 65 percent of all suffixed words. However, 87 percent of all words can be learned simply by including the following suffixes in the child's repertoire: *ly, er/or, ion/tion, ible/able, al, y, ness, ity,* and *ment* (Cunningham 2000). However, suffixes are not as consistent and are more difficult to learn and remember because they tend to be more abstract. It is

FIGURE 6-5

Idiomatic phrases

Idiomatic expressions cannot be understood from the literal meanings of their words. Idiomatic expressions are used often in conversation and informal writing; however, most are not suitable for formal writing. Students who are English language learners find idiomatic expressions particularly difficult. The following expressions should be taught in the same way that vocabulary words can be taught.

Kathryn *caught a cold* during vacation.
Fred and Jack don't *see eye to eye* on everything.
Sue has always been *afraid of her own shadow*.
Jim finished the paper *ahead of time*.
It cost *an arm and a leg* to buy a new television.
Dad is a *backseat driver*.
We need to *clear the air* after our fight.
Jane *got cold feet* when it was her turn to present.
We each *coughed up* a dollar.
Paul did not *crack a book* all weekend.
Samantha was *dead to the world* after a busy night.
Dave was *down in the dumps* all day.
Have Gary *drop me a line*.
Alicia *drove a hard bargain*.
The math quiz was *duck soup*.
The price goes up *every time I turn around*.
Joe's *eyes popped out* when he saw the bill.
We have *a fat chance* of earning enough to buy this.
Dot's *head was in the clouds*.
Sam was *fishing* for the answer during the test.
It takes Tom *forever and a day* to get out the door.
The party was *for the birds*.
I'd *give my right arm* to own a boat.
That was a *half-baked idea!*

We all saw the *writing on the wall*.
We're all *in the same boat*.
Keep your *eye on the ball* and you'll do fine.
Jane *lost her marbles* after her father yelled at her.
Adam kept his *nose in a book* before the test.
His *days were numbered*.
He's not *playing with a full deck*.
Dinner was *on the house*.
Alex *got up on the wrong side of the bed*.
That movie really *opened my eyes*.
The car *came out of nowhere* and almost hit us.
The teacher gave us a *song and dance* about doing our homework.
We need to *stick together* to finish this project.
John *took the rap* for the others.
Do you *get the picture?*
He didn't *know the ropes* yet as he was new.
Keep it under your hat and don't tell anybody.
She's been *walking on air* all day after hearing the news.
We're not *out of the woods* yet.
He *lost his temper* for no reason.
Straighten up the house before you leave.
Don't *get hung up* on the problem.
She got *hung up* on one problem.
Frank's grandmother has a *green thumb*.

(Adapted from Fry, E. B., & Kress, J. E. (2006). The Reading Teacher's Book of Lists, 5th edition. New York: Jossey-Bass.)

recommended that teachers use a variety of hands-on word sorts and games such as Greek and Latin Jeopardy that are highly motivational and provide many opportunities to use suffixes with different base and root words (Bear et al., 2000). As children see these word parts in a variety of contexts and are introduced to their various meanings, they can learn to use and distinguish them in figuring out the meanings of new words. Cunningham (2000) explains that teaching about suffixes is different from teaching how prefixes change the meaning of words. Instead, she demonstrates how suffixes indicate a change in what part of speech the designated word becomes rather than in meaning; that is, *compose* is what you do (verb), the *composer* is the person doing it (noun), and a *composition* is what you have once you have composed (noun). Students must learn how suffixes signal changes in such relationships and also learn how these added suffixes may signal changes in the pronunciation of the root words.

Games can be played during which students work in collaborative groups to form as many words as they can. First, the students use the list of prefixes. Later, they practice using the list of suffixes to build on to base and root words they already know and on to those that the teacher introduces. After forming the words, the students should: (1) define the prefix for each word, (2) write the newly formed word correctly in a sentence, and then (3) define each of the whole words that they produce.

Word tree

FIGURE 6-6

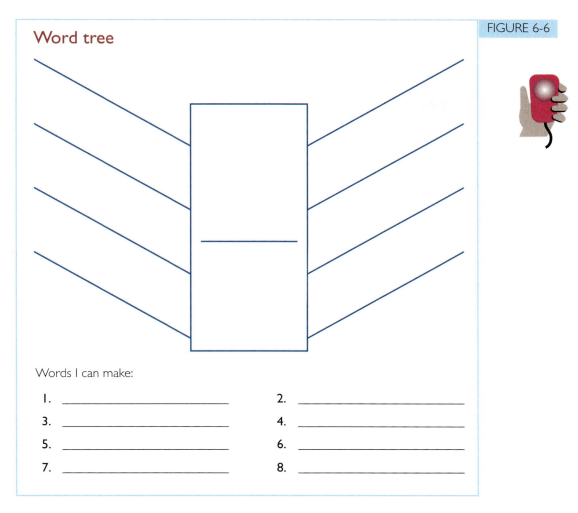

Words I can make:

1. _____ 2. _____

3. _____ 4. _____

5. _____ 6. _____

7. _____ 8. _____

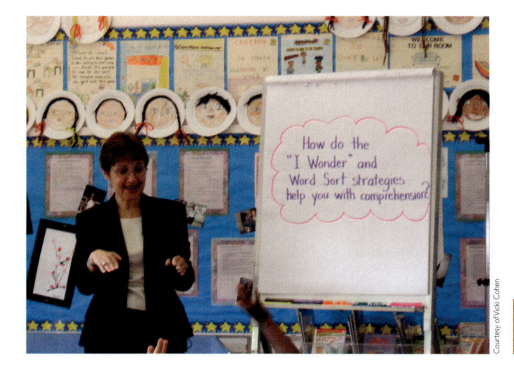

Courtesy of Vicki Cohen

Using vocabulary words in the context of meaningful sentences and word sorts helps improve comprehension.

Labeling

Labeling is an important skill for thinking and reading comprehension. Labels play an important role in helping every child learn words, no matter what language he or she is learning. In fact, children start to label important things with single words during their first year of life and continue to learn words for the rest of their lives. By applying a label to an object, a child will repeatedly associate the object with its graphical configuration and eventually will learn to automatically visualize the object when the label appears. Labels are important in helping children learn sight vocabulary words, and they also help children learn the referent meaning behind the word. Labeling is an excellent way for children to learn defined concepts.

Using Word Walls and Word Banks

A "word wall" is a systematically organized collection of words displayed in large letters on a wall or other area in the classroom. Teachers have reported that the use of word walls is a successful instructional strategy for teaching vocabulary words (Berne & Blachowica, 2008/2009). Using the word wall as an interactive activity helps ensure that children learn new words. By providing review and repetition of these new words, teachers provide enough practice and exposure that the children learn to read and spell the words instantly and automatically. A more indepth description of word walls is included in Chapter 5.

Some activities for interactive word walls are as follows:

Classifying: This task requires students to group or classify words under the same label. A child first identifies the family pet as a pussycat and later learns that *cat* belongs to the *feline family*. This labeling and classifying task not only provides a way of broadening word meanings but is an obvious way to broaden a child's thinking system, which is also used to retrieve words when speaking or writing. Following is an example of a classification task:

Directions:

Place the following words from our word wall into groups that you think would be the best, and then label each group:

tiger, lion, wolf, sheepdog, rat, puppy, mouse, kitten, hamster

Response:

CATS	DOGS	RODENTS
tiger	wolf	rat
lion	sheepdog	mouse
kitten	puppy	hamster

Word Banks: A **"word bank"** is a collection of words taken from the word wall that becomes a student's own personal collection of words. Often the words are written on a note card and placed into a container where the student can then review the new words, classify the new words, and use them in writing. Word banks can grow over time or be refreshed as the student learns the words. Each student's word bank is unique and comprises those words that the student needs to learn.

Walking the Wall: A teacher will want to work with the word wall by "walking the wall" periodically. In this activity, the teacher will go to the word wall and carefully go over each word, asking students to contribute to the discussion about what the word means personally. Different activities can take place during this walk: students can create personal statements about the word; students can offer synonyms, antonyms, homonyms, or homographs; students can write down clues as to what the word means; and students can play games with the words. The important point is that the teacher takes the students through this walk for review and repetition of the words on the wall.

Using the Dictionary

By the turn of the nineteenth century, the dictionary was thought to be the best way to teach vocabulary instruction. This prevalent belief continued until the 1980s, when vocabulary studies demonstrated that traditional approaches to learning vocabulary by simply looking up words in the dictionary, writing them down, and memorizing them were not adequate for improving a rich vocabulary.

Denotation – **Denotation** is dependent on definitions; that is, it is the act of marking down plainly or recording what is given or stated as the dictionary meaning. Definitions are also inadequate in teaching the underlying concept of words such as *osmosis* or *photosynthesis*. Much more explanation and text information is required to learn concept vocabulary, which is usually encountered in content-area instruction. In other words, telling children to "look it up in the dictionary" without following up this activity by illustrating how the word is used in context often leads to faulty usage and miscomprehension.

Does this mean that dictionary usage should be avoided or not taught as a viable alternative in the elementary and middle schools? Not at all! As suggested earlier, it is necessary to use dictionary study as an initial step that is basic for learning word definitions and for verifying word predictions or guesses. The dictionary is an excellent tool that can be used to help students continue their lifelong pursuit of improving vocabulary independently, either through reading or writing at home. The dictionary is a useful alternative to finding the meaning of an unknown word that cannot be derived using context clues, or a tool to help students verify meanings that they have predicted based on their analysis of a given word.

It is extremely important, however, that the teacher model how to use the dictionary to students when introducing the concept of word definitions. Using the overhead projector, a large visual, a computer, or a personal dictionary displaying a typical word entry is helpful for modeling how to use the dictionary efficiently and effectively to learn the meanings and origins of new or difficult words. Modeling is an important instructional procedure to use to point out the various parts of a dictionary entry.

The more familiar students become with the dictionary, the more proficient they will be when taught how to use dictionaries found online. The use of an electronic dictionary can improve vocabulary usage in a variety of ways, including spelling words, identifying a variety of definitions from which to choose, identifying word origins, and checking grammatical usage or parts of speech, all of which—together with background knowledge, vocabulary instruction, dictionary study, recreational reading, and writing experiences—can help students use and understand the new vocabulary word.

Connotation – Words can be defined in two distinct ways: (1) by using the denotation or exact dictionary meaning; or (2) by using the connotative meaning, which tells more about the feeling or emotionality the word conveys. For example, the denotation of the word *skinny* is quite similar in definition to the word *slim*; however, when students are asked whether they would prefer to be called *skinny* or *slim* they usually answer *slim*. Naturally, it is because the **connotation** of the word *skinny* is negative, or less flattering, than the feeling caused from the sound of the word *slim*. Connotation, therefore, may cause individuals to react to the sound or pronunciation of a word, causing either a negative or a favorable response. For example, *pulchritude* is an odd-sounding word. The first syllable sounds rather harsh and ugly (that is, *pulk*); therefore, someone hearing or reading this word for the first time might think the meaning is also ugly. To the contrary, its denotative meaning is "beautiful."

Using Graphic Organizers to Teach Vocabulary Development

Graphic organizers, in the form of semantic maps and other visual tools (Hyerle, 1996), serve as frameworks for interactive learning, enabling students to make connections between their prior knowledge and unknown words or texts. Mapping has proved to successfully teach students the meaning of new words they encounter by linking them and by categorizing and/or comparing and contrasting them with other known words (Cowen, 2003b). Mapping and other graphic organizers are most helpful in scaffolding the learning of struggling readers, including children with learning disabilities and ELLs, who use these visual tools to guide them on the way to a better vocabulary and toward independent reading (Cowen, 2003b).

According to the *Report of the National Reading Panel* (NICHD, 2000), a **semantic map** is an effective tool that can be used to illustrate instructional strategies. Mapping is valuable in helping students construct deeper understanding of new vocabulary words, which, in turn, empower them to read with greater confidence, increased organization, and improved categorization of ideas, resulting in better comprehension.

The following vocabulary mapping strategies provide students with a visual way to identify the attributes of a vocabulary word and help students examine the word's relationship to other words and concepts.

Brainstorming Using Semantic Maps

Semantic mapping uses a structure or framework to help students visualize and relate new words to familiar words and concepts. A brainstorming activity often is used together with semantic mapping to teach students how these new vocabulary words relate to familiar words and concepts derived from literature, themes, and other topics known from the child's background and prior knowledge (Figure 6–7). Therefore, the use of brainstorming and semantic mapping helps students integrate learning about words with other background knowledge. By mapping out how new information relates to what they already know, students are able to use this background knowledge as a basis for learning new words. For example, if a student knows the word *fear,* and the teacher

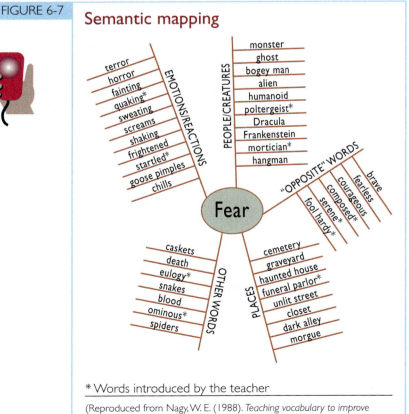

FIGURE 6-7 Semantic mapping

* Words introduced by the teacher

(Reproduced from Nagy, W. E. (1988). *Teaching vocabulary to improve reading comprehension.* Newark, DE: International Reading Association, by permission.)

uses the semantic map to link the word *fear* graphically to the word *ominous*, defined as "threatening," the student is able to understand the relationship and, therefore, the distinction necessary for learning how these two words are similar in meaning. As students brainstorm and generate other words for *fear*, they build vocabulary knowledge by learning synonyms. The teacher can redirect student thinking using the semantic map to generate other related words that are antonyms, the opposite meaning of the word *fear*, which is "bravery." The semantic map related to the theme *fear* is structured so that the student is required to categorize words related to *fear* by the following groupings: emotions/reactions, people/creatures, "opposite" words, places, and other words. This method of categorizing helps students identify the attributes of the concept and identify examples and nonexamples. This use of categorization can be introduced as a prereading activity, with the idea that the student is integrating learning words with other knowledge.

The National Reading Panel researchers have concluded that semantic mapping is one of the most effective vocabulary instructional methods whereby students can learn new words by categorizing them into familiar topics (NICHD, 2000).

Word Map

Research indicates that when students encounter a new word for the first time, they need more than a simple reference from the dictionary definition to learn that word, to remember it, or to use it correctly in speaking or writing (Schwartz & Raphael, 1985). Therefore, the researchers developed the "concept of definition," a word map that provides a visual representation of the word's definition (Figure 6–8). The purpose of the word map is to teach students how to use context clues independently by learning and using the components of a definition.

Carr and Wixson (1986) explain that students follow a simple procedure in which the teacher guides them in using context clues to define a word with the word map

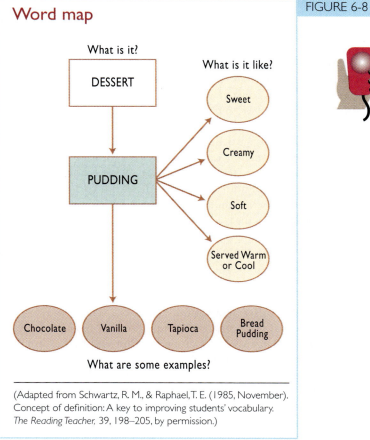

Word map

FIGURE 6-8

What is it?

DESSERT

What is it like?

PUDDING

Sweet

Creamy

Soft

Served Warm or Cool

Chocolate   Vanilla   Tapioca   Bread Pudding

What are some examples?

(Adapted from Schwartz, R. M., & Raphael, T. E. (1985, November). Concept of definition: A key to improving students' vocabulary. *The Reading Teacher, 39,* 198–205, by permission.)

until the responsibility for learning the new word shifts from the teacher to the student. The teacher introduces the word map by modeling aloud how to use it. The procedure enabling the student to use this strategy independently involves the following steps:

1. *Categorization tasks:* The student must answer the following questions about the target word: What are some examples? What is it like? The student tries to fit the target word into a category that is familiar and helps define the target word.

2. *Practice with complete contexts:* The student works with context-rich sentences where there are many clues to provide the meaning of the target word.

3. *Practice with incomplete contexts:* The student works with sentences that provide some clues, but the student must use much more inference.

4. *Learning to use context clues:* The student learns to use context clues independently to define the new target word.

The word map shown in Figure 6–8 introduces the word *pudding* and asks, "What is it?" (dessert). The student then categorizes the word by answering the following questions: "What are some examples?" (chocolate, vanilla, tapioca, bread pudding); "What is it like?" (sweet, creamy, soft, served cool or warm). The teacher can model how to use the word map first, through brainstorming, then by filling in the keywords or answers once the students agree which responses best fit the categories. For example, the teacher asks, "What is it?" Students may suggest several answers, such as, "It's yummy!" "It tastes like chocolate candy." "It's a snack." Some examples they could give are "thick," "gooey," or "tasty." After the brief brainstorming session, the teacher may ask students to consider the best choices and have them share the pen to complete the task of filling in the word map. With enough practice using word maps, students grow accustomed to using context clues independently, learning the components of a definition for building their own vocabulary knowledge as a lifetime skill. In brief, this map provides confirmation to students, letting them know when they really know the meaning and use of a new word.

Semantic Feature Analysis Chart

Semantic feature analysis goes further than semantic mapping because it can use a chart format or matrix that is more visually discriminating, allowing students to focus on analyzing a group of closely related words that, at the same time, have distinguishing features or attributes (Figure 6–9). A matrix helps students learn related new words in a category by identifying the attributes that define the target word, and then allowing students to compare those attributes to words that share similar attributes. In Figure 6–9, the key term is *shelter*. Listed in the first column are words related to shelter: *house, shack, shed, barn, tent,* and *mansion*. Most second and third graders should know the words *barn* and *tent*. Others might not know the distinctions or descriptions among words such as *shack, shed,* or *mansion*. Going across the first row are different semantic features that all of these words might share, such as *for people, for animals,* and *for storage;* these features are generated by the teacher. The plus sign designates that the word does share that feature, the minus sign designates that the word does not share that feature, and the circle designates that the word shares that feature sometimes. The question mark designates that the class is not sure if the words share that feature. The matrix can help students identify *semantic features,* or phrases to describe or distinguish different attributes, such as, "The *barn* does not shelter people, but is used instead for animals." "A *house* may or may not be *fancy,* but a *mansion* is certainly *big* and *fancy*." An open-ended approach to this semantic feature analysis activity could be used by the teacher to brainstorm other related words, such as *hangar, garage, hogan,* or *igloo* (Nagy, 1988). Therefore, further analysis and introduction to new words are possible by introducing an additional "semantic feature" by showing how the relationship of tents, hogans, and igloos are related to natives or indigenous people.

FIGURE 6-9

Semantic feature analysis using matrix

Target word: shelter

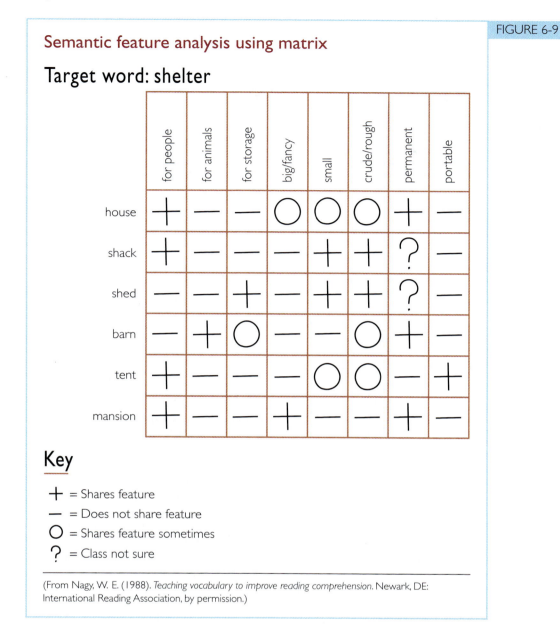

	for people	for animals	for storage	big/fancy	small	crude/rough	permanent	portable
house	+	−	−	○	○	○	+	−
shack	+	−	−	−	+	+	?	−
shed	−	−	+	−	+	+	?	−
barn	−	+	○	−	−	○	+	−
tent	+	−	−	−	○	○	−	+
mansion	+	−	−	+	−	−	+	−

Key

+ = Shares feature

− = Does not share feature

○ = Shares feature sometimes

? = Class not sure

(From Nagy, W. E. (1988). *Teaching vocabulary to improve reading comprehension.* Newark, DE: International Reading Association, by permission.)

Hierarchical Array

Science is often described by showing how names, organisms, or taxonomies fit into certain classifications or organizational frameworks. The **hierarchical array** is a useful organizer for teaching students how to categorize information by illustrating key words or terms in a hierarchy that starts with the most general term at the top and becomes more detailed at the lower levels. Figure 6–10 is an example of a hierarchical array for the word *shelter* and shows how the targeted word can be divided into different categories (*permanent* and *temporary*), which, in turn, are subdivided into lower categories (*for people, for animals, for storage*). Hierarchical arrays can be used for most activities that help students organize words in categories that are easier to learn and remember; nevertheless, the Hierarchical Array is particularly useful for instructing students in learning concept words in the content areas (Nagy, 1988).

Word Family Tree

Buehl (2001) recommends that teachers use the analogy of a family tree when introducing the **word family tree** graphic organizer to students. He suggests that most students have prior knowledge about how family trees are used to illustrate the family's relatives,

FIGURE 6-10

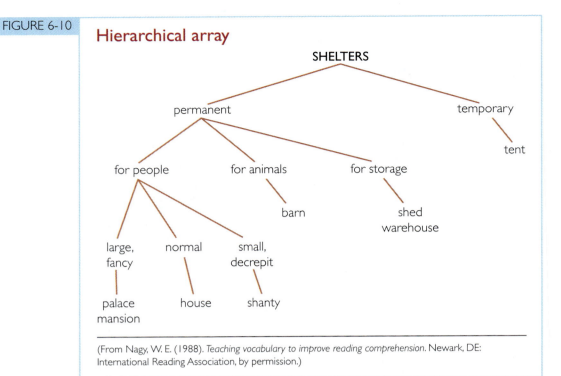

Hierarchical array

(From Nagy, W. E. (1988). *Teaching vocabulary to improve reading comprehension.* Newark, DE: International Reading Association, by permission.)

or ancestors. Similarly, the Word Family Tree is used to illustrate the word's relatives, or the origins of its family. In this way, the student learns more about the new word by discovering information about its family relatives, origins, or genealogy. By grade 3, students are learning about prefixes, suffixes, and roots, so this is an opportunity to use the Word Family Tree to reinforce their understanding and use of this valuable concept and visual tool for learning words in depth. By learning to use parts of words when encountering new words while reading independently, the student develops habits for learning that are self-instructive. Naturally, the teacher must introduce the concept by placing the keyword at the center of the graphic organizer. In Figure 6–11, the teacher selects *spectator*, which is the new word that will appear in the text that the children are going to read. Next, the teacher shows how the keyword is related to a meaningful root, *spec-*, meaning "to see." Students are asked, "What words are relatives to *spectator*?" They are also asked what words are similar. Based on these learning experiences, the children are asked to give their own definition of the keyword. They must find the keyword in context and write it in the proper cell. Finally, the students are asked to use the word in a sentence, by indicating which three kinds of people might say this word. Buehl (2001) concludes that use of the Word Family Tree teaches students to use word parts as they see connections among words with similar origins. Consequently, students remember new words better, begin to use this method independently, and become more confident in using the new words in their speech and writing.

Semantic Gradient

Semantic gradients show how words differ gradually or in gradations, for example, from *beautiful* to *ugly*. The student is told to arrange such words from beautiful to ugly graphically, using the semantic gradient vertical ladder-like structure; this allows students to see the various gradations of words, making connections between words that they know and those that are not known. Figure 6–12 shows a semantic gradient, in which students arrange words related to appearance from beautiful to ugly. Blachowicz and Fisher (2002) have introduced other valuable semantic gradients that can be used in teaching terms related to social studies by exploring scales or degrees of difference related to government, such as *democracy/dictatorship* or *wealth/poverty*, or descriptions related to characters from literature, such as *pride/humility* or *courage/cowardice*.

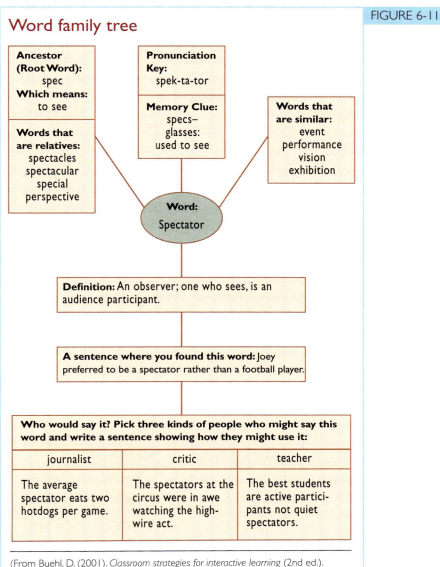

FIGURE 6-11

Word family tree

Ancestor (Root Word): spec	Pronunciation Key: spek-ta-tor	
Which means: to see	Memory Clue: specs– glasses: used to see	Words that are similar: event performance vision exhibition
Words that are relatives: spectacles spectacular special perspective		

Word: Spectator

Definition: An observer; one who sees, is an audience participant.

A sentence where you found this word: Joey preferred to be a spectator rather than a football player.

Who would say it? Pick three kinds of people who might say this word and write a sentence showing how they might use it:

journalist	critic	teacher
The average spectator eats two hotdogs per game.	The spectators at the circus were in awe watching the high-wire act.	The best students are active partici-pants not quiet spectators.

(From Buehl, D. (2001). *Classroom strategies for interactive learning* (2nd ed.). Newark, DE: International Reading Association, used with permission.)

Said Web

Kathryn L. Laframboise (2000) developed the **said web** as a remedy for tired words, such as the word *said*, while creating a strategy for students to learn new and interesting vocabulary in meaningful groups, rather than as a list of isolated words (Figure 6–13). Said webs provide students with a deeper processing approach to learning vocabulary in keeping with recent research findings; that is, they develop an understanding of new words that shows real ownership and facilitates proper word usage in reading, writing, and speaking. Laframboise (2000) recommends the following modified instructional steps for implementing this effective strategy:

◆   The teacher leads a two- to three-minute brainstorming session with the class to come up with a "start list" of synonyms, antonyms, and related words for *said* (that is, *shouted, yelled, whispered, explained,* and *exclaimed*).

◆   The class selects words, agreed to be the most common words, which should be kept for the web; students signify these words by circling them with a blue marker.

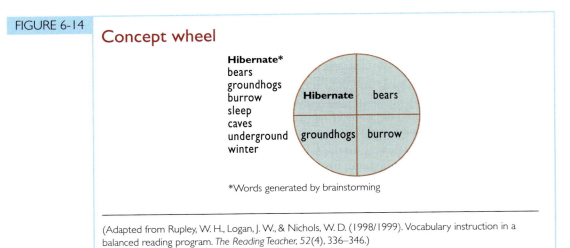

FIGURE 6-14

Concept wheel

*Words generated by brainstorming

(Adapted from Rupley, W. H., Logan, J. W., & Nichols, W. D. (1998/1999). Vocabulary instruction in a balanced reading program. *The Reading Teacher, 52*(4), 336–346.)

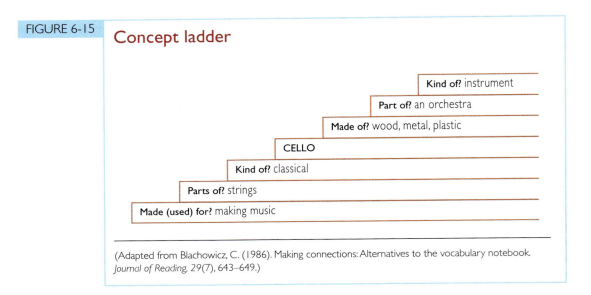

FIGURE 6-15

Concept ladder

(Adapted from Blachowicz, C. (1986). Making connections: Alternatives to the vocabulary notebook. *Journal of Reading, 29*(7), 643–649.)

musical instrument such as the *cello* and to know its properties or distinguishing features. With a concept ladder, the student places the target word, *cello,* at the center of the ladder and responds to key questions, which, when answered adequately, demonstrate that the student fully understands the word, as well as its properties, characteristics, and qualities. Questions are asked that show how much the child really knows about the word or concept, such as: "What is it made (used) for?" "What are some parts of . . .?" "What are some kinds of . . .?"

Blachowicz (1986) indicates that children can create their own concept ladder that presents information in a hierarchical way, demonstrating how the concept word is related to other words they know already. Children using this hierarchical ladder are able to associate other related known vocabulary to reinforce their understanding of the concept being learned. Therefore, the concept ladder is used to help children focus on one important concept word by relating that major word to other known words that are of lesser importance on the rungs of the ladder. In this way, children can concentrate on learning about a main idea or major concept thoroughly, rather than diverting their attention by learning minor details. Consequently, Blachowicz (1986) concludes that children, through the use of the concept ladder, can learn to gauge their own levels of knowledge. Having identified their own shortcomings, children begin to set purposes for improving their knowledge by citing specific areas in which they need to do more reading.

The Frayer Model

The **Frayer model** (Buehl, 2001) is a visual framework for recording concept words, and it is like the concept wheel in that it is divided into four compartments. However, only this framework takes the shape of a square or rectangle. The Frayer model is used to record and display pertinent information for helping students understand a new concept by distinguishing between essential and nonessential characteristics representing the concept (Buehl, 1995). For example, the Frayer model in Figure 6–16 uses a compare-and-contrast approach by illustrating what a vegetable is and what it is not. The Frayer model does so by listing key words and phrases that describe the "essential characteristics" of a vegetable (see Figure 6–16, top left quadrant). "Nonessential characteristics" are listed so that the student can readily compare and contrast those characteristics that are displayed visually (see Figure 6–16, top right quadrant). "Examples" of vegetables (see Figure 6–16, bottom left quadrant) also are listed, as well as a list of "nonexamples" (see Figure 6–16, bottom right quadrant). The information is organized in a user-friendly format that encourages students to study the model and to construct a meaningful understanding of the concepts being introduced.

Buehl (1995) recommends that, when introducing a concept, the teacher should ask questions that require brainstorming, such as "What is a vegetable?" or "What is a reptile?" Students should be actively involved in generating examples and brainstorming in small, cooperative groups. Students should also be asked to identify key characteristics and examples, as well as nonessential characteristics and nonexamples. Naturally, the teacher begins by modeling, using an overhead transparency, or by recording suggested concept words or examples on a word wall or on an easel pad. By encouraging student inquiry and by being responsive to student questions, a variety of pertinent questions will emerge. With "sharing the pen," students begin by recording key concepts, and after much discussion and analysis, they learn how to record the concepts in the appropriate quadrants that may later require further analysis. The advantage of using this strategy is that students are active learners and are noticeably highly motivated. Consequently, students exposed to the Frayer model tend to go far beyond learning mere

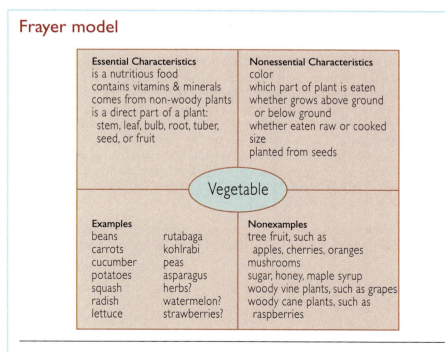

Frayer model

FIGURE 6-16

Essential Characteristics	Nonessential Characteristics
is a nutritious food	color
contains vitamins & minerals	which part of plant is eaten
comes from non-woody plants	whether grows above ground
is a direct part of a plant:	or below ground
stem, leaf, bulb, root, tuber,	whether eaten raw or cooked
seed, or fruit	size
	planted from seeds

Vegetable

Examples		Nonexamples
beans	rutabaga	tree fruit, such as
carrots	kohlrabi	apples, cherries, oranges
cucumber	peas	mushrooms
potatoes	asparagus	sugar, honey, maple syrup
squash	herbs?	woody vine plants, such as grapes
radish	watermelon?	woody cane plants, such as
lettuce	strawberries?	raspberries

(Adapted from Buehl, D. (2001). *Classroom Strategies for Interactive Learning* (Second Edition, p. 158). Copyright by International Reading Association. Originally published by Frayer & Klausmeiser (1969), Wisconsin Research and Development Center.)

definitions of words; instead, they develop a far deeper understanding of concepts. As a result, the use of the Frayer model increases the students' understanding of new vocabulary, and they show a deeper and more complex understanding of concepts.

Games and Wordplay for Learning Words

Games and wordplay have been around as long as humankind has spoken and used words. Play is a common outgrowth of language and is readily observed in our youngest children, who laugh uninhibitedly when they hear strange combinations of sounds. Nursery rhymes and poetry advance the playfulness and lyrical qualities of language as Dylan Thomas, the great Welsh poet, once acknowledged in an interview several years before his death. Dylan stated:

> The first poems I knew were nursery rhymes and before I could read them myself I had come to love just the words of them, the words alone . . . I did not care what the words said, overmuch, nor what happened to Jack and Jill and the Mother Goose rest of them; I cared for the shapes of sound that their names and the words describing their actions made in my ears; I cared for the colors the words cast on my eyes. (Thomas, 1961)

From Thomas's remarks, it seems obvious that children who become fascinated with language first come to love the sounds of words and the shapes of sound that somehow describe things colorfully and magically for them. Wordplay, therefore, is not just an important instructional approach; from Thomas's viewpoint, wordplay means a great deal to a writer and especially to a poet. Wordplay and games that are played with words should be done for the "sheer fun" of playing with words, their sounds, their shapes, and their meanings. Because wordplay is a natural outgrowth of language usage, the classroom is a natural place to see that word games and playfulness with words flourish. It is important that teachers carefully evaluate the games being used in the literacy classroom to ensure that they are meaningful and support vocabulary development. Many puzzles and games should be used only for reinforcement, and not as the primary instructional strategy.

Rivet

The Rivet word strategy that Patricia Cunningham (2000) developed is an excellent prereading game that keeps students focused on predicting target words from texts that are preselected by the teacher in anticipation that these new words will probably be challenging. As in most predicting word games such as Hangman, the format is simple. In Hangman, the exact number of spaces are drawn, signifying the number of letters in the word; for instance, if the word was *decomposed*, there would be 10 blank spaces: _ _ _ _ _ _ _ _ _ _. The teacher should select several large, multisyllabic words or terms such as *decomposed*, containing the most frequently used prefixes and suffixes (*de-, ex-, re-, -ed, -s, -ing*), as well as stem or base words (that is, *compos, expect, rely, spec*). The procedures for Rivet are as follows:

◆ Begin by numbering the words that the student will be asked to predict (from 5–10) and by drawing the exact lines for the targeted words as illustrated below:

  1. _ _ _ _ _ _ _ _ _
  2. _ _ _ _ _ _ _ _ _ _
  3. _ _ _ _ _ _ _ _ _ _ _
  4. _ _ _ _ _ _ _ _
  5. _ _ _ _ _ _ _ _

◆ As the students watch, the teacher begins to fill in one letter at a time, encouraging them to guess the word as soon as they think they know it. Most students will not be able to guess the word at this point:

  unr_ _ _ _ _ _ _

◆ The students' eyes are now riveted on the given three letters (hence the name of the game) in anticipation of new letters to help them predict the word:

unreli_ _ _ _

Many guess that the word is *unreliable*. Some students have guessed *unreligious*; a good prediction, but when the teacher spells the word and asks the students to count the remaining spaces, they see that *unreligious* has one more letter than *unreliable*.

◆ The teacher (or designated student) should continue writing in the letters, one at a time, until all of the words have been written out as the students have correctly predicted the target word.

◆ The final Rivet words should be written out as follows:

unreliable

examinations

decomposition

retrieving

disability

◆ Students should use the 5 to10 target words to predict how these words might reveal events in the story they are about to read. More importantly, the students have focused on reading and spelling each of these words and, as a result, will be more aware of them when they are encountered during reading.

Hink Pink and Hinky Pinky Families

Johnson (2001) indicates that the Hink Pink and Hinky Pinky games are rhyming brainteasers or riddles that use many variations of wordplay that can be manipulated syllabically or by rhyming. These brainteasers are used to introduce children to a variety of words, from easy to difficult, through the use of larger, multisyllabic, rhyming word games.

Hink Pinks are one-syllable rhyming words used to solve a riddle. A student moderator, known as the "big wig," chooses words from a predetermined word list and asks peers to solve riddles, such as:

"Who steals steaks?"
Answer: A beef thief.

Hinky Pinkies are two-syllable rhyming word riddles; for example:

"What is a better cafe?"
Answer: A finer diner.

Hinkety Pinketies are three-syllable rhyming riddles, for example:

"What is it called when you get permission to take something away?"
Answer: Removal approval (Johnson 2001).

Commercial Word Games

Many commercial word games are readily adapted to be used in the classroom. Teachers often design these games, and depending on the age group, some of the more sophisticated children are often quite adept at creating their own board games, card games, match games, bingo games, and guessing games. Most of these games can be created using index cards, oak tag, and pencil and paper. Movers, dice, and spinners are available at most teacher supply stores, which can aid teachers and students in modifying many commercial games to make them more educationally and age-level appropriate. It is also necessary that several resources be made accessible to the children, such as dictionaries, thesauruses, or electronic dictionaries to be used whenever a student challenges a definition or questionable interpretation of a word meaning. Just a few of these games are introduced below to serve as springboards for other instructional ideas.

Go Fish is an adapted card game that uses 20 cards (up to 40 cards can be used with older children); at the start, the cards are dealt to all of the players. The object of the game is to pair vocabulary words with the correct definitions. Vocabulary words are preselected and written on the front of the cards; definitions with examples or illustrations are written on the opposite side of the cards. The first student to pair all of the words is the champion.

Ol' Big Fish is an adaptation of Old Maid, which is played like Go Fish. An extra card, with a drawing or a decal of an Ol' Big Fish, is placed in the deck of cards, and the student left holding this card at the end of the game is the Ol' Big Fish.

Guessing games such as Hangman, Wheel Game, and 20 Questions are age-old favorite word games that are readily adaptable for classroom use, similar to the examples shown above. The basis of these guessing games is that given a subject or concept and opportunities to guess letters (limited to either the number of questions, as in the case of 20 Questions, or limited to a set time [for example, three–four minutes]) creates just enough tension to remain exciting, challenging, and competitive. It is valuable for the teacher to model how each of these games is played and to set rules to eliminate unruly or unsportsmanship behavior. To illustrate how most guessing games are played, a modified 20 Questions game (Blachowicz & Fisher, 2002) is presented below to illustrate how a game can help students think about words they are learning:

> **20 Questions:** One player is "It." That player chooses a word from a stack of word cards. A team can ask up to 20 questions to guess the word. Approximately three to five players make up a team, and each player can ask a number of questions (requiring yes or no answers) until receiving a "no" answer. Types of questions are: "Is the word a person, place, or thing?" ("Yes.") Is it a place? ("No.") The next player then asks questions. If a given player guesses the word, that player becomes "It" for the next round. If the team does not guess the word in 20 guesses, the player who is "It" remains "It" for another round.

Other commercial word games that can be easily modified (or purchased) for classroom and age-appropriate use are as follows:

> *Blurt! The Webster's Game of Word Racing* (Riverside Publishing Company): The player reads a definition aloud as the other players race to guess the appropriate word. The first player to say the word is the winner. A junior level of Blurt is available for kindergartners and first graders.

> *Boggle Master* (Parker Brothers): Within a time limit of three minutes, players compete by forming as many words as possible, linking them up, down, sideways, or diagonally. A Boggle Junior level with pictures is available for kindergartners and first graders.

> *Hangman* (Milton Bradley): The original pencil-and-paper guessing game, in which one student plays the Hangman while the other student tries to minimize the number of incorrect guesses to avoid exposing parts (such as arm, hand, fingers, and so forth). The game is played similarly to Rivet and 20 Questions.

> *Pictionary Junior* (Golden and Design): A card game in which the word is drawn and teammates sketch clues to help guess the drawn word within a given timeframe. Somewhat reminiscent of the word game Charades, which is played by giving nonverbal clues.

> *Scrabble Crossword Game* (Milton Bradley): This classic game is a crossword puzzle used with manipulative, lettered wooden tiles, in which the player forms words by connecting the letter tiles up, down, and across. The letters each have a value that is added up and totaled; the player with the highest total wins.

Vocabulary Strategies for Diverse Learners

Vocabulary Instruction for English Language Learners

The limited vocabulary of ELLs in their nonnative language is an obvious obstacle to reading comprehension; therefore, vocabulary skills are especially important for students who are at risk for learning to read and those who are ELLs. Native speakers typically know at least 5,000 to 7,000 English words before kindergarten, which is a large number of words to know especially when someone is trying to learn a new language (Hart & Risely, 1995). ELLs must not only close this gap but also try to keep pace with the native speakers as they continue to expand their vocabularies. This is a daunting task, and ELLs are likely to perform poorly on assessments and to fall increasingly behind in school. Continuous instruction must be planned using a realistic timeline and should be delivered through a multifaceted approach.

Instruction in vocabulary development for diverse learners should begin with establishing a **sheltered language approach,** or low-risk environment in which to raise questions about new word meanings, word usage, and interesting new words encountered in texts and in oral communications (Bear, Templeton, Helm, & Baren, 2003). It is important that instruction begin with the students' own background knowledge and their personal experiences, including their native cultural and linguistic experiences. When learning vocabulary, diverse learners often need additional support including the aid of visuals, concrete examples, and field trips to ensure their success in using the target language. This sheltered language approach is useful in a number of ways: (1) It enables the targeted group to feel more confident, creating a community of learners whereby the children are more likely to participate in learning activities; (2) it provides interaction through peer participation and collaborative learning, which facilitates the children's ability to communicate by trying out newly learned vocabulary words and phrases; and (3) communication-based instruction is necessary for meeting the diverse levels of linguistic development leading to improved vocabulary and reading comprehension.

ELLs appear to rely more on word meaning than on knowledge of the subject or syntax. Therefore, it is quite important that vocabulary development be stressed before reading a text. It is recommended that vocabulary learning be through direct instruction; while native speakers learn a majority of their vocabulary through **incidental learning** (through context clues and reading different texts), ELLs must review the words until they know their meanings. Intentional vocabulary learning is more effective for retention and comprehension (Koren, 1999). Therefore, explicit instruction of vocabulary words is needed for ELL students.

One strategy to increase vocabulary with ELL students is the use of cognates to infer word meaning (August, Carlo, Dressler, & Snow, 2005; Bravo, Hiebert, & Pearson, 2005; Carlo et al., 2004; Lehr, Osborn, & Hiebert, 2004). **Cognates** are words that are related in origin, as certain words in genetically related languages are descended from the same ancestral root. This is especially true with English, Latin, and Spanish, which share many of the same cognates. For students who are native Spanish speakers, an important resource is the presence of many words in school texts that have a Latin origin, especially in science texts. Because Spanish is closely tied to Latin, students who are native Spanish speakers may draw on their knowledge of these shared root words or cognates as they learn to read English. Some examples are:

English word	Latin root	Spanish word
first, primary	primus (first)	primero
moon, lunar	luna (moon)	luna
sell, vendor	venus (sale)	vender

Another strategy to teach vocabulary to ELLs is through the *use of literature*. In the Vocabulary Improvement Project that Carlo and colleagues (2004) developed, books were chosen carefully to focus on particular words and word study strategies. The focus of each lesson was on teaching specific vocabulary words from the chosen books. The literature included informational texts and narrative stories. One example used with fifth grade children was to have them choose a book that many of the children could relate to, such as a book about immigration. Furthermore, many of the Spanish speakers learned how to use the Spanish–English shared cognates found in this book. The teacher read the book to the students and the students also read the texts independently and with classmates. The vocabulary became a jumping off point for further lessons and activities such as Word Wizard, in which students look for targeted words in other texts and analyze the words according to prefixes, suffixes, roots, and derivations. Such structured vocabulary activities increased reading comprehension for this group of Spanish-speaking students.

Another strategy to increase vocabulary words of ELL children is through **structured talk.** When teachers engage children in academically relevant content, students can learn words needed to engage in class discussions and to comprehend what they read in various subjects. Words are learned and used in meaningful context, and children have opportunities to use those words in context and to "make them their own." What is important is that teachers must have deliberate strategies for clarifying word meanings and teaching them directly to the class.

Hernandez (2003) recommends that ELLs need to be taught **content-area vocabulary** that is supported by social studies, science, music, art, and literature curriculum. However, Hernandez cautions that content words should be taught gradually, using a rich language environment together with many opportunities for learning new words in highly contextual ways. Otherwise, she admonishes, unrealistic intentions in teaching vocabulary often create an overload, resulting in frustrating diverse learners, while unintentionally delaying otherwise meaningful growth.

Concrete aids should be used to help ELLs in vocabulary acquisition. Content vocabulary charts and word walls are excellent tools that serve as important references for diverse learners to use whenever they are writing or in need of a prompt for oral communication. Authentic pictures, magazines, and newspapers related to new vocabulary words are also advisable to display, especially when introducing concept vocabulary terms to older students, such as *photosynthesis* or *metamorphosis*. Other useful concrete aids for learning abstract vocabulary terms include illustrations, diagrams, manipulatives, graphic organizers, as well as having students create their own visual tools.

Dutro and Moran (2003) recommend that teachers of ELLs think of vocabulary development by considering two major categories: **content-specific** and **general-utility** (or "brick" and "mortar") **words**. "Brick" words refer to content-specific words that are pretaught before a unit or before reading a text; for example, words such as *mitosis, revolution, habitat,* or *climate* are general-utility words and should be pretaught. "Mortar" words are necessary for comprehension and are general-utility words that hold a sentence together. For example, connecting words such as *and, but,* and *then*; prepositions/prepositional phrases such as *of, about, for, next to,* and *in front of*; pronouns such as *his, her,* and *their*; and verbs such as *eat, use, saw,* and *go* are all necessary for comprehension and need to be emphasized. These mortar words should be taught through direct instruction using flash cards, word games, memorization games, and repetition. They are difficult to learn because they are abstract and not easily visualized or defined (try to define *about* or *for*). Many of these general-utility words should be on a word wall with model sentences that demonstrate their use, which is helpful for diverse learners in their reading, writing, and speech development.

It is essential that the ELLs receive instruction on **homonyms** (*to/too/two* and *their/there/they're*) and **homographs** (*bank* for my money and *bank* of the river), which can be quite confusing to them (see Figures 6–3 and 6–4). It is also essential that ELLs are introduced to **idiomatic language,** which can be confusing and does not have any direct translation for the phrases. Examples of idiomatic language include: "It's raining cats and dogs." "He's the top dog of the class." "I caught a cab today." Figure 6–5 lists common idiomatic phrases.

ELLs have special needs that must be addressed in the classroom using direct vocabulary instruction. Emphasizing oral language and engaging in social activities are essential components of vocabulary instruction that build understanding and higher order thinking skills.

Vocabulary Instruction for Students with Learning Disabilities

Vocabulary knowledge varies greatly in students with learning disabilities. For some students with learning disabilities, vocabulary development can be an area of great strength, despite having phonological weaknesses (that is, their ability to associate a letter with its sound) that adversely affect the development of decoding skills. These students may have excellent listening comprehension, as well as the ability to dictate stories with strong verbal content. For other children with learning disabilities, weaknesses in vocabulary development can be part of a broader language impairment. Just as for all children, vocabulary knowledge for students with learning disabilities is affected by previous literacy experiences, such as being read to at home and exposure to effective strategies to learn new vocabulary words in the classroom (Spear-Swerling, 2006).

Many students with learning disabilities show poor performance on tests that require them to name a series of repeating objects, letters, or colors. Performance on these tests is directly related to problems in reading and predicts future reading ability (Mann, 2003). It has also been found that students with learning disabilities take longer to name randomized letters and are particularly prone to difficulties in recognizing many high-frequency vocabulary words (Mann, 2003). This rate-of-processing problem affects their ability to retrieve vocabulary words and remember their meanings.

Many of the same techniques that are effective in the classroom to promote vocabulary acquisition can be used for students with learning disabilities. What works best is when the child is actively involved in making connections with the new word. The more connections the child can make between the new word and the words he or she already knows, the more meaningful the new word will become. The child should be encouraged to use the word as much as possible and to have repeated encounters with the same word to ensure that the meaning is tightly woven into the automatic reading circuits within the child's brain, so that the word can be retrieved quickly (Shaywitz, 2003).

Both teachers and parents should choose new words carefully so that the child is not overwhelmed. Words should be chosen that are most likely to stretch the child's mind and those that the child may not be able to learn independently. Words that are integral to the reading should be pretaught and become the focus of the vocabulary lesson. It is often recommended to focus on a group of words that are tied together by a common theme or topic so that learning each single word reinforces learning the other words in the group as well. For example, if the theme is the *rain forest*, some words that may be taught connected to this theme might be *canopy, poachers, illegal, abundance,* and *diversity.*

The key to instruction is that it must be flexible and depend on the word itself. If the word is abstract such as *democracy*, it might demand a discussion together with many different examples. If the word is concrete, such as *hammock*, a picture and concrete example can be used. If the word is *transportation*, an analysis of prefixes, suffixes, and roots is warranted. The important point for all children is that new words require repetition and reinforcement and repetition again.

STRATEGIES FOR TEACHING DIVERSE LEARNERS

Ideas to Develop Vocabulary for English Language Learners

1. Provide structured academic conversation built around books and other subject matter activities to build vocabulary and comprehension.

2. Provide direct instruction in vocabulary words: preteach vocabulary words before reading text, provide definitions of the words while reading, and discuss the targeted words after reading.

3. Focus on words children are unlikely to learn on their own through exposure to English oral discourse; it is also important to focus on words children will encounter frequently in text and oral language (August, Carlo, Dressler, & Snow, 2005).

4. Ensure that ELLs know the meaning of Tier 1 words. Tier 1 words are basic words, such as *clock*, *baby*, and *happy*, which are rarely taught in school. However, for ELLs, these words do require instruction; moreover, it is not so easy to teach these words because many of them are not concrete, such as *which*, *that*, and *over*.

5. Focus follow-up activities for the lesson on studying vocabulary words and having students use these words in multiple ways.

6. Choose books purposefully that can reinforce certain vocabulary words that you want to teach and to which the students can relate.

7. Build on children's prior knowledge by using texts that relate to their background culture.

8. Capitalize on students' first language knowledge if this language shares cognates with English. Teach cognates, if possible, especially with Spanish-speaking students, by having students learn words that have similar roots as their native language.

9. Use concrete visual aids to assist students in remembering vocabulary words. Such things as word walls, visuals, photographs, and graphic organizers can help children acquire vocabulary words.

10. Be sure to teach content-area vocabulary words, because they can pose extra problems in comprehension of text.

11. Support ELLs with their native language, if possible. Provide text summaries and word meanings in native language.

12. Be patient and provide a supportive environment in which to learn. Remember that repetition and consistency in a comfortable and engaging environment is best. Studies (Hakuta, Butler, & Witt, 2000) show that oral proficiency can take three to five years to develop, and academic English proficiency can take four to seven years.

13. Stress higher order thinking and strive for excellence.

Explicit vocabulary instruction is recommended for all children but is essential for students with learning disabilities. Vocabulary instruction should provide many opportunities for children to use new words, to discuss words, and to compare new words with previously learned words so that the children can "make the words their own." In addition, children need to learn how to use classroom resources such as glossaries, dictionaries, and thesauruses, including electronic and online resources. Students with learning disabilities can also benefit from learning to use context to determine word meanings and to determine how words are used in sentences to imply certain meanings. For example, the words *clever* and *sly* are both synonyms usually used to connote someone who is smart; however, *clever* is usually a compliment, while *sly* implies that someone is not quite honest and has a negative connotation. Children with learning disabilities need instruction on how to use context to determine the implied meanings of words.

Direct, explicit instruction of vocabulary words, which includes repetition and reinforcement, is recommended for all children.

Courtesy of Bill Lisenby

STRATEGIES FOR TEACHING DIVERSE LEARNERS

Tips for Working with Students with Learning Disabilities: Vocabulary Acquisition

1. Use direct instruction to teach specific vocabulary words. Do not assume that children with learning disabilities will understand the word from the context of the paragraph. Be sure to preteach the vocabulary words before reading the text and to carefully go over new words after the students have read it. Continue to reinforce and maintain these words in word banks, in word sorts, and in the children's writing.

2. Have the child make as many connections as possible with the new word by relating it to his or her prior experiences and interests.

3. Provide concrete examples when possible.

4. Provide repetition and reinforcement of the new word(s), which are essential.

5. Involve the parents in helping the child learn new words at home. Have them pick out new words from readings, and then see how many times they can see or hear the word in the next 24 hours.

6. Use semantic maps and graphic organizers to help the child visualize the word and understand its meaning.

7. Choose vocabulary words selectively so that they add to the child's overall growth and contribute to comprehension of the text.

8. Be flexible in teaching new words to the child and vary techniques so that the child remains motivated and engaged.

9. Use mnemonic strategies to reinforce vocabulary words. Mnemonic strategies are systematic procedures for enhancing memory. Using keywords is often beneficial; that is, the learner makes a connection between the new word and an image involving a related word that serves as a "key" to remember the new word. For example, a student of French could remember that *pain* is the French word for bread by vividly picturing a loaf of bread in a pan. Another example is when one student learned the capital of Florida because she had linked it to things with which she was familiar. For example, Florida sounds like flower (the keyword), and it was easy to teach her to make an automatic connection between Florida and flower. She also linked Tallahassee and television, because television was very familiar to the student, and the two words have similar sounds (Mastropieri & Scruggs, 1998).

10. As students advance beyond beginning levels of reading, vocabulary instruction should be integrated with decoding and spelling instruction. For example, at the same time that students learn that the prefix tele- means distant (as in telephone, telegram, telepathy, and telemarketing), they should also encounter the prefix in their reading and learn that its spelling is generally the same each time it is used; therefore, the word for the object that broadcasts their favorite shows must be television, not telivision or telavision (Spear-Swerling, 2006).

Technology and Vocabulary Instruction

Research has shown that technology has been used effectively to teach vocabulary instruction, and that use of technology facilitates learning, resulting in significantly higher vocabulary achievement over traditional methods (NICHD, 2000). Following are some examples of the many different ways that technology can be used to enhance vocabulary instruction:

◆ Using software programs that provide an easy way to create semantic maps and visual tools
◆ Using hypertext to create nonlinear documents
◆ Using the Internet to reinforce vocabulary instruction
◆ Using commercially purchased software programs to reinforce vocabulary instruction

Software to Create Visual Tools

Computer software such as Kidspiration and Inspiration allow children as young as kindergarten age to create their own semantic maps. These programs provide basic tools to allow the teacher and the students to create visually appealing semantic maps and webs. Children can use pictures easily in these programs to enhance their webs and associate the vocabulary word with key visual images.

Hypertext in Vocabulary Instruction

Hyptertext allows the reader to click on a word or phrase in a document and be brought to a different location within the document or to a different site altogether. Hypertext can be beneficial to vocabulary instruction because it allows the teacher or student to develop a document where vocabulary words can be made into links that bring the reader to an elaboration of that word. The elaboration could be a definition, a picture of the word, a sentence, a discussion about the concepts and issues behind the word, or even a video clip. For instance, while reading an electronic document on democracy, the student can click on the word *constitution* and be redirected to a page that contains a definition of the word, a picture of the United States Constitution, and a link to the National Archives, which has the U.S. Constitution archived in digital format. The link can also provide a structural analysis of the word to explain its prefixes, suffixes, and roots. Reinking and Rickman (1990) found that elementary students reading science texts independently explored the meanings of more difficult words, recalled more of their meanings, and comprehended more content when they read passages displayed by a computer that provided immediate, context-specific assistance with vocabulary.

Hypertext technology has been beneficial to ELLs and to children with learning disabilities who are able to access meanings and other visual and interactive aids in a quicker and more convenient way. Hypertext can also be beneficial to the teacher, who can then determine how often readers look up the meanings of unfamiliar words and identify which words were looked up. Students find such programs motivating and attractive when they incorporate rich graphics and animation. However, many children can be easily distracted by the use of hypertext and get "lost" as they explore different links, losing their original path through the material. Care needs to be taken that when using hypertext with ELLs there is a clear return button, and that there are not any diversions to other sites that would confuse the learners.

Children can learn how to create their own hypertext documents, which would be an excellent way to reinforce the meanings of unknown words and to have them develop graphic tools to visually depict the relationship of the word to other concepts. These documents can then be shared with the class and published as an "electronic book." See Figure 8–10 to create a hypertext document.

The Internet for Vocabulary Instruction

The Internet is an excellent resource for teachers to find the latest research regarding vocabulary instruction, to locate ideas that can be used in lesson plans, and to find sites that children can use for vocabulary instruction. The following sites are recommended sites for teachers (many more sites are listed on this textbook's website). As always, it is essential that the teacher preview each site first to ensure it meets the goals and objectives of the lesson, and to ensure that the site is current and all links are working properly. Some of the sites will allow teachers to make their own puzzles using students' vocabulary or spelling words. Although many students may find these activities motivating, puzzles and word search activities alone do not provide effective instruction in vocabulary. Such puzzles should be used only as reinforcement for more meaningful vocabulary activities.

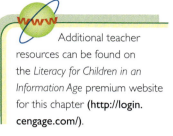

Additional teacher resources can be found on the *Literacy for Children in an Information Age* premium website for this chapter (**http://login. cengage.com/**).

sites that promote professional development for teachers in vocabulary instruction

put reading first: k—3 (vocabulary)

http://www.nifl.gov/partnershipforreading/publications/reading_first1vocab.html

This chapter on vocabulary from the publication *Put Reading First: The Research Building Blocks for Teaching Children to Read* was developed by the Center for the Improvement of Early Reading Achievement (CIERA) and funded by the National Institute for Literacy (NIFL).

National Writing Project

http://www.writingproject.org/pub/nwpr/quarterly/Q2002no3/simmons.html

This is a lesson from the National Writing Project, in which students are instructed on how to visualize vocabulary words that contain prefixes, suffixes, and roots.

Vocabulary Acquisition: A Synthesis of the Research

http://idea.uoregon.edu/~ncite/documents/techrep/tech13.html

The National Center to Improve the Tools of Educators (NCITE) offers an excellent synthesis of the research related to vocabulary instruction. Report authors Scott Baker, Deborah Simmons, and Ed Kameenui are highly regarded educators and researchers, and their insights are well worth a look.

sites for use in the classroom

Discovery School's Puzzle Maker

http://puzzlemaker.school.discovery.com

The Discovery School's Puzzlemaker site allows teachers to make their own puzzles using students' vocabulary or spelling words.

Personal Educational Press

http://www.educationalpress.org/

The Personal Educational Press site allows a teacher to create free educational games, flash cards, and worksheets that can be printed out. The teacher can choose which words to include on the games.

Vocabulary University

http://www.vocabulary.com

Vocabulary University offers free vocabulary puzzles to enhance vocabulary mastery and is designed for upper primary, middle school, and high school levels. Exercises include fill-in-the-blanks, definition match, synonym and antonym encounters, crosswords, word finds, true/false, and word stories.

Sufficient Suffixes: Four in a Row

http://www.collaborativelearning.org/suffixconnect4.pdf

This site allows teachers to print out a board game designed for upper elementary children to practice suffixes. The game challenges students to add suffixes to change a word to a different part of speech.

Commercial Software for Vocabulary Instruction

Clicker 5 by Crick Software (http://www.cricksoft.com) is an excellent program that promotes vocabulary development, as well as writing. This writing support tool has built-in text-to-speech technology, so that once a student writes a word, phrase, or sentence, Clicker will read it back to the student. It allows a student to hear the words in a special grid before actually writing them in the Clicker Writer, and the student can hear the sentence after it is written. This allows students to try out words and see what they look like before actually using them in writing. The program also has add-ons that allow a student to hear the words in a different language, which can support ELLs. Clicker comes with a built-in library of pictures so that children can illustrate common words or use the pictures in their writing. This program is beneficial to students with learning disabilities and provides needed support and scaffolding for learning new words.

There are many different educational software programs on the market that can be used in the classroom to reinforce vocabulary development. Many of these programs use a "drill and practice" approach, which would reinforce the denotative meaning of the word, rather than its connotative meaning. Most of the programs do not stress learning vocabulary through the context of the sentence; the *deep processing* of word meanings that is mandatory for children to "make the word their own" may not occur. Nevertheless, these programs can be useful in a computer center where students can practice and reinforce new vocabulary words.

The use of computer technology is extremely promising for at least two significant reasons: (1) It serves to reinforce direct instruction in vocabulary, so students can receive substantially more practice, thereby developing a deeper understanding of new vocabulary words; and (2) it takes advantage of several sources of media and different modalities that are tapped, ensuring that the student has a greater opportunity to acquire word knowledge using a multisensory approach to learning. Both online access to vocabulary and opportunities for repeated practice are important factors for overall improvement in reading comprehension. Technology serves an important role in vocabulary acquisition; it is highly motivating for young people, and it provides constant accessibility. One cannot underestimate the importance of using technology within the literacy classroom, which research studies support (Reinking & Rickman, 1990; Davidson, Elcock, & Noyes, 1996, cited in NICHD, 2000).

Assessing Vocabulary Development

Assessing Your Student's Vocabulary Development

Vocabulary plays a key role in comprehending text; therefore, it is important that teachers assess children's vocabulary development on a continuous basis. Assessment of vocabulary is critical for identifying children at risk for reading problems and designing appropriate instruction. Vocabulary development is strongly correlated to reading achievement; therefore, any student who is deficient in vocabulary development will need an intensive program in developing background knowledge and vocabulary instruction. When assessing vocabulary, it is essential that oral measures are used. Tests that require reading or writing make it difficult to differentiate other problems children may have, such as difficulties in word decoding or spelling, from lack of vocabulary knowledge. Children with suspected learning disabilities and ELLs should be assessed individually on measures that include both receptive and expressive oral vocabulary. **Receptive vocabulary** involves understanding of spoken words, for instance, asking a child to point to a picture that represents a word spoken by the teacher. **Expressive vocabulary** involves using a word in speech or naming a word, as when the examiner shows a picture to a child and asks the child to name it. Expressive vocabulary appears to be a stronger predictor of beginning reading achievement than receptive vocabulary. Therefore, both areas should be included in a comprehensive assessment (Spear-Swerling, 2006).

Although standardized testing provides educators with a baseline for assessing vocabulary, it is too general and, therefore, not particularly useful for providing pedagogical information in determining what approaches or strategies to use for improving student vocabulary. As a group test, standardized formats are not likely to provide accurate individual student diagnosis. Standardized testing generally provides a section that assesses student knowledge of vocabulary; however, the greatest disadvantage of using standardized instruments to evaluate student vocabulary is the limited number of words that can be assessed during any one examination. Multiple-choice questions or fill-in questions based on high-frequency word lists are generally used for measuring student vocabulary knowledge. Other types of words examined usually include frequently used content words in social studies and science texts (Cooter, 1990). Most evaluators, therefore, do not believe that standardized tests provide enough substantial evidence to determine what the student's vocabulary knowledge is or is not. Also, most summative approaches to vocabulary assessments are rarely used for improving vocabulary instruction. Researchers indicate that there are so many approaches used to assess word knowledge that there is no single standard. Nevertheless, a multiple assessment is still required for a meaningful evaluation of vocabulary according to most evaluation experts (NICHD, 2000).

The best way to assess a student's vocabulary development is informally in the classroom, using multiple measures such as:

◆ Informal Reading Inventories
◆ Answers to comprehension questions after reading a passage
◆ Anecdotal records in guided reading groups
◆ Writing samples
◆ Semantic maps

Informal Reading Inventories (see detailed description in Chapter 9) provide teachers with practical information about individual student reading and vocabulary ability. Although there is a limited number of vocabulary words in any informal inventory word list, teachers can probe student knowledge of individual words to get further insight into their usage limitations. The teacher can even create her own informal measure based on content-area instruction or the use of keywords selected from social studies, science, or other content-area texts used by students. This personalized testing procedure is one feature of the teacher-made informal inventories, which can be much more useful than the vocabulary section of a standardized test.

After a student reads a passage, comprehension questions can often target vocabulary words and give a teacher an idea whether the student is familiar with a word. By focusing carefully on targeted words in a reading passage, a teacher can get a good idea of a student's understanding of the unknown words and level of comprehension.

Guided reading groups allow a teacher to work closely with a small number of students and to conduct quick, informal assessments. At this time, the teacher should listen closely to the student's conversation and note the extent of vocabulary usage in speech. This can be recorded in a log and placed in the child's individual folder to show growth over time. In a similar way, the teacher can start to obtain an informal assessment of reading comprehension and the extent to which lack of vocabulary development is interfering with comprehension. The guided reading session can focus on building vocabulary knowledge, and the teacher should take the opportunity to have each child develop his or her own word bank of vocabulary words that reflects those words each child needs to know.

Writing samples are an excellent way to determine whether the child has "ownership" over the word. Often, children will use vocabulary words incorrectly in writing, demonstrating a lack of deep processing of the word, which can be noted. Vocabulary development will enhance a child's writing ability, and use of quality words will contribute to the child's ability to express thoughts and ideas. Writing samples can be assessed based on word usage, and children should be encouraged to use the words they are learning in their own writing.

Many teachers use the standard multiple-choice test to assess the week's 20 vocabulary words. Although this will give the teacher a quantitative score to record, it does not assess whether the child has only memorized a meaning or, in fact, knows how to use the word effectively in speech and writing, or whether the child will understand what it means when it is read in a passage. Multiple-choice tests usually are based on memorization and, therefore, are not a recommended assessment strategy to use in the classroom.

Another way to assess a child's vocabulary development is through semantic mapping. Teachers and students can keep dated samples of a child's semantic map on given vocabulary words to provide valuable evidence of the child's growth in breadth of understanding, especially if the word is a complex concept, such as *transportation, democracy, economics,* or *sustenance.* The teacher can ask the child to develop a map about the vocabulary word, sharing everything currently known. Later, with the child, the teacher can analyze the semantic map and look for accuracy of details, the logical flow of ideas, and the child's overall knowledge of the word and how it is connected to other related concepts. This should be paired with having the child use the word within the context of writing about a topic.

Assessing Your Classroom Vocabulary Program

It is important to be able to assess a good vocabulary program when you see one (Figure 6–17). This is especially helpful in developing an interactive, long-term, effective vocabulary program, such as the one that Mr. Crow established for his third graders. This checklist is an excellent reminder to preservice and veteran classroom teachers that they must continue to use only the best researched-based instructional practices to ensure that their students build their vocabularies to the best of their abilities. Teachers have always known the importance of building a rich vocabulary, but not all of these past practices have been successful. To avoid the pitfalls of the past, Blachowicz and Fisher (2002) believe that it is possible to identify such a good vocabulary program using the following criteria: an environment that is word-rich; an environment that builds the base for independence; a teacher who models, supports, and develops good strategies; and a teacher who uses varied assessments.

How Will I Know a Good Vocabulary Program When I See One? A classroom checklist

I. Teacher shows enthusiasm for words and word learning by having:
___ Daily read-aloud
___ Word-of-day or word-activity-of-day
___ Students engaged in activities involving words and wordplay
___ Activities involved in spelling, phonics, and vocabulary

II. Classroom shows physical signs of word awareness by displaying:
___ Word charts or word walls (showing student input)
___ Books on words, wordplay, specialized dictionaries (where students can access them)
___ Labels in classroom
___ Word games
___ Puzzle books and software
___ Student-made wordbooks, alphabet books, dictionaries, PowerPoint presentations

III. Teacher builds the base for independence by having students:
___ Show enthusiasm for words and word learning
___ Spend part of each day reading on appropriate level
___ Name a favorite word book, puzzle activity, and/or word game
___ Own a personal dictionary or word logs
___ Use a dictionary written on an appropriate level
___ Use a strategy for dealing with unknown words
___ Use strategies for self-selection and self-study
___ Develop a knowledge base for independent strategies (word parts, context, word references, etc.)
___ Develop strategies for using their own knowledge base before reading

IV. Teacher models, supports, and develops Good Strategies by having:
___ Rich instruction on content area vocabulary words where definitional and contextual information is provided
___ Activities that use mapping, webbing, and other graphics to show word relationships
___ Multiple exposures and chances to see, hear, write, and use new words
___ Focus on students using strategies
___ Wordplay and motivational activities
___ Activities on the computer that support word learning and wordplay

V. Teacher varies assessment by using:
___ Different assessment depending on goal
___ Different assessment depending on entry knowledge level of learners
___ Assessments that measure both depth and breadth
___ Multiple sources of assessment
___ Data from multiple sources to design instruction of each child

(Adapted from Blachowicz, C., & Fisher, P. J. (2002). *Teaching vocabulary in all classrooms* (2nd ed.). Upper Saddle River, NJ: Pearson Education, Inc.)

FIGURE 6-17

STRATEGY BOX

Helping Children Acquire Vocabulary Words

Mr. Crow used the following strategies when he taught his vocabulary lesson to the class:

1. Preteach vocabulary before a student starts reading the text.

2. Activate the readers' background knowledge so they can relate to the word; make connections with the students' interests, previous experiences, and knowledge so that the new word becomes meaningful.

3. Read, read, read. Have the students encounter the new word in multiple contexts and in different texts.

4. Use direct instruction to teach the vocabulary words. Do not assume that the children will "get" the word; instead, carefully and systematically incorporate vocabulary instruction into the literacy classroom.

5. Focus lessons on learning new words and provide activities that support and reinforce the acquisition of new vocabulary words.

6. Use multiple strategies/activities to teach and reinforce new words. Be flexible and vary the type of activities that children use to learn new words. Try to make the activities fun and engaging.

7. Use the word wall to reinforce new words. Be sure to use the word wall within lessons so that the words are not just "sitting there."

8. Group words by themes. This will help students associate new words to other words with which they are familiar.

9. Have children "make the words their own" through writing activities, discussion, games, and hands-on activities.

10. Do not teach vocabulary words in isolation; choose words that come from readings or activities.

11. Do not use drill and practice to reinforce. Stay away from pure memorization because these words do not remain in short-term memory for long.

12. Use graphic organizers to help children visualize and remember the words.

13. Engage children in using technology to learn new words through software to create visual tools, through the use of Internet sites, and through commercial software packages.

Final Thoughts

The best way for children to learn new vocabulary words is by reading rich, quality literature and by being exposed to new words through listening, talking, and interacting with words. Children build vocabulary understanding through context, or what is called incidental learning. Therefore, engage children in quality reading, writing, and conversation.

As stated earlier, active student participation with multiple exposures and approaches to learning new word meanings results in optimal learning. Vocabulary acquisition is directly related to children being exposed to new words found in the context of rich, quality reading material. Integration, repetition, and meaningful use are important points to remember when developing a vocabulary program in the balanced literacy classroom.

EXPLORATION   Application of Concepts

Activities

1. Using a list of context-rich sentences taken from literature (see Figure 7–3), in a group try to figure out what each targeted word means and explain the process you went through to determine the word's meaning. Each group can find its own context-rich sentences with targeted unknown words and give them to another group to infer meanings.

2. Create meaningful vocabulary games that can be used in the classroom with a specific age group and or with ELLs. Also, develop your own word games to play that are based on Bingo, Chutes and Ladders, Hangman, 20 Questions, Matching, or Wheel of Fortune.

3. Choose a "tired" word such as the word *nice*. Break into small groups to brainstorm, using a word web to add synonyms that are more interesting words compared with the word *nice*. After several synonyms have been generated, develop a list of antonyms for *nice*, such as *ugly* or *wicked*.

4. Develop a different graphic organizer for each of five targeted words from a children's book. You can choose any five graphic organizers described in this chapter. Present them to a group and explain which you like best.

5. Explore different websites listed in this chapter and on the companion website with a partner. Evaluate the websites and discuss which ones you like best. Many additional teacher resources on vocabulary instruction can be found on the companion website for this chapter (http://login.cengage.com/).

6. Develop a content-area lesson plan that emphasizes development of key vocabulary words. Develop prereading, during-reading, and postreading strategies to support vocabulary development.

HOME–SCHOOL CONNECTION   Word Banks for Making Deposits at Home

Parents and guardians can augment their child's vocabulary by use of word banks and by following several of the tips below:

- Encourage the child to read silently every day in a self-chosen book that is easy or slightly challenging.

- Have the child write unknown words on a word card stored in a word bank container.

- Read with the child daily, recording difficult words to add to the child's word bank.

- Preread books the child is reading and select difficult words to preteach so these words are easily learned when read in context.

- Use an "I wonder what this word means?" technique for learning new words in context.

- Have the child write new words in sentences to reinforce learning and to show understanding.

- Use the words from the word bank to form spelling lists, sorting activities, word games, word webs and other learning activities.

- Praise the child for his or her accomplishments. Keeping a mastery list of newly learned words is highly motivational (see Chapter 5 for details).

Adapted from: Rasinski, T. and Padak, N. D. (2001). *From phonics to fluency: Effective teaching of decoding and reading fluency in the elementary school*, New York:NY: Addison-Wesley Educational Publishers Inc.

7 READING COMPREHENSION: AN INTERACTIVE PROCESS

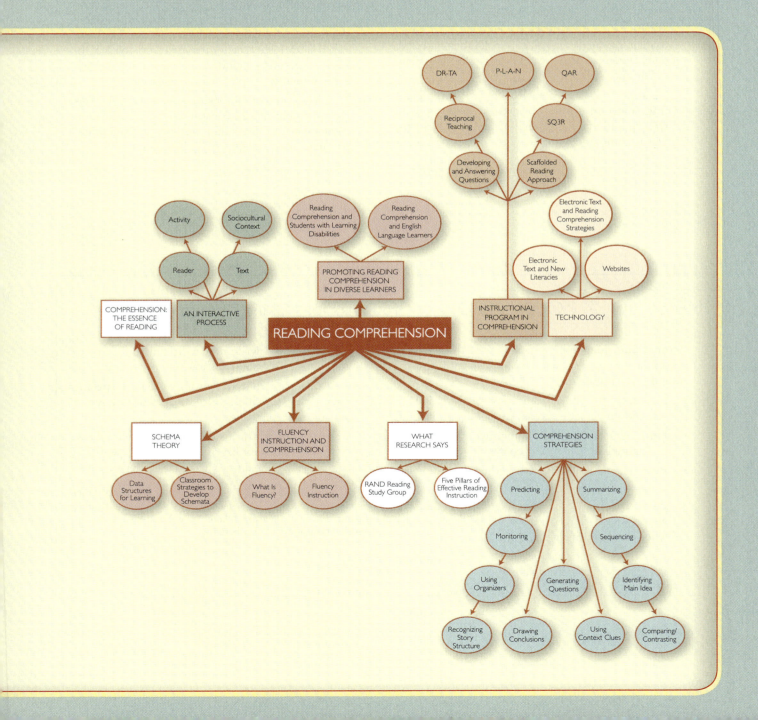

International Reading Association Professional Standards Addressed in this Chapter:

IRA STANDARD 1:   FOUNDATIONAL KNOWLEDGE

Candidates:

1.4 Demonstrate knowledge of the major components of reading (phonemic awareness, word identification and phonics, vocabulary and background knowledge, fluency, comprehension strategies, and motivation) and how they are integrated in fluent reading.

IRA STANDARD 2:   INSTRUCTIONAL STRATEGIES AND CURRICULUM MATERIAL

Candidates:

2.2 Use a wide range of instructional practices, approaches, and methods, including technology-based practices, for learners at differing stages of development and from differing cultural and linguistic backgrounds.

Key Terms

comprehension strategies

schemata

sociocultural context

schema theory

data structures

fluency

Automaticity

prediction

flexibility

self-monitoring

metacognitive strategies

story structure

literal comprehension questions

interpretive comprehension questions

creative comprehension questions

scaffolded reading approach

reciprocal teaching

SQ3R (survey, question, read, retell, review)

DR-TA (directed reading and thinking activity)

QAR

P-L-A-N (predict, locate, add, note)

electronic text

Focus Questions

1. What is reading comprehension and why is it so important to beginning readers? What does the phrase *comprehending text is an interactive process* mean and what is involved in this interaction?

2. Why is schema theory so important in reading comprehension and what can the classroom teacher do to activate or develop background knowledge?

3. What is fluency and what impact does it have on comprehension? What can a classroom teacher do to develop fluent readers?

4. What are the five pillars of effective reading instruction? What are the five missing pillars of reading instruction and why are these so important?

5. What are comprehension strategies? How should teachers instruct readers in using comprehension strategies? What are eleven important comprehension strategies that all readers should be using when reading?

6. What are three types of questions teachers should be developing to assess comprehension of students?

7. What are some instructional strategies that teachers can use in the classroom to promote comprehension?

8. How can you promote comprehension in students with learning disabilities? In English language learners?

9. How can technology support reading comprehension in the classroom? Why is it important that electronic text be included in the literacy program?

Welcome to Mrs. Ghali's Second Grade: Helping Students Comprehend Text

Alex Mares-Manton/Asia Images RM/PhotoLibrary

Mrs. Ghali, a second grade teacher, informs her class that it is "reading time" and asks the class to join her in the reading corner. The class quickly assembles on the floor, sitting in a carpeted area, with Mrs. Ghali sitting in a chair next to an easel. As Mrs. Ghali starts reading the book aloud, some of the children listen attentively and are highly motivated to follow along. Other children seem to pay attention sporadically, while a few others show no interest at all; their eyes wander around the room and they are clearly not paying attention. Mrs. Ghali finishes reading the story, then engages the students in a discussion about it. Those who paid attention are most actively engaged in the discussion; others do not contribute to the postreading activity at all. After about five minutes of discussion, Mrs. Ghali asks the students to go back to their seats and assigns them three questions to answer in

writing. The children work at their desks independently; some students work on task, while many others are off task, talking to their neighbors and fidgeting at their desks.

Afterwards, Mrs. Ghali asks, "How do I get all the children involved and motivated to read? Why do some children pay attention, others are clearly not interested?" A major reason for this disparity in motivation is in the students' ability to comprehend what they read. What can Mrs. Ghali do to improve her reading time and help ensure all students are engaged in the reading process? Let us look at the scenario again after Mrs. Ghali's peer mentor and her literacy coach gave her some feedback on her teaching strategies.

At reading time, Mrs. Ghali sits in a chair next to an easel in front of the children. She starts by discussing the theme they have been studying in class for the past week: how families are important to us. She talks about grandparents, assuring the class that not all children have grandparents, and asks any student to discuss a visit with a grandparent. After many students volunteer their experiences, Mrs. Ghali takes out the book *The Hello, Goodbye Window* by Norton Juster and illustrated by Chris Raschka, a 2006 award winner of the prestigious Caldecott Medal. She has the students look at the cover and a few of the illustrations. She asks the students what they think the book will be about. She writes their predictions down on the easel, telling them to pay attention to whether they are correct. She elicits comments from all students, calling on those who do not appear to be paying attention and giving positive feedback to all. Mrs. Ghali now tells the students that as they read, they need to be *investigators* and to pay attention to *clues* that will help them understand the book. She then asks the students to list different types of clues they used to help them understand the story. She writes down their responses, trying to elicit such things as picture clues, word clues, and phonic clues.

Mrs. Ghali starts reading the book out loud, pausing at certain points to model how she is using clues to help her gather meaning. She does this at strategic points to maintain the flow of the story. She carefully monitors all students while she is reading and will call on a student who is not attending to answer a comprehension-monitoring question. Mrs. Ghali finishes reading, then asks the class to go back to their predictions and see whether they were correct. They discuss the clues used to help them comprehend the story, and Mrs. Ghali adds to the list of clues posted on the easel. The class discusses the story for a few minutes. Mrs. Ghali tells the children they will now create a story about visiting a relative or a friend. The students can illustrate their story by finding pictures on the computer, cutting out pictures from a magazine, or creating original drawings. The students can write their story by hand, by using a multimedia software or word-processing program, or dictating into a tape recorder. In this way, Mrs. Ghali is accommodating all learners in her class, including struggling readers, English language learners, and children with learning disabilities. All of the children are excited and go off to do their project. She tells them that when they are finished, they should read a book of their choice independently or find a partner and reread the book together a few times.

This chapter explores how a teacher such as Mrs. Ghali can promote comprehension in a literacy classroom and help motivate students to read text. The following sections give specific methods a teacher can use in the classroom to promote comprehension as a student reads text.

During reading time, a teacher asks students to confirm and discuss story predictions.

Courtesy of Guilherme Cunha

Comprehension: The Essence of Reading

Comprehension has come to be viewed as the "essence of reading" (National Institute of Child Health and Human Development [NICHD], 2000), which is essential for achievement in school as well as success in the world. Reading comprehension has been defined as "intentional thinking during which meaning is constructed through interactions between text and reader" (Durkin, 1993). Reading comprehension is the end goal of all reading—it is the understanding gained from reading text. However, there can be many levels of comprehending text: Readers can have a surface or literal understanding of what they have read, or they can gain a deeper understanding involving inferring meaning from what is not explicitly stated, analyzing information, and synthesizing the meaning into a new and deeper meaning.

In the 1970s, new theories about reading comprehension emerged that suggested that meaning is an interactive process that is constructed through interactions between the text and the reader. In other words, comprehension is not a static process that resides exclusively within the reader, but rather is a complex process that involves a reciprocal interchange of ideas between the reader and the message in a particular text (NICHD, 2000; Snow, 2002). Comprehension begins before actual reading of the text while the reader scans the title and looks at the book to make predictions; it occurs during reading while the reader is processing information and asking questions; and it occurs after the reading process when the reader analyzes what was read and synthesizes the reading into the reader's existing knowledge base. Comprehension is an active process in which readers construct mental representations of what they read, store them in their memories, and then use these representations for subsequent applications when desired.

Before the 1970s, comprehension was taught almost exclusively in the content areas, and not in formal instruction of a literacy classroom. This view has now changed, and recent research indicates that comprehension can be improved by teaching students to use specific cognitive strategies while reading. **Comprehension strategies** are specific procedures that guide students to become aware of how well they comprehend as they attempt to read and write. Explicit teaching of comprehension strategies is believed to improve text comprehension and reading achievement. Instruction of comprehension strategies is performed by the teacher who models them and then provides guidance, feedback, and support for the reader to use them, ultimately resulting in the reader using the strategies independently and effectively interacting with the text. Readers who are not taught these strategies are unlikely to apply them consistently or use them spontaneously in reading.

Reading Comprehension: An Interactive Process

As mentioned earlier, reading is an *interactive process* that involves the reader and the text. Successful readers are capable of engaging in the act of reading as an interactive process; that is, they generally have a personal interest or a specifically defined purpose for reading. They are more likely to read nonfiction texts successfully if they are highly motivated to research or learn more about a given subject, idea, or category that is meaningful, interesting, or useful.

The RAND Reading Study Group (Snow, 2002) suggests that reading comprehension must include at least three central elements: (1) the reader, (2) the text, and (3) the activity (purpose) for reading. These three central elements must also occur within a larger sociocultural context according to this definition (Figure 7–1).

The Reader

The reader must have the appropriate background knowledge, be motivated to read the text, and have a purpose and interest in reading a variety of genres or the various content areas. The reader must attend to the task of reading the text and engage in reading in an interactive, involved manner. In so doing, the reader begins by obtaining meaning from the words that he or she learns to read with automaticity—that is, being able to recognize words quickly and with ease. The reader's ability to decode words and to read fluently at an accelerated rate is based on preexisting structures within the reader's memory. When this memory is activated, the reader is able to remember and to critically analyze the words, sentences, paragraphs, and ideas with greater understanding. From these interactions with the text and by virtue of the reader's cognitive abilities,

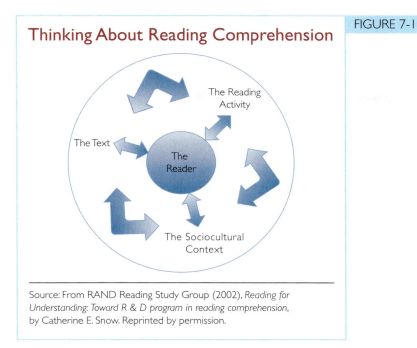

Thinking About Reading Comprehension

FIGURE 7-1

Source: From RAND Reading Study Group (2002), *Reading for Understanding: Toward R & D program in reading comprehension*, by Catherine E. Snow. Reprinted by permission.

he or she is able to visualize and draw inferences and meaning; however, this ability is dependent on whether the text is written within the reader's comfort level. For instance, does the reader have the background knowledge or cognitive ability to understand the reading material? Does the reader have the ability to decode unknown words, unlock the meaning of the text's vocabulary, or apply the specific reading comprehension strategies required to understand a given text? Finally, does the reader have the **schemata** (plural for schema) or experiences that are prerequisites for reading successfully?

How do all of the above attributes affect the learning of an English language learner or a student with learning disabilities? All readers must be given texts that are within their grasp to read and understand. That is, no student should be expected to read any materials independently or be required to comprehend any text that is written at or above his or her frustration level, or the level that the reader shows signs of being frustrated and is no longer comprehending the material. All readers first must be able to decode and comprehend text with at least 90 percent reading accuracy to develop the necessary confidence, knowledge, and ability to become a successful reader.

The Text

Younger readers are dependent on key features of the text that help scaffold the reading process for them. Beginning readers feel comfortable with books in which they can recognize and decode a few words. This is especially important for English language learners who may do best starting with decodable texts that use phonetically regular words to tell a story and have only a minimum number of words on the page. Dr. Seuss books are a good example of how such predictable language can be both enjoyable and informative for young readers.

Beginning readers also rely heavily on the size and boldness of the print in the text. They use print and illustrations almost referentially to guide their reading of individual words, as well as the physical layout, design, and artistic use of corresponding colors that aid in constructing their own meaning from the text. The author's style of writing and use of text structure are guideposts that readers learn to use to construct meaning.

The visual literacy aspects of the text are of greater importance now more than ever before, evidenced by the fact that visual literacy standards are now incorporated into many statewide and national assessments. Students now also must learn how to read nonlinear and hypertext materials by scanning sections of text in ways that are unknown to prior generations of readers. Electronic text, such as reading from the Internet or on a cell phone, create new challenges for today's readers, including the reading of e-mail and instant messages. Students must learn different strategies for comprehending these new textual formats.

The Activity

The reading activity requires that the student read for one or more purposes, although it is possible that the original purpose for reading might change due to the content or multifaceted meanings of the text. The reading activity generally includes decoding words, recognizing vocabulary meanings, reading for higher order thinking, and applying comprehension strategies to help comprehend what is being read. Therefore, the goal of the reading activity should be to produce at least four main outcomes as follows:

◆ To increase knowledge
◆ To find solutions to real and imagined problems
◆ To engage with the text for one or more purposes
◆ To realize that intended outcomes may or may not be fulfilled

According to the RAND Reading Study Group (Snow, 2002), identifying instructional strategies that help develop long-term reading comprehension improvement and that promote effective reading across the curriculum in the various content areas should be the major priorities of reading instruction.

The Sociocultural Context

As our schools continue to reflect a major shift in demographics across the nation, schools must teach diverse learners how to improve their immediate and long-term reading comprehension skills to succeed both academically and socioeconomically in a rather inequitable, polarized society influenced by politics, economics, society, culture, ethnicity, race, and linguistics. Students are influenced by the cultural background they come from and the **sociocultural context** within which they operate at home. Teachers need to examine the external social world where an individual child has developed. Through participation in activities that require cognitive and communicative functions, that child will learn to use language and comprehend it in ways that the culture has nurtured and supported. In a global society that continues to shrink dramatically more each generation, it is necessary to take all of these sociocultural elements into consideration when planning for the long-term improvement of our diverse students' reading comprehension development.

More specifically, a number of studies have focused on how culture shapes children's assumptions about being able to read and the value of reading (Field & Aebersold, 1998; Gee, 2001; Strickland, 1998). Culture influences children's attitudes toward reading and literacy instruction. Students learn how literacy is used and how knowledge is communicated, both at home and at school. Background experiences and culture help determine how people interpret and mentally organize the world, and these factors impact literacy learning. Both teachers and students must learn that individuals construct meanings from different perspectives, and they need to understand how one's own interpretation of meaning may be different from others. Gee (2001) claims that language in use always comes not in some generic "English," but in some *specific variety* of English *customized* to and used within a specific context. Only when we understand a child's "multiple literacies," or different ways in which the child communicates in different social contexts, can we really understand and assess a child's language and literacy development. Teachers need to understand children's culturally specific ways of communicating at home, which may not be "school aligned." Teachers may need to bridge the gap between a child's primary way of communicating at home and school-based literacy practices occurring in the classroom to develop a meaningful program for all students and to allow each student to build his or her own sense of self (Gee, 2001). Teachers need to use materials and experiences that students can relate to and that will expand their conceptual framework. Teachers should use multicultural literature and become sensitive to the cultural background of students in the classroom and its potential impact on learning (Strickland, 1998).

A report from the National Literacy Panel on Language—*Minority Children and Youth* (August & Shanahan, 2006)—suggests that it is important to become familiar with the home environment of students and their home culture; bridging the home–school differences in interaction patterns or styles can enhance students' engagement, motivation, and participation in classroom instruction. This report also suggests that students perform better when they read or use material that is written in the language they know best. Culturally meaningful or familiar reading material also appears to facilitate comprehension.

Teachers' VOICES   Classroom Observation of a Fourth Grade Classroom

On September 13, I visited Mrs. K's fourth grade class, which consisted of 26 students. The children were seated in groups of four and one group of five; each group included boys and girls. The classroom itself was a colorful room decorated with many different stimulating pieces of artwork and quotes. When I arrived, the students were seated in their groups, getting ready to start the language arts portion of the day. About an hour and a half is usually devoted to language arts each day, and it is taught across the curriculum all day long as well.

After the students had completed an assignment that involved writing an original poem, Mrs. K asked everyone to meet in the back of the classroom on the rug in front of their in-class library. When the students met in the back of the classroom, they discussed the book that they were reading yesterday for about five minutes, then Mrs. K reviewed the appropriate way to read with a partner and modeled the proper way to share a book while reading together. After debriefing the previous day's reading, the class broke into pairs and found a place to read away from everyone else. Some children chose to read at their desks, others

chose to sit on the floor. One group even asked to sit at Mrs. K's desk, and of course, she allowed them. As the children read, they discussed different elements of the story and helped each other further understand difficult excerpts. Occasionally, I would even overhear students quizzing each other on the paragraphs or pages they had just read to their partner.

Mrs. K had chosen a fictional book about the ocean that correlated with the unit the children were studying in their science class. She informed me that she has a handful of students who are below their grade level for reading. She usually places them into their guided reading groups according to skill level, but other times places them according to social group. For the first novel they read that year, she chose students who would have the opportunity to get to know each other. Mrs. K focuses on the children being able to comprehend what they are reading as a whole. It was interesting to see children working together to comprehend what they were reading.

—*Jennifer Bane, Future Teacher*

Mrs. Ghali needs to understand that students are only one part of the interactive process of reading. She needs to ask herself whether the reader has the appropriate background, skills, and knowledge to fully comprehend and understand the material. Can the reader interact with the text appropriately? Is the font too big, too small, and written clearly? Does the reader understand the author's writing style? Is the author effectively communicating to the reader? Does the reader have the appropriate strategies to engage successfully in this particular reading activity? Can the reader relate to the content and cultural background of the material? These are questions Mrs. Ghali needs to consider before she starts reading a book with the class. She needs to understand that reading is an interactive process that involves many different components, not just the reader, and if there is a problem, she needs to examine the different components involved in this interaction—what the reader brings to the process, what the author and text bring to this process, and the actual activity itself. She needs to analyze what part of the interactive process can be adjusted and supported to help make the interactive process a successful one.

Schema Theory

Although there is much yet to be learned about how to teach reading comprehension to students of all ages, one of the major breakthroughs to reading comprehension occurred in the early 1980s when theorists showed the importance of activating children's background knowledge and prior experiences for developing critical understanding of texts. **Schema theory** prepares children for learning new information that builds on that which they already know. For instance, children will be much better able to read a new book about spiders if they are reminded by their teacher that they learned about the characteristics of spiders when reading a recent science unit, and that they had learned how spiders differ from insects in that they have a two-part body, eight legs, and two or more abdominal organs for spinning thread to make their webs. Children now know that they can compare and contrast spiders with insects, which they have learned have only six legs. Similarly, adult readers would have difficulty reading a physics book if they did not have a background in physics. For example, a teacher might inform adult readers about their *schemata* or knowledge, including such things as motion, force, pulleys, and inclines, that could be put to use in understanding a text written about how the ancient Egyptians used their knowledge of physics to build their pyramids thousands of years ago.

Data Structures for Learning

Learners rely on memory for building connections that not only help them remember and recall information stored away but also to use this memory bank to build on what they know as they learn new things. Rumelhart (1981) reports that knowledge comes in little bundles of memories or *schemata* that enable us to know objects, sequences of events, and actions or experiences, and that we can match one against the other, helping us confirm that we know something because we've experienced it or something like it through real experiences, vicarious experiences such as reading, or through similar, mediated experiences taught by a teacher, parent, or surrogate. Feurerstein theorizes, for instance, that we learn things in basically two ways: either through direct experience or through mediated experience that is taught as a simulated, representative, or vicarious event (Feurerstein, Rand, Hoffman, & Miller, 1980).

The ease of learning, therefore, largely depends on our schemata; the more we know about something beforehand, the faster we will be able to learn new things by relating to this prior knowledge. As schemata build up, they form into data structures that help keep related items together to facilitate organization and recall of the many items each person stores in his or her memory. **Data structures** are networks of interrelated concepts that help people interpret information; they are essential to comprehension. Schemata are always organized meaningfully, and, as an individual gains experience, they branch out to become more developed. Schemata change moment by moment as information is received and can be reorganized with the addition of new experiences and concepts. These mental representations combine to form a whole which is greater than the sum of its parts (Anderson, 1977). Schema theory is important for teachers to take into account each time new material or a new text is introduced. If a child does not have the appropriate schemata built up or the appropriate background knowledge on the topic, the child will not be able to comprehend the new material; it will "fall on deaf ears." A good analogy is that the teacher is a fisherman (or fisherwoman) each time a new topic or text is introduced. At the end of the fishing pole is a hook that the teacher must cast out; hopefully, the hook will catch on to an existing data structure of schemata, and then the teacher can reel the line back in, extending the data structure, and building up schemata through the reading and exploration of new material. If, however, existing schemata do not exist, the teacher will come up empty-handed and the student will not totally comprehend the material read.

Classroom Strategies to Develop Schemata

How do classroom teachers develop background knowledge and build schemata within their students? There are many different ways that a teacher should build up background knowledge before a selection is read. The process of comprehension does not occur only after a book is read, but rather is an active process that occurs during all phases of the reading process. Developing background knowledge is an essential prereading activity that will promote reading comprehension and literacy achievement. Before the students read a selection, the following activities will help build schemata:

- ◆ *Discussion:* A class discussion on the topic to be introduced will generate many ideas and help students activate prior knowledge. Students also will learn from each other as the topic is discussed. The teacher will learn about the level of prior knowledge that the class has before starting the reading selection.

- ◆ *Background-generating activity:* Involve the class in a hands-on activity that will build prior knowledge and prepare the students for the reading.

- ◆ *Prequestions and stating objectives:* By writing questions on the board or stating objectives of a lesson, a student can start to draw on prior knowledge and build on background experiences.

- ◆ *Story previews:* Have the class preview the book or text selection by looking at the title and discussing what it might mean, looking at the pictures, and discussing what headings or chapters might be about.

- ◆ *Field trips:* A wonderful way to build prior knowledge is to encourage children to become actively involved in the topic. For many children who are English language learners, direct experience is an excellent way to build literacy skills. For example, before reading a book about a farm, Mrs. Person's multilingual, urban kindergarten class visited a farm. When it came time to read the book, the class had a great deal of background knowledge stored up, which greatly increased students' comprehension of the material. Classes can also take virtual field-trips using the Internet to explore places and sites they might not be able to physically visit, such as the Louvre Museum in Paris, France.

- ◆ *Semantic mapping/brainstorming:* Semantic mapping/brainstorming is a wonderful way to activate prior knowledge and build up schemata. The children can share what they know about a topic, and they all learn from each other. It is also helpful to keep adding to the semantic map as the book or selection is read.

- ◆ *Video/film/pictures:* Another wonderful way to introduce a topic and build background knowledge is to show a video or film. It is also helpful to provide access to pictures of the concepts that will be covered in the text material. The Internet offers many primary resources and wonderful images, such as the Declaration of Independence and orginial photographs of historic events. Anything that makes the material more concrete and helps students relate to it is beneficial to their comprehension.

- ◆ *Quick Write:* An excellent way to activate prior knowledge is to have students write (or draw) what they know about a topic before reading the selection; when students share their ideas, other students learn about the topic.

- ◆ *Role-playing:* Have the students enact a scene or situation that the book deals with; this will help the students relate to the upcoming reading. For example, before reading a book about a boy who is having a bad day, the teacher might have two students role-play a scenario where one boy is having a bad day at school and the other child is his friend.

- ◆ *Internet sites:* Many Internet sites can provide excellent information to build background knowledge about a concept or theme. Students find these sites very motivating; they allow the user to explore the information at his/her own pace.

- ◆ *Podcasts:* Teachers can develop podcasts that can be played on children's iPods or MP3 players . These podcasts can help students build background knowledge or activate prior understandings.

A teacher can develop student background knowledge by previewing, prequestioning, and discussing a story.

The activities outlined above are excellent ways for the teacher to develop background knowledge by using schemata theory to help students better comprehend text materials. These activities are helpful for children with learning disabilities because they are more concrete experiences and help prepare the student for the upcoming reading. They provide scaffolding for the students to use while reading, as well as the essential background to facilitate comprehension.

In the introductory scenario, Mrs. Ghali helped her students build schemata before the reading process began. At reading time, she supported her students in activating prior knowledge about grandparents to help her students relate to the book *The Hello, Goodbye Window*. It is essential that Mrs. Ghali prepare her students for the upcoming reading by incorporating activities that develop schema and provide the necessary support so that the students can grasp what is being read. Before the actual reading occurs, teachers need to activate, develop, and build children's prior knowledge to help ensure success.

Fluency Instruction and Comprehension

What Is Fluency?

Researchers have discovered that fluency is a critical factor in comprehension. Fluent readers spend much less time laboring over text, resulting in more time to read for understanding. Even though fluency is a critical component of reading comprehension, it is often neglected in classrooms as a crucial instructional strategy (Adams, 1990; Chall, 1967; NICHD, 2000). During a nationwide assessment of fourth grade students, it was discovered that 44 percent of students do not read fluently. The National Assessment of Educational Progress (NAEP) researchers found a close relationship between fluency and reading comprehension, concluding that by providing instruction in fluency, together with vocabulary development and specific reading comprehension strategies, student achievement in reading comprehension will improve. In addition, instruction in phonemic awareness, phonics, and automaticity in sight-word recognition has shown to produce a positive effect in building reading comprehension (NICHD, 2000). However, the terms *fluency* and *automaticity* often are used interchangeably, but they are not identical and must, therefore, be defined carefully to avoid confusion (Figure 7–2). Research also indicates that fluency of reading is highly correlated with improved

FIGURE 7-2

Definition of Terms to Describe Fluency

FLUENCY—Reading text with speed, accuracy, and expression.

AUTOMATICITY—Recognizing words quickly and with ease; necessary, but not sufficient, for fluency.

To Assess Fluency—Calculate the student's oral reading rate on a passage for 1 minute; then, count the number of words read and record the WPM. Students should read faster than 90 words per minute. To assess accuracy, count the number of miscues (should read 95+% at their Independent Level).

comprehension, and that fluency is taught best through guided interaction with direct feedback given by the teacher or surrogate (Cowen, 2003).

Fluency is fast, expressive reading that involves both rate of reading words and the phrasing that good readers use when reading out loud (Cunningham, 2000; Pinnell & Fountas, 1998; Samuels, 1979). Fluency refers to how readers put words together in phrases so that they have a good pace to the reading, they read with expression, and they read easily, reflecting comprehension of the material. Fluency is highly correlated with comprehension scores on the standardized tests of the NAEP (Fountas & Pinnell, 1996; NICHD, 2000). Fluency is a critical component of skilled reading, which nevertheless often is neglected in classroom instruction (Rasinski, 2003).

Fluency provides the bridge between word identification and comprehension because readers do not have to concentrate on decoding words and can focus their attention on what the text means. More fluent readers can concentrate on making connections between what they are reading and their background knowledge, instantaneously constructing meaning as they are reading text. However, less fluent readers must concentrate on word identification and are unable to focus on what the text means (Adams, 1990; Chall, 1967; Snow, Burns, & Griffin, 1998).

Fluency develops slowly over time with readers going through various stages before attaining fluency. One of the first steps in reading is "being glued to the print," whereby young readers focus all their attention on word identification and read word by word. This is a normal stage for beginning readers who have not learned to quickly identify many words. They read in a slow and labored manner as they learn to "break the code"—that is, associate sounds with letters and blend them together into a meaningful word.

Strategies that contribute to fluency in reading include the following:

Automaticity—recognizing words and spelling patterns quickly and instantaneously while keeping the flow of the text going

Prediction—predicting what is coming next

Flexibility—changing directions at any point in time, catching a mistake and quickly self-correcting and go on, and quickly adapting to what the text calls for in terms of expression, phrasing, and continuity of thought

Self-monitoring—checking that what is being read makes sense for pronunciation, meaning, and phrasing (Fountas & Pinnell, 1996)

Even when students can read words automatically, this does not mean that they are fluent readers. Many readers fail to read with expression by dividing text into meaningful chunks; these chunks usually translate into phrases and clauses that correspond to pauses during the reading. Fluent readers must know how to pause appropriately within and at the ends of sentences and when to change emphasis and tone so that they are not reading in a monotone voice. Automaticity refers only to accurate, speedy word recognition, not to reading with expression; automaticity is necessary, but not sufficient, for fluency.

Fluency Instruction

Researchers (Bukovec, 1982; Samuels, 1979; NICHD, 2000) have investigated two major instructional approaches used to increase fluency: (1) repeated and monitored oral reading (commonly referred to as *repeated reading*), where students read text aloud several times; and (2) independent silent reading, where students are given time during the day to read independently on their own. The following findings are suggested from research on fluency:

Repeated and monitored oral reading improves reading fluency and overall reading achievement (NICHD, 2000).

Students who read and reread passages orally while receiving guidance and feedback from the teacher become better readers. Repeated oral reading significantly improves word recognition, rate of reading, and fluency. It also affects reading comprehension, but to a lesser extent. This instructional approach improves reading ability of all children throughout every grade level and is especially effective for struggling readers.

Sometimes teachers think that giving students a turn reading aloud from a text or reader *(round-robin reading)* will help fluency; in fact, this type of reading aloud can be harmful to readers, especially those who are struggling. In round-robin reading, students usually read only a small section once and do not get a chance to repeat the reading and receive guidance and support in a nonthreatening situation. Findings regarding the use of the round-robin approach show that such procedures of having children alternate reading text aloud to the class is boring, anxiety provoking, disruptive of fluency, and a waste of classroom time (Stallings, 1980).

Rather, the following two techniques are suggested to increase fluency:

- Students read and reread text out loud to the teacher, to peers, or at home until a certain level of fluency is reached. Four rereadings are sufficient for most students.
- Students use audiotapes, tutors, and peer guidance to practice reading out loud with instructive feedback.

It is unclear whether instructional time spent on silent, independent reading with minimal guidance and feedback improves fluency and overall reading achievement.

Teachers have long encouraged their students to choose their own reading material and spend time reading it independently. Programs such as "Drop Everything and Read (DEAR)" or "Silent Sustained Reading (SSR)" have been common components of the daily literacy lesson. Many studies have found a strong relation between reading ability and how much time a student spends reading. However, the National Reading Panel (NRP) suggests that there may be more beneficial ways to spend time in the classroom than with independent reading because there has been no proven relation that reading independently without guidance or feedback improves reading achievement and fluency (NICHD, 2000). This is not to say that children should not be choosing their own reading material and reading independently on their own; literacy classrooms should always encourage this in children. However, it does suggest that further studies are needed to investigate more thoroughly in-class reading approaches that are widely used in the classroom. In contrast with the NRP conclusions, Block and Mangieri's study (2002) on recreational reading shows that students who spent more time in recreational reading scored higher on comprehension tests, obtained higher grade point averages, and developed more sophisticated writing styles than those children who did not engage in recreational reading. Teachers need to provide opportunities for children to interact and discuss their independent reading experiences with their peers. For example, peer-directed discussion groups and literature circles appear to be effective in motivating children to read for pleasure while developing comprehension and life-long reading skills in a supportive environment (Cowen, 2003).

Teachers can help their students become fluent readers through the following two methods:

1. *Model fluent reading and have students reread text on their own.* The teacher should read out loud to the students on a daily basis. By reading with fluency, the teacher is modeling how the students should sound when they are reading. Choral reading—in which the whole group reads together—is also helpful. After the student has listened to the teacher and participated in choral reading, the student should practice reading the same text out loud at least four times. Have other adults read aloud to students and encourage parents, friends, and other family members to read to their children at home. The more models the child hears, the more beneficial it will be.

2. *Have students repeatedly read passages aloud while providing guidance and feedback.* Students need to practice reading the same text over again with support from the teacher. It is important that the text the student is reading is on the correct level and is reasonably easy for him or her. The student should know or be able to easily learn most of the words contained in the text, and the text should be relatively short. Use a variety of reading materials that the student finds interesting, including stories, nonfiction, and poetry. Some recommended approaches for students to practice reading fluently are:

Teachers' VOICES Repeated Reading

Repeated readings can be done silently or orally, although oral repeated reading is my most favored form for developing fluency. Oral repeated readings can be practiced individually with my guidance or performed with a partner. In a partner or paired reading setting, my students take turns reading aloud to each other. Most often, fluent readers are paired with nonfluent readers. Paired reading can also take place between student and teacher and student and parent, with the fluent reader serving as a model.

*—Kristin Crisafi, First Grade
Reading Recovery Teacher*

Repeated reading: The student reads and rereads a text one-on-one with an adult (see Figure 7–3 for a repeated reading technique to improve fluency).

Choral reading: Students read along as a group while the teacher models fluent reading.

Tape-assisted reading: Students read along in their books as they listen to a fluent reader on an audiotape.

Computer-assisted instruction: The student reads along with the computer in such software programs as Living Books, in which the software uses synthesized speech to read the text of the story.

Partner reading: Students are paired into teams of two, and they take turns reading to each other. More fluent readers can be paired with less fluent readers.

Readers' Theatre Workshop: Students rehearse and perform a play for peers while they read from scripts that have been developed from books that are rich in dialogue. A student will choose a character and read that character's lines throughout the script.

Echo reading: The student repeats the teacher's dictated words, phrases, and/or sentences immediately after they are uttered, as if the student is "echoing" what the teacher is saying.

Neurological impress: Neurological impress has been used with children with learning disabilities and is an excellent strategy for struggling readers. Here, the teacher is positioned directly in back of the child, so that the teacher can read right into the child's ear. The child is encouraged to repeat the words simultaneously: as soon as the teacher says a word, the child repeats it as if he or she were actually reading the word(s)

FIGURE 7-3

Repeated Reading Technique

1. Give the student a short reading selection of 50–200 words.

2. Have the student read the selection to the teacher.

3. The teacher records the reading speed and the number of words pronounced incorrectly.

4. The student practices reading the selection independently until she or he feels capable of reading it fluently (at a predetermined rate).

5. The student rereads the selection to the teacher (the teacher records his or her reading rate and mistakes again).

6. This procedure is repeated until the criterion rate has been achieved.

7. Once the student achieves the desired rate and accuracy criterion, she or he proceeds to the next selection.

8. The teacher graphically charts the student's improvement in both rate and accuracy.

9. The teacher can have the student read to a paired reading buddy for practice sessions, but students seem more highly motivated and engaged when the teacher monitors and records initial and ending scores.

Source: Bukovec, J. A. (1982). Improving reading skills through auricular reading techniques. *The Reading Instruction Journal, 25*(2, 3), 32–37.

To increase student fluency, teachers often monitor students' oral reading.

without teacher assistance. Although somewhat like the echo reading technique, in this instance, the student repeats the teacher's words but does not wait to hear a given phrase or sentence. Instead, the student repeats the teacher's spoken words simultaneously, almost before the words are spoken. The purpose of the neurological impress method is to actively engage the student by releasing more responsibility at once, and to activate and to impress the auditory and visual perceptions at once.

Fluency instruction should begin as soon as reading instruction begins. It should become the overall goal of the literacy program. If a student is reading text word by word, is not reading with expression, is demonstrating labored and slow reading, or is having difficulty with comprehension after reading aloud, the teacher should emphasize fluency instruction with that student. The fluent reader is one who can perform multiple tasks at the same time—for example, recognizing words while comprehending material while predicting the phrasing and grouping of the upcoming words. The nonfluent reader can perform only one task at a time. Practice helps the reader multitask by reducing cognitive demands needed for reading processes.

Mrs. Ghali needs to keep in mind that for her students to fully comprehend the text they are reading, they must have a degree of fluency, or the reading process will be laborious, difficult, and frustrating. She needs to concentrate on increasing fluency in her students by incorporating many of the activities listed earlier into her classroom literacy program. She should include activities that use repeated readings such as echo, choral, and assisted reading. These activities will help struggling readers become familiar with the process of reading and ultimately assist them in comprehending the material to be read. Mrs. Ghali could assign a passage to struggling readers as a homework assignment to read with their parents or read the text in a guided reading session *before* reading time so that these students are familiar with the passage and have developed fluency with it before they encounter it with the whole class. This would increase their motivation, confidence, and ability to comprehend the passage.

What Research Says About Reading Comprehension

RAND Reading Study Group Report on Reading Comprehension

The RAND Reading Study Group (Snow, 2002) investigated major issues about reading for understanding to determine what we still need to learn about reading comprehension. The researchers also investigated comprehension issues related to low-achieving students and English language learners who attend schools with high poverty rates. The researchers' preliminary findings show that far more information needs to be known in three specific domains of reading comprehension: (1) instruction, (2) teacher preparation, and (3) assessment.

Good comprehension instruction demands that teachers need to learn how to choreograph the readers' knowledge with appropriate motivating activities and text, within a variety of sociocultural contexts, including but not limited to the following:

◆ Community
◆ Cultural/linguistic student differences
◆ Culture of the school
◆ Culture of the classroom
◆ Specific curriculum design
◆ Instructional activities
◆ Teacher–student interactions

RAND (Snow, 2002) also provides a list of a number of research findings that tell us what we currently know about reading comprehension and what teachers should know. These findings are as follows:

◆ Instruction that is designed to enhance reading fluency leads to fairly significant gains in word recognition and fluency and to moderate gains in comprehension.
◆ Instruction can be effective in providing students with a repertoire of strategies that promote comprehension monitoring and foster comprehension.
◆ The explicitness with which teachers teach comprehension strategies makes a difference in learning outcomes, especially for low-achieving students.

◆ Instruction plays a critical role in addressing the problems of students with poor comprehension results, and comprehension can be taught.

◆ The role of vocabulary instruction in enhancing comprehension is complex.

◆ Teachers who provide comprehension strategy instruction that is deeply connected within the context of subject matter learning, such as history and science, foster comprehension development.

◆ Using various genres of text (that is, stories and informational text) diversifies instructional opportunities, as assessed by teacher and student discourse.

◆ Teachers who give students choices, challenging tasks, and collaborative learning structures increase their motivation to read and comprehend text.

◆ Despite the well-developed knowledge base that supports the value of instruction designed to enhance comprehension, comprehension instruction continues to receive inadequate time and attention in typical classroom instruction across the primary and upper elementary grades.

The Five Pillars of Effective Reading Instruction

The National Reading Panel (NRP) report (NICHD, 2000) set forth five areas that all reading programs should include to promote reading:

(1) Phonological and Phonemic awareness

(2) Phonics

(3) Vocabulary

(4) Fluency

(5) Comprehension

These areas have been called the "five pillars of effective reading instruction," and teachers should provide explicit instruction to students in these key pillars.

According to the NRP (NICHD, 2000), most reading programs do not provide enough instructional time in teaching comprehension, and there is greater need for explicit instruction in helping students read for understanding. The RAND report (Snow, 2002) corroborates the need for further reading comprehension instruction in classrooms, including (1) word attack and fluency, (2) reading in the content areas, (3) specific reading strategies, (4) vocabulary knowledge and use in reading, (5) recreational reading pursuits, (6) writing about reading, and (7) linking literacy and technology to support reading and writing. Similarly, Pressley's (2000) synthesis of comprehension instruction research concludes that reading comprehension is "multicomponential and developmental"; therefore, it depends on instructing students in the following areas:

◆ Developing their word-level competencies

◆ Activating their background knowledge

◆ Developing their metacognition (see later for definition)

◆ Self-regulating their use of comprehension strategies

Pressley (2000) further concludes that the development of reading comprehension is dependent on instruction in sight words—that is, vocabulary, fluency, and extensive opportunities for the student to *read, read, read*. He encourages students to ask themselves why the ideas related in a text make sense.

Five Missing Pillars of Scientific Reading Instruction

Although educators agree on the importance of teaching the five pillars that the NRP outlined, the NRP report has been criticized for its narrowly focused research review that ignores the substantive and broad experimental research on other aspects of effective reading instruction (Allington, 2005). Many researchers believe that these five

When children are encouraged to read their own selections from a classroom collection of interesting books, reading comprehension increases.

Courtesy of Becky Stovall

pillars are too narrow and do not cover other important aspects of reading. Allington (2005) recommends five other areas that directly impact reading instruction:

1. *Classroom organization:* Classroom organization includes effective reading instruction that provides a balance of whole-group, small-group, and individualized instruction every day. The whole-class, single curriculum in reading instruction with the whole class reading one book is ineffective; this approach does not promote reading comprehension.

2. *Matching pupils and text:* All pupils need texts that are matched to their appropriate level of reading development all day long. This is especially critical with struggling readers who need differentiated instruction. English language learners and students with learning disabilities should be given books to which they can relate and that are on an appropriate level of comprehension.

3. *Access to interesting texts, choice, and collaboration:* Students need easy access to a wide variety of interesting texts, they need choices as to what they read, and they need opportunities to collaborate with other children while reading. These options will impact their comprehension of the material they are reading.

4. *Writing and reading throughout the curriculum and throughout the day:* Reading and writing are reciprocal processes and enhance each other. Writing enhances reading, and reading enhances writing. This concept is covered in more detail in Chapter 8.

5. *Expert tutoring:* Struggling readers benefit enormously from access to quality tutoring. Research shows strikingly positive effects of tutoring on reading achievement. This is especially true with struggling readers such as English language learners and children with dyslexia.

Metacognitive Comprehension Strategies for Students to Apply

Comprehension strategies are different processes that students can apply to derive meaning from text. These strategies can not only be directly taught in the classroom to benefit student achievement in literacy, but they also should become **metacognitive strategies.** *Metacognition* literally means "thinking about thinking" or having students become aware of how they learn, how they read, and what strategies they use to help them solve problems during their thinking process. When a strategy is metacognitive, the student has become aware of the benefit of that strategy and can now apply it at the appropriate time to help derive meaning from the text. Students learn to think about how to read best, and they learn to think about strategies they can use to comprehend text. Students are thinking about cognitive processes; that is, they are applying metacognition.

Researchers have found that when these strategies are explicitly and directly taught in the classroom, reading comprehension improves (Adams, 1990; Gambrell, Pfeiffer, & Wilson, 1985; NICHD, 2000; Pressley, 2000; Wenglinsky, 2004). Although there are dozens of important reading comprehension strategies that are used daily with degrees of success in elementary and middle school classrooms across the United States, scientific research recommends several specific reading comprehension strategies. When readers are taught how to use these strategies explicitly and directly through modeling, guided practice, and cooperative learning, students' abilities to comprehend texts improve dramatically (NICHD, 2000). These important reading strategies are: (1) prediction, (2) monitoring comprehension, (3) using graphic and semantic organizers, (4) generating student questions, (5) recognizing story structure, (6) summarizing, (7) sequencing of events, (8) identifying main idea, (9) using context clues, (10) comparing and contrasting, and (11) drawing conclusions. These strategies apply to reading all types of text from narrative (stories) to informational (nonfiction) text. They are explained in detail in the following sections.

Prediction

Prediction encourages readers to speculate about the text based on the collection and analysis of "clues" from the book: illustrations, titles or subtitles, keywords from the text, character names or descriptions, or short excerpts from the text (Graves & Graves, 1994). Prediction allows students to think reflectively about what the book or text might be about and helps the reader ask questions that will guide the reading process. For example, when a student examines the cover of *Where the Wild Things Are* by Maurice Sendak (1963), the student will make note of the title, picture, and author and might predict that the book will be about monsters that live in far-off lands. This prediction is based on the systematic gathering of clues and information available and is not a wild guess. This prediction will help the student develop questions about the book before it is read, thereby facilitating comprehension.

Prediction is an important strategy to teach readers before they start to read. Not only does it focus their attention and give them a purpose for reading, it helps them during the reading process by making them think about what just happened and infer what might happen next. As part of this process, it is important that teachers not encourage wild guessing, but rather help students attend to salient details that will give the reader clues as to what the book will be about. It is therefore important that after a prediction activity the teacher goes back to the reader's initial prediction and confirm whether it was on target or analyze why the prediction was off base (Richardson, Morgan, & Fleener, 2006).

As a during-reading strategy, prediction involves stopping at key points in the story to ask what will happen next. In all stories, there are times right before the resolution of the problem when the reader stops and thinks about what will happen next. This is when the reader asks questions concerning the book and formulates conclusions as to what has occurred to date. A self-monitoring process is actually occurring, with new information being added to help direct prediction questions.

Some educators believe that prediction is the most important strategy a reader can use to comprehend text (Smith, 1985). According to Frank Smith, prediction is the prior elimination of unlikely alternatives; it is not reckless guessing, and it is not a matter of taking a chance on some likely outcome. Prediction is a matter of asking questions, and those questions are significant for gaining meaning from text. As Smith points out, without the ability to ask the right questions, there will be no way to answer them. According to Smith, asking appropriate questions and finding relevant answers lies at the heart of reading; prediction is a critical strategy that readers must use to comprehend material, which is the ultimate goal of reading.

Teachers can model the strategy of prediction with "think alouds," whereby before reading a book, the teacher will demonstrate how to make accurate predictions based on the cover illustrations, the title, the cover page, and background knowledge. These predictions should be written down on an easel or the board. After reading the book, the teacher can go back to the initial predictions and show how they were on target or off base; then the class can discuss and reflect on why this is so and how predictions can lead to understanding the text. Children can then practice this strategy in pairs and individually by sharing predictions with each other.

One strategy that teachers can use is a *Predicting and confirming activity* (PACA). This strategy helps students improve predictions by following a systematic procedure for predicting and confirming:

1. Ask students: "Predict what content will follow as you preview the text. Log your predictions or include them on a piece of paper."

2. Tell the students: "Confirm your predictions as you read the actual text and/or add important information that was not part of your predictions."

3. Tell the students to check their correct predictions. Have them draw a star next to any additional predictions they made as they read and cross out any incorrect predictions.

4. Have students confirm their predictions by writing supporting evidence in their log.

Teachers also use a "book walk" as a means to teach prediction strategies. During shared reading, the teacher will "walk" the students through the book, showing the students the illustrations, discussing them, and reviewing key concepts that may be incorporated in the book. Book walks are excellent activities to demonstrate how readers can preview texts before reading them, and then ask relevant questions that should be answered during the reading process.

Monitoring Comprehension

Self-monitoring is a strategy that readers use during the reading process that lets them know whether they are reading correctly and provides them with strategies if they do not comprehend what they have read. The key to self-monitoring is that students must think about how they read and be aware when they do not comprehend text. This strategy is therefore metacognitive: it is a strategy in which students must think about how they learn and read. Self-monitoring therefore empowers children by teaching them how to use "fix-up strategies" during their reading. For example, while reading the book *Where the Wild Things Are*, if the reader notes that the main character is in a far-off land with monsters and the reader does not understand why or how this occurred, the reader is using a self-monitoring strategy and will go back a few pages and reread the text to solve the confusion.

This strategy is important for children to learn, because readers need to know when they are not comprehending, and they need to stop themselves and do something to rectify the situation. Often when a person is reading, he or she will start thinking about something else—perhaps dinner or plans for the evening—but continue reading. Suddenly, the reader becomes aware that the last few pages are a blur, and that he or she has not understood the text. A good reader will stop, think about what was the last thing he or she comprehended, and then go back to reread and reprocess the text. Poor readers do not use this strategy and just go on reading, not even aware that their comprehension has been compromised and not taking any action to rectify the problem. Poor readers' main goal in reading is just to finish the text, not to pay attention to whether comprehension has occurred.

According to Fountas and Pinnell (1996), teachers can use a variety of cueing-strategy prompts to support the reader's use of monitoring strategies. These prompts include the following:

To support self-monitoring or self-checking behavior: *Were you right?*

To support reader's use of all sources of information: *What else could you try?*

To support self-correction behavior: *I liked the way you worked that out.*

To support phrased, fluent reading: *Can you read this quickly and with expression?*

Older readers, including capable adult readers, also must constantly monitor and self-correct their own reading behaviors. Comprehension is greatly dependent on reading for accuracy; as Marie Clay (1993) states: "Literacy activities can become self-managed, self-monitored, self-corrected and self-extending for most [readers], even those who initially find the transition into literacy hard and confusing" (p. 345).

Using Graphic and Semantic Organizers

Graphic organizers are visual diagrams that portray the relations among concepts and help readers organize, classify, and structure information from a text, whether it be stories (narrative text) or content-based materials (expository or informational text). Examples of graphic organizers are semantic maps or webs, charts such as flowcharts, story maps, and Venn diagrams. Graphic organizers should eventually be a metacognitive strategy for students to use during reading, in that students should be constructing their own graphic representations of the material to help visualize and comprehend the material. Graphic organizers can be used as a prereading, during-reading, or postreading activity, depending on how the teacher would like to support the reader during the reading process (Cowen, 2003b).

As a prereading activity, the most frequently used graphic organizer is the semantic map, whereby an inner circle contains the primary concept to be learned and smaller circles leading off the main circle like spokes become the attributes or preconceptions the readers know about the concept before reading. This graphic organizer is an excellent way for students to activate their prior knowledge before the reading takes place. The student places the topic in the middle of the circle, then fills in the outer circles with anything he or she knows about the topic. In a similar way, a semantic map can be used as a prewriting tool to help organize thoughts and structure ideas. Figure 7–4 is an example of a semantic map that Mrs. Ghali generated with her students as a prereading activity before starting reading the book *The Hello, Goodbye Window*. This map models the process that the students should be developing before they begin reading.

As a during-reading activity, graphic organizers help a student keep track of events and act as an ongoing conceptual organizer. They can help students reinforce important concepts by visually representing them, thereby facilitating short-term memory for

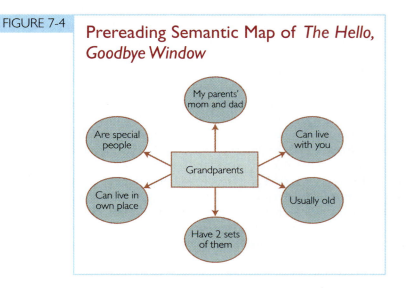

FIGURE 7-4

Prereading Semantic Map of *The Hello, Goodbye Window*

retrieval purposes. This type of activity helps students with learning disabilities who need support in focusing on the main ideas and order of events by providing them with a visual representation from which to work. It also helps English language learners who need reinforcement of the semantic and orthographic structure of the concepts being taught. It is recommended that during-reading activities be done with longer, more complex material, which can help students track the important events and concepts and not distract from the overall flow of the reading, thereby interfering with comprehension.

As a postreading activity, graphic organizers promote long-term comprehension of conceptual information because the information is organized graphically and structured in such a way that it is much easier for children to remember and subsequently recall. Graphic organizers are excellent ways for children to respond to literature, because children usually find them fun and helpful in organizing material.

Research in reading since the early 1980s has led to some major inroads in helping readers comprehend more effectively. This research shows that building on a learner's schema, or prior knowledge, together with scaffolding, or support mechanisms, enable readers to make the necessary connections that improve comprehension. The graphic organizer, used in tandem with a reader's background knowledge, provides the necessary support that allows learners to bridge gaps in their understanding. According to David Hyerle (1996), graphic organizers foster a collaborative, interactive style of learning. Hyerle introduced the term *visual tools*, which he believes broadens the concept of the term *organizer* beyond the sole purpose of helping students organize information. Indeed, visual tools can be used for brainstorming and facilitating dialogue, open-ended thinking, mediation, metacognition, theory development, and self-assessment.

The real value of introducing graphic organizers or visual tools is to provide students with a lifetime set of skills that they can use independently to become problem solvers and to learn to read, write, and think with greater facility and meaning. Once students begin internalizing these organizers, they can learn to use them as their own visual tools when encountering similar reading and thinking problem-solving situations. Some examples of graphic organizers can be found in Chapter 12, which describes visual tools in more detail. These organizers are particularly useful for struggling readers and English language learners who will learn to use them as a guide to independent reading, learning, and problem solving.

Generating Student Questions

It is also important that students themselves learn how to develop different types of questions as they read text. By asking many different types of questions, a student will learn how to monitor his or her own reading and comprehend the text through a deeper, more thoughtful approach. It is therefore important that teachers give direct instruction to their students on how to develop different types of questions. This can be done in a pair-share, where after reading a passage, two students pair up and write down different types of questions to ask each other. The teacher can monitor this process and give feedback to the students on the types of questions they are asking.

In more recent years, Louise M. Rosenblatt (1978) introduced the *transactional reading* approach, which requires students to think actively as they read and to acquire meaning by generating their own questions about what a given text means to them from a personal or aesthetic stance. Once students have experienced the real purpose of reading a story or narrative, they usually proceed to raise questions about what the text means from a cognitive or efferent stance, which, according to Rosenblatt (1978), is a natural progression in a typical transactional reading experience driven by student curiosity and interest, and not driven by the curriculum or a need to move on to the next learning objective.

J. T. Dillon (1988), in his influential book on student questioning, *Questioning and Teaching: A Manual of Practice*, points out the importance of students being actively involved in the reading and thinking process and the need to create a safe, positive environment that encourages student questioning in which the author demonstrates how students learn more effectively. Recent research (NICHD, 2000) supports Dillon's theoretical position. For example, Dillon (1988) recommends that teachers use the following approach to encouraging student questions:

- Provide for student questions.
- Create an atmosphere of systemic acceptance.
- Make use of questions for further teaching and learning.
- Welcome student questions when they come.
- Keep an open invitation for student questions.
- Create a wait time to be granted to students for speaking or writing.
- Sustain and extend student questioning.

Dillon indicates that teachers, by and large, tend to do most of their questioning related to teaching reading; therefore, he points out that teachers must create an environment in which students are welcome to raise questions.

The "dirty dozen" (Dillon, 1988) is an approach that teachers can use to ensure that students are encouraged to ask questions in the classroom.

1. Start the first class by asking for student questions, oral or written.
2. Have students ask and answer questions (while teacher listens).
3. Use student questions as an alternate to teacher questions in class.
4. Teach a questioning approach to text and content.
5. Let students construct test questions.
6. Reward and reinforce students' asking questions.
7. Sustain the questioning by empowering the students.
8. Help students formulate their unasked questions.
9. Understand and clarify student questions.
10. Help students reformulate questions.
11. Help students elaborate on questions.
12. Help students question by respecting their knowledge.

When students are encouraged to ask questions during the reading of the text, they become more reflective readers and tend to better understand what they are reading. Students can be taught strategies that help them ask questions that teach them how to read the text structure or, for example, to distinguish between main ideas and supporting details.

Recognizing Story Structure

Usually some of the first books children read at an early age are stories or *narrative* text. Narrative texts all contain similar elements, or **story structures,** that define them as a "story":

Setting usually includes two elements: time and place. *Time* refers to when the story is occurring—that is, present day, the future, or during a historic period. *Place* refers to where the story is taking place—that is, in a city, in a rural area, in a particular place.

Main character(s) are who the story usually focuses on.

Plot refers to the sequence of events of the story and how a conflict is resolved. The plot usually involves a *conflict* and a *resolution.*

Theme is the central message that the author is trying to convey, the overriding idea that the story revolves around.

Style is often considered one of the literary elements, although it is not always included. It refers to the way that the author writes—for example, in a humorous fashion, in a serious style, in a highly descriptive manner.

By identifying these narrative elements, children improve their comprehension of narrative text and become familiar with the structure of narrative prose.

Research findings support that when children are taught how to read for aesthetic pleasure and meaning at an early age, their reading comprehension improves dramatically (NICHD, 2000). Therefore, it is important to teach children how to recognize the various story elements. Searfross, Readence, and Mallette (2001) recommend, for example, that teachers use a guide that revolves around story structure. This guide encourages children to make predictions about how they think the story to be read will unfold shortly after the teacher has activated their background knowledge about the story. The children then learn how to think reflectively by creating questions about the story's setting, plot, characters, time, and motives. Some of Searfross and colleagues' (2001) questions to help children internalize what these story structural elements may include are as follows:

◆ Where does the story take place? (setting)
◆ When does the story take place? (time)
◆ Who is the story mainly about? (main character)
◆ Who else is in the story? (minor characters)
◆ What happens first? (plot, episode 1)
◆ What happens next? Next? (plot, episode 2, 3, and so forth)
◆ What problem does the character have? (conflict)
◆ How does the character solve the problem? (resolution)
◆ Did you like the way the story ends? (motives)

The "story map" is another tool that teachers can use as a postreading activity to help children recognize story structure and to help them better understand narratives. In Figure 7–5, a story map is used for the book *Amistad Rising: A Story of Freedom* by Veronica Chambers to help students identify the different elements of the story. This book tells the true story of Joseph Cinque, who was kidnapped from his African homeland and imprisoned on the slave ship *Amistad* with 52 other Africans. The book tells the story of how this courageous man fought for his freedom and in so doing changed the course of history.

Summarizing

Summarizing is when the reader is asked to restate what the author has said in a concise format. The reader needs to state only the main ideas of the text, and not retell every detail about the text. Summaries are brief restatements that include only important ideas, not trivial and minor details.

Summarizing is an important strategy for all children to perform as a during-reading and postreading activity. When good readers read text, they are constantly stopping and summarizing the material, mentally identifying the main ideas and deleting the trivial and unimportant details. When they feel they have gotten the main point, they go on. This also is an important strategy to perform after finishing the text because it allows the reader to condense the material into a shorter version that is easier to remember and comprehend. Good readers summarize as they read a passage and after they finish. Poor readers fail to do this and frequently get bogged down with details and minutia, failing to see the "big picture."

Summarizing is a difficult process for children to learn, particularly for those below the fourth-grade level. Primary-grade students often have difficulty identifying central ideas of a passage and condensing the material down into concise capsules. If you ask a first grader to summarize the short story just read, the summary often will be longer than the actual passage, including every last detail and even mentioning details that refer to the child's own life as well.

Story Map

Title: *Amistad Rising: A Story of Freedom*
Author: Veronica Chambers
Illustrator: Paul Lee

Setting:
Time: 1839
Place: On board the ship *Amistad* and later in New London, Connecticut

Characters:
1. Joseph Cinque, a kidnapped African
2. John Quincy Adams

Problem:
Joseph Cinque was put in prison after landing in Connecticut and was fighting for his freedom.

Action:
Joseph Cinque killed the captain of the *Amistad* and was tricked into believing they were sailing for Africa. When they landed in Connecticut, he was arrested. John Quincy Adams argued for Cinque's freedom in front of the Supreme Court and won the case.

Outcome:
Joseph Cinque won his freedom and returned to Africa a free man.

Theme:
It is important to fight for what you believe in.

FIGURE 7-5

It is important to make summarizing activities as easy as possible. The following guidelines can be used in teaching summarizing:

1. Use a brief passage at first. Simple narratives—that the children are familiar with—are recommended at the beginning.

2. The text should be written on an easel or in view when younger students start to write summaries. This reduces the burden of having the student remember what was in the text. Later, when the students become more proficient with summarizing, the text should be removed.

3. The texts to be summarized should be well organized and written at the appropriate readability level. Vocabulary and content should be familiar so that the children do not have to try to remember unfamiliar words or work with unfamiliar content.

4. Initial summaries should be just slightly shorter than the original, involving the retelling of the story with the deletion of only the most trivial details. The teacher can model this by using a marker to cross out any details that are not important. Shorter summaries can come later when the children are more proficient.

5. These initial summaries should be written for the student, not the teacher. The summaries should be similar to journal entries where the main focus is on the skill of

summarizing, and not on the writing style or grammar. The important point is whether the student is able to identify the main ideas and delete the unimportant details.

Summarizing should be initially modeled by the teacher; then children should be given a chance to practice the techniques in groups. The teacher can give students short passages and ask them to summarize them using the same process demonstrated above. Students can also do pair-shares by reading the same passage, writing a summary on it, and then sharing their individual summaries with a partner, comparing each other's summary and giving feedback.

Sequencing of Events

Sequencing is a basic strategy that allows the reader to order the events of the text in a logical order, usually chronologically. It is one of the first strategies required for full comprehension of the material, and it allows the reader to then use more complex strategies, such as drawing conclusions and inferring. Before the reader is able to extend the comprehension process to higher order thinking, a basic recall of the events as they took place sequentially in the text must occur. In many instances, this process is straightforward and direct. In other instances, where there is a complex storyline or a great deal of material to process, this strategy becomes much more difficult for the reader and requires the effective use of memory strategies to facilitate the ordering of events.

Sequencing is for the most part a postreading activity that the reader should use after he or she has finished reading the text. However, sequencing can be a during-reading strategy as well, when the material is complex and there are a great many events to remember. Effective readers will rehearse the sequence of events while reading to help them recall the previous details of the story, realizing that final comprehension of the story will depend on keeping these events in order. Poor readers will just read without any self-monitoring or pausing to rehearse; when they have finished reading, they fail to fully remember and thus understand the material they have read.

Sequencing can be a critical strategy to emphasize depending on the story or material to be read. Many children's books are based on a simple chain of events in which one character influences another character, who influences another, until the ultimate conclusion is brought about. For this type of story, sequencing of events is a critical activity for the teacher to stress. Such activities as rehearsal of events and drawing of pictures, timelines, flowcharts, and graphic organizers that help the reader see the chain of events sequentially all help the reader to learn the strategy of sequencing.

Teachers' VOICES   Teaching Tip on Comprehension: Sequencing

The *retelling wheel* is a great strategy that can be used with the whole class or in small groups such as literature circles. The strategy helps the children to sequence and retell stories. It can be modified and used in kindergarten through fifth grade.

DAY 1

1. Read a story aloud or have the students read the same text independently.

2. Discuss the story within the group, talking about events, connections, and themes.

DAY 2

1. Reread the story.

2. Explain to the students that they are going to make a wheel to help them retell the story to a friend.

   Review the time order words (for example, *first, next, then, after that, finally*).

3. Discuss the important parts that should be included in the retelling.

4. Tell students to assign parts (events) to each other within small groups that they will write down and illustrate. If you are doing a whole-class wheel, assign events to small groups to work on together.

5. Glue each event to the wheel in sequential order according to the story.

6. Ask students to retell the story to each other or the class, using the wheel as a guide.

—Dana Carloni, First Grade Teacher

Identifying the Main Idea

Teaching children how to identify the main idea of a text is difficult; however, unless the reader can distinguish between essential and nonessential information in contrast with knowing what the central idea of a selection is, he or she cannot become a successful reader. Teachers can model how to find the main idea by using *think alouds*, during which time the teacher demonstrates (by talking out loud) how he or she goes about locating the central or main idea, and then how he or she locates supporting details that further explain the main idea. Teachers can also help students identify the main idea of a passage, first by highlighting the big ideas in a specific color (for example, in red), then by highlighting minor or supportive details in contrasting color(s) (for example, in blue or green).

When teaching how to identify the main idea, teachers should remember that it is helpful for students to learn how to write a topic sentence that contains the main idea of a writing assignment. It is always beneficial to teach a comprehension strategy in two ways: have the student learn to apply the strategy as a reader, and have the student use the strategy as a writer. In this way, the reciprocal processes of reading and writing are reinforced.

Graphic organizers can also be used to help students visually distinguish main ideas from supportive details by having students fill in a semantic map or web with the main idea in the inner circle and the supporting details branching out as spokes. This visually represents what the main idea is about and will help the student focus on the important concepts. In this way, the semantic map or web can be used to help students identify their own main idea and supporting details in the prewriting stage (Cowen, 2003b).

Using Context Clues

Inferring the meaning of a word using the context of the sentence is an essential strategy that readers use constantly as they process print. When a reader comes across a word that he or she does not know, the reader must identify clues in the sentence that will unlock the meaning of that word. In context-rich sentences, there are many synonyms and clues provided to help unlock the unknown word. These sentences should be targeted to teach a student this skill. For example, in the following sentence from *Saint George and the Dragon* by Margaret Hodges, try to find the clue words that would unlock the meaning of the word *hideous*.

> Then they heard a hideous roaring that filled the air with terror and seemed to shake the ground.

In analyzing this sentence to determine meaning, it is quite obvious that something bad is occurring. "Roaring" and "terror" both connote something frightening, and the phrase "seemed to shake the ground" further clarifies this awful roar. There is no doubt that "hideous" can be only a terrible and frightening thing that fills one with fear. This is the type of thinking a reader must do when using context clues to infer meaning from the sentence.

There are many different clues that a reader can use to infer the meaning of an unknown word. First, the reader can use semantic clues, such as other words that may be synonyms or antonyms that signify what the meaning might be. For example, in the sentence above from *Saint George and the Dragon*, "roaring" and "terror" are both synonyms that can help unlock the meaning of "hideous." Second, the reader can use syntax or grammar clues to help infer the meaning. For example, if the student knows that the word "hideous" is describing the word "roaring," then "hideous" must be an adjective that describes some sort of sound, probably not a pleasant one. The student is then using the syntax or grammar of the sentence as a clue to unlock meaning. Third, the reader can use the phonologic structure of the word. The student may be able to sound out the word by using phonic analysis, or the student may be able to use structural analysis and identify prefixes, suffixes, or roots that could unlock the meaning of the word.

Teachers should directly teach this strategy as part of the literacy program. Children need to learn how to determine the meaning of unknown words and phrases without constantly stopping and asking an adult or finding a dictionary. As Adams (1990) points out, the best way to build children's visual vocabulary is to have them read meaningful words in meaningful contexts. Learning from context is an important component of comprehension and should be taught explicitly in the classroom. Sometimes the meaning of an unknown word can be inferred from the context of the sentence or text, and sometimes it cannot. However, Adams concludes that a student's ability to use the contextual clues that follow or precede a word is not automatic, giving credence to the benefits of directly teaching such strategies.

The cloze method (discussed in detail in Chapter 5) is an excellent way to teach children how to decide which keywords or key phrases are necessary to understand a passage. This is accomplished by leaving out every fifth or tenth word of a text (not accounting for dates, proper names, or numerals). Teachers often use variations of the cloze method and leave out key terms and ask the students to use the context of the passage to figure out the missing words. Teachers who teach English language learners find that leaving out noncontent words helps these students—who are not reading in their native language—learn the new abstract words through the use of the surrounding context.

Content area teachers can also delete keywords from passages that they want students to learn by using clues from the context of the textbook passage selected for this purpose. Sometimes the student is asked to identify the missing concept word, using context clues by reading and by considering the remaining words of the passage. Other context clues to help the student uncover text meaning can be used by covering a word and asking the child to use the surrounding text to reveal the masked word's meaning. When a child cannot figure out a word, the teacher might give the student one of the following context clues: *Can you guess the unknown word if I give you a synonym, the prefix, the suffix, or root?* Figure 7–6 provides an example of the cloze method, which was used with the book *Zen Shorts* by Jon J. Muth, a 2006 Caldecott honor award winner. As this example shows, the child must use context clues to determine the exact word that should be written in the blank space. The teacher chose which words to leave out based on context clues in the story.

Comparing and Contrasting

Showing how things are alike and how things are different is one of the most important ways to help students develop their understanding of comparing and contrasting information. The use of graphic organizers such as a Venn diagram or a compare/contrast chart (see Chapter 10 for an example) enables students to visualize differences. Figure 7–7 shows a compare/contrast visual tool for the book *Aunt Harriet's Underground Railroad in the Sky* by Faith Ringgold that was developed using the software program *Inspiration*. This tool was used to help students compare and contrast—by visualizing—the two main characters in the book, Cassie and Be Be, who explore what the Underground Railroad was all about. Students learn how to be more

FIGURE 7-6

Cloze Technique

Book: *Zen Shorts*
Author: Jon J. Muth

The next _____, Addy went to have tea with Stillwater.

"Hello?" Addy said as she stepped _____.

"Come in! Come in!" a faraway _____ called.

Then she heard the voice ___, "Oh, yes. . . . Come out! Come out!"

Stillwater was in the backyard.

He was in a tent.

"This is the birthday present _____ my Uncle Ry," Stillwater said.

"He always gives presents on his birthday, to celebrate the _____ he was born.

I like it so much, that I'm not staying in my house _____ now."

Stillwater invited Addy to _____ with him.

Answers:
day, inside, voice, say, from, day, right, sit or go

Compare/Contrast Chart

Book: *Aunt Harriet's Underground Railroad in the Sky*
Author: Faith Ringgold

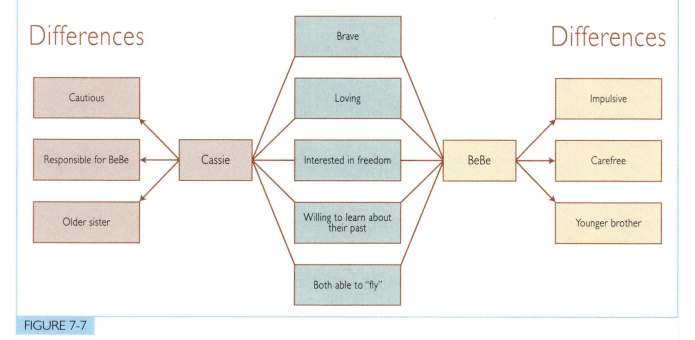

FIGURE 7-7

discriminating, critical, judgmental, and evaluative, which, according to researchers (Silver, Strong, & Perini, 2000; Bloom, 1956), develops their ability to read for high order thinking skills, increasing their reading comprehension development. Comparing and contrasting as a reading strategy is one of the best ways to improve a student's reading comprehension (Marzano, Pickering, & Pollock, 2001; NICHD, 2000).

Drawing Conclusions

Drawing conclusions is a strategy that is based on the effective use of other strategies previously described. For a reader to effectively draw conclusions, he or she first needs to be able to predict, sequence the material, and summarize. Drawing conclusions depends on the reader synthesizing all the derived information into a conclusion that the author intended the reader to understand. If many other strategies are not being used effectively, this conclusion may be inaccurate, incorrect, or missing altogether. In drawing conclusions, there is an underlying message that the author intends the reader to learn by the end of the selection. A subtle process occurs between the author and the reader, and within this interaction, the reader must start picking up threads of a hidden message. The conclusion that the reader finally draws from the text is based on this interaction and how effectively the author conveyed his or her message on paper and how effectively the reader used various strategies to detect this message. For most text selections, a reader may be able to predict, sequence, summarize, and infer words from the context of a sentence, but still miss the whole point of the text. If the reader cannot draw the correct conclusion from the reading, the moral or theme is still hidden and only a shallow depth of understanding is reached. This is the difference between a good reader and one who is struggling with comprehension. The one who is struggling may enjoy a story but not draw the correct conclusions from the book. At this point, discussion, questioning, and prompting can help this student start drawing conclusions.

Teachers can teach this strategy by purposely choosing books that have significant conclusions to be drawn. Through "think alouds," in which the teacher models the process she or he goes through in drawing conclusions, this strategy can first be modeled to students. Through guided questions designed to prompt the students, the teacher can guide students to draw the appropriate conclusions. Often, literature discussion groups or literature circles can help students by having them discuss with other students books that they have read. This discussion can be an enlightening experience for these students by helping them see different perspectives on the same book, and thereby expand the conclusions they might have drawn.

The Importance of Comprehension Strategies

In summary, it is essential that teachers focus on teaching the comprehension strategies listed earlier explicitly and directly in the classroom as part of the instructional program in literacy. Teachers should model these strategies and show students how to be aware of the strategies they are using during the reading process. These metacognitive strategies should be practiced and openly discussed as part of everyday instruction in literacy, so that students become familiar with them and use them as part of their vocabulary during discussion of the reading process. Figure 7–8 lists a summary of all the comprehension strategies discussed.

After consulting with the literacy coach, Mrs. Ghali modeled certain strategies to her students during reading time and discussed how she found these strategies useful to understanding the story. She also could have asked students to discuss these strategies during the postreading discussion. One strategy she used was prediction; she had students discuss what their prediction of the book would be before the reading began. She then verified whether the students' predictions were correct or needed revising, focusing on the struggling readers and English language learners to involve them in the process of reading.

Summary of Comprehension Strategies

Strategy	Description	Purpose	Example
PREDICTION	The reader makes an educated "guess" about what the text will be before reading it based upon the collection and analysis of "clues" from the book. The reader then confirms or refutes this prediction after reading the text.	To help the student ask questions about what the book will be about so that these questions can be answered during the reading process.	The student will do a "walk through" of a book, looking at the title, cover page, and pictures, and then will write down what the book will be about. After reading the book, the student will check to see if the prediction was accurate.
MONITORING COMPREHENSION	A reader knows whether he is reading correctly and applies strategies to help comprehend what has been read.	To let the reader know when to use "fix up strategies" to comprehend the text being read.	The student thinks, "I do not understand what I just read . . ." The student then thinks, "Let me go back and reread this passage, trying to figure out what this means. That might help." If it doesn't help, the student can apply another strategy or may ask a teacher, adult, or another student for help.
USING GRAPHIC AND SEMANTIC ORGANIZERS	Visual diagrams the student develops that portray the relationships among concepts and help readers organize, classify, and structure information from a text.	To help visualize and comprehend the material through graphic representations.	After reading a book on hurricanes, the student develops a graphic organizer to help organize and classify the information that will help her remember the content.
GENERATING STUDENT QUESTIONS	The reader develops different types of questions during reading that will help the student monitor comprehension and read for meaning.	To help guide the reader by asking questions and answering them while reading the text.	As the student is reading a Harry Potter book, the student asks what will Harry do next? Will Dumbledore help him? Will his friends come to his aid?
RECONIZING STORY STRUCTURE	The reader recognizes the story elements while reading: setting, characters, plot, theme, and style. This helps the reader comprehend the text and anticipate what is coming next.	To become familiar with the structure of narrative prose, which will help in overall comprehension.	While reading, the student instantly recognizes the setting as Hogwarts; the main characters as Harry, Ron, and Hermione; the plot with its conflict and resolution; and the theme, which helps the student keep track of what is going on.
SUMMARIZING	The reader is asked to restate what the author has said in a very concise format.	To condense the text into a shorter version, which is easier to remember and comprehend.	After reading a book, the reader writes or tells the teacher or class a concise version of the text, mentioning only the important details.

FIGURE 7-8

continued

Stratergy	Description	Purpose	Example
SEQUENCING OF EVENTS	The reader orders the events of the text in a logical order, usually chronologically.	To recall the events as they took place sequentially in the text so that full comprehension can occur.	The reader records the major sequence of events onto a graphic organizer to better remember what occurred, and then infers what the theme is and draws a conclusion about the text.
IDENTIFYING MAIN IDEA	The reader identifies the primary topic or idea that the text is about; often used in informational text and writing.	To distinguish important ideas from supportive details, which will aid in comprehension.	The student reads a passage in a textbook and identifies the main idea that the author is trying to convey. The reader can also identify supporting details that support this main idea.
USING CONTEXT CLUES	The reader infers the meaning of a word using the context of the sentence or the passage. The user can use semantic clues, syntactic clues, or phonological clues.	To unlock the meaning of unknown words by searching for various clues in the surrounding passage of the text.	The student comes across the word *malevolently* and searches the passage to see if there are any clues. The student notices that the passage has the words *furious* and *panic* in it, and when studying the word knows that the prefix *mal-* means *bad* or *not good*. The student therefore deduces that *malevolently* must be something evil.
COMPARING AND CONTRASTING	The reader shows how things are alike and how things are different.	To learn how to judge and value differences, and thereby be more discriminating, critical, and evaluative, which leads to higher-order thinking.	The student is asked to compare and contrast two characters in a book: Harry Potter and his friend Ron. Using a Venn diagram, the student compares and contrasts them using the following criteria: physical attributes, personality traits, likes, and dislikes.
DRAWING CONCLUSIONS	The reader synthesizes all the information that was read into a conclusion that the author intended the reader to see.	To help the reader see the "deeper" meaning of a text that the author might not have clearly stated but intended to convey.	After reading the text *Number the Stars* by Lois Lowry, the reader joins a literacy circle where the themes of friendship and sacrifice are discussed. The student starts to obtain a deeper understanding of what the book's message and theme is.

FIGURE 7-8

Teachers' VOICES   Teaching Tip on Comprehension: Drawing Conclusions

Drawing conclusions is an important facet to reading comprehension. So, instead of boring questions, I came across a fun activity involving comic strips. The materials for "concluding comics" are easy to collect, and the setup is virtually painless. Teachers can place this activity into their reading center for reinforcement of comprehension skills, and it can be adapted to other grade levels as well.

- Search through newspapers and cut out several comic strips with at least three sequence boxes.
- Cover up the caption of each box.
- Add a new caption that gives a humorous clue about what is happening in each box, leaving the last one empty. (Each strip should be done the same way!)

- Next, glue the comic strips that you have collected onto a piece of construction paper and laminate each one.
- Model with the class how to use the clues in the captions to write a "concluding caption" for the last box.
- If using in a learning center, place laminated strips with an erasable marker in a folder for the students to use again and again.
- Once the children are comfortable using comic strips, you can have them create their own.

—*Heather DiSerio, Third Grade Teacher*

The following section focuses on specific instructional approaches that teachers can use in the classroom to help support reading comprehension. Try to determine which approaches will continue to help Mrs. Ghali have a more successful literacy program with her students.

Instructional Program in Comprehension

Teachers can help students become "better comprehenders" or better readers through instructional approaches that they use in the classroom. Through direct instruction of these approaches, teachers can have a positive impact on student achievement in literacy. This section describes various instructional approaches that teachers and students can use in the classroom to promote comprehension of text and improve students' reading ability.

The RAND report (Snow, 2002) indicates that there is a great deal to investigate about improving instruction in reading comprehension; nevertheless, major research reports (NICHD, 2000; Snow, Burns, & Griffin, 1998) recently have established that there is a body of knowledge that is now accessible that informs teachers how to improve reading comprehension, and that through proper preparation, teachers can have a positive influence on student literacy achievement. Searfross, Readence, and Mallette (2001) state quite simply that "comprehension can be taught." These researchers indicate that not enough attention has been given to the teaching of reading comprehension, and they recommend that adequate time must be devoted to ensuring that the following strategies are taught:

- Teachers must model the comprehension processes for students.
- Guidance in comprehension processes must be scaffolded for readers before, during, and after their reading experiences.
- Teachers must provide feedback to children about their ongoing progress.
- Students must practice comprehension using a variety of texts to gain independence and confidence.

The following sections describe different instructional approaches that should be incorporated into the balanced literacy program to promote comprehension of text.

These approaches are oriented toward reading both narrative and informational text; however, Chapter 12 covers in detail instructional approaches specifically designed for comprehending informational text.

Developing and Answering Questions

Asking questions after a student reads text is perhaps one of the more popular strategies that teachers use to assess students' comprehension of material. Asking questions is an excellent and effective way to assess quickly whether a student has fully comprehended the material or, in fact, has missed some significant aspects of the text. Developing excellent questions is an important skill that all teachers need to learn.

Questioning students before, during, and after they have read text is an effective strategy to enhance comprehension of material. Teachers need to learn how to ask questions that make students think about the material in different ways and encourage them to go beyond merely recalling information and facts from the text. Through carefully developed questions, teachers can guide students to understand deeper meanings of the passage, and to look beyond what is merely stated to infer what the author meant and analyze subtle details. Teachers can also help students relate personally to the text through questioning, which will help build schemata from which students can draw on in later readings. Questions can help students tap into and build on prior knowledge.

Research indicates that teachers must vary the kinds of questions that they ask students, and that higher order thinking type questions tend to produce higher level responses (Marzano, Pickering, & Pollock, 2001). In fact, teachers' questions that require students to analyze or synthesize information result in improved student learning and reading comprehension. Bloom (1956), as well as Silver, Strong, and Perini (2000), found that when questions require only rote level or mastery level responses, student thinking remains unchallenged. Bloom's research indicates that there are at least six levels that a teacher should try to have students work at, starting at a basic recall of knowledge and working up a hierarchy toward analysis, synthesis, and evaluation. Silver, Strong, and Perini (2000) suggest that questions that require students to respond by using analysis, synthesis, and creativity produce higher achievement, resulting in higher level student artifacts or products.

There are three basic types of questions that teachers can use to assess comprehension of students' reading ability: literal, interpretive, and creative. Each type of question requires the student to think differently about the material and draw on different cognitive skills.

***Literal Comprehension Questions* – Literal comprehension questions** involve recognition of that which the author specifically stated in the selection. These types of questions identify stated details in the passage such as specific names, places, events, and dates. These questions can also ask the student to identify the main ideas of the text or to identify the genre of the reading selection, such as if it is fiction, nonfiction, or biography.

Research shows that teachers tend to ask students more literal, mastery, or lower level questions that do not require the students to analyze or apply information, to make inferences, or to restructure information in any way. After students have read a story, for instance, there is a tendency for teachers to ask questions that can be found as direct statements in the text. Questions that ask "What?" "Who?" or "Where?" tend to elicit rote, or lower level, literal comprehension responses. Although such questions and responses are valuable for helping students recall important details of the text, they should not dominate teacher-questioning techniques (see Figures 7–9a and 7–9b for examples of literal comprehension questions).

***Interpretive/Inferential Comprehension Questions* – Interpretive comprehension questions** involve the recognition of the many alternatives that the author may have meant but did not state specifically. In these types of questions, students must draw inferences by separating facts from opinions, drawing conclusions, and predicting outcomes. These questions can be difficult to answer because they involve inferring what is not overtly stated, but rather what is implied. It means that students must read between the lines and ascertain subtle clues as to what the meaning of the text involves. This type of question can also be more difficult for the teacher to formulate because it involves leading students to infer meaning.

Questions that require students to interpret information or to draw inferences are more likely located in more than one part of the text, and more likely, the answer will be derived by forming an opinion about the text based on a complete reading or rereading of the selection. Raphael (1982, 1986; Raphael & Au, 2005) uses the Question–Answer Relationship (QAR) reading strategy approach (discussed in detail later in this chapter) to show students that information is not always found directly in the text, but that some responses are often drawn from the reader's prior knowledge, which helps form the opinions drawn from an overall understanding of the text (see Figures 7–9a and 7–9b for examples of interpretive comprehension questions).

Creative Comprehension Questions – **Creative comprehension questions** require students to draw on their background of information and experiences, values system, and originality to demonstrate that they relate to that which is specifically stated or implied in a selection. In answering this type of question, the student must project himself or herself into the situation that the text is describing and draw on background knowledge to make a judgment. This type of question begins with, for example, "If you were the main character . . ." or "If you had a similar opportunity . . ."; these questions end with, for example, ". . . what would you have done?" In constructing this type of question, it is important that the teacher remembers to refer back to specific events in the selection so that comprehension of the text is assessed, not just pure background knowledge; comprehension is not being assessed if the student can answer the question

---

Levels of Reading Comprehension Questions

The paragraphs below are graded passages written on second and third grade levels. The questions that follow are examples from the three different levels of reading comprehension questions: literal, interpretive, and creative.

Second Grade Level

The Crab and His Mother

An Old Crab said to her son, "Why do you walk sideways like that, my son? You ought to walk straight." The Young Crab replied, "Show me how, dear mother, and I'll follow your example." The Old Crab tried and tried, but then she saw how foolish she had been to find fault with her own child.

Literal Questions (all the answers can be found in the passage):
1. What did Old Crab ask her son?
2. How did Young Crab answer her?
3. What did Old Crab try to do?
4. Why did Old Crab feel foolish?

Interpretive Questions (all the answers are not explicitly stated in the passage, but must be inferred):
1. Why did Old Crab want her son to walk differently?
2. Why did Young Crab ask his mother to show him how?
3. Why couldn't Old Crab walk straight?

Creative Questions (all the answers are based upon the student's placing himself or herself into the situation and personally relating to the passage):
1. If you were Young Crab, how would you have reacted to your mother asking you to walk differently?
2. Do you think that it was right for Old Crab to ask her son to walk straight? Why or why not?

FIGURE 7-9a   *continued*

Third Grade Level

The Desert: What Lives There

The desert is a place that gets very little rainfall. The ground is often sandy and rocky. When the sun beats down, the sand and rocks grow hot and dry. It is hard to imagine that a place like this is full of living things.

All living things need food, water, and some kind of shelter to survive. Some plants and animals are well suited to survive in the desert. They can live off the food, water, and shelter that are there.

The cactus is one kind of plant that is suited to survive in the desert. The cactus has a special way of getting water in the dry desert. It spreads its roots out close to the top of the ground. When rain comes, the cactus roots soak up the water quickly before it drains deep into the sand.

Once a cactus plant gets water, it can store it for the dry days ahead. A cactus can store enough water from one rainstorm to last a long time.

Literal Questions (all the answers can be found in the passage):
1. What kind of a place is the desert?
2. What do living things need to survive?
3. Why is the cactus well suited to survive in the desert?
4. How do the roots help the cactus survive?
5. How long can a cactus store water?

Interpretive Questions (all the answers are not explicitly stated in the passage, but must be inferred):
1. Why is it hard to imagine living things surviving in the desert?
2. How often does the sun beat down in the desert?
3. Why can some plants and animals live in the desert?

Creative Questions (all the answers are based upon the student's placing himself or herself into the situation and personally relating to the passage):
1. If you were a cactus, how would you survive in the desert?
2. If you lived in the desert, what other living things might you see surviving there?
3. What advice might you give someone who is going to visit a desert?

FIGURE 7-9b

without ever really having read the selection (see Figures 7–9a and 7–9b for examples of creative comprehension questions).

In summary, it is important that teachers learn how to develop many different types of questions that encourage students to think and assess material critically. Questioning is a skill that can take many years of practice to perfect, but it is a powerful tool in the classroom to promote deep and rich comprehension of material. Questioning is also an effective way to assess student comprehension of text.

Scaffolded Reading Approach

The **scaffolded reading approach** (Graves & Graves, 2003) is a nurturing strategy that has proved to be a successful way to improve reading comprehension by implementing three phases in the instructional reading process: prereading, during-reading, and postreading activities. These scaffolded reading activities begin with the teacher taking on the greatest amount of instructional responsibility; however, once the student shows improvement, the teacher gradually releases this responsibility for learning over to the student. The teacher can plan an instructional approach to comprehension that focuses on these three distinct parts of a lesson: prereading, during-reading, and postreading. These three different activities are described briefly later in this chapter and in detail in Chapter 13.

Prereading Activities – Prereading activities currently are viewed by most elementary and middle school teachers and researchers as being extremely important for preparing all students to comprehend upcoming reading selections (Graves & Graves, 2003; Rand Reading Study Group, 2002; Snow, 2002). The prereading activities recommended below are widely used and have proved to be effective in preparing students to read challenging texts.

Activating prior knowledge: It is important that teachers take the time to activate prior knowledge before the students read the text. Most students come with some background knowledge or information about what they are going to read. However, struggling readers or English language learners are not always confident or aware that they, too, have background knowledge that will help prepare them in advance to relate what they know to new material or information. Therefore, it is important to prompt students so they bring what they do know to their own consciousness to help them learn new information. For example, the use of multicultural literature that is set in the native country of several students in the classroom can be used to great advantage by helping the students recall background information from their earlier experiences; recall of background information will help them read, enjoy reading, and contribute rich and pertinent information to understand a narrative story, historical event, or description.

Building background knowledge: As mentioned earlier, it is important that teachers develop students' background knowledge before the reading occurs. This can be done by discussion, field trips, hands-on activities, visiting websites that introduce the topic, going on virtual field trips on the Internet, and viewing videos/films/ pictures related to the upcoming reading.

Preteaching vocabulary: Preteaching vocabulary words allows the teacher to introduce new synonyms, antonyms, or unfamiliar words to children before they actually begin to read a given selection or assignment. Because key vocabulary words may influence the student's understanding of some key ideas that are being read, it is extremely helpful to preteach and elaborate on the meaning of keywords (about five or six) that are preselected by the teacher.

Motivating and interest: If students are not interested in what they are reading, then the reading activity will literally be meaningless to the students. Technology and computer-assisted programs for teaching reading can be used in the prereading stage to motivate an interest in the text. It is also beneficial to allow students to select their own reading material because this will inherently motivate them to read more than when text is assigned. Involving students in a variety of prereading motivational activities on an ongoing basis is a necessary component of ongoing comprehension.

Predicting, prequestioning, and direction setting: As mentioned earlier, prediction occurs when the reader makes specific "guesses" about the text based on the collection and analysis of "clues" from the illustrations, titles, keywords, character names, or short excerpts from the text. Prediction is a way of involving the reader—creating active reading participation—and at the same time teaching students to attend to what is important as they read. Predicting, prequestioning, and direction setting focus the reader on what the upcoming text may be about and help the reader answer questions posed during the prereading stage.

During-Reading Activities – During-reading activities support readers during the process of reading. As students read, they are taught how to ask questions, clarify meaning as they proceed, and reflect on what they are reading by checking to see what they remember. Thoughtful readers monitor their understanding of the text *during reading*, and they adjust or reread certain parts of the text once they determine that they do not comprehend what they have been reading. Teachers can aid the reader by providing thoughtful *during-reading activities* to support comprehension of text. Examples of during-reading activities include:

Mapping: An excellent during-reading activity for students that supports comprehension of text is mapping out important concepts, events, and characters during the reading process. Students can use graphic organizers such as story maps, timelines, and outlines to help comprehension.

Making connections (text-to-text, text-to-self, text-to-world): Good readers think about how a book reminds them of their own lives, and while they are reading they make connections to their own personal experiences that are similar to what they just read. Good readers also make connections to other texts that they have read that may be by the same author, have the same theme, or discuss a similar topic. Lastly, good readers make connections while they are reading with events that occurred in the world, such as a recent current event or something that happened at home or at school. These connections are an important during-reading (and postreading) strategy that the teacher can model for the student. It is helpful to have the students place sticky notes on the page of the book about the connection they made. That way, they can discuss this strategy after they have completed reading the text.

Guided reading and teacher modeling: Teachers can scaffold reading strategies during the reading process by reading aloud to students to ease them into a difficult passage or to provide a pleasurable, meaningful reading experience. Reading aloud to students can also serve as a way to model fluency that students can emulate and practice. Teachers can also model how to ask questions and provide students with helpful hints or insights to help them comprehend passages. Small groups of students can be brought together to form guided reading lessons (see Chapter 3 for more information), which will support students in their reading comprehension strategies.

Modifying texts: Modifying texts, assignments, or both is an extremely important option for aiding struggling readers; this activity enables the classroom teacher to alter a reading assignment along the way. In some situations, the teacher may modify specific paragraphs by reading aloud or by rewriting the text for students with special needs. Such intervention may be reserved for English language learners or students with learning disabilities who require text modifications and close teacher guidance and intervention.

Postreading Activities – The postreading stage should be viewed as the final stage of an ongoing reading process and should serve as an opportunity for students to reflect or write, or both, about the reading experience. Postreading activities should provide opportunities for the teacher and student to exchange ideas about the text, for the student to pose unanswered questions about the text, and for the student to synthesize and assess the content as a way of crystallizing his or her personal understanding. These activities should not be viewed simply as the aftermath of an assignment on which the teacher can base a summative evaluation of the student's reading progress. The following activities should be used during postreading:

Retelling, summarizing, synthesizing: Retelling is a simple instructional approach that helps children develop reading comprehension; it also can be used by the teacher as a form of assessment to determine how well students understand a story or nonfictional text. Retelling is a widely used and favored approach with teachers of younger readers; however, teachers of older readers often use the retelling strategy. *Summarizing* is when the reader is asked to restate what the author has said in a concise format (see earlier). *Synthesizing* requires the reader to apply higher order thinking skills to derive an original thesis or statement about the reading. It requires the reader to come up with an original idea and relate it directly to the text.

Making connections: Making connections allows students to connect what they read to their own lives (text-to-self), to other texts they have read (text-to-text), and to the outside world (text-to-world). Students can use sticky notes to mark locations in the book where they made such connections while they were reading; then after they finish reading, they can fill in a graphic organizer or discuss their connections with the class. Figure 7–10 presents graphic organizers that students can use as a postreading strategy to help them make connections.

Making Connections Graphic Organizer: Text-To-Text, Text-To-Self, and Text-To-World

Name: _____   Date: _____

Making Text-to-Text Connections

Title: _____
Author: _____

What I read in the book:	What I read in another book:

Making Text-to-Self Connections

Title: _____
Author: _____

What I read in the book:	What it reminds me of in my own life:

Making Text-to-World Connections

Title: _____
Author: _____

What I read in the book:	What it reminds me of in the world:

FIGURE 7-10

Hands-on activities, discussion, and writing: This activity allows the reader to think about the text in creative ways and to reflect on what the text meant. The teacher can help students comprehend text by having them respond to what they read in creative, meaningful, and motivating ways.

The scaffolded reading approach is an excellent instructional strategy that teachers can use to promote comprehension of text. It allows them to systematically approach reading instruction through three phases: prereading, during-reading, and postreading activities. These activities support readers in different phases of the reading process and provide necessary reinforcement to help readers comprehend text. You can see an example of a teacher, Ms. Cowen, using the scaffolded reading approach in the Video Case below.

Reciprocal Teaching

Reciprocal teaching (Palincsar & Brown, 1984) is an excellent strategy that teachers can use to promote comprehension and comprehension monitoring. In this technique, the teacher and students take turns instructing each other and being the "teacher." The "teacher" guides the students through the text they are reading and leads the discussion. There are four steps to the process of reciprocal teaching: prediction, question generating, summarizing, and clarifying. It is suggested that the teacher model the process first, which demonstrates to the students how an effective reader uses different strategies at different times during the reading process. The modeling will also introduce the different steps to the students and show them how to apply these strategies to difficult text. Gradually, as the students become more competent in using these strategies, the students should model strategic reading themselves and take on the role of the "teacher." This process then becomes a highly interactive one, where students and teacher reciprocate between modeling the process and being guided through it.

Research has shown that reciprocal teaching is highly effective in helping students increase their reading achievement. This strategy has been most effective in helping struggling readers, including English language learners and students with learning disabilities, increase their level of comprehension at a rapid rate (Rosenshine & Meister, 1994).

TEACHSOURCE VIDEO CASE

A Visit to Ms. Cowen's Classroom: The Scaffolded Reading Approach

As we enter Ms. Cowen's classroom, we see a brightly decorated room with posters describing different reading strategies placed strategically around the room. The far wall is covered with student artwork depicting different original characters that the students have created from a previous lesson. The colorful and imaginative characters are on large poster board, adding a sense of humor and whimsy to the classroom atmosphere. There is a word wall in the front of the room over the whiteboard, and the desks are clustered into small tables so that four students sit at each cluster facing each other.

Ms. Cowen is seated in front of the room next to an easel. Once all students are gathered around her, she does a prereading exercise: She asks them to visualize what their bedroom would be like if they could have it look any way they want. She asks the students to close their eyes and gives them a few minutes to reflect and imagine. Ms. Cowen then takes out the book *Where the Wild Things Are* by Maurice Sendak. She then shows them the cover and has them predict what the book will be about, calling only on those who have not read the book before.

After the prereading strategies, she starts reading the book, modeling fluent, expressive reading. She pauses at

(continues)

TEACHSOURCE VIDEO CASE (CONTINUED)

certain points in the story to ask questions and to review certain words that she thinks the students may need help with, using the context of the sentence to generate meaning. She also makes continual connections back to the children's original predictions and asks the students to make further predictions as to what will occur next.

After Ms. Cowen has completed the reading of *Where the Wild Things Are*, she discusses the book with the students, generating interest and responses from all the students. She then describes what they are to do next: They will take the original characters they have created from a previous lesson and place them into the story. They will then rewrite part of the book with their characters in the story. She models for them how one of the original characters can be placed onto a page and how the story can be rewritten. The students go back to their desks, and one distributes the miniature stick versions of their characters that they created another time. The children work at their desks for the next 20 minutes, actively engaged in this activity. In the last 10 minutes of the lesson, a few students share their work with the class and read their new story.

In reviewing this lesson, Ms. Cowen used the scaffolded reading approach during her read-aloud. She used the following prereading strategies:

- Activating prior knowledge by having students make connections to their own lives
- Predicting what the book will be about by discussing its cover and title
- She used the following during-reading strategies:
- Modeling of fluent, expressive reading
- Questioning during reading

- Making connections back to original predictions
- Making new predictions during the reading process
- Reviewing vocabulary words within the context of the story
- Discussing the story
- Writing about the story
- Relating the book to previous lessons
- Making connections (text-to-self)
- Using imagination and creativity to actively engage all students in the construction of meaning through a hands-on activity and writing

Questions:

1. How could Ms. Cowen integrate technology into the scaffolded reading approach?
2. What other strategies could you use in the prereading, during-reading and postreading phases of Ms. Cowen's lesson?

Go to www.cengage.com/ login to register your access code for the premium website for *Literacy for Children in an Information Age*, where you can watch an in-depth video exploration of Ms. Cowen's classroom and to see how she used these valuable strategies.

The steps to reciprocal teaching are:

1. *Prediction:* The "teacher" asks the group to *predict* what happens in the text. These predictions can be written on a flip chart or in notebooks, or a visual tool can be generated by the cooperative group. The predictions that the students make help them set a purpose for reading: to test their predictions. The "teacher" should focus on headings and subheadings to help students frame their predictions.

2. *Question Generating:* The "teacher" or student leader poses specific questions about the content and ideas in the passage to which the students in the group try to respond.

3. *Summarizing:* After students read a short passage orally or silently, the "teacher" summarizes what was read (students in the cooperative group may add to the summary). Students may add to the summary as they move through the steps, or they may receive guidance from the teacher.

4. *Clarifying:* The "teacher" tries to clarify any confusing points in the passage by either pointing them out or asking the other students to help clear up the confusion. Students may need to reread parts for clarification. (The teacher may be called on for help.)

SQ3R: Survey, Question, Read, Retell, Review

SQ3R (survey, question, read, retell, review) (Robinson, 1946) is one of the earliest and longest-lasting strategies that serves as a model for almost all of the specific reading strategies currently in use. Basically, this approach deals with previewing, questioning, predicting, reviewing, clarifying, and summarizing techniques. This historical strategy has been used for many decades by knowledgeable, comprehension-savvy classroom teachers and reading specialists. Also notable is that graphic organizers can be used to help students generate their own student-made visual tools to help them make the necessary connections from text to understanding.

The student learns to preview the text, ask questions about the text, and answer questions after reviewing the text by following these steps:

1. *Survey*/preview the text before actually reading.
2. Generate *questions* about the text before actually reading and write them down.
3. *Read* to answer your questions and to add other information.
4. *Retell* what you learned by writing a summary.
5. *Review* what you have learned by discussing it with a classmate or by answering questions asked in step 2.

This strategy is quite helpful with informational text such as textbooks and has been shown to improve comprehension of difficult material. The teacher should first model this strategy with the class by conducting "think alouds" to show how the process works. Students then should apply this strategy with the guidance and help of the teacher, practicing it in groups and pairs.

DR-TA: Directed Reading and Thinking Activity

DR-TA (directed reading and thinking activity) (Stauffer, 1969) is also a historical strategy that has helped students to comprehend expository texts such as textbooks. Both the SQ3R and DR-TA strategies have been used quite successfully in improving reading comprehension with diverse populations of struggling readers and English language learners, who often struggle with textbook comprehension.

In DR-TA, the student learns how to predict reading a given text and how to make notes about what is actually learned. The student performs the following actions:

1. *Previews text* to predict what will be learned (then writes down predictions)
2. *Reads text* and takes notes
3. *Writes* about the accuracy of predictions, *adding important ideas*
4. *Reviews* text and *writes a summary* about what was learned

Preservice and in-service teachers can use the successful DR-TA and SQ3R strategies to help students improve their reading comprehension ability of informational text, as well as narrative stories.

QAR: Question–Answer Relationship

In the 1980s, Raphael (1982, 1986) developed the **QAR** strategy to help children find answers in text. QAR instruction encourages readers to use information that they find in their readings, while also considering their background knowledge. Raphael and Au (2005) believe that the QAR strategy provides a framework that offers teachers a straightforward approach for reading comprehension instruction for all children in kindergarten through grade 12. They claim that research has shown that QAR can reliably improve students' comprehension, and that this approach provides teachers and students with a common language for talking about the "invisible" processes that comprise listening and reading comprehension (Raphael & Au, 2005).

Many students have difficulty answering questions, and this strategy helps readers locate answers to questions. Often, answers to questions can be located in different places in the text: Sometimes a reader can find the answers straight from the text almost word for word, other times a reader must search for the answers, and still other times the reader must infer the answers from clues in the text.

There are two types of QARs that a student should look for when searching for an answer: (1) "In the book" (literal meanings) and (2) "In my head" (implied meanings).

In the book (QAR): This includes two categories of answers that are located right in the book and do not ask the student to infer the answer.

Right there: This type of QAR asks students to look for words in the question and read the sentence containing those words to locate the answer. The teacher can model this by pointing out that some questions can be answered by finding statements that are directly stated, or are "in the book."

Think and search: This type of QAR asks students to search for the answer from multiple sentences or paragraphs. The teacher can model how the reader sometimes locates information in more than one sentence found in different parts of the text and must put more than one piece of information together to create the answer. In other words, the reader must "think and search."

In my head (QAR): This includes two categories of answers where the information had to come from the reader's own knowledge and ability to infer information.

Author and me: This type of QAR asks students to use clues that the author provides to infer answers not explicitly stated in the text. Here the teacher can model how to infer meaning from the text, pointing out clues the author provided and showing the student how to use his or her own personal knowledge to answer questions.

On my own: This type of QAR requires the student to use background knowledge, personal insight, and comprehension of what was read to answer the question. The teacher can model how readers are really *on their own* in answering questions that require responses that are more like "opinions" rather than "facts." Students are taught to read for general impressions to form opinions about what they read. Students learn that some "on my own" questions can be answered without reading the text, by using their own personal experiences.

Modeling is an important part of this strategy so that the teacher is demonstrating how students can effectively answer different types of questions. Gradually students can start working in pairs or in small groups to apply these two different types of QARs. A helpful technique is to give a group of students four different types of questions and have them classify the questions into the four different categories. Figure 7–11 provides a summary of the question–answer relationships framework.

P-L-A-N: Predict, Locate, Add, Note

P-L-A-N (predict, locate, add, note) (Caverly, Mandeville, & Nicholson, 1995) is a four-step strategy that is used to increase comprehension of expository text such as nonfiction and textbooks. This research-based approach is usually taught to students in middle school through college. However, P-L-A-N is also widely used with students in grades 2 through 6, whereby the teacher models this strategy for the students and provides the support, guidance, and practice needed to apply it.

The Question-Answer Response Framework

QAR Relationship	Category of Answers	Explanation	Comprehension Stratergy(ies) Used	Questions Asked by Reader
IN THE BOOK	Right There	The answer is in one place in the text. Words from the question and words that answer the question are often identical and are "right there" in the text.	1. Scanning to locate information 2. Note-taking to recall key information 3. Using context clues for creating definitions 4. Sequencing events	1. Who is the main character? 2. What is the setting? 3. What are the important details? 4. What is the sequence of events?
	Think and Search	The answer is in the text. Readers need to "think and search," or read different parts of the text to find the answer. The answer can be within a paragraph, across paragraphs, or even across chapters.	1. Scanning to locate important information 2. Summarizing 3. Visualizing to identify setting, mood, and themes 4. Making inferences from the text 5. Recognizing story structure 6. Comparing and contrasting 7. Making text-to-text connections	1. What is the problem and how is it resolved? 2. What role do the characters play in the text? 3. What are the important events?
IN MY HEAD	On my Own	The answer is not in the text. Readers need to use their own ideas and background knowledge to answer the question.	1. Activating prior knowledge 2. Making self-to-text connections	1. How can I relate to what I just read? 2. How do my experiences compare to what I just read? 3. If I was the main character, how would I feel?
	Author & Me	The answer is not in the text. To answer the question, readers need to think about what they already know and how it fits together with what they just read.	1. Predicting 2. Making inferences 3. Comparing and contrasting 4. Drawing conclusions 5. Making text-to-self connections	1. What is the author's purpose for writing this? 2. What is the theme of the text and how do I relate to it? 3. What is the author's writing style and do I like it? 4. How does this text compare to other books I have read? Other experiences I have had?

Adapted from Raphael, T., and Au, K. (2005). QAR: Enhancing comprehension and test taking across the grades and content areas. *The Reading Teacher* 59(3), 206–221.

FIGURE 7-11

The P-L-A-N strategy has the following steps:

1. The student *predicts* what will be learned after a preview (or "book walk") of the text. The student will preview the title, subtitles, table of contents, headings, charts, maps, illustrations, and index. The student then will construct a visual tool such as a prediction map or semantic web, making tentative predictions about the content and the text.

2. The student *locates* and checks familiar and unfamiliar information and/or concepts by adding checkmarks next to what is known and question marks next to what is unknown.

3. The student *adds* words or phrases to the prediction map or semantic web, trying to explain questions or confirm known information previously indicated by checkmarks or question marks. Fix-up strategies can be used at this point to help students clear up any during-reading problems or confusion.

4. The student *notes* what has been learned after reading the text by writing a summary or completing a visual tool.

The P-L-A-N strategy is an excellent way to promote study skills and should be taught as part of the literacy curriculum. Such study strategies have been shown to improve comprehension of expository material and are especially effective for English language learners and children with learning disabilities. These children often have an especially difficult time with reading, remembering, and comprehending content area textbooks. Such a systematic method helps scaffold their comprehension abilities and provides the necessary support they need to approach content area material.

It is important that teachers use the most current and research-based instructional strategies in the classroom that will help students become better readers by comprehending text. The scaffolded reading approach gives teachers a structured approach to incorporate prereading, during-reading, and postreading activities into an instructional lesson. By developing appropriate questions, teachers will ensure that readers are thinking and reflecting on the text that they have read at three different levels: literal comprehension, interpretive or inferential comprehension, and creative comprehension. Such instructional approaches as reciprocal teaching, QAR, and P-L-A-N are research-based comprehension strategies that help readers to comprehend both narrative and expository text. Teachers should incorporate these research-based strategies into their instructional program in comprehension.

Promoting Reading Comprehension in Diverse Learners

Many diverse learners such as students with learning disabilities and English language learners have trouble understanding what they are reading. They frequently have trouble answering questions about what the book is about, and they cannot relate what they read to their own personal experiences. The goal in any classroom is to encourage each student to be an active listener, as well as an active reader. Words and the ideas they represent need to take on meaning for children. Teachers need to look for ways to connect what is happening in the pages of a book to what is familiar or meaningful to the children. An excellent way to promote this process is by developing prereading, during-reading, and postreading activities that support all readers (see earlier).

It is also important to remember that when a student is having trouble comprehending, the difficulty can be based on many different factors that contribute to effective comprehension. The child could have difficulty with word recognition and is unable to read fluently because of lack of automaticity. In other cases, the child may not understand what is being read because of difficulty recognizing word meanings and understanding vocabulary words. Other times the student may not be effectively using comprehension strategies and is not predicting, inferring, self-monitoring, and drawing conclusions. The child may not have the appropriate background knowledge to understand what the text is about or be unable to relate to the material because of sociocultural differences. All of these factors need to be considered when working with diverse learners who are struggling to understand what is read.

Explicitly teaching reading comprehension strategies has become the main approach to comprehension instruction for struggling readers (Pressley, 2000). As described earlier, strategy instruction should have a strong emphasis on metacognition and emphasize when and how the student should use each strategy during the reading process. Students are taught to take steps to ensure their understanding by rereading, trying to connect the material to be learned with what they already know, asking themselves questions during the reading, and trying to summarize. They are explicitly taught to self-monitor their comprehension by stopping occasionally to ask themselves whether they understand what they read. This approach may be considered remedial in that good readers seem to use these strategies without being specifically taught how to use them and, in fact, often are not even aware that they use them (Williams, 2003). This approach should be used with all struggling readers, including children with learning disabilities and English language learners.

Struggling readers often have difficulty in comprehension because they fail to identify the "theme" or main idea of a passage (Williams, 2003). The theme is usually expressed by a concept such as "friendship" and can be defined as the overall message that the author wishes to convey in a story. As such, it is similar to the "main idea" of expository or informational text found in magazine articles or textbook passages, and identifying the theme or main idea is a critical component of reading comprehension.

Reading Comprehension and Students with Learning Disabilities

Research has shown that students with learning disabilities have much more difficulty in building up accurate representations of a story, and this interferes with their getting the point. They include much more irrelevant and implausible information into summaries of stories than do students without disabilities (Williams, 2003). This inability to identify important information and to become distracted with irrelevant details contributes to students with learning disabilities not fully comprehending what they are reading and seeing the "big picture." In fact, students without disabilities can also have a difficult time identifying the theme. The theme usually is the most difficult story component to teach (Williams, 2003).

Teachers' VOICES   Reading Comprehension

I tutor a third grade student with learning disabilities whose greatest area of difficulty is reading comprehension. Some of the strategies I have used that have helped her are as follows:

1. I have her use sticky notes as she reads to identify characters, setting, problem, events, solution, and outcome. I then provide her with a question or story map for which she uses the sticky notes to help her fill in the correct responses.

2. At the end of each chapter, she records on an index card one or two sentences about the chapter, any difficult words she encountered, or any characters she read about. After she has read the chapter silently, we review the card. On

conclusion of the book, the cards really help her to organize her thoughts.

3. Graphic organizers also help her organize her thoughts while she is reading. The organizer includes sections on predicting, clarifying, questioning, and summarizing; she fills in the sections as she reads.

4. I also use a retelling activity that requires us to throw a ball to one another. As each of us catches the ball, we say one sequential thing about the story. She loves to retell the story in this way and it truly helps her comprehend the material.

—*Nicole Zecchino, Special Education Teacher*

Fluency instruction should be a component of comprehension instruction for diverse learners. Struggling readers should take part in repeated readings in the classroom and at home. Parents should become involved in working with the students at home and supporting their repeated readings of text. The teacher should also carefully activate prior knowledge and build background knowledge before the students read the text. Many students with learning disabilities have a rich and varied background in many different areas and are quite articulate and knowledgeable about a wide range of subjects. This will help the students to comprehend the text, especially if they can personally relate to it (Shaywitz, 2003).

Reading Comprehension and English Language Learners

When evaluating teaching approaches for English language learners, there have been acrimonious debates about bilingual education (teaching children in their native language while transitioning them to classes taught exclusively in English) versus immersion (placing children directly into classes taught exclusively in English while they receive support). Proponents of bilingual education want to ensure success for English language learners while maintaining and valuing the language the students speak at home. Opponents are concerned about delaying the use of English while wanting to maintain the use of the native language.

There is a good deal of support for the idea that native language instruction can be beneficial for English language learners who are learning how to read English (Gersten & Geva, 2003; International Reading Association, 2001; Slavin & Cheung, 2003). Many studies show positive effects of bilingual education that uses paired bilingual strategies that teach reading in English and in the native language at the same time (at different times of the day), or that use a fast transition (for example, one year in Spanish before beginning transition) (Slavin & Cheung, 2003). English language learners who are receiving reading instruction in their native language in their early years of English schooling need to wait before beginning English reading instruction.

Many creative and useful techniques exist for fostering comprehension in English language readers. It is important that teachers focus on building comprehension as the primary goal of reading instruction and not concentrate on only correct pronunciation and vocabulary instruction of isolated words. Strong home–school links with students' families is also helpful, even with those with limited or no English-language proficiency. Children can take "keywords" or even books home from the classroom reading sessions and have their family work with them in learning new words. This transforms the child into the "expert" in the new language, while honoring the native language. This practice, when explained to parents, fosters comprehension and encourages transfer skills between the two languages (Lenters, 2004).

Research supports the value of combining cooperative learning and comprehension strategy instruction, especially in helping children actively use English as they transition from Spanish to English reading (Slavin & Cheung, 2003). One-to-one tutoring for English language learners who are struggling in reading is also beneficial, as is direct teaching of English vocabulary. Encouraging children to read a wide range of grade-appropriate books helps build their reading skills.

In summary, it is important that teachers consistently and continuously assess students throughout the school year to identify those readers who are having trouble comprehending what they read. During guided reading sessions, teachers should have students orally read passages to ensure that they fully comprehended the text. Teachers should develop different types of questions to ask the students and encourage them to develop their own questions to ask themselves during the reading process. In addition, teachers need to explicitly teach specific reading comprehension strategies to struggling readers and monitor how the students are using those strategies to comprehend text. Comprehension skills generally will progress when a child has all the prerequisite skills in place, that is, decoding accuracy, fluency, vocabulary, background knowledge, and comprehension strategies. A weakness in any of these skills will affect overall comprehension (Shaywitz, 2003). Figure 7–12 provides a list of questions that will help teachers identify those students who may be having difficulty with reading comprehension.

FIGURE 7-12

Recognizing Signs of Trouble in Reading Comprehension

Ask the following questions for a student who may be having difficulty comprehending text. If you answer "No" for any of the questions, you will want to probe further to determine the comprehension problem.

1. Can the student answer the question, "What was the book about?"
2. Does the student enjoy reading?
3. Does the student vary the amount of time spent reading easy passages as on difficult ones?
4. Does the student usually finish what he begins to read?
5. Does the student relate the book to things she is familiar with?
6. Does the student have trouble drawing inferences from the reading? Do his interpretations go beyond the literal level?
7. Can the student summarize what she read?
8. Can the student tell you what the main idea of the reading was?
9. Can the student identify important details of the text from the incidental details?
10. Can the student make accurate predictions?
11. Does the student check back to earlier pages to monitor his reading?
12. Does the student stay interested in the reading and find it interesting?
13. Does the student ask to read books and show an interest in reading?

STRATEGIES FOR TEACHING DIVERSE LEARNERS

Ideas to Develop Reading Comprehension for Students with Learning Disabilities

- Build background knowledge using as many concrete experiences as possible. This will provide the necessary scaffolding for students to use while reading, as well as the essential background to facilitate comprehension.

- Have students work on prediction skills before they read the text. Have them study the cover illustrations and try to point out what the pictures mean and what the book might be about.

- Explicitly teach comprehension strategies and provide sustained support through modeling, guided practice, and independent practice to ensure that the students can effectively use the strategies.

- Provide continuous and ongoing feedback to the students to help them monitor and regulate their comprehension.

- Give students texts that are on the correct reading level within their grasp to read and understand. Students with disabilities should not be expected to read any materials that are written at or above their frustration levels.

- Modify texts and assignments to aid struggling readers. In some situations, the teacher may modify specific paragraphs by reading aloud or rewriting the text for students with special needs. The teacher can also record the text while reading it aloud and then have the students listen to the recording.

- Ensure that students are self-monitoring. When a student with learning disabilities is reading to you in guided reading, be sure to model how to self-monitor and then apply appropriate strategies to support comprehension.

- Use strategies such as SQ3R and P-L-A-N when reading expository text.
- Use graphic organizers to present material visually; this will help students with learning disabilities process the information. Have students develop their own graphic organizers to take notes and present to the teacher. Having the student develop graphic organizers is an excellent way to modify an assignment that requires comprehension of information. Often, students with learning disabilities will know the information and can present it either orally or

graphically, but have a difficult time putting it into writing.
- Never have a student with learning disabilities read aloud to the class unless the student has had sufficient chances to practice reading and rereading the text and feels comfortable reading a short passage.
- Work on fluency training in the classroom through guided, repeated oral reading whereby you are providing guidance and feedback each time the child reads out loud.

Technology and Reading Comprehension

Electronic Text and New Literacies

Digital technology is quickly transforming how we read and write to communicate with others. Students spend more time reading **electronic text** over the Internet than they do reading books, and with the advent of instant messaging (IM) and text messaging over cell phones, electronic text is becoming pervasive and common. While listening to an iPod, downloading music from the Internet, or finding a phone number in a cell phone, we are reading electronic text and need to comprehend what we read. Lewis and Fabos (2005) argue that we need to reconceptualize literacy in digitally mediated times. This type of reading and writing is complex, can promote higher order thinking, and can foster complex reading and writing that is useful in the world of work or global communication.

STRATEGIES FOR TEACHING DIVERSE STUDENTS

Ideas to Develop Reading Comprehension for English Language Learners

- Activate prior knowledge and build background knowledge of the topic to be covered in the text before reading. Often, English language learners are not aware that they have the knowledge to relate to what they are about to read.
- Ensure that English language learners see the connection between oral and written language, especially in the early stages of their reading development. Use techniques in which you transcribe their sentences and stories down on an easel or in their own "book." Have the students read their stories or sentences back to you.
- Type or print the child's simple dictated stories. Then, with the help of a native English speaker, have the child cut the sentences into individual

words and glue them into a premade blank booklet, which is later illustrated by the child. Have the child read each word.
- Involve parents or older siblings in creating translations of favorite simple stories. These translations may be illustrated by the student for placement alongside the English version of the classroom library.
- Encourage English language learners of the same language background to discuss stories in their native language that they are reading in English. Together, they will naturally support one another to address gaps in comprehension.
- Use the cloze technique to teach high-frequency words commonly used in English. This helps

students learn these new abstract words through the use of the surrounding context.

- Use multicultural literature from your students' native countries and have the students share their knowledge, customs, and experiences with this culture.

- Pair the English language learner with a native speaking student. Have them write and illustrate a book. The text on one side of the page could be written in English, and the other side could be written in the native language of the English language learner. "Publish" the book by sharing it with other children, making it a part of the classroom library.

- Use teacher-developed graphic organizers such as charts, graphs, Venn diagrams, and semantic maps to help students identify the important points of text. Use the students' native language to label the

important points they are to identify. For example, if the students are to identify the components of narrative text (setting, main characters, plot, and theme), label these sections in both English and their native language.

- Have students develop their own graphic organizers using their native language, if necessary, to demonstrate their understanding of the text.

- Have students read text repeatedly to each other, checking for speed and accuracy.

- Have students "read along" using tape recordings of texts; check each student's ability to reread orally, checking for miscues.

- Have students use electronic talking books to practice repeated readings for improvement of fluency and reading comprehension.

Electronic text provides new text formats for readers to comprehend and new ways to interact with the information. Reading and comprehending material on the Internet often can confuse and overwhelm readers who have been taught to derive meaning from print-based materials only. It is important that students learn the new literacies involved in reading electronic media such as the Internet, and that teachers incorporate these new media into their curriculum so that students learn the vital skills necessary to comprehend electronic text. Proficiency in the new literacies of the Internet will become essential to our students' literacy future (International Reading Association, 2001).

The different types of electronic text that readers will need to comprehend can be characterized as hypertextual networks that explore new types of story grammar and a variety of new formats (Coiro, 2004). Web-based texts are typically nonlinear, interactive, and include multiple media formats. Each of these formats presents a range of challenges for the reader that may require new comprehension strategies for deriving meaning because they require skills and abilities that go beyond those required for the comprehension of print-based, linear text, which currently is being taught in schools.

Some of the different types of electronic text a student may encounter on the Internet, in a software program, or on a digital device are as follows (Coiro, 2004):

Nonlinear hypertext: In this type of text, which is often found on the Internet, readers must navigate their own path through the information that may be different from the path that other readers chose, or follow a different path each time the reader rereads the material. Hyperlinks bring the reader to a location that provides more information about a particular or related topic. A reader must understand the advantages and disadvantages associated with having control of the direction in which text progresses and must use inferential reasoning skills and context clues to discern one type of hyperlink from another (Coiro, 2004).

Multimedia texts: Print-based text usually includes a combination of print and graphics or illustrations. Electronic texts can integrate a range of multimedia formats including hypertext print written in different font size and color, icons, animation, photographs, advertisements, audio and video clips, and virtual reality environments. Images and sounds are used to create new ways of conveying meaning, explaining procedures, and communicating interactively. Readers must apply new ways of thinking about how to access, manipulate, and respond to information (Coiro, 2004).

Interactive texts: Many sites on the Internet invite readers to participate in the sharing of information by either posting their comments on a bulletin board or by uploading their work, which can then be published. There are many "blogs" and "wikis" on the Internet, in which the author keeps an online diary of events, and readers are invited to participate by sharing their thoughts. E-mail and instant messaging (IM) have allowed the reader to instantly engage with text that can be shaped instantaneously and transmitted with a push of a button. Many software programs on CDs also invite the readers to participate in and interact with the program, such as Living Books, which provide children with a popular children's story (such as the *Arthur* series or Dr. Seuss books), in which the story is read to the child and the child can interact with the pictures to find animated objects and surprises.

New comprehension processes are required for these electronic text environments. Such strategies as previewing text and asking prereading questions change dramatically with such instantaneous interaction with the author. Traditional prediction questions might ask: What is this text going to be about? What will happen next? What do I know about this topic? What is the author's purpose? These types of questions need to be asked with interactive text. However, proficient readers also need to ask questions about their role in the reading process: How should I navigate this information? Do I need to interact with this environment? What is my role or task in this activity? How can I add to this body of knowledge (Coiro, 2004)? Readers must constantly self-monitor as they go through these interactive texts to ensure that they understand what the author means, and also to figure out what their role is in the interactive process, and whether they feel comfortable in contributing to the interaction.

Online communication networking text: Online communication networking text is becoming more and more prevalent today with IM, social networking sites such as Facebook, and text messaging on electronic devices such as cell phones. This type of text often is truncated and cryptic, deploying special characters, colors, font types, and abbreviations to convey messages. IM requires a user to read and respond to a message while performing other tasks on the computer, and it often requires the user to address multiple audiences simultaneously. It actually blends spoken and written textuality into a hybrid language representing casual, insider exchanges of informal speech (Lewis & Fabos, 2005). Text messaging requires the reader to interpret truncated, casual messages written in a hybrid language as well; messages often are read on a small LCD (liquid crystal device) screen. In addition,

Silvia Jansen/istockphoto.com

students are being inundated with electronic text found on other digital devices such as iPods and handheld devices. These all require new comprehension strategies to interpret the meaning of the written text.

Electronic Text and Reading Comprehension Strategies

When students work on the Internet, whether it is to search a site for information, read an article of interest, or scan an article for a class assignment, they must apply reading comprehension strategies just as when they read print-based text. The ultimate goal is for the students to understand what they read and to apply the information that they learned in an effective way. Many of the same skills used to comprehend text are used when students search the Internet for an answer to a question or browse a website. They must be adept at seeking, evaluating, and using the information they find, and they must apply their knowledge of the reading process. Although reading on the Internet requires the student to navigate different types of interactive formats, readers appear to apply similar reading strategies as those used with print-based text reading, but in a different context and in different ways (Schmar-Dobler, 2004). Reading electronic text online is almost always a problem-solving activity in which the student is reading to locate information and then must critically evaluate its usefulness in answering the question that has generated the search (Mokhtari, Kymes, & Edwards, 2008/2009).

Comprehension strategies that readers use while reading text online are listed below. Although some of these are similar to strategies required when reading print-based material, they are applied in a different context and used in different ways. An important aspect of reading online is that readers regularly communicate with others about the problem being investigated (Mokhtari, Kymes, & Edwards, 2008/2009).

Activating prior knowledge: It is extremely important that readers recall information and experiences related to the topic. On the Internet, this can be done by having students examine sites to build prior knowledge.

Generating student questions: This is usually the first strategy a student must apply in conducting an online investigation, and this question will guide the subsequent search to locate relevant information. The student must constantly keep the question in mind while exploring different sites. It is very easy for readers to become distracted and start browsing sites that are not relevant to the question at hand. By the same token, oftentimes the reader will have to refine the question and may come up with new ones as the search continues. It is recommended that students write these questions down before starting their search and keep them next to the computer to remind them of what they are looking for.

Monitoring comprehension: The reader must constantly monitor reading on the Internet and determine whether it is too difficult to read and whether the reader comprehends the material. This is extremely important on the Internet where there is little oversight to ensure that the material is on the correct reading level. Students need to constantly self-monitor, and if the website is inappropriate, they need to continue their search for sites that provide information at a reading level at which they can derive meaning.

Locating information and identifying the main idea: Locating information online and identifying the main idea is one of the key strategies in reading text online. The reader must process expository text that will be used to answer a question or solve a problem (such as what is the best snowboard to buy, or how do I decrease my carbon footprint?). Readers must be able to locate information in the text, identify the main idea and determine whether it matches with the question that they are trying to answer.

Critically evaluating information: Readers must be able to determine if the information is appropriate to answer the question or solve the problem. In addition, the reader must evaluate if the information comes from a reliable and trustworthy source and thereby is accurate and unbiased. Therefore, the reader must evaluate the information, itself, and the site from where it is coming.

Synthesizing from multiple sources: The student must not only identify the main idea but generate new theories of how this information applies to the topic; in addition, the reader must combine many different sources together to form the big picture and apply this synthesis to the unanswered question.

Inferring: The reader must read between the lines to determine what is not explicitly stated but rather implied, and use background knowledge to determine what the author is trying to convey. This strategy must be applied constantly when reading text on the Internet because there is no oversight as to what sites the student is reading, and many of the sites may require a great deal of inferential skill to comprehend.

Navigating: While reading the Internet, students must become adept at navigating through a series of links, icons, pop-up windows, and addresses that may or may not be current. Students need to learn how to navigate through all the information and learn how to keep multiple windows open to conduct an efficient search. Navigation becomes a key part of the comprehension process while reading on the Internet; it is unique to computer-based text material, which is not linear in approach.

Other key comprehension processes that are required when using electronic text on the Internet are the abilities to search, locate, and draw connections between resources of diverse and multiple perspectives (Coiro, 2003). With Internet searches becoming a predominant activity of students at home and as part of schoolwork, students need to build on traditional research and summarizing skills to conduct effective searches. New literacies such as manipulating electronic databases, using multiple search engines, and navigating many different sites at once to obtain key information are vital skills for educators to teach so that students can comprehend and use information effectively.

Web-based environments also can cause cognitive overload and frustration even to competent readers of conventional text. Many websites offer too many choices and provide too much stimulation; thus, they are distracting and disorienting to readers. Many readers can be confused by the layout of the screen, distracted by animations, and unable to read the text because of the colors and style of the font and background. Teachers need to carefully choose and monitor websites that students are using and provide the necessary scaffolding and guidance in supporting comprehension.

Comprehending text on the Internet requires readers to apply reading processes and strategies within a new context. Some tasks require readers to extend their use of traditional comprehension strategies to obtain meaning from electronic text, while other tasks, such as conducting searches or participating in online communication and collaboration projects, demand fundamentally different strategies not currently addressed in most literacy classrooms. Teachers should model and discuss key strategies used in comprehending electronic text to ensure that students are learning the new literacies. Teachers must help students explore digital information environments and provide them with the necessary skills so that they are able to comprehend and apply the information that they learn. As electronic text, such as what can be seen on the Internet, proliferates as a major source of entertainment and education, we as educators must ensure that our students are learning how to apply appropriate comprehension strategies to derive meaning and become successful citizens of the twenty-first century.

Websites That Promote Reading Comprehension

The following websites and software packages are excellent resources for the classroom teacher to learn more about reading comprehension, use as resources to develop lessons, or use with students during a literacy lesson. Many additional resources on reading comprehension can be found on the *Literacy for Children in an Information Age* premium website: http://www.cengage.com/login

websites to learn more about how to teach reading comprehension

University of Connecticut Literacy Page

http://www.literacy.uconn.edu/compre.htm

Within this web page, the complex processes involved in reading comprehension are divided into three categories (much like the NRP report): vocabulary instruction, text comprehension instruction, and teacher preparation and comprehension strategies instruction. Also available are links to useful websites that students can visit to practice their use of comprehension strategies with fiction and nonfiction texts at a variety of reading levels.

Southwest Educational Development Laboratory

http://www.sedl.org/reading/framework/nonflash/reading.html

The Southwest Educational Development Laboratory has an excellent site that is devoted to reading comprehension. Under Instructional Activities, there is an Instructional Resources Database for reading, with interesting activities that promote comprehension. The activities are for emergent and developing readers and are available in English or Spanish.

Center for the Improvement of Early Reading Achievement

http://www.ciera.org/library/reports

This site has excellent articles on reading and comprehension. Explore some of the research reports under their library link.

websites and software that teachers can use to reinforce reading comprehension strategies

School–Home Links Reading Kit

http://www.ed.gov/pubs/CompactforReading/kitcover.html

This is an excellent site for the home–school connection, and was developed to provide resources for family involvement in education.

Resource Room

http://www.resourceroom.net/Comprehension/index.asp

The Resource Room website functions as a "resource room" for structured multisensory learning. It has excellent lessons to build comprehension for special needs learners.

Arthur Online

http://pbskids.org/arthur

This site is from the Public Broadcasting Service (PBS) and provides different activities and games for children to improve reading comprehension.

WiggleWorks (Scholastic)

http://teacher.scholastic.com/products/wiggleworks/

WiggleWorks, an early literacy program for kindergarten through grade 2, addresses five areas: phonemic awareness, phonics, fluency, vocabulary, and comprehension. Students

www

Additional teacher resources can be found on the *Literacy for Children in an Information Age* premium website for this chapter (**http://www.cengage.com/login**).

can listen to modeled reading by a book's narrator, and then record their own reading for comparison. The program also includes emphasis on writing and word study.

Reading for Meaning (Tom Snyder Productions)

http://www.tomsnyder.com

This software package or Internet subscription service targets five reading strategies: main idea, inference, sequence, cause and effect, and compare and contrast. Students read literature selections, complete graphic organizers and then answer comprehension questions.

Destination Reading (Houghton Mifflin Harcourt Learning Technology)

http://www.hmlt.hmco.com/DR.php

This popular reading program spans preK through middle school and focuses on building reading comprehension.

websites and programs that assess reading comprehension

BookAdventure

http://www.bookadventure.org

BookAdventure is a free website by Sylvan Learning Foundation that allows children to create their own booklists, then provides a quiz to assess their comprehension. It is an excellent site for struggling readers who need motivation to read a book.

Accelerated Reader by Renaissance Learning

http://www.renlearn.com

Accelerated Reader by Renaissance Learning is a popular program in schools for motivating students to read books and for assessing their comprehension. Students choose a book from a specified list; after reading the book, students take a quiz on the computer and find out immediately whether they passed the quiz. The system keeps track of the number of books the student has read and his or her quiz scores to track each student's performance in comprehension.

As the Internet becomes a major source of information, communication, education, and entertainment within our society and around the world, teachers need to incorporate new literacies into their curriculum. Students are spending more time reading on the Internet than reading books. They need to learn how to apply strategies to comprehend the material they are reading. This requires teaching students comprehension strategies that are not only applicable to print-based text, but also to text found in electronic formats such as hypertext, interactive media text, and multimedia text. It also means that literacy classrooms should focus on strategies to comprehend expository text, the most frequently found structure on the Internet.

STRATEGY BOX

Helping Students Comprehend Text

Mrs. Ghali was much more successful during her reading time after meeting with her literacy coach and mentor. The following strategies helped her support all her students in becoming better "comprehenders" of text.

1. Develop, build, and activate prior knowledge of the students before reading the text. This is a key strategy that cannot be overemphasized.

2. Examine the interactive process of reading to ensure that there is a "perfect fit" in all elements involved. Does the reader bring the appropriate background, knowledge, and skills to be successful with this particular text? Is the text appropriate for the student? Is the font too big, too small, clear? Are there pictures to support the reader, or do the pictures make the book appear too "babyish" for older readers? Does the author communicate clearly and in a way the reader understands? Is the author's message appropriate and on target with the reader? Is the reading activity itself supported and appropriate for the text?

3. Explicitly and directly teach and model comprehension strategies that all children should be applying during the reading process.

4. Build in prereading, during-reading, and postreading activities.

5. Develop questions for students that ensure they are comprehending text at the literal, interpretive, and creative levels. Have students create questions at these levels to assess themselves and other students.

6. Use different strategies such as SQ3R and reciprocal teaching to support comprehension of text.

7. Use the computer and different Internet sites to support the instructional program in reading. These programs are motivating for students. These resources are also an excellent way for Mrs. Ghali to keep current in the latest research and theories regarding how to teach comprehension and reading.

Final Thoughts

Perhaps one of the most important things that teachers should remember about reading comprehension is that they must develop their students' background knowledge before students start reading text. Readers must be able to relate personally to what they read, and they must be able to draw actively on their previous experiences and knowledge about what they are reading. Otherwise, readers will not fully comprehend the text or will not be motivated to try.

Another important point about reading comprehension is that specific reading strategies can be taught in the classroom through direct instruction. These strategies should be modeled by the teacher, and readers need guided practice in applying them. Students need to become aware that they are using these strategies and know when it is appropriate to apply a specific strategy to help them comprehend the text. By doing so, the students are learning metacognitive strategies.

Other important points to remember concerning comprehension are:

◆ Fluency is a critical factor in comprehension.

◆ Teachers need to ensure that they are asking a wide variety of questions that encourage students to think on many different levels.

◆ It is important that students learn the new literacies involved in reading electronic media such as the Internet and software programs.

Too little instructional time is provided in the vital area of comprehension, and there is greater need for explicit instruction in helping students read for understanding.

EXPLORATION   Application of Concepts

Activities

1. Choose a piece of children's literature. In a group, discuss how you could build background knowledge before the book is read. Write down different activities that you could introduce in the classroom to help develop, build, and activate prior knowledge. Have the group explain why they chose those activities and why they are important as a future or current reading teacher.

2. Now take the same piece of literature and develop prereading, during-reading, and postreading activities to help support comprehension. Present these activities to the class.

3. Prepare a lesson to teach a specific comprehension strategy using a piece of children's literature. Present this to the group and have each of the other members present a lesson on a different strategy to the group.

    With another preservice teacher, design a series of cloze passages that can be used with English language learners and for the following purposes: identifying frequently used words such as "that," "which," and "said"; identifying adjectives; and identifying concept words in science and social studies (for example, *osmosis, photosynthesis, transportation, economy*).

4. Select a series of poems that can be read orally and dramatically for the purpose of developing patterns of fluency while creating an interest or motivation in enjoying poetry as a medium.

5. Select a series of passages written on different grade levels. Create three types of questions for each passage: literal, interpretive, and creative. Share these questions with the rest of the class and give feedback on whether these are good questions.

    Explore the additional resources on reading comprehension found on the *Literacy for Children in an Information Age* premium website: http://www. cengage.com/login. Evaluate these sites using the Literary Website Evaluation Form provided in Chapter 1. Compile a log of quality websites that promote comprehension.

6. Do a Quick Write: Explain why explicit teaching of reading comprehension strategies is so important. How does knowledge of reading comprehension contribute to your professional growth? Which Professional Standards for Reading Professionals by the International Reading Association (found at the beginning of each chapter) are being addressed?

Visit the websites listed in this chapter and on the *Literacy for Children in an Information Age* premium website for this chapter (http://www.cengage.com/ login). Choose two of your favorite websites and present them to the class, explaining how these sites can be used to promote reading comprehension in the classroom.

HOME–SCHOOL CONNECTION Improving Fluency

Research shows that fluency is an essential skill in developing reading comprehension. It is a skill that parents can help their struggling children improve using repeated readings at home. Parents can do this by:

1) Using a reading program such as Read Naturally (http://www.readnaturally.com). The child reads a story played on an audiotape or CD-ROM, then repeats reading aloud 3–4 times. The parent and child can calculate the fluency rate by timing the child's independent oral reading and counting the number of errors. Both the child and the parent can monitor progress, also giving the parent the opportunity to provide immediate and valuable feedback.

2) Parents can go to the library and take out audiobooks, books-on-tape, or electronic talking books on CD's. This will also allow the child to listen to a story being read and read along with the text as it is being read.

3) There are many e-books available online for free which also provide options for the text to be read out loud electronically. The child can practice fluency by using these books. See chapter 10 for a list of sites that allow you to download free e-books.

4) The parent and child can practice reading books out loud together. Repeated readings will promote fluency. It is especially helpful if the parent works with the child on books that are being used in the classroom.

Parents should reinforce reading comprehension by encouraging the child to make predictions before reading, to generate questions during reading, and then to answer the questions together after reading the text. It is also helpful to discuss the text after reading it, and to be very open and tolerant of the child's interpretation of the text, supporting deeper comprehension and higher order thinking.

8 THE PROCESS OF WRITING, LISTENING, AND SPEAKING

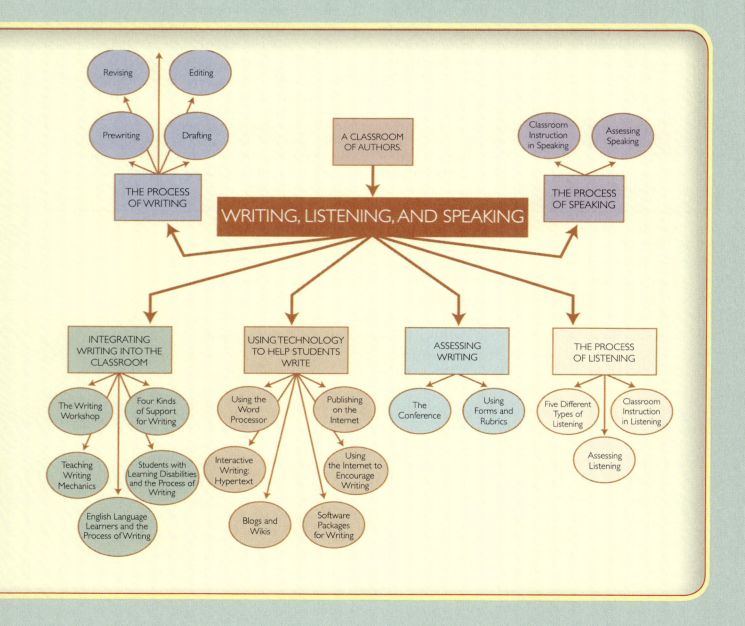

International Reading Association Professional Standards Addressed in this Chapter:

IRA STANDARD 1: FOUNDATIONAL KNOWLEDGE

Candidates have knowledge of the foundations of reading and writing processes and instruction. Candidates:

1.1 Demonstrate knowledge of psychological, sociological, and linguistic foundations of reading and writing processes and instruction.

1.2 Demonstrate knowledge of reading research and histories of reading.

1.3 Demonstrate knowledge of language development and reading acquisition and the variations related to cultural and linguistic diversity.

1.4 Demonstrate knowledge of the major components of reading (phonemic awareness, word identification and phonics, vocabulary and background knowledge, fluency, comprehension strategies, and motivation) and how they are integrated in fluent reading.

IRA STANDARD 2: INSTRUCTIONAL STRATEGIES AND CURRICULUM MATERIALS

Candidates use a wide range of instructional practices, approaches, methods, and curriculum materials to support reading and writing instruction. Candidates:

2.2. Use a wide range of instructional practices, approaches, and methods, including technology-based practices, for learners at differing stages of development and from differing cultural and linguistic backgrounds.

2.3 Use a wide range of curriculum materials in effective reading instruction for learners at different stages of reading and writing development and from different cultural and linguistic backgrounds.

IRA STANDARD 3: ASSESSMENT, DIAGNOSIS, AND EVALUATION

Candidates use a variety of assessment tools and practices to plan and evaluate effective reading instruction. Candidates:

3.1 Use a wide range of assessment tools and practices that range from individual and group standardized tests to individual and group informal classroom assessment strategies, including technology-based assessment tools.

3.2 Place students along a developmental continuum and identify students' proficiencies and difficulties.

3.3 Use assessment information to plan, evaluate, and revise effective instruction that meets the needs of all students, including those at different developmental stages and those from different cultural and linguistic backgrounds.

IRA STANDARD 4: CREATING A LITERATE ENVIRONMENT

Candidates create a literate environment that fosters reading and writing by integrating foundational knowledge, use of instructional practices, approaches and methods, curriculum materials, and the appropriate use of assessments. Candidates:

4.1 Use students' interests, reading abilities, and backgrounds as foundations for the reading and writing program.

4.2 Use a large supply of books, technology-based information, and nonprint materials representing multiple levels, broad interests, and cultural and linguistic backgrounds.

4.3 Model reading and writing enthusiastically as valued lifelong activities.

4.4 Motivate learners to be lifelong readers.

Key Terms

writing as a process
prewriting
drafting
revising
editing
postwriting

Focus Questions

1. What are the different stages in the writing process? Give an example of an activity you would do in the classroom for each stage.

Focus Questions (continued)

writing workshop

shared writing

interactive writing

guided writing

independent writing

content and organization

mechanics

language usage

sentence construction

instructional conversations

word processor

publishing

blog

wiki

writing conference

receptive skills

expressive skills

discriminative listening

listening for details

strategic listening

critical listening

appreciative listening

capacity level

2. What is the reading/writing workshop? How can it be implemented in an elementary classroom? What are the four types of support that a teacher can provide in the classroom?

3. Describe the four areas of skills/strategies that develop children's writing: content and organization, mechanics, language usage, and sentence construction.

4. What are strategies for promoting the writing process with English language learners? students with learning disabilities?

5. Describe how technology can be used to support writing in the classroom. What does the research say about using word processors in writing?

6. How can writing be assessed in the classroom?

7. How can a classroom teacher promote listening skills in the classroom?

8. How can a classroom teacher promote speaking and oral language development in the classroom?

Welcome to Miss Kim's Second Grade Class: Conducting A Writing Workshop

Alex Mares-Manton/Asia Images RM/PhotoLibrary

The children in Miss Kim's second grade class are gathered around her on the floor while she is sitting next to a large easel. The children are wearing their "thinking caps," which are made out of paper plates that tie under their chin with string, and they are engaged with the lesson. Miss Kim is busy writing down the children's comments and sentences about a field trip they took to a farm yesterday. She is focusing on writing a topic sentence that clearly states what the topic of the paragraph will be, and then writing supporting sentences with details about that topic. Miss Kim keeps flipping back to the previous page on the easel, which has a semantic map drawn on it with the word *barn* in the middle and four different spokes describing what animals are. She shows the students how the topic sentence is about a barn and the supporting details are sentences that describe the animals. She reinforces how sentences always start with a capital letter and end with a period.

Using different-colored markers, she writes the topic sentence in one color and then the supporting sentences in another color. The children are all sharing in this writing experience and are highly engaged in contributing to it. When she comes across a difficult word to spell, she prompts different students to decode the word for her and to try to spell it phonetically, emphasizing various phonic patterns

that are listed on the word wall. At one point, Miss Kim asks one student to come to the easel and write the word *goat*, emphasizing that it belongs to the *oat* family and pointing to the word wall. As the student writes the word in a different-colored marker, Miss Kim helps him by prompting and sharing the marker with him, when necessary.

After about 10 minutes, when a paragraph has been written and the mini-lesson on how to write topic sentences is over, she talks about her expectations for their writing assignment. The students must write their own story about the field trip, which should have one paragraph with a topic sentence and three supporting details. First, she expects them to develop a little web that has the topic sentence listed in the middle and three supporting ideas going out as spokes. She has them take out their writing checklists and goes over the criteria that they are expected to follow when writing. She also explains where the dictionaries are and points to the word walls, encouraging the students to use them when needed. The children then spread out over the room and work independently on writing their own story about the field trip.

Miss Kim proceeds to call a student to her table and conference with her on her story. Miss Kim uses the writing checklist to show the student where she needs to focus to improve her writing. After conferencing with a few more students, she travels around the room, giving feedback and help when needed. If a child needs more individualized help, she invites the student to the table for a conference. After about 25 minutes, she tells the class to finish up with their work because they now need to share what they have accomplished. After another five minutes, Miss Kim tells the class to put down their pencils and look at her. As a class, she has individual students talk about what they have accomplished. She encourages them to talk about the process of writing, including their frustrations and successes. She encourages each student to ask the class for help or suggestions. After about 10 minutes of this sharing, Miss Kim has the students put their writing in a folder and tells them that they will continue their writing tomorrow and that all their work will eventually be published in a class book entitled *Our Trip to the Farm*. This book will be laminated and placed in the class library for the children to check out and take home if they wish.

This scenario outlines a writing workshop in which children are actively engaged in being "authors who will publish their work. They are actively involved in a hands-on activity during which writing is seen as a process that involves children listening, conversing, and applying literacy skills. The teacher guides the students through the process, encouraging collaboration, sharing, and independent seat work. She is committed to having her students write well and learn the appropriate mechanics, as well as the joys and frustrations of being a writer.

A Classroom of Authors

In a classroom, one of the most important factors that contribute to developing writing ability in students is having the teacher perceive himself or herself as writer. Teachers need to model a love for writing in the classroom and embrace reading and writing as a fun activity in which everyone in the classroom is learning, sharing, reading, and writing. Students need to learn that literacy is fun and enjoyable. One reason some students do not like to write is because they see it as a chore, as dreaded work, and as something to "get done"; they do not perceive themselves as writers. One of the first steps to encouraging writing in the classroom is by having teachers think of themselves as writers, thereby modeling the love for written expression. How many of you consider yourself an author? How many of you take pleasure in expressing yourself through writing and write frequently in your free time?

The classroom needs to be a place where a community of learners exists that includes the students and the teacher. The teacher needs to structure the curriculum so that it focuses on the behaviors that students engage in as language learners. According to Atwell (1998), children learn to write by exercising the options available to real-world authors, including daily time for writing, conferences with teachers and peers during drafting, pacing set by the writer, and opportunities to publish what they have written. Atwell suggests that students, not the teacher, should decide what they will write about. Another important point is that teachers need to sit down to write with their students so that they are modeling the process of writing; they need to listen to and learn from young writers. Writing becomes a process that all can engage in, share, learn from, and ultimately, enjoy.

Perhaps out of all of the literacy skills, technology has had the greatest impact on writing and how we craft this art form. Children love to use the computer to write and find it motivating and exciting to see their ideas expressed in such a professional-looking format. Technology is now an integral part of the writing process, whether it is done on a computer with a word processor, on a cell phone with text messaging, or through instant messaging.

Reading, writing, speaking, and listening are reciprocal processes that involve learning about literacy and language. That is, many of the strategies involved in reading and comprehending a piece of text can be applied in a reciprocal fashion when writing a piece of text or learning to give a speech. For example, if a teacher is giving instruction on how to summarize what was read, it is helpful to teach students how to write summaries. If a teacher is instructing children how to identify the topic sentence and supporting details of a paragraph, it is beneficial to teach children how to write a topic sentence with supporting details. Good readers usually become good writers because they become familiar with how writers effectively express themselves and they become comfortable with the use of rich vocabulary words and excellent sentence structure to convey meaning. The more readers are exposed to new words in contextually rich and meaningful ways, the more likely they are to use these words in their own speech and writing. The more readers are exposed to complex, well-structured sentences, the more apt they are to articulate themselves using more sophisticated sentences and to write using more complex sentence structures. These four processes of reading, writing, speaking, and listening are reciprocal in nature, and teachers should strive for comprehensive instruction that ties these processes together.

This chapter explores the processes of writing, listening, and speaking as part of the literacy curriculum. These three processes are emphasized in state and professional language arts/English standards, and teachers need to emphasize each process through explicit modeling of best practices, providing direct instruction, giving support and guidance to students as they develop their literacy skills, using technology to support these processes, and continuously assessing each child. Each process is discussed below, starting with an examination of writing.

The Process of Writing

Most educators today agree that integrating reading and writing benefits the development of literacy. Studies (National Writing Project, 1999) have shown that reading development does not take place in isolation; children develop simultaneously as readers, listeners, speakers, and writers. One study asked students and teachers questions about the ways in which reading and writing are combined in their classrooms. Students were asked how frequently in school they were asked to write long answers to questions on tests or assignments that involved reading. Students who said they wrote long answers on a weekly basis had higher reading scores than those who said they never or rarely did so. Writing supports children's reading development in at least three ways (National Writing Project, 1999):

1. Readers and writers use the same intellectual strategies, including organizing, monitoring, questioning, and revising meaning, and children grow in their ability to use these strategies through both reading and writing activities. The biggest difference between good and poor readers and good and poor writers is their strategy use, not their skill use.

2. The reading and writing processes are similar. The first step in both processes, for example, involves activating prior knowledge and setting purposes. Because the two processes are so similar, students learn literacy concepts and procedures through both reading and writing.

3. Children use many of the same skills in both reading and writing. Phonics is a good example of this transfer. Children use phonic skills to decode words to become fluent readers, and they also use their phonics knowledge to sound out the spelling of words and to apply spelling rules.

Courtesy of Bill Lisenby

Integrating reading and writing is an important part of literacy development.

Readers need to learn how to be authors and how to express themselves through written language. Authors need to learn how to be good readers and how readers interpret language and become involved in story structure, ideas, and sentence construction. As Jane Hansen states in her book *When Writers Read* (2001), "When writers read their own work, they realize how much their readers don't know. Later when writers read something written by another writer, they know how much is missing and wonder about the decisions that writer made. When writers read, they ask multitudes of questions and feel a sense of appreciation for the many decisions the writer made" (p. 2).

Authors learn to recognize *voice* when they are readers; and readers learn to write with *voice* when they are authors. As Jane Hansen (2001) points out, as teachers we decide whether our classroom honors our students' voices or forces them to remain quiet. Students must find value in themselves, in others, and in their expression through individual voices. In the same fashion, when students give oral presentations, they learn how to involve their audience in the spoken word and how to articulate their voice through expression, intonation, and the message they are delivering. They learn how to use language to convey verbal messages and develop their self through voice.

In recent years, the focus of writing has shifted from thinking about writing as a perfectly finished product that should be graded, to viewing writing as a process that emerges through various stages of self-discovery. Most high school students believe that the way to write is to sit down at the computer, and type up an essay as quickly as possible with at least three paragraphs, all of which should have a topic sentence and three supporting ideas. Most elementary school students also believe that writing means sitting down and quickly getting words onto paper with a huge burst of energy. The problem with this approach is that once students "get it all down," they feel that their writing is complete, and they greatly resist any attempt at structural revision. They will edit their paper by changing individual words and correcting any "typos," but will highly resist any further modification. This is not the way authors compose or write. Authors spend much time thinking, brainstorming, trying out ideas and giving them up, and modifying and throwing away unsuccessful drafts. They start, stop, and try again. It is not a smooth, one-time process.

Writing as a process involves many stages, each of which is as valuable as the next, each focusing on the overall design and purpose of the final product. Lucy Calkins (1986) claims that when we, as teachers, understand the writing process, we can help each of our students use and adapt effective writing strategies. The stages are not linear and hierarchical, but rather circle back and overlap with each other. These stages are *prewriting, drafting, revising, editing,* and *postwriting.* Each stage builds on the next, but teachers should not interpret the stages as though the whole class can be working on one stage in unison, such as Monday is for picking a topic, Tuesdays are for first drafts, Wednesdays are for rewrites, and so on. The writing process does not work that way; it is not a smooth, step-by-step linear process. Rather, writing is a process of dialogue between the writer and the emerging text (Calkins, 1986). It is a process of focusing on what to write, pulling back to ask questions, and then commencing to write again. The writer is always asking, "What am I trying to say?" "How does this sound?" and "Where am I going with this?" These are the same questions that teachers should be asking their students during writing conferences so that the children internalize these questions and actually start questioning themselves as they write. Teacher–student conferences are at the heart of the writing process, and it is through them that students learn the effective strategies needed to interact with their own text (Calkins, 1986).

Prewriting Stage

The **prewriting** stage is perhaps the most important stage in writing. During this stage, the student explores and focuses on the purpose, audience, topic, and form that the writing task could take. This is the "getting-ready-to-write" stage where writers take the time to explore thoughts and feelings, organize and jot down ideas, and develop a strategy for how they will approach the writing. This stage has three activities:

◆ *Identifying the purpose and audience:* The writer needs to ask, "Why am I writing the text? Am I writing to entertain? To persuade? To inform?" The writer also needs to ask, "Who is the audience? Am I writing for my teacher? A group of legislators? My friends?"

◆ *Determining the content:* The writer needs to decide the topic and what content needs to be included. Often, the topic is assigned to the students and there is no choice, but sometimes the topic can be more open-ended and the student must narrow down the topic.

◆ *Developing an organization plan:* The writer must design an overall plan for organizing the information to be presented and the composition in general. This phase is usually the most neglected by children, who often see little need to organize their thoughts; yet, this is the phase that most writers will agree is the most significant and important aspect of a successful piece of writing.

Several different activities can facilitate a successful prewriting stage:

◆ *Brainstorming:* This prewriting activity involves allowing students to generate and develop ideas for writing. Any idea is written down and is not considered "good" or "bad." Each student participating in a group or the student working individually should write down as many ideas as possible, trying to "think outside the box." This is an excellent way to explore ideas for a topic or to narrow down a topic. It is also an excellent way to get started trying to figure out what content should be included.

◆ *Webbing:* This technique uses a visual tool to start organizing ideas and concepts that have been generated in brainstorming. Usually, a central idea or concept will go into a circle in the middle and all supporting ideas will stem from that circle. Each supporting idea can have more details branching off from that circle. In this way, the writing assignment can be represented visually, with each supporting idea becoming a new paragraph with supporting details to substantiate it. Inspiration is a wonderful software package that supports the use of webbing in writing. Figure 8–1 presents an example of a writers brainstorming web on the topic of the narwhal that was done in Inspiration. Note that there are four main ideas about the narwhal: what it looks like, that it is a member of the whale family, its tusk, and where it lives. These main ideas become the topic sentence of each paragraph. Each paragraph has at least three supporting details to support each main idea. Webbing becomes a graphic way to "outline" a topic and can be easily converted to an outline. Inspiration allows you to view your map as a graphical web or as a standard outline, which is a wonderful way to bridge that gap for children who are accustomed to the visual configuration of presenting ideas.

◆ *Drawing/doodling:* Drawing or doodling is an excellent prewriting activity for all ages, because it might help to focus the writer on key ideas and concepts that need to be covered. This is especially important for very young children who are just starting their journey into the writing process.

◆ *Prompts:* Prompt writing means listening to or reading someone's idea or question, thinking about it, and responding (Angelillo, 2005). State assessment tests in writing, as well as standardized tests such as the SAT, usually include prompts in which students must respond to a given question or picture. Additional prewriting stimuli, such as visual prompts like photographs or pictures (picture prompts), can help a writer start to focus on an idea and think about what should be covered in the writing. Prompts can also come from reading books, newspapers, websites, magazines, poetry, and playing music in the classroom. In all cases, students must comprehend what is presented and carefully plan and organize their thoughts to respond correctly and completely. Writing prompts for ELLs should include clear directions and should describe the context or situation to be written about. The prompts need to be carefully construed, taking into account cultural and linguistic factors. The prompts should be based on the cultural knowledge the students possess, as well as the knowledge they have gained as part of their academic schooling. Teachers should try to avoid prompts in which students are expected to write about their new culture. For example, the

FIGURE 8-1

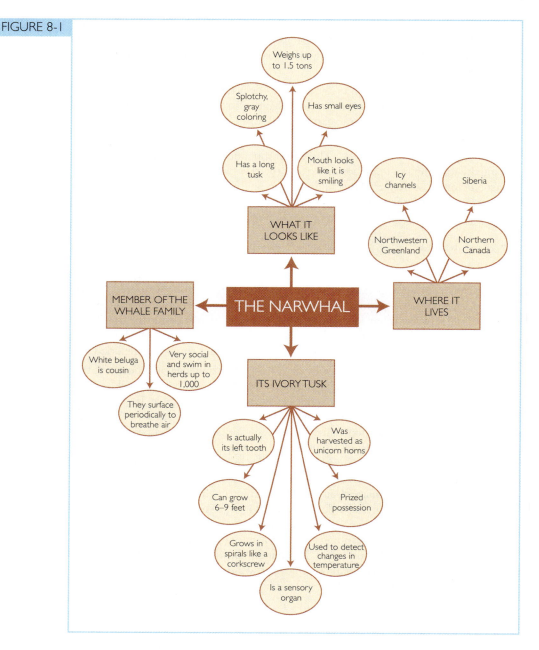

following prompt could be confusing for an ELL: "Write about how your family celebrates Thanksgiving." If the child's family is new to the country and does not celebrate Thanksgiving or has no background with this holiday, the child will not know what to write. A better prompt is: "We will have no school on Thursday and Friday this week because of Thanksgiving. Write about what you would like to do during your time off" (Education Alliance at Brown University, 2006).

◆ *Outlining:* Children should learn how to structure their ideas into a formal outline. As children learn how to web, a natural step is to convert this to an outline. By the time children are in fourth and fifth grade, they should be using simple outlines to help organize their writing assignments.

The prewriting stage allows writers the time to be reflective, to rehearse, to explore their own thoughts and feelings regarding the topic they are to write about, and to organize their ideas. Students need to know that this is a stage that they may and should return to as they start writing; once they move on to the next stage, they still need to go back and revise their outline or their web or even start over again. Writers often start to write, and then say that this is not working and begin again. Students need to know that it is all right to start over, and that it is not a mistake or a waste of time. However, students also need to know that at a certain point in time, they need to move ahead with the topic that they have chosen and invest their time and energy by putting their best effort into their writing.

Drafting Stage

The **drafting** stage uses the results of the prewriting stage to have students begin writing a rough draft of their piece. In this stage, the focus should be on getting the message across with regard to purpose, audience, content, and organization, not on conventions of writing such as spelling and sentence structure. It is recommended that children skip a line or double-space the text as they write to allow the teacher space to write in comments for revision. It is also advisable for children to write a "rough" draft so that everybody knows that this piece is in the process of being written and the mechanics have not been emphasized yet. With the advent of computers in the classroom, this is the time for children to use word processors to start typing their pieces. This is helpful for children who have learning disabilities (LD) and for ELLs. The computer allows children to publish what looks like a professional piece of writing without penmanship or handwriting skills interfering with their ability to express themselves. Computers also demand a level of proficiency with keyboarding, but peers can work together with one dictating the writing to another who has more proficiency at typing. Also, many software programs exist that allow students to write and illustrate their piece using multimedia technology right on the computer (see the Software Packages for Writing section later in this chapter for a list of software programs that promote writing). These are excellent motivating tools for children to start their first draft.

During the first draft stage, children may need to go back and revise their initial map or outline and work on the organizational structure. They should be concentrating on writing a topic sentence for each paragraph and supporting it with details. Students need to understand that writing is an iterative process of going back and forth between getting those ideas down on paper as quickly as possible and reviewing the outline or map and asking, "Does this make sense?"

Children also should be focusing on a composition's lead or opening sentence at this time. This is when students need to grab the attention of their audience. This can be done through asking questions, such as "When is the last time you swam with dolphins?" or "Did you know that the narwhal's tusk grows eight feet long, and it is really its left tooth that functions as a sensory organ?" Donald Graves (1994) and Lucy Calkins (1996) recommend that students create several leads and read them to other students, trying them out for their peers' reactions. As students work on their leads, they learn valuable lessons about language and how to motivate their readers to read more (Tompkins, 2000).

The teacher should be available for short conferences during this stage. Students will need guidance and feedback now; often, novice writers just need a short confirmation to be reassured that what they have written is truly on target. Other students may need more help to develop their ideas and express themselves properly. ELLs can sit next to a student who is proficient in writing so that they are peer-coached as they go through the process. It may also be helpful to have ELLs use a tape recorder to express their ideas before they write them down on paper. ELL students should be encouraged to express themselves in English as soon as possible; but if necessary, have the students use the tape recorder to express their ideas in their native language first, and then convert it to English. Conferences are an important part of this process, but they should be short. Children should be encouraged to write independently, using dictionaries, word walls, and word banks available to the class.

The teacher should have available a variety of materials to help the children at this time. Class dictionaries should be accessible and written at the appropriate level of the children. Older children should have a thesaurus available to help derive the correct

Teachers need to continually conference with students during the writing process.

word usage. Word walls of frequently used words are helpful to writers who need assistance spelling these words. If the writing assignment is on a specific topic, it is useful to have word walls that contain key concepts, ideas, and words about this topic. Students' individual word banks (note cards of selected words placed in a small box on the students' desks) and individually created dictionaries written in journals are also helpful materials. Children should be encouraged to use the "ask two rule," where they must first ask two students for help before coming to the teacher.

Revising Stage

The **revising** stage is one of the most important and difficult stages for writers to go through. In this stage, the writer revisits the text and evaluates the content, the organization, the form, and the mechanics of the piece, and makes the necessary revisions. Students should write several drafts in order to improve both the content and the language of the message they are communicating. Students should work collaboratively in teams during this stage to get feedback and support from their writing partner.

An essential feature of the revising stage is a writing rubric. This rubric should specify the skills and processes the writer should be following during writing and be at the appropriate level of the grade (see Figure 8–7). Children should have this rubric or a checklist before they begin writing so they know what is expected of them, and they should use this checklist as part of the revision process when working with their writing partner or in teams. Finally, the teacher should use this rubric to evaluate the children's writing.

Most children are resistant to making major structural revisions. As they write, many children believe that this will be their final piece. They also become attached to what is written and develop "ownership" over everything that they put down on paper. The computer can exacerbate this problem, because once children see their words in print, they feel their job is done. The teacher needs to constantly remind children that revision might mean tearing their piece apart and starting over on a section of it or from the beginning. The teacher must work patiently and consistently with the children until they see that this process is a necessary step in the writing process.

The steps for revising a rough draft are as follows:

◆ *Reread the rough draft.* Writers need to put their text down for a while and then come back to it with a fresh point of view. They should read it silently first and make revisions based on this new perspective.

◆ *Have another student read the draft.* Next, it is helpful if the writer reads the piece to another student or asks that student to read it silently. Peer editing is helpful in the revision process, and the peer editor should use the checklist that the class is using to do the revising. Most children are not adept at revising another person's work and can make only minor suggestions in the process. This is quite acceptable because part of the process of being a writer is learning how to read and revise other's work. The teacher needs to work with the class on teaching them the correct process for revising and what it entails.

◆ *Have a conference with the teacher.* The conference with the teacher is an extremely important part of the revision process. Students need feedback from their teacher on the good qualities of the written piece and what needs revising. The teacher needs to be sensitive to the writer's feelings and perspective about the written piece and offer suggestions as to how the piece can be improved. Revision should be a collaborative effort involving the student and the teacher, not a dictatorial command that needs to be followed. The checklist should be used as a means of assessing the rough draft, and the prewriting outline and/or web should be referenced to determine what the initial thoughts were about the writing.

The revising stage is an important one in the writing process, during which the student goes back and reworks the rough draft so that it reflects the criteria outlined on a writing checklist. A student might revise his or her writing many, many times before the teacher and the student are satisfied that it is satisfactory.

Editing Stage

During the **editing** stage, the student works on correcting and proofreading the writing for usage, mechanics, and spelling. Although this stage can follow the revision stage, the two often occur simultaneously. In this stage, students take a final look at their writing and correct misspellings, check their grammar, and change words to convey the appropriate meanings. The teacher should provide instruction on sentence formation, word usage, and use of dictionaries and other reference materials to help students in the correct mechanics of standard written English. Students should receive instruction on how to proof the revised composition. The teacher should model how to do this using an easel or overhead projector. The teacher corrects possible errors as they are located and marks up the composition using special proofreaders' marks. Figure 8–2 presents a list of proofreaders' marks that elementary school students can learn to use during the editing of their own work. It is helpful to have children proof each other's work using these proofreading marks. The teacher should ensure that the proofing is correct before the student continues with the editing. Once a composition is proofed by the teacher, the writer needs to go back and make the necessary changes. During this stage, the writer is actively working toward handing in a final draft that is free of errors and that looks like a "publishable" piece of work. This final draft will be the one that is ultimately given a grade.

Teachers should be aware that in kindergarten through about second grade, invented spelling probably will be used in children's writing. This is quite acceptable and should be encouraged within the first draft. As children move toward their final draft, the teacher can show the students how the correct spellings look and instruct the children in the correct letter–sound correspondence so that they are moving from invented spelling to standard written English in their final draft.

Postwriting Stage

The **postwriting** stage focuses on the publication and sharing of students' writing with an appropriate audience. This stage is particularly important because it provides feedback to the writer, motivates the writer to continue writing, and takes the piece of writing and puts it into the "public domain" for an audience to read. This last stage is sometimes overlooked in the classroom but is an important aspect of the writing process.

FIGURE 8-2

Proofreaders' Marks

Delete	ℓ	James was upset because his cat had run away from his home.
Insert	∧	His cat was last seen at the corner of Maple Ave. and Main Street.
Indent paragraph	¶	¶The cat was from his sister who had gone to the shelter and picked out a yellow and black kitten. She gave it to him on his birthday.
Capitalize	≡	James decided to call his cat april because that is the month they were both born.
Change to lowercase	/	April was a good Cat and easy to take care of.
Add period	⊙	James was worried that he would not be able to find her ⊙
Add comma	∧	He looked in his backyard in his neighbor's yard and on his porch.
Add apostrophe	∨	James finally found his cat sleeping in his dads car!

Editing Checklist

Author   Editor

_____   _____   1. I have checked to make sure that all words are spelled correctly. I circled all misspelled words.

_____   _____   2. I have checked that all sentences begin with capital letters.

_____   _____   3. I have checked that all proper nouns begin with a capital letter.

_____   _____   4. I have checked that all sentences end with the proper punctuation mark.

_____   _____   5. I have read through to make sure that all errors have been fixed.

Signatures:

Author: _____   Editor: _____

One of the most popular ways to publish students' work is to make it into a book by laminating the pages and binding them into a booklet with a cover. This can be done with either an individual student's piece or by compiling all children's writing into a class booklet. Children love to see their work in a book format and find this highly motivating. It is also a wonderful way to display work for parents and other classes in the school. This book can then become part of the class library and a card can be attached to it so children can take it out and read it independently.

Another popular way to introduce a book to the class is by having an "author's chair"; in this approach, while the other students gather around, the child who just had a book published sits in a special chair and reads the book to the students, presenting it to the class for their library. This is also a wonderful way to involve parents and members of the community who have similar interests as the student who wrote the book. For children who are ELLs, this experience can be beneficial in building confidence, in encouraging the use of standard English, and in having their families participate in school activities.

Other ways that children's work can be published are:

◆ Submit pieces to writing contests.
◆ Display the writing on the wall or bulletin board.
◆ Publish children's writing online. There are many sites where children can publish their work (see list of websites later in this chapter).
◆ Submit children's writing to a local newspaper or children's magazine.

An important part of the postwriting stage is that the writer receives feedback from an interested reader. Such feedback is important to the writer to further improve that student's writing ability. The teacher needs to be sensitive to the writer's feelings and place any feedback within the context of positive feelings and praise for the finished piece. During the author's chair, students can also offer feedback and their opinions on the piece to the author. This will also help the author reflect back on the writing and motivate him or her to continue writing.

Instructional practices such as writing as a process have been found to be useful with ELLs (Anderson, 2003). A process-oriented approach teaches students to see writing as a cyclical process and encourages them to write for an audience and to compose messages for real reasons, as opposed to writing because they were told to. The students become aware of and consider, on some level, audience, purpose, and context of writing. In addition, although ELLs are in the process of learning English, they can provide considerable support to other children, especially others who are learning English, by offering feedback, seeking feedback on their own writing, and sharing their success and difficulties as writers. In addition to being responsible for their own writing, ELLs are also responsible for helping each other grow as writers.

Courtesy of Guilherme Cunha

In the Writing Workshop, students actively work together with the teacher—and with each other—to develop literacy skills.

The writing process concentrates not so much on the final draft, but on ensuring that all students achieve success in expressing themselves and feel encouraged to write more. The focus is not only on what is produced, but that students find joy and satisfaction in writing, as well as learn how to write a well-constructed and organized piece of text.

Integrating Writing into the Classroom

The Writing Workshop

The **writing workshop** is exactly what its name connotes—a workshop type of environment is created where children have the opportunity to engage in enjoyable writing and reading activities. The writing workshop is student-centered in the sense that each student's development and expression of an idea is the primary goal of this phase of literacy. It demands participation of all involved because it exists to serve each student's needs. A literate environment is established where students are writing and reading; it is the process that is emphasized, not the skills learned in doing it. Students learn that skills help them become better at the process, and that the curriculum does not revolve around a subset of isolated skills to be mastered.

The four steps of a writing workshop are described in the paragraphs below:

1. *Introduction (5 minutes):* During the introduction, the teacher gathers the students around her at the writing corner to look at yesterday's work on the easel. She provides background information, activates prior knowledge, and offers motivational comments to get them ready for their writing workshop.

2. *Mini-lesson (10 minutes):* During this step, the teacher reviews what the students wrote yesterday and gives them a mini-lesson on a specific writing skill or strategy. For example she provides them with a short lesson on how to use descriptive words such as *big, yellow, pink,* and *crunchy* to enhance their writing. She reinforces the need to use descriptive words in the students' own writing by modeling the strategy in a paragraph written on the easel. At the end of the mini-lesson, she carefully goes over what their writing assignment is and gives them all the cue words and directions they will need to successfully write on their own. She points out where the necesssary reources are located, such as dictionaries, writing tools, the word wall, and the computer center.

3. *Independent writing and conferring (30 minutes):* The teacher confers with individual students and small groups on their writing.

4. *Wrap-up and sharing of personal experiences (5 minutes):* Students share personal experiences involved with their writing. This can occur at their desks with their writing in front of them or at the reading/writing corner in the classroom.

In setting up a writing workshop, Atwell (1998) suggests that the following factors need to be considered in the beginning of the school year before any student enters the classroom:

Making time: Writers need regular, frequent chunks of time for writing. Graves (1994) suggests allotting at least three class periods a week for students to be able to develop and refine their ideas. Regular, frequent time for writing also helps students write well. For upper primary and middle school teachers, the workshop is not an add-on; rather, it is part of the English program. If the period lasts for 45 minutes, the bulk of the time can be spent on writing workshops three to four days per week. Atwell (1998) claims that of any discipline, writing needs the most attention because this is where students need more hands-on help, teacher demonstrations, and structured time.

Creating the context: Graves (1994) compares a classroom organized as a workshop to an artist's studio. The studio is set up to help the artist create, just as the writing and reading classroom should be set up to encourage students to write and read. The supplies needed for a writing workshop are pencils and ballpoint pens, lined paper, colored pens for editing, stapler, paper clips, and correction fluid. Sticky notes, rulers, index cards, clipboards for writing outside the classroom, construction paper, and art supplies all help the writer as well. Reference books such as dictionaries, a thesaurus, and writer's guides should be located in a reference center. The room should be structured so that students have comfortable areas to write quietly and individually. There should also be an area where students can confer together or groups can collaborate. Often, just grouping tables together into "centers" is sufficient.

Keeping track: A teacher will need to develop a system for keeping records and collecting students' work throughout the year. The following forms are recommended (Atwell, 1998):

♦ *Writing Survey*—given once at the beginning of the year to learn about each student's experiences and attitudes as a writer (Figure 8–3)

♦ *Reading Survey*—given once at the beginning of the year to learn about each student's experiences and attitudes as a reader, which will help inform the teacher about the student's attitudes toward writing as well (Figure 8–4)

♦ *Student Writing Record*—a record of finished pieces of writing that a student keeps track of throughout the year (Figure 8–5)

♦ *Student Reading Record*—a record of finished pieces of reading that a student keeps track of throughout the year (Figure 8–6)

♦ *Writing Rubric*—a rubric/checklist that all students must have when they write, which is to be completed by the writer and attached to each piece of writing submitted; this is probably one of the most important tools a writer needs to work with because it specifies criteria that will be used to assess the student's writing (Figure 8–7)

♦ *Writing Conference Record*—a record of the conferences between a teacher and a student, which would include any comments made by the teacher; this form could be used in a peer conference (Figure 8–8)

FIGURE 8-3

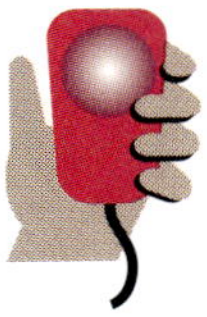

Writing Survey

DATE:_____ NAME:_____

1. Do you like to write? Why or why not?

2. What kinds of things do you like to write best?

3. How often do you write at home?

4. What things do you think are easy about writing? What things do you think are hard about writing?

5. Do you consider yourself an author or a writer? Why or why not?

6. How could your teacher help you write better?

7. Describe one piece of writing you are proud of. What did you write about?

FIGURE 8-6

Student Reading Record

NAME:_____

#	TITLE	AUTHOR	GENRE	DATE COMPLETED	DATE ABANDONED

The different levels of support given to children as they write are shown in p. 338 (Fountas & Pinnell, 1996):

Shared writing is when the teacher provides full support by writing down what the children dictate. The writing usually is done at an easel or on a large chart where the class is gathered around the teacher as she uses markers to compose the message. As the teacher models the writing process, children contribute spellings and word usage while the teacher writes down the ideas. The teacher will use a think-aloud approach, correcting her own mistakes as the children follow along, demonstrating that writing is a process of trying out ideas and revising them. Once the text is complete, the teacher will first read the message to the class; then the class will read the message together. They will reread it several times, and revisit it in the next few days to review its message. This rereading helps develop concepts of print and reinforces the grapheme–phoneme connection between letters and correspond-ing sounds, and between written words and their corresponding pronunciation. An example of this is presented in the earlier scenario when Miss Kim writes down the children's story about going to the farm. She starts out by modeling the process of writing a topic sentence with the children contributing ideas, phrases, and words. She often did "think alouds," in which she would try out ideas and revise them as she wrote, thinking out loud so the children could hear her. In this example, Miss Kim provides full support for the writing process.

Interactive writing allows children to start taking part in the actual physical writ-ing of the message by sharing the pen with the teacher. While composing a message with the class, the teacher selects letters, words, or sentences for selected children to

FIGURE 8-7

Writing Rubric

NAME:_____ DATE:_____

WRITING ASSIGNMENT:_____ GRADE:_____

Writing Rubric

Areas	Skills	1 Needs Much Improvement	2 Needs Some Improvement	3 Good	4 Excellent	Total
Content and Organization	Opening and closing are evident					
	Keeps to central idea					
	Supports ideas with details					
	States ideas in a clear sequence					
	Clear paragraphs with topic sentence					
Usage	Subject-verb agreement					
	Effective and varied word choice					
Sentence Construction	Complete sentences					
	Varied length and structure					
Mechanics	Spelling					
	Capitalization					
	Punctuation					
Total						

share the pen and guide them through this writing process. The teacher provides a high level of support. Each sentence is written word by word, with the teacher "stretching" out each word as the children pronounce it slowly. The teacher chooses which child will write the letters that represent each sound or spell the entire word, depending on the child's knowledge of phonics and spelling. Often, teachers will use a different-colored marker for the letters that the children write. In this way, the teacher can keep track of how much writing the children have done. Posters of the upper and lowercase letters of the alphabet should be in view to help children form the letters. Correction tape is used when students write a letter incorrectly or write the wrong letter. Once completed, the writing is displayed in the room and is read many times by the group for shared reading. There are four purposes to interactive writing (Tompkins, 2000): (1) to demonstrate how to write words and sentences; (2) to teach how to use capital letters and punctuation marks; (3) to demonstrate how to use phonics and spelling patterns to spell words; (4) to create written texts for the classroom that children could not write independently. An example of this is when Miss Kim in the scenario presented earlier had a student come to the easel and prompted him to write the word *goat* in a different-colored marker, sharing the pen. In this way, Miss Kim was demonstrating the phonic pattern *oat*, while having the student refer to the word wall where that particular rime was listed.

FIGURE 8-8

Writing Conference Record

Writing Conference Record
(to be stapled to the student's writing folder)

NAME: _____ GRADE: _____

Date	Writing Piece	Suggestions	Mini-Lesson Needed	Goals/ Comments

Guided writing is when children are starting to write independently but still need a great deal of support from the teacher. The teacher provides instruction and assistance to children during the writing process, either individually or in small groups. Teachers work closely with the children throughout all phases of the writing process, helping them choose a topic, organize their thoughts, write a first draft, and revise and compose a finished copy. Teacher conferences provide the scaffolding needed at this stage. An example is the writing workshop approach that Miss Kim used in the earlier scenario. Children were writing independently but received a great deal of support from Miss Kim, who helped individual and small groups of students and conferred with those who needed more intensive, individualized help. During the conferences, Miss Kim helped one student choose a topic, another student construct a semantic map so that his thoughts were organized before he started writing, and another student compose a topic sentence. Guided writing allows students to work at the level they feel comfortable with, while providing the necessary support when they need it.

Type of Writing	Description	Purpose(s)	Types of Written Text
SHARED WRITING	The teacher provides full support for the children by writing down what the children dictate. The children can assist the teacher by helping with the spelling and wording of the sentences. The teacher then reads it back to the children and the text is reread over and over again.	◆ Provides a model of phrased, fluent writing ◆ Promotes language development ◆ Develops concepts of print ◆ Allows children to share in the process of writing text and becoming authors at a very young age ◆ Involves children in an enjoyable literacy experience	◆ Large-print piece on a large chart and written with markers ◆ Poems ◆ Stories after field trips ◆ Postreading discussion charts ◆ Holiday descriptions ◆ K-W-L charts ◆ Biographies ◆ Descriptions of events ◆ Brainstorming maps
INTERACTIVE WRITING	The teacher provides a high level of support by writing most of the text but will share the pen with individual children who will write letters, words, and phrases. Often, the teacher will hold the pen with the child and help form the letters together. The message or story is composed by the whole class and then reread.	◆ Allows the class to partake in an enjoyable shared literacy experience ◆ Allows teacher to model specific writing strategies ◆ Increases children's knowledge of print ◆ All children partake in composing and constructing the written piece	◆ Large-print piece written with markers ◆ Poetry ◆ Lists of things ◆ Retelling a story from a book ◆ Postreading discussion charts ◆ Familiar stories ◆ Summary of events from the day
GUIDED WRITING	The teacher provides some support, but children are starting to work independently to master writing strategies. The teacher gives a mini-lesson to the whole class or small group on a specific aspect of writing and then guides students as they write on their own. The teacher may work with small groups of students to provide support. The teacher will give individual conferences to students as they work. Specific skills and strategies are taught in a supportive session.	◆ Provides the opportunity for students to receive help on specific needs and to write independently while still receiving support ◆ Provides the opportunity for students to receive "scaffolding" or support on writing strategies ◆ Allows teacher to individualize instruction ◆ Children select their own topics or have a range of choices to write about	◆ Children can choose from an array of topics on which to write ◆ Prompts such as photographs and interesting picture can be provided ◆ Word walls, dictionaries should be provided ◆ A print-rich environment should be available for children to write
INDEPENDENT WRITING	Children write independently on topics with little support from the teacher except when needed.	◆ Allows students to practice writing independently ◆ Children know how to use the resources available to compose and spell	◆ A variety of prompts should be available to help children choose a topic ◆ Many different types of writing are provided as a model

Teachers' VOICES The Workshop Approach

In a writing workshop, I follow a process in which students gather seeds in a writer's notebook (one new seed each day for 7–10 days); they pick a seed they can live with for the next five to seven days, and they nurture that seed, revise, draft, edit, and publish. The format is similar to a reading workshop in that I begin each lesson with a 10- to 20-minute mini-lesson, followed by 30 minutes of conferring with individuals while they "try it" (some aspect of the mini-lesson), followed by a 10- to 20-minute conclusion. The units of study focus on craft, process, and leading a "writerly life," individually at times and as an overlapping, interwoven process of writing.

In a reading workshop, I focus on six reading strategies throughout the year. They are connections, questioning, visualizing, inferring, determining importance, and synthesizing. My reading class is a solid 60-minute block each day. Each class begins with a mini-lesson (10–20 minutes long), usually a discussion and teacher modeling a facet of the strategy in the spotlight. Students read independently for 30 minutes while I "coach" or confer with individual students (and later on with groups in book clubs), and there is a closure of 10 to 20 minutes to share and debrief what has been tried. During the 30-minute read, students are expected to record on sticky notes the strategies they had used to assist the sharing and reflection process.

Missing from the brief explanation above is the element of *passion*. I am passionate about reading and passionate about writing, and I believe in what I do so much that it nearly scares me. . . . If I love something, even the most resistant learner comes along "liking" it. It has been wonderful.

A bridge exists between reading and writing that must be spanned in the classroom. I am constantly reading children's literature to my third grade class during their mini-lesson—books they have heard before since kindergarten, books they shouldn't read by themselves until fifth grade, and everything in between. In each book, I stop and make a big deal about ordinary things—ordinary things that authors are able to convey in an extraordinary manner, such as an author looking at his twin brother and describing him. In reading, we point out great writing, or poor writing, or exemplary writing of any kind. The students do the same. In writing, we look for examples of great writing that makes, of course, great reading.

The above technique works for me. It would work for any teacher who is willing to put the effort and time in. Failures within the framework above would probably come in the form of trying too much or spending too much time on one area. If you feel the literacy ideas for your mini-lessons are getting thin, they probably are. It is time to bring another strategy into the spotlight.

—*Chuck Nebbia, Third Grade Teacher*

Independent writing is when children are working on their own piece of writing without much support from the teacher. They are learning how to use writing as a tool and to write for a variety of purposes, whether it be to write a letter, a story, or an article about something interesting. They are capable of working independently on their own with limited support from the teacher. This does not mean that they do not need mini-lessons on different aspects of writing, nor does it mean they do not receive help and guidance to improve their writing. Independent writing allows the children and teacher to work efficiently in a writing workshop environment. While children are working on independent writing, the teacher can be conferencing with other children and working with small groups in guided writing. In the earlier scenario, Miss Kim's goal was to develop a classroom environment in which independent writing is an ongoing, daily activity that allows children the opportunity to pursue writing as a form of expression and personal growth. The writing workshop provides the structure that allows teachers to provide the type of writing support students will need, whether it be full support through shared writing, high-level support through interactive writing, partial support through guided writing, or little support in independent writing. The writing workshop is the foundation of the writing curriculum in the literacy classroom, allowing children to grow as authors who enjoy written expression in a supportive environment.

Teaching Writing Mechanics

During the elementary grades, children need to learn how to use different types of writing skills and strategies in each of the four broad areas listed below:

1. Content and organization
2. Mechanics: spelling, punctuation, and capitalization
3. Language usage
4. Sentence construction

Teachers need to focus instruction on each of these broad areas in a writing workshop through mini-lessons, modeling of the strategy, guided writing with teacher support, and feedback via conferencing. Direct instruction should occur in the mini-lessons in which teachers provide strategies on how to write effectively. In addition, each of these areas should be represented on a Writing Rubric (see Figure 8–7), which each child should have. This Writing Rubric should be used as an integral part of the writing classroom: for children to use as a guide as they go through the writing process, for the teacher to use to provide guidance and feedback during conferencing, for the writer to use for editing and revision, for peer editors to use to proofread papers, and ultimately, for the teacher to use to assess the student's final draft.

Content and organization refers to the extent to which the writer is focused on the purpose and audience and organizes the paper into a clear and logical piece with relevant and supporting details. The purpose refers to why the writer is engaged in this exercise: Is it to write a persuasive letter, tell a story, present research about a specific topic, or discuss the writer's views on an issue? The purpose will influence who the audience or reader of the student's writing will be—a teacher, a parent, a friend, or someone in the community. The organization of the piece should have a clear opening and closing, should be focused on the purpose at hand and not wander from it, and have a logical progression of ideas where key ideas are developed. The content consists of the ideas a writer uses and presents.

Content concerns cannot be taken for granted with elementary students (Bratcher, 1994). This involves identifying the main idea and articulating it clearly. Students often need a great deal of practice in finding and writing main ideas. Once they have identified the main idea, students often have difficulty describing the details that support the main idea. The details need to focus on the content of the writing piece; therefore, the student may need to do further research to fill in the missing pieces. Students usually have difficulty realizing that writing is an iterative process of expressing ideas, doing more research, and then going back to fill in the details. Students often resist learning more content in order to write.

A software program such as Inspiration can help students map out their ideas before they begin their first draft. The central bubble becomes their main idea, then supporting details can be filled in to sufficient levels, depending on the age of the student and the purpose of the writing task. This will help the student identify the main idea and supporting details, and encourage him or her to do the required research before writing the actual first draft.

Mechanics refers to the extent to which the message is written in standard, grammatically correct English. In the early primary grades, teachers should focus on correct spelling, punctuation, and capitalization. In kindergarten and first grade, children should be encouraged to use invented spelling in their writing. Depending on the purpose of the task and the developmental level of the child, the teacher can encourage the student to move from invented spelling to standard spelling as he or she goes through the writing process by having the teacher or another adult transcribe the correct spelling underneath the invented writing, encouraging the use of word walls, and working with the child to sound out the word. In the upper primary grades and middle school, the teacher should start focusing on correct tense formation, subject–verb agreement, and correct pronoun usage and agreement.

Language usage refers to the extent to which the response includes sentences that are complete, correct, and varied in length and structure. Writing involves choosing precise and imaginative language, and children must learn how to make their writing more interesting during the elementary grades. In all grade levels, the teacher should concentrate on having students use a variety of words in their writing by developing their vocabulary. A dictionary and thesaurus should be part of every classroom in every grade level. In kindergarten, the teacher can use these books to model how to spell a word or how to vary word usage. These reference books should be age appropriate and easily accessible to all. In addition, starting in the upper primary grades, children should learn different types of figurative language. For example:

- Alliteration—when several words that begin with the same sound are written side by side in a sentence. Example: The *s*oftly *s*etting *s*un is *s*hining on the *s*idewalk where the dog is *s*itting.
- Onomatopoeia—when the sound of the word corresponds to its meaning. Example: We heard the *woosh* of the water splashing against the boat.
- Personification—when human characteristics are given to inanimate objects. Example: The rock stared silently back at me.
- Similes—when *like* or *as* is used to compare two unlike things. Example: The leaves on the trees were like paper confetti drifting slowly down from the sky.
- Metaphors—when two unlike things are compared without using *like* or *as*. Example: The leaves were snowflakes falling from the sky.

Sentence construction refers to the extent that the response includes sentences that are complete, correct, and varied in length and structure. The teacher needs to concentrate on correct grammar and sentence construction. Children need to know what a complete sentence, fragment, and run-on sentence are. Many children have difficulty differentiating between these in the early primary grades; however, children need to learn how to write a complete sentence in the upper primary grades. Grammar can be taught in mini-lessons during a writing workshop so that it is integrated into the writing process and not just taught in isolation of writing skills. Children also need to be taught how to vary their syntax so that it is interesting to read and is effective in communicating to their audience. Reading rich children's literature helps develop the use of inventive and interesting writing styles that the children can emulate and use as a reference during the writing process.

Students with Learning Disabilities and the Process of Writing

Most students with learning disabilities (LD) have difficulties in writing text that is organized, fluent, and well written. Most students with LD use a "condensed" or simplified model to writing—that is, their written product is usually short and focused on retelling what they know about a topic, using as few words as possible. They have a tendency to use a simplified version of the writing process, basically generating ideas and writing them down without any planning, revising, or editing. Therefore, the basic goal in writing instruction for students with LD is to help them develop a more strategic and planned approach to composing, applying the same types of processes used by more skilled writers (Graham & Harris, 2003).

One reason students with LD have difficulty writing is that they have trouble sustaining the writing effort. According to Graham and Harris (2003), one study involving fourth and sixth grade students with LD found that they spent an average of six minutes writing an essay. Their essays usually started with a simple statement, followed by one or two briefly stated reasons to support their statement, and then abruptly ended without a concluding sentence. Students with LD have trouble focusing on the task for a prolonged period, and "complete" their writing in a much shorter period than skilled writers.

Another reason students with LD have trouble writing is that they have difficulty tapping into their own background knowledge. When the same fourth and sixth grade students were prompted by the teacher to write more about an assigned topic, their written text doubled or tripled in length. The students needed constant prompting to tap into their own knowledge about a topic, and they needed encouragement to elaborate and write more. Many students with LD are not confident about their own knowledge and feel their voice is not valuable or worthwhile.

A third reason children with LD have trouble writing is because of their difficulties in mastering the mechanics of writing. Usually, the writing of students with LD has numerous spelling errors, syntax errors, errors in punctuation and capitalization, and incomplete sentences. In addition, many children with LD have difficulty in actually forming the letters and mastering the mechanics of handwriting. Many students may lose ideas or plans because they cannot write down their thoughts quickly enough or feel frustrated by the mechanics of putting their thoughts down on paper (Graham & Harris, 2003).

One way to help students with LD to become more skilled writers is to teach them to use the same types of strategies that more skilled writers use, namely, to systematically apply the stages in writing: planning, writing, revising, and rewriting. It is important that teachers spend time carefully modeling, teaching, and reinforcing each stage of the writing process and providing the necessary support and guidance that these students need at each stage. Students with LD need to learn how to self-regulate or self-monitor their own progress as they move through the writing process. They need to be taught that each stage is an important component of writing, and that with effort and focus on the task, they can succeed (Graham & Harris, 2003). Figure 8–9 shows a comparison of skilled and unskilled writers during the writing process.

Other approaches that will help students with LD in the writing process include:

◆ Constructing an environment in the classroom that is supportive, pleasant, and nonthreatening

◆ Assigning writing topics that serve real purposes (such as writing letters and constructing speeches) and that promote their interest

◆ Allowing students to work on topics of their own choosing

◆ Encouraging children to share their writing with others

◆ Establishing predictable classroom routines where planning and revising are expected and reinforced

◆ Letting students arrange their writing environment and work at their own pace

Teachers need to keep in mind that accommodations in the classroom will help students with LD succeed in the writing process. Many software packages are currently available that will support struggling writers by providing them with tools to assist their writing. Some software programs have text-to-speech capability, which will allow the student to write a sentence and then have the computer read it back. There are also software programs that have speech-to-text capability that enables a student to talk to the computer and have his or her speech translated into text on the screen. Clicker 5 by Crick Software (http://www.cricksoft.com) allows a student to hear the words in a special grid before actually writing them in the Clicker Writer, and the student can hear the sentence after it is written. This allows students to try out words and see what they look like before using them in writing. (Other programs to support struggling writers are described later in the Using Technology to Help Students Write section.)

Word processing programs are of great benefit to children with LD because they free these children from the frustrations of poor handwriting and the painstaking formation of letters. Many children with LD use laptops or handheld devices in class to take notes and as a substitute for pencil and paper. This is a wonderful accommodation for struggling writers, although they still must learn how to keyboard properly.

English Language Learners and the Process of Writing

Researchers claim that the same strategies used to promote reading and writing in native speakers of English are appropriate for ELLs, as well (Boyle & Peregoy, 1998; Doyle, 1998). However, teachers need to be aware that all learners actively construct meaning using their linguistic knowledge, as well as their social and cultural world

Comparison of Skilled and Unskilled Writers

Process/Stratergy	Skilled Writer	Unskilled Writer
PREWRITING	Jots down ideas and takes notes Organizes thoughts carefully Discusses ideas with others and does preliminary research Thinks about purpose of writing and intended audience Constructs visual tool and/or outline	Does not write down ideas or take notes Does not participate in prewriting discussion with others Might consult one source to do research Does not think about the audience nor the purpose for writing Does not construct any outline or use any visual tool to help organize thoughts
DRAFTING	Writes in style appropriate for audience Stops frequently to reread and rewrite Works carefully with the outline to organize the text Takes time to get ideas down on paper	Writes in an informal style without thinking of intended audience Does not reread text Does not consult an outline Works with little organization of thoughts Overemphasizes spelling and mechanics Completes writing in a short period of time without rereading it
REVISING AND EDITING	Makes corrections for all detected errors Rereads text repeatedly and revises and edits Makes structural revisions if text is not organized properly May ask another to edit work	Does not review or make any structural revisions to text Editing consists of changing a few words Recopies to make a neat version in ink Feels that first draft is the final draft Spends little time on this stage
FLUENCY	Writes many words in allotted time Writing is easy to read and focused on topic Writes well-crafted paragraphs	Writes few words in allotted time Writing is stilted and difficult to follow Paragraphs are not well formed
CONTENT AND ORGANIZATION	Writes a clear opening and closing Uses logical progression of ideas to develop content	Has no opening or closing Abruptly ends text Text is not organized properly and content is not developed
MECHANICS	Makes few or no errors Writes neatly Uses punctuation and capitalization effectively	Makes many errors Handwriting is difficult to read with misformed letters Many misspelled words
LANGUAGE USAGE	Uses many different words Avoids overuse of certain words Has a rich vocabulary	Repeats favorite words many times Uses high-frequency words throughout paper
SENTENCE CONSTRUCTION	Writes in complete sentences Varies types of sentences used	Writes incomplete or simple sentences Sentences are not well crafted

(Adapted from Meese, R. L. (2001). Teaching Learners with Mild Disabilities: Integrating Research and Practice. Belmont, CA: Wadsworth.)

FIGURE 8-9

Strategies for Teaching Diverse Learners

Tips for Working with Students with Learning Disabilities: The Writing Process

1. Teach students with learning disabilities to systematically apply the stages in writing: planning, writing, revising, and rewriting. Be sure to model, teach, and reinforce each stage of the writing process and provide the necessary support and guidance needed at each stage.

2. Assign topics that are interesting to the student and that will motivate him or her to write.

3. Give students ample time to write. Let them work at their own pace. Encourage them to write for a longer time, and provide prompting and encouragement when necessary.

4. Provide accommodations to help students with learning disabilities, such as allowing them to use the computer to take notes and tape record their first draft, and giving them graphic organizers to organize their thoughts.

5. Use technological tools that improve writing performance, such as mapping software, multimedia applications, and word processors that provide spell checking, word prediction, grammar and style checkers, and text-to-speech capability.

6. Use the COPS acronym to help students monitor their errors (Mercer & Mercer, 2005):

   C—Have I *capitalized* the first word and proper nouns?

   O—How is the *overall* appearance? (Look at spacing, legibility, indention of paragraphs, neatness, and complete sentences.)

   P—Have I put in commas, semicolons, and end *punctuation*?

   S—Have I *spelled* all words correctly?

7. Create a social climate conducive to writing and sharing of writing ideas.

8. Provide support and guidance through frequent teacher–student conferences.

knowledge. For ELLs, teachers need to become familiar with their students' cultural backgrounds and develop literacy instruction that addresses their students' strengths and background knowledge. Teachers can support all students by linking reading and writing experiences at all stages of development. There is no need to wait for a specific level of oral language or reading proficiency to emerge before engaging ELLs in meaningful writing experiences that reinforce understandings needed for reading. Writing activities that address specific readings contribute to student engagement and promote comprehension (Doyle, 1998).

Writing gives ELLs an opportunity to develop their own voice and to tell their own story. Teachers need to provide ELLs with reading material related to their lives and interests; sometimes this can best be accomplished by having them read their own writing and having them become authors. This helps students improve their own reading and writing in English and contributes to a sense of pride and confidence in their abilities. It also allows native speakers of English the chance to read about what it is like to be an immigrant in this country and what experiences the student went through to get here. Instructional conversations are beneficial in teaching ELLs literacy skills.

Instructional conversations are interactions that occur between teacher and student and between students and students that are centered on discussing instructional activities, ideas, and concepts. Meaningful negotiation requires conversation between partners to clarify and elaborate on the content being discussed. When used in conjunction with literature logs, instructional conversations have been shown to be beneficial to ELLs (Saunders & Goldenberg, 1999). Another way to promote instructional conversations is through a dialogue journal: an ongoing, written conversation in which the partners exchange their journals daily or at least weekly. Each participant makes an entry in a spiral notebook and returns it to the partner, who addresses questions and makes comments before introducing new material (Dolly, 1998). The partner can be either the teacher or another student. This activity has been found to involve ELLs actively in the reading and writing of English. Although some students may not write in English as proficiently as others, the dialogue journal requires writer–reader transactions that engage the student in both the reading and writing of English. This type of dialogue journal helps learners become aware of the collaborative process of reading and writing and that writing is not just putting words on paper to an unknown audience.

Teachers' VOICES   I'm a Writer Now

For the past 19 years, *Silver International* has grown and flourished as a publication for ELLs in our school and many other schools around the world that subscribe to it. It is called a newspaper, but there is not much news in it. Yes, there are a few articles about things happening in our school and other schools, but there are also a lot of essays, poems, drawings, personal messages, and letters written by ELLs—students who rarely have the opportunity to see their written work in print. Writers enjoy sharing their personal stories, full of pain and hope. Readers love skimming the paper, looking for something about their country or an article written by a friend.

Originally intended for our school's ELLs only, the paper now has a circulation of 4,200. It is distributed to 3,500 students and staff in my high school, Montgomery Blair High School in Silver Spring, Maryland, and is mailed to more than 700 students, teachers, parents, and friends around the world. A number of teachers in other schools have class subscriptions and submit their own students' writing for publication.

I was not thinking about how getting published in a newspaper would give students such positive feelings about themselves and their lives in this country. One day after school, I was paged over the intercom to go to the office to take a phone call from a teacher in Arizona. As I walked to the office, I wondered what the teacher would be calling about. She had had a subscription to the paper for a number of years, and we had communicated in letters, but we rarely spoke on the phone. "I had to call you," she said, "to tell you an amazing thing that just happened." She started to tell me about one of her students, whom she referred to as a "do-nothing." He would come to school but rarely completed assignments. However, she had noticed that he was starting to do his work after a poem he had written was published in *Silver International*. That morning, she saw him with a pen in his hand, surrounded by a group of girls. "I asked him what he was doing," she said. "He answered, 'I'm giving them my autograph. I'm a writer now!'"

—*Joe Bellino, High School Teacher and Teacher-Consultant with the Maryland Writing Project*

Source: Bellino, J. (2005). *"I'm a Writer Now!" The Who, Where, and When of an ELL Newspaper.* The National Writing Project. Retrieved June 4, 2006, from http://www.writingproject.org/cs/nwpp/print/nwpr/2192.

Several writing techniques can be used to help ELLs compose and comprehend text. One way is by using story maps and graphic organizers to scaffold the writing process. Story maps and graphic organizers help students organize their thoughts during the prewriting stage and move through the writing process. Another approach focuses on visual literacy, and uses images such as pictures, photographs, film, art, and graphic design to support the writing process. Because ELLs generally have difficulty speaking and writing standard English, photo essays developed from their environment provide a universal way to communicate (Sinatra, Beaudry, Stahl-Gemake, & Guastello, 1998). The images and ideas that students compile in an essay using photographs transcend any language differences, and students are able to express themselves creatively using minimal language.

STRATEGIES FOR TEACHING DIVERSE STUDENTS

Working with English Language Learners: The Writing Process

1. Link reading and writing experiences for ELLs throughout the day. There is no need to wait for a specific level of oral language or reading proficiency to emerge before engaging students in meaningful writing experiences.

2. Assign writing activities that address specific readings; this will contribute to student engagement and will promote comprehension.

3. Provide ELLs with writing assignments that relate to their own lives and interests. Allow them to tell stories about their own culture, background, and experiences.

4. Encourage ELLs to develop their own voice. Have them write meaningful text in English and in their own native language. Encourage them to become authors and to express themselves through their sociocultural context.

5. Promote instructional conversations within the classroom and encourage interactive dialogue with the students through journal writing and interactive written experiences.

6. Use story maps and graphic organizers to help scaffold the writing process.

7. Use visual literacy to encourage written communication through such activities as photo essays, video presentations, and multimedia presentations.

8. Teach grammar, but do not put too much emphasis on it at first; provide students with opportunities to build confidence in their ability to express themselves.

9. Use patterned writing to model written text in English. Repeated phrases, refrains, and rhymes help ELLs model correct usage. Students can create poems based on the patterns, sharing them with one another in peer editing groups and in classroom publications. An example of a sentence pattern is, "I used to be . . . , but now I am . . . ." followed by "I am the one who . . . ." (Boyle & Peregoy, 1998).

10. Writing prompts should include clear directions and describe the context or situation to be written about. The prompts need to be carefully construed to take into account cultural and linguistic factors. The prompts should be based on the cultural knowledge the students possess, as well as the knowledge they have gained as part of their academic schooling.

11. Give constant feedback to the students. Try not to use only holistic scoring while assessing writing assignments. Give a more analytical breakdown of the scores so students know their strengths and weaknesses on each of the different traits listed on the rubric.

ELLs will certainly make many more grammatical errors than their native English-speaking peers, who may have already acquired the structural conventions of oral English. Teachers need to work consistently on improving the grammar and sentence structure of students, but be careful not to be too overly critical and expect too much too quickly. The important point is that all students need to learn how to express themselves without feeling they will be stigmatized or criticized; their voice needs to develop while their grammatical errors are slowly corrected.

Using Technology to Help Students Write

Using the Word Processor

The **word processor** has drastically changed the way that text is now written. Perhaps of all of the literacy skills, technology has had the greatest impact on writing and how we craft this art form. Computers have not made the process of writing or the generation of ideas any easier. What it has done is allow authors to:

- Revise easily
- Edit instantaneously
- Move text quickly from one place to another
- Access online resources and databases
- Have text spell-checked and grammar-proofed
- Access a built-in thesaurus that generates synonyms
- Produce professional-looking documents that are ready for publishing

Although many authors still use paper and pencil—or perhaps a typewriter—to compose, most authors sit at the computer and compose as they write. If, in fact, authors compose right at the computer, how does this affect the writing process? Does technology help or hinder children in developing writing skills? What role should computers play during writing?

In general, recent research (Goldberg, Russell, & Cook, 2003) has consistently found that when students write on computers, writing becomes a more social process in which students share their work with others. Using computers in the writing process encourages students to make revisions while writing, rather than after writing the text. Between initial and final drafts, students also tend to make more revisions when they write with computers. In most cases, students also tend to produce longer passages when they write with computers.

For educators questioning whether computers should be used to help students develop writing skills, research suggests that, on average, students who use computers produce written work that is better than students who develop writing skills on paper (Goldberg, Russell, & Cook, 2003). Although teachers undoubtedly play an important role in helping students develop their writing skills, research suggests that computers are valuable tools for helping students develop writing skills: students engage in the revising of their work throughout the writing process, more frequently share and receive feedback from their peers, and benefit from teacher input earlier in the writing process.

Given that computers are beneficial for writing, when is the best time to use them in the writing process? As noted previously, mapping programs such as Inspiration are excellent tools to use in the prewriting stage, in which students can brainstorm and organize their ideas into an initial map. It is important that students develop a map or outline of their intended writing before they use the computer to compose their work. It is detrimental to let a student start composing on the computer without having an outline or map to help direct the composition. Students become so eager to type on the computer they might be tempted to skip the first prewriting stage.

If there are enough computers to accommodate all students in the class, then students can start composing their first draft on the computer. If the classroom only has a few computers, then students can write their first draft with pencil and paper. Computers are beneficial to students with LD and particularly to those who do not like to write because of poor handwriting. Computers are wonderful tools to motivate students to express their thoughts without the impediment of illegible writing. A few computers can be reserved for those students who greatly benefit from composing their first draft on the computer.

After the first draft is written, initially revised, and edited, students can type the composition on the computer, either at home, in class, or in a computer lab. Additional editing and revising should be done at this stage as the student should print out the text and reread what has been written. Revisions and editing become much easier now. Conferencing can be done either at a desk with the teacher reviewing a printed copy of the piece or done at the computer while the teacher instructs the student on how to make structural changes by moving text around and deleting words or passages.

The final draft should be typed and presented for **publishing**. This can be done in the computer lab or classroom or at home. Depending on the purpose of the writing assignment, the student may want to illustrate the text by adding clip art, photos, or images, and use different fonts for different purposes.

Publishing on the Internet

A wonderful way to integrate technology into the writing process is by having children publish their work on the Internet. The sites listed below provide a safe, interactive place for children to post their stories and poems, and they allow students to read other children's posted work. Children find it motivating to post their stories and poems online and have others read their work.

Teachers can use this as part of the publishing phase of the writing process by enabling students to experience what it is like to publish written material. Not all children will feel comfortable with submitting their work to be published online, and the teacher should carefully select and work with those children who choose to do so. It is helpful for the teacher to initially introduce the websites as part of a literacy lesson, so that children can first read other students' published work and the class can start to feel comfortable with the layout and navigation of the website.

recommended websites for children to share stories and poems online

Scholastic: Writing with Writers

http://teacher.scholastic.com/writewit/

Published authors describe how they write. Students can submit their work for publication and comments.

MidLink Magazine

http://www.ncsu.edu/midlink/

MidLink Magazine is a digital magazine written by students for students.

Poetry.com

http://www.poetry.com

Poetry.com allows students and adults to post their poetry and to read others' poems. Students can enter their poems in a contest by submitting an original poem, 20 lines or less, on any subject, in any style.

Publishing with Students

http://www.publishingstudents.com

This site has many different resources for teachers interested in helping students publish their writing. When publishing online, it is important that teachers consider the security issues involved. Sites should comply with the Children's Online Privacy Protection Act by providing a safe platform on the World Wide Web for children:

◆ The teacher should make sure that the children do not divulge personal information. Visitors to the site should not see anything that would allow them to contact the author, directly or indirectly. Only the first name and age of the author should be used.

◆ The site should not use "cookies," or markers that collect information from visitors.

◆ All material at the site should be reviewed for proper language, topic, and content before it is posted. This will protect young readers from inappropriate material.

Teachers may want to publish children's work using their own website. This can be done by using a digital camera to take pictures of the work if it includes pictures, scanning in pictures or large text of younger children's work, or saving text as an HTML document. These documents can then be uploaded directly to the teacher's website. There are many different examples of this being done in classrooms throughout the world from kindergarten through high school, and it is an excellent alternative to using an existing site, because the teacher can ensure that the child's piece is being viewed on a secure and safe site.

Using the Internet to Encourage Writing

The Internet can be used in many ways to promote writing and literacy in the classroom. Many sites have interesting and motivating activities that involve writing. For example, at *Weekly Reader*, students can write about how they feel about a specific issue, or their feelings on a particular singer, or answer a survey. Each one of the sites listed below involves literacy activities that children will find motivating.

recommended sites and examples of literacy activities

ePals

http://www.epals.com

The ePals site helps teachers find an "e-pal" for their students. Established in 1996, ePals has classroom profiles in more than 150 countries, which allow teachers to communicate with cross-cultural learning partners and friends. This is a wonderful way for teachers to build writing skills into the classroom through an exciting and interdisciplinary writing assignment.

ReadWriteThink Postcard Creator

http://readwritethink.org/materials/postcard

The Postcard Creator site allows students to create electronic postcards. This is a great resource for a fun literacy activity. Students can create a fun postcard using a theme or on a specific topic and send it to someone else.

Weekly Reader

http://www.weeklyreader.com

Weekly Reader Galaxy is another good site to use with younger grades that promotes reading and writing literacy and also has great online activities. Each grade has an interesting and fun writing activity the students can explore.

Software Packages for Writing

Many commercial software packages are on the market to improve writing skills. The software packages includes many diverse features, including some that:

- Are predominately skill-based and focus on grammar, spelling, and word usage
- Encourage creative expression through prompts and creative ideas to which children can respond
- Offer a word processing program customized to support children in their writing and publishing
- Incorporate multimedia features such as graphics, animation, and audio so that children can create their own illustrated stories
- Integrate many of the above features into a total package that functions as a comprehensive language arts writing program

Software packages can benefit a classroom teacher greatly by providing a rich array of activities to reinforce the writing process. If the classroom has only a few computers available, the software programs can become part of a writing center that the teacher develops and uses during either the writing workshop or specified periods of the day. Many of these programs are excellent for ELLs and children with LD because they have an audio component built into them and the computer can read the text back to the student after it has been written. This helps the student make the grapheme–phoneme connection and serves as a means to edit what has been written.

The software packages listed below are not endorsed or recommended, but are listed as examples of the types of programs that a classroom teacher can purchase to support the writing process. Some companies issue new editions each year; all of the programs are designed to run on both PC and MAC platforms.

Skill-Based Software Programs – Skill-based software programs are probably the most limited in scope and need to be assessed carefully before purchase to make sure that they conform to the school's reading program and philosophy. These programs usually focus on a few skills and provide a simple "skill-and-drill" format. This can be beneficial for those students who need to reinforce specific skills in a motivating way.

◆ Word Munchers for the 21st Century (PCI Education) is a reading, grammar, and vocabulary skill builder in a game format. Designed for grades 1 through 5.

◆ Carmen Sandiego Word Detective (Broderbund) is a language arts program that focuses on parts of speech, sentence structure, punctuation, using words in context, spelling rules, word definitions, and dictionary skills. Designed for grades 3 to 7.

◆ Plurals—No Problem!; The Punctuation Marks; and Antonyms, Synonyms, and Homonyms (Thomas S. Klise Company) are programs that focus on specific writing skills and how to use different types of antonyms, synonyms, and homonyms in writing. Designed for grades 4 through 12.

◆ Accelerated Grammar & Spelling (Renaissance Learning) helps teachers build language skills in grammar, usage, spelling, and mechanics. It provides detailed reports that allow teachers to closely monitor each student's progress in these skill areas. Designed for grades 3 through 12.

Creative Expression Software Programs – Creative expression software encourages children to write creatively by providing prompts and incentives for writing. These often include page-layout templates that provide an easy way for children to write and illustrate their work. Teachers need to make sure that these programs are easy to use, and that students can navigate from screen to screen without difficulty.

◆ Storybook Weaver Deluxe (Riverdeep) provides an array of multimedia tools that allows children to create an original story. It combines the use of music, graphics, and sound effects so that children can create and hear their story read aloud in either English or Spanish. Designed for grades 1 through 6.

◆ The Amazing Writing Machine (Broderbund) is a program that allows students to express themselves in five formats: story, letter, journal, essay, and poem. These projects can be illustrated using various tools. Designed for grades 1 through 5.

◆ Ultimate Writing & Creativity Center (The Learning Company) coaches children through the five stages of the writing process and allows them to illustrate them as well. Designed for grades 2 to 5.

◆ Clicker 5 (Crick Software) allows students to use an easy-to-use talking word processor with multimedia presentation functions. It is a good program for students with LD. Designed for preK through grade 8.

◆ Creative Writer 2 (Microsoft) allows students to create their own art and illustrate an original story. This program allows you to select clip art, set backgrounds, and add music.

Word Processing and Assistive Technology Programs – Word processing programs provide a word processor especially designed for children and can also provide add-on features that support and assist children as they write. Many of these programs allow struggling writers to express themselves through technological tools such as text-to-speech, word prediction, and on-screen support. Students with learning disabilities and English language learners find these tools quite helpful.

- Write On! Plus the Writer's Resource Library (Sunburst) allows students to use different reference resources, such as a dictionary, photo library, thesaurus, and rhyming dictionary. It is designed for fourth graders to adult users with on-screen resources that can be used throughout the writing process. Kurtzweil 3000 (Kurtzweil Educational Systems) is a comprehensive reading and writing program for struggling readers and writers that speaks each letter and word as a student types.
- WriteOnline (Crick Software) offers a range of writing support features such as text-to-speech so students can hear what they have written, word prediction, Wordbar (which gives students point-and-click access to a word vocabulary), and a document analysis tool so teachers can analyze a student's writing.
- Co-Writer (Don Johnston Incorporated) seamlessly adds linguistic word prediction to any word processing or e-mail program. It uses linguistic word prediction to provide word choices that are grammatically correct. Students compose grammatically correct sentences containing rich, topic-specific words.
- Dragon Naturally Speaking 10 (Nuance Communications) is a tool that allows students to dictate their sentences into the computer. This type of program is ideal for students with LD and for ELLs.

Multimedia Programs – Many programs that are not specifically designed to promote writing are still excellent programs to promote writing development. By using these programs, children get a chance to express themselves through visual and textual means as they incorporate many of the multimedia features into their composition. These programs are highly motivating and allow teachers to provide instruction that is suited for many different learning styles. Students with LD or ELLs may find that they can express themselves through visual representations and graphics to support their writing skills.

- Roger Wagner's HyperStudio 5 (Mackiev.com) is a multimedia program in which students develop interactive projects that incorporate graphics, photos, clip art, text, video, and audio. The program contains project ideas, templates, and lesson plans that meet state curriculum standards and International Society for Technology in Education (ISTE) standards. Designed for all grade levels.
- KidPix 3 (Mackiev.com) is a versatile graphics program that allows students to expand their writing skills while they interweave art, text, and sounds into multimedia SlideShows. Designed for kindergarten through grade 8.
- PowerPoint (Microsoft) is a presentation tool that allows students to create slide shows that can incorporate text, graphics, video, sound, and animation. It is wonderful tool to use in the classroom as an alternative to a paper-and-pencil assignment. Students can be creative with their slides, and then present them to the class. Designed for fourth graders to adult users.
- The Print Shop (Broderbund) allows students to create and print a wide array of different products—from cards to newsletters to flyers to posters. Children love this program and find it highly motivating to develop attractive cards and posters. Designed for grades 2 to 12.

Commercial software programs offer the teacher an excellent way to integrate technology into the writing process. The programs can provide reinforcement on basic writing skills, motivate students to write on a specific topic, and provide guidance on the different stages of writing. The teacher needs to carefully evaluate any program that is purchased to ensure that it supports school, district, and state standards in the area of writing. The software also needs to comply with federal standards to support handicapped and disabled students.

Interactive Writing: Hypertext

As Reinking (1997) points out, printed documents such as this book and articles read for class have beginnings, middles, and endings that physically and conceptually segment the piece into sequential sections. Technology allows the writer to redefine these conventions because there is no such thing as a linear sequence in cyberspace. Technology allows the reader and writer to develop a nonsequential path through the material by using the concept of links and "hotspots." Reinking points out how hypertext is a particularly good example of how a technology of reading and writing always affects the way we communicate and disseminate information, how we approach the task of reading and writing, and how we think about helping people become literate. Writing hypertext allows the writer to digress down a different path and assume that readers will be willing to explore the idea that the author is expanding. With hypertext, a writer can allow the reader to explore a concept or to stay on the straight and narrow path that is developing right on the page. Reinking found that elementary school students reading science texts explored the meanings of more difficult words, recalled more of their meanings, and comprehended more content when they read passages displayed by a computer that provided immediate, context-specific assistance with vocabulary. Technology now allows the author to compose in three-dimensional writing—across, down, and out through the links that the author has developed.

Teachers can show their students how to create hyperlinks using a word processing program such as Microsoft Word. Figure 8–10 shows how to create hypertext using Word. Students can use this type of writing for research reports and for creative essays. It is a motivating and fun learning activity for children.

Blogs and Wikis

A **blog** (short for *weblog*) is an interactive web page where individuals can post entries, articles, links, and pictures, and ask others to join in conversations. Blogs have proliferated over the Internet because anyone can post an online journal without needing to learn hypertext markup language or special programming skills. Blogs have become very popular, especially with high school students, and are quickly being adapted as useful tools within the classroom to promote writing. Blogs can be useful tools for sharing ideas among students who are seeking peer review or who need help developing their ideas. For many students, blogging can be a useful method to improve writing. Some students and teachers use them as vehicles to develop critical thinking, reading, and writing skills. For example, in one high school, students have used blogs to collaborate with authors of the books they are reading in literature class, contact professional mentors in journalism classes, and communicate with other schools overseas as part of a unit on the Holocaust (Richardson, 2006).

Educators can use blogs in a multitude of ways:

1. *Information/communication tools:* Teachers can post student writing, artwork, information about homework, upcoming events.
2. *Online filing cabinets:* Students and teachers can use a blog as a place to store assignments, links, plans, and handouts.
3. *Collaborative tools:* Students can extend conversations outside of the classroom and collaborate with invited guests from around the world and from within the community.
4. *Literature circles:* Book clubs can involve students and parents or students from other communities.
5. *Online discussions:* Blogs can work as a discussion group for students and staff in every discipline.
6. *Writing tools:* Students can have interactive electronic journals or post completed works to an authentic audience.

Creating Hypertext using Microsoft Word

1. Start a new document in Word.

2. Start typing your document and save it before starting to add hyperlinks. Go to **File** and click **Save As**. Name and save your file.

3. When you come across a word you would like to have your readers explore further, you can create a hyperlink.

4. You should put your links below your document on another page. You can create a new page for the link by clicking **Ctrl-Enter** (hold down the **Ctrl** key, then quickly depress the **Enter** key at the same time). You have just created another page at the end of your document.

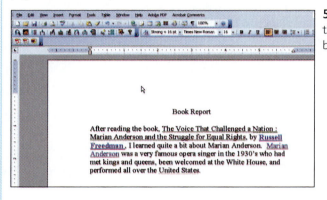

5. When you look at the example on the left, Book Report, this author wanted to make *Russell Freedman* a hyperlink because he had read other books by this author.

6. To make *Russell Freedman* into a hyperlink, you go to the second page and type the information you wish to include here to provide the reader with more detail.

Copy these words to make a hyperlink

Russell Freedman has written many biographies and books. The book, Lincoln: A Photobiography, won the Newbery Medal. His book, Eleanor Roosevelt: A Life of Discovery, won the Newbery Honor Award and his most recent book, The Voice That Challenged a Nation: Marian Anderson and the Struggle for Equal Rights, received both a Newbery Honor and the Robert F. Sibert Informational Book Award.

7. Now you are going to copy the two words that will become the link, *Russell Freedman*. Highlight the word on the second page, making sure you highlight only the words and not any spaces before or after the words. You can do this by pointing to the first letter, clicking, and carefully dragging to the right. Once the word (or words, *Russell Freedman*) is highlighted, go to the menu bar, click **Edit**, and then **Copy**. You have now copied this to your clipboard.

8. Now go back to the main document where the Book Report is written. Find the place where you wish to create the hyperlink, in this case, the two words *Russell Freedman*. You need to erase these two words so you can insert it as a hyperlink. Highlight these two words and press the **Delete** key.

9. On the menu bar, click on **Edit**, then **Paste as Hyperlink**.

FIGURE 8-10

continued

Creating Hypertext using Microsoft Word—cont'd

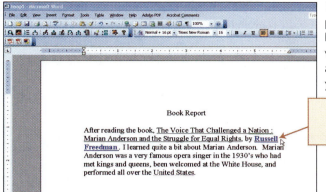

10. You should now see a blue underlined word. When you point to the word and hold down the **Ctrl** key, the cursor becomes a hand. You can now click on the word and you will see the expanded information you wrote. Use the back arrow on the menu bar to return to your main document. If you want to make more hyperlinks within your document, continue expanding on different words on that additional page underneath the information on *Russell Freedman*.

11. If you want to make a link to a site on the Internet, you can do that easily. Choose the word you would like to create a hyperlink for, in this case, *Marian Anderson*. Now find the website you would like to link to. Place your cursor into the area that says **Address** and has the URL (it will start with http://). Click once in this box and the whole address should be highlighted blue. If you are using Microsoft Windows, right-click using your mouse and drag down to **Copy**, or go to the **Edit** menu and click on **Copy**. This will copy the URL into the computer's clipboard to use later.

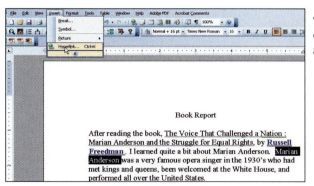

12. Now go back to your Word document and highlight the words you would like to make a hyperlink, *Marian Anderson*, by dragging your cursor over the words. Go to the **Insert** menu and click on **Hyperlink**.

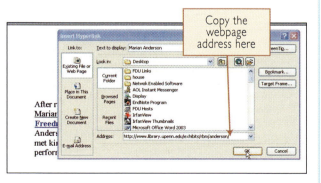

13. Where it says **Address**, either right-click and press paste, or press **Ctrl-V** (press the **Ctrl** key and the **V** key at the same time). The URL you copied to your clipboard should appear there. Click OK.

14. The word that is hyperlinked should now be underlined. When you drag your cursor over the word and press the **Ctrl** key, it should link to the website you chose.

15. You should now have two links, one that links to further information within the Word document and the other that links to an Internet site.

Book Report

After reading the book, The Voice That Challenged a Nation : Marian Anderson and the Struggle for Equal Rights, by Russell Freedman, I learned quite a bit about Marian Anderson. Marian Anderson was a very famous opera singer in the 1930's who had met kings and queens, been welcomed at the White House, and performed all over the United States.

FIGURE 8-10

The best way to become familiar with blogs is by visiting some sites that host educational blogs, such as:

Pembina Trails School Division, Canada

http://www.pembinatrails.ca/program/EducationTechnology/Link 1/ EducationalWikis & Blogs.html

The Pembina Trails site is an interesting site that explains many uses of wikis (see below) and blogs in education.

Visit My Class

http://www.visitmyclass.com/blogs

Visit My Class is a good site for teachers who wish to share experiences.

Poetry Hut Blog

http://www.poetryhut.com/wordpress

Poetry Hut Blog is a blog site for those who want to read and share in poetry.

MyBlogSite

http://www.myblogsite.com

MyBlogSite provides free tools to bloggers.

Blogger

http://www.blogger.com

A site that offers free blogging software and hosting services.

A **wiki** is a collaborative tool that allows users to create and edit content that is online. *Wiki* is the Hawaiian word for "quick." The best known example of a wiki is Wikipedia.org, the online encyclopedia which contains more than 2,943,000 articles written by users across the world (wikipedia.org, 2009). Each entry is continuously developed by anonymous contributors who log on to the encyclopedia and add new information when they see a need. There is no way of knowing if the information is correct or falsified; however, the wiki is maintained by a community of people who are committed to keeping the entries accurate. If erroneous information is entered, or the site has been vandalized, another user usually repairs the damage or corrects the error. The wiki community usually maintains a high degree of accuracy and appropriateness (Richardson, 2006). Students and teachers are building their own wikis that contain lists of annotated resources and links relevant to the class they are in, which can be shared with other classes. This is another example of how new and innovative tools on the Internet can foster creative writing and motivate students to become authors.

For every assignment that asks students to research a topic, teachers can use a wiki to supplement the lesson. With a wiki, students from one class, multiple classes, or even multiple schools can post their writing samples and research on the wiki for comment and review. The wiki structure makes it possible for several students to work on an assignment concurrently. Most wiki software programs track changes to a page so that students and teachers can monitor what changes have been made, when they were made, and by whom. Parents and community members can be invited to add detail, correct errors, and comment on what has been posted, engaging the community in the learning experience.

Wickicities

http://wikicities.com

A free hosting site where teachers can create their own class page.

Wikipedia.org

http://en.wikipedia.org/wiki/Main_Page

To experience the full value of a wiki, try wikipeida.org. It is truly inspiring.

PBWiki

http://pbwiki.com

A free hosting site where a user can set up a wiki.

In summary, there are many ways that technology enhances the process of writing through word processing, publishing on the Internet, interactive writing, using software packages especially adapted to support writing, and exploring new innovations such as blogs and wikis. Students are quite motivated to use technology to support their writing, and literacy classrooms need to adapt these tools as part of the curriculum. More and more students use technology to write, whether it be through e-mail, instant messaging, or blogs, and educators need to harness this creative activity to teach students how to be better writers and readers.

Assessing Writing

The Conference

Perhaps the most important aspect about teaching and assessing writing is the **writing conference**. Teachers must conference with writers all the time. Writers must conference with other writers. Every child has a story to tell, but it is the teacher's responsibility to create a climate and classroom that encourages children to tell their stories. According to Lucy Calkins in her book *The Art of Teaching Writing* (1986), in good writing classrooms, clusters of children are everywhere writing and sharing stories with each other. They confer with each other while the teacher is conferencing with individual students. Because of these conferences, stories grow longer and more detailed. At first, length comes from revisions, but soon children approach their drafts with plans to include more detail. They start envisioning longer stories that do not end in two or three sentences. Then they bring their masterpieces to the teachers to share.

Cynthia Johnson/Time Life Pictures/Getty Images

Teachers can approach each conference as a celebration of what each child has written. We can congratulate the child on what has already been said. We also need to guard against revision for revision's sake. There is nothing worse than someone who edits a paper just to edit, when in fact the changes do not inherently add any quality or substance to what has already been said. In a conference, the child's energy for writing increases, so that the child leaves the conference wanting to write more.

In writing conferences, the main task of the teacher is to find out what excites the writer, to talk about that, and to find out what is not going well (Hansen, 2001). The main task of the student is to evaluate the writing process so far and to discover how to move forward. The teacher should respond with instruction based on the student's self-evaluation. The important role of the "student as evaluator" is the heart of literacy instruction.

Content conferences focus on the content of what has been written. Children not only realize that the details about their topic matter but they also learn that to write well, they must focus on their subject matter as well. Content conferences should help children focus on their subjects, and their writing usually improves as a result. As part of the writing process, students need to know what is expected of them.

Using Forms and Rubrics to Keep Track of Writing

A teacher must keep track of many different aspects of a student's writing development. Different types of forms are needed as part of the assessment process. These forms should be available to the students from the first week of class and explained carefully as part of the classroom rules and procedures. The forms can then be made readily available, even posted on the bulletin board or wall to remind children how to use them.

A writing rubric is a mandatory part of a writing classroom (see Figure 8–7). Children should know what criteria they will be judged on, and they should be fluent in the terminology used to assess writing. They should understand what "content and organization" means when it comes to writing. They should be able to discuss what "usage," "sentence structure," and "mechanics" are when conferring with another student or a teacher. This terminology should become part of the classroom vocabulary and discussed openly.

Each grade level should have a rubric and a corresponding checklist that students use to assess their own writing. It should be based on the state's core curriculum content standards. This rubric and checklist will then be used in peer conferencing and in eventual scoring of the writing sample by the teacher. Writing is an open process in which all writers—students and teachers—are using the same criteria to improve writing skills.

Most states use writing rubrics to score students' performance in writing on state assessment tests. Rubrics are frequently referred to as scoring guides and are used to determine the quality of the students' writing sample. In state assessments, rubrics are crucial in current implementations of academic standards. Many of these rubrics use holistic scoring, a method in which one number is assigned to the total writing sample, usually 1 to 4, with 1 showing the lowest level of writing competency and 4 showing the highest level of competency. In holistic scoring, a single score is produced based on assessing the writing sample on the different criteria specified in the rubric. Figure 8–11 shows an example of a holistic scoring rubric and its corresponding author's checklist, which uses four criteria to assess writing: content and organization, usage (which includes tense formation, subject–verb agreement, pronoun usage and agreement, and word choice), sentence structure, and mechanics. This rubric uses six different performance levels to assess students, with 1 being "inadequate command" and 6 being "superior command."

Because the holistic approach to evaluating student writing samples yields a single overall score for the written piece, this can be problematic for diverse learners who struggle with writing. They need detailed feedback to improve their English writing skills, and raters can assign too much weight to grammatical conventions that may take years for ELLs to master. A more analytical approach to evaluating writing samples of ELLs and students with LD is recommended. In this approach, each criteria item or trait is weighted separately and the student is given a breakdown on specific features of the writing sample. For example, students are evaluated separately on such criteria as ideas, organization, voice, word choice, sentence fluency, grammatical conventions, and presentation. This allows the teacher to provide specific feedback to students and allows the student to feel that the paper is not being graded solely on grammar or sentence structure (Education Alliance at Brown University, 2006).

Teachers' VOICES   Story Writing Matrix used by a Fifth Grade Teacher

Category	Excellent (10 points)	Good (7.5 points)	Satisfactory (5 points)	Needs Improvement (2.5 points)
Writing Process*	Student devotes a lot of time and effort to the writing process (prewriting, drafting, reviewing, and editing). Works hard to make the story wonderful.	Student devotes sufficient time and effort to writing process (prewriting, drafting, reviewing, and editing). Works and gets the job done.	Student devotes some time and effort to the writing process, but was not very thorough. Does enough to get by.	Student devotes little time and effort to the writing process. Does not work hard.
Setting	Many vivid, descriptive words are used to tell when and where the story took place.	Some vivid descriptive words are used to tell the audience when and where the story took place.	The reader can figure out when and where the story took place, but the author did not supply much detail.	The reader has trouble figuring out when and where the story took place.
Characters	The main characters are named and clearly described in text and pictures. Most readers could describe the characters accurately.	The main characters are named and described. Most readers would have some idea of what the characters looked like.	The main characters are named. The reader knows little about the characters.	It is hard to tell who the main characters are.
Introduction (Organization)	The introduction is inviting and previews the plot of the paper.	The introduction previews the plot of the paper, but is not particularly inviting to the reader.	The introduction has nothing to do with the plot, nor is it particularly inviting to the reader.	There is no clear introduction.
Sequencing (Organization)	Details are placed in a logical order and the way they are presented effectively keeps the interest of the reader.	Details are placed in a logical order, but the way in which they are presented or introduced sometimes makes the writing less interesting.	Some details are not in a logical or expected order, and this distracts the reader.	Many details are not in a logical or expected order. There is little sense that the writing is organized.
Transitions (Organization)	A variety of thoughtful transitions are used. They clearly show how ideas are connected.	Transitions clearly show how ideas are connected, but there is little variety.	Some transitions work well, but connections between other ideas are fuzzy.	The transitions between ideas are unclear or nonexistent.
Conclusion (Organization)	The conclusion is strong and leaves the reader with a feeling that they understand what the writer is "getting at."	The conclusion is recognizable and ties up almost all the loose ends.	The conclusion is recognizable but does not tie up several loose ends.	There is no conclusion, the paper just ends.
Grammar and Spelling	Writer makes none or only one error in grammar or spelling and it does not distract the reader from the content.	Writer makes two errors in grammar or spelling that distract the reader from the content.	Writer makes three to four errors in grammar or spelling that distract the reader from the content.	Writer makes more than four errors in grammar or spelling that distract the reader from the content.
Capitalization and Punctuation	Writer makes no errors in capitalization or punctuation; thus, the paper is exceptionally easy to read.	Writer makes one or two errors in capitalization or punctuation, but the paper is still easy to read.	Writer makes a few errors in capitalization and/or punctuation that catch the reader's attention and interrupt the flow.	Writer makes several errors in capitalization and/or punctuation that catch the reader's attention and greatly interrupt the flow.

*Worth double points.

Holistic Scoring Rubric

In scoring, consider the criteria for each feature.	Inadequate Command	Limited Command	Partial Command
Score	1	2	3
Content and Organization	• May lack opening and/or closing	• May lack opening and/or closing	• May lack opening and/or closing
	• Minimal response to topic; uncertain focus	• Attempts to focus • May drift or shift focus	• Usually has single focus
	• No planning evident; disorganized	• Attempts organization • Few, if any, transitions	• Some lapses or flaws • May lack some transitions
	• Details random, inappropriate, barely apparent	• Details lack elaboration, i.e., highlight paper	• Repetitious details • Several unelaborated details
Usage	• No apparent control • Severe/numerous errors	• Numerous errors	• Errors/patterns of errors evident
Sentence Construction	• Assortment of incomplete and/or incorrect sentences	• Excessive monotony • Numerous errors	• Little variety in syntax • Some errors
Mechanics	• Errors so severe they detract from meaning	• Numerous serious errors	• Patterns of errors evident

Non-Scorable Response	(FR)	Fragment	Student wrote too little to allow a reliable judgment of his/her writing.
	(OT)	Off Topic/Off Task	The response was not on the assigned topic/task.
	(NE)	Not English	The response was written in a language other than English.
	(NR)	No Response	The writing task folder was blank, or the student refused to write on the topic.

FIGURE 8-11

continued

Holistic Scoring Rubric—cont'd

Adequate Command	Strong Command	Superior Command
4	5	6
• Generally has opening and closing	• Opening and closing	• Opening and closing
• Single focus	• Single focus • Sense of unity and coherence • Key ideas developed	• Single, distinct focus • Unified and coherent • Well-developed
• Ideas loosely connected • Transitions evident	• Logical progression of ideas • Moderately fluent • Attempts compositional risks	• Logical progression of ideas • Fluent, cohesive • Compositional risks successful
• Uneven development of details	• Details appropriate and varied	• Details effective, vivid, explicit, and/or pertinent
• Some errors that do not interfere with meaning	• Few errors	• Very few, if any, errors
• Some variety • Generally correct	• Variety in syntax appropriate and effective • Few errors	• Precision and/or sophistication in syntax • Very few, if any, errors
• No consistent pattern of errors • Some errors that do not interfere with meaning	• Few errors	• Very few, if any, errors

Content/Organization	Usage	Sentence Construction	Mechanics
• Communicates intended message to intended audience • Relates to topic • Opening and closing • Focused • Logical progression of ideas • Transitions • Appropriate details and information	• Tense formation • Subject-verb agreement • Pronouns-usage/agreement • Word choice • Proper modifiers	• Variety of type, structure, and length • Correct construction	• Spelling • Capitalization • Punctuation

FIGURE 8-11

continued

Holistic Scoring Rubric: Author's Checklist

Student: _____

Score: _____ Date: _____

Features	Overview	Criteria
Content/Organization	Extent to which the response is • focused on task, purpose, and audience • supported by relevant and elaborated details • clearly and logically ordered	1. Opening and closing evident
		2. Single focus maintained
		3. Sense of unity and coherence
		4. Key ideas developed
		5. Logical progression of ideas
		6. Transitions evident
		7. Fluent, cohesive
		8. Appropriate and varied details
		9. Compositional risks evident
Usage	Extent to which the response is written in standard written English	10. Correct tense formation
		11. Subject-verb agreement evident
		12. Correct pronoun usage and agreement
		13. Effective and varied word choice
		14. Use of proper modifiers
Sentence Construction	Extent to which the response includes sentences that are: • complete and correct • varied in length and structure	15. Correct sentence construction (syntax)
		16. Variety in structure
		17. Appropriate and effective in syntax
Mechanics	Extent to which the response is technically correct: • spelling • capitalization • punctuation	18. Few errors in spelling
		19. Few errors in capitalization
		20. Few errors in punctuation

FIGURE 8-11

continued

FIGURE 8-11

Holistic Scoring Rubric: Author's Checklist—cont'd

CONFERENCE RECORD

STUDENT   DATE

TEACHER   DATE

ANNOTATION GUIDE

Strengths +	Needs −	Comments About Writing Strengths and Needs

In addition to assessing a student's writing, a literacy teacher should be collecting data on different aspects of the student's writing and reading. A writing survey and reading survey (see Figures 8–3 and 8–4) can be administered to all students during the first few weeks of school. This survey will help determine whether the child likes to write, what he or she likes to write about, how often he or she is writing, and how the teacher can best approach the child to motivate him or her. A writing record and a reading record (see Figures 8–5 and 8–6) will help the teacher keep track of the quantity and type of writing each student has completed. A writing conference record (see Figure 8–8) should be kept to record the number of conferences the teacher had with each student, when the conference was held, and whether further reinforcement of a skill is needed through a mini-lesson. These records help a teacher determine the best instruction to help develop children's writing skills.

A portfolio of each student's writing should be maintained throughout the year. It is best to keep a variety of different pieces in the portfolio to track a student's growth over the course of the year. Samples from each stage of the writing process can be kept in the portfolio to demonstrate that writing is a continuous process, and that although the final product is important, the other steps along the way are as well. The writing rubric, writing checklist, writing survey, writing conference record, and writing record can all be kept in the portfolio as well.

Teachers' VOICES   Writing Strategies

As part of a writing unit in my fifth grade classroom, I am using the official writing rubric of my school to help my students learn to become better writers and incorporate new vocabulary into their work. One of the categories on this school-wide rubric is "word choice." We have gone through several days of lessons on how to improve word choice in writing. I want the students to use a greater variety of words to more accurately express their thoughts and be more descriptive.

First, we had a "contest" with the six different tables of students to see who could come up with the greatest number of synonyms for a particular word spontaneously, after practicing this together as a class. Then they had some time to look for words or places in their writing where they may want to revise their choice of words.

On the next day, we reviewed how to use a thesaurus. I gave the students the opportunity to use this writing tool to find better, more descriptive, or more sophisticated words to incorporate into their writing pieces. They continued to revise their first draft.

Finally, on the third day, I had the students work in a fun activity called "synonym rolls." This activity is based on a drawn outline of a cinnamon roll or cinnamon bun and the students are to pick a word, maybe one from their writing pieces that they need some help with, and write it in the center of the "synonym roll." They then have to write synonyms for that word in a circular pattern all the way around the "synonym roll." These are then shared with the class and hung on one of our bulletin boards.

These activities not only help students learn (and learn to use) new words and expand their vocabulary, but they also help the students learn how to recognize areas of their writing that might need improvement and incorporate new vocabulary into their writing. Some of the students now seem less intimidated when they come across difficult words in the books that they are reading and are more inclined to look them up in a dictionary (or thesaurus) to learn the meaning. Sometimes they even write the words down as good words they may want to use in their own writing some day.

—*Kim Dunleavy-Visconti, Fifth Grade Teacher*

The Process of Listening

Listening is a primary component of many states' English/Language Arts Standards, yet it is rarely taught in the classroom. For example, the California State Board of Education English Language Arts Content Standards for Grade Four under Listening and Speaking states, "Students listen critically and respond appropriately to oral communication. They speak in a manner that guides the listener to understand important ideas by using proper phrasing, pitch, and modulation" (California State Board of Education, 2007). Teachers assume that when they are talking, reading, giving directions, or discussing a topic, that children will automatically "listen"; however, they often find that, in fact, a number of children who appear to be "paying attention" have not followed directions or "tuned in" to what was being communicated. Reading, writing, speaking, and listening are all reciprocal processes that function as interdependent components as children develop language and literacy skills.

In defining literacy, Opitz and Zbaracki (2004) suggest that listening is the process by which spoken language is converted to meaning in the mind. They say that listening involves the following factors:

1. *Listening is a complex process that is far different from hearing.* Listening is an active process in which the listener is focused on trying to figure out what the speaker means. Hearing is a process that involves sensing incoming sound, while listening requires interpretation of that sound and attributing meaning to the complex aural patterns that are being heard.

2. *Many internal and external factors influence listening.* Internal factors include the child's motivation to listen, past habits (which may be good or bad), neurological influences such as attention disorders, the degree of language development, background knowledge on what is being communicated, and overall cognitive abilities of the child. External factors include the context in which the communication is being conducted (have you ever found that a student listens *carefully* to what his or her friends are saying but does not appear to "tune in" during class time?), the topic (many students will "tune out" a topic they find boring), the speaker's ability to communicate (many speakers have a speaking style that can cause one to "tune out"), and the sociocultural background associated with the communication (many cultures have different ways of responding to speech and interacting with one another).

3. *Listening happens in a pragmatic, specific context that will influence how we interpret what we hear and subsequently respond.* The context often determines how the listener is interpreting what is being communicated and deciding how to respond. A person will respond to the same question quite differently if it is posed by a total stranger or by a close friend, or if it is asked in a classroom or in a cafeteria.

There are many reasons a teacher should teach listening in the classroom as part of the literacy classroom. A student's initial language learning develops through listening, as does receptive vocabulary (vocabulary words we understand). Listening helps children learn sounds and develops phonological awareness. As children listen to stories being told in shared literacy experiences and through read-alouds, children learn to discriminate sounds and learn how language is used to convey a message. In addition, research has shown that children who comprehend well while listening also comprehend well when reading, and vice versa (Opitz & Zbaracki, 2004). Lastly, those children who listen well are usually successful in school—they follow directions, are actively involved in discussions, are able to articulate clearly, and are responsive during conversations. It is important that teachers integrate listening activities into the classroom and teach children the significance of becoming a good listener.

Listening is also important in the development of ELLs and needs to be cultivated in the classroom. ELLs need to develop both receptive and expressive oral language skills in English. **Receptive skills** are needed to understand what has been said, and **expressive skills** are needed to speak and communicate thoughts and ideas to others. Without a solid foundation of receptive skills, students will not be able to develop strong expressive skills.

Courtesy of Vicki Cohen

Listening is an active process that should be taught in the classroom.

Five Different Types of Listening

Opitz and Zbaracki (2004) suggest that there are different purposes for listening and that teachers can develop activities to help develop five different types of listening: discriminative listening, listening for details, listening for understanding, critical listening, and appreciative listening.

Discriminative Listening – **Discriminative listening** is important because students need to learn to discriminate among different sounds and develop phonological awareness as they develop literacy skills. The listener must be able to tell the difference between sounds in order to focus on specific identified sounds. Such tasks as having children focus on words within a sentence that begin with the same sound (alliteration) help develop discriminative listening. During read-alouds, teachers should choose books that use rhyme, repetition, alliteration, and encourage students to play with phonemes in words (such as in Dr. Seuss books) to help children aurally discriminate sounds.

Listening for Details – Students need to pay attention and to remember details of what they hear. **Listening for details** becomes extremely important as students get older and need to take notes in class and remember what they hear. Part of listening for details is learning good listening behavior, which many students may not practice. They need to look at the speaker, remain quiet when another is speaking, and think about what the speaker is saying. Visual organizers such as semantic maps, printouts of lectures, and specific note-taking strategies all help students focus on recalling the details of what is being said. Giving students direct instruction with the primary goal of teaching them to note important details during a conversation or lecture will help them develop their precise listening skills.

Listening for Understanding (Strategic Listening) – Students must learn to listen for understanding, and **strategic listening** helps children develop these cognitive abilities. The listener must concentrate on the intended meaning of what is being heard and synthesize many of the details into a coherent understanding of what the overall message is. This differs from listening for details because the student must recall what the speaker said and then make sense of it to ascertain the "big picture." This involves connecting what is being heard to prior knowledge, summarizing, comparing, contrasting, and making inferences. Read-alouds are important in teaching strategic listening as the teacher reads a book out loud and then discusses the meaning and overall theme as part of the lesson. For older children, chapter books can be read over a period of time with the teacher having continuous discussion with the class about the book and the comprehension strategies needed to understand it. The teacher should choose specific books to read aloud that emphasize different comprehension strategies, such as a book that requires inference skills, a book that creates strong visualization of the story, or a book that carefully the develops characterization and uses dialogue effectively. The teacher can then emphasize these strategies as part of the read-aloud to ensure that students develop strategic thinking.

Critical Listening – Students need to go beyond recalling details and understanding what is heard to analyzing the message and critically evaluating it for validity. This is especially true in today's media-saturated world, where many different types of messages are presented on television, the radio, and the Internet. It is extremely important that students are able to distinguish between what is fact and what is opinion, what is objective and what is subjective, what is really "news" and what is a newscaster's biased interpretation of an event (which is not such an easy task, given today's "edutainment" news). Part of developing **critical listening** is using criteria that can be used to evaluate the speaker: Is the speaker stating an opinion, or is he or she presenting the message as fact? Does the speaker present a bias or slant on the material? Does the speaker appear to have an agenda, bias, or perspective on the material? A teacher can use television shows and radio shows to teach this skill by having students try to evaluate a news broadcast or a children's show. The teacher could also choose a book that has a specific perspective on a topic and read the book to the children, asking them to note what perspective this author may have. The teacher can then choose a second book about the same topic that is written from a different perspective and have the children compare the two books. Another excellent activity to teach critical listening is to have children evaluate commercials on television or radio and try to determine what message is being conveyed and if that message is true.

Appreciative Listening – Children will quickly learn to listen to music that they enjoy, which may be quite different from what the teacher appreciates. **Appreciative listening** is subjective and differs from person to person; however, students can learn to expand their appreciative listening to many different types of music and many different things. We listen appreciatively to six different things: the way a speaker presents material (oral style); environmental sounds (birds singing, the sound of the ocean, whales calling); oral reading of literature; radio, television, and film; live theater; and music. A wonderful way to enrich children is to expose them to many different types of music while they are working. Classical music can be a wonderful way to set the stage and provide a relaxing background for writing or group work. Poetry and humorous literature is also a wonderful choice for read-alouds. Children can watch videos or films of live theater productions or go on field trips to enjoy live productions. After each of these, the teacher needs to discuss what feelings the children had while listening to these events and what these events meant to the students.

Classroom Instruction in Listening

Teachers should engage students in listening for a purpose by creating opportunities where listening skills and strategies are incorporated into daily classroom instruction. Teachers should give explicit instruction in listening skills and provide support and guidance to students as they develop their listening skills. The following activities can be built into the classroom to support students listening for a purpose:

◆ *Read-alouds:* Teachers should read aloud to students every day. This is an important means of teaching listening and a powerful vehicle for expanding language development and vocabulary growth. This is beneficial for ELLs who need to develop proficiency in listening and speaking English as the foundation of second-language acquisition. Teachers should read a variety of books, both fiction and nonfiction, and choose books that reflect different cultural backgrounds. It is helpful for ELLs if they can relate to the book being read and place it within the context of their social and cultural background.

◆ *Sharing circles or show-and-tell:* Teachers should give students a chance to share and discuss their ideas, stories, and favorite items with the class or a small group. The students should listen carefully and formulate questions to ask each presenter.

◆ *Listening and media centers:* Listening centers can provide students with the opportunities to listen to taped stories. Teachers can use a range of commercially prepared tapes, as well as those prepared by students, the teacher, or the school community. Students can also tape themselves reading and listen to their tape to assess themselves.

◆ *Listening games:* Listening games can provide a fun way for students to focus on their listening skills and learn a number of strategies (see Figure 8–12 for a list of some favorite listening games).

◆ *Guided listening instruction:* Teachers should model and discuss effective listening strategies. A useful framework to teach students is to present behaviors they should follow before listening, during listening, and after listening. This is a similar strategy used in the scaffolded reading approach. The charts below can be posted

Listening Games

I Packed My Bag: Each student "packs a bag" by naming an article beginning with successive alphabet letters. Students try to repeat in order each item previously packed (e.g., "I packed my bag and in it I put an apple, a banana, a car, a dog, an elephant, and a fridge.")

I Spy: Students can be seated on the floor. One is elected to begin. That student looks around the room, decides on one object, and then says to the others, "I spy with my little eye something beginning with P (or a letter that starts the word of the object sighted)." The others look around the room and guess what the object might be. Whoever guesses correctly chooses the next object, and so on.

Telephone: Everyone sits in a circle. The teacher whispers to one student a statement or short series of statements that are part of a story. The first student then passes the statement or story to the next student by whispering it. This continues around the circle until the last student has heard it. The last student then tells the group what he or she heard, and this is compared to the original. A useful starting stem is: *One day a little bird landed on my shoulder and began to talk with me. He said it was a good day for playing baseball in the park.*

Place Names: Students focus on sounds in the words for places and take turns giving another place name that begins with the last letter of the previous name (e.g., New York-Kentucky-Yellowstone).

Progressive Story (or Add-a-Sentence): Students sit around a circle and build a group story as each student adds successive sentences to a starter sentence (e.g., "It was a dark and stormy night."). Alternatively, students can develop summaries of special events, field trips, experiments, and so on. Students can also work in pairs. One student composes a sentence orally while the partner transcribes it; then, the first transcriber composes the next sentence and the partner writes it down. This continues until the story is concluded.

Simon Says: The leader gives a series of commands such as "Clap your hands; hop three times; stand up." If the leader inserts "Simon says" before the command, students are to obey. If the leader does not say "Simon says," students must not follow the directions. Students can take turns being the leader. As a variation, students can pantomime actions (e.g., "pat the dog") or respond to rhyming directions ("Says Pat, bring the bat") while ignoring nonrhyming directions (e.g., "Says Simon, hit the ball.")

Twenty Questions: The teacher chooses a word and gives students its category (i.e., animal, vegetable, or mineral), and then the students can ask a maximum of 20 questions to see if they can guess the word. The teacher answers only "yes" or "no." Students have to listen carefully to what responses have been given to the previous questions.

Yes, I Can: A student asks a question such as "John, you can bounce a ball?" and John then responds, "Yes, I can bounce a ball," and mimes the action. John then poses a new question to another student, and so on.

(Adapted from Saskatchewan Education. (2002). English Language Arts: A curriculum guide for the elementary level. Saskatchewan, Canada. Retrieved December 12, 2004, from http://www.sasked.gov.sk.ca/docs/ela/listening01.html)

FIGURE 8-12

on the walls of the class to help students remember each stage (Saskatchewan Education, 2002):

sample grades 1—3 chart

When I listen I:

- Concentrate on what the speaker is saying
- Think of questions about what I hear
- Make pictures in my mind about what I hear
- Go over what the speaker just said

sample grades 4—6 chart

Before listening:

- Do I review the purpose for listening?
- What prior knowledge do I have on the topic?
- Am I prepared to take notes?

◆ Do I know what type of listening I will be doing (pleasure, informational, directions)?

During listening:

◆ Do I understand what the speaker is talking about?

◆ Can I organize the information?

◆ Am I taking notes that make sense?

◆ Am I paying attention?

After listening:

◆ Did I review what was said?

◆ Do I have any questions?

◆ Did I review my notes?

◆ Do I understand what was said?

◆ Do I need more information?

Assessing Listening

It is important that teachers not only directly teach listening skills but also assess students' achievement of this literacy area. One way that a teacher can assess a student's listening ability is by determining his or her **capacity level**, which can be taken in place of administering an Informal Reading Inventory (IRI; see Chapter 9. In an IRI, the student reads a graded passage and the teacher asks comprehension questions at the end to determine the student's level of comprehension of the passage; in finding the capacity level, the teacher reads a series of graded passages to the student, and then asks comprehension questions to determine the listening level of understanding. Each time the student demonstrates understanding of the passage, a more difficult passage is administered until the student reaches his or her frustration level. This type of assessment is excellent for ELLs and children with LD, who may be able to understand more material by listening to it than by reading it.

The teacher can also assess the student by using an observation checklist during listening activities (see Figure 8–13 for an example of a listening checklist). During the course of the day, the teacher should make notes concerning the development of listening skills for each individual student and use the observation form periodically to record how each student is developing in each of the five areas of listening.

The teacher can also conduct a self-assessment on his or her own classroom and listening behaviors. By being a good listener, the teacher can model the appropriate behavior to the class and create an environment that promotes language development. Figure 8–14 contains a Teacher Self-Assessment Form that is helpful to teachers in determining how well they promote listening in their classroom.

Listening skills should be assessed at all stages of language acquisitions for ELLs. Students who are just learning English can demonstrate comprehension nonverbally; teachers can observe how well students follow simple commands such as "Stand," "Sit down," and "Take out your book." Teachers can also ask ELLs to hold up pictures in response to simple questions, such as "Show me something you eat" (the child will hold up a picture of an apple), or "Show me how you get to school" (the child will hold up a picture of a car). Teachers also can keep anecdotal records to record what each student is capable of understanding and can keep a continuous update on the child's receptive development.

The Process of Speaking

Oral language is the basis for the development of cognition and is an essential part of communicating, thinking, and learning. The development of language skills is a uniquely human characteristic that allows us to negotiate relationships with others, give

Listening Checklist

Name: _____ Date: _____

Fill in each number below with a checkmark if the student displays the described behavior listed in the item. Use NA (not applicable) if the item is not appropriate for the student or class. Add comments when needed.

Discriminative Listening:

_____ 1. The student demonstrates awareness of different phonemes in words.

_____ 2. The student can discriminate between different sounds in words, such as the difference between "b" and "d" and "ing" and "ink."

_____ 3. During dictation of spelling words, the student discriminates between the different sounds that are similar and writes down the appropriate letters.

_____ 4. The student can successfully "play" with words and isolate different phonemes in words.

_____ 5. The student listens carefully to different sounds and can identify different common sounds in the environment, such as water running, car horns honking, dogs barking.

Comments:_____

_____

Listening for Details:

_____ 6. The student remembers details after listening to a story read to him/her.

_____ 7. The student follows directions successfully when they are first given.

_____ 8. The student displays good listening behavior: he/she looks at the speaker, remains quiet when another is speaking, and appears to be thinking about what the speaker is saying.

_____ 9. The student successfully writes down what is written on the board or easel.

_____ 10. The student takes notes (or fills in a graphic organizer) while the teacher or speaker is talking.

Comments:_____

_____

Listening for Understanding (Strategic Listening):

_____ 11. The student connects what is being heard to his/her background knowledge by talking about how the topic relates to his/her life.

_____ 12. The student appears to understand what he/she is listening to.

_____ 13. The student is capable of summarizing or retelling what he/she was listening to.

_____ 14. The student responds successfully to questions regarding what he/she just heard.

_____ 15. The student engages in discussion/conversation about the topic he/she was listening to.

Comments:_____

_____

_____

(Adapted from Opitz, M. F., & Zbaracki, M. D. (2004). *Listen hear! Twenty-five effective listening comprehension strategies.* Portsmouth, NH: Heinemann.)

FIGURE 8-13   *continued*

Listening Checklist—cont'd

Critical Listening:

_____ 16.   The student is able to distinguish between "fact" and "opinion" when listening to a speaker.

_____ 17.   The student is able to determine that two speakers may be coming from different perspectives when they speak.

_____ 18.   The student is able to evaluate and rate a speaker's lecture/speech/talk and state why he/she gave it that rating.

_____ 19.   The student appears to be aware that many commercials and advertisements may not be telling "the whole story."

_____ 20.   The student discusses why it is important to listen critically and understands what it means to be an effective listener.

Comments:_____

_____

Appreciative Listening:

_____ 21.   The student enjoys listening to many different types of music, books, speakers.

_____ 22.   The student displays a wide range of enjoyment in choosing material to listen to.

_____ 23.   The student listens attentively to poetry and humorous stories.

_____ 24.   The student listens attentively and seems to be enjoying read-alouds.

_____ 25.   The student displays enjoyment when listening to books on tape, listening to records or audio tapes, or television.

Comments:_____

_____

FIGURE 8-13

definition to our thoughts, and learn about ourselves and others in the world around us. Oral language is the foundation on which reading and writing is based, and all students need many different opportunities to talk in a linguistically rich environment. Researchers have found that students' learning is enhanced when they can share ideas and talk to others in a collaborative, socially engaging environment (Saskatchewan Education, 2002). Teachers need to go beyond providing opportunities for children to engage in social activities together and plan regular periods of close interaction with children to model effective language skills and draw children into meaningful conversations. Clay (1991) suggests that children, especially those with limited language abilities, need periods of close interaction with an adult who shows interest in their ideas and concerns.

When working with ELLs it is important to check that they understand the key-words needed for any topic being discussed and to help them generalize their knowledge of words from their native language to English. It has been noted that ELLs have little opportunity within the classroom to simply converse with others (Lenters, 2004). Teachers need to provide opportunities for meaningful interactions with children to foster vocabulary acquisition that is essential for language growth. It is particularly important to develop young ELLs' comprehension of oral speech, which will assist in their learning vocabulary simultaneously with their reading development. It is also recommended that teachers be flexible in accepting pronunciation and grammar with young ELLs because too much emphasis on accuracy can be detrimental to rate of literacy growth and self-confidence (Lenters, 2004). It is also recommended that teachers give direct instruction to children on vocabulary words and not rely exclusively on incidental learning as the only way that ELLs will learn new words. The techniques discussed in this chapter such as explicit modeling of effective use of language, providing

Teacher Listening Self-Assessment Form

Think about the degree to which you actively try to incorporate each task into your classroom. Then select the appropriate number on the scale, with 1 being seldom and 5 being frequently.

		Seldom				Frequently
1.	I listen to students without interrupting them.	1	2	3	4	5
2.	I give my students complete attention when they talk to me.	1	2	3	4	5
3.	I give nonverbal signs that I am listening to my students such as eye contact, nodding my head, smiling, and other facial expressions that show interest.	1	2	3	4	5
4.	I state directions clearly and make sure all students understand what they are to do. I repeat directions, if necessary, especially for English language learners and students with learning disabilities.	1	2	3	4	5
5.	I speak slowly and enunciate clearly. I explain all words that may cause my students problems in understanding what I am saying.	1	2	3	4	5
6.	I discuss the importance of being a good listener with my students. I post these ideas on the wall.	1	2	3	4	5
7.	I spend time teaching my students how to listen. I show them different purposes for listening.	1	2	3	4	5
8.	I integrate listening into all subject areas and throughout the day.	1	2	3	4	5
9.	I provide my students with tools to help them remember what they heard, such as graphic organizers, notes, and charts on the wall.	1	2	3	4	5
10.	I provide the necessary background information so that my students are prepared to remember what they hear.	1	2	3	4	5
11.	I encourage my students to listen to each other and reinforce good listening behavior in the class.	1	2	3	4	5
12.	I assess my students on their ability to understand what they heard (receptive language).	1	2	3	4	5
13.	I provide necessary accommodations to help diverse learners understand what I said and remember what I told them.	1	2	3	4	5

(Adapted from Opitz, M. F., & Zbaracki, M. D. (2004). *Listen hear! Twenty-five effective listening comprehension strategies.* Portsmouth, NH: Heinemann.)

FIGURE 8-14

STRATEGIES FOR TEACHING DIVERSE STUDENTS

Strategies to Promote Oral Language for English Language Learners

- Have a prereading activity where children take turns with proficient English speakers to discuss a story's illustrations and title to predict its content before reading it. Have the children use specific vocabulary words in their discussion about what they think the book will be about and encourage them to use the words in their prediction.

- Engage in repeated reading of simple, predictable texts. New vocabulary and important text structures may be internalized through this method.

- Tape recordings of simple stories and graded readers will allow second language learners to engage independently in shared and repeated reading.

- Pair-share with an English-speaking buddy and take turns reading and rereading the text together, independently and chorally.

- Highlight the vocabulary and story structure of favorite simple stories the children are learning to read and have them reconstruct the stories in book-making activities. The activity will provide second language learners with a growing library of personal texts they may read and reread for oral vocabulary and sight word development.

- Engage in literary discussions with second language learners, encouraging them to use their English and to answer in full sentences. Read books from their own culture and have them share a custom, food, or tradition with the class.

Source: Lenters, K. (2004). No half measures: Reading instruction for young second language learners. *The Reading Teacher, 58*(4), 328–336.

opportunities for children to engage in speaking, use of cooperative learning, and providing support and guidance are all helpful in providing differentiated instruction for new learners of English.

Halliday (1975) posits that there are different functions of language, and that students need to learn how to use language effectively for each function. These functions are as follows:

Instrumental function of language: People use language to communicate preferences, choices, wants, or needs, such as "I want to . . ." Classroom activities to support this function might be problem-solving activities, in which children have a choice of the role they may play within the group, or are given a series of choices within the activity and must choose one alternative. Role-playing and persuasive speeches also reinforce this function of language.

Personal function of language: People use language to express individuality, such as "I am . . ." This type of communication is largely done in personal conversations, but teachers can reinforce this through projects that emphasize children describing themselves or allowing them to express their feelings about a particular topic or activity. Children can create posters about themselves that can be displayed, and they can talk about themselves to the class.

Social relationships/interactional function of language: People use language to interact and plan, develop, or maintain a group activity, such as "You and me . . ." or "I'll be the recorder . . ." Group activities and collaborative teamwork help reinforce this function of language. Teachers should encourage class dialogue with others through group discussions, literature circles, cooperative learning, and structured social or play activities.

Regulatory function of language: People use language to control others, such as "You need to . . ." or "You should. . . ." Activities to reinforce this function could be to have children create rules for a game or take turns giving instructions on how to do something. An excellent way for children to practice using language in this way is to give them the opportunity to teach a class or a small group. In group work, children can rotate being a leader and, thus, have the opportunity to use regulatory language.

Representational function of language: People use language to explain things, such as "I'll tell you . . ." or "Let me explain. . . ." A good way to reinforce this type of language is by having students give oral presentations where they must explain a topic or express an opinion to the class. Children can also explain a topic in cooperative learning groups, in which each group learns about one topic in-depth, and then members of one group go to other groups and explain the topic they just learned.

Heuristic function of language: People use language to find things out or to hypothesize why things happen, such as, "Why did that happen?" or "I hypothesize that . . ." Inquiry-based activities and research are excellent ways to reinforce this function of language. A question-and-answer activity whereby children must ask the questions and answer them is another excellent activity.

Imaginative function of language: People use language to create, explore, and imagine various ideas and to express themselves, such as "Let's pretend . . . ," "I wish that . . . ," or "Once upon a time . . ." Children love to use language in this way, which involves telling stories; creating rhymes, poems, and riddles; and putting on plays.

Classroom Instruction in Speaking

Teachers need to provide many opportunities for students to speak daily. This can be in classroom routines such as the morning talk/sharing circle time when teachers discuss the daily calendar, weather, and take attendance. Students can make short oral presentations to the class each day on a rotational basis where they present book reviews; news reports; demonstrations; or their favorite joke, movie, or television show. Students can also be encouraged to contribute to class and group discussions. Students can be paired together and encouraged to work together for the day, which is often beneficial to ELLs who find the informal support of a peer to be helpful.

Students should also receive guidance and explicit instruction that help develop effective speaking skills. Charts such as the ones below can be posted on the walls of the classroom and help specify the rules that students should follow (Saskatchewan Education, 2002).

sample grades 1—3 chart

When we speak, we:

- Share our thoughts
- Speak loudly so everyone can hear
- Pay attention to each other
- Speak clearly
- Are always polite to others
- Tell about important things
- Let others speak

sample grades 4—6 chart

When we speak, we:

- Are prepared
- Speak loudly, slowly, and clearly so others can hear us
- Make sure everyone is paying attention before beginning
- Organize our thoughts into a logical sequence
- Provide clear reasons for our main points
- Look up at the audience to make eye contact

Other classroom activities that help children use language effectively are as follows:

◆ **Group work:** Teachers should provide frequent opportunities for students to work in pairs or small groups to solve problems, create projects, and share ideas. Literature circles, in which students form small groups to read and discuss a text are an excellent vehicle to promote discussion and use of language.

◆ **Storytelling:** Storytelling stimulates the imagination and helps students learn the elements of stories while expanding their language abilities. When students tell stories, they should consider their facial expression, intonation of voice, body language, and ways to engage the listeners in their story. Teachers can give explicit instruction, modeling, and guided practice in helping students create the appropriate mood to present a story.

◆ **Choral speaking:** Like choral reading, choral speaking helps develop students' fluency, increases self-confidence, and provides a model for oral presentations. Students read or chant, together with the teacher, a piece of poetry, story, script, or poem, modeling appropriate phrasing, expression, and body language. This can be done as a class, in a small group, or with pairs.

◆ **Drama:** Dramatic activities help students explore language in a context that they usually find exciting and motivating. Students can practice reading and "playing" with the script, exploring a character's personality through oral expression of dialogue. Performing can take the form of role-playing, character interview, performing a favorite story, and Readers Theatre Workshop, whereby students read a script of a story to the class without props or costumes.

◆ **Structured play:** Giving young children the freedom to explore their environment is an important part of language development. Structured play develops children's ability to communicate with others and to use language to express themselves in an informal setting. Structured play should not stop in first grade but should extend in the lower primary and even upper primary years in different forms.

◆ **Learning centers:** Learning centers are an excellent vehicle to support a structured but informal setting for children to interact with each other. Learning centers allow children to explore different subjects using hands-on and creative activities, such as in reading centers, listening centers, drama centers, sand play centers, computer centers, and mathematics centers. For older children, social problem solving can contribute to students' language growth and help students communicate their needs and ideas within a structured environment.

◆ **Oral reports and presentations:** Oral presentations have become an important part of the classroom, with many states implementing oral reports as part of standardized testing. It is important that students learn how to give a focused, well-developed presentation to the class on a topic of interest to them. Students need explicit instructions on how to prepare a speech, including choosing the topic, researching information on the topic, organizing the information to be presented, creating visuals to support the presentation, and giving the speech. Figure 8–15 shows some of the guidelines that should be followed in developing an effective speech.

Assessing Speaking

It is important that teachers assess a student's speaking ability on a continuous and systematic basis. Oral presentations should be assessed carefully, and feedback should be given to the students after they give a presentation. Rubrics to assess oral presentations will help a student know what criteria should be considered in the preparation and delivery of the oral presentation and help the teacher focus on providing necessary feedback to the student for growth and development. Figure 8–16 shows a rubric for oral presentations based on the following criteria, which can be adapted for lower primary grades:

◆ **Speech development:** A good speech has an opening, body, and conclusion. It immediately engages the audience's attention, then moves forward toward a significant

FIGURE 8-15

Developing an Effective Speech

1. Choose a topic that:
   - Is interesting for you
   - You can personally relate to
   - You know something about

2. Create content that shows:
   - Development of ideas
   - Originality of thought
   - Logical flow of ideas
   - Sense of oneself

3. Organize ideas:
   - In a clear and logical manner
   - With a clear introduction and conclusion
   - With details to support the speech

4. Express ideas:
   - Using effective vocabulary
   - Using formal language (no slang or idioms)
   - Slowly and clearly (purposely slow down speech so the audience can hear you)

5. Present yourself:
   - By standing erect on both feet
   - By dressing nicely
   - By using body language (hands and gestures) to support your ideas
   - With confidence

6. Use voice:
   - To project yourself so everybody can hear you
   - To keep everyone's attention by varying pitch, volume, and expression
   - To express yourself clearly
   - To command the audience's attention and keep it

conclusion. The introduction should contain a clear topic sentence so that the listener knows what the speech is going to be about. The speech is supported by relevant examples and illustrations, facts, and figures, which are blended into the framework of the speech as a unified whole. The speech ends with a good conclusion that ties all the parts of the speech together.

- *Effectiveness:* An effective speech allows the audience to determine the speaker's purpose, and the speech should meet its overall goal. The speaker should be able to hold the interest of the audience, and the speech should be appropriate for the particular audience listening to it.

- *Correctness:* The speaker should use correct language, including proper use of grammar and correct punctuation, which ensures that attention will be directed toward what the speaker says, not how it is said.

- *Appropriateness:* The speaker's choice of words should relate to the speech's purpose and be appropriate for the audience listening to the speech. The language used promotes clear understanding of the speech and fits the occasion.

- *Speech value:* The speaker has something meaningful and original to tell the audience. The listeners should feel the speaker has made a contribution to their thinking.

- *Voice:* The speaker's voice is flexible, moving from one pitch to another for emphasis and has variety in rate and volume. The speaker can be clearly heard and the words are easily understood.

Rubric for a Prepared Speech

FIGURE 8-16

Criteria		Excellent	Very Good	Good	Fair	Poor
SPEECH DEVELOPMENT	- Organization - Body - Opening/closing	10 9	8 7	6 5	4 3	2 1
EFFECTIVENESS	- Achievement of purpose - Interest - Reception	10 9	8 7	6 5	4 3	2 1
CORRECTNESS	- Grammar - Pronunciation - Word selection	10 9	8 7	6 5	4 3	2 1
APPROPRIATENESS	- Word selection and style appropriate to the audience	10 9	8 7	6 5	4 3	2 1
SPEECH VALUE	- Ideas - Logic - Originality	10 9	8 7	6 5	4 3	2 1
VOICE	- Flexibility - Volume - Variety	10 9	8 7	6 5	4 3	2 1
NONVERBAL	- Appearance - Movement - Assurance	10 9	8 7	6 5	4 3	2 1

Score each item with 10 being the highest and 1 being the lowest for each criteria listed above.

◆ *Nonverbal:* The speaker's appearance should reinforce the speech. Body language should support points through gestures, expressions, and body positioning. The speaker's manner should indicate an interest in the topic, in the audience, and in their reactions.

In addition to assessing the student during oral presentations, the teacher can also assess the extent to which speaking is supported in his or her classroom. Figure 8–17 provides a "Teacher Checklist to Support Speaking" that a teacher can use to conduct a self-assessment.

It is important to carefully assess how ELLs use expressive language. Rubrics and checklists help teachers pinpoint the different strengths and weaknesses of the student's language development. It is also helpful to answer some of the questions listed below (Education Alliance at Brown University, 2006) that focus on the student's expressive oral language skills and to record these in the student's portfolio:

◆ Does the student understand what is being said?

◆ Can others easily understand what the ELL says, or does pronunciation interfere with communication?

◆ Does the ELL speak at a natural pace or haltingly?

◆ Does the ELL make many grammatical errors? What types of errors are made? Are these errors typical of a beginning language learner or of someone who is at a higher level of language acquisition?

◆ What types of vocabulary words does the student use? Does the student use academic vocabulary appropriately? Is the vocabulary used appropriate to the message being conveyed?

Teacher Checklist to Support Speaking

_____ 1. I provide many opportunities for my students to speak for different purposes.

_____ 2. I encourage my students to share their thoughts, opinions, and feelings.

_____ 3. I provide a supportive classroom environment so my students can develop a sense of community and build relationships with other students.

_____ 4. I provide instructional activities in which my students need to inform and persuade others.

_____ 5. I conduct mini-lessons on specific speaking strategies to help support them in speaking.

_____ 6. I emphasize language usage and form in the classroom on a regular basis.

_____ 7. I model specific strategies for speaking effectively and give the students guided support to use the strategy.

_____ 8. I provide instruction on the different purposes of speaking and discuss how the use of language varies depending on the purpose of the speaking (formal vs. informal situations).

_____ 9. I provide opportunities for my students to present formal speeches to the class.

_____ 10. I emphasize the need for a formal introduction, well-organized body of the speech, and clear summary when giving a formal speech.

_____ 11. I support my students in allowing a speaker to finish without interrupting or being rude.

_____ 12. I encourage my students to share their thoughts with others when working in small groups.

_____ 13. I support my students in accepting many different roles in a group and making a positive contribution in that role.

_____ 14. I provide students with checklists, rubrics, and clear directions as to what is expected when speaking.

_____ 15. I discuss with students their strengths and needs in speaking.

_____ 16. I assess my students regularly on speaking.

_____ 17. I provide feedback to my students on their speaking abilities and behaviors.

_____ 18. I involve the students in developing their own criteria to assess the development of speaking.

_____ 19. I involve students in self-assessment and determining their own goals for instruction.

_____ 20. I value speaking in the classroom and constantly try to incorporate speaking across the curriculum.

_____ Total of 20 points

FIGURE 8-17

Oral language is the foundation on which reading and writing is based, and teachers need to provide many different opportunities for children to develop both receptive and expressive skills in a linguistically rich environment. Oral language is an essential part of communicating, thinking, and learning, and it should be a major focus in all literacy classrooms.

STRATEGY BOX

Writing, Listening, and Speaking

Miss Kim used the following strategies to teach writing, listening, and speaking to her students:

1. She modeled writing strategies to the class in mini-lessons, and then reinforced this strategy when students were writing.

2. She held conferences with individual students on a regular basis to improve their writing.

3. She emphasized that writing is a process and that each stage of the process is an important part of successful writing.

4. She made writing an important part of everyday classroom activities. She made writing fun and meaningful.

5. She created a supportive environment that encouraged creative thinking, risk taking, and sharing. Students had all the necessary tools to write and the appropriate space for independent writing.

6. She used a writing rubric and checklist in the class as an essential tool for writing. Students used it during planning, revising, and peer editing. The same rubric was used for assessment.

7. She provided accommodations for struggling writers, such as software programs and alternate ways of taking tests that require writing.

8. She emphasized the importance of listening and integrated listening activities into the classroom curriculum through read-alouds and other listening lessons.

9. Children gave oral presentations to the class in which they used language to express their ideas, opinions, and research.

10. She had meaningful interactions with students to foster language development.

11. She provided many opportunities for students to speak daily and to develop effective speaking skills.

Final Thoughts

This chapter focuses on three processes that are an integral part of literacy: writing, speaking, and listening. These three processes are emphasized in state and professional language arts/English standards, and teachers need to emphasize each one through explicit modeling of best practices, providing direct instruction, giving support and guidance to students as they develop their literacy skills, and continuously assessing each child. Reading, writing, speaking, and listening are considered to be reciprocal processes and are all integrally tied to language development and literacy skills. These processes promote achievement in all children and help them become productive members of our society.

EXPLORATION   Application of Concepts

Activities

1. *Observe a writing workshop.* Note which part of the writing process the children are working on. Critique the class and determine whether all different stages of the writing workshop were being followed.

2. *Collect writing samples from elementary school children and, using an appropriate grade-level rubric, assess the writing.* Give the elementary school students feedback by commenting on their assessment.

3. *Using an easel, role-play shared and interactive writing with the class.* First model the strategies an elementary classroom teacher would use to provide this type of support, and then let another candidate act as the teacher.

4. *Visit the websites listed in this chapter and on the Literacy for Children in an Information Age premium website of this chapter (http://www.cengage.com/login).*

Many additional teacher resources on writing can be found on our companion website. Review the website for use in the classroom. Rate the sites using the Website Evaluation Form found in Chapter 1 or using the following criteria: (a) usefulness in the classroom, (b) motivates students, (c) encourages student writing, (d) ease of use, (e) kid friendly, and (f) age appropriate. This same activity can be done with various software packages mentioned in this chapter.

5. In a group, discuss whether you think technology can enhance the development of writing. Make two columns and label them "How Technology Helps Writing" and "How Technology Hinders Writing." Then have each group choose one side and carry on a reasoned debate about the issue. Try to summarize the main points and devise a list of generalizations about the use of technology in writing.

6. Discuss different strategies that can be used in the classroom to support ELLs. Make a list on the board. Discuss strategies that support children with special needs and make another list on the board. How are these two lists similar and how are they different? Are they any different from best practices in the classroom for teaching writing?

HOME–SCHOOL CONNECTION Writing Together

Parents and guardians frequently express frustration that they want to help their child become a better writer, but they don't know how. Children often learn how to write in the classroom using interactive and guided writing. Parents and guardians can follow the teacher's tips listed below to learn how to help their own children improve writing at home:

1. The parent or guardian should encourage the child to write frequently and not pay attention to spelling, helping the child "get the ideas down."

2. The parent or guardian can encourage writing by using the computer. Children love to work at the computer. There are many software programs that incorporate colorful graphics, enabling the child to create a picture and write a sentence to explain the picture. Older children can use the same word processor program that adults use, such as Mircrosoft Word. This is a good way for students to learn keyboarding skills and how to navigate a word processor, and it encourages writing. The parent or guardian and child can sit at the computer together, taking turns writing the words (parts of words), and sentences.

3. For younger children, the parent or guardian can write down what the child dictates, based upon a common experience, like *apple picking*.

4. The parent/guardian and child can take turns thinking about what to write. The parent or guardian should encourage the child to write down ideas first, before beginning the actual writing process.

5. The parent or guardian can show the child how to use such programs as Inspiration, a mapping software program, that allows a writer to map out ideas before the writing process begins. Children will find this fun to do while sitting at the computer alongside a parent.

6. The parent or guardian can encourage the child to use proper mechanics by asking a younger child to show where the comma or the period should go, or an older children about more advanced mechanics.

7. The parent or guardian can model and conduct think alouds so that the child sees authentic writing at home and can follow along, learning how to use writing as a tool.

8. The child can reread to the parent or guardian what is written to make sure it makes sense. With older children, the parent or guardian can reread what the child wrote to make sure it makes sense.

9. The child and parent or guardian can edit the writing together, checking to see that younger children punctuated each sentence correctly, and that older children did not make any grammatical mistakes.

10. Parents or guardians should always provide positive feedback and praise the child's writing. It is important that the child does not feel as if the parent is interfering or being overly critical. This will discourage the child from writing and interfere with the intended sense of fun and companionship.

(Adapted from McCarrier, A., Pinnell, S. G., & I. C. Fountas (2000). *Interactive writing: How language and literacy come together, K–2.* Portsmouth, NH: Heinemann.)

9 ASSESSMENT IN THE LITERACY CLASSROOM

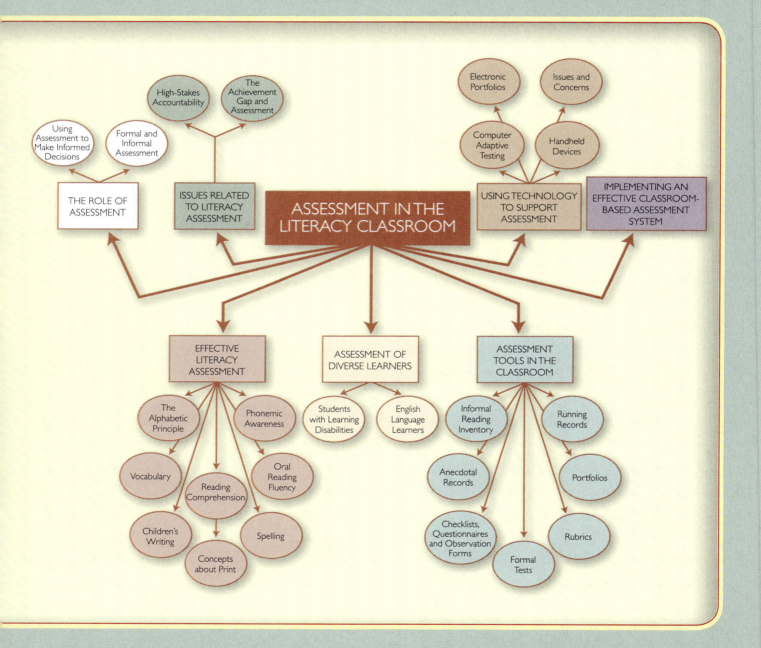

ASSESSMENT IN THE LITERACY CLASSROOM

THE ROLE OF ASSESSMENT
- Using Assessment to Make Informed Decisions
- Formal and Informal Assessment

ISSUES RELATED TO LITERACY ASSESSMENT
- High-Stakes Accountability
- The Achievement Gap and Assessment

USING TECHNOLOGY TO SUPPORT ASSESSMENT
- Electronic Portfolios
- Issues and Concerns
- Computer Adaptive Testing
- Handheld Devices

IMPLEMENTING AN EFFECTIVE CLASSROOM-BASED ASSESSMENT SYSTEM

EFFECTIVE LITERACY ASSESSMENT
- The Alphabetic Principle
- Phonemic Awareness
- Vocabulary
- Reading Comprehension
- Oral Reading Fluency
- Children's Writing
- Concepts about Print
- Spelling

ASSESSMENT OF DIVERSE LEARNERS
- Students with Learning Disabilities
- English Language Learners

ASSESSMENT TOOLS IN THE CLASSROOM
- Informal Reading Inventory
- Running Records
- Anecdotal Records
- Portfolios
- Checklists, Questionnaires and Observation Forms
- Rubrics
- Formal Tests

International Reading Association Professional Standards Addressed in this Chapter:

IRA STANDARD 1: FOUNDATIONAL KNOWLEDGE

Candidates have knowledge of the foundations of reading and writing processes and instruction. Candidates:

1.1 Demonstrate knowledge of psychological, sociological, and linguistic foundations of reading and writing processes and instruction.

1.2 Demonstrate knowledge of reading research and histories of reading.

1.3 Demonstrate knowledge of language development and reading acquisition and the variations related to cultural and linguistic diversity.

1.4 Demonstrate knowledge of the major components of reading (phonemic awareness, word identification and phonics, vocabulary and background knowledge, fluency, comprehension strategies, and motivation) and how they are integrated in fluent reading.

IRA STANDARD 3: ASSESSMENT, DIAGNOSIS, AND EVALUATION

Candidates use a variety of assessment tools and practices to plan and evaluate effective reading instruction. Candidates:

3.1 Use a wide range of assessment tools and practices that range from individual and group standardized tests to individual and group informal classroom assessment strategies, including technology-based assessment tools.

3.2 Place students along a developmental continuum and identify students' proficiencies and difficulties.

3.3 Use assessment information to plan, evaluate, and revise effective instruction that meets the needs of all students, including those at different developmental stages and those from different cultural and linguistic backgrounds.

IRA STANDARD 4: CREATING A LITERATE ENVIRONMENT

Candidates create a literate environment that fosters reading and writing by integrating foundational knowledge, use of instructional practices, approaches and methods, curriculum materials, and the appropriate use of assessments. Candidates:

4.1 Use students' interests, reading abilities, and backgrounds as foundations for the reading and writing program.

4.4 Motivate learners to be lifelong readers.

Key Terms

assessment
diagnosis
prescription
formal test
informal test
No Child Left Behind Act (NCLB)
retelling
holistic scoring
anchor papers
inter-rater reliability
test accommodations
test modifications
independent level
instruction level

Focus Questions

1. What is the primary purpose of assessment in the classroom? Why is it so important that a teacher set up an effective literacy assessment system?

2. What major assessment issues are classroom teachers and educators dealing with at this point in time?

3. What key areas need to be assessed in literacy? Explain techniques to assess each area.

Focus Questions *(continued)*

4. What accomodations can help support the assessment of students with learning disabilities? What methods can be used to assess English language learners?

5. What are the primary tools a teacher can use to assess literacy in the classroom?

6. How can technology be used to promote assessment in the classroom?

7. What are the basic principles a teacher should follow in implementing an effective classroom–based assessment system?

Welcome to Miss Chen's Third Grade Classroom: Assessing Each Child For Effective Instruction

WizData, Inc. 2009/Used under license from Shutterstock.com

In September, Miss Chen was anxious for all the students in her third grade class to be reading texts on an appropriate level for them. She needed to know the strengths and weaknesses of each student so that she could design instruction to meet their needs. She did not want to make the mistake of giving a student a text that was too difficult to read, causing frustration, anxiety, and behavioral problems; nor did she want to give a student material that was too easy to read, causing boredom, distraction, and other behavioral problems. Her goal was to match students with the right level of reading material, and then have each progress at his or her individual pace of learning to more challenging material. Miss Chen wanted to form guided reading groups, and needed to be sure that the students in each group were reading at a similar level so that she could address their needs. She needed to gather some initial information about her students.

Starting in September, Miss Chen began collecting information and data about each child's literacy skills. She administered a reading questionnaire to the class that asked the children how often they read, what types of books they like to read, and what they like and dislike about reading. She also collected a writing sample from the students and found out about each one's interests in writing. In mid-September, she administered an Informal

Reading Inventory (IRI) to each student in the class. While the other children were working on independent seat work or group work, she called each student over to a table in the back of the room. While she faced the class to monitor them closely, she had each student read aloud progressively more difficult passages from a graded reader or leveled text. She recorded any mistakes they made in reading aloud (commonly referred to as miscues) on a copy of the passage the student was reading. She then had the student retell the story and answer a few questions to assess comprehension. She quickly determined his or her reading level. Each student's assessment took approximately 15 minutes, and Miss Chen was able to assess two to three students each day. After approximately one month of initial assessment, Miss Chen had an excellent idea as to how each student was reading.

Miss Chen now felt much better prepared to plan her literacy program and develop an instructional program for each student. She had data on which she could base her decisions regarding placement into guided groups, reading material to give each student, mini-lessons that individual students needed, and an instructional program that would support each student in her class. She also had an individual folder set up for each student so that when she met with parents or made recommendations to her reading specialist or principal, she had data to support her comments. Miss Chen would continue assessing her students all year long using both informal methods such as the IRI, running records, and ongoing observation, as well as through more formal evaluations such as the standardized tests given to her students each year. Miss Chen knew that her decisions needed to be based on multiple assessment results and the collection of data on a continuous and systematic basis.

Miss Chen has shown that assessment is an essential daily activity in her classroom, the purpose of which is to collect data to inform her about the current strengths and weaknesses of each child. She has used a variety of assessment instruments to help her know each child and plan an individualized reading and writing program for him or her. This chapter focuses on the various techniques that teachers such as Miss Chen use to assess literacy. It will examine the different roles that assessment can play in the classroom. It will also explain what an IRI is and how it can be used in the classroom. Lastly, it will examine how technology is impacting the field of assessment, and how it is being used in the classroom to facilitate assessment procedures.

The Role of Assessment

Using Assessment to Make Informed Decisions

Classroom teachers must rely on assessment data to make important decisions about curriculum, classroom management, and daily activities. The phrase "assessment drives instruction" means that **assessment** is an integral part of the classroom teacher's responsibility, and that all instructional decisions should be based on careful collection and analysis of information gathered from the student; it is also essential that the student receives constant feedback from assessment results regarding daily progress. This feedback will help the student keep striving toward attainable goals set by the teacher.

Assessment is the broad process of collecting, synthesizing, and interpreting information to measure achievement, plan instruction, and improve student performance (Airasian, 1997; Tucker & Strong, 2005). It refers to all teacher observations, student surveys, homework assignments, writing samples, oral reading samples, and comprehension questions answered by the student. Once the data are collected, teachers need to use it to make decisions about classroom instruction and meeting the needs of students. Evaluation is the process of making those decisions or judgments about what is good or desirable, such as determining the quality of a student's writing sample or collecting information on a student's fluency in reading a text. The key point here is that data must be collected for the process to be considered assessment. That is, when a teacher observes a student reading independently, the teacher should record certain behaviors in a notebook or on a standard form (such as time spent on task, interest in the book); this would then be valid assessment data. If a teacher just observes a student during the course of the day without making notes, this is valuable information, but is not considered assessment data. The teacher must collect data on the student in the form of questionnaires, observation forms, writing samples, homework assignments, rubrics from projects, checklists, and recording sheets for noting miscues from oral reading. Perhaps the biggest misconception regarding assessment is in the area of data collection: Student work should be collected or student behavior should be recorded for decision-making purposes.

The purpose of collecting assessment data in literacy is so that the teacher can derive a **diagnosis** or determine a child's strengths and weaknesses. Assessment data allow a teacher to develop a profile of a particular student that specifies that child's areas of strength and areas for improvement. Once this is determined, the teacher can develop a **prescription,** or blueprint for instruction. The prescription is based on the child's diagnosis and becomes an instructional plan that builds on strengths while focusing on areas that need improvement. A diagnosis and prescription can be developed for every child in the class, whether the child is an accelerated reader who needs more challenging and advanced material or a struggling reader who needs more work on word study and phonic analysis. A diagnosis and prescription will help the teacher place students into guided reading groups and provide guidance for the type of reading material that should be used, the mini-lessons that need to be taught, and the individualized work the child should be doing independently.

In the "Five-Stage Early Literacy Documentation-Assessment Cycle" (Jones, 2003) (Figure 9–1), classroom-based literacy assessment is an integral part of the daily

FIGURE 9-1

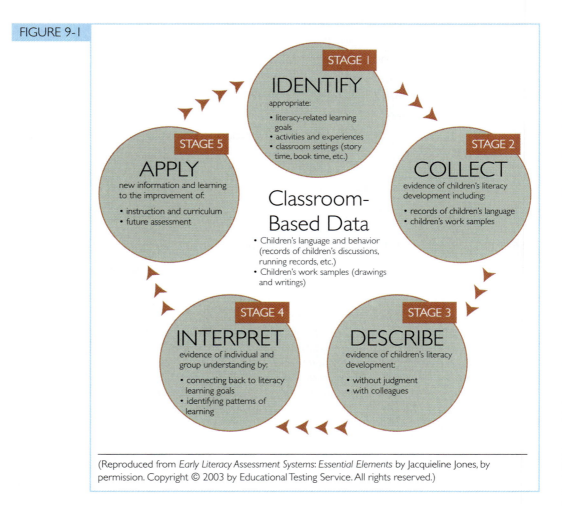

(Reproduced from *Early Literacy Assessment Systems: Essential Elements* by Jacqueline Jones, by permission. Copyright © 2003 by Educational Testing Service. All rights reserved.)

classroom routine. In Stage 1, *Identify*, the teacher must identify the learning goals and determine what evidence can be collected to show that the students have mastered the goals. In Stage 2, *Collect*, the teacher must collect the evidence over time. This evidence can be in the form of observations, checklists, rubrics, samples of students' work such as drawings and writings, and hands-on projects. In Stage 3, *Describe*, the teacher works to describe the evidence; this is often done collaboratively where teachers share their evidence and observations. In Stage 4, *Interpret*, the teacher weighs the evidence against the goals and interprets the evidence to determine whether the child has mastered the literacy goals. In Stage 5, *Apply*, the teacher uses the information to plan classroom instruction that will benefit each child and, if the goals have been mastered, to identify new goals for each child. At the heart of this five-step model of assessment is the teacher's ability to become an astute observer and systematic collector of information about each child in the classroom.

Assessment plays a key role in the classroom, and a teacher needs to be knowledgeable about the type of data that can be collected daily to help make decisions. With the emphasis on state and national standards, it has become mandatory that a teacher is accountable and has the data to back up decisions. A teacher will depend on two different types of assessments on which to base decisions: formal and informal assessments.

Formal and Informal Assessments

A **formal test** usually is given to a group of students and is generally known as a standardized test, or statewide assessment, that provides clear and direct but inflexible directions for administering. Generally, these tests are scored in a prescribed manner, usually by the publisher, the state, or by using the publisher's software package. The main purpose of giving formal, standardized tests to groups of students is to provide an efficient way to determine how well school districts and/or particular grade levels are meeting district-wide or statewide standards and benchmarks. Formal tests do not provide specific information about individual student learning styles or about individual student's learning strengths, nor do formal tests usually prescribe how to improve instruction. They give little feedback to the teacher concerning whether the literacy instruction in the classroom is being implemented effectively.

Formal tests give a general guideline as to how an individual child is faring compared with a normative group, or a group of students that the publishers used to determine the statistical validity of the test. Formal tests yield valuable information to administrators, who need to determine whether their school, district, or population of students is scoring on comparable levels with other populations of similar students. If a school is scoring lower than the normative group in a particular subject area, then the administrator knows that some remedial action needs to be taken in that school. Formal tests are excellent tools for comparing large groups of students with other groups across the country. However, they are not effective tools for determining what one individual student needs in the classroom.

Formal assessment scores yield such statistics as percentiles, grade levels, normal curve equivalents, and stanines, which do not provide the teacher with much feedback about the curriculum being taught, the amount of information that the student knows, the skills and strategies the student is using, or the actual material in the classroom that the student can read. Because formal tests usually require students to attempt successively more difficult questions, the score does not really tell the teacher the level the student is functioning at successfully, but rather the level that the student can reach with much frustration. The scores of formal tests, therefore, yield a general picture about the student's performance and give the teacher an idea about how well the student is reading and testing under stressful circumstances, but they do not help develop an accurate and specific diagnosis or prescription.

An **informal test** is used to test individual students or small informal groups of students with specific strengths or needs. Informal tests usually provide more valuable results for the teacher because they are designed to assess individual students' strengths and weaknesses in a number of specified reading skills areas. Teacher discretion can

Courtesy of Guilherme Cunha

Informal assessment should be continuous and ongoing throughout the year.

play a part in informal testing so that portions of the test can be modified to meet the diagnostic needs of individual students. For example, a teacher has greater latitude with interpreting the results of a test or in deciding to end a particular test if a student is showing signs of frustration. Conversely, a teacher may decide to add an authentic writing portion to a given student's informal test based on earlier responses in which he or she showed signs of weak language usage.

Informal assessments usually take place in a natural setting within the classroom; therefore, they are much more relaxed and stress free than formal assessments. The teacher usually designs the assessment based on the curriculum; therefore, there is a close match between what is being taught in the classroom and what is assessed. The results can provide the teacher and the student with important feedback about instructional methods and the curriculum, allowing the teacher to modify instruction and reteach if necessary. The informal assessment is usually subjective in nature, whereby the teacher is the decision maker and can modify the assessment at any given time, modify the administration to suit the needs of the student, and interpret the data based on the teacher's perception of the student.

Informal assessments use scores that teachers can easily read and interpret: percentage correct, scores on a rubric, number of miscues out of 100 words, number of questions answered correctly, and even how many items were checked off on a checklist. The scores can be easily converted to a grade or a criterion that will tell the teacher whether the student mastered the knowledge, skills, or processes being taught. The scores, therefore, yield specific information about how a student is achieving in a particular subject area, skill area, or literacy skill, which is quite useful to a teacher during the year. Figure 9–2 summarizes the differences between formal and informal assessments.

Issues Related to Literacy Assessment

High-Stakes Accountability

One of the most pressing issues in today's schools is the legal imposition of high-stakes assessment as a method to ensure that children are not left behind. The **No Child Left Behind Act** (NCLB) of 2002 stipulates that all reading materials used in the classroom must be based on scientific reading research, and that early reading instruction must include attention to early, systematic, explicit phonics instruction. The federal

Differences Between Formal and Informal Assessments

	Formal Assessments	Informal Assessments
Purpose	To determine how well school districts and/or particular grade levels are meeting districtwide or statewide standards and benchmarks	To determine achievement of individual students on specific skills, content, and processes so that instructional decisions within the classroom can be made
Development	Developed by large publishing companies such as Educational Testing Services (ETS) or State Department of Education	Developed by the teacher or a publishing company to assist the teacher in determining levels of achievement related to the curriculum being taught
Examples	Standardized tests such as TerraNova Reading, state-wide tests, published tests that accompany a reading series	Teacher-made tests, Informal Reading Inventories, running records, projects, observation forms
Relationship to the Curriculum	Is not developed to align with a district's curriculum and may or may not reflect what is taught in the classroom	Relates directly to the curriculum being taught in the classroom and is designed to determine whether the student is achieving within the classroom
Setting	Usually formal setting with careful monitoring under a timed administration	Usually within the classroom in a more relaxed atmosphere; flexible setting; teacher can impose "testlike" conditions
Administration	Strict and prescribed way to administer the assessment with no flexibility; usually given once or twice a year	Much more flexible; teacher has opportunity to vary the assessment based on students' needs; given continuously throughout the year
Student Reaction	Stressful and anxiety-provoking	Much more relaxed; often student is not aware that an assessment is occurring
Scores	Percentiles, grade levels, stanines; gives a general overview of how a student fared compared with a group of students	Usually based on percentage correct but can be "pass/fail" or with a checkmark to show successful completion of item
Interpretation of Scores	Usually based on a normed group of students, and scores reflect how a student achieved on a test compared to the normed group; the scores are based on a bell curve and there is no flexibility regarding interpretation	Teacher has much subjectivity in interpreting the scores; the teacher bases interpretation on multiple assessments over a continuous period of time; interpretation relates directly to what is taught in the classroom
Decisions Made From Score	Usually high-stakes assessment whereby if a student does not pass, he/she will be held back a grade, put in a remedial group, or given special educational services	The scores will provide information on the student's strengths and weaknesses and lead to a prescription or blueprint for instruction; usually a student's grade in a subject area is based on informal assessments

FIGURE 9-2

government set up a website, What Works Clearinghouse (http://ies.ed.gov/ncee/wwc/), that provides information on those acceptable reading programs that have provided studies to support their effectiveness as an intervention. This law requires a new federal intervention into state and local education that has never been seen before and includes a long list of mandates to which schools must adhere. One of these mandates is that schools must annually assess students to ensure that yearly progress goals are met, and it imposes consequences on the schools if they do not collect, analyze, and respond to the data about student learning (Reutzel & Mitchell, 2005). Schools that do not meet federally mandated goals of performance are considered "failing schools."

One of the most controversial aspects of the law is the mandate that all special education students and English language learners (ELLs) are included in the yearly testing and their scores are counted as part of the general population of students. Therefore, a school with a high percentage of students with diverse needs could be considered a "failing school" because of this practice. This provision was included to ensure that all students make yearly progress and are "not left behind."

Students with learning disabilities (LD) have special needs and require specific accommodations during testing. Critics question whether it is fair to administer formal assessments to this population of students without considering their special needs, and then to aggregate the results into one result. One stated concern is that high-stakes tests are stressful, and the information gathered from them may not be a valid source of information either for the teacher to base instructional decisions on or for the school district to monitor its population of students.

Another major concern of critics is the use of high-stakes accountability to make valid decisions with ELLs who are not yet proficient in English and cannot demonstrate what they know when the test is written in English. It is suggested that a child from a minority culture may not understand certain test items that reflect a different cultural perspective. Although students may demonstrate proficiency in conversational English, it takes much longer to develop academic literacy skills required for such tests. It may take five to nine years for ELLs to reach grade level on many standardized tests (Cooper & Kiger, 2005).

Although there are many beneficial goals outlined in NCLB with its focus on achieving equity in educational opportunities for all children, critics point out that the emphasis on testing has caused classroom teachers to often focus on a narrowly defined curriculum that will be assessed and on the need to "cover the material." Hence, many teachers spend considerable time teaching "test-taking skills" and preparing children for these tests, taking valuable time away from the literacy curriculum. However, the emphasis on having all children attain higher standards in all subject areas and the requirement to provide evidence of this achievement has been praised as an excellent direction to improve educational quality.

The Achievement Gap and Assessing Young Children

A major issue related to literacy instruction is the assessment of children younger than third grade. Traditionally, teachers have used informal assessments to evaluate young children's literacy skills, such as observations of language development, writing samples, drawings, and records of children's attitudes toward books and reading. Recently, however, there has been recognition of fundamental differences in reading achievement and language development based on socioeconomic status (SES). A report from the National Center for Education Statistics (West, Denton, & Geronimo-Hausken, 2000) examined differences in the reading readiness of kindergartners grouped by sex, race/ethnicity, SES, and age. The study reported statistically significant differences in reading readiness among different subgroups of kindergartners. SES was strongly related to reading proficiency, because children in higher SES groups were more likely to be proficient in reading than children in lower SES groups. The study also reported that Asian and white children were more likely than children in other racial/ethnic groups to be proficient across all reading tasks measured. However, nearly all racial/ethnic differences in reading disappeared when children were grouped into similar SES levels (Jones, 2003).

In the PIRLS (Progress in International Reading Literacy) study (Ogle, Sen, Pahlke, Jocelyn, Kastberg, Roey, & Williams, 2003) a reading assessment was administered to 9- and 10-year-olds in 35 nations. The mean score in literacy in schools where more than 75 percent of the children are on free and reduced lunch was 100 points below the scores of other students, and well below those of many other nations. The PIRLS study points to the fact that social class affects achievement levels in the U.S. (Berliner, 2006).

This study helped educators realize that SES has a major impact on early childhood development and educational opportunities. Economically advantaged children often demonstrate significantly better language skills over their less economically privileged peers. Most disturbing has been the finding that these differences in language development based on SES can persist throughout the school years, resulting in overall poor literacy development and impacting educational performance and transition to the workforce (West, Denton, & Geronimo-Hausken, 2000). Identifying such discrepancies in early childhood literacy development has created great concern that our public education system may not be effective in teaching all children to read and write, especially those from lower socioeconomic levels.

One reaction to the achievement gap in kindergartners was the passage of the NCLB Act with its demand for more accountability and the requirement of using standardized formal assessments to determine children's literacy achievement over time. This act authorized two new reading programs that all states have adopted, "Reading First" and "Early Reading First," both of which are intended to enhance the language and literacy skills of all children to help eliminate the achievement gaps identified among racial/ethnic and socioeconomic groups. Both programs require formal standardized testing of reading skills to receive federal funding. States must show that they have a high-quality, effective reading program that includes rigorous assessments with proven validity and reliability.

Much of the controversy that surrounds the NCLB Act focuses on the requirement to use formal standardized tests to assess preK students in the nationally funded Head Start program and all children in every grade, including kindergarten. Critics of this requirement claim that the effective assessment of young children does not merely require a new set of standardized instruments to measure literacy development, but also multiple approaches to assessment that inform classroom practice and monitor children's progress.

Lorrie Shepard and her colleagues claim that assessment of children younger than third grade should focus on classroom-based evidence of learning rather than standardized tests. This information can then be used to guide and improve instruction (Shepard, Kagan, & Wirtz, 1998). In addition, the National Association for the Education of Young Children (NAEYC) and the National Association of Early Childhood

Courtesy of Becky Stovall

Assessment of young children should focus on classroom-based evidence of learning.

Specialists in State Departments of Education (NAECS/SDE, 2003) developed a joint position statement outlining a set of principles for appropriate assessment of young children. Their focus on assessment is to make sound decisions about teaching and learning, identify significant concerns that may require focused intervention for individual children, and help programs improve their educational and developmental interventions. They feel that the use of formal standardized testing of young children should be limited to situations in which such measures are appropriate and potentially beneficial, such as to identify potential disabilities.

Literacy assessments should focus on diagnosing children's strengths and weaknesses and should be connected to classroom instruction, materials, and school-wide curricula. Most educators agree that high-stakes testing is not appropriate for beginning readers (Jones, 2003; NAEYC and NAECS/SDE, 2004; NAECS/SDE, 2003; Paris, 2003; Shepard et al., 1998). Closing the literacy gap for all children will require a commitment to ongoing professional development within the field of literacy, strong leadership in the field, and coherent use of multiple literacy assessments. Teachers should collect information on many different aspects of literacy using many different instruments and methods.

Effective Literacy Assessment

When implementing an effective assessment system within the literacy classroom, teachers need to know what literacy skills to assess. The *Report of the National Reading Panel* (NICHD, 2000) identified five essential skills to assess and teach in primary grades: (1) the alphabetic principle, (2) phonemic awareness, (3) vocabulary, (4) oral reading fluency, and (5) comprehension. The same five skills were endorsed in the Reading First part of the NCLB Act (2002) as fundamental skills that all children need in the classroom. Thus, it is important to know how these five reading skills can be assessed in the classroom. In addition, there are other literacy skills and processes that a teacher should also assess, including concepts about print, children's writing, and spelling. These skills are covered in detail in other chapters in this book, but are discussed briefly in the following sections with a focus only on assessment. Although these skills are discussed separately, literacy skills are intricately tied together into the complete process of fluent reading and writing. Therefore, teachers need to make connections to each essential skill because they all contribute to development and achievement in literacy.

The Alphabetic Principle

The alphabetic principle involves having children associate the individual grapheme or letter with its phoneme or sound, so that there is an automatic connection between the letter and its sound. This requires not only that children identify the individual letters of the alphabet but that they associate sounds with the letter as well. These skills normally are assessed informally during shared reading, when teachers ask students to identify individual letter patterns and sounds or during guided reading, when children are reading beginning texts aloud to the teacher. Teachers often use alphabet books with many different pictures and few words to help assess the alphabetic principle.

Teachers can also assess these skills in isolation by asking children to:

◆ Name letters that are shown to them
◆ Pronounce letter sounds
◆ Choose letters that have specific names and sounds

Such assessments can be relatively quick and can be recorded to show progress over time.

Assessment Tip: Pay attention to how a child writes. For the purposes of assessing the child's understanding of the alphabetic principle, it does not matter whether the child writes accurately. What matters is that the child writes one symbol per sound. The symbols do not even have to be letters, as long as words with three phonemes are represented in writing by three symbols (Southwest Education Development Laboratory [SEDL], 2005).

Phonemic Awareness

Phonemic awareness is the ability to hear, to identify, and to manipulate sounds in spoken language. As discussed in Chapter 4, it refers to the specific understanding that spoken words are made up of individual phonemes—not just sounds in general, but phonemes. Children with phoneme awareness know that the word *wait* is made up of three phonemes, and that the words *pill* and *map* both contain the phoneme /p/. In short, they know that phonemes are the building blocks of spoken words, and that these building blocks can be rearranged and substituted to make different words (SEDL, 2005). Researchers have shown that the two greatest predictors of young children's ability to learn how to read are their understanding of the alphabetic principle and phonemic awareness (Adams, 1990; Snow, Burns, & Griffin, 1998). Some key features of phonemic and phonological awareness that teachers should assess in kindergarten through grade 2 are as follows (Paris, 2003):

◆ Can children recognize consonants at the beginning and end of words?

◆ Can children recognize vowels and their sounds in words?

◆ Can children identify and produce rhyming words?

◆ Can children identify and segment distinct sounds in words?

◆ Can children blend phonemes to create words?

◆ Can children manipulate phonemes in words, for example, knowing that dropping the "f" sound from the word *feel* leaves the phoneme *eel*?

Other aspects of phonemic awareness that teachers should look for are distinguishing long and short vowels, recognizing alternative spellings of the same phonemes (for example, *meet/meat*), and identifying double vowel sounds in diphthongs (for example, *mouse*). By the end of first grade, most children acquire many aspects of phonemic awareness, but some children with more serious reading disabilities may need explicit instruction about phonemes in second grade and beyond (Paris, 2003).

A number of ways a teacher can assess phonemic awareness exist. Adams (1990) identifies the following tasks as strong predictors of early reading achievement, and each task can be used in daily reading activities and recorded for each child:

◆ Nursery rhymes or familiar books (for example, *Brown Bear, Brown Bear*) provide excellent vehicles to assess rhyming. Can children recognize words that rhyme in text (for example, *see–me*), and can they supply words that rhyme with a target or group of words (for example, *sad–bad* or *hit–fit*)? Identifying rhyming words is easier than generating them.

◆ Another task requires children to identify which word is different from several others; the group may include words with the same initial, final, or medial sounds (for example, *sit, fit, light*). This task requires children to compare and contrast the words to identify how one word is different from the others.

◆ A different assessment task requires children to segment syllables into phonemes; for example, given the word *mud*, children need to say the individual sounds of /m/-/u/-/d/ or, perhaps, to clap their hands for each distinct phoneme. Segmenting words begins with one familiar word and requires children to identify the component sounds. This is easier than the next method, blending phonemes.

◆ Blending phonemes is a difficult task because children must remember and blend individual sounds they are given, such as /s/-/a/-/t/ into the word *sat*.

◆ Adding, deleting, and moving phonemes are more difficult tasks because they require the student to "cut off" a phoneme and to identify the sounds that remain. For example, if the /f/ sound is taken away from the word *fish*, what do you have left? The answer is *ish*.

◆ Can a child produce words that start with the same sound (alliteration), such as *milk, more, man,* or match words based on alliteration (*man, more, fish*)?

◆ Another task to assess phonemic awareness is to have a child count the number of phonemes in a word (for example, How many phonemes are in the word *pin*?), or asking the child to delete a phoneme from a word (for example, What would *pin* be if you took out the /p/ sound?), or add a phoneme (add an /s/ sound to the beginning of *pin*), or substitute a phoneme (replace the /i/ in *pin* with an /a/ sound).

Assessment Tip: Use the Turtle Talk game to assess the child's phoneme segmentation ability. Sit one-on-one with a child; tell him or her that, in addition to walking slowly, turtles talk slowly. Ask the child to take a breath after every sound he or she makes. Demonstrate for the child how a turtle would say the word *man* (/m/ /a/ /n/), taking a clear breath between each sound. Try to use words that have phonemes that are easy to say in isolation, such as /t/, /m/, and /f/. Avoid words that contain phonemes such as the hard /g/ and /b/ because they cannot be said without adding a vowel to the end (so they sound like /guh/ and /buh/). Also, start with simple words; then build up to more difficult words (SEDL, 2005).

Vocabulary

Vocabulary acquisition is an important part of reading proficiency and should be assessed regularly. Many basal reading programs come with assessment tests that include vocabulary words used in the readers. Teachers can assess vocabulary informally throughout the year and collect this information on a continuous basis.

For the young child who is at the emergent literacy stage of reading, assessments should not be given in print because this becomes more of a decoding task than a test of semantics or determining the meaning of a word. For young children, it is common to use pictures in vocabulary or semantic assessments. A child might be asked to provide a name for a particular picture, or to match spoken words with pictures as a test of receptive vocabulary. Another task is to ask the child to rearrange a set of pictures to reflect a logical sequence of events (SEDL, 2005). To assess expressive vocabulary (those words the child can use in his or her own speech), the child can be asked to provide a word that best matches a definition or a picture presented. An issue in testing for vocabulary with young children is that many assessments require that the child be familiar with more than the word being tested. For instance, if a child is asked to select a word that does not belong in a group of words (for example, *thread, string, rope, knot*), the child must know the meaning of most, if not all, of the words in each sequence to be successful.

For children who are beyond the emergent literacy stage, teachers may ask them to read, define, and use words in sentences, either verbally or in writing. These words can be drawn from the students' reading selections, content area reading, or based on a theme the class is studying. Students may be assigned vocabulary words in isolation from the curriculum, which are assessed on a weekly basis. Thus, informal vocabulary assessments can be used by teachers on a continuous basis and allow the assessments to be flexible, brief, and focused on words found in the current curriculum. Many teachers use vocabulary assessments before reading a text to help build students' background knowledge (Paris, 2003).

Assessment Tip: For ELLs and children with LD, you want to assess their knowledge of word meanings and not their ability to read the words. Therefore, the teacher can read the word choices to the student and have them point to the correct picture or draw a picture of what the vocabulary word means. Students may know what the word means but be incapable of identifying it in text.

Oral Reading Fluency

Fluency is fast, expressive reading that involves both rate of reading words and the phrasing that good readers use when reading out loud (Cunningham, 2000; Pinnell & Fountas, 1998; NICHD, 2000). Fluency refers to how readers put words together in phrases so that they have a good pace to the reading, read with expression, and read easily, reflecting comprehension of the material. Fluency is highly correlated with comprehension scores on the standardized tests of the National Assessment of Educational Progress (NAEP) (Fountas & Pinell, 1996; NICHD, 2000).

The most common way in which teachers assess children's ability to read out loud and decode words accurately is to use an IRI, which will assess a child's reading rate together with accuracy and comprehension of the text read. Such assessments can help teachers give children materials that are at their instructional levels, as well as diagnose problems such as guessing words based on initial letters or substituting similar-looking words that are inconsistent with the text meaning. Rate, accuracy, and intonation together provide a more comprehensive assessment of fluency than any single measure (Paris, 2003). The IRI is described in detail later.

Oral reading fluency measures are by far the most popular assessments in kindergarten through grade 3. The information is relatively easy to collect, chart, and interpret because beginning readers make steady progress in reading faster with fewer errors and with more expression. All these measures reflect the development of automatic decoding processes; thus, they are good measures of increasing fluency or potential problems.

To assess fluency, the NAEP developed a fluency scale to help measure elementary students' oral reading ability (Figure 9–3). The key elements they used to assess children's fluency include: (1) grouping or *phrasing* of words as demonstrated through the intonation, stress, and pauses exhibited by readers; (2) adherence to author's *syntax*, or grammatical structure used in the text; and (3) *expressiveness* of the oral reading, or the ability of the reader to interject a sense of feeling, anticipation, or characterization. Students at levels 3 and 4 are generally considered to be fluent, and those at levels 1 and 2 are nonfluent.

Oral reading fluency is an important benchmark of reading ability, and teachers need to become proficient in collecting data to document student growth over time. Fluency indicates that a student has mastered automatic word recognition, established effective strategies for decoding words, and can recognize syntactic and semantic units in text (Paris, 2003). Teachers should use this information to provide appropriate

National Assessment of Educational Progress Oral Reading Fluency Scale

FIGURE 9-3

Level 4 Reads primarily in larger, meaningful phrase groups. Although some regressions, repetitions, and deviations from text may be present, these do not appear to detract from the overall structure of the story. Preservation of the author's syntax is consistent. Some or most of the story is read with expressive interpretation.

Level 3 Reads primarily in three- or four-word phrase groups. Some smaller groupings may be present. However, the majority of phrasing seems appropriate and preserves the syntax of the author. Little or no expressive interpretation is present.

Level 2 Reads primarily in two-word phrases with some three- or four-word groupings. Some word-by-word reading may be present. Word groupings may seem awkward and unrelated to larger context of sentence or passage.

Level 1 Reads primarily word by word. Occasional two-word or three-word phrases may occur, but these are infrequent and/or they do not preserve meaningful syntax.

(Reproduced from U.S. Department of Education, National Center for Education Statistics [NCES]. (1995). *Listening to children read aloud*, 15. Washington, DC: NCES.)

instruction and to diagnose the strengths and weaknesses of all children in the classroom, especially when teaching children younger than third grade. It is also important that teachers of upper primary grades collect these data on those children who may be struggling, so that they can receive the necessary support to succeed in school.

Assessment Tip: Use Readers Theatre Workshop—where groups of students practice reading a script developed from children's literature and perform it to the class (see Chapter 11 for a detailed description of this reading activity)—as an instructional approach to increase fluency in children. After a struggling reader has practiced the text to be performed, use the NAEP fluency scale to assess fluency. Compare this with a text that the reader has not read before. Make sure both texts are at the student's appropriate reading level. This will give you an idea of the student's potential for fluency with repeated readings.

Teachers' VOICES   Assessing Fluency Problems

Nonfluent readers fall behind quickly and need to be identified early on. I measure my students' levels of fluency through the use of both informal and formal assessments methods. To different degrees, either type of assessment can provide me with the information I need to properly identify students for supplemental instruction and assignments. Regardless of assessment method, it is critical that I assess my students often and on a recurring basis. The most informal type of assessment is simply listening to students read aloud at their independent reading level while the teacher records observations regarding word recognition errors, rate of reading, and use of expression. Comprehension is measured by asking the student to respond to several questions about the passage. A formal fluency assessment method is a timed reading of a grade level passage. Through this type of assessment, teachers can evaluate both speed and accuracy by examining the student's oral reading rate. At the end of the time period, typically one minute, reading fluency can be measured by calculating the total number of words read, minus the number of errors, to derive words correct per minute fluency score.

—Kristin Crisafi, First Grade Reading Recovery Teacher

Reading Comprehension

Assessment of reading comprehension is probably the most frequently assessed literacy skill in today's classrooms. Comprehension requires the reader to apply many different types of strategies—from prediction to inference to self-monitoring—and it is sometimes difficult to assess which strategy is being used effectively by the reader. For the most part, assessments of comprehension tend to be more global in nature, and they try to ascertain the extent to which the text material being read is understood.

The most common reading comprehension assessment asks a child to read a passage of text that is leveled appropriately for him or her, and then asking some explicit, detailed questions about the content of the text. Some questions may ask the child to recall factual material, while others require that the child infer information that was implied by the text. It is important that teachers construct many different types of questions that go beyond recalling factual material to assess whether the student fully comprehends the deeper meaning of the text, such as drawing conclusions, inferring meanings that are not explicitly stated, and relating the information to one's own experiences.

Another way to assess comprehension is by having the child retell the story in his or her own words. **Retelling** is when the student reconstructs the whole story in sequence. The teacher then evaluates the student's understanding of the story by analyzing whether the retelling included the story's basic elements: the main character(s), the setting, the problem, the solution, and the ending. The teacher also evaluates whether the retelling is a cohesive and sequential summary of the text (Hansen, 2004). Sometimes, the retelling is tape-recorded or transcribed to assist in analysis and evaluation.

Retelling may be unaided (the student reconstructs the story without any prompting) or it can be aided (the teacher uses questions to probe the reader's understanding). The teacher may ask specific questions without giving the student information that has not already been mentioned. The questions below can be adapted and used as probes during retelling (Johns, 2005):

◆ Tell me more about what you have read.
◆ Tell me more about what happened.
◆ Tell me more about the people in the story.
◆ Tell me more about where this happened.

Although retelling is a viable option to assess comprehension, the information gained from retelling may not be valid. Retelling is not an easy procedure for young children; it requires a great amount of teacher judgment to assess the level of comprehension of the student. There are generally no accepted criteria for judging student retellings of passages, and they place a heavy demand on the student's ability to retrieve and organize information in the passage, placing students with learning disabilities at a disadvantage (Johns, 2005). When children have been taught how to retell and have practiced it, their scores generally go up as they learn how to "perform" well (Fountas & Pinnell, 1996). However, if a teacher keeps these caveats in mind, retellings can provide useful information about how a reader approaches and comprehends text. See Figure 9–12 for a retelling checklist.

Many teachers informally assess comprehension by having a discussion with the child or with the whole class after a reading. Questioning after a read-aloud is an effective way to assess comprehension, especially when the questions probe for more information than just recall of facts. Many basal readers have review questions at the end of the selection, which teachers use as informal assessments of comprehension.

Reading comprehension can also be assessed more formally using the IRI. This reading assessment is administered individually, which is time-consuming for teachers, but it can show more details about children's comprehension strategies than group-administered tests. (The IRI is described in detail later in this chapter.)

Commercial software programs exist that assess reading comprehension, such as Accelerated Reader (Renaissance Software). Accelerated Reader is a popular program in schools for motivating students to read books and assessing their comprehension. Students choose a book from a specified list; after reading the book, they take a quiz on the computer and find out immediately if they have passed the comprehension test.

Courtesy of Becky Stovall

Retelling is one way to assess children's reading comprehension.

The system keeps track of the number of books students have read and the score on the quiz that they took to track their performance in comprehension. Reading comprehension assessments are the most common type of published reading test that is available.

Assessment Tip: After a child has read a text, take the passage away and ask, "What would be a good title for this story?" This will help the child focus on what the main idea of the story is and not become distracted by the details of the text. Then have the child retell the story to you. You may have to prompt struggling readers to continue with the retelling because they may know the sequence of the story but be reluctant to articulate it or stray from the main idea.

Concepts About Print

Experienced teachers will collect more information than the five essential skills listed above. Kindergarten and first grade teachers often assess children's emerging knowledge about concepts of print. As children mature, they start to engage in "play-reading" behavior, where they model the reading behaviors they see with siblings and other adults. Children who are developing healthy concepts about print flip through books from beginning to end, holding them right-side up, and they point to the text they are "reading" (even though they may be telling a story unrelated to the actual text). As they point, they may even demonstrate the understanding that text is read from top to bottom and from left to right, and they may point at the individual words in the passage (as opposed to pointing at random locations in the line) (SEDL, 2005).

Teachers can assess a child's concept of print by observing children at play and during "independent reading time." The teacher should note the following questions:

- Does the child know where the cover of the book is?
- Does the child hold the book right-side up?
- Does the child turn the pages appropriately?
- Does the child know that the message of the book is contained in the text?
- For older children, does the child have one-to-one correspondence between printed words and spoken words?
- Does the child know what a sentence is? What punctuation is?
- Can the child identify capital and lowercase letters?

A child's writing is a good way to reveal his or her understanding of the concepts of print. Very young children who have some experience with text "write" on a page starting at the top left corner, writing in parallel, horizontal lines from left to right and from the top of the page to the bottom of the page. The "words" the child forms are separated by spaces and may even contain letter-like symbols. Sometimes children even insert some attempts at punctuation into their creations (SEDL, 2005).

Assessment Tip: Hand a book, closed and facedown, to a child and ask him or her to open it and point to the words so that you can read them. Read each word as the child points. The child should move from word to word as you do. Ask older children to find uppercase and lowercase letters in the text and to describe the function of the punctuation (SEDL, 2005).

Children's Writing

Children do a great deal of writing in the classroom throughout the day in all subject areas, and it is important that teachers collect data on their progress in written communication. Teachers can concentrate on assessing three main areas of children's writing: (1) the process they use to write; (2) the product that they produce; and (3) the conventions of writing that they use—grammar, mechanics, and spelling (Cooper & Kiger, 2005).

In looking at the process of writing, the teacher should collect evidence from each stage of the writing process: prewriting, drafting, revising, editing, and postwriting or publishing. Children should have individual writing folders where teachers keep evidence of each stage of the process. Each piece of work should have the child's name on it and be clearly dated to show the progression of work throughout the writing process and evidence of growth throughout the year. The folder itself can be organized so that all prewriting techniques such as semantic maps, drawings, and outlines are stored in one compartment; all first drafts are stored in another compartment; and so on. There should also be a record kept of all conferences that were held with the teacher or a peer. If a checklist is used as part of the editing process, notes about revisions and feedback can be made on the checklist and stored in the folder with a clearly marked date. The teacher should then periodically check each child's folder and note which children are having troubles with specific steps of the process. For example, if a child is not writing clearly or organizing the paper in a logical way, the teacher might note that the prewriting stage is missing or not well developed, and start helping the child work on a semantic map before he or she begins writing. If a child is using a word processor to write the paper, a printed copy of the paper with the date on it can be placed in the folder before revisions are done; this will trace the development of the child's writing as the paper develops.

When assessing the product of writing, usually a writing checklist or rubric is used (for example, see Figure 8–7). One assessment technique that is being used widely, especially at the state and district levels, is to assess writing using holistic scoring. **Holistic scoring** of writing involves assigning a single score to a piece of writing based on the overall quality of both the content and mechanics (Cooper & Kiger, 2005). The score is usually based on a rubric that has been developed, and usually it is accompanied by **anchor papers** or sample responses that represent each score that an assessor can give. For example, if number 1 indicates the lowest score a paper can be given, an anchor paper will represent the sample writing of that type of paper. There will be an anchor paper representing each numeric score given so that the teacher can compare an individual student's paper to the anchor paper to ensure appropriate scoring. In this type of assessment, teachers are trained in applying the rubrics to ensure a high degree of **inter-rater reliability**—that is, that a given paper will be assigned the same score no matter who reads the paper. Holistic scoring is an excellent technique for assessing writing, but it does require training and careful development of a rubric of which the district is in agreement.

A teacher can assess many different types of writing products, one of the most common being a written report. Usually reports are the culmination of many different activities that were implemented over time. Two of the most common assigned reports are book reports and research reports. If a report is to be assessed, children need to know ahead of time what criteria will be used to assess the report. Either the teacher can develop a rubric with the class or hand it out as a guideline to follow while the students are writing the report. Checklists can also be used to ensure that the students are following the appropriate steps and that all components are handed in. Figure 9–4 shows a sample of a checklist that can be used to help organize a research report, and Figure 9–15 shows a rubric that can be used to assess a report.

Such writing activities as journals and learning logs are also used frequently in the classroom; however, it is not recommended that these be formally assessed by the teacher because that would undermine the purpose of these informal writings, which is to encourage children to write freely and creatively without fear of grades or negative feedback. Cooper and Kiger (2005) suggest that the teacher notes growth in students' writing through discussion or an informal questionnaire , and by having the students talk about their writing and what they like to write about.

Mechanics in writing can be assessed by using writing rubrics and checklists. Figure 9–5 shows a checklist that can be used to assess mechanics of writing. A teacher can develop an individual rubric just to assess such things as capitalization, punctuation, grammar, and sentence structure. The rubric can be used to help children concentrate on those skills being learned, and it can become a cumulative index of all the skills that the class has worked on throughout the year. A large poster of the skills listed on the rubric can be displayed in the classroom; children can use this list to improve their mechanics as they write.

Assessment Tip: When having children compose writing samples that will be formally assessed using a rubric, be sure that they are using the rubric/checklist during the entire process of writing. You should have them discuss each of the criteria during

FIGURE 9-4

Report Checklist

Name: _____   Date: _____

Title of Report: _____

My report includes the following:

_____ 1. An appropriate topic

_____ 2. Pictures, graphics, illustrations

_____ 3. Three or more references (at least two books)

_____ 4. Information synthesized into my own original words

_____ 5. A good introduction (one paragraph)

_____ 6. At least four supporting paragraphs

_____ 7. A good concluding paragraph

_____ 8. A rough draft showing revisions

_____ 9. A cover page with name, date, and title

_____ 10. A bibliography

_____ 11. A neat, finished copy that was handed in on time

(Adapted from Cooper, J. D., & Kiger, N. D. (2005). *Literacy assessment: Helping teachers plan instruction.* Boston: Houghton Mifflin Company.)

teacher conferences so that you are sure they understand what each factor means and they understand how to use it in their own writing. Then the assessment will come as no surprise to them, and they will know exactly what areas they need to improve.

Spelling

When assessing spelling, teachers usually implement weekly spelling lists with the end-of-the-week spelling test. Many schools use a published reading program that has its own spelling component built into it. Other schools use a separate spelling program that specifies the spelling words and provides the assessment tools. Many teachers organize their spelling lists by using a phonetic rule that is being taught (for example, spelling words for one week will belong to the *eat* word family and may include *beat, cheat, heat*) or by theme (for example, all words will relate to the theme "Saving Our Wetlands"). The "Instant Word List" is also used for assessment because this list specifies the 100 most frequently used words in English (see Figure 5–2).

Another way to assess spelling is to determine the child's developmental spelling stage by analyzing the type of mistakes the child is making in spelling words. Gentry and Gillet (1993) identify five stages of spelling development: precommunicative, semiphonetic, phonetic, transitional, and correct. These stages are described below:

◆ The *precommunicative stage* is used to describe spelling that cannot be read by others and is often called the babbling stage of spelling. This stage is characterized by random strings of symbols, shapes, and mock letters—characters that look like certain letters. Children do not yet know the alphabetic principle that letters represent sounds and letters may or may not follow a left-to-right progression. Usually, the writing includes a mix of both capital and lowercase letters.

◆ In the *semiphonetic* or prephonetic stage, evidence of the alphabetic principle is demonstrated. Spellers know that there are letters in words, but they spell words in an abbreviated way. The semiphonetic speller also illustrates a beginning

Writing Mechanics Checklist

FIGURE 9-5

Skill	Mastered	In Process	Not Mastered
Period			
End of sentence			
After a number in list (1. 2. 3.)			
After abbreviations (except states)			
After initials (J. S. C.)			
Question Mark			
After asking a question			
Exclamation Point			
After an exclamatory sentence			
Comma			
To separate a series of 3 or more items			
Between the name of a city and state			
Between the month and the year			
After the greeting of a letter			
After the closing of a letter			
To separate a quote from the speaker			
Before the conjunction (*and, or, but*) in a compound sentence			
Capital Letters			
At the beginning of a sentence			
For the beginning letter of names			
For the first letter of the names of cities, states, countries, and rivers			
For the titles of books			
For titles such as Mrs. and Mr.			
For the greeting in a letter			
Apostrophe			
In contractions			
To show possession			
Quotation Marks			
Before and after a direct quote			
Around the title of a poem, story, or TV program			

understanding of phonemes—the sounds that correspond to the graphemes, the written letters. Outsiders have difficulty reading the words at this stage. This stage is characterized by words that are represented by one, two, or sometimes three letters. Often, only consonants are used to spell a word, and letter names sometimes are used to spell a word, such as *r u d = are you deaf.* The child is becoming more sophisticated of the grapheme–phoneme connection or the letter–sound correspondence.

◆ In the *phonetic* stage, the spelling of words does not conform to our standard adult spellings, but the spelling is close and an outsider can interpret the written work. In this stage, students become aware of the idea that the sounds in words can be represented phonetically; therefore, they spell words the way they sound. This is the stage that represents invented spelling: spelling a word the way it sounds. The spelling is usually close enough that others can read it at this stage. Fluency in writing usually increases, and although students may memorize the spellings of certain words, they use the sounds or phonemes to guide their spelling. See Chapter 4 for a detailed discussion of invented spelling.

◆ The *transitional stage* is the point at which writers start to pay attention to what words look like, as well as to the sounds. This is the stage in which the writer realizes that words must be spelled not only on the basis of how they sound but also how they look. Writers at this stage start to use vowel sounds in every syllable and words look like "real" words. Common patterns start to appear, and sight words are spelled correctly. Words are represented by syllables, and writers learn about prefixes, suffixes, and root words.

◆ *Conventional* or *correct spelling* is the stage in which the writer is spelling 90 percent of the words in a written piece correctly. It is at this stage of spelling that formal instruction in spelling can begin. Writers have developed the ability to detect when a word does not look right and can correct its spelling. These spellers have developed an awareness of the English orthographic system and how it works. This knowledge of the English orthography develops over many years with exposure to reading and writing. They apply not only the sound system but also the visual and morphological components of words.

To assess the developmental spelling level that a student is on, Gentry and Gillet (1993) have developed a developmental spelling test that allows the teacher to use 10 words to determine an individual child's stage. Figure 9–6 presents the 10 words together with possible responses from the student representative of each spelling stage. A teacher can also collect a spelling sample at the beginning and end of the year. The teacher should make a list of the misspelled words and match them to the characteristics of each stage. The stage that has the greatest number of words representing it will be the child's current stage.

Assessment Tip: Giving students a "spelling test" on a list of 10 words may not be the most reliable way to assess how your students are progressing with spelling. Many students get nervous during a test, and sometimes a student will forget the word immediately after a test. A more reliable way to assess spelling is to note how children are using the selected words in their writing. It is beneficial to have the children use the words in a written passage, and then to calculate how many of the 10 words the student spelled correctly. The assessment should concentrate on the 10 spelling words, although the writing sample might yield other words that the child should be learning as well. This type of assessment allows the child to spell words in the context of a passage and not in isolation.

Figure 9–7 summarizes effective literacy assessments that classroom teachers should be using in their classroom literacy program. It is important that teachers

Student Spelling Responses Indicating Stage of Development

Word	Precommunicative	Semiphonetic	Phonetic	Transitional	Conventional
1. monster	random letters	MTR	MOSTR	MONSTUR	monster
2. united	random letters	U	UNITD	YOUNIGHTED	united
3. dress	random letters	JRS	JRAS	DRES	dress
4. bottom	random letters	BT	BODM	BOTTUM	bottom
5. hiked	random letters	H	HIKT	HICKED	hiked
6. human	random letters	UM	HUMN	HUMUM	human
7. eagle	random letters	EL	EGL	EGUL	eagle
8. closed	random letters	KD	KLOSD	CLOSSED	closed
9. bumped	random letters	B	BOPT	BUMPPED	bumped
10. type	random letters	TP	TIP	TIPE	type

(From Gentry, J. R. (May 1985). You can analyze developmental spelling and here's how to do it! *Teaching* K–8, 44–45, by permission.)

FIGURE 9-6

Summary of Effective Literacy Assessments

Literacy Area to Assess	Description	Informal Assessments	Instruments
ALPHABETIC PRINCIPLE	Children automatically associate the individual letter with its sound	Teacher asks child to: • Name letters that are shown • Pronounce letter sounds • Choose letters that have specific names and sounds	Checklists Observation instrument
PHONEMIC AWARENESS/ PHONOLOGICAL AWARENESS	Ability to hear, to identify, and to manipulate sounds in spoken language	Teacher asks child to: • Recognize words that rhyme in text • Identify a word that is different from several others • Segment syllables into phonemes • Blend phonemes into a word • Produce words that start with the same sound • Count the number of phonemes in a word • Add, delete, and move phonemes around in words	Checklists Observation instrument
ORAL READING FLUENCY	Fast, expressive reading that involves both rate of reading words and the phrasing that good readers use when reading out loud	Teacher administers: • Informal Reading Inventory (IRI) • Miscue Analysis • Running Record • Fluency Scale	IRI recording sheets Running record Fluency scale
VOCABULARY	Understanding the meaning of words	The emergent reader is asked to: • Provide a name for a picture • Rearrange a set of pictures to reflect logical sequence of events • Provide a word that best matches a definition or a picture The more mature reader is asked to: • Read, define, and use words in sentences • Take a vocabulary test • Define words before reading	Written sample Tests Observation instruments
COMPREHENSION	Ability to understand what has been read	The child is asked to: • Retell the text • Answer questions • Discuss • Take a test	Checklists Observation instruments Answers to comprehension questions Interest inventories

FIGURE 9-7

continued

Summary of Effective Literacy Assessments—cont'd

Literacy Area to Assess	Description	Informal Assessments	Instruments
CONCEPTS ABOUT PRINT	Knowledge about books and print that emerging readers demonstrate as they mature	The child is asked to: • Identify the cover of a book • Point to the top, bottom of a book • Identify a word • Identify a sentence • Identify capital and lowercase letters • "Write" across a page	Checklists Observation instruments Surveys
WRITING	Ability to write	Child is asked to: • Compose a writing sample • Answer questions about interest in writing	Writing samples Questionnaires Checklists Rubrics Holistic scoring
SPELLING	Ability to spell	Child is asked to: • Spell words for a weekly quiz • Give a writing sample and the teacher analyzes spelling mistakes	Quizzes Checklist of developmental spelling stages

FIGURE 9-7

become familiar with these assessments and apply them in a continuous and systematic way so that they can document student progress and achievement over the school year. Teachers should use the results of these assessments to inform classroom practices and instructional decisions. They should provide the necessary feedback to the students so that the students take ownership and pride over their own progress and hard work. Assessment should drive instruction, and teachers must make assessment an integral part of their classroom.

Assessment of Diverse Learners

The passage of the NCLB Act (2002) requires that all students in grades 3 through 8, including students with LD and ELLs, be tested every year in reading and math. If schools and districts are unable to demonstrate adequate yearly progress, which is typically measured as a percentage of students who pass standardized tests, corrective actions may be imposed and these schools are designated as "failing" schools. Sanctions include school-wide restructuring or requiring schools to provide students the option of transferring to another school.

This can have both positive and negative effects for students with LD and ELLs. Because high-stakes tests are meant to raise standards for student learning, diverse learners—together with all other students who are tested—may be challenged to meet higher levels of academic achievement than before. However, many tests are timed and require students to recall a great deal of information, which could be detrimental to struggling readers. In addition, most high-stakes tests are written and administered only in English, often leaving ELLs at a disadvantage and raising questions as to how the test results should be interpreted. With issues such as school funding, grade-level promotion, and graduation at stake, using standardized test scores as a basis for major decisions could potentially be detrimental to the population of diverse learners and to the schools that serve them (Coltrane, 2002).

A classroom teacher can implement different methods to fairly assess diverse learners and address their different learning styles and needs. One way is through test accommodations and modifications. **Test accommodations** are methods that provide access to, but do not change, a test. **Test modifications** are any changes or adaptations that are made to an assessment or test for a given student that will still provide a valid assessment of the student's achievement (Meese, 2001). Test accommodations and modifications may be necessary for students with LD and ELLs.

Students with Learning Disabilities

It may be necessary for the classroom teacher to make certain accommodations in the classroom for students with LD. Frequently, the student with LD knows the content but, because of reading and/or writing disabilities, is unable to respond appropriately and quickly enough to receive a passing score. If the classroom teacher is going to assess knowledge of content, or administer a standardized test, accommodations and modifications may be necessary.

According to Shaywitz (2003), accommodations represent the bridge that connects dyslexic readers to their strengths and allows them to reach their potential. By themselves, accommodations do not produce success, but rather are a catalyst for success. Test accommodations and modifications are among the more important support services a teacher can provide to students with LD.

Test modifications are now required on the Individualized Education Program (IEP) for students with special needs. An IEP describes the educational program that has been designed to meet that child's unique needs. Among other things, the IEP must state: (1) how the child is currently doing in school; (2) annual goals that the child can reasonably accomplish in a year; and (3) the special education and related services to be provided to the child, including any modifications or supports that will assist the child in the classroom (LD Online Newsletter, 2006).

According to Shaywitz (2003), *the most critical accommodation for the dyslexic reader is the provision of extra time.* Recent studies confirm a dyslexic reader's "physiologic" need for extra time. Research shows that good readers and dyslexic readers follow very different pathways to mature, fluent reading. Good readers' skills increase with age, and by the time they are in fourth grade, they no longer rely on context to identify words, and their reading becomes more accurate and automatic. In contrast, because of a phonological weakness, the dyslexic reader will eventually learn to read accurately, but it will take a lot longer. Dyslexics read more slowly and with great effort, struggling to recognize words automatically (automaticity). Consequently, if a dyslexic is to identify many of the words on the page, he must pause and rely on the context of the passage to obtain the word's meaning, which is a much slower and indirect process.

With this in mind, it becomes critical for students with LD to have more time when taking tests. This becomes especially important for high-stakes standardized tests that districts and states administer regularly now and upon which many significant decisions are based. This type of accommodation should become part of the planning process routinely held within each school, and not be conducted as a spur-of-the-moment decision (Shaywitz, 2003). It should be coordinated with the LD specialist, the child's parents, and all members of the child study team (CST).

There are ways in which teachers can implement instructional support for struggling readers that are excellent accommodations that benefit all students. For example, teachers can give frequent, short tests that alleviate "test anxiety" and assess students on a smaller amount of content, alleviating "cognitive overload" and reducing the amount to be retained for one test. Practice tests help review essential information and improve grades, thus reducing anxiety. In addition, informing students of the types of questions that will be on the test (multiple-choice, fill-in-the-blank, or essay questions) and providing a study guide helps all students prepare for tests (Meese, 2001).

Test accommodations that support the student while being assessed and that do not change the test are:

1. Provide extra time for the student.
2. Read important directions to the student.
3. Minimize distractions in the location that the test will take place.
4. Allow the student to take the test in a different location, where there are few distractions.
5. Assist the student in understanding writing prompts.
6. Provide several sessions for students to take longer assessments.
7. Provide a dictionary, an electronic speller, or both.
8. Allow the student to dictate responses to the teacher or proctor.

Test modifications that are effective and easy to implement yet still maintain academic integrity are (Meese, 2001):

1. Permit the student to tape-record answers to essay test questions.
2. Underline important directions and keywords on the student's test paper.
3. Allow the student to use a computer to write answers on the test, especially if the test contains essay responses.
4. Use multiple-choice items with fewer choices (that is, three responses instead of four or five).
5. Arrange matching items so that related information is grouped together with no more than five or six items in a group.
6. Allow the student to be assessed in an alternate format (that is, use a performance assessment or project instead of a test).

Special education teachers can collaborate with classroom teachers to provide support for students with LD during testing. By providing test accommodations and modifications, students with LD can be fairly assessed on their knowledge of content without having their reading or writing disability compromise their responses. With high-stakes testing becoming increasingly important in a student's schooling, starting with the primary grades and extending through college, it is important that appropriate support and guidance are given to all students so accurate and valid decisions can be made.

English Language Learners

Assessment plays a key role in every aspect of the educational program for ELLs. It identifies the students who need special programs, placing them into appropriate levels of service; it monitors their progress; it provides feedback on the programs that serve them; it decides when the student no longer needs special services; and it provides the classroom teacher with invaluable information on which to base instructional needs. Valid assessment of ELLs is problematic in that it is frequently difficult to determine the achievement level of students because of the language barrier. Another complication beyond the level of English proficiency is the student's proficiency in the native language. It is important to remember that ELLs may not necessarily perform better when assessed in their native language if most of their schooling has been in English. Although standardized tests are used to determine whether students have met state and local standards, classroom-based assessments are an integral part of the ELLs' instruction, helping teachers make instructional decisions and providing specific feedback to students that support their learning.

Many researchers support authentic performance-based assessments for ELLs (Hargett, 1998; Hurley & Tinajero, 2001; Mantero, 2002; Valdez Pierce, 2002). Students engage in tasks that are useful outside of the classroom and these tasks show what students know and can do without relying on proficiency in English. Examples of performance tasks include oral reports, skits, demonstrations, multimedia presentations, hands-on projects, and scientific experiments. Products, performances, and process-oriented assessments can all be used to generate rich information on ELLs' ability to apply knowledge and skills while meeting state and local standards (Valdez Pierce, 2001). Authentic performance-based assessments require a more cognitively demanding method of assessment that includes more discourse and reliance on emergent language processes by the students because they become engaged in collaboration with others, planning with the teacher and their peers, and interacting within a supportive environment (Mantero, 2002).

Teachers can also use the following methods to assess various literacy skills of ELLs:

Observing oral language: A teacher can assess students' command of oral language from what they observe on a continual basis in a variety of situations: class, discussions, playground interactions, and interactions with other students in class. Using the student oral language rubric (Figure 9–8), the teacher rates the student's language proficiency in five areas: listening comprehension, vocabulary, oral fluency, grammar, and pronunciation.

Writing samples: It is important that the teacher carefully assess the ELLs' proficiency in writing. A writing rubric should be used (see Chapter 8), and teachers should assess the writing frequently.

Dictation: Dictations should be used periodically to assess student reading and writing levels. Teachers can construct a dictation by taking a reading passage written at the students' instructional level and reading it once to the students all the way through. The students are instructed to listen at first, and then are asked to write what they hear. The teacher breaks the passage into short phrases, relying on natural phrasing and giving the students ample time to write each phrase. Finally, the teacher reads the whole passage through at a normal rate to let students double-check their work (Hargett, 1998). Dictation is an excellent diagnostic assessment used on an occasional basis.

Test accommodations and modifications: Frequently, ELLs need accommodations or modifications on tests as a method for assessment. ELLs often enter into our schooling system with a great amount of background knowledge in many different subjects, but are unable to adequately articulate it orally or through writing. Therefore, it is important that the classroom teacher carefully plan the best way to assess children on content knowledge and provide the support necessary to evaluate each child fairly.

Test accommodations and modifications recommended to assess ELLs are as follows (Coltrane, 2002):

1. *Lighten the language load of the test.* Provide glossaries, dictionaries, translated assessments, and other ways to help the ELL demonstrate proficiency without language interfering with the results.

2. *Alter the timing/scheduling.* Provide additional time to take the test or additional time for breaks during the test.

3. *Provide an alternate setting.* Have the test administered in another location that the student is familiar with to ensure that the ELL feels comfortable and at ease.

4. *Modify the presentation.* Have the test administrator repeat or explain test items and directions in the native language; have the test translated into the students' native language and administered by an English as a Second Language/bilingual administrator.

5. *Modify the response.* ELLs may respond to test items in their native language, or they may dictate their responses to a test administrator.

Student Oral Language Rubric

Student's Name:			Grade:	Date:

Language Observed:		Administered by (signature):		

	1	2	3	4	5
A. Comprehension	Has trouble understanding even simple conversation.	Has trouble following what is said. Can comprehend social conversation spoken slowly and with frequent repetitions.	Comprehends most of what is said at slower-than-normal speed with repetitions.	Comprehends nearly everything at normal speech; however occasional repetition may be necessary.	Comprehends everyday conversation and normal classroom discussions.
B. Fluency	Speech is halting, slow, and fragmentary so that conversation is difficult.	Speech is hesitant; often forced into silence by language limitations.	Speech in everyday conversation and classroom discussion frequently disrupted by the student's search for the correct manner of expression.	Speech in everyday conversation and classroom discussions generally fluent, with occasional lapses while the student searches for the correct manner of expression.	Speech is fluent in everyday conversation and classroom discussions, approximating that of a native speaker.
C. Vocabulary	Vocabulary limitations are extreme so that conversation is difficult.	Misuses many words; comprehension quite difficult.	Frequently uses wrong words; conversation somewhat limited because of inadequate vocabulary.	Occasionally uses inappropriate terms and/or must rephrase ideas because of lexical inadequacies.	Use of vocabulary and idioms approximate that of a native speaker.
D. Pronunciation	Pronunciation problems are severe so it is difficult to understand speech.	Difficult to understand due to pronunciation problems. Must frequently repeat in order to make him/herself understood.	Has difficulty with pronunciation, occasionally leading to misunderstanding.	Always intelligible, although the listener is conscious of a definite accent and occasional inappropriate intonation patterns.	Pronunciation and intonation approximate that of a native speaker.
E. Grammar	Errors in grammar and word order are severe, so it is difficult to understand speech.	Makes many grammar and word order errors. Often rephrases and/or restricts him/herself to basic patterns.	Makes frequent errors of grammar and word order that occasionally obscure meaning.	Occasionally makes grammatical and/or word order errors that do not obscure meaning.	Grammar and word order approximate that of a native speaker.

Adapted from the San Jose Unified School District, San Jose, California.

FIGURE 9-8

The most effective method to find out what students know is to ask them in the language they can best understand. In fact, the Improving America's Schools Act of 1994 (U.S. Department of Education, 1994) states that "limited English proficient students shall be assessed, to the extent practicable, in the language and form most likely to yield accurate and reliable information on what such students know and can do, to determine such students' mastery of skills in subjects other than English" (sec. 111(b)(3)(F)(iii)). In a national review of state assessment policies, Rivera and her colleagues found that the types of accommodations least frequently offered and most frequently prohibited were those that lighten the language load of the test for ELLs (Rivera, Stansfield, Scialdone, & Sharkey, 2000).

STRATEGIES FOR TEACHING DIVERSE STUDENTS

Assessment

1. Assess frequently and continuously throughout the day. Collect information and data on each student, and create a profile of that student's strengths and weaknesses.
2. Provide frequent and continuous feedback on all aspects of learning. This will help diverse learners build confidence and self-esteem while giving them the necessary support for continuous growth and development.
3. Make sure that the assessment is a fair and valid indicator of what the student knows and is able to do. The assessment should reflect what has been taught and practiced in the classroom.
4. Select appropriate test accommodations and modifications to meet the needs of the diverse learners.
5. Use authentic performance-based assessments as the primary way of assessing diverse learners.

6. Implement portfolio assessments as a means of demonstrating what the students can do in the classroom. Make sure that the artifacts or assignments collected in the portfolio incorporate both oral and written literacy exercises designed to promote both academic skills and English language development.
7. Teach diverse learners test-taking skills so that they can prepare for standardized tests.
8. Be sure to assess both receptive (one's ability to comprehend what another says) and expressive (one's ability to speak clearly) oral language skills for diverse learners.
9. When assessing content, focus on what the student knows, not how the student is expressing his or her ideas in writing.
10. Use multiple assessments to evaluate diverse students. Important decisions should not be based on one test score.

Assessment Tools in the Classroom

A teacher can use many different tools to assess the different areas of literacy. These tools can include IRIs, running records, portfolios, anecdotal records, checklists, questionnaires, observation forms, rubrics, and formal tests. Some of these can be purchased from commercial vendors, others can be accessed online, and still others can easily be developed by the teacher to meet specific class and student needs. Each tool is described briefly below.

Informal Reading Inventory

The IRI is an informal assessment that allows a teacher to determine a child's strengths and weaknesses in reading, thereby making appropriate decisions regarding classroom instruction. The IRI requires children to read from graded word lists and passages, and then answer comprehension questions to determine their reading levels. Often, the IRI is administered at the beginning of the year, then is followed up on later in the year with a second or third administration, especially for struggling readers. It is an excellent instrument to assess progress in oral reading fluency, reading comprehension, and silent reading.

One result of administering the IRI is that the teacher can determine the estimated reading level at which the child is functioning. The teacher needs to determine the following three levels for each child:

1. **Independent level:** The highest level of material that the child can read fluently and accurately, while requiring little or no instructional assistance from the teacher.
2. **Instructional level:** Material that the child can read with approximately 90 percent accuracy and, therefore, requiring limited instructional assistance from the teacher. This is the most important level for a teacher to determine, because this is the level at which instruction in the classroom should be targeted.

3. **Frustration level:** Material that the child cannot read fluently or with understanding, and material that is too difficult for the child to handle, even with instructional support. At this level, the child displays evident frustration with the material, showing stress, anxiety, and tension; reading is characterized by slow, word-by-word reading.

The IRI is a valuable tool that can be used by the classroom teacher in a number of ways, including:

◆ To select the appropriate level of texts and materials so that each child is reading material that is not too easy or too difficult

◆ To identify each child's instructional level so that appropriate learning opportunities can be designed and implemented for each child

◆ To confirm or redirect instructional decision making

◆ To help group students for instruction in vocabulary and reading comprehension activities

◆ To help place students into appropriate groups for guided reading

◆ To determine a student's fluency at various intervals in the school year

◆ To document changes in reading levels and reading ability at different intervals in the school year

◆ To identify struggling readers who may be working at their frustration level in certain texts and materials

◆ To provide ongoing, continuous assessment of each child's reading progress

Administration of the Informal Reading Inventory – Teachers can construct their own IRI using the material out of their own classroom, or they can purchase a commercial IRI. Whether teacher made or commercially purchased, an IRI is usually administered following the steps listed below.

First, the child reads **graded word lists** orally. These word lists are composed of words usually taken from the reading passages and are divided into grade levels. The student starts reading word lists comprising usually 20 words at a much lower grade level than the student is currently in to ensure that the child has success. As the child reads these words, the teacher makes notes of each word the child reads incorrectly. If the child does well on the word lists, he or she will go on to the next list, moving up grade levels until the words become so difficult that the child is struggling and showing signs of frustration. The teacher will then stop and, using this information, place the child in the appropriate level of a reading passage. The word lists are used only for placement in the reading passage levels because they indicate only how a child reads words in isolation, not how well the child can actually read passages. Many children are excellent word readers but are poor comprehenders; thus, no real generalization can be made regarding reading the graded word lists.

Second, the child starts to read the **graded reading passages.** These passages have been leveled according to grade level and increase in difficulty as they go up in grades; they are usually approximately 100 words in length. The teacher will have a copy of the reading passage, and as the child reads, the teacher will conduct a miscue analysis. A **miscue analysis** is where the teacher notes each **miscue,** or mistake, that the child makes when reading the passage. Miscues include such errors as substitutions (whereby one word is substituted for another), omissions (whereby a word is omitted), insertions (whereby the reader inserts a new word into the sentence), repetition (whereby the reader repeats a word or phrase), and reversal (whereby the reader reverses two words in their order while reading). As the teacher notes the child's miscues during oral reading, specific notations for each miscue are recorded on the teacher's copy so that the teacher can go back later and analyze the type of miscues the child is making and provide necessary instruction to help the child. Figure 9–9 provides a list of the different types of miscues and the specific markings for each. These marked miscue notations help the teacher observe the child's strengths and weaknesses in word recognition, phonic strategies, and overall fluency.

Types of Miscues and Their Corresponding Markings*

How to Code Miscues:

Example

Omission: Circle the omitted word.

Jackie was excited about (playing) the drums.

Insertion: Write the inserted word or words above the sentence with a carrot mark.

She knew that she wanted to be in a band *loud* someday and play rock and roll music.

Substitution: Write the substituted word above the actual text.

She practiced different *exciting* exercises every day.

Mispronunciation: This results in a nonsense word. Write the mispronounced word above the actual text.

Jackie became very *adop* adept at playing before long.

Aided Word: Draw a line through the word that is pronounced for the student. Pronouncing the word for the student should be used as little as possible. Try not to pronounce the words for the student.

A few acquaintances from school asked her if she would like to join a band.

Repetitions: Put a line under the repeated word or words. Record only if two or more words are repeated. Repetitions can interfere with fluency and cause the student to lose comprehension.

Jackie was thrilled to be part of a band.

Reversal: If two words or letters have been reversed, use a curved line to show that they have been reversed.

She knew that the band would work hard.

The following miscues are to be marked but not always added into the final count.

Self-correction: If a student self-corrects, write SC above the word. If a reader is constantly self-correcting, it may interfere with fluency, but it also means that the reader is self-monitoring for comprehension.

The band was *composed SC* comprised of two boys and two girls.

Hesitation: If a student hesitates after words, it interferes with fluency and comprehension. If the hesitation is longer than 7 seconds, the examiner should pronounce the word and consider it an aided word. Put a / at the end of the word or lines where the hesitation occurred.

Jackie and another band member/composed original music and wrote the/lyrics.

Punctuation: If a student ignores punctuation, place an "x" over the punctuation mark. This miscue could interfere with comprehension and often means that the reader is not monitoring for meaning. If this miscue is prevalent, the examiner should count it as a miscue in the final tally.

After a few months the band was ready to perform. The members decided to call themselves "The Misfits" and wore clothes that were either too big or too small.

*There are many different variations on how to code miscues. Many books give different markings for miscues than what is presented here. The important point is to be consistent in how you mark so that you can recognize what type of miscue the reader made during an informal reading inventory or running record. The purpose of coding miscues is to obtain a full picture of how the reader interacted with text so that you can plan for instruction that meets the specific needs of each reader.

FIGURE 9-9

Third, after the child finishes reading each graded passage, the teacher asks the child comprehension questions to determine the child's degree of understanding. Usually, the questions are coded according to type of question: recall of details, inference, vocabulary, drawing conclusions, and creativity. These questions help the teacher evaluate the child's comprehension strategies. The teacher might also ask the child to retell the story in his or her own words instead of, or in addition to, the comprehension questions.

Fourth, based on the child's combined score on the oral reading (which determines the child's level of word identification) and the comprehension questions (which determines the child's level of comprehension), the teacher will move the child up to the next hardest level of reading passage. If the child has reached frustration on either oral reading (as evidenced by having 10 or more miscues out of 100 words) or comprehension questions (by missing more than 50 percent of the questions), the teacher will stop the test.

At the fifth step, the teacher can assess the reader's silent reading ability by giving the student a new reading passage that is again lower than the current grade level of the child. This time, the student is asked to read the passage silently, and then to answer comprehension questions. If the student can answer more than 80 percent of the questions correctly, the child moves up to successively harder passages until the frustration level is reached. Often in upper primary grades, students can read silently at a higher level than they can orally. In first and second grades, children do not usually know how to read silently or are just beginning to transition into silent reading, and thus this part of the assessment is not suggested. In upper primary grades, silent reading is an important skill that all children need to master, and this part of the assessment may yield invaluable information, especially if it is timed, because rate becomes an extremely important factor in successful silent reading of text.

An extra sixth step can be added for ELLs and for children with LD: administering the IRI to obtain the capacity level (sometimes called listening level). This level is used when a teacher feels that the student's capacity for understanding material that is read to him or her is higher than the child's ability to read the material aloud. In this case, the teacher would read the graded passages to the student out loud and give the comprehension questions to the student. The student would progress to successively harder material until frustration is reached. This is an important assessment to help teachers determine how much material the child understands in the classroom, and it gives the teacher an opportunity to observe the discrepancy between the child's receptive language and reading abilities.

Analyzing the Data – Once all the above steps in administering the IRI are completed, the teacher analyzes the data and fills out various forms to help in the analysis. The teacher records how many miscues were made under each type of miscue listed and analyzes whether the student needs help in one specific area. For example, if a student had a preponderance of repetition miscues, the teacher would need to work with the student on fluency and confidence to reduce constant repetitions. If the student had a preponderance of substitutions, this might indicate that the student needs more phonic skills and word identification strategies.

The teacher should carefully analyze all of the child's miscues and try to determine whether there is a pattern that emerges in the child's oral reading. This should help the teacher design an instructional plan that will help the child become more proficient at recognizing unknown words and comprehending text.

Interpreting the Results – As the teacher analyzes the data, he or she needs to keep in mind the question, "Is this child reading on grade level?" The way to determine this is through the simple generalization that at the beginning of a school year, a child should be reading material at the instructional level that is at his or her own grade level. At the end of the school year, a child should be reading material at the independent level at his or her own grade level. Thus, a child in third grade should be reading third grade material at the instructional level in September; in May, the same student should be reading third grade material at the independent level. This is an important consideration for teachers to keep in mind as they interpret the findings from an IRI because it gives a baseline from which to develop a blueprint for instruction for each child and for the class as a whole.

In reviewing the data from an IRI, a teacher should consider the whole child and construct a diagnosis and prescription to meet individual needs. This means creating a list of each student's strengths and weaknesses, and formulating an instructional plan that builds on strengths and focuses on areas of improvement. In this way, the teacher can record a student's progress during the year and document growth and achievement through specific activities and interventions. If a student is an accelerated reader and is reading material three or four levels above grade level, he or she should also have a prescription that specifies how he or she will be accelerated and challenged to become a better reader. Ultimately, the IRI is an excellent tool for the classroom teacher to use as an ongoing, continuous assessment of fluency, word recognition, and reading comprehension.

Running Records

The **running record,** originally devised by Marie M. Clay (1993) as the basic assessment tool for her early intervention Reading Recovery Program, is used as the basic guided reading assessment tool. The running record is fast becoming a popular assessment tool, used by most balanced reading primary teachers. Running records provide a systematic way to observe and monitor individual student reading behavior by recording and collecting pertinent data and analyzing these data to make strategic instructional decisions. According to Clay (1993), the running record is more than an assessment instrument used to collect and analyze data: it is integral to teaching, in that it sharpens the teacher's observation skills and gives a deeper insight and understanding into the reading process. While the child is reading a familiar text, the teacher records patterns of reading behaviors, stressing how the child uses strategies of self-monitoring, searching for cues, and self-correcting. The teacher also observes and records how the child uses sources of information, which, according to Clay's analysis, are related to the three cue systems: graphophonic (grapheme–phoneme), syntax (grammar and sentence structure), and semantic (meaning). In other words, children who are good readers develop an internal system that enables them to self-monitor their reading to confirm that what they are reading makes sense, sounds right, and looks right. The running record is an assessment tool that helps teachers identify how a child is using these sources of information, and that will, ultimately, determine his or her future reading growth (Fountas & Pinnell, 1996).

The running record, like a miscue analysis, is based on noting and analyzing samples of individual students' reading errors during oral reading. The teacher listens to the child's oral reading, keeping a running record of each word read correctly by use of a checkmark, or as Clay calls them, "ticks," and notes reading errors with a symbol or by noting the mistaken word. Coding a running record is done systematically, so that when a student's running records are forwarded to the next grade level, they can help inform that new classroom teacher or reading specialist. Figure 9–10 provides an example of a running record and how it is scored.

Anecdotal Records

An **anecdotal record** is a written accounts of events and behaviors the teacher has observed in the classroom (Airasian, 1997). Teachers' daily observations give them a wealth of information regarding their students' learning and achievement. For example, a second grade teacher observes that Sue mispronounces words from the -*aid* family during oral reading, Ed does not seem to be paying attention during shared literacy, and Sydney is not using punctuation correctly in her writing. Such daily observations have special evaluative significance in that they allow teachers to assess how students perform in many different situations and at many different times. They allow teachers to develop a profile of student learning that, in many ways, is more valid than a "one-shot" test or assessment. These observations should be written down on a daily basis and used as a supplement to support data obtained from other assessments. In some instances, anecdotal records may be the primary means of assessment for determining specific literacy outcomes, such as increasing the frequency and quality of using conversational English for an ELL.

Sample Text with Running Record Examples

Sample text read orally by a student to the teacher:

For animals that live in the north, winter can be hard. Some animals sleep through the winter, but others stay busy.

Running record recorded on lined notebook paper for a student reading orally to the teacher:

✓ | ✓ ✓ ✓ ✓ ✓ ✓ ✓ ✓ ✓
✓ | ✓ ✓ ✓ ✓ ✓ ✓ ✓
✓ ✓ ✓

Excellent reader. No problems. Move to more difficult text

In the above example, this student had no reading errors.

Running record for a different student reading orally the same text to the teacher:

Made many errors. Needs help on final blends (har**d**, nor**th**) and sight words. Move down to easier text.

In the above example, this student made many errors.

Key:

✓ = correct pronunciation   X = error

(Adapted from Flippo, R. F. (2003). *Assessing readers: Qualitative diagnosis and instruction.* Portsmouth, NH: Heinemann.)

FIGURE 9-10

Anecdotal records should be written down shortly after the event occurs. The descriptions should be recorded on separate cards, one for each pupil, or on separate pages in a notebook. A good anecdotal record will keep the objective description of an incident separate from the interpretation of the event or behavior. It is also helpful to have a separate space for recommendations and comments concerning the student's outcome that is being assessed.

A major advantage of using anecdotal records is that they depict actual behavior in natural classroom situations, and thereby contribute to the overall evaluation of students when used in conjunction with other assessment tools. Records of actual literacy events occurring in the classroom provide a valuable comprehensive picture of the child and enable teachers to determine the extent of change in the student's typical patterns of behavior (Linn & Miller, 2005). In addition, anecdotal records allow teachers to record events that normally cannot be captured in a formal assessment, such as a quiet student who speaks out for the first time or a student who starts interacting with other children in a positive manner.

Some of the disadvantages of anecdotal records are that they are time-consuming and subjective in nature. It is often difficult for teachers to constantly maintain quality records on a daily basis, and these records can be biased in the manner that they are written. Therefore, teachers need to take care that the records are written as objectively as possible. In addition, teachers need to specify exactly which literacy outcomes they wish to document; otherwise, they can be recording every incident and become overwhelmed.

Anecdotal records should be maintained for each student at least once per week as part of a teacher's formal observation of individual students. It is helpful for teachers to limit observations to just a few types of behaviors for each student and to use other forms of assessment to capture a complete picture of each child's growth and development.

Portfolios

A portfolio that contains samples of student work should be kept for each child in the class. The literacy portfolio is a collection of student exemplars or original student products that may include special projects, student writing, charts, lists, inventories, teacher notations, records, and even testing results. It provides opportunities for the student to share his or her work by showing progress and achievement; it also provides the student with the opportunity to reflect on a body of work that can be considered as evidence

Courtesy of Bill Lisenby

Anecdotal records are important tools for assessing children's literacy development in the classroom.

to be judged intermittently over several periods during the school year. The portfolio enables the child to collect exemplars over time as evidence of academic and creative accomplishments and is an excellent vehicle to teach reflection about personal growth. Portfolios can function as a valuable tool in self-evaluation (Glazer & Brown, 1993).

The child is encouraged to share his or her best work, in a collaborative way, with the teacher and, in some cases, with the parent or guardian. In this way, there are opportunities to share, discuss, and evaluate the portfolio contents retrospectively by reviewing evidence of growth from the beginning to the end of the school year. At the end of the year, the child, teacher, and parents or other family members can meet to discuss what should be forwarded to next year's teacher and what should be taken home.

An important part of implementing portfolios in the classroom is the teacher–student conference—this is when the evidence of progress that the student has attained to date is discussed. During regularly scheduled reading-portfolio conferences, the student and teacher can go over the strengths and weaknesses of certain samples contained in the portfolio and decide on needed changes to establish continued growth. This reading-portfolio conference enables the teacher to document the history of the child's development in a range of literacy areas such as reading fluency or persuasive writing, and it helps link assessment and teaching to learning (Searfoss, Readence, & Mallette, 2001).

Children should be part of the decision-making process as to what items to include in the portfolio. Students need to feel ownership over the development of the portfolio and be a real partner in the assessment of the work in it. The more opportunities that children have in making decisions regarding assessment, the more independent, responsible, and reflective they become.

Some possible items, samples, and data collections that a teacher and student might consider including in a portfolio are:

- Student-written narratives
- Student nonfiction writings
- Self-reflections
- Student creative poetry
- Student-created children's books
- Project inquiries
- Teacher graphic organizers (completed by student)
- Visual tools created by the student for a project
- Student journals entries
- Teacher journal entries
- Student interest inventories
- Running records
- Samples of oral readings with miscues, retelling, and questions
- Daily student work packets
- Reading and book lists
- Results from IRIs

The above list is a basic sampling of the types of portfolio documents and student work that is accumulated over time. Therefore, this should not be thought of as an exhaustive, comprehensive list, but rather a representative sampling of possible student/teacher evidence used to determine student growth.

It is important that a teacher use a systematic set of guidelines when implementing the portfolio:

- Date all documents so that progress can be reviewed over time.
- Use two different types of portfolios: a **conference portfolio** to select and show the best work of the child during teacher/student/parent conferences and grade reviews, and a **working portfolio** to use by the child on a daily basis.

- Help children see the value of the portfolio so that it is seen as a positive supportive document rather than as a chore.

- Introduce the concept of portfolios by showing prototypes.

- Show children how to select their best work and how to place materials in the portfolio.

- Demonstrate how to use portfolios for conferences and grade reviews.

- Explain to the children when to weed out, when to review their working folder, and when and how to choose their best work for the conference folder.

- Set specific times, on a rotating basis, for meeting with children to review their portfolios (portfolio conferences or reading-portfolio conferences).

- Explain to the child how portfolios bridge communications between teachers and parents.

- Explain to parents the purpose and the process of using portfolios.

- Praise children for assuming the responsibility of collecting and reflecting on their work.

Implementing portfolios into the classroom can be a time-consuming and often overwhelming task, especially for new teachers. There is the problem of organizing the portfolios so that the teacher and students have easy access to them, yet they need to be kept secure so that private information is not shared with everyone. It is recommended that the working portfolio be kept within easy access to the students in the class and the conference portfolio be kept in a private, secure location. In addition, portfolios can take quite a bit of time to review and assess. Once the portfolios are set up, the teacher needs to periodically go through each child's portfolio carefully and determine progress over time, developing an instructional plan to benefit each child. It is recommended that teachers move slowly into this process so that they and the children feel comfortable with portfolio assessment.

Portfolios provide an excellent and valuable source of assessment data for the teacher, the parent, and the student. The process of collecting samples of work throughout the year can show the initial proficiency level of a child at the beginning of the year and how the child developed and progressed over time. They provide an authentic means of assessing each student by allowing a teacher to make instructional decisions based on multiple sources of data, and thereby develop a profile of each child over time.

Checklists, Questionnaires, and Observation Forms

Checklists are an excellent tool for quickly collecting data on a specific objective in the classroom. Some teachers prefer using checklists in combination with narrative and observational anecdotal records, for fear that they will miss important *kid watching* opportunities because they are too busy looking at and marking off the checklist. Routman (1994) suggests using checklists for the following literacy objectives:

- Check concepts about print.

- Check letters known and word knowledge.

- Check to see whether children are monitoring their own learning.

- Use as a proofreading tool before handing in written work.

- Check children's introduction and mastery of an inventory of skills, including initial and ending consonants, two- and three-letter consonant blends, phonograms, irregular vowels, homonyms, and compound words.

- Check students' use of comprehension strategies such as predicting, inferring, and summarizing.

There are a number of advantages to using developmental checklists in literacy. Student attitudes and behaviors are described so that teachers can use this information to help them monitor and structure the observations of their students' reading skills. Checklists identify key literacy areas that teachers must be aware of, and by using these checklists as guides, teachers will develop a clearer understanding of the reading process. The reading checklist, together with anecdotal records, helps teachers develop instructional goals and objectives for improving literacy instruction. Checklists also help simplify the process of identifying struggling readers who have specific needs, a necessary requirement for setting up guided reading groups. In fact, when combined with other sources of assessment information, checklists are one of the most effective assessment tools in the classroom. Figures 9–11 and 9–12 provide examples of checklists used in the classroom to assess different literacy skills.

Checklists also can be used for self-assessment by the teacher. If the teacher desires to institute a certain instructional strategy or to use a particular approach to reading, a checklist can give the teacher guidance and feedback by determining which features are being used successfully and which features need improvement. Because most checklists do not provide a gradient of responses from which to choose from, but require an absolute "yes" designated by a checkmark or "no" designated by the absence of a checkmark, checklists can be limited in the feedback they give. However, they do give the teacher feedback about areas that need improvement, whether it be the teacher's own instruction or the students' skills. Figure 9–13 presents an example of a checklist a teacher could use to determine whether her classroom is using differentiated instruction.

Questionnaires or surveys can help a teacher assess student attitudes toward a particular skill or activity that will be useful in determining an instructional plan. The questionnaire can find out how a child feels about reading, how often the child reads, if the child reads at home, if the child goes to the public library, and what the child's favorite activities are outside of school. This information can help determine whether

FIGURE 9-11

Checklist for Assessing Student Use of Internal Comprehension Strategies

Name:_____ Date:_____

_____ 1. Is the reader using meaning, structure, and visual information to confirm reading accurately?

_____ 2. Does the reader self-monitor by asking: Does this make sense? Does this sound right? Does this look right?

_____ 3. Is the child searching actively for information sources, such as meaning, visual information, or knowledge of sentence structure that will assist problem solving?

_____ 4. Does the child cross-check, by checking one cue against another by relating one source of information to another?

_____ 5. Does the child make attempts to reread when unsure?

_____ 6. Does the child show signs that he or she is actively monitoring by searching and making self-corrections when she misreads text?

_____ 7. Does the child rely on many kinds of information or cues?

_____ 8. Does the reader actively search for cues when coming to new words?

_____ 9. Is the reader reading fluently?

_____ 10. Does the reader reread the entire sentence when he or she is cross-checking?

_____ 11. Is the child showing signs of growth by self-monitoring, cross-checking, and self-correcting in reading for meaning?

Retelling Checklist

Name: _____ Date: _____

Text: _____

Indicate the degree to which the reader's retelling reflects comprehension of the text.

	Not At All		Somewhat		High Degree
The student's retelling:					
1. Included information that came directly from the text.	1	2	3	4	5
2. Included important content, concepts, and facts.	1	2	3	4	5
3. Mentioned main characters and their role in the text.	1	2	3	4	5
4. Included a coherent sequence of what happened.	1	2	3	4	5
5. Recounted the plot or main idea of the text.	1	2	3	4	5
6. Inferred the important theme, moral, or message.	1	2	3	4	5
7. Was succinct and to the point.	1	2	3	4	5
8. Reflected a good understanding about what the text was about.	1	2	3	4	5
9. Indicated the reader's ability to make connections with the text (background knowledge, personal feelings, etc.)	1	2	3	4	5
10. Summarized the main points in a fluent and organized way.	1	2	3	4	5

Additional comments:

Total Points: _____

50 – 43 = high
42 – 36 = medium
35 – 0 = low

Interpretation of Retelling:

FIGURE 9-12

the child is motivated to read or write and what type of support the child has outside of the classroom. It is recommended that this type of survey be given at the beginning of the year for both reading and writing to help the teacher gauge the overall attitudes that the class has toward literacy activities and to help build on individual student's interests. It is also recommended that a questionnaire be given to a child before administering the IRI. The time spent asking the student questions will put the child at ease, relax the administrator, and help to establish a rapport between the child and the administrator. See Figure 8–4 for an example of a reading survey that is used to learn about a student's attitude and background toward reading.

FIGURE 9-13

Checklist of Authentic Assessment

Name: _____ Date: _____

Give yourself 1 point for each item you check off below. See how many points you accumulate after analyzing your classroom.

_____ 1. Do I focus my assessment on the most important outcomes in the curriculum?

_____ 2. Is assessment ongoing and diagnostic in my classroom (is it every day and is the information helpful to me in planning my lessons)?

_____ 3. Do I clearly explain to my students how I will assess them?

_____ 4. Do I clearly show my students the relationship between what they are learning in class and how they are being assessed?

_____ 5. Do I assess my students in many different ways so that decisions are not based on only one test or assessment?

_____ 6. Do I collect data continuously on each student and then analyze it to see where the student's strengths and weaknesses are?

_____ 7. Do my students do self-assessment on different activities?

_____ 8. Do I conference individually with my students at varying times during a unit to provide feedback and guidance?

_____ 9. Are my assessments performance-based and actual tasks that students would perform in the outside world?

_____ 10. Do I use multiple forms of assessment and make instructional decisions based upon the collection of data?

_____ Total points

Comments about my classroom:

Observation forms are similar to checklists in that they allow the teacher to assess the student in a natural, authentic manner during the regular classroom routine. They can give the classroom teacher valuable information regarding students' current and developing interests, motivation, strategies, and work habits. Numerous opportunities exist during the school day for the teacher to observe how individual children are performing. It is important that the teacher decide the purpose or objective for the observation, decide which time or assignment during the school day would be best, and choose one or two children to observe initially during the specified time. The teacher should keep careful notes on what he or she observed and write them down on a standard observation form so that the observation of each student is consistent. The teacher should write down anything that would be helpful in understanding the child, including developmental observations, strategy use, motivations, interactions with other children, and work habits (Flippo, 2003). These anecdotal notes are a powerful tool for collecting information on an ongoing basis during reading and writing. Figure 9–14 provides an example of an observation form that teachers can use in the classroom to observe literacy behaviors.

Rubrics

A **rubric** is a scoring tool that lists the criteria for a piece of work and specifies how students' work will be judged by using several levels of performance. For example, a rubric for a writing assignment might tell students that their work will be judged on the following criteria: *statement of purpose, organization, details, voice,* and *mechanics.* A good

Observation for Assessing Literacy Behaviors in 1st Grade

Circle the response that you believe is appropriate for the child. Write in comments below each item.

Student's Name: _____ Date: _____

		Rarely		Sometimes		Often
1.	The child is eager to read books during school hours. Comments:	1	2	3	4	5
2.	The child has self-selected his/her own book to read. Comments:	1	2	3	4	5
3.	The child settles down quickly to read the book on his/her own without any prompting. Comments:	1	2	3	4	5
4.	The child stays "on-task" and focuses on the book, "reading" it or looking at the pictures. Comments:	1	2	3	4	5
5.	The child asks to read more books. Comments:	1	2	3	4	5
6.	The child appears eager to choose his/her own books. Comments:	1	2	3	4	5
7.	The child likes to "write" on his/her own. Comments:	1	2	3	4	5
8.	The child attempts to "spell" words using invented spelling. Comments:	1	2	3	4	5
9.	The child requests paper and pencils to draw, write and "doodle" in his/her spare time. Comments:	1	2	3	4	5
10.	The child seems interested in the printed word. Comments:	1	2	3	4	5

Other comments regarding the child's literacy behaviors in the classroom:

FIGURE 9-14

rubric also describes levels of performance for each of the criteria, which are usually written as different ratings such as "Excellent," "Good," and "Needs Improvement," or as numerical scores such as 4, 3, 2, 1. Each level of performance provides descriptors to enable the teacher to assess students in a more reliable and unbiased way. These descriptors should explain specific examples of performances that the teacher should look for.

The rubric provides the child, parent, and teacher with objective criteria that can be mutually agreed on and set up at the start of a grading period. A rubric can be used like a contract to which both child and parent can agree (some teachers ask a parent and the child to sign the rubric), because its purpose is to objectify the evaluation of the child's completed project or products. Teachers can involve the students in the formation of the rubric as part of a collaborative grading process, which can be a valuable learning experience. Conferences can be held using the rubric to evaluate student strengths and weaknesses, to discuss differences in perceptions, and to identify areas where student improvement is needed based on mutually agreed on goals and expectations. Teachers need to be careful that in constructing the rubric, the levels of performance and criteria for success are specific enough that children are quite clear as to what is expected of them and they know exactly what they need to accomplish to obtain a certain grade.

Rubrics are used in various ways in the literacy classroom. They can be used to judge a more general type of performance such as an essay, speech, writing assignment, or oral report as forms of communication. These rubrics are used as general guidelines for the literacy process being taught and are used for an extended period to assess the process (see Figures 9–15, 9–16, and 9–17 for examples of these types of rubrics). Rubrics also can be used to judge a specific task or assignment and can be unique to that specific activity (see Figure 9–18 for an example of this type of rubric).

There are many websites that provide teachers with tools for constructing rubrics. These websites are helpful in laying out the rubric, but the teacher needs to carefully consider what the criteria are to assess the performance and what comprises the different levels of performance that students achieve. Three websites that can help a teacher construct a rubric are:

◆ RubiStar: http://rubistar.4teachers.org/index.php
◆ Teach-nology: http://www.teach-nology.com/web_tools/rubrics
◆ Kathy Schrock's Guide for Educators: http://school.discovery.com/schrockguide/assess.html

Rubric for a Written Report

	Beginning 1	Developing 2	Accomplished 3	Exemplary 4	Score
Topic	Totally unrelated to the assignment and not appropriate	Topic is somewhat related to the assignment and appropriate	Stated in the paper, relates fairly well to the assignment, and is appropriate	Clearly stated, relates directly to the assignment, and a very appropriate topic to choose	
Organization	Not organized, the events make no sense	Some organization; events jump around; start and end are unclear	Organized; events are somewhat jumpy	Good organization; events are logically ordered; sharp sense of beginning and end	
Quality of Information	Unable to find specific details	Details are somewhat sketchy	Some details are nonsupporting to the subject	Supporting details specific to subject	
Grammar & Spelling	Many grammar and/or spelling errors	More than two errors	Only one or two errors	All grammar and spelling are correct	
Interest Level	Needs descriptive words	Vocabulary is constant, details lack "color"	Vocabulary is varied; supporting details need work	Vocabulary varied; supporting details vivid	
Neatness	Illegible writing; loose pages	Legible writing; some ill-formed letters; print too small or too large; papers stapled together	Legible writing; well-formed characters; clean and neatly bound in a report cover; illustrations provided	Word processed or typed; clean and neatly bound in a report cover; illustrations provided	
Timeliness	Report handed in more than one week late	Up to one week late	Up to two days late	Report handed in on time	
				Total	

FIGURE 9-15

Collaboration Rubric

	1 Needs Improvement	2 Satisfactory Understanding	3 Good Understanding	5 Thorough Understanding
GROUP GOALS	Works toward group goals only when prompted	Works toward group goals with occasional prompting	Works toward group goals without prompting	Always works toward group goals consistently and actively
CONTRIBUTION TO GROUP	Works with group well only when prompted	Contributes to the group with occasional prompting	Contributes knowledge, skills, and opinions without prompting	Consistently and actively contributes knowledge, skills, and opinions
SENSITIVITY TO OTHERS	Needs reminders to be sensitive to team members	Shows sensitivity to others with occasional prompting	Shows sensitivity to feelings of others	Consistently shows sensitivity to feelings of others
INDIVIDUAL ROLE IN TEAM	Does not assume responsibility for role in the group	Assumes role in the group with occasional prompting	Assumes role in the group and fulfills all responsibilities	Willingly and enthusiastically assumes all responsibilities for role in the group
GROUP BEHAVIOR	Does not take an active role in supporting team members	Occasionally makes comments to support a team member	Supports team members with helpful comments, and is open to each member's ideas and comments	Actively supports all team members throughout the project and willingly accepts each member's ideas and comments
TEAMWORK	Participates in working together as a team and making changes when prompted and encouraged	Participates in working together and making changes when occasionally prompted	Willingly participates in working together as a team and helps make identified changes	Actively helps the group work together as a team and identifies necessary changes to make the project a success

FIGURE 9-16

Formal Tests

Formal tests will continue to have a major impact on the literacy classroom and the decisions that are made about our students. It is therefore important that teachers are aware of what tests can be used to assess literacy and how to prepare students to take formal tests. It is also important that teachers help families understand what the scores mean and how they will affect their child's educational future.

Evaluating Student Presentations

	1	2	3	4	Score
Organization	Audience cannot understand presentation because there is no sequence of information.	Audience has difficulty following presentation because student jumps around.	Student presents information in logical sequence that audience can follow.	Student presents information in logical, interesting sequence that audience can follow.	
Subject Knowledge	Student does not have grasp of information; student cannot answer questions about subject.	Student is uncomfortable with information and is able to answer only rudimentary questions.	Student is at ease with expected answers to all questions, but fails to elaborate.	Student demonstrates full knowledge (more than required) by answering all class questions with explanations and elaboration.	
Graphics	Student uses superfluous graphics or no graphics.	Student occasionally uses graphics that rarely support text and presentation.	Student's graphics relate to text and presentation.	Student's graphics explain and reinforce screen text and presentation.	
Mechanics	Student's presentation has four or more spelling errors and/or grammatical errors.	Student's presentation has three misspellings and/or grammatical errors.	Student's presentation has no more than two misspellings and/or grammatical errors.	Student's presentation has no misspellings or grammatical errors.	
Eye Contact	Student reads all of report with no eye contact.	Student occasionally uses eye contact, but still reads most of report.	Student maintains eye contact most of the time but frequently returns to notes.	Student maintains eye contact with audience, seldom returning to notes.	
Delivery	Student mumbles, incorrectly pronounces terms, and speaks too quietly for students in the back of class to hear.	Student's voice is low. Student incorrectly pronounces terms. Audience members have difficulty hearing presentation.	Student's voice is clear. Student pronounces most words correctly. Most audience members can hear presentation.	Student uses a clear voice and correct, precise pronunciation of terms so that all audience members can hear presentation.	
				Total Points:	

FIGURE 9-17

With states now mandated to institute the Reading First program, different formal assessments have been developed to ensure that children be assessed annually so districts can identify at-risk children and implement intervention programs. Formal assessments that states use to assess reading skills to qualify for the Reading First program are:

◆ The TPRI (Texas Primary Reading Inventory) developed by the Texas Education Agency and revised by the University of Texas (http://www.tpri.org/)

◆ Tejas LEE to assess reading skills of children whose primary language is Spanish, developed by the Texas Education Agency and revised by the University of Texas (http://www.tpri.org/)

◆ PALS (Phonological Awareness Literacy Screening) developed by the University of Virginia (http://pals.virginia.edu/)

◆ DIBELS (Dynamic Indicators of Basic Early Literacy Skills) developed by the University of Oregon (https://dibels.uoregon.edu/)

Task-specific Rubric

Your town has decided to hold a campaign to clean up the local river. They have enlisted the fourth grade class to create brochures to pass out to other students on ways that they can help in this effort. The brochure must contain specific problems that affect the river and clear-cut steps as to what students can do to help. The brochure should also mention books that students can read to find out more about cleaning up the environment and having a clean river nearby. Your team will work together to create a brochure. It will be presented to a group of judges made up of parents, teachers, and local businesspeople who will use the rubric below to choose the winning brochure.

	Novice	Apprentice	Practitioner	Expert
SPECIFIC PROBLEMS OF THE RIVER	The brochure mentions a few problems with the river and briefly explains them with no research to support the reasons.	The brochure mentions 3-4 problems and contains brief reasons why these are important to solve.	The brochure mentions at least 4 problems and contains reasons why these are important to solve. Some are supported by research.	The brochure mentions 4-5 problems and contains detailed reasons why these are important to solve. Each problem is supported by research.
STEPS TO HELP THE RIVER	The brochure mentions some steps that students can take to help clean the river. They might not be directly related to the problems mentioned in the brochure.	The brochure mentions 3-4 steps that students can take to help clean the river. Each step is explained.	The brochure mentions at least 4 steps that students can take to help clean the river. Each step is explained in detail and makes sense.	For each problem mentioned, the brochure lists specific ways that students can help clean the river. Each step is well thought out, explained in detail, and easy to accomplish.
BOOKS TO READ	The brochure mentions 1 or 2 books that students can read to learn more about the environment.	The brochure mentions 1-2 books that students can read to learn more about the environment. A short summary is given of each.	The brochure mentions 2-3 books that students can read to learn more about the environment. The books are well chosen and a summary is given of each.	The brochure mentions at least 3-4 books that students can read to learn more about the environment. The books are well chosen, and students would enjoy reading them. They are summarized in detail.
WRITING MECHANICS	The writing style needs improvement and there are enough errors in spelling, grammar, and sentence structure to interfere with the flow of ideas.	The writing style is good. There are a few errors in spelling, grammar and/or sentence structure.	The writing style is very good. It is interesting to read. There are very few errors in spelling, grammar, or sentence structure.	The writing style is excellent. It is interesting to read and has its own "voice." There are no errors in spelling, grammar or sentence structure.
BROCHURE LAYOUT	The brochure is arranged in an unorganized way and is difficult to read. The layout uses some photos and graphics.	The brochure is put together in a pleasing way. Most of the content is organized. The layout uses some photos and graphics.	The brochure is put together in a professional-looking way. Most of the content is organized in an easy-to-read format. The layout is eye-catching with use of photos and graphics.	The brochure is put together in a very professional-looking way. All content is organized in an easy-to-read format. Headings are used. The layout is eye-catching with use of photos and graphics.

FIGURE 9-18

Using Technology to Support Assessment

Computer Adaptive Testing

Technology is greatly impacting the field of assessment and drastically changing the way in which tests are constructed. In the traditional paper-and-pencil tests, all students answer the same questions, which wastes students' time because they give students a large number of items that are either too easy or too difficult. As a result, the tests give little information about the particular level of ability of each student. With recent advancements in measurement theory and the increased availability of microcomputers in schools, the practice of using these tests may change. Computerized tests are starting to replace paper-and-pencil tests in many instances.

With computerized tests, each student's ability level can be estimated during the testing process, and items can be tailored to this estimate of ability. Consequently, students can take different versions of the same test. These tests are called **computerized adaptive tests (CATs).**

CATs work in the following way: Every student starts the assessment by answering an item of medium difficulty; if the student answers correctly, then he or she would receive a more difficult item; if the student does not answer correctly, then he or she would move to a less difficult item. This process continues until the student has answered enough items to give him or her a score on the test scale or determine whether he or she has met a certain standard. CATs allow schools and districts to administer on-demand assessments to students and track their progress across a particular school year and throughout their academic careers. The data can be easily aggregated at the school and district levels to check accountability (Asp, 2000).

Computer technology will likely make assessment more flexible and allow assessments to be tailored to student and teacher needs. Although the computer adaptive testing can customize the assessment process to accommodate the needs of diverse learners, it is still considered to be a high-cost item for widespread use.

Many commercial companies are using CAT to deliver assessments. CAT is used to administer the GRE and GMAT, where the user will get one question at a time and each subsequent question depends on how the previous question was answered. Students can elect to take the SAT and PSAT using CAT, as well. Other companies such as Renaissance Software, which produces Accelerated Reading and Accelerated Writing, use adaptive branching in their assessment system.

Students find computer adaptive testing (CAT) to be motivating.

Courtesy of Bill Lisenby

Handheld Devices

Handheld devices, commonly called Personal Digital Assistants (PDAs), have become a common tool in the classroom to facilitate the collection of data and support assessment. The Palm, Blackberry, and smart phones such as the iPhone can all be used to access calendars, documents, presentations, photos, and videos. In addition, most of them can wirelessly connect to the Internet and have the capability of being a Global Positioning System (GPS). Cell phone technology has become similar to PDAs and much of technology is merging into small, portable, wireless "mini-computers" and "netbooks."

An increasing number of applications for PDAs have been developed for teachers and students in the classroom. Because they are inexpensive compared with laptop computers, many schools are finding that a mixture of desktop, laptop, and handheld devices can be used to meet a variety of educational needs. PDAs allow students to use their handheld as a graphing calculator, word processor, database, test prep tool, and reference resource.

Teachers' VOICES   Using Technology in Literacy Assessment

My district uses an adaptive branching assessment system known as STAR Early Literacy (Renaissance, 2002; http://www.renlearn.com). I really like this program because it customizes a literacy test to meet each of my student's needs. This computer software is capable of assessing several literacy skills of a group of children during a 25-minute time frame, and it provides timely feedback to me with a diagnostic report. STAR Early Literacy provides specific diagnostic information in several literacy areas, including:

· Graphophonemic knowledge

· Phonemic awareness

· Phonics

· Comprehension

· Structural analysis

· Vocabulary

Each test question begins with dictated instructions, using a digitized audio recording, and is presented in a graphical format. Some of the important diagnostic features that accommodate the needs of all my children are:

· Assessment in early literacy skills preK through grade 3

· Identification of skills where students need additional practice or instruction

· Provision of individual and classroom diagnostic measures

· Provision of timely, accurate information to plan instruction and intervention

· Help monitor individual student progress based on each child's specific literacy needs

—*Melissa Begley, First Grade Teacher*

In the area of assessment, teachers are using handheld devices for record keeping, scheduling, and other administrative applications. An example of this is, during the 2004–2005 school year, the Chicago Public Schools' Office of Technology Services eLearning (OTS eLearning) and the Office of Literacy began collaborating to administer early literacy screening and diagnostic assessments using PDAs and a web-based data management tool. The project goal was to streamline assessments so teachers can make data-driven decisions to improve instruction and enhance student achievement. The assessment tools used were: DIBELS, TPRI, and Tejas Lee (National Educational Technology Plan, 2004).

Wireless Generation (http://www.wirelessgeneration.com/) has developed an online assessment process using a handheld device that facilitates administration of the DIBELS assessment test. Class lists are entered into the handheld devices and most of the test's scoring is done using these devices, which also provide an easy-to-use stop-watch for recording timed running records. All directions are on the device and teachers can write notes about the child's assessment during the test administration. The device will automatically calculate the number and type of miscues that the child made and his or her reading rate. When teachers synchronize their devices with a computer, their scores are tabulated automatically and they have access to tables and charts showing how their class has fared in comparison with other groups of students. This process has greatly reduced the amount of time teachers need to spend on the administration, scoring, and interpretation of results. Many states, including Florida and Indiana, have adopted this approach to literacy assessment.

Electronic Portfolios

The electronic portfolio **(e-portfolio)** is used in higher education and being instituted in K–12 schools. An e-portfolio is a collection of authentic and diverse evidence that is drawn from a larger archive representing what a student has learned over time, on which the student has reflected, and is designed for presentation to one or more audiences for a particular purpose (Cohen, 2005). The portfolio will involve a careful process of thinking, planning, reflecting, and organizing and will reflect pieces that the student chose for a specific reason from a larger body of stored work.

An e-portfolio allows students to choose which artifacts they can include in their portfolio collection and they facilitate reflective thinking. They also help students develop new literacies and become more technologically adept. When developed as a means of assessing students' development over time, an e-portfolio allows students to tell a story of their own personal growth and what they value as part of this process.

E-portfolios are gaining in popularity and are used by preservice teachers in a number of colleges. A number of school districts have begun using them as part of their tiered evaluation system for nontenured teachers, with the intent of creating authentic accountability measures that new teachers can use for self-evaluation and reflection to bolster their tenure chances. Some school districts are beginning to make strides in this area by converting student file-folder-crate portfolios into electronic-style portfolios that are readily accessible and easier to store and retrieve.

Issues and Concerns of Using Technology to Assess Students

Although there is a great deal of promise in assessment practices that include present and future of technological advances, there are realistic concerns and cautions that we as educators must continue to safeguard against (Asp, 2000):

- Technology is only a tool if students and teachers have access to it.
- Equity issues regarding fairness for individuals and schools will most assuredly arise.
- Computer assessments could be considered as biased if used with less computer-literate students.
- Districts whose test scores are ranked and judged in public and who lack the resources, training, and students to use computer technology may be unfairly judged.
- Computer-based technology assessments may begin to perform too many functions and not do any of them well enough.

Classroom assessment should be based on the collection of many forms of data throughout the entire year, so that teachers can make wise instructional decisions about their students. This could include collection of data from technological devices such as handheld devices, CATs, and e-portfolios, as well as from such simple tools as observation forms for "kid watching," checklists, running records, and rubrics. The current technology can help provide classroom teachers with immediate, ongoing assessment information to help determine when it is necessary to intervene with individual students.

We already have the assessment procedures; what we need now is the opportunity for teaching and technology to interface so that these possibilities can soon become realities for daily classroom use.

Implementing an Effective Classroom-Based Assessment System

Teachers need practice and time to implement an effective classroom-based assessment system. Some suggestions to teachers for implementing effective classroom literacy assessments are:

◆ Focus assessment on the most important outcomes in the curriculum. Determine the most important goals you have for each unit. Determine what evidence you need to collect and what instruments you will use to collect the evidence. Be sure to date everything that you collect.

◆ Be clear about the goals of instruction and make them explicit to the students. For example, if students will be reading a story and you are focusing on comprehension, discuss what strategies they will need to use to comprehend the text and model how to use these strategies. Both you and the students have a better chance of achieving your goals if you make clear to them the relationship between the strategies they are learning and the task they are completing.

◆ Make self-assessment a dependable, integral part of your classroom. Begin with nonacademic activities, such as judging how well the class is working in collaborative groups or discussing a favorite television show. This requires students to step back from their normal classroom routine to think reflectively. This type of self-assessment needs to develop over time and facilitates higher order thinking skills.

◆ Help students understand what good reading and good writing look like by providing them with examples, examining work, reviewing portfolios, and discussing criteria. For example, help the class develop criteria for a good research report or oral presentation, and then have students use the criteria to evaluate their work. Use criteria and scoring rubrics as part of your instruction to guide students in improving their performance, instead of using them just for grading.

◆ Schedule portfolio conferences with your students. Set up times when you meet with individual students to review their artifacts collected in their portfolios. By doing this weekly, you will be able to systematically track the growth of your students and ensure that students are keeping up. Use portfolios to celebrate accomplishments, as well as to identify needs. In addition, use this time to self-reflect on your own instruction by identifying goals and activities with which students need more help. This process will help with your grading: to save time you do not have to grade everything in the portfolio.

◆ Begin classroom assessment slowly. Start with those tasks with which you feel comfortable and confident in collecting evidence. As the year progresses it will get easier and you will develop a more thorough system to track students' progress. The time you and your students take to review classroom work and reflect on their performance is a valuable and worthwhile classroom activity. This will help you and your students learn about quality performance and exemplary work.

It is important that teachers implement a classroom-based assessment system that effectively uses data to inform instructional decisions within the classroom. Students should receive constant feedback about their performance and should know what criteria are being used to assess their performance. Effective assessment drives effective instruction and establishes a strong literacy program so that children can continuously improve their literacy skills. Using a variety of tools explained in this chapter, teachers will become more effective practitioners who use data wisely to help all children learn.

STRATEGY BOX

Using Assessment Data

Miss Chen was anxious to use assessment data wisely so that she could make good instructional decisions about her students' needs. Miss Chen used the following strategies in her class:

1. She started collecting information and data about each child's literacy skills at the beginning of the year so that she could base her decisions on a profile of each child's strengths and weaknesses.

2. She used assessment data to focus on one goal: to match each student with the appropriate level of reading material, and then have each student progress at his or her individual pace of learning, always trying to move her students to more challenging and difficult material.

3. She used assessment data to place students into guided reading groups, determine which reading material to give each student, develop mini-lessons that individual students needed, and develop an instructional program that would support each student in her class.

4. When necessary, she would provide accommodations for diverse learners so that she could accurately assess what their achievement level was and what they knew.

5. She was organized in how she collected and recorded data, setting up an individual folder for each student, so that when she met with parents or made recommendations to her reading specialist or principal, she had data to support her comments.

6. She used multiple assessment results and the collection of data on a continuous and systematic basis. She did not base instructional decisions on one test alone, but used many different types of assessments in literacy.

7. She made assessment a daily activity and built it into her total literacy program. Assessment was an integral part of her daily classroom routine.

Final Thoughts

Assessment plays a key role in the classroom, and a teacher needs to be knowledgeable about the type of data that can be collected on a daily basis to help make decisions. With the emphasis on state and national standards, it becomes mandatory that a teacher is accountable and has the data to back up decisions. The primary purpose of assessment is to make careful and wise decisions about instruction in the classroom. Assessment should be an ongoing, continuous process throughout the day, and teachers should collect data from multiple sources to build a profile of each child in order to meet individual needs.

EXPLORATION   Application of Concepts

Activities

1. In groups, discuss issues regarding the No Child Left Behind Act. Discuss the goals of the act based on the achievement gap and the controversies about high-stakes testing of all children. List the pros and cons of this act and write a short paragraph describing at least three implications for the classroom teacher since it was passed.

2. Develop an informal assessment tool such as a checklist, observation form, or questionnaire for two areas of literacy that need to be assessed and are listed in this chapter. Share your tools with the rest of the class.

3. Develop a rubric to assess a specific literacy task that accompanies a lesson plan. Use the *Literacy for Children in an Information Age* premium website (http://www.cengage.com/login) to explore tools offered on the Internet. The rubrics should list specific criteria for the task and have performance indicators. Have other candidates assess the rubrics and give feedback.

4. Administer an IRI to one elementary school student using a commercially available inventory. Write up a diagnosis and prescription based on the findings.

5. Research the use of handheld devices in the classroom to facilitate assessment. Present your information to the class.

   or

   Research computer adaptive testing. Have you ever taken a computer-adapted test? What was your experience? Did you like it? Discuss the pros and cons of this new advancement and how it can change assessment strategies.

HOME–SCHOOL CONNECTION   Making Sense of Assessment

Assessment and testing can be very confusing for parents and guardians, especially the high-stakes tests required by school districts. Parents and guardians often have little idea how these tests are given, how they are interpreted, and what the results might mean for their child's education. Teachers should communicate regularly with parents and guardians and help them understand the importance of these tests and interpret their results. Parents and guardians can help prepare their children by ensuring that they have sufficient sleep the night before the test, that there is a minimum of stress, and that a good breakfast is served the morning of the test. Children should know that they are supported no matter how they do on the test, and parents and guardians should know that they are an integral part of their children's educational process.

Teachers should inform parents and guardians about how they assess students on an ongoing basis in the classroom, as well. Being informed is a confidence-builder for the parents: they know that the teacher is monitoring their child's progress. Also, parents and guardians should be aware that assessment is much more than a standardized test score that is only administered annually. At parent–teacher conferences, the teacher can share the results of ongoing literacy assessments such as running records, IRI's, portfolios, writing samples, questionnaires and checklists.

Parents and guardians can also check on how their child's school is faring with regard to its standardized testing. All testing data is reported in the local newspapers and posted online. Each state is required to post school report cards, which contain demographic data, school profiles, and test results. The parents and guardians can either ask the school for the URL, or use a search engine to find their school's "report card."

10 APPROACHES AND STRATEGIES THAT PROMOTE LITERACY

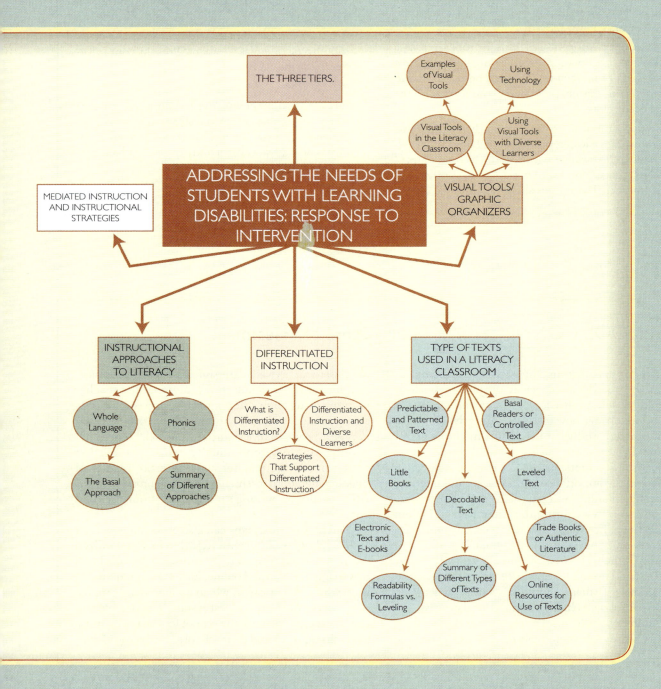

THE THREE TIERS.

Examples of Visual Tools

Using Technology

Visual Tools in the Literacy Classroom

Using Visual Tools with Diverse Learners

ADDRESSING THE NEEDS OF STUDENTS WITH LEARNING DISABILITIES: RESPONSE TO INTERVENTION

VISUAL TOOLS/ GRAPHIC ORGANIZERS

MEDIATED INSTRUCTION AND INSTRUCTIONAL STRATEGIES

INSTRUCTIONAL APPROACHES TO LITERACY

Whole Language

Phonics

The Basal Approach

Summary of Different Approaches

DIFFERENTIATED INSTRUCTION

What is Differentiated Instruction?

Differentiated Instruction and Diverse Learners

Strategies That Support Differentiated Instruction

TYPE OF TEXTS USED IN A LITERACY CLASSROOM

Predictable and Patterned Text

Basal Readers or Controlled Text

Little Books

Leveled Text

Decodable Text

Electronic Text and E-books

Trade Books or Authentic Literature

Readability Formulas vs. Leveling

Summary of Different Types of Texts

Online Resources for Use of Texts

International Reading Association Professional Standards Addressed in this Chapter:

IRA STANDARD 1: FOUNDATIONAL KNOWLEDGE

Candidates have knowledge of the foundations of reading and writing processes and instruction. Candidates:

1.1 Demonstrate knowledge of psychological, sociological, and linguistic foundations of reading and writing processes and instruction.

1.2 Demonstrate knowledge of reading research and histories of reading.

1.3 Demonstrate knowledge of language development and reading acquisition and the variations related to cultural and linguistic diversity.

1.4 Demonstrate knowledge of the major components of reading (phonemic awareness, word identification and phonics, vocabulary and background knowledge, fluency, comprehension strategies, and motivation) and how they are integrated in fluent reading.

IRA STANDARD 2: INSTRUCTIONAL STRATEGIES AND CURRICULUM MATERIAL

Candidates use a wide range of instructional practices, approaches, methods, and curriculum materials to support reading and writing instruction. Candidates:

2.1 Use instructional grouping options (individual, small-group, whole-class, and computer-based) as appropriate for accomplishing given purposes.

2.2. Use a wide range of instructional practices, approaches, and methods, including technology-based practices, for learners at differing stages of development and from differing cultural and linguistic backgrounds.

2.3 Use a wide range of curriculum materials in effective reading instruction for learners at different stages of reading and writing development and from different cultural and linguistic backgrounds.

IRA STANDARD 4: CREATING A LITERATE ENVIRONMENT

Candidates create a literate environment that fosters reading and writing by integrating foundational knowledge, use of instructional practices, approaches and methods, curriculum materials, and the appropriate use of assessments. Candidates:

4.1 Use students' interests, reading abilities, and backgrounds as foundations for the reading and writing program.

4.2 Use a large supply of books, technology-based information, and nonprint materials representing multiple levels, broad interests, and cultural and linguistic backgrounds.

4.3 Model reading and writing enthusiastically as valued lifelong activities.

4.4 Motivate learners to be lifelong readers.

Key Terms

literacy is a socially mediated process
mediated instruction
scaffolding
whole-language
systematic phonics instruction
basal readers
high-frequency words
predictable and patterned text
decodable text
trade books

Focus Questions

1. What is mediated instruction and why is it so important in the literacy classroom? Explain and give a concrete example of the zone of proximal development.

2. What are the characteristics, advantages, and disadvantages of each approach: (a) whole language, (b) phonics, (c) basal, (d) balanced literacy?

authentic literature

leveled text

e-book

visual tool

response to intervention (RTI)

discrepancy model

three-tier model

3. What are the characteristics and uses in the classroom for each type of text: (a) predictable and patterned text, (b) decodable text, (c) basal readers or controlled text, (d) little books, (e) trade books or authentic literature? What is leveled text, and what is the purpose of leveling texts?

4. What are visual tools and how can they be used in the classroom? How can visual tools benefit diverse learners?

5. What is response to intervention (RTI) and how can it address the needs of students with learning disabilities?

Welcome to Mr. O'Neil's Fourth Grade Class: Using Different Strategies to Support Literacy

Steve Gorton/Dorling Kindersley/Getty images

Mr. O'Neil is about to do a read-aloud of the book *Smoky Night* by Eve Bunting for his fourth grade class. He is using a trade book about the race riots in Los Angeles in the1990s to explore the theme the class is investigating: "What does tolerance mean and how can we promote it within our classroom?" *Smoky Night* is about a young boy who loses his cat one night during the riots and discovers that his neighbor's cat is also lost. It takes this one night of crisis and two lost cats to bring together neighbors and have them learn to appreciate each other even though they are from different cultures. Mr. O'Neil starts the reading lesson by asking the students to look at the pictures, which are collages made up of items that are depicted on each page; for example, one page displays a collage made from clear plastic used for covering clothes, while the text describes how a neighborhood cleaner's store is broken into and looted. Mr. O'Neil has the children look at the pictures and predict what the book will be about. He discusses what the title *Smoky Night* might mean. He writes their predictions on the board and proceeds to read the book with expression. At key points, he stops to point out the pictures and to ask key questions about the narrative elements, such as setting, characters, problem, action, and outcome. After the reading is finished, Mr. O'Neil has his class use a visual tool, a story map, to help emphasize the story line and theme of tolerance. The students work individually to fill in the story map, and after they have completed them, the students discuss the answers and hand in their story maps. Mr. O'Neil has copied the story map onto an easel pad, and as he goes over each student's response, he writes it on the large pad. Mr. O'Neil keeps emphasizing the theme of *tolerance* and how this book demonstrates what tolerance is. He then tries to have the students relate the book to their own lives and think about how tolerance can be demonstrated in this class.

This scenario shows different strategies that Mr. O'Neil uses to promote literacy in his classroom.

One strategy is the use of a read-aloud that is tied into the theme his class is exploring. The read-aloud is an effective strategy used by teachers who promote literature in the classroom. This scenario also shows how using fiction and nonfiction texts can be motivating to students. The scenario also shows the use of visual tools as a key strategy to support reading comprehension.

This chapter reviews various instructional approaches that promote literacy in the classroom. Throughout this book we have referenced different approaches that teachers historically have used to teach literacy: whole language, phonics, and the basal reader. The upcoming sections briefly review each of these approaches and discuss their strengths and limitations in teaching literacy in today's classrooms. The balanced approach to literacy is covered in-depth in Chapter 3 and throughout this book.

In addition, this chapter reviews different types of texts that can be used in a literacy classroom. Choosing the correct text for students is an important strategy to help the teacher meet the needs of the students and provide support for their literacy development. Different types of texts can support different students as they develop into fluent readers. A teacher has options when choosing a book that is best suited for a specific child, and the teacher should choose a text that will scaffold the child's reading strategies.

This chapter also introduces an important strategy for promoting literacy in the classroom: visual tools. It describes them, explains how they can support literacy development, and gives examples of different types that teachers can use.

Many of the strategies and approaches discussed in this chapter are based on the influential work of Lev Vygotsky (1978), whose theories led to the formation of mediated instruction. This theory is reviewed below because it is an important component of literacy instruction that beginning teachers should understand and know how to apply in the classroom.

Mediated Instruction and Instructional Strategies

Vygotsky (1978) is one of the most influential cognitive psychologists in recent time. His work has changed the way educators look at a child's development of language and concepts. He claimed that **literacy is a socially mediated process,** a process in which children learn language and literacy experiences through the process of interacting and sharing language with others. In Vygotsky's view of learning, literacy moves from social interaction to internalized independent activity (Combs, 1996), in which the child can take on the activity as an independent learner only after he or she has become familiar with it through the socially mediated experiences provided. Therefore, **mediated instruction** is based on the notion that children learn best through social interaction and sharing ideas, and that learning is mediated through this process. Vygotsky's notion of mediated instruction is quite different from what occurs in many classrooms—children sitting quietly at desks working independently with little social interaction. To Vygotsky, socially mediated instruction is an essential component of how children learn.

One of Vygotsky's most popular theories is the *zone of proximal development.* He described the zone of proximal development as being that zone encompassing the gap between the child's level of actual development and level of potential development. Children can demonstrate their zone of proximal development through problem-solving activities, which they can do either independently or with support provided by an adult through collaboration and feedback. Vygotsky believed that the child's optimal learning occurs when he is working in the zone of proximal development, and thereby engaged in an activity that is slightly too difficult to perform independently (his instructional level). The child, therefore, should be supported by an adult or capable peer who is providing the needed **scaffolding** (or support and guidance) so that the challenging

Courtesy of Guilherme Cunha

Teacher-provided mediated instruction helps support a student in her zone of proximal development.

task can be accomplished. Vygotsky believed that much of a child's learning in the zone of proximal development is socially mediated, and that interaction and shared social activities form the basis of effective instruction. Learning is a social matter, and interaction between student and teacher and between student and student is essential for a child to internalize concepts and thereby work independently.

The role of the teacher becomes essential when working in the zone of proximal development. The teacher must mediate or support the child's ability to perform various learning tasks through social interaction and cooperative guidance. The teacher's mediational role must be flexible, depending on the feedback received from the child while he or she is engaged in the problem-solving activity. If the child indicates a need for more support, then the teacher must provide it. If the child indicates the need for more independence, then the teacher must retreat and provide less mediation. The teacher's support can range from modeling the activity and giving explicit direction to providing only vague hints.

Mediated instruction becomes an important part of teaching reading. Literacy is very much a shared, social experience between readers. As such, younger readers need to develop the reading strategies that will allow them to derive meaning from the text. Teachers need to use mediated instruction when teaching these strategies. They need to consider each child's zone of proximal development, work within this zone, and provide the support, scaffolding, and guidance required of mediated learning so that their students become better readers.

Teachers' VOICES   Working in the Zone of Proximal Development

To teach effectively, teachers need to "meet the students where they are." Put another way, teachers need to establish the zone of proximal development for each student and find ways to build upward from the zone. Implementation of reading inventories and the creation and analysis of running records are keys to this building process.

I assessed two students whose reading performance was fairly low in comparison with their classmates. I met individually with them three times each to assess where their reading abilities were, with the hope of gaining further insight into making them into better readers. I gave each student three reading passages ranging from easy (grade 2) to hard (grade 4).

I used a duplicate passage on a separate page to make notations on their performance. In their reading of a passage at the second grade level, each of my two selected students self-corrected their one error. Both students had apparently used visual information in arriving at their initial error. Over the course of the six observations, I was able to gain important insight into two of the weaker readers in my classroom so I could teach them in their zone of proximal development.

—*Parker Winston, Fourth Grade Teacher*

The next section reviews different instructional approaches. As you read through them, it is important to keep in mind what role mediated instruction plays in each approach, and whether the approach supports readers' development of literacy through a shared, social context of learning.

Instructional Approaches to Literacy

Since the 1980s, the proper method for teaching children to read and write has been debated and divided into two powerful schools of thought: whole-language instruction and phonics-based or skills-based instruction. These so-called reading wars have driven educators into two warring camps. Fortunately, the debate has evolved, and instead of focusing on the "either/or" of the phonics versus whole-language approaches to teaching reading, it now centers on the essential components of a comprehensive, balanced reading program. This chapter reviews the basic components of these two instructional approaches, as well as other instructional approaches that should be included in a balanced literacy approach. These approaches were discussed in other chapters, while the intent of this chapter is to review the basic components of each approach so that you may see the big picture concerning how elements from each approach are incorporated into a comprehensive literacy program. It is important that the beginning teacher understand what comprises each approach so that the balanced literacy classroom reflects a combination of each, that is, a literature-rich approach with a phonics, skill-based approach.

Whole-Language Approach

Whole-language instruction is based on several sources of research: research demonstrating the social nature of the reading process such as the theories espoused by Vygotsky (see earlier); research in language acquisition of young children, which claims that acquiring language is a similar process to learning how to read and write; and research on how humans learn. This philosophy believes that learning is not passive but active, and that when learners are presented with whole, natural language (not unnatural language patterns such as "Run Dan Run. Nan can fan Dan," which is used in some reading programs), they will form concepts about written and oral language that will contribute to their overall literacy development.

In the United States, the advent of whole language can be traced to the mid-to-late 1970s when Kenneth Goodman and other educators developed interest in the development of literacy (Goodman, 1986). Many of the whole-language theories are derived from New Zealand and Australia, where whole language is known as "natural" learning. Whole-language instruction as we think of it today did not become widely known in the United States until the late 1980s and even in the early 1990s, when it became quite popular in many classrooms across the country and transformed literacy instruction into a more child-centered, flexible approach to teaching (Weaver, 1996).

In 1987, whole-language instruction was incorporated into California's reading framework and adopted throughout the state. Whole language became the accepted instructional approach that was used in many districts throughout the country. Unfortunately, many classrooms adopted its philosophy but did not implement it effectively. In 1994, California saw a steep decline in the reading test scores of its students on the National Assessment of Educational Progress (NAEP) assessment compared with test scores from two years earlier. This caused increased concern among educators and parents, and in 1995, the state superintendent of public instruction issued a report from the Reading Task Force that called for balance in the way reading is taught throughout the state. Since that report, school districts across the country have redesigned and implemented literacy programs that call for more balance and are more comprehensive in approach (Institute for Education Reform, 1996). In fact, whole-language instruction has fallen into disfavor with many educators who believe that its approach was too limited and did not effectively teach all children to read. Yet, whole language has had profound and positive effects on elementary literacy instruction since the early 1990s, and many whole-language practices should be incorporated into an elementary literacy program (Pressley, 1998).

Whole-language instruction stresses that children learn to read and write much in the same way they learn to speak—as a natural developmental process. Whole-language instruction centers on a top-down approach in which comprehension is stressed as the overall goal in reading. Students are immersed in reading quality literature and daily writing. During shared reading, children will concentrate on the whole text and draw meaning from the text first. Skills are not explicitly taught unless the teacher deems it necessary, and then skills are taught only within the context of authentic reading and writing, not in isolation. Whole-language classrooms are print-rich environments centered on providing time and opportunity for children to read rich and enjoyable literature, with the teacher providing feedback, guidance, and support along the way. This is a child-centered approach where the emphasis is on learning and using language in natural settings to communicate and share.

Whole language can be summarized in the following points (Goodman, 1986):

- Whole language focuses on meaning and on language itself, in authentic speech and literacy events.
- Whole language builds on the whole child learning whole language in whole literacy-rich environments.
- Learners are encouraged to take risks.
- Whole language emphasizes oral and written language and activities that are authentic, real, and enjoyable.
- Readers use strategies such as prediction, confirmation, self-correction, and self-monitoring to make sense of text.

As Goodman (1986) points out, whole language is ***not:***

- Isolating skill sequences
- Breaking up reading and writing into a series of skills or grades or objectives to be mastered
- Reading simple, controlled texts that have been formulated around phonic patterns
- Receiving scores on standardized tests or test of "subskills"
- Teaching reading or writing outside of its true application as a tool to accomplish everyday life goals

How does this transform into classroom instruction? What would a visitor to a whole-language classroom observe?

- A reading corner with a chair for the teacher, an easel to write on, a stand for big books, and a rug for children to sit on
- A teacher reading big books that are predictable and enjoyable for children to share

◆ A class engaged in frequent shared reading experiences through read-alouds, read-alongs, paired reading, and independent reading

◆ A class that is print-rich, with a large library of quality literature books, print materials from home, and writing corners

◆ A class of children that is engaged in reading and writing and speaking all day long

◆ A class where there are usually "themes" to guide the selection of books

◆ A class where there is constant assessment based on miscue analysis, running records, portfolios, writing samples, and hands-on projects

◆ Children using invented spelling in their writing if they are in the second grade or younger

◆ A class where children can explore many different topics and rotate to centers based on interest

◆ A noisy classroom where all children are engaged in learning, using language and enjoying shared literacy experiences

Although whole language is a student-centered, literature-based program that has brought many benefits to the elementary literacy classroom, it has lost favor during this politically charged, high-stakes testing climate, most notably because its advocates have claimed that skills instruction is not necessary, and that children will learn how to read by reading, reading, and more reading (Pressley, 1998). The philosophy has been beneficial to language arts instruction for encouraging the development of reading and writing competencies and motivating students to read. Many of the theorists advocating this approach (Goodman, 1986, 1996; Holdaway, 1979; Routman, 1988, 1991; Smith, 1973, 1985; Weaver, 1994) have greatly contributed to the field of literacy and brought great changes to the old methods of teaching reading through the Dick and Jane basal readers. The whole-language approach has transformed literacy instruction into a literature-rich curriculum where reading, writing, speaking, listening, and comprehending are all valued ways to communicate, stressing children's literature, the writing process, and inquiry learning.

Phonics Approach

Phonics instruction stresses the need for beginning readers to recognize individual words by associating each letter with its specific sound. In this approach, beginning readers need to learn the alphabetic system—the letter–sound correspondences and spelling patterns (National Reading Panel [NRP], 2000). Systematic phonics instruction is used to teach the acquisition of letter–sound correspondences explicitly through direct instruction and in a systematic way. Researchers (Adams, 1990; Chall, 1967; Cunningham, 2002; Foorman, Francis, Fletcher, Schatschneider, & Mehta, 1998; NRP, 2000; Pressley, 1998; Snow, Burns, & Griffin, 1998) claim that **systematic phonics instruction** makes a larger contribution to children's growth in reading than do those programs that provide little or no phonics instruction. Systematic phonics instruction in kindergarten and first grade is highly beneficial, and children at these developmental levels are developmentally ready to learn phonemic and phonics concepts (NRP, 2000). Research also supports that systematic phonics instruction is significantly more effective than nonphonics instruction in helping to prevent reading difficulties among at-risk students and remediate reading difficulties in children with learning disabilities (NRP, 2000).

Following is a listing of some of the many different approaches to teaching systematic phonics:

◆ *Analytic phonics*—sounds are taught within the context of whole words so that individual sounds are not pronounced in isolation to identify words. Once a word is identified, children analyze letter–sound relations and learn phonics rules and generalizations based on those words. Phonics is taught gradually over a longer period, and children are encouraged to read all types of text and write about all kinds of topics. Their reading and writing are not controlled by or limited to the sounds they have been taught.

◆ *Synthetic phonics*—sounds are taught first and children read words that contain those sounds. As more sounds are added, children are capable of reading more "decodable" words. For example, after children learn the short vowel sound for *a* and the consonant sounds *m, t,* and *b,* they can read the words *am, at, mat, tab, tam,* and *bam.* The children usually read only decodable text whose vocabulary is controlled by words that contain the sounds that have been taught. Children's writing is also limited to the words that contain the sounds they have already learned. Authentic literature is read aloud to the students, but the primary aim of reading instruction is to practice decoding (Cunningham, 2000).

◆ *Embedded phonics*—teachers present a word that contains the target spelling pattern and, by deleting the word's initial consonant or consonant cluster, directs attention to the spelling and sound of its remaining letter patterns or rime. By substituting different beginning sounds and spellings (or onsets), students are led to generalize the pattern to new words. Children read books that contain these patterns, and these spelling patterns are then practiced by the children in context through repeated readings of these books. This instruction is complemented with writing activities to reinforce the patterns being taught.

Research has shown that direct, systematic phonics programs are all significantly more effective than nonphonics programs, and that they do not appear to differ significantly from each other in their effectiveness, although more evidence is needed to substantiate these findings (NRP, 2000).

The phonics approach to teaching reading can be summarized in the following points:

◆ This is a skill-based approach in which careful and systematic attention is paid to teaching the alphabetic system—the letter–sound correspondences.

◆ Children need tools to be able to recognize an unknown word when they come across one while reading. Phonics provides them with the ability to break down a word into its component sounds in order to decode it.

◆ Children need multiple and varied opportunities to decode and spell words.

◆ There is no best way to teach phonics, but it must be taught explicitly and systematically in the primary grades, especially kindergarten and first grade.

◆ Children who engage in a variety of phonics activities and in daily reading and writing become better readers and writers.

◆ Phonic activities must stress transfer, because the only phonics knowledge that matters is what children actually do with that knowledge when they are reading and writing.

The Basal Approach

The basal approach is based on the purchase of comprehensive commercial packages that constitute the core reading programs in the majority of school districts throughout the United States. These reading programs generally include instructional manuals (the teacher's guide) for teachers with detailed lesson plans and activities for the whole school year and accompanying **basal readers** for students who have been graded to specific grade levels. In addition, the packages typically include supplementary material for the teacher and student, which often include such things as big books, games, workbooks, manipulatives for the students, assessment forms, puppets, wall charts, posters, audiotapes of songs, books on tape, and many other types of materials to provide a comprehensive reading program "in a box." Basal reading series are published by commercial publishing houses and are therefore sensitive to market needs and state adoption schedules. States such as California, Texas, and Florida, which conduct state adoptions, have great influence over the publishers' decisions about which objectives to emphasize in each new edition. Basal programs are revised and reissued approximately every two to five years; therefore, content, objectives, and philosophy may lag behind current instructional preferences and practices, although the programs do try to reflect current best practices and methodology being purported by educational researchers (Snow et al., 1998).

In using the basal approach in the classroom, teachers are limited to the accompanying readers as the basis for their reading program. The total class of students will be assigned to the same reader, although some grades may have as many as three different leveled readers per grade, usually for grouping students into low, medium, or high reading groups. The limitations of this system are self-evident. When you have a class of diverse children reading at many different levels, it becomes difficult to accommodate each child's needs with a limited selection of graded books to assign. This is especially detrimental to the accelerated students, who become bored with the basal reader very quickly, and the students with reading difficulties, who find the text is not at their level and feel increasingly frustrated. If a teacher moves a child up to the next grade level reader, there is the problem that the same level text will be repeated the following year as the student moves up a grade. If the teacher moves a student down to a lower reader, there is the problem that the student probably struggled through the same book the previous year. Currently, one of the more popular ways in which teachers are accommodating the range of student needs is to include many optional activities within a lesson and give students supplemental materials to read. Many of the teacher's guides outline plans that allow classroom time for individuals or small groups to work at their respective instructional levels.

The basal series reading texts are generally composed of different stories, poems, and short narratives. They are usually put together attractively with bright, colorful photographs and illustrations. Careful attention is given to the level that the text is written on; to ensure that the text is written at a certain grade level, original stories are often edited so that they have shorter sentences and smaller words (not as many syllables). In essence, these books become edited anthologies of different stories, many of them excerpted from award-winning literature. After each story or section, there are usually a series of questions and activities to assess comprehension. Usually, there will be an accompanying workbook to reinforce skills taught during the reading lesson.

One of the advantages to a basal approach is the care that the authors have taken in sequencing skills and strategies across the whole program. There is usually a scope and sequence chart located in the teacher's guide that lays out all of the skills and strategies to be covered for the year and for the duration of the whole series, usually preK through grade 8. This is helpful to teachers (especially new teachers) for daily lesson planning, as well as long-range units. The teacher's guide provides specific directions on what skills and strategies to emphasize during the year; it also provides background information about skills that were taught in previous years and what skills should be introduced and reinforced in upcoming years. In this sense, basal series are advantageous to teachers, especially beginning ones, for organization, planning, and classroom management because of its clarity of presentation and ability to lay out a progression of learning that will occur in the future. The teacher's guides are exceptionally thorough in spelling out what a lesson plan should encompass and in providing the background knowledge a teacher should know. Many beginning teachers find basal series to be extremely helpful in developing a comprehensive literacy program.

All of the above advantages, however, can prove to be a disadvantage for a more experienced teacher. A major concern of teachers who have used basal series for many years is that it inhibits creativity and initiative. The lesson plans are structured in the same format throughout the whole year, and teachers often find themselves becoming bored with the replication of procedures lesson after lesson. Everything is spelled out for the teacher; thus, a teacher is left little room to try new ideas and pursue other activities and topics. It is also difficult to meet the varied levels and needs of so many diverse children, including struggling readers, English language learners, and students with learning disabilities.

The basal approach to teaching reading can be summarized in the following points:

- This approach is based on the purchase, adoption, and implementation of a commercial reading series that usually spans from kindergarten through eighth grade.
- It is a comprehensive program that includes many different types of materials, from a teacher's guide to student readers to workbooks and assessment tests.
- The teacher's guide contains extensive and carefully developed lesson plans covering the whole year for the teacher to follow. The lesson plans follow the same format and emphasize a skills-based approach to reading.
- The basal approach ensures that skills are taught throughout the year and contains a scope and sequence chart outlining every skill covered for one year and for the whole series.
- This is probably the most popular approach that districts have implemented throughout the United States. More districts use a basal approach than any other reading approach (Snow et al., 1998).
- All children in a class are assigned the same reader, which is written on that grade level; however, in some grades, the teacher may have a choice of two or three readers for the class for placing students into low, medium, and high reading groups.

Summary of Different Approaches

The following chart summarizes the different approaches to literacy instruction described in this section:

Instructional Approach	Philosophy	Books Used	Activities	Advantages	Disadvantages	What Research Says
WHOLE LANGUAGE	Comprehension is primary goal; Child-centered; Focus on language development	Trade books; Authentic reading materials; Quality literature; Big books	Shared reading; Children read and write throughout day; hands-on activities to reinforce text	Children become motivated to read; Children are engaged in learning activities; Stress on comprehension and quality literature	Skills not directly taught; Children with reading problems can be "overlooked"	Children have more positive attitudes toward reading; not associated with higher performance in beginning reading; may enable students to sustain an interest in reading through the upper grades (Foorman, et al., 1998)

Instructional Approach	Philosophy	Books Used	Activities	Advantages	Disadvantages	What Research Says
PHONICS	Emphasis is on recognizing individual word Decoding is primary goal Need to know how to decode unknown word using alphabetic system	Decodable texts Text with controlled vocabulary	Skill-based work reinforcing alphabetic system Worksheets reinforcing skills Oral repetition and dictation of sounds and words Reading of controlled texts	Children learn the tools to unlock an unknown word Children learn skills needed to read Often essential for children with reading difficulties	Reading can be seen as a series of skills to be mastered Children can become bored with the repetition of skills Often reading becomes a chore and loses its fun and enjoyment; texts are not as interesting to read	Improvement in reading appears to be associated with degree of explicitness in teaching phonics; systematic and explicit phonics instruction increases reading achievement, especially in early instructional intervention (Foorman et al., 1998; NRP, 2000; Snow et al., 1998)
BASAL	Adoption and implementation of a commercial reading program Skills-based and comprehensive to ensure that skills and strategies are taught throughout the year; a total reading program is provided for the teacher	Readers that the publisher provides are usually graded with a controlled vocabulary	Prescribed activities as described in the teacher's guide; includes reading the story, follow-up activities, and workbook lessons on skills reinforcement	A district can be assured that a total comprehensive reading program has been adopted throughout the schools; beginning teachers are provided with support and lessons to guide their reading instruction; skills are built into the program	All students are assigned the same level reader; accelerated readers and at-risk students can become bored and frustrated; teachers can become bored with the program; there is little room for creativity and variation; often, the textbooks are not composed of quality literature that engages students	Strategies for teaching students to manipulate sounds are not explicitly taught and do not address students with special needs (Snow et al., 1998); not enough research on effectiveness of basal programs in reading instruction
BALANCED APPROACH	Incorporates elements from both whole language and phonics Implement balance in the literacy classroom	Authentic literature Big books Leveled texts	Read-alouds Shared reading Guided reading Independent reading Writing and reading workshops Hands-on activities	Motivates students to read and also teaches them the skills necessary to recognize unknown words	Teachers need to be carefully trained in both approaches	Most researchers support a balanced approach to teaching reading

There are resources available online that can help a teacher learn about these different approaches. A few of these links are described below:

Southwest Educational Development Laboratory (SEDL)

http://www.sedl.org/reading/topics/balancedliteracy.pdf

SEDL provides an overview of phonics, whole language, and balanced approaches at this site, which is helpful to educators.

The National Right to Read Foundation Website

http://www.nrrf.org/caq_rdg_instr.htm

The National Right to Read Foundation site provides frequently asked questions about reading instruction, which is a helpful resource to help explain the different approaches.

Information on Basal Reading Programs

http://www.readingprograms.info/basal.html

This site provides some useful information about basal reading programs.

Major Basal Reading Program Publishers

http://www.readingprograms.info/ed_pubs.html

This site provides teachers with a list of companies that publish basal reading programs.

It is important that teachers understand what comprises different instructional approaches to literacy, so that a comprehensive, balanced literacy program can be adopted in the classroom. Using technology is an important factor in supporting children's literacy acquisition while also providing invaluable resources for the teacher. As you progress through this chapter, you will also learn about the different types of texts that can be used in the classroom to support literacy development.

A balanced literacy approach is a literature-rich curriculum where children are actively engaged in learning.

Courtesy of Becky Stovall

Differentiated Instruction

What Is Differentiation of Instruction?

Differentiation of instruction occurs when teachers begin instruction at the level that each student needs, rather than starting from what the curriculum dictates for all. In differentiated classrooms, teachers provide specific ways for each individual to learn as much as possible and as quickly as possible, individualizing according to student need. Teachers in differentiated classrooms begin with a clear and solid sense of what constitutes a powerful and engaging curriculum. They then modify that instruction so that each learner comes away with a more complete understanding of what the subject is all about. These types of classrooms can be difficult to achieve and involve much planning and careful analysis of each individual student's needs. Differentiated instruction promotes literacy across the curriculum because each student is working within his or her zone of proximal development. Each student is reading material that is on his or her correct level and is engaged in activities that push the zone of proximal development toward more challenging areas. What this means is that a teacher needs to differentiate each curricular area—literacy, social studies, science, mathematics—by offering each student a chance to learn at his or her own pace, read materials that are appropriate, and engage in activities that are challenging and absorbing.

Principles that guide differentiated classrooms are as follows (Tomlinson, 1999; Tomlinson & McTighe, 2006):

◆ *The teacher attends to teacher–student relationships and students' backgrounds.* When a teacher develops a positive teacher–student relationship, student motivation and self-esteem increases. Each student feels that he or she is valued by the teacher. The teacher can also make connections between the student's linguistic and cultural background and the material that is to be presented so that the curriculum becomes more relevant and engaging to the student. The teacher can build bridges that connect learners to important content.

◆ *The teacher focuses on the essentials of the content area.* Rather than trying to "cover all of the material," the teacher focuses on what is essential and ensures that the students are spending their time grappling with important complexities, rather than repeating work that is already known or covering every detail in a chapter that a student will never remember anyway.

◆ *Assessment and instruction are inseparable.* Teachers need to know exactly what the student's readiness level is for each lesson. They need to know whether the student can read the material and comprehend what is being read. This means day-to-day assessment that is closely tied to the instruction. Assessment is not viewed as the "test" that comes at the end of the chapter, but rather as an ongoing process in which the teacher constantly assesses and determines each student's zone of proximal development and pushes it to a new level.

◆ *The teacher modifies content, process, and products.* Using assessment data, the teacher modifies the content, process, or expected outcome (product) for students. Teachers adapt the curriculum when the need arises.

◆ *The teacher and students collaborate in learning.* A differentiated classroom is student-centered, and together, teacher and students plan, set goals, monitor progress, and work to provide quality instruction.

◆ *The teacher draws on a wide range of instructional strategies that help focus on individuals and small groups, not just the whole class.* Many different types of approaches are used in a differentiated classroom. There are times when the teacher will focus on the whole class, and there are times when the teacher will focus on small groups and individuals. The class works flexibly together.

Differentiation does not mean that the teacher needs to individualize instruction for every student in the class, which is an overwhelming task. Rather, the teacher needs to develop a classroom environment that allows students to learn at their own pace, connect to content using their background knowledge, and ensure that each student is working at his or her own level of instruction. Teachers can use different grouping arrangements to provide differentiated instruction; for example:

- Small flexible homogeneous groups that are based on the needs of the students and focus on developing specific skills
- Small heterogeneous groups for collaborative learning
- Whole-group learning to facilitate class discussions and to introduce new concepts
- Independent learning where the student works at his or her own pace on an individual academic task.

Differentiated Instruction and Diverse Learners

Differentiated instruction is essential when working with diverse learners such as students with learning disabilities and English language learners. Students come into the classroom wanting to learn about the world around them and they are looking for connections, engagement, and affirmation as to who they are. Teachers need to practice responsive teaching so that they are sensitive to their students' learning styles, varied needs, and linguistic and cultural backgrounds. Responsive teaching requires that teachers work to establish positive relationships with each student and design a learning plan that can accommodate the great differences that they display. Differentiated learning allows teachers to develop classrooms that reflect responsive teaching.

Tomlinson and McTighe (2006) have outlined different ways in which teachers can practice responsive teaching within a differentiated classroom:

- Establish teacher–student relationships.
- Develop a learning environment that is inclusive and supportive.
- Be sensitive to students' backgrounds and needs.
- Attend to student readiness and make adjustments to the curriculum when appropriate.
- Develop lesson plans based on student interest.

In differentiated instruction, the teacher meets the needs of individual students.

Courtesy of Vicki Cohen

- Pay attention to student learning profiles and their preferred mode of learning.
- Provide challenges for all students that promote complex and creative thinking.

For English language learners entering the U.S. school culture, they must not only adjust to a new language but to different assumptions about how children are supposed to learn within the educational system. Some teachers assume that all students are able to accomplish the academic assignments, and that those who do not succeed need to seek outside help. In fact, some students are capable of performing but are unable to do so because they are not clear about the cultural expectations within the classroom. Other students might need extra support and accommodations because of language barriers.

For students with learning disabilities, teachers need to be sensitive to their learning needs as specified in their Individualized Education Program (IEP). Differentiated instruction provides students with the opportunity to work at their own pace, to receive alternate methods of learning the content, and to develop their skills in a supportive environment. They can work in small groups based on similar needs to receive additional, more intensive support, as well as work in collaborative groups with their classmates for long-range projects. Differentiated instruction allows the teacher to break tasks into smaller, more manageable units so that students with learning disabilities are able to attain success and continue improving their skills, thereby building self-esteem and confidence.

Strategies That Support Differentiated Instruction

It is important that teachers incorporate strategies that support the needs of all students, including diverse learners. Strategies that support differentiation are as follows (Tomlinson, 1999):

- *Learning Centers:* Learning centers are stations set up with specific tasks and activities that students must complete at their appropriate level.
- *Agendas:* Teachers can develop personalized agendas for each student, specifying the list of tasks that a particular student must complete in a specified time.
- *Orbital studies:* Orbital studies are independent investigations, done individually or in groups, generally over three to six weeks, that revolve around some facet of the curriculum in which students must complete some project, activity, investigation, or research.
- *Differentiated activities:* The teacher provides different activities for different students that are interesting, foster high level thinking, and are of varying degrees of difficulty, all revolving around the same topic or concept.
- *Learning contracts:* The teacher provides an opportunity for students to negotiate an agreement between the teacher and student that gives the student some freedom in determining what activities, readings, and concepts will be learned within a certain duration of time.
- *Cooperative learning:* Cooperative learning encompasses group investigations that guide students through the process of doing research and presenting it.
- *Use of multiple materials:* Instead of using just one textbook, the text becomes supplemental and many different types of materials are available and used to study the concept or topic, including trade books, primary source materials, pictures, photos, computer software, and art materials. Readings are assigned to a student based on the appropriateness of the fit to the student's needs.
- *Flexible groupings:* Different type of groupings should be used daily to facilitate instruction based on the type of instruction that is being given—whole-class, small homogeneous groups, small heterogeneous groups, and individualized instruction.

Differentiated instruction is not just a strategy, but rather a philosophy about how each teacher approaches teaching and learning. It is based on the assumption that teachers start with the individual student rather than with a prescribed plan of action for

FIGURE 10-1

Differentiated Instruction Checklist

IS DIFFERENTIATED INSTRUCTION BEING USED IN THIS CLASSROOM?

Name: _____   Date: _____

Give the classroom 1 point for each item you check off below. See how many points the classroom accumulates after analyzing it.

_____ 1. Are student differences used as a basis for beginning the planning of a lesson?

_____ 2. Is assessment ongoing and diagnostic in the classroom (is it every day and is the information used in planning lessons)?

_____ 3. Are many different instructional groupings used during the course of the day such as whole class, cooperative learning, and small homogeneous groups?

_____ 4. Are different students allowed to learn the material in different ways that address each student's needs?

_____ 5. Are a wide range of materials made available that can be used in a content-based lesson such as trade books, textbooks, pictures, videos, software?

_____ 6. Are students included in the planning of goals, strategies, and methods for learning the material?

_____ 7. Do students have a choice on how they can learn in the classroom?

_____ 8. Are there individual conferences with students at varying times to provide individualized instruction?

_____ 9. Does the teacher make sure that each student is capable of reading and understanding the material required, and does the teacher provide alternative readings for those students who need them?

_____ 10. Are each student's needs being met in the classroom? Does the teacher provide enough time, resources, and planning to ensure that all students are being challenged?

_____ Total points

Comments about the observed classroom:

the whole class. It assumes that the teacher will take into account student readiness, student learning styles, student interests, and each individual profile. As schools become more diverse, it becomes increasingly important that we take the time, resources, and guidance needed for all teachers to move away from "teaching to the middle." We must move toward meeting the individual needs of every student in our classroom.

Figure 10–1 is a "Differentiated Instruction Checklist" that teacher candidates and teachers can use to assess whether differentiated instruction is being used. By analyzing the classroom on the 10 different items listed, the teacher can become aware of how the classroom is set up and whether there needs to be a shift in philosophy about how teaching and learning occurs.

Type of Texts Used in a Literacy Classroom

Not only does the instructional approach affect the type of literacy instruction that young children are exposed to, but the type of text they read will also be a large factor that affects their reading achievement. As noted in the previous summary chart, different approaches to reading use different types of texts with beginning readers. Until the past decade, the texts used for beginning readers had a controlled vocabulary based on using **high-frequency words,** or those words that appear most frequently in printed materials. At points in time, texts that have phonetically regular words have also been proposed and used in the classroom for beginning readers. It is only recently that literature-based beginning readers were created that are neither controlled for vocabulary nor phonetically regular (Hiebert, 1999). Through experiences with particular texts, readers may be acquiring some skills and not others (Hiebert, 1999). It has been suggested (Brown, 2000) that as students progress as readers, teachers should provide texts that support and expand their capabilities to become effective readers. By matching different types of texts with students' developmental needs, teachers are able to scaffold their instruction and work in the students' zone of proximal development and support their readers' literacy development.

Teachers should choose books that will help students develop fluency, which is the ability to read a text accurately and quickly. As discussed in Chapter 7, fluency is important because it provides a bridge between word recognition and comprehension. Because fluent readers do not have to concentrate on decoding the words, they can focus their attention on what the text means. Less fluent readers must focus on decoding words, and their attention is not on understanding the text, but figuring out individual words (NICHD, 2000). Students should practice reading texts that contain mostly words that they know or can decode easily and that are relatively short—about 50 to 200 words, depending on the age of the students. A variety of reading materials should be used, including stories, nonfiction, and poetry.

The different types of text materials described below can be useful in promoting fluency. The following paragraphs briefly describe the different types of texts available to teachers in a literacy classroom, starting with a description of the simplest type of text for beginning readers and progressing to more challenging text that requires greater competencies from the reader.

Predictable and Patterned Text

Predictable and patterned text is often found in big books, which teachers use with beginning readers during shared reading. The text is controlled to emphasize repetition, rhythm, and rhyme (Brown, 2000). It contains simple sentence structures and usually has bright, colorful illustrations that support the text so that children can use contextual features of the pictures to infer meaning from the text. The plot is often limited and there is a restricted amount of text per page. These books are often used by teachers to model "print concepts": that books have a cover page, an illustrator, text written from left to right, and contain words that have spaces between them. They are used by the teacher to first read aloud, and then have the children join in and repeat the phrases when appropriate with the intent to develop oral reading fluency and expression. Big books are meant to be read in an enjoyable setting, and through repeated readings they help children recognize words and start to read through the constant repetition and predictability of the text.

The disadvantage of predictable and patterned text is that often there is little plot and the constant rereading of the text can become boring and repetitious for some children. Many of the children who sit in reading corners on the floor, especially those toward the outer perimeter, do not pay attention and do not read along. Another problem is that the vocabulary is not controlled in these books; multisyllabic words are used, as well as words the children may not come across very frequently (low-frequency words). This may make it difficult for some children to read these books independently.

However, these types of books are excellent choices for children who are just learning about print and just starting to learn the alphabetic system. These books emphasize phonological structures through rhyme and repetition and help children reinforce phonemic awareness. For those children who have not progressed to decoding words and applying the letter–sound correspondence in reading, these books will increase their motivation to read (Brown, 2000). Once students hear a predictable text read aloud a few times, they can rely on memory, effective prediction of what will occur next, and illustrations to negotiate the text independently.

Examples of predictable and patterned texts are:

◆ *Have You Seen My Cat?* by Eric Carle
◆ *Frightened* by Joy Cowley
◆ *Breakfast* by Virginia King
◆ *Can You Find It?* by Amy John Casey

Decodable Text

With the new emphasis on teaching systematic and explicit phonics instruction, there is renewed interest in decodable text. **Decodable text** is controlled to emphasize letter–sound correspondence, spelling patterns, and graphophonemic connections. It usually introduces a phonic element, such as the word family "at," so that many of the words will reinforce that family (The *bat sat* on the *mat*). It usually has simple sentence structures, a simple, familiar story line, and limited plot.

Research shows that children in programs that emphasize the alphabetic nature of written English have an advantage over children in programs where other features, such as high-frequency words, were emphasized (Hiebert, 1999). Texts that are connected to the phonic skills that children are learning in the classroom will reinforce those skills in the context of reading and help children use phonics strategies to recognize words (Hiebert, 1999). Therefore, decodable texts are useful with beginning readers, and the questions that need to be answered are which children should use them and when should they be assigned (Jenkins, Vadasy, Peyton, & Sanders, 2003).

Reading practice with decodable text is thought to help struggling readers in three ways (Jenkins et al., 2003):

1. Decodable text reminds readers that all letters in a word are important and that there are no shortcuts to learning words.

2. Reading texts that contain specific graphophonemic connections helps children remember patterns that are seen frequently in words, thereby allowing beginning readers to decode unfamiliar words, as well as sight words.

3. Reading decodable texts enhances motivation for beginning readers and builds confidence, especially for those children who are at risk for reading problems.

Decodable text has the following characteristics (Jenkins et al., 2003):

◆ Text is controlled to emphasize letter–sound correspondences, spelling patterns, and high-frequency irregular sight words.
◆ Text has simple sentence structures.
◆ Text has simple, familiar story line.
◆ Illustrations support and extend the text.
◆ Text has limited plot and offers limited information on a topic.
◆ Each page has a limited amount of text.

These texts have been somewhat controversial because of their limited plot line and ability to motivate students. When text is controlled for a limited amount of spelling patterns, the story line becomes quite limited and narrow. Educators have criticized these texts for their lack of authenticity and creativity, believe that they stifle and bore many children and cause readers to be turned off to reading books. Children are not being exposed to rich and vivid language or involved in an exciting and engaging story.

Examples of decodable texts are:

◆ *The Snow Game* by Patricia Griffith
◆ *Fun with Zip and Zap* by John Shefelbine
◆ *All about Bats* by Jennifer Jacobson
◆ *The Cat in the Hat* by Dr. Seuss

It is usually recommended that students with learning disabilities work with decodable texts to support their ability to decode unfamiliar words, as well as sight words. Students with learning disabilities often have phonological processing difficulties, need to analyze phonemic structure, and are slower in word recognition (Soifer, 1999). Therefore, controlling the amount of words that need to be processed and providing easily decodable words is beneficial to students with learning disabilities; this allows them to gain confidence in reading without being overwhelmed by an abundance of new words all at once.

Decodable text also can be beneficial to English language learners, who need support in learning a new language. Decodable text allows English language learners to progress at a slower pace, using a phonics-based approach to language, and it helps them to concentrate on a smaller number of phonetic patterns to learn. Although authentic literature is highly motivating, especially when discussing the student's own culture, the text can be overwhelming and use many multisyllable words that are unfamiliar to the student. English language learners need the support and scaffolding to learn a new language, and decodable text allows them to feel success with a limited number of words and word patterns so they can progress at a pace with which they feel comfortable.

Basal Readers or Controlled Text

Basal readers were really the first textbooks that children used in the classroom, starting off with the McGuffey readers in the 1800s and progressing to the Dick and Jane series in the 1950s, with which many generations of children grew up. In the past, basal readers had what is known as a controlled vocabulary. These books were "stripped down" stories, created not so much for aesthetic purposes as for a means of focusing on and practicing skills and learning sight words (Cole, 1998). The stories in these texts had a certain amount of words that were used, and the teacher could follow in the teacher's guide which words were being introduced and reinforced for each selection. These anthologies of stories were basically plotless and authorless. They had a few characters, a simple text structure, and progressed from very simple to more difficult. Each text was carefully controlled, not only for vocabulary, but for the grade level it was written on; thus, the teacher could be assured that the children in the class were reading a book at their own grade level. In this way, the teacher would know what books they had read in previous years and what book they would move up to in the following year.

Textbook companies have incorporated a "literature-based" approach to their basal readers and have been using stories and other genres that have been created primarily for what Cole (1998) calls "aesthetic purposes," that is, for the pure sense of enjoyment and entertainment, as well as for information. By using this material, publishing companies have "tuned in" to a trend in reading that promotes literature as a way to learn how to read. Through the use of such material, it is hoped that children will enjoy reading this material and thereby be more highly motivated to continue reading.

Some educators believe that the controlled vocabulary structure of basal texts actually functions as a scaffold for struggling readers who need a more "beginner-oriented text" (Cole, 1998) to meet their needs while reading. The difficulty of the text increases gradually from year to year, and usually the illustrations provide support for comprehending the text. Basal readers tend to be more difficult to read than either predictable or decodable text, with more words per page and text that uses more polysyllabic words, more difficult high-frequency words, and more complex sentence structures. However, because of a controlled vocabulary, basal texts can be more accessible, yet also challenging to beginning or struggling readers, such as students with learning disabilities and English language learners.

Little Books

Many beginning reading programs are now using little book programs for reading instruction. These programs usually consist of many little books that are short in length (8–24 pages rather than the usual thick anthologies of the basal readers) and presented in a series of levels. Many basal literature-based programs now include little books as part of their components (Hiebert, 1999). These little books were initially published in Australia and New Zealand, where many of our literacy "trends" have originated, but they have become part of the mainstream of literacy classrooms in the United States.

Each of the books is leveled so that they progressively get more difficult. The beginning texts usually contain a phrase or sentence that names an item in a category such as zoo or farm animals. The illustrations directly support the text so there is a close picture–text match. This allows beginning readers to recognize the high-content words that appear and help them make meaning of these words (Hiebert, 1999). These books are used frequently in guided reading, where it is possible to read the book in one short sitting and to subsequently have time to reinforce specific skills on which the students are working.

Leveled readers are extremely useful in helping struggling readers make progressive skill improvement by scaffolding them at their appropriate reading level and allowing them to work within their zone of proximal development. Leveled readers also greatly benefit English language learners and students with learning disabilities whose feelings of self-worth are enhanced by their apparent improvement in reading.

Trade Books or Authentic Literature

Trade books are those books that are published for the general public rather than specifically for the classroom, whether they are novels or informational texts. It has become quite popular for teachers to use trade books in their literacy program, and usually a classroom library includes many different types of trade books.

Using **authentic literature** to teach reading is a direct outgrowth of the whole-language approach, which emphasizes the joy and richness of good literature and focuses on comprehension as the main goal of reading. Authentic literature is not controlled for word choice or sentence structure; as a result, authors can develop complex plots and provide a quantity of information that is unavailable in most of the other types of texts discussed earlier in this chapter. There also can be much more text per page than other types of controlled texts.

One distinguishing characteristic of literature is the use of colorful and engaging illustrations by renowned artists. Children's literature has spawned a whole industry of artists who now specialize in—or have branched out to—illustrating children's books. Usually the illustrations support and extend the text, but the illustrator can be very creative and does not have to follow any formula, hence the beauty and engagement of this type of text.

Beginning readers need to use advanced word identification strategies while reading these types of texts. They must rely on a strong sight word vocabulary, and they must be able to chunk unfamiliar words into manageable phonetic units to decode. They must use prior knowledge to construct meaning because many of the topics covered in the plot or text may be advanced and complex. Readers must constantly self-monitor their reading strategies to make sure the text is making sense (Brown, 2000).

Examples of authentic literature are:

- *Snowflake Bentley* by Jacqueline Briggs Martin, illustrated by Mary Azarian
- *Golem* by David Wisniewski
- *Smoky Night* by Eve Bunting
- *So You Want to Be President?* by Judith St. George, illustrated by David Small

Leveled Text

A critical aspect of guided reading in a balanced reading program is to match the reader's individual needs with the appropriate text level. According to Fountas and Pinnell (1996), it is necessary to organize books used in the classroom into specific levels so that teachers' decisions can be easier, faster, and more effective. Usually the type of books used in this leveling procedure range from predictable and patterned texts to decodable texts to easy readers to more advanced chapter trade books. The focus should be on enjoyment, meaning, and connection to children's lives—books that engage children through humor and interesting stories. Therefore, the heart of the leveled book library would be authentic literature.

Fountas and Pinnell (1996) provide detailed guidelines for leveling books in a classroom. Whether the text is easy or hard for a particular student depends on the structure and characteristics of the text, as well as how the teacher introduces the text and supports the reading process in the classroom. Some of the characteristics of text that guide a teacher who is trying to determine whether a book fits into a particular level are:

◆ Language structure and vocabulary
◆ Amount of picture support
◆ Size and placement of print on the page
◆ Complexity of concepts
◆ Nonfiction text features

For *emergent readers*, a teacher should look for the following characteristics in a text:

◆ Text has large print.
◆ Text is consistently placed on page throughout book.
◆ Repetition of phrases and patterns is used.
◆ High-frequency words are introduced.
◆ Text is predictable.
◆ Illustrations have strong support.
◆ Simple books have one line of one to six words per page, are easy to read, and have ample space between words.
◆ Children can focus on print and gradually increase their control over words.
◆ Most books focus on topics familiar with children.

For *beginner readers*, a teacher would want the following text characteristics:

◆ Longer sentences are used with more lines of text on the page.
◆ There is a change in sentence patterns.
◆ There is a change in punctuation.
◆ Illustrations provide support.
◆ There is some repetition of text.
◆ More attention to print is needed.
◆ Larger range of high-frequency words is used.
◆ Book increases use of vocabulary words.
◆ Stories explore familiar topics in a variety of ways to offer new viewpoints to readers.
◆ Text contains more compound and multisyllable words in a full range of punctuation.

For *transitional readers*, or those who are transitioning to fluency, a teacher would want the following text characteristics:

◆ Medium- to small-print size is used.
◆ Variety of fonts are used.
◆ More complete story is presented.
◆ Illustrations do not support text as significantly.
◆ Story contains a problem and solution.
◆ Use of descriptive language is used.
◆ Concepts and themes are familiar.
◆ Complex sentences are used.
◆ Language changes on each page, rather than repeating patterns.

- Books offer challenges in ideas and vocabulary, with some introduction to technical language.
- Variety of print styles and text layout requires reader's close attention and flexibility.

For *fluent readers*, a teacher likely prefers the following text characteristics:

- Medium to small print size is used.
- Variety of fonts and text patterns are used.
- The book increases the use of multisyllabic and compound words.
- Wide range of sentence patterns is used.
- The story has episodes.
- The story has a problem and a solution.
- The illustrations give little support.
- Characters are beginning to develop.
- Wide range of punctuation is used.
- The author presents a point of view.
- Descriptive and literary language is used.
- Stories are longer and may be divided into chapters.
- Wide range of genres are represented.
- Some chapter books include whole pages of text with fewer illustrations.

According to Fountas and Pinnell (1996), each of the levels of books described above are divided into many different gradients within that level, so that, for example, the emergent literacy reader has 4 different levels to choose books from, while the fluent reader has 10 different levels, each level progressing slowly in difficulty and complexity according to text characteristics.

Recently, a few commercial publishing companies began publishing what is called **leveled text** for use in the guided reading session. These books are already leveled and a district can purchase the series without teachers having to spend extensive time and energy to level texts within their own classrooms. However, these books do not conform to what Fountas and Pinnell (1996) originally recommended when instituting leveled readers in the classroom: using authentic literature based on enjoyment and engagement with the text.

Electronic Text and E-Books

As technology becomes increasingly accessible to children and adolescents, more and more students are reading electronic text at home and in school. Electronic text is any text that is being displayed digitally via an electronic source, whether it be a computer, iPod, cell phone, personal organizer, or e-book reader such as the Kindle. A survey by the Henry J. Kaiser Family Foundation (Rideout, Roberts, & Foehr, 2005) found that young people, aged 8 to 18, are using electronic media for an average of more than six hours a day. This survey reported that many of these young people are "multitasking": listening to music on an MP3 player, while surfing the web and instant messaging friends, while doing their homework on a word processor. The Pew Internet & American Life Project (2009) found that 93 percent of teens use the Internet; most of them are treating it as a venue for social interaction—a place where they can share creations, tell stories, and interact with others. Electronic text has become pervasive, and teachers need to consider the most effective use of it in the classroom.

Electronic text has also become a part of the literacy curriculum in many classrooms; children are going online to conduct searches for a specific topic, reading e-books, reading electronic talking books (electronic books that have text written at the bottom with interactive, animated illustrations), playing educational games, using educational software, or using a word processor. As with other types of text, teachers need

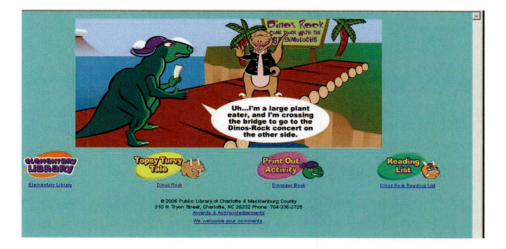

E-books are becoming increasingly popular in the classroom, and can be accessed via the Internet.

to be sure that electronic text is written on the appropriate reading level, and that it supports the student in developing literacy skills. Chapter 7 discusses how students need to apply comprehension strategies to comprehend electronic text in a similar way to print-based text. The ultimate goal is for students to understand what they read and to apply the information that they learned in an effective way. Because of the large amount of time students spend searching for sites on the Internet, they are reading more informational text than they did five years ago. In many cases, the sites might not be written on the children's appropriate reading level and usually contain a dense amount of challenging information. Increasingly, students must be adept at seeking, evaluating, and using information found on the Internet, and they must apply their knowledge of the reading process. They must learn to navigate links that bring them to other parts of the text or to different sites, and they need to learn how to comprehend information that is not necessarily presented in a linear manner.

E-books are one form of electronic text that is becoming increasingly popular. An **e-book** is an electronic (or digital) version of a book that is displayed on a computer or a handheld device. The term is used to refer to both the electronic text of the book and the handheld hardware device used to read books in digital format. The advantages of an e-book are: (1) text can be searched; (2) the books take up little space; (3) hundreds (or thousands) of e-books may be carried together on one device or a CD-ROM; and (4) there are many e-books that are available free on the Internet. Because they take up little space, e-books do not go "out of print," allowing readers to find older works by favorite authors. Also, e-books may be read in low light, or even total darkness, with a back-lit device.

As mentioned earlier, e-books can be read on PDAs (personal digital assistants, which can function as a cell phone, fax sender, web browser, and personal organizer), Pocket PCs, laptops, and cell phones. E-books can be read on any of these devices, but the e-book devices, such as the Kindle, are increasingly becoming popular. These devices have large displays and backlights to facilitate reading electronic text. To read e-books, you usually must download the e-book onto the device that shows the electronic text. Many sites charge for the e-books, such as Amazon.com; however, many provide them for free.

Many sources on the Internet provide e-books for children that can be used in the literacy classroom and displayed over the Internet. Many of these resources are excellent for English language learners and students with learning disabilities because they provide color illustrations and audio features, such as narration and individually "clickable" words. This provides support and motivation for struggling readers who enjoy logging on to the computer to read. Many e-books are written in different languages and can support English language learners within the classroom.

The following list provides resources of free e-books teachers can use in the literacy classroom. Most of the resources can be accessed using the Internet; others may need to be downloaded to the teacher's own computer. Some provide excellent graphics and illustrations with audio provided to support students as they read the text. Many more resources are available on this textbook's website.

Children's Storybooks Online

http://www.magickeys.com/books/index.html#books

Children's Storybooks Online has e-books written and illustrated by various authors, all available via the Internet. Stories are categorized for young children, older children, and young adults.

Lil' Fingers Storybooks

http://www.lil-fingers.com/storybooks/index.html

The Lil' Fingers Storybooks site hosts simple e-books about colors, shapes, and making faces. These stories feature small animated illustrations and large text. (Note that each ends with a book recommendation and an advertising link to an online bookstore.)

Ohio University's Telecommunications Center

http://wiredforbooks.org/kids.htm

Ohio University's site, Kids' Corner, provides several illustrated Peter Rabbit stories. *The Tale of Peter Rabbit* has an audio slide show, and *Two Bad Mice Alice's Adventures in Wonderland* is a recent addition.

Story Place

http://www.storyplace.org/

Story Place is sponsored by the Public Library of Charlotte and Mecklenburg County and includes such resources as the e-book *Topsy-Turvy Tale*, an interactive, animated text available in both English and Spanish. Many of the stories are read aloud.

Between the Lions

http://pbskids.org/lions

This site, hosted by the Public Broadcasting Service, has e-books that are read out loud and many different games to go along with the television show *Between the Lions*.

Project Gutenberg

http://www.gutenberg.org

Project Gutenberg is the oldest producer of free e-books on the Internet. Its collection has been produced by hundreds of volunteers. More than 17,000 free books are available, some of which are for children and young adults.

Free e-Books.Net

http://www.free-ebooks.net/

This site provides a variety of free, downloadable e-books (in pdf format). A "youth" category has a variety of books for children.

Etext Center

http://etext.virginia.edu/ebooks/

This site contains over 2,100 publicly available e-books from the University of Virginia Library's Etext Center, including children's literature.

Additional teacher resources can be found on the *Literacy for Children in an Information Age* premium website for this chapter (**http://www. cengage.com/login**).

The websites listed above are excellent resources that teachers can use to incorporate electronic text into the literacy classroom.

Teachers need to carefully monitor the use of electronic text in the classroom to ensure that students can read it properly. The text needs to be on the appropriate reading level; often this is difficult to assess when students are conducting a search for a topic. The text also needs to be large enough for students to read easily and presented in a professional manner. Some Internet sites use colored text in the background: this is extremely difficult to read and may be frustrating for children. The web page should not have distracting images moving on and off the screen, or animated, flashing images. This may be distracting and frustrating for students with learning disabilities, as these images can interfere with their comprehension.

Readability Formulas versus Leveling

The readability formula has traditionally been used in determining the level that a particular text is written on so that a teacher can match it to a student's literacy needs. Readability formulas give a numerical score to rank books and texts in order of difficulty and level. This numerical score usually corresponds to a particular grade level and is derived by applying an objective formula to all texts.

The McGuffey Readers, famous reading textbooks in the 1840s, did not use grade-level designations, but rather a simple numerical ranking (book 4 was more advanced than book 3) (Fry, 2002). By the 1930s, there were a great number of different reading series, and these books were graded according to difficulty (with a 4 designating fourth grade). Recently, basal series have moved away from controlled text toward a "literature-based" approach; however, most readers still carry designations of the grade level (usually hidden in some format for the teacher to interpret).

Most readability formulas are objective in that they can be done by computers; word processors also can give the user a readability level for the written text. These formulas provide a fairly accurate and consistent comparison of books so that the teacher can be assured that books graded by this formula are all on the same level.

The Fry Readability Formula is commonly used in classrooms (Figure 10–2). It is worthwhile to apply this formula to a book or text that you are using to determine its grade level. Often, you will find that the grade level is surprising—it is either too high to be appropriate or too low to be used with that level of student. You can find the Fry Readability Formula online at these two sites:

◆ Kathy Schrock's Guide to Educators: http://school.discoveryeducation.com/schrockguide/fry/fry.html
◆ Fry Text Readability Assessment: http://www.berghuis.co.nz/abiator/rdg/fry-readability-assessment-tool.html

Most traditional readability formulas are based on two measures that have been verified by research studies (Fry, 2002):

1. *Syntactic difficulty* (grammatical complexity) is measured by the length of the sentence (that is, how many sentences in 100 words).
2. *Semantic difficulty* (meaning of the words) is measured by the length of the word (that is, how many syllables there are in 100 words).

Both of these measures make assumptions that sometimes cause a level to be inaccurate. If a text contains long sentences, it is assumed that the difficulty level is higher, yet there are many simple sentences that can be very long and easy to comprehend. Conversely, there are many complex sentences that are short and difficult to understand. Therefore, using sentence length as an indicator of difficulty may not always be accurate. The same holds true for word length, another measure used to determine the level of text. It is assumed that the longer the word (more syllables), the more difficult the word is to understand. However, there are many long words that are simple to understand (*transportation* has four syllables) and very short words that are difficult to

FIGURE 10-2

Fry Readability Formula

Graph for Estimating Readability—Extended by Edward Fry

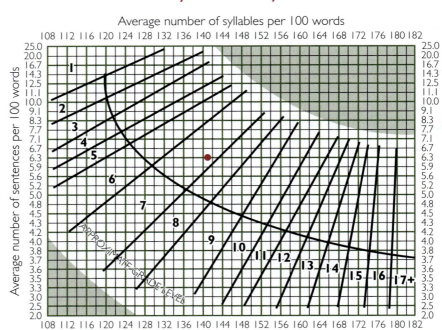

Directions:

Randomly select 3 one hundred word passages from a book or an article. Plot average number of syllables and average number of sentences per 100 words on graph to determine the grade level of the material. Choose more passages per book if great variability is observed and conclude that the book has uneven readability. Few books will fall in gray area but when they do grade level scores are invalid.

Count proper nouns, numerals, and initialization as words. Count a syllable for each symbol. For example, "1945" is 1 word and 4 syllables and "IRA" is 1 word and 3 syllables.

Examples:

	Syllables	Sentences
First hundred words	124	6.6
Second hundred words	141	5.5
Third hundred words	158	6.8
Average	141	6.3

Readability seventh grade (see dot plotted on graph)

Reproduced from *Elementary Reading Instruction* by Fry, © 1977, by permission of The McGraw-Hill Companies.

understand (*nuance* has two syllables). Therefore, using word length as an indicator of difficulty also may not be accurate.

Leveling is a technique that takes into account more diverse and subjective measures of difficulty. Leveling cannot be done by a computer and it takes a teacher a significant amount of time to level the books in a classroom. There is no assurance that the books placed in the same level are consistently the same or would be placed in the same level in another teacher's classroom.

Teachers can use this criteria when leveling a book:

1. *Content:* Is it appropriate for the age group and do students have prior knowledge of the information?

2. *Sentence structure:* Are the sentences easy to understand or complex and dense, with much information packed into each one?

3. *Writing style:* What is the author's writing style like? Is it easy to follow, or is it more complex, with subtle meanings and inferences throughout?

4. *Illustrations:* Do the illustrations support the content of the text? Do they provide visual clues as to what the text is about?

5. *Format:* How is the text formatted on the page? Is the text big or smaller? How much text is there on a page?

These measures are very subjective; however, the teacher can make judgments based on his or her knowledge of the students and the curriculum of the school. The leveling can be adjusted as the teacher tries out the books in the classroom with various students and fine tunes this process.

Both techniques—readability formulas and leveling—are valuable resources for a literacy teacher to use with texts in the classroom. Used together, they both yield valuable information. They help classroom teachers select books for their students and ensure that their students will have a successful literacy experience.

Online Resources for Use of Texts

4 Blocks Literacy Framework

http://www.k111.k12.il.us/lafayette/fourblocks/book_levels.htm

This site contains excellent links for leveled texts, including a leveled books database, which is a list of more than 1,100 picture books created by the Portland (Oregon) Public Schools. The books in the database are a great resource for teachers who are attempting to level texts.

Busy Teacher's Café

http://www.busyteacherscafe.com/teacher_resources/literacy_pages/leveled_books.htm

This site provides information, resources, and links on leveling books for a classroom library.

Summary of Different Types of Texts

The following table summarizes the different features found in each type of text described:

Text	Characteristics	Reading Strategies Required	Use in the Classroom
PREDICTABLE AND PATTERNED TEXT	◆ Text contains repetitive and predictable phrases ◆ Text has simple sentence structure ◆ Illustrations support and extend text ◆ Text has limited plot/information ◆ Text has restricted amount of text per page	◆ Predicting what comes next ◆ Reading of whole words ◆ Using context clues to predict ◆ Using prior knowledge to construct meaning ◆ Using print tracking and knowledge of print/books	◆ Used with emergent readers ◆ Used in shared literacy experience ◆ Models the concept that print has meaning ◆ Helps develop students' oral reading and fluency ◆ Reinforces enjoyable literacy experience

(continues)

Text	Characteristics	Reading Strategies Required	Use in the Classroom
DECODABLE TEXT	◆ Text is controlled to emphasize phonic patterns and letter–sound correspondence ◆ Text has simple sentence structure ◆ Text has simple, familiar story line ◆ Illustrations support and extend the text ◆ Text has limited plot/information ◆ Each page has limited amount of text on it	◆ Decoding of phonetically regular words ◆ Blending of letter and sounds ◆ Associating letters and letter patterns with sounds to unlock unknown words ◆ Using sight words (*said, thought, was*)	◆ Used with beginner readers ◆ Used to support children with learning disabilities and English language learners ◆ Used to reinforce phonic elements taught in class ◆ Used to provide practice in applying phonic strategies ◆ Develops students' oral reading fluency ◆ Builds struggling readers' confidence ◆ Scaffolds students' reading ability
BASAL READERS	◆ Anthologies of stories are collected into a graded reader ◆ Vocabulary is often controlled ◆ Stories usually have questions afterward ◆ Basal programs are skill-based and usually cover K–6 reading levels ◆ Teacher follows a teacher's guide, which has a prescribed set of lessons for each day of the week ◆ Reader is usually accompanied by workbooks, skills assessments, and other materials ◆ Difficulty of text increases as a student moves up through the levels	◆ Using sight words ◆ Using prior knowledge to construct meaning ◆ Emphasizing skills such as grammar, sentence structure, comprehension strategies ◆ Using automaticity to identify words	◆ Basal texts are used with emergent readers, beginner readers, and all the way up through highly fluent readers ◆ One or two readers are used in a classroom for every student ◆ Controlled set of readers is used throughout the school so teacher knows what was previously covered and what will be covered in future years ◆ Teacher is ensured that skills will be taught and emphasized ◆ Teacher has little flexibility to adapt more creative approaches ◆ All students must read the same book(s) for the whole year
LITTLE BOOKS	◆ Small books that are short in length ◆ Series of books that get progressively more difficult ◆ Beginning texts contain only a word or phrase on each page ◆ Illustrations support text ◆ Focuses on reinforcing high-content words	◆ Using sight words ◆ Using prior knowledge to construct meaning ◆ Using context clues to predict ◆ Using prior knowledge to construct meaning	◆ Used primarily with beginner readers ◆ Used in guided reading sessions ◆ Allows teacher to read one book per guided reading session ◆ Allows a student to quickly finish a book and not be overwhelmed with long books
AUTHENTIC LITERATURE	◆ Text is not controlled for vocabulary, sentence structure or content	◆ Using advanced word identification skills ◆ Using sight word knowledge	◆ Used primarily with fluent readers or those who are transitioning from beginning reading to more fluent reading

Text	Characteristics	Reading Strategies Required	Use in the Classroom
	• Text contains very colorful, engaging illustrations that usually support and extend text • Text can have very complex plot/information • Text can have more words per page than other types of books • Books are usually engaging, enjoyable, and motivating to read	• Using prior knowledge to construct meaning • Using self-monitoring strategies to ensure comprehension • Using prediction strategies to infer meaning	• Used for enjoyment and engagement of students • Used for read-alouds by teacher • Used to motivate students to read more • Used to expose children to multicultural literature • Used to motivate English language learners • Used to model rich sentence structure and authentic writing • Used to teach complex storytelling and structure of plots • Used to teach complex language structure and literary devices
LEVELED TEXT	• Books in a classroom have been divided into different levels based on characteristics of the text • All types of books and genres are included, with the majority being authentic literature • Leveling is based on language structure and vocabulary, amount of picture support, size and placement of print on the page, and complexity of concepts	• All skills mentioned above are used because all types of books are part of the leveled classroom library	• Used with emergent readers through highly fluent readers • Used for guided reading, as well as independent reading • Texts are leveled into many different gradients and students are matched with their appropriate level of text • Teacher assigns students books to read based on constant assessment of students' needs
ELECTRONIC TEXT	• Text is displayed digitally from an electronic source such as a laptop or handheld device • Electronic text includes text read on cell phones, computer software programs, games, PDAs, and the Internet • An e-book is a digital version of a book that is displayed on a computer or a handheld device	• Being able to navigate links • Comprehending nonlinear presentation of text and information • Manipulating many different windows with text displayed • Synthesizing information from many different sources	• Used with all readers • Used to motivate struggling readers • Teacher needs to be careful that text is at the appropriate reading level and presents appropriate content • Teacher needs to carefully monitor reading of electronic text to make sure it is clear, large enough, and easy to read

Many different types of texts exist that a teacher can use to promote literacy in a classroom. At times, district policy will determine what type of text will be used predominantly in a classroom; often, large districts adopt a total program to implement within the district. It is important that the beginning teacher is aware of the different types of texts and their benefits. Each different type of text can support different types of students as they develop into fluent readers. A teacher has options in the type of book that is best suited for a specific child and should be aware of these options as an alternative that will scaffold the child's reading strategies.

The best approach is to have many different types of texts within a classroom that allow a teacher to meet the needs of all children. Hiebert (1999) believes the ideal situation would be to use texts that have more engaging content and language than many of the phonetically regular texts and that provide more opportunities to apply phonics strategies than do most of the current little books and literature-based programs. An optimum goal of a teacher should be to find texts that not only engage children but give them sufficient experience in applying the phonics skills that are being taught. Currently, this combination of textual features is not present in most books. Either a book is authentic literature with an engaging story and rich language construction but does not provide the scaffolding needed for beginning or struggling readers, or it has decodable text or carefully controlled vocabulary and lacks the excitement and complexity of story structure to make it motivating to read.

The most important point is that teachers must balance the needs of the students with the type of texts that they are reading. Perhaps this is a good rationalization for why leveled texts make the most sense within a balanced literacy program: this leveling allows a teacher to use all different types of books in the literacy classroom, meeting the needs of English language learners, children with learning disabilities, emergent readers, as well as with fluent readers. Leveled texts allow a teacher the flexibility to choose from many different types of texts and provide a basis for which to assign a given book—text features of the book matched to a specific reading level of the student. The goal is for the perfect "fit" so that readers can comprehend what they read, and leveled texts provide for that outcome.

Choosing the correct text for each student is only one way that the teacher can help meet the needs of the students and provide support for their emerging literacy. Providing support for the student while reading the text is also important, whether that be during shared, guided, or independent reading. The teacher can help the student construct meaning by providing aids that model effective reading strategies during the reading process. Instructional strategies such as visual tools are an important aid to the student while rehearsing appropriate comprehension strategies.

The next section describes the use of visual tools in a balanced literacy classroom as a valuable instructional strategy that all teachers should use to help support readers as they construct meaning from text.

Visual Tools/Graphic Organizers

Visual Tools in the Literacy Classroom

A **visual tool,** or a graphic organizer, is a graphical diagram that portrays the relationships among concepts and creates a pattern of information that is constructed by an individual or group on paper, board, or computer screen (Hyerle, 1996). Visual tools have been known as graphic organizers and semantic maps; however, the term *visual tool* connotes a more active application, in which the student uses the visual representation as a tool to actively make sense of the material to be learned. Visual tools help students build their own knowledge base, much like a carpenter builds a house (Hyerle, 1996).

Research has shown that visual tools or graphic organizers can improve reading comprehension (NICHD, 2000). The main effect of using visual tools appears to be on the improvement of the reader's memory for the content that has been read. Teaching students to organize the ideas that they are reading about in a systematic, visual representation helps them to remember what they read and improves their comprehension and achievement in all subject areas.

According to Hyerle (1996), visual tools foster a collaborative, interactive style of learning. Indeed, visual tools can be used for brainstorming and facilitating dialogue, open-ended thinking, mediation, metacognition, theory development, and self-assessment. For example, Hyerle points out that there are three types of visual tools: brainstorming webs (useful for generating ideas), task-specific organizers (helpful for organizing information specifically for a learning purpose), and thinking process maps

Characteristics of Three Types of Visual Tools

	Brainstorming Webs	Task-Specific Organizers	Thinking Process Maps
TYPES OF VISUAL TOOLS	Mapping of ideas Clustering Webbing	Story maps Flow charts Venn diagrams	Bubble maps Tree maps Brace maps Flow maps Multiflow maps
CHARACTERISTICS	Free-form Any response accepted Represents rapid-fire response to topic in question Idiosyncratic in form	Highly structured Usually teacher-generated Students must fill in boxes and responses provided Usually applies to a specific task or book	Visually designed to reflect fundamental thinking Somewhat similar to task-specific organizers
USES	Excellent prereading and prewriting strategy Promotes connection between ideas Allows all ideas to be considered	Excellent postreading activity Reinforces specific skills and reading strategies Good reinforcement of comprehension	To improve thinking ability To improve metacognition To allow students to be reflective To increase comprehension and enable transfer to other areas
INDIVIDUAL APPLICATION	Useful before reading and writing to get all ideas down on paper	Can be completed individually to reinforce concepts	Allows student to analyze and organize conceptual structure of a discipline
APPLICATION IN COOPERATIVE GROUPS	Allows all students to voice ideas Students gain respect for each other	Groups can fill out together to reinforce concepts	Good collaborative tools for communication in group problem solving
ASSESSMENT ISSUES	Not a valid instrument for formal assessment	Excellent to assess comprehension and reading strategies	Excellent to assess students' organization of concepts and connection of ideas

FIGURE 10-3

(enabling students to apply thinking processes, such as comparing or contrasting events or characters). Figure 10–3 describes these three types of visual tools and how they can be used in the classroom for all students.

According to Hyerle (1996), *brainstorming webs* are used to generate ideas and develop students' fluency with thinking. They are usually guided by focus questions such as "What is a community?" or centered around a specific objective such as the topic "whales." As brainstorming webs develop, it is important for the teacher to model how to link related ideas and connected concepts by clustering them. Brainstorming webs are very open-ended, and there should be no "wrong" response, being very unstructured and idiosyncratic. They are useful as a vehicle that allows students to articulate and verbalize ideas in a safe and supportive environment where they will not be criticized because "anything goes." Figure 10–4 shows an example of a brainstorming web that a graduate-level literacy class developed using the software program Inspiration to describe its philosophy of a balanced literacy class. Note how the different strands are clustered according to topic.

Hyerle (1996) explains *task-specific organizers* as visual tools for managing and displaying information that relates directly to a specific learning skill, a defined task, or

Brainstorming Web

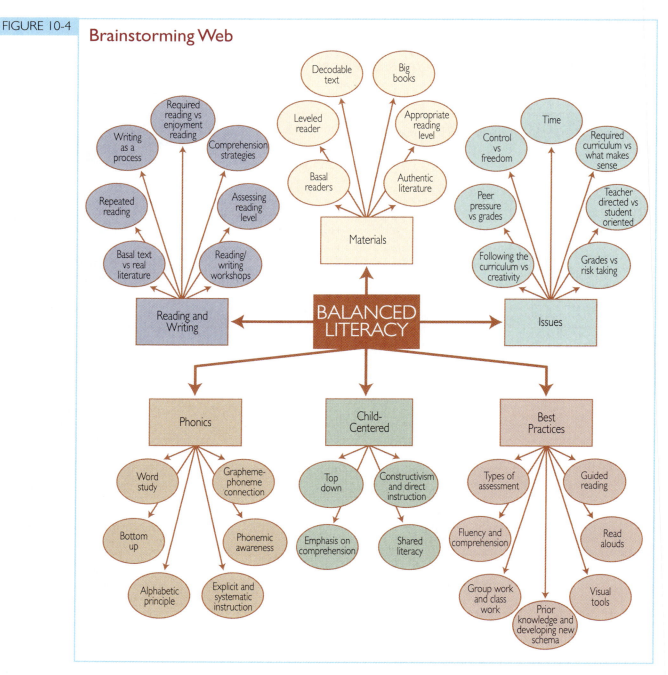

specific book that is being read. Examples of task-specific organizers range from story maps, flowcharts, and diagrams outlining a specific procedure or skill. Two task-specific organizers developed by a teacher to help students comprehend the books are shown in Figures 10–5 and 10–6. Figure 10–5 is a literary poster and was developed for the book *Saint George and the Dragon* by Margaret Hodges. Figure 10–6 was developed for the book *Why Mosquitoes Buzz in People's Ears* by Verna Aardema and helps readers to sequence events. These tools were developed for specific books so students could accomplish specific tasks and are, therefore, what Hyerle would term "task-specific." They are powerful tools for visually representing the interrelationships of concepts and ideas. They support students as they apply strategies to comprehend text and allow teachers to see how students organize ideas and information gathered from text; these visual tools are useful in assessing students' comprehension.

According to Hyerle (1996), the third type of visual tool allows students to develop thinking processes and improve their metacognitive abilities and reflectiveness. These

FIGURE 10-5

Task-Specific Organizer: *Saint George and the Dragon*

Wanted: A brave knight to fight the dragon.

List what characteristics this knight should have.

The Knight must be:

1. _____
2. _____
3. _____
4. _____
5. _____

The Knight must do the following:

1. _____
2. _____
3. _____
4. _____
5. _____

thinking process maps support the improvement of students' overall thinking abilities over time. Once a student learns how to construct and analyze these tools, they become lifelong tools for independent learning and problem solving. The thinking process maps themselves need to be consistent graphic tools that are the same across tasks and disciplines, they must be flexible in use, and they must promote understanding and reflection of the content or skills to be learned. Figure 10–7 provides an example of a tree map based on the book *Aunt Harriet's Underground Railroad in the Sky* by Faith Ringgold. This type of visual tool can be used in many different activities in many different disciplines, and it promotes higher order thinking skills. By learning how to construct tree maps, students learn how to break a general topic down into subtopics and elaborate on aspects of each subtopic. This type of activity facilitates higher order thinking skills and is generalizable to other subject areas and tasks.

The real value of introducing graphic organizers or visual tools is to provide students with a lifetime set of skills that they can use to read, write, and think with greater facility and meaning. Once students begin internalizing these organizers, they can learn to use them as their own visual tools when encountering similar reading and thinking problem-solving situations.

There are many ways in which students and teachers can use visual tools in a literacy class. The teacher can construct a visual tool to accompany a lesson or a book, and then have the students fill it in as the lesson progresses. This is probably the simplest and most basic way that visual tools are used in the classroom. The teacher can construct a visual tool with the class to demonstrate the relationship of concepts and to graphically organize information with the class's input. One of the most effective ways to use visual tools is to have the students construct their own to represent their patterns

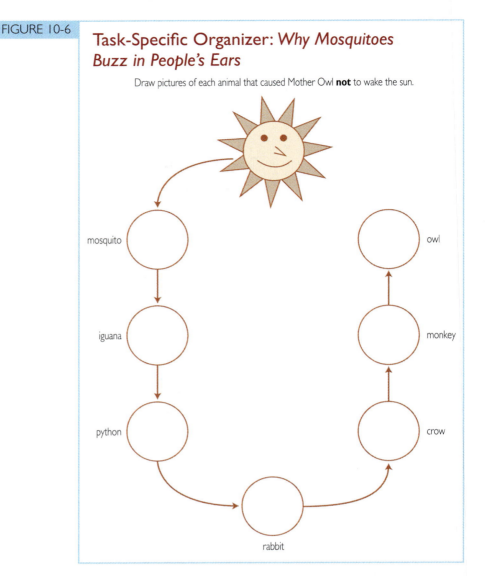

FIGURE 10-6

Task-Specific Organizer: *Why Mosquitoes Buzz in People's Ears*

Draw pictures of each animal that caused Mother Owl **not** to wake the sun.

mosquito

iguana

python

rabbit

owl

monkey

crow

of thinking and conceptualization of the topic. In all the ways just mentioned, the visual tool is used to reinforce or build instructional knowledge.

Visual tools also can be used for assessment. They provide teachers with a picture of student thinking, and as such allow the teacher to assess depth of knowledge and how that information is organized. The teacher can see the supporting connections that underlie the students' knowledge base and evaluate not only the actual product of learning but also the hidden processes that the student went through in learning the material.

Teachers' VOICES   Using Graphic Organizers in the Classroom

I am a teacher who wants to improve the reading comprehension levels of second language learners. When contemplating a technique to improve reading comprehension, I thought about my own learning style and the techniques I use to grasp information presented in articles and books. I understand concepts and ideas better when information is categorized and organized; therefore, I center my lesson plans on various types of graphic organizers. I use sequence chains, description guides, and compare/contrast charts. I have found that graphic organizers that are more specific and structured aid the learning of my students.

—*Jennifer M. Cavanaugh, Fourth Grade Teacher*

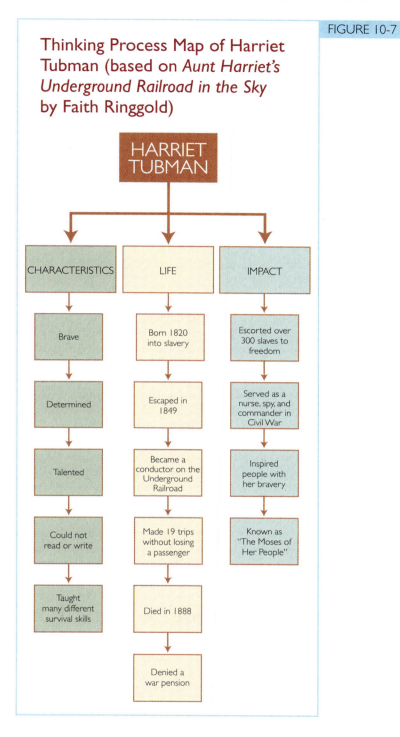

FIGURE 10-7

Thinking Process Map of Harriet Tubman (based on *Aunt Harriet's Underground Railroad in the Sky* by Faith Ringgold)

When students construct their own visual tools, they develop metacognitive behaviors. They have the opportunity to see their own thinking develop through visual representations and they learn to think about their own thinking, to assess their own learning. Students can step back and literally view their own work to determine whether it is clear and whether they understood the material (Hyerle, 1996). They can see the holistic picture of what they have learned and think about whether it makes sense. The development of metacognition is one of the more valuable aspects of using visual tools.

Visual tools increase reading comprehension by allowing students to represent their understandings of the text visually. It helps them to organize their thoughts into a coherent pattern and to examine whether that pattern makes sense. It reinforces what they remember from the text and allows them to better retain this visual image as a representation of their understanding. The old adage "a picture is worth a thousand words" often holds true when students are trying to process and retain information from text. Visual tools act as a scaffolding tool by supporting students' comprehension and retention of material.

In teaching students how to use visual tools in the classroom, Hyerle (1996) recommends the following steps:

1. Present at least one good example of a completed visual tool to the class.

2. Model how to construct either the same visual tool or one similar to it.

3. Provide knowledge on how to construct the visual tool, doing a "think-aloud" and showing students the procedural knowledge necessary to proceed independently.

4. Give the students opportunities to practice constructing their own visual tools with support and feedback from the teacher.

5. Coach the students as they proceed to work independently on constructing their own visual tools.

In a reading lesson, visual tools can be a prereading, during-reading, or postreading activity. As a prereading activity, students can construct brainstorming webs on the topic to activate prior knowledge. They can also fill in visual tools that will assess their prior knowledge of the topic or motivate them to learn more about it. As a during-reading activity, visual tools can help students keep track of events and act as an ongoing conceptual organizer. Visual tools can help students reinforce important concepts by visually representing them, thereby facilitating storage in short-term memory for retrieval purposes. It is recommended that during-reading activities be done with longer, more complex material, rather than with short, simple stories. It is often better to complete a story and focus on comprehension rather than interrupt the story to complete an activity and thereby disrupt the development of comprehension. However, if the story is long, complex, or expository text (nonfiction), during-reading visual tools can help students keep track of the important events, as long as the tool does not distract from the overall flow of the text. As a postreading activity, visual tools promote long-term comprehension of conceptual information because the information is graphically organized and structured in such a way that it is much easier for children to remember and subsequently recall (Dixon-Krauss, 1996a). Visual tools are an excellent way to have children respond to literature because children usually find them fun and helpful in organizing material.

Using Visual Tools with Diverse Learners

Visual tools have been found to be beneficial to students with learning disabilities. The interactive nature of these tools may help students with learning disabilities overcome their "passive" approach to learning, as well as to facilitate storage and retrieval of information from memory (Meese, 2001). As students progress into the higher grades, reading increasingly involves comprehending informational text such as textbooks; however, this type of text can pose more challenges than reading narrative fiction. Informational text (see a detailed discussion in Chapter 12) is structured differently than fiction and may contain many technical vocabulary words. This type of text requires students to apply different comprehension strategies, and many students with learning disabilities who already have difficulty with reading may be further challenged by informational text. Using a graphic organizer is one strategy that has often been recommended to support students with learning disabilities (Kim, Vaughn, Wanzek, & Wei, 2004).

Graphic organizers can help struggling readers graphically represent the meaning of the material and the relationships of the ideas, while developing their visual style of learning. Often, visual tools are an excellent way to help students with learning disabilities take notes when the mechanics of writing can prevent them from getting their ideas down fast enough. Visual tools are also an excellent way to assess those students who may know the content but find that language problems interfere with their expression of ideas and communication of content. Thus, visual displays of information provided by graphic organizers enhance the reading comprehension of students with learning disabilities, possibly by helping them organize the verbal information and thereby improving their recall of it (Kim et al., 2004).

Visual tools can also benefit English language learners by providing a means of conveying information without having to rely on knowing the grammatical structure of English. Visual tools allow English language learners to concentrate on the main ideas and concepts being taught, and they provide a visual means to learning new information and communicating ideas. One recommendation is to create visual tools that have words in the child's native language to represent the ideas being taught, thereby scaffolding the process of learning a new language and helping the student remember both the content and the new words that represent the content in a more visual and effective way.

STRATEGIES FOR TEACHING DIVERSE STUDENTS

Approaches and Strategies that Promote Literacy

1. Make sure that all students are working in their zone of proximal development. This is especially important for diverse learners, such as students with learning disabilities and English language learners, who need the support and guidance of working at their appropriate instructional level in the classroom.

2. Teach direct, systematic phonics instruction for struggling readers. Students with learning disabilities greatly benefit from this type of instruction due to a phonological weakness and need the systematic approach to decoding words. English language learners may also benefit from this type of instruction, especially native Spanish-speaking students whose language is also phonetically based.

3. To motivate struggling readers, incorporate read-alouds, shared reading, and guided reading into the balanced literacy classroom. English language learners will be especially motivated to read multicultural literature that addresses their own culture.

4. Use decodable texts with students with learning disabilities. These books allow students to progress at a slower pace using a phonics-based approach to language, and it helps them concentrate on a smaller number of phonetic patterns. Decodable texts may also be beneficial to English language learners, who need to work on decoding skills.

Decodable books can be used in guided reading sessions and during independent reading, but they should not replace authentic literature during read-alouds that will motivate students.

5. When assigning reading material to struggling readers, be sure that the text is on the student's correct level of reading. Leveled texts help the teacher match the appropriate text with the student's literacy needs.

6. Carefully monitor the use of electronic text in the classroom to ensure that all students can read it properly. This is especially important for struggling readers.

7. If using a basal series, make sure these texts meet the needs of diverse learners: (1) make sure that they are on the appropriate reading level, (2) make sure that English language learners can relate to the material and illustrations, and (3) adapt instruction so that students with learning disabilities and English language learners are not becoming frustrated and falling increasingly further behind.

8. Use visual tools and graphic organizers to support comprehension of text for students with learning disabilities and English language learners. These tools have been shown to increase comprehension and are an important strategy to increase literacy achievement in the classroom.

Examples of Visual Tools

The following visual tools reinforce the use of children's literature in the literacy classroom. Each tool is designed to help students use specific reading strategies to effectively respond to and comprehend a piece of literature. These visual tools can be used as a postreading activity to reinforce the concepts in the book. Many of the activities require the students to go back and reread the book or remember specific details of the book; therefore, the book should be available for students to refer back to if necessary.

Visual Tools for Prereading – The following visual tools can be used in a literacy classroom to support students' comprehension of text. They serve as excellent tools for prereading activities. The Story Map Prediction Chart (Figure 10–8) can be used in two different ways: (1) After doing a walk-through of the book, the student can predict the setting, characters, and problem; (2) after the book is read, the student can go back to

FIGURE 10-8

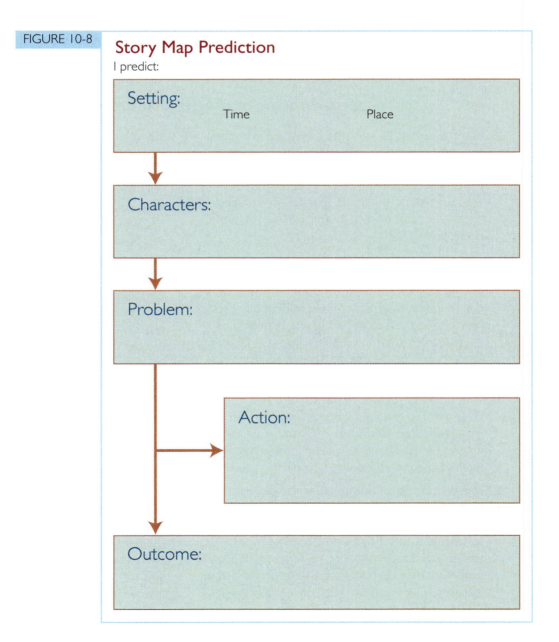

Story Map Prediction

I predict:

Setting:
             Time   Place

Characters:

Problem:

Action:

Outcome:

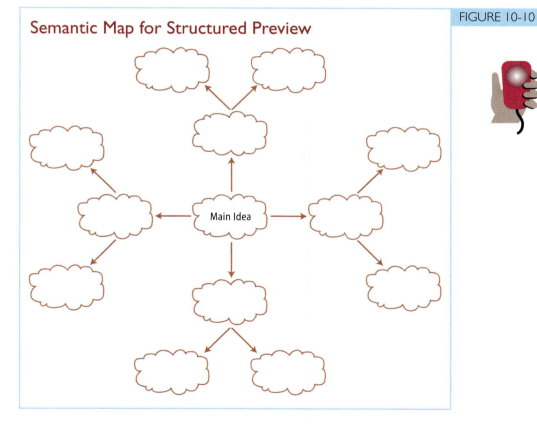

K-W-L Chart

FIGURE 10-9

K-W-L Strategy Chart

K	W	L
What we KNOW	What we WANT to learn	What we LEARNED

Semantic Map for Structured Preview

FIGURE 10-10

Main Idea

revise the original predictions and fill in the action and outcome. The K-W-L Chart (Figure 10–9) can be used before a topic is introduced. The student fills in the K (what we Know about the topic) and the W (what we Want to learn about the topic). After the text has been read, the student completes the final L column (what we Learned about the topic). The Semantic Map for Previewing Text (Figure 10–10) can be used before a text is read to preview the main idea or topic. It is also a good way to generate ideas from the students about what they might already know about the story or topic to be read.

Visual Tools for Postreading – The following visual tools are excellent postreading activities, once a text has been read to reinforce comprehension strategies. The Story Map Chart (Figure 10–11) is similar to the Story Map Prediction Chart; however, it

FIGURE 10-11

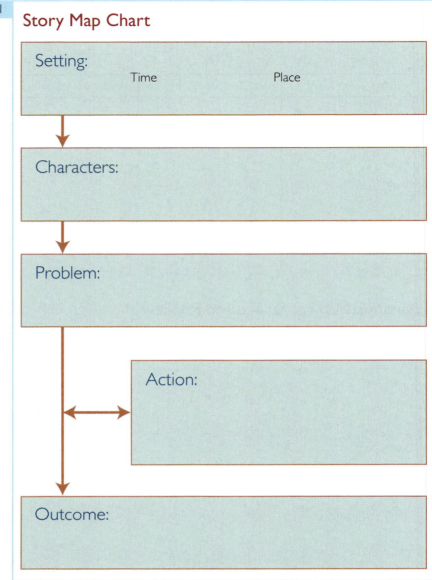

Story Map Chart

Setting:

Time   Place

Characters:

Problem:

Action:

Outcome:

is used as a postreading activity to summarize the key points of a story. The Semantic Map can also be used to reinforce ideas after the text is read to have students organize and recall events in the story or to analyze a character in a story. Figure 10–12 shows how a semantic map can be used to analyze a character in a story. The Venn diagram (Figure 10–13) is an excellent visual tool to compare and contrast ideas for kindergarten through grade 3. In the middle circle, the student writes down all those attributes that are similar to the two objects, events, or characters being compared. In the outer circles, the student identifies all those attributes that are unique to the individual object, event, or character being contrasted. The Three Main Ideas Chart (Figure 10–14) is an excellent tool to organize a student's writing; it can be used as a postreading strategy for students to write down three main ideas from the text and three supporting details. It is the precursor to outlining and can be used to help students organize their thoughts before they start writing a composition. The Compare and Contrast Chart (Figure 10–15) is an excellent tool of grades 4 through 12. It is a more advanced tool than the Venn diagram because it requires the student to develop criteria to contrast the attributes of the two objects, events, or characters being evaluated. Figure 10–15a shows how this tool can be used to compare the whole-language and balanced reading approaches to literacy. They are compared using the criteria of *skills, grouping, readings,* and *phonics.*

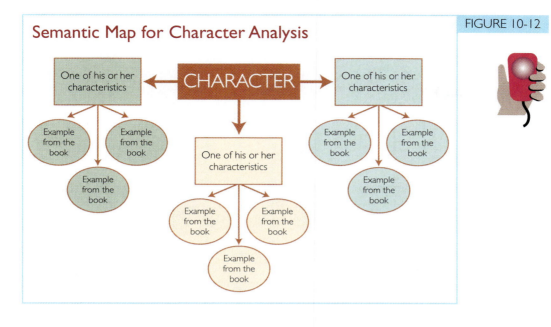

Semantic Map for Character Analysis

FIGURE 10-12

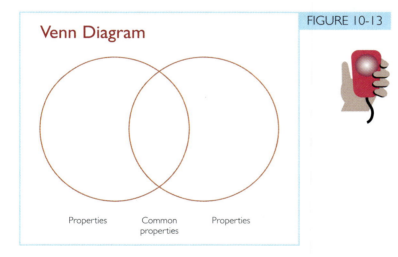

Venn Diagram

FIGURE 10-13

Using Technology to Promote the Use of Visual Tools

Many wonderful sites on the Internet provide excellent visual tools or graphic organizers for teachers to use in the classroom. A simple search on the Internet using the term *graphic organizers* will yield a multitude of sites with ready-made tools. A few of these sites are given below, and more can be found on this chapter's website.

The following sites offer ready-made graphic organizers that a teacher can use in the literacy classroom. Many of these tools are pdf files, which will allow the teacher to quickly download and print them out. Most of these organizers are generic visual tools that can be used in many different ways. Some of the visual tools available are Venn diagrams, K-W-L charts, and organizers to help students identify story elements.

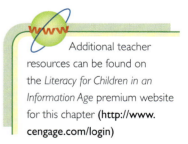

Additional teacher resources can be found on the *Literacy for Children in an Information Age* premium website for this chapter (**http://www. cengage.com/login**)

- http://edhelper.com/teachers/graphic_organizers.htm
- http://www.eduplace.com/graphicorganizer
- http://www.sdcoe.k12.ca.us/score/actbank/torganiz.htm
- http://www.region15.org/curriculum/graphicorg.html (in English and Spanish)
- http://www.writedesignonline.com/organizers

FIGURE 10-14

Three Main Ideas Chart

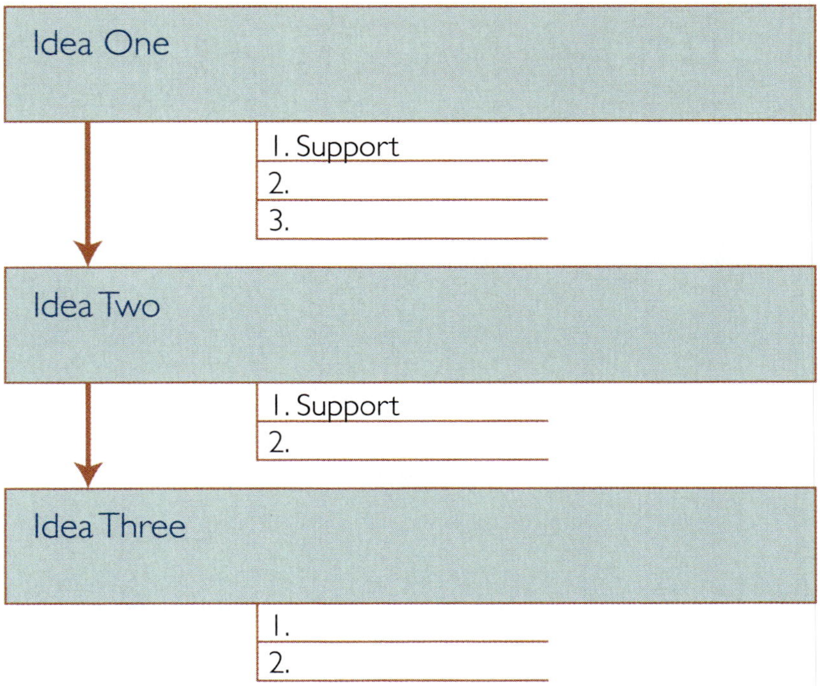

Idea One

1. Support
2.
3.

Idea Two

1. Support
2.

Idea Three

1.
2.

FIGURE 10-15a

Compare and Contrast Chart

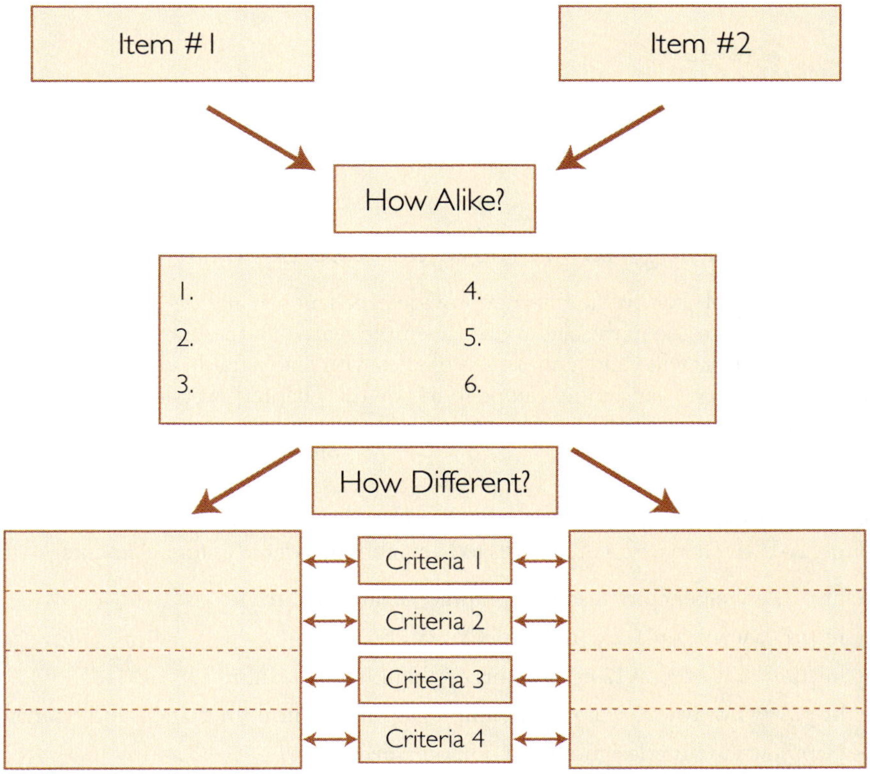

Item #1   Item #2

How Alike?

1.   4.
2.   5.
3.   6.

How Different?

| Criteria 1 |
| Criteria 2 |
| Criteria 3 |
| Criteria 4 |

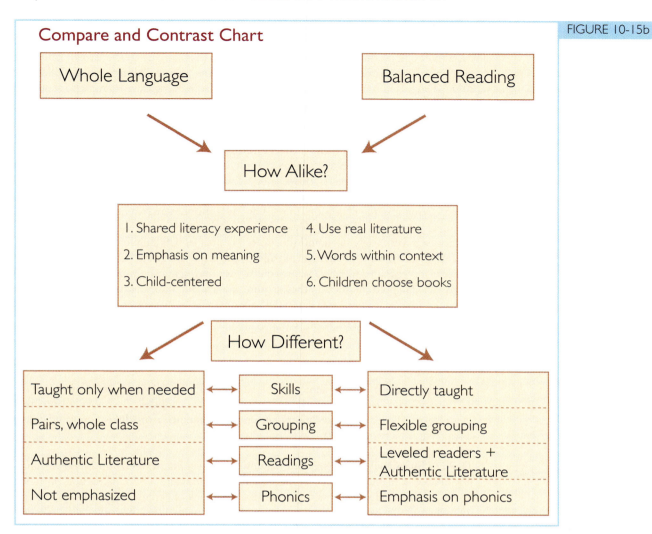

Compare and Contrast Chart

FIGURE 10-15b

Whole Language

Balanced Reading

How Alike?

1. Shared literacy experience   4. Use real literature

2. Emphasis on meaning   5. Words within context

3. Child-centered   6. Children choose books

How Different?

Taught only when needed	Skills	Directly taught
Pairs, whole class	Grouping	Flexible grouping
Authentic Literature	Readings	Leveled readers + Authentic Literature
Not emphasized	Phonics	Emphasis on phonics

Response to Intervention: Addressing the Needs of Struggling Readers

Response to Intervention (RTI) is an alternative approach to identifying struggling readers by providing intensive, timely, and necessary instruction based upon continuous diagnosis of student needs. This new approach shifts the emphasis of the identification process toward providing support and intervention to struggling students in an effort to reduce the growing numbers of children receiving special education services (Allington & Walmsley, 2007; Lipson & Wixson, August/September, 2008).

Mesmer and Mesmer (December 2008/January 2009) indicate that this new identification process is an important change in special education law, citing the reauthorization of the 2004 federal legislation known as the Individuals with Disabilities Education Act (IDEA). This recent initiative provides language that enables RTI to be "a process based on the child's response to scientific research-based intervention" (34 C.F.R. 300.307, 2006). RTI is also viewed by policy makers, educators and parents as a safeguard, ensuring, "that underachievement in a child suspected of having a specific learning disability is not due to lack of appropriate instruction" (34 C.F.R. 300 & 301, 2006).

The importance of expert, intensive tutoring in producing dramatic results in struggling readers is presented in the experimental research by Frank Vellutino and colleagues (1996), which was conducted nearly a decade before RTI was introduced. Results of this seminal research study argue convincingly that approximately two-thirds of at-risk first graders were found not to have specific learning disabilities but were, instead, "instructionally disabled." More recent research findings by Vellutino and Fletcher (2005) show that beginning readers' difficulties may not be cognitive deficits that are biologically based but may be due to the lack of intensive instructional opportunities children have in learning to read (Allington and Walmsley, 2007). Thus, RTI is a way of preventing children from being over-identified for special education when, in fact, these at-risk children may actually be deprived of appropriate reading interventions.

Prior to the RTI initiative, and dating back to 1977, students with learning disabilities have been identified using a **discrepancy model.** This assessment method uses the discrepancy between a student's IQ test scores and the student's achievement in the classroom as the basis for diagnosing a learning disability. If a student has normal cognitive functioning based upon IQ scores, but does not perform at the expected level of achievement in the classroom in reading, then the student can be referred for formal testing to determine eligibility for special education services. This discrepancy model continues to be widely used and most often results in delaying instructional interventions for students with learning disabilities until second grade. In contrast, RTI uses an early screening prevention approach by identifying and helping struggling readers receive the targeted instruction they require. As a result, many of these children will no longer be in jeopardy of "waiting to fail" (Fuchs, Fuchs, & Vaughn, 2008; Mesmer and Mesmer, December 2008/January 2009).

The Three Tiers

Although there is no single, thoroughly researched and widely practiced "model" of the RTI process, it is generally implemented in a three tier model of school supports that uses research-based academic interventions. The **three-tier model** is described below (RTI Action Network, 2009).

Tier 1: High-Quality Classroom Instruction, Screening, and Group Interventions – Within tier 1, all students receive high quality, scientifically based instruction provided by the teacher and specialists to ensure that their lack of achievement is not due to inadequate instruction. All students in a school are screened on a periodic basis to establish an academic and behavioral baseline, and this screening identifies those students who are struggling and who need additional support. This screening can take place in kindergarten or first grade, but preferably in all grades. Students identified as being "at risk" through the screenings and/or results on state- or district-wide tests receive supplemental instruction during the school day in the regular classroom. The length of time for this step generally does not exceed eight weeks. During this time, student progress is closely monitored using a curriculum-based assessment. At the end of this period, students showing significant progress are returned to the regular classroom program. Students not showing adequate progress are moved to tier 2.

Tier 2: Targeted Interventions – Students not making adequate progress in the regular classroom in tier 1 are provided with increasingly intensive instruction matched to their needs based upon their performance and rates of progress. These services and interventions are provided in small-group and tutorial settings in addition to instruction in the general classroom. In the early grades (kindergarten through grade 3), interventions are usually in the area of reading. A longer period of time may be required for this tier, but it should generally not exceed eight weeks. Students who continue to show too little progress at this level of intervention are then considered for more intensive interventions as part of tier 3.

Tier 3: Intensive Interventions and Comprehensive Evaluation – At this level, students receive individualized, intensive interventions that target the students' skill deficits. Students who do not achieve the desired level of progress in response to these targeted interventions are then referred for a comprehensive evaluation and considered eligible for special education services under the IDEA 2004. The data collected during tiers 1, 2, and 3 are included and used to make the eligibility decision.

It should be noted that at any point in an RTI process, IDEA 2004 allows parents and guardians to request a formal evaluation to determine eligibility for special education. An RTI process cannot be used to deny or delay a formal evaluation for special education.

Implementing RTI – Staff development is essential in implementing RTI successfully, particularly in helping classroom teachers differentiate and monitor instruction (Fuchs, Fuchs, & Vaughn, 2008). High costs attributed to staff development in the past, may be eased somewhat, in that IDEA legislation allows school districts to use 15 percent of monies earmarked for students with learning disabilities, to be used in general education. This money can be used to increase the reading achievement of at-risk children, thereby, preventing them from being classified. Consequently, local school districts can use this funding source for staff development and increased staffing to provide smaller student–teacher ratios in tier 2 and tier 3 settings for the purpose of limiting the numbers of children identified for special education. Once policy makers and district leaders realize that RTI is not solely a special education initiative, and that funding can be used to improve targeted at-risk students in regular education, it is likely that greater interest in this valuable alternative process will become a long, overdue reality (Allington, R. L. and Walmsley, S. A., 2007; Fuchs, Fuchs, & Vaughn, 2008).

STRATEGY BOX

Using Different Approaches That Promote Literacy

In the introductory scenario, Mr. O'Neil incorporated literature into his literacy program by using many different approaches. Through a shared literacy experience, he read a quality award-winning book about a topic they were investigating in class: *tolerance*. Mr. O'Neil used the following strategies in his classroom:

1. He used authentic literature to motivate the students in the class.

2. During the read-aloud session, he modeled fluent reading to motivate students.

3. He used visual tools to help students visualize the content being presented and comprehend the material more effectively.

4. He had students develop their own visual tools to communicate what they had learned of the material presented.

5. He used visual tools as a means of assessment, especially for students with learning disabilities and English language learners.

6. He used a variety of texts within the classroom to support different types of readers.

7. He taught specific strategies for comprehending different types of text.

8. He taught students strategies for reading and comprehending electronic text.

9. He provided a library with leveled books for students to read so that students are reading texts at their appropriate level.

10. He selected texts that the children could relate to and that were culturally sensitive to their native culture.

11. He used many different approaches to teaching literacy in the classroom.

Final Thoughts

Teachers need to know about different instructional approaches and philosophies to implement a balanced literacy program. Elements from each approach can be incorporated into a comprehensive program and support children's literacy growth. The most important thing teachers should remember is that there is not *one* approach that works for all children; the teacher needs to know a variety of approaches and techniques to meet the diverse needs and backgrounds of students. Teachers must see the big picture that all children need support and guidance in their literacy development while working in their zone of proximal development. Teachers, therefore, need to know a multitude of approaches, techniques, and strategies to support each child.

EXPLORATION   Application of Concepts

Activities

1. *Collect a few examples of each type of text used in literacy classrooms: predictable text, decodable text, basal readers, little books, and authentic literature.* In groups, look over each type of text, make up a list of distinguishing features for each type of text, and give the group's impressions of each type. Conduct Fry's readability formula on each one. Then have each group try to level the books. Have each group present its findings to the class.

2. *Bring in a basal reading program with its readers, teacher's guide, and supplemental materials.* In groups, pick out one grade level. Have the groups carefully analyze the program according to the following criteria:

   - Does it provide a balanced approach to literacy?

   - Does it support mediated instruction and Vygotsky's theory of literacy as a socially mediated process?

   - Are the readers interesting? Are they controlled or literature-based text? Do they promote higher order thinking?

   - What is the basic philosophy of the basal program?

   - What types of lesson plans are included in the teacher's guide? Are they consistent across the year? Do they allow for flexibility and creativity?

   - Is there a scope and sequence chart in the package? Does it lay out all the skills covered for the year?

   - What supplemental material is provided? Do they support literacy in the classroom? Are they valuable?

3. *Visit a classroom that is using leveled readers as part of its literacy program.* Question the teacher as to how difficult it was to level the texts in the classroom and what the advantages/disadvantages of this system are. As a follow-up, pick out 10 children's texts of all levels and try to level them in groups.

4. *Develop lesson plans that use a visual tool as an integral part of the instruction.* Hand in a blank one and a filled-in version to ensure that it works well. Explain how it would support diverse learners in your classroom.

5. *Explore the resources available on the companion website for this chapter that can help a teacher learn about different approaches to teaching literacy.* Many additional teacher resources are available on the *Literacy for Children in an Information Age* premium website (http://www.cengage.com/login).

HOME–SCHOOL CONNECTION Staying Informed about Current Approaches to Literacy

Parents and guardians should be well informed about the different approaches to literacy that are being implemented in their child's classroom. This can be accomplished by the teacher sending home periodic handouts updating the parents and guardians on the approaches and strategies being used. The handouts can also recommend additonal readings and websites that the parents and guardians can access for further information. Teachers can also recommend different types of books that the students can read at home, based upon the students' individual needs.

Keeping parents and guardians informed about response to intervention (RTI), and how it works is extremely important because:

1. Parents and guardians need to be personally involved at key points in the RTI process
2. Parents and guardians whose children are considered for more intensive phases of RTI (tiers 2 and 3) must be part of the team of decision makers
3. In order for RTI to be successful, the schools will need parental support and involvement.

There are a variety of ways in which parents and guardians can be informed about the process of RTI:

- District-wide dissemination of information about RTI through newsletters
- RTI workshops held by the school or district
- RTI websites for parents and guardians
- Back-to-school night
- Parent–Teacher Association meetings

Several important educational associations and research organizations have posted websites about RTI that are an excellent way for parents, guardians, and teachers to obtain important information, support materials, and resources.

• RTI Action Network
http://www.rtinetwork.org/Learn/What/ar/WhatIsRTI

• National Research Center on Learning Disabilities
http://www.nrcld.org/topics/rti.html

11 USING LITERATURE TO PROMOTE LITERACY

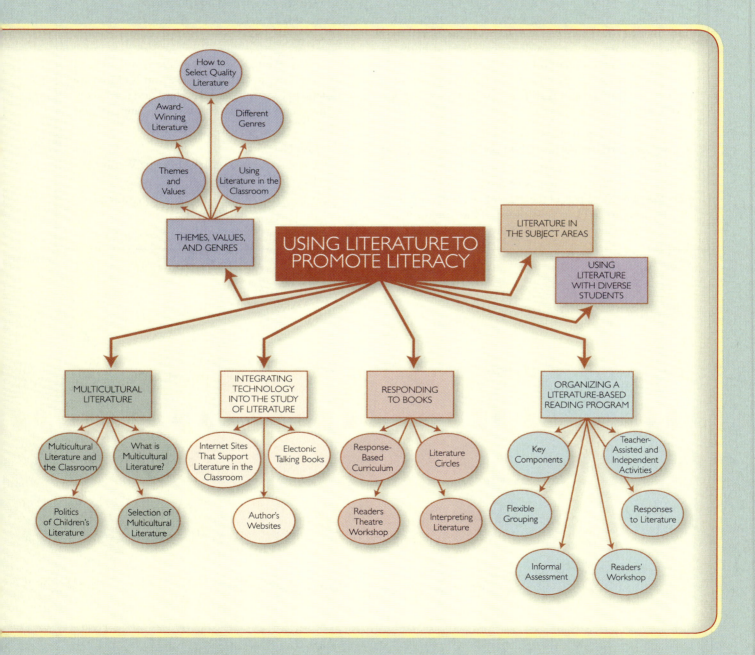

How to Select Quality Literature

Award-Winning Literature

Different Genres

Themes and Values

Using Literature in the Classroom

THEMES, VALUES, AND GENRES

USING LITERATURE TO PROMOTE LITERACY

LITERATURE IN THE SUBJECT AREAS

USING LITERATURE WITH DIVERSE STUDENTS

MULTICULTURAL LITERATURE

Multicultural Literature and the Classroom

What is Multicultural Literature?

Politics of Children's Literature

Selection of Multicultural Literature

INTEGRATING TECHNOLOGY INTO THE STUDY OF LITERATURE

Internet Sites That Support Literature in the Classroom

Electonic Talking Books

Author's Websites

RESPONDING TO BOOKS

Response-Based Curriculum

Literature Circles

Readers Theatre Workshop

Interpreting Literature

ORGANIZING A LITERATURE-BASED READING PROGRAM

Key Components

Teacher-Assisted and Independent Activities

Flexible Grouping

Responses to Literature

Informal Assessment

Readers' Workshop

International Reading Association Professional Standards Addressed in this Chapter:

IRA STANDARD 1: FOUNDATIONAL KNOWLEDGE

Candidates have knowledge of the foundations of reading and writing processes and instruction.

1.1 Demonstrate knowledge of psychological, sociological, and linguistic foundations of reading and writing processes and instruction.

1.2 Demonstrate knowledge of reading research and histories of reading.

1.3 Demonstrate knowledge of language development and reading acquisition and the variations related to cultural and linguistic diversity.

1.4 Demonstrate knowledge of the major components of reading (phonemic awareness, word identification and phonics, vocabulary and background knowledge, fluency, comprehension strategies, and motivation) and how they are integrated in fluent reading.

IRA STANDARD 2: INSTRUCTIONAL STRATEGIES AND CURRICULUM MATERIAL

Candidates use a wide range of instructional practices, approaches, methods, and curriculum materials to support reading and writing instruction.

2.1 Use instructional grouping options (individual, small-group, whole-class, and computer-based) as appropriate for accomplishing given purposes.

2.2 Use a wide range of instructional practices, approaches, and methods, including technology-based practices, for learners at differing stages of development and from differing cultural and linguistic backgrounds.

2.3 Use a wide range of curriculum materials in effective reading instruction for learners at different stages of reading and writing development and from different cultural and linguistic backgrounds.

IRA STANDARD 4: CREATING A LITERATE ENVIRONMENT

Candidates create a literate environment that fosters reading and writing by integrating foundational knowledge, use of instructional practices, approaches and methods, curriculum materials, and the appropriate use of assessments.

4.1 Use students' interests, reading abilities, and backgrounds as foundations for the reading and writing program.

4.2 Use a large supply of books, technology-based information, and nonprint materials representing multiple levels, broad interests, and cultural and linguistic backgrounds.

4.3 Model reading and writing enthusiastically as valued lifelong activities.

4.4 Motivate learners to be lifelong readers.

Key Terms

Caldecott Medal
Newbery Medal
narrative text
expository text
genre
picture book
poetry
verse
folklore

Focus Questions

1. Why is it important to read quality children's literature in the classroom?

2. How can multicultural literature be used in the classroom to promote literacy?

Focus Questions *(continued)*

3. How can technology enhance the study of children's literature?

4. What is a response-based curriculum? Describe at least five ways in which children can respond to literature.

5. How can you use literature with diverse learners, such as students with learning disabilities and English language learners?

6. What are the key components in organizing a literature-based curriculum?

7. How can teachers integrate literature into the subject areas?

Welcome to Mrs. Santos' Third Grade Classroom: Using Literature to Promote Literacy

David Young-Wolff/PhotoEdit

Mrs. Santos has her third grade class sit in the reading corner on a rug while she sits on a comfortable chair. They are involved in Reader's Workshop, a workshop approach to teaching, reading, and Mrs. Santos is going to conduct a read-aloud. She holds up the book *The Other Side* by Jacqueline Woodson and asks the students to look at the cover of the book and to think about the title. The book tells the story of Clover, a black girl, and Annie, a white girl, and a fence that separates their houses. The story is about how Clover and Annie learn to sit on the fence together and become friends, overcoming the racial tension that divides them. Mrs. Santos asks the class about the fence on the cover and what they think it might mean. She elicits their predictions and comments about what the book might be about. She then reads the book out loud, modeling expressive and fluent reading. When she is finished, the class discusses the book and the different themes that emerged from the reading. Mrs. Santos calls on different children, especially those who might not be eager to volunteer comments, and encourages all children to talk.

After the read-aloud, Mrs. Santos gives a short 10-minute mini-lesson, the second part of Readers' Workshop, on the literary elements of a story: the setting, main characters, problem, and solution. She has already drawn a story map on the easel, and together with the class, she models how to fill in the different elements of *The Other Side* on the story map.

She also adds the heading "Theme" to it, and they discuss the different themes of the book.

After the mini-lesson, Mrs. Santos asks the children to go to the class library with their partner to choose a book or to take out a book they have been previously reading. She now has the partners read a book out loud: the children read it together first and then one student reads it alone while the other provides feedback. They practice rereading the books several times, which helps develop fluency. The students are paired heterogeneously. Mrs. Santos walks around the room to make sure they are reading books that are on their appropriate level, and she also conferences with some students. She provides feedback and help when students are having trouble identifying words and she refers them to the word wall, which has many high-frequency words and word families listed on it. She administers a running record to some of the students and systematically writes anecdotal records as she observes them. Three days a week, Mrs. Santos works with guided reading groups when the students are reading independently.

After about 20 minutes, Mrs. Santos tells the children it is now time to respond to what they have read. The children get into literature circles, sitting at desks clustered together; each circle is based on common topics, authors, or books. Again, Mrs. Santos roams around the classroom, joining in the literature circles and helping direct the discussion. After about 10 minutes, Mrs. Santos calls on one student from each circle to briefly share what they have discussed. She then has the children go back to their desks and write a brief paragraph or draw a picture in their journals about what they have read today and how it relates to their own lives. She asks them to comment on the book *The Other Side* and write about an experience that they might have had with a friend.

This scenario shows how Mrs. Santos incorporates literature-based instruction into her classroom. It describes Readers' Workshop (see the detailed discussion later in this chapter), and it shows how Mrs. Santos uses literature to promote comprehension and fluency. Mrs. Santos has her children respond to literature in many different ways: through class discussion, through a story map, through literature circles, through sharing of ideas with the whole class, and through writing in literary journals. A response-based curriculum is an essential component of a balanced literacy classroom. This chapter describes how literature can be incorporated into the classroom and discusses many different ways children can respond to what they have read.

Themes, Values, and Genres

The following passage vividly describes an account of one of the most feared and hated villains of the twenty-first century, a villain who has captured the imagination of youths around the world.

> Voldemort raised his wand again and whirled it through the air. A streak of what looked like molten silver hung shining in the wand's wake. Momentarily shapeless, it writhed and then formed itself into a gleaming replica of a human hand, bright as moonlight, which soared downwards and fixed itself upon Wormtail's bleeding wrist.
>
> Wormtail's sobbing stopped abruptly. His breathing harsh and ragged, he raised his head and stared in disbelief at the silver hand, now attached seamlessly to his arm, as though he were wearing a dazzling glove. He flexed the shining fingers, then, trembling, picked up a small twig on the ground, and crushed it into powder. "My Lord," he whispered. "Master . . . it is beautiful . . . thank you . . . *thank you* . . ." (J. K. Rowling, *Harry Potter and the Goblet of Fire*, p. 563)

The *Harry Potter* series has become a phenomenon for our youth, reawakening the joy and anticipation of reading a good book and becoming immersed in its story-telling. For our children, who are growing up in a computerized world of role-playing games and technical wizardry, J. K. Rowling has conjured a world that is as exciting, far-reaching, and imaginative as any website. Like Oliver Twist or Dorothy from *The Wizard of Oz*, Harry Potter is an orphan who must make his way alone in a confusing world, fighting to preserve goodness against evil and willing to bend adults' rules to do so. Many universal themes abound in these books, as they do in other classic tales, and J. K. Rowling has inspired a new generation of children to read books and explore these themes.

A large number of young adults do not read for pleasure anymore. The literary read-ing rates of 18- to 24-year-olds fell significantly from 1992 to 2002. The portion of young people reading at least one poem, play, or work of fiction for pleasure fell from 53 to 43 percent (National Endowment for the Arts, 2004). In addition, the number of books sold that was purchased by people younger than 25 declined from 5 to 3.9 percent from 2000 to 2003. With so much time spent on e-mail, instant messaging, and browsing the Internet, our children quickly make the transition from reading for pleasure to reading for homework. *Harry Potter* has helped overcome this resistance to reading for many children and has encouraged parents to sit and read the books aloud to those not yet capable of reading them independently. As entertaining as a *Harry Potter* character is, there are many, many other books that can capture the imagination of our youth and enrich their lives.

Young children are usually introduced to the concept of literacy through children's literature. They sit by a parent's side and share the beauty and emotions conveyed through the text. They look at the pictures together, laugh at the jokes, alternate in the reading, and mutually share in the emotional journey that the book takes its readers on. The joy of holding those books, leafing through the pages, and examining the illustra-tions is an experience that stays with children throughout their whole lives. This is one reason children's literature makes so much sense in the classroom.

Literacy development begins to evolve when the child is very young and progresses through the process of sharing and interacting with a parent, grandparent, older sibling, aunt, or uncle. Children develop their ability to construct meaning by sharing books with others and by responding to what they have read. In a shared literacy experience, chil-dren share the process of reading good literature and learn how to relate these meanings to their own lives. Shared literacy should continue in the classroom for all age groups.

Reading children's literature is highly motivating.

Courtesy of Guilherme Cunha

Themes and Values

Many of the themes in children's literature are universal; they transcend age, race, and gender. Children's literature addresses issues of growing up, being homeless, searching for lost parents, dealing with divorce, contending with death in the family, finding inner strength, and persevering during adversity and hardships. Many of these themes may be difficult to discuss in class, but through a protagonist's personal tale, they can be discussed and explored openly. A story gives personal and emotional significance to a topic and often adds much humor, something desperately missing from our classrooms today.

An example of this is *Bud, Not Buddy* by Christopher Paul Curtis, a funny, heartwarming tale of a young boy growing up in Flint, Michigan, during the Great Depression who is determined to find his unknown father. It is a book with wonderful characters, funny situations, themes that deal with friendship, loss, and perseverance, and emotional depth that teaches readers about what it is like to be African American in 1936. It is a book that could tie into so many different themes, such as an exploration of the Great Depression, the history of American music (Bud joins a jazz band while searching for his father), the geography of Michigan, and the importance of family in growing up. Readers learn directly about Bud's emotional needs, and learn values and morals through his eyes, as the following passage shows.

> I went back up to the librarian at the lending desk. . . .
>
> "I'm looking for Miss Hill." The librarian looked surprised. "Miss Hill? My goodness, haven't you heard?" Uh-oh! That's Number 16 of Bud Caldwell's Rules and Things for Having a Funner Life and Making a Better Liar Out of Yourself, that's one of the worst ones.
>
> **RULES AND THINGS NUMBER 16**
>
> **If a Grown-up Ever Starts a Sentence by Saying**
>
> **"Haven't You Heard," Get Ready, 'Cause**
>
> **What's About to Come Out of Their Mouth Is Gonna**
>
> **Drop You Headfirst into a Boiling Tragedy.**
>
> It seems like the answer to 'Haven't you heard' always has something to do with someone kicking the bucket. And not kicking the bucket in a calm, peaceful way like a heart attack at home in bed either, it usually is some kind of dying that will make your eyes buck out of your head when you hear about it, it's usually the kind of thing that will run you out of a room with your hands over your ears and your mouth wide open. Something like hearing that your grandmother got her whole body pulled through the wringer on a washing machine, or something like hearing about a horse slipping on the ice and landing on some kid you went to school with.
>
> (C. P. Curtis, *Bud, Not Buddy*, pp. 55–56)

Children's literature is an excellent way to convey values and morals of a culture. Without lecturing or talking about moral reasoning, readers learn to experience it by being placed in situations to which they can relate. Many folktales and stories about a culture have a definite message or moral to teach. In Japan, popular American children's fairy tales are changed to reflect the values that the culture desires to convey to its young population. In the Japanese version of *Little Red Riding Hood*, the wolf apologizes to Little Red Riding Hood and grandma for his immoral behavior, thereby teaching children that it is important to acknowledge one's misdeeds, show remorse, and hopefully change for the better (Kristof, 1996). In the same way, the morals of folktales are a means of teaching beliefs and reaffirming the significance of those beliefs. The moral and ethical dimension of children's literature is an excellent vehicle for introducing ethics into the classroom and teaching students how to analyze different cultures' values and views of the world.

Children's literature presents a concept in a simple and accessible way, becoming an excellent way to introduce a new theme or topic. It can be integrated into every subject area and enhance and enrich the subject matter for students of all ages. The themes and values that are conveyed in children's literature will add a new dimension to any class and will promote literacy through a motivating and interesting context.

Using Literature in the Classroom

One of the most important reasons children's literature should be used in a literacy classroom is that it is so highly motivating for children. Children of all ages, of all abilities, and of all cultures read the *Harry Potter* series because they are motivated to do so. Motivation is the key element to success in anything undertaken, and good literature can be a highly motivating factor to get children to read. When children are presented with an alluring picture book with wonderful illustrations, captivating plot and memorable characters, they will want to read on.

Using rich literature in the classroom promotes literacy development. Frequent and positive contact with books creates interest in reading, increased interest results in more reading, and more reading results in better reading (Cullinan, 1992). Even if young children are just browsing through a book and enjoying the pictures, they are partaking in reading behaviors that display an interest in reading. They are learning how to predict a story from studying the illustrations, they are learning how to use pictures as a clue to gather information, they are following a sequence of ideas, and they are learning that books are enjoyable and interesting objects that are worthwhile to spend time with. When children learn to enjoy spending time with a book, chances are they will read more and become better readers. There is no secret to becoming a good reader; those who read become *good* readers.

Children's literature contributes to language growth and development (Galda & Cullinan, 2010). When children are exposed to rich language through literature, it shapes their thought processes and cognitive development. Through literature, children encounter a greater variety of new words and become familiar with the syntax of complex sentences. Their vocabulary becomes richer and their ability to express themselves improves. The language of literature differs from the language of conversation; often, literary language is lyrical, poetic, and uses many different techniques to convey a message. Look back at the excerpt from *Harry Potter and the Goblet of Fire* that introduces this chapter. Note how J. K. Rowling describes the force coming out of Voldemort's wand: "molten silver hung shining in the wand's wake . . . it writhed and formed itself into a gleaming replica of a human hand, bright as moonlight." These are not phrases or words that an ordinary 8-year-old would be exposed to in normal conversation at home. These words enable young people to have a broader range of experiences to call on in the future; rich figurative language enables them to draw on resources that nonreaders would never have.

Using literature in the classroom helps students become better writers. The variety of narrative structures children see in quality literature helps them become better writers by adding to the resources they can call on. Literature can cause a reader to think about not only *what* is said but *how* it is said (Cullinan, 1992). This will help children think about not only what to write but how it should be written. They will mimic many of the styles that they encounter while reading and try to write like a favorite author, trying out new styles.

Lastly, one of the major reasons literature should be used in the classroom is the emotional appeal of a good story. Literature deals with the whole range of human emotions and enables the reader to empathize with characters they never would relate to if not through reading. This type of emotional connection is such an important part of human growth and development; children need to develop empathy, sympathy, and relate to others from other cultures, races, and ways of life. The human experience is revealed and explored in good literature in a way that textbooks, videos, and films will never be able to replicate. Good literature can touch the soul and make you laugh and cry.

Award-Winning Literature

Each year in mid-January, there is great excitement in children's book publishing: educators wait for the winners of two different awards that are given to outstanding children's literature to be announced. Among the awards given out by the American Library Association (ALA) are two separate categories: the Caldecott Medal and the Newbery Medal.

The **Caldecott Medal** was named in honor of nineteenth-century English illustrator Randolph Caldecott. It is awarded annually to the illustrator of the most distinguished American picture book for children. Although the award is given to one book, the "runners-up" are also given a medal known as the Caldecott Honor Book. A list of all the Caldecott books and recent winners is available at the ALA website (http://www.ala.org/alsc/caldecott.html).

The **Newbery Medal** is awarded to the most distinguished American children's book published the previous year. It is awarded to what is commonly called "chapter books" in the classroom, that is, books geared for an older audience of readers. On June 21, 1921, Frederic G. Melcher proposed the award to the ALA meeting of the Children's Librarians' Section and suggested that it be named for the eighteenth-century English bookseller John Newbery. The Newbery Medal thereby became the first children's book award in the world, and it continues to be the best known and most discussed children's book award in this country. Like the Caldecott Medal, the "runners-up" are awarded the Newbery Honor Book award. A list of the previous winners, as well as this year's winner, is available at the ALA website (http://www.ala.org/alsc/newbery.html).

The Coretta Scott King Book Award is presented annually by the Coretta Scott King Task Force of the American Library Association's Social Responsibilities Round Table. Recipients are authors and illustrators of African descent whose distinguished books promote an understanding and appreciation of the "American Dream." The award commemorates the life and work of Dr. Martin Luther King, Jr., and honors his deceased widow, Coretta Scott King, for her courage and determination in continuing the work for peace and world brotherhood in her lifetime. A list of previous winners is available at the ALA website (http://www.ala.org/ala/mgrps/rts/emiert/cskbookawards/index.cfm).

Teachers should be aware of the different books that have won the awards mentioned above; the selection is of high quality and contains a variety of books that will enrich literacy activities. Children will enjoy the varied selections that these books can bring to the classroom and will find them motivating and fun to read.

Different Genres of Literature

Books can be broken into two very broad categories: narrative and informational (often called expository) texts. **Narrative text** tells a story and is usually fiction. Narrative books have characters who encounter a problem and resolve it; therefore, a narrative contains certain literary elements. These include setting, characterization, plot, theme, and style (see Figure 11–1 for an explanation of the literary elements). **Expository text** includes informational books or nonfiction, such as a book written about a historical event or one that describes a specific topic or subject, such as dolphins. Informational texts are described in detail in Chapter 12.

Literature can also be categorized into different genres. A **genre** is a type of book that is distinguished by its use of a specific setting, type of characters, plot, and overall form or structure (Galda & Cullinan, 2010). This categorization helps readers distinguish among different types of books and provides a framework for discussion and teaching strategies. For example, poetry is made up of a distinctive form or structure, with its short sentences or lines, often rhythmic pattern and rhyming words, and word repetition.

A **picture book** presents a story or concept that is told through a combination of text and illustration. Picture books include small books made out of cardboard for

Literary Elements in Narrative Text

Setting: Setting usually includes two elements: time and place. *Time* refers to when the story is occurring, i.e., present day, the future, or during a historic period. *Place* refers to where the story is taking place, i.e., in a city, in a rural area, in a particular place. Many narrative texts revolve around the setting, which becomes an extremely important part of the story. Other stories do not elaborate on the setting quite as much, tending to emphasize characterizations and plot development much more. Teachers should focus on the setting, pointing out how it is important to the development of the author's message, or how it is purposely not emphasized and how other literary elements are.

Books that emphasize setting are: *Smoky Night* by Eve Bunting and illustrated by David Diaz; *Strega Nona* by Tomie dePaola; and *Island of the Blue Dolphin* by Scott O'Dell.

Main Characters: In narrative text, stories have main characters, those on which the story focuses. How the author develops the main character is an important feature for teachers to note. Characters can be multidimensional, showing strengths and weaknesses and developing over time. The characters can also be one-dimensional, showing little emotion and not bringing much depth to the story. Teachers should choose books that have strong characterization; the characters are portrayed dealing with conflict in resolving problems and show realistic emotions during the story.

Books that have strong main characters include: *Bud, Not Buddy* by Christopher Paul Curtis; *Mirette on the High Wire* by Emily Arnold McCully; *Sam, Bangs and Moonshine* by Evaline Ness; and *The Invention of Hugo Cabret* by Brian Selznick.

Plot: Plot refers to the sequence of events of the story and how a conflict is resolved. The plot usually revolves around a conflict and how the main character can resolve it. The plot can be subdivided into:

    Problem: The primary conflict that the main character needs to contend with can be self against self in which the main character must deal with a struggle within him or herself; self against others in which the main character must contend with a struggle against other people or another character; self against society in which the character must struggle with some sort of societal issue like racism or values; and self against nature in which the character must battle the forces of nature.

    Resolution: The main character must resolve the problem in some way, and this resolution is a major part of how the plot plays itself out.

Teachers should point out the sequence of events that makes the plot interesting and show how all stories don't have to be action-packed to have an interesting plot.

Books that have strong plots are: *Hey, Al* by Arthur Yorinks; *Lon Po Po: A Red Riding Hood Story from China* adapted and illustrated by Ed Young; and *Number the Stars* by Lois Lowry.

Theme: The theme is the central message that the author is conveying. It is the overriding idea around which the story revolves. Often, a story can have a number of interrelated themes that the author is trying to communicate. Teachers should point out and discuss the theme of the book with the class and encourage different interpretations of what the theme might be. Usually the theme can convey a moral of the story.

Books that have strong themes are: *The Giver* and *Number the Stars* both by Lois Lowry; *Roll of Thunder, Hear My Cry* by Mildred B. Taylor; and *Grandfather's Journey* by Allen Say.

Style: Often, style is considered one of the literary elements. This is the way that the author writes—in a humorous fashion, in a serious style, in a highly descriptive manner. Often, the style will reflect the time and place in which the story is occurring; for example, if it is historical fiction, it might be written in a manner similar to that period. The author's style will also help develop the characters through description and dialogue used. Style also includes the point of view that the author is writing in—first-person narrative in which the story is told directly by one character and "I" and "we" are used to tell the story, or third-person narrative in which the characters are described as if someone was watching from the outside and telling the story using "he," "she," and "they." Teachers should point out defining features of the author's style and how the author used words to effectively tell the story, develop characters, and convey a specific message.

Books that have distinctive writing styles are: *Holes* by Louis Sachar which is told in a very humorous style; *Golum* by David Wisniewski, which is told in a very serious style; *Tuesday* by David Wiesner, which although there are few words, has a definite style of writing.

FIGURE 11-1

young children to the elaborate illustrations of a book like *Rapunzel* by Paul Zelinsky. Picture books have become a major industry and have inspired such artists as Eric Carle, who wrote such noteworthy books as *The Very Hungry Caterpillar* and *The Very Busy Spider,* to open up a museum dedicated to his artwork. In the book *Smokey Night,* a story about the Los Angeles race riots, the illustrator, David Diaz, created collages out of common objects found at the riot such as paper bags, beans, rice, and the plastic that dry cleaners wrap around clothes. Picture books have become a rich source of excellent literature for all ages, not just for children. Many books, such as *So You Want to Be President?* by Judith St. George and illustrated by David Small, are appropriate for an older audience, even high school students, who can grasp the difficult concepts and sequence of events. It is no longer true that picture books are for primary grade children only. Picture books are defined as a genre through structural form—the combination of text and illustration. Every genre is represented in picture books.

Poetry and **verse** are a wonderful form of literature that children naturally love, perhaps due to their exposure to rhymes and verse from a very young age. Poetry is defined through its musical language, rhythm, and structural form, often distinguished by short, condensed lines and use of metaphor that convey meaning in creative and unusual ways. The normal rules and structures of grammar do not apply to poems; therefore, children find reading and writing poetry especially motivating. Rhyme, rhythmic patterns, repeating words and phrases, expressive words, and creative combinations of language are all features that comprise poetry as a unique structural form. Poetry is not emphasized enough in the classroom, especially with older children. Poetry can help teach reading and writing skills in a motivating way. Researchers have found that poetry learned by heart in childhood stays with a person for the remainder of his or her lifetime (Galda & Cullinan, 2006). There are many wonderful books of poetry out on the market. Such poets as Shel Silverstein, who wrote *A Light in the Attic*, *Falling Up*, and *Where the Sidewalk Ends*, Jack Prelutsky who wrote *For Laughing Out Loud*, Bill Martin Jr. who edited *The Bill Martin Jr Big Book of Poetry*, and many other books, are children's favorites due to their humorous and irreverent attitude toward life.

Folklore is composed of stories that were passed down by word of mouth through the generations. The stories are not attributed to authors, but rather to the storytellers who finally wrote them down. Charles Perrault and the Brothers Grimm wrote volumes of fairy tales that reflected the culture and value of their time. Modern storytellers continue to pass along many of these aural stories and change them to reflect the current culture. Examples of folklore are nursery rhymes from Mother Goose, tall tales such as Paul Bunyan, fairy tales such as Cinderella, folktales such as Anansi stories from Africa, and mythology from Greek, Roman, and Native American cultures. Recently, many of the picture books that have been published fall into this genre; for example, *Joseph Had a Little Overcoat* by Simms Taback, *Rapunzel* by Paul O. Zelinsky, *Golem* by David Wisniewski, *Lon Po Po: A Red Riding Hood Story from China* adapted and illustrated by Ed Young, *St. George and the Dragon* retold by Margaret Hodges, and *Why Mosquitoes Buzz in People's Ears* retold by Verna Aardema are all rich and wonderful examples of folklore from many different cultures.

Fantasy is based on its unique setting of imaginative worlds and make-believe places. Fantasy books usually involve characters and creatures that could not exist and that live in fantastical lands. Dragons, wizards, and magic are often common in fantasy books. This genre has become increasingly popular with the advent of the *Harry Potter* series of books and movies and the making of the Tolkien trilogy, *Lord of the Rings*, into popular movies. Many readers become involved with this particular genre and specifically choose books from this category as the predominant books they read. They love to be transported to fantasy lands, to read about heroes who slay dragons and use supernatural powers to overcome enemies. Because authors develop complete worlds with imaginary characters, they tend to create series of books that continue the theme and adventures of these characters. Philip Pullman's trilogy *The Golden Compass*, *The Subtle Knife*, and *The Amber Spyglass* are wonderful, rich stories about two young children who battle evil forces to save their world. Susan Cooper's books are based on Celtic myth and include *Over Sea, Under Stone*, and continue with *The Dark Is Rising*, *Greenwitch*, *Silver on the Tree*, and *The Grey King*. Lloyd Alexander has a wonderful award-winning set of books based on old English lore, *The Prydain Chronicles*, which include five books and follows the adventures of its young hero, Taran. Tamora Pierce with her *Alanna, the First Adventure* series is loved by young girls because of the strong, adventurous main character, Alanna. C. S. Lewis wrote *The Chronicles of Narnia*, with the first book being *The Lion, the Witch and the Wardrobe*, which has been loved by children for years. Fantasy is a wonderful imaginative genre for children of all ages that has many rich and powerful books written about alluring lands and classic themes. Usually those children who become involved in this genre need encouragement to explore other books from different genres.

Science fiction is close to fantasy except that the imaginative worlds and unique characters live in the future. Often, science fiction melds scientific theories with fictional worlds and presents "what-if" scenarios using these theories as the basis for its story. Unfortunately, teachers do not often use this genre in the classroom. Like fantasy, many children prefer only this type of genre to read, while other children have not been exposed to it and will shun it if given the chance. There are many good science fiction books from which to choose. Madeleine L'Engle has written a series including *Wrinkle in Time*, in which children search for their father, who has been taken to a far-off galaxy. Lois Lowry explores the notion of tight control of communities and thoughts in her classic *The Giver* and its sequel, *Gathering Blue*. Science fiction is well-suited for readers in the upper elementary grades who are exploring scientific concepts in class and can expand their connections of science to good literature.

Realistic fiction is based on telling stories that could happen today, using characters that could exist in our world. Realistic fiction addresses the problems that plague the human condition—hunger, death, divorce, homelessness, growing up and making friends. Such books as Beverly Cleary's *Ramona* series and Judy Blume's *Tales of a Fourth-Grade Nothing* and *Superfudge* are wonderful and humorous stories about the problems of growing up. These books are used frequently in classroom libraries for independent reading and as part of the literacy curriculum for read-alouds and class reading. This genre gives children an opportunity to connect with experiences similar to their own and allows children to discuss issues that may be difficult to express. This genre includes mystery stories, adventure/survival stories, stories about animals, sports stories, humorous stories, romance stories, stories about other cultures, and stories about growing up.

Historical fiction is based on telling a story whose setting is in the past and telling of events that occurred (or might have occurred) in the past. The story basically weaves historical facts into a fictional story, usually with fictional characters. These books are an excellent way to integrate literacy into the social studies curriculum and help make often boring accounts into realistic, exciting, and motivating tales of adventure and daring. *Bud, Not Buddy* (see earlier) is historical fiction that takes place during the Great Depression. Mildred Taylor's *Roll of Thunder, Hear My Cry* is another book written about an African American family growing up in the 1930s and the racism and hatred that they must endure. Elizabeth George Speare has written two award-winning historical fiction books, *The Sign of the Beaver* and *The Witch of Blackbird Pond*. *My Brother Sam is Dead* by Colier and Colier is a wonderful tale of the American Revolution that has powerful themes of war and loyalty running throughout its story line. Historical fiction is an excellent way to relate many historical events to children's lives through a compelling story that makes the historical period and event meaningful and relevant. Readers get a chance to travel back through time and place to explore an event they might never be exposed to otherwise.

A **biography** tells the story of someone's life and achievements. It gives children a chance to read about a person who made an impact on the world in some way. It expands the vision of their own lives by letting them view how one person accomplished something noteworthy, and hopefully will inspire them to try to achieve and attain more themselves. Many different biographies exist that have been written by a wide range of people who have achieved notable accomplishments, from sports stars to singers to politicians to historical figures to artists to scientists. *The Invention of Hugo Cabret* by Brian Selznick, the 2008 winner of the Caldecott award, is an amazing book about Georges Méliès, the father of science-fiction movies. Russell Freedman has written many excellent award-winning biographies, such as *Lincoln: A Photobiography*, *The Wright Brothers: How They Invented the Airplane*, *Eleanor Roosevelt: A Life of*

Discovery, and *The Voice That Challenged a Nation: Marian Anderson and the Struggle for Equal Rights*. An autobiography is written in the first person by the author. A few authors have written autobiographies that children may find interesting after becoming familiar with their books. Tomie dePaola, a favorite author of children's picture books, writes about his own life in four different books: *26 Fairmount Avenue, Here We All Are, What a Year*, and *On My Way*, all slim chapter books that allow children to read about dePaola's childhood. Often, children are required to read a biography or autobiography as part of the social studies or science curriculum, which allows the children to personalize that subject area through an emotional story. Through exploring someone's life, children can understand many of the obstacles and hardships that the person had to overcome. They learn that life is not so easy or glamorous, and that one must work hard to attain any degree of success. Biographies are not usually among children's most favorite genres to read, but they are excellent books to teach about famous people and events.

Nonfiction books are those that present facts, ideas, and concepts in order to teach about something. The book may tell a story, but the facts must be true and the emphasis on presenting a realistic and factual account of what occurred. Some popular nonfiction books are the *Magic School Bus* series. These books present factual knowledge in a fun, humorous, and exciting way to children. Nonfiction books are an excellent resource in all subject areas and greatly enhance the curriculum with motivating and enriching material. Many nonfiction books for children contain excellent illustrations and detailed information presented in a much more accessible manner than traditional textbooks. Any classroom library should have a rich collection of nonfiction books to help students expand their knowledge of many different subject areas. When a specific topic is being covered in social studies or science, the classroom library should also feature nonfiction books on that specific theme or topic. Some of the 2009 winners of the National Council of Teachers of English Orbis Pictus Nonfiction award are: *Amelia Earhart: The Legend of the Lost Aviator* by Shelley Tanaka, illustrated by David Craig (which won the award); *George Washington Carver* by Tonya Bolden (an Honor Book); and *When the Wolves Returned: Restoring Nature's Balance in Yellowstone* by Dorothy Hinshaw Patent, illustrated by Dan and Cassie Hartman (an Honor Book). Other nonfiction books that children have chosen as favorites are *Crocodiles* by Sandra Markle, which is about "the perfect predator who can hold his breath underwater for a full hour," and *Dogs: How to Choose and Care for a Dog* by Laura S. Jeffrey. Many children prefer reading nonfiction books such as these, and there is a wide variety of quality books written for children and adolescents that teachers can choose. Chapter 12 covers informational text in detail and contains a more in-depth discussion of nonfiction literature.

How to Select Quality Literature

Children's literature provides us with the opportunity to build background knowledge about a topic and learn about the world around us. Selecting books for the classroom is a multidimensional process that depends on what topics and themes the curriculum will be covering and the teacher's goals on how to enrich the curriculum. There is a wide diversity of quality books on the market today from which teachers can choose for their students.

One of the most important qualities to look for in children's literature is the richness of the story line and its emotional connection to the teacher and students. If the book matches closely with curriculum goals and it contains suitable, nonbiased material that presents its material in a fair and honest manner, then the book might be an appropriate selection. Once a teacher becomes familiar with the various genres in contemporary children's and adolescent literature, and knows the types of books her students connect with, then choosing books becomes easier. The most important points are that the book should not present any characters in stereotypical fashion, the content should be accurate and nonbiased, the message should be one that is appropriate for children or adolescents, and students should be able to make a connection with the book.

Courtesy of Becky Stovall

Effective teachers encourage students to choose quality books from a variety of genres.

The collection of books in the classroom should be culturally diverse and portray many different cultures in a rich and sensitive manner. This helps children understand and appreciate the similarities and celebrate the uniqueness of different cultural groups. All genres of children's and adolescent literature can promote cultural diversity and be shared and discussed in the classroom.

Currently, there are so many high-quality children's and adolescent books on the market that making a selection can be quite overwhelming. Teachers can use the resources listed below to help them make their choices:

◆ *Book awards:* An excellent place to start is with the books that have won awards recently and in years past. Children's book awards include the Caldecott Medal (given to the illustrator of a picture book), the Newbery Medal (given to the author of children's or adolescent literature), the King Award (given to an African American author and illustrator whose work exemplifies world peace), and the Pura Belpre Award (given to a Latino/Latina writer and illustrator whose work celebrates Hispanic culture). To find out which books have won awards, visit the ALA website (http://www.ala.org).

◆ *Electronic databases:* There are many electronic websites that can help teachers select books and offer a wealth of resources.

BookWire

http://www.bookwire.com

BookWire is an online portal used by the book industry to access the latest industry news, literary journals, reviews, and a directory of book sites around the world. There is also a link to children's books: "BookWire Presents" at http://bookwire.com/bookwire/BowkerRecommends/Feb2006/childrens.htm. This is an interesting site to explore for book enthusiasts.

The Children's Book Council

http://www.cbcbooks.org

The Children's Book Council, Inc., is the nonprofit trade association of publishers of trade books for children and young adults. This site is an excellent resource for the selection of quality children's literature.

www

Additional teacher resources can be found on the *Literacy for Children in an Information Age* premium website for this chapter (http://www.cengage.com/login).

Children's Literature Network

http://www.childrensliteraturenetwork.org

Children's Literature Network is a wonderful site to explore children's literature; it offers extensive information, resources, and links.

The Cooperative Children's Book Center (CCBC)

http://www.education.wisc.edu/ccbc

The CCBC site is part of the research library for Wisconsin schools and is devoted to children's literature. It recommends books for children and young adults on many themes and topics (see "Book of the Week"). It also grants awards to quality literature.

Library of Congress

http://www.lcweb.loc.gov

The Library of Congress has a section for kids and families and for teachers. You can search for a book by last name of author or by book title.

Teachers' VOICES Self-selecting Literature

Most of the time, students in my classroom self-select their novels/reading books. There are a few times when I bring them back together to read a whole class book (like the fabulous *Charlotte's Web*: I am committed to making sure every child who leaves my class has read this on his or her own!), but this happens only two to three times a year. When self-selecting, the students are given a range of five to seven books, all related by a central theme, that will be explored throughout the reading (transformations, challenges, identity, and so forth). I think back to my first year of teaching, when the students were not self-selecting their books and I am immediately struck by the change in their motivation to read. When they are given the opportunity to choose what they read, they thrive (for the most part). I have found that the challenge is how to help the child who does not thrive and love reading to become interested and intrigued by a great book. I am still looking for the answer.

—*Donna Friedrich, Third Grade Teacher*

◆ *Professional Associations:* The International Reading Association (IRA), the National Council of Teachers of English (NCTE), and the ALA are wonderful resources for discovering the quality books that are published each year. Each year, the IRA (http://www.reading.org) publishes two lists of recommended books: (1) "Teacher's Choices" are outstanding trade books published for children and adolescents that teachers find to be exceptional in curriculum use; and (2) "Children's Choices" are books that children evaluate, providing reviews of their favorites. Both lists are divided into age groups and genres to help in the selection process. The ALA (http://www.ala.org) publishes "Children's Notable Lists," which recommend exemplary books, videos, recordings, and computer software for children. This is an excellent resource for quality selection of classroom materials. The NCTE (http://www.ncte.org) also grants awards for excellence in children's and adolescent literature. The Orbis Pictus Nonfiction Award is given to only one book, with up to five Honor Books recognized. The NCTE also grants the NCTE Poetry Award for Children and is an excellent resource for selecting quality children's poetry.

Classroom teachers need to explore the richness and variety of quality books that are constantly being published. It is worthwhile for teachers to stay current with professional associations, electronic databases, and children's awards to provide a wide array of books for children to read in the classroom.

Multicultural Literature

Multicultural Literature and the Classroom

Literature can develop and extend understandings and attitudes important to living in our multicultural society. In our increasingly diverse classrooms, it is important that youngsters begin to understand the effects of social and economic problems on the lives of ordinary individuals and learn to appreciate and understand cultural differences. Literature can show us how we are connected to one another through emotions, needs, and desires, all experiences common to humankind. Literature can help all of us appreciate and celebrate our differences.

Minorities, now roughly one-third of the U.S. population, are expected to become the majority in 2042, with the nation projected to be 54 percent minority in 2050. By 2023, minorities will comprise more than half of all children (U.S. Census Bureau News, 2008). **Multicultural literature** is literature of all children, not just of a certain group. Multicultural studies should be woven into the curriculum with books that emphasize multicultural issues and themes. Children need to see themselves reflected in literature at all ages, and they must also be exposed to every race, ethnicity, and culture that is present in our society. Through literature, children will come to know and respect their own heritage and that of other children.

The teacher's role is vital in introducing multicultural books to children, in making them enjoyable, and in facilitating discussion about them in a natural and supportive way. Their treatment of multicultural issues should not be superficial, covering only holidays, famous people, and customs. Rather, teachers need a more integrated approach in which they reexamine the curriculum and focus on students viewing problems, themes, concerns, and concepts from the perspective of different ethnic and cultural groups. For example, after reading *Aunt Harriet's Underground Railroad in the Sky* by Faith Ringgold, children learn what it was like to be a slave escaping along the Underground Railroad by experiencing the journey through the eyes of the main character, a young girl named Cassie. It is important that children receive different perspectives on events that occurred in history, because many different cultural groups view historical events differently—some in a positive way and some as having a negative impact on their culture.

Before the 1980s, few multicultural books were available. In 1965, Larrick surveyed 5,206 children's books published between 1962 and 1964. Of those books, only 6.7 percent included one or more African American characters in the text or illustrations. Furthermore, many of those characters were portrayed in biased and stereotypical ways. By 1979, Jeanne Chall and her colleagues tried to replicate this survey and found that of the 4,775 children's trade books published by the 51 responding publishers between 1973 and 1975, only 14.4 percent included one or more African American characters in the text or illustrations (Micklos, 1996). This represented more than a 100 percent increase from the prior survey, although many of the books still included stereotypical depictions of African Americans. Neither study focused on any other minority group.

In the 1960s, the Council on Interracial books for Children (CIBC) played a key role in increasing the number of children's literature books published by African Americans. The CBIC sponsored a number of literary contests that helped launch the careers of notable African American authors, such as Mildred Taylor (*Roll of Thunder, Hear My Cry*). In response to the civil rights movement, the federal government provided funding to school districts to purchase books created by African American authors. During this period, the Coretta Scott King Book Award, which honors African American authors and illustrators of outstanding books for children, was established (Brooks and McNair, 2009).

In the late 1980s and early 1990s, multicultural publishing experienced a spurt, as did children's book publishing in general. Almost all major publishers increased their multicultural book lists, and the number of smaller presses specializing in multicultural titles grew. This increase was due not only to a growing awareness and sensitivity on the part of book publishers, but also to the need to purchase these books as the school population changed demographically. Today, you can find an increased number of books about African, Asian, Latino, and Native American cultures. Children need to see themselves reflected in the books that they read and feel like they are important and valued members of society.

What Is Multicultural Literature?

What exactly is multicultural literature? If a book has illustrations of African-American children in it, but the plot and setting refer to no particular culture or traditions, is this multicultural? If the book is about a small town on an island in northern Maine that depicts specific values, cultural differences, and customs of these people, is this multicultural? Bishop (1993) claims that multicultural literature is literature by and about people who are members of groups considered to be outside the sociopolitical mainstream of the United States. Frequently, books featuring such groups have not been a part of the mainstream of children's literature in any significantly positive way. Usually, the term *multicultural literature* refers to books about people of color in this country—African Americans, Asian Americans, Native Americans, and Hispanics. Most lists of multicultural literature also include books about people of color outside the United States—for example, folktales from Africa and Asia. Multicultural books can also include books about regional groups in the United States, such as people from the Appalachians, or different religious groups, such as Amish or Jewish people, who have at times been misrepresented or portrayed inaccurately in literature.

Bishop (1993) claims that there are three general categories of multicultural literature: specific, generic, and neutral. A "culturally specific" children's book illuminates the experience of growing up as a member of a particular nonwhite cultural group; it details the particulars of daily living within that group using such specifics as language styles, religious beliefs, musical preferences, family configurations and relationships, attitudes and values, and social mores. A book such as Mildred Taylor's *Roll of Thunder, Hear My Cry* or Faith Ringgold's books *Tar Beach* and *Aunt Harriet's Underground Railroad in the Sky* are examples of culturally specific books.

"Generic" multicultural children's literature features characters who are members of so-called minority groups, but they contain few specific details that might serve to define those characters culturally. These books contain plots that have universal themes and experiences that are common to the world. Many picture books are generic in that the illustrations portray culturally diverse characters, but the plot and situations could occur within any cultural group. A well-known example of this is Ezra Jack Keats's Caldecott Medal winner *The Snowy Day* (1962). In this book, the characters are depicted in the illustrations as being African American, but the story is about one little boy's encounter with snow and could be about any little boy throughout the world.

The third category of multicultural books, known as "culturally neutral," predominantly includes picture books or books with illustrations that contain information about a topic and depict the characters as being culturally diverse. A textbook might portray culturally diverse children in its photographs, but its intent is to teach a specific topic in math, science, social studies, and so on. The writers and illustrators of these books have a strong commitment to cultural diversity, but cultural authenticity is not likely to be a major consideration when evaluating these books.

Many websites support teaching multicultural books in the classroom. After reading *Aunt Harriet's Underground Railroad in the Sky* by Faith Ringgold, children can visit a website that children in a second grade class developed about this book (http://www.pocanticohills.org/tubman/tubman.html). The following websites for children also support reading of multicultural literature:

www Additional teacher resources can be found on the *Literacy for Children in an Information Age* premium website for this chapter **(http://www.cengage.com/login).**

International Children's Digital Library (ICDL)

http://www.icdlbooks.org/index.shtml

The mission of the ICDL is to select, collect, digitize, and organize children's materials in their original languages and to create appropriate technologies for access and use by children 3 to 13 years old. This library includes 904 free children's books written in 34 different languages.

Multicultural Pavilion

http://www.edchange.org/multicultural

Multicultural Pavilion is an excellent site to learn more about multicultural education and to access current resources.

Folk and Fairy Tales from Around the World

http://www.unc.edu/~rwilkers/title.htm

http://www.topics-mag.com/folk-tales/page.htm

Both these sites contain a collection of folk and fairy tales from different countries.

Politics of Children's Literature

There is no doubt that quality children's literature brings enjoyment and aesthetic pleasure to the classroom, enriching the curriculum and motivating students to read. It should also be recognized that children's literature conveys messages, whether explicitly or implicitly, about many important social and political questions. Children's literature teaches our children from a young age about what a culture values and how social mores and customs should be followed. For example, children's literature will depict what it means to be a "good human being"; the relative worth of boys and girls; the value of a particular action; how we should treat people from different cultures; how we should react to stealing, lying, and other negative behaviors; and much more. If you examine folktales from different cultures, you can see how the characters react to similar circumstances in different ways. Because of the implicit messages that children's literature conveys, there have been criticisms of nursery rhymes and suggestions that they do not portray human behavior in a way that children should model.

A perfect example of the political implications of children's literature is through an examination of different books on Christopher Columbus. As Taxol (1993) points out, one cannot refute that Christopher Columbus's journey to the New World was of major historical significance, changing the course of history forever. His exploration marked the beginning of the Great Age of Exploration. However, what most teachers do not realize as they commemorate Columbus Day in the classroom by reading about his journey is that most books ignore the fact that Columbus's arrival on the coast of San Salvador on October 12, 1492, initiated what Taxol calls an "American holocaust" that resulted in the virtual genocide of the hemisphere's native population. It also helped set in motion the migration of European people all over the globe, including the initiation of the Atlantic slave trade, which resulted in death and enslavement for millions of Africans.

Most children's books about Christopher Columbus depict him as a great hero and, perhaps, the greatest sailor of all time. They show him as a superhuman, who despite great adversity and horrendous conditions overcame his challenges to begin a new, wonderful world in America. As Taxol (1993) points out, there are great political implications in this message in that we are perpetuating a myth instead of retelling history accurately. We are virtually ignoring the peoples and civilizations that had lived in America for millennia before Columbus "discovered" it. We are also ignoring the peoples who "lived on the other side of history" and suffered for generations from the slave trade that began due to his sea explorations. To indigenous people, Columbus's arrival on the shores of the Western Hemisphere was perhaps an initial step toward a European invasion.

Teachers should not stop reading books and commemorating Christopher Columbus or other holidays or heroes. However, they need to ensure that history is accurately portrayed in the books they choose to read, and they need to be aware of the political messages conveyed by their choice of books. By ignoring different perspectives on history, whether it be the desecration of the indigenous population after Columbus's arrival, the slave trade, or the internment of Japanese Americans, we are perpetuating a cultural group's powerlessness and making them invisible. Teachers need to carefully examine whether a message is being conveyed in the books chosen for classroom reading, and they must begin to help our children ask important questions about what the books are and are not about.

Selection of Multicultural Literature

In selecting books suitable for the classroom, teachers need to maintain high standards for evaluating all books. Form and content are equally important. Children's books should be well written, tell a good story, have strong characterization, and offer a worthwhile theme or issue children can understand. A picture book should have rich illustrations that enhance the story. A nonfiction book should be accurate, current, and represent the information in a nonbiased manner.

As the number of multicultural books increases, it is also important to include specific criteria for selection of these books (Bishop, 1993), such as:

◆ Have available a variety of books that show diversity within and across human cultures.

◆ Select a variety of books that helps counter subtle stereotyping. For example, some books may have pictures of African-American mothers wearing aprons and being in the kitchen; this portrayal of African-American women may be a subtle reinforcement of a stereotype.

◆ Have books available that present different perspectives on issues and events. For example, if you have books on Columbus that present him as a hero, choose additional books that show the Native American perspective on his journey and its effects on their population.

◆ Search for books that correct distortions or omissions of significant information. For example, if some books about the United States' involvement in World War II do not cover the internment of Japanese Americans in camps, then choose additional books that do.

◆ Look for the point of view that the author takes toward his or her subject. Ask whether the author is showing any bias or paternalistic attitude toward one culture.

◆ Analyze the way people of color are characterized. Are the main characters well developed? Do they show leadership qualities? Do they solve their own problems? Are stereotypes avoided?

◆ Examine the language of the author, the narrator, and the characters. Offensive terms such as *brutal, conniving, primitive, savage,* and *backward* should be avoided as descriptors of people of color. Colloquial speech or dialect may be used to enrich characterizations, but it should not be used to show inferiority or ridicule of the characters.

◆ Consider the possible effect of the book on a child's self-esteem. Put yourself in the children's perspective and try to imagine how they would feel after reading this story. Would the book evoke empathy and understanding? Can it be used with a group of mixed-race children? Is there anything that might offend a child in the class?

◆ Ask the following questions when examining the book: What perspectives and values are represented? Which are missing? For what purpose is the text written? Whose interests are being served and why? What evidence is provided (if any) that supports the author's perspective? What are the social, historical, and political circumstances shaping the content of the text?

Integrating Technology into the Study of Literature

Technology is a wonderful way to support the study of literature in the classroom. It can directly link the class with valuable resources that it may not ordinarily have access to, including author's web pages and lessons involving the use of literature. Technology can even enable students to select books from the library from their classroom or home. Although many people may believe that technology might diminish the role of literature in the classroom, in fact, it helps enhance quality literature. Technology can:

◆ Allow students and teachers to use online libraries and databases to search for books and quality literature, including multicultural literature.

◆ Allow students to listen to podcasts from their favorite authors or of a favorite book.

◆ Provide students with creative tools to develop artistic and professional-looking documents when they are responding to a book.

◆ Allow students to develop creative responses to books through multimedia presentations.

◆ Help teachers and students develop tables and charts so they can do author and genre studies and compare/contrast books.

◆ Help teachers and students develop visual tools—such as maps and webs—to accompany literature and support reading comprehension.

◆ Allow students to visit an author's home page and further explore that author's body of work.

◆ Allow students to communicate with other classes all over the world that are involved with reading the same book.

◆ Allow students to publish their ideas and responses to literature on the Internet and share them with the community.

◆ Allow students to do research on a topic that extends or reinforces the theme of the book.

◆ Allow students to use online library "card catalogs" to search and select a book to read.

◆ Provide students with an opportunity to access primary sources of material, such as original documents and original texts, that they may not ordinarily have an opportunity to see or read. Such sites as the Library of Congress (http://www.lcweb.loc.gov) allow students to browse a library they may never get a chance to visit in person.

Internet Sites That Support Literature in the Classroom

Many excellent websites are available on the Internet that teachers can use to support using literature in the classroom. Some of these are listed below.

Children's Literature Web Guide (CLWB)

http://www.acs.ucalgary.ca/~dkbrown

CLWB is an excellent site to start exploring children's literature on the web. This site provides many links to quality literature.

Carol Hurst's Children's Literature Site

http://www.carolhurst.com

Carol Hurst's site is devoted to children's literature, including how to integrate literature into the subject areas. You can pick a theme for a subject area, such as "Colonial

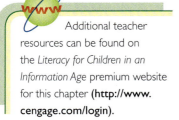
Additional teacher resources can be found on the *Literacy for Children in an Information Age* premium website for this chapter (**http://www. cengage.com/login**).

America" for social studies, and find curricular ideas and books for use in studying this theme.

SCORE CyberGuides

http://www.sdcoe.k12.ca.us/score/cyberguide.html

SCORE CyberGuides is an excellent site that contains lesson plan ideas and activities for scores of K–12 literature. CyberGuides are supplementary, standards-based, web-delivered units of instruction centered on core works of literature. Each CyberGuide contains a student and teacher edition, standards, a task and a process by which it may be completed, teacher-selected websites, and a rubric, based on California Language Arts Content Standards.

Aaron Shepard's Home Page

http://www.aaronshep.com

Aaron Shepard's site provides many different resources for integrating children's literature into the classroom. This site can provide you with actual scripts that you can use in the classroom for Readers Theatre Workshop.

American Library Association

http://www.ala.org/alsc

The ALA site lists the Newbery and Caldecott award winners and it allows you to explore how the ALA is promoting literacy.

Authors' Websites

One of the wonderful ways in which technology can enrich the language arts classroom is by connecting students to their favorite authors and providing insight into authors whose books they have read. Authors' websites often provide biographical information and additional materials that can be used in the classroom to reinforce literacy skills after a particular book is read. For example, Jan Brett—who has written picture numerous books and is a favorite author of young children—has developed a rich site with many resources that teachers can use to supplement classroom activities. It is worthwhile to visit the sites listed below and become familiar with the authors' books (if you are not already familiar). These websites provide numerous ways to reinforce the readings, from exploring the author's life to printing out illustrations of the book to color in.

◆ Jan Brett: http://www.janbrett.com

◆ Eric Carle: http://www.eric-carle.com

◆ Avi: http://www.avi-writer.com

◆ Faith Ringgold: http://www.faithringgold.com

◆ Judy Blume: http://www.judyblume.com

◆ Katherine Paterson: http://www.terabithia.com

◆ Dav Pilkey: http://www.pilkey.com

◆ Audrey Wood: http://www.audreywood.com

◆ Adopt-an-Author: http://adoptanauthor.com—This is a free, web-based, nationwide, nonprofit program designed to excite students about reading and writing through the use of literature. This site allows students to contact authors via personal appearances, classroom phone calls, e-mails, and interactive websites.

◆ Kidsread: http://www.kidsreads.com—This is a good site for students to learn more about authors.

Electronic Talking Books

Electronic talking books (also called Living Books or CD-ROM storybooks) present children's literature with text and animated illustrations on a CD-ROM to be presented on a computer. It is similar to a traditional book in that it has text on each "page" or screen with an accompanying illustration. However, many of its features support young readers, including audio reading of the text and graphic animations where book characters talk and settings come alive. For example, on each screen there is a "hotspot" where children can activate certain sound effects, cause a picture to animate, and manipulate certain elements. In addition, the reader can choose to highlight a word or phase to hear an audio pronunciation or access a definition. Electronic talking books can also read the entire story, simulating a read-aloud experience for the student.

Studies have found several benefits to using electronic talking books in the class to promote literacy (Lefever-Davis & Pearman, 2005). These storybooks allow children to choose when they need assistance, thereby giving them more control over their learning. When they cannot identify a word, they can click on it to have the computer read the word to them. Students do not have to struggle decoding words, nor do they need to define every word because they have definitions available. This allows children to devote their attention to comprehending the story.

The animations also promote comprehension of the story by providing the context within which the story takes place. In the electronic talking book *Just Grandma and Me* by Mercer Mayer (Broderbund), the reader can join Critter for a day at the beach with Grandma. The reader can click on many hotspots on the screen and interact with different objects found on the beach. The reader can choose to have the story read to him or her, and play with stickers on each page. Studies show that students gave richer story retellings and scored higher on comprehension questions after reading electronic talking books (Lefever-Davis & Pearman, 2005).

Vocabulary also is enhanced through children viewing and hearing the animated characters speaking sentences and phrases that are written in the book. This reinforces the development of the vocabulary introduced in the story and helps children make a three-way connection—the visual image to the spoken word to the written word. The vocabulary is additionally clarified when needed by clicking on the word and being able to hear the definition.

Lefever-Davis and Pearman (2005) outline some of the disadvantages in using electronic talking books. They discuss how children may become dependent on the embedded features in these electronic books, and instead of reading the text, they will passively listen to the story being read to them. Without practicing decoding skills, students may not develop literacy skills on their own. An over-reliance on the support features provided in the electronic talking books may hinder literacy development, because students are not practicing the reading strategies necessary for future success. When the computer immediately supplies an unknown word to the reader, a built-in reliance develops and the child becomes accustomed to being provided full support. In a classroom setting, the teacher will provide assistance usually by prompting the reader to use a specific cuing system or reading strategy, not just pronouncing the words to the child. Computers are not capable of making instructional decisions regarding the type of assistance needed and, therefore, cannot scaffold the child's literacy development. In addition, children can become too engaged in the animation features and will be distracted from following the story line, which will detract from comprehension. They will also have less time available for reading actual print-based materials.

Nevertheless, electronic talking books offer much potential in the classroom with beginning readers. They are highly appealing, engaging, and motivating to children. They can also support struggling readers' attempts to read literature and increase their confidence in reading. They provide a positive experience for English language learners (ELLs) and students with learning disabilities (LD) who can successfully interact with text. Many electronic talking books also provide text in different languages such as Spanish, German, and French, which may support children trying to learn a new language or who need instruction in their native language. Electronic talking books are an excellent resource to engage children in successful reading and provide a unique way for beginning readers to develop their literacy skills.

Responding to Books

Response-Based Curriculum

When children read books, a significant component of the curriculum should ask students to respond to what they have read. Readers need to articulate and formulate responses about how they interpreted a story; through this process of responding, students learn to share and organize their thoughts about the text, thereby clarifying within their own minds what the text is about. As Cullinan (1992) reports, the reading curriculum should not be centered around content, but on responding. Schools should develop a response-centered curriculum that actively engages the reader in thinking about what was read.

In a **response-based curriculum**, teachers view readers as active meaning-makers whose personal experiences affect their interpretations of literature. Therefore, there is no one "correct" interpretation of the story, but each reader may have a very different, very valid interpretation of the story. A response-based curriculum will also encourage student-generated questions as the center of learning, using a problem-solving approach to develop critical thinking skills. Comprehension is seen as a *process*, not as one single right answer, which is derived through social and personal examination of the text.

Children can respond to text in many different ways, sometimes formally through assignments they hand in and sometimes informally through fun activities that are not graded. It is important that both ways of responding are used in the classroom. Listed below are different ways children can respond to text.

Technology is a wonderful tool to help children respond to literature. Word processing programs such as Microsoft Word can be used to create classroom newspapers about books that have been read. Word can be used to create tables and charts, add clip art for illustrations, and create professional-looking documents. Children can create narratives with hyperlinks to develop a nonlinear document in which certain words have been made into "links" that bring the reader to a different part of the article. For example, a student may develop a hyperlinked narrative in Word, in which each main character's name is linked to another page that contains a description and picture of him or her. Programs such as PowerPoint or KidPix are a wonderful way to develop a multimedia presentation to the class on a book that the student just read. PowerPoint is also an excellent program for developing graphic organizers and visual tools that the teacher can use to help children respond to literature. The software program Inspiration is a wonderful tool for webbing or mapping concepts about a book or describing characters. There are also many terrific websites on the Internet that will allow children to explore a book further. As mentioned above, some authors have their own websites, which are excellent resources for both the teacher and student to further explore the author and his or her work.

Role-playing and drama are an excellent way to emphasize characterization and to help children feel empathy with the characters in a story. It also helps children learn how to understand different perspectives. Readers Theatre Workshop, which is described below, is a wonderful way to incoporate drama into your literacy classroom.

Writing is another way children can respond to text. Formal written assignments such as book reports or summaries can be used. Informal writing in journals can also help children become sensitive to their feelings about a book. Structured writing assignments that answer specific questions about the book help guide students to extract the author's meaning. Reading guides developed by the teacher that guide the reader through the whole book in a step-by-step fashion are another helpful device. Sharing letters with a pen pal about books is another way to have children respond to literature.

Arts and crafts and hands-on activities associated with the book are fun ways for children to respond and think about the meaning of the book. Such activities can include creating:

- Murals
- Dioramas
- Puppet shows
- Student-produced videos
- Interviews with characters
- Talk-show simulations
- Multimedia productions
- Posters
- Book covers
- Travel brochures describing the setting
- Advertisements
- Models of structures described in the book
- Costumes of the period in the book

The following specific activities are examples of ways in which students can come to appreciate an author's craft, and thereby increase the potential for pleasure and understanding.

A Topic/Theme Study: A topic/theme study activity is designed to help children notice how different authors treat the same topic or theme. Over a short period of about a week, read at least three different books on the same topic or theme written by different authors. Then, using a large easel or a computer hooked up to a projector system, make a table like the one below. List the three books across the top, and down the columns list various ways the books can be compared.

Illustrations	Book 1	Book 2	Book 3
Objects Illustrated			
Colors Used			
Content About the Topic			

Author Study: Author study is designed to help students notice the differences in one author's styles. Over a short period, the teacher (or students) would read at least three books by the same author. Using an easel or a computer hooked up to a projector screen, make a table like the one below and compare the three books based on genre, theme/topic, and any other special element you wish to point out, such as writing style, illustrations, or any special features.

Books by Jane Yolen	Owl Moon	Commander Toad in Space	Greyling
Genre	Picture book	Chapter book; fantasy/adventure	Picture book; Scottish folktale
Theme/ Topic	Child goes looking for an owl in snow with her dad	Commander Toad and his crew of "Star Warts"	A seal turns into a human and lives with fisherman
Writing Style	Serious, descriptive	Funny; toads and frogs that talk	Serious folktale with moral

Graphing a Book: Graphing a book helps students recall the sequence of events in a story and evaluate the effect of each event on one of the main characters. This activity is suitable for any book with action and an adventuresome plot. One can use this activity with younger primary children if the teacher develops the graph first and has them fill it in, or if the class fills in the graph together. This is a good activity for upper primary children and middle school children who can construct the graph themselves using PowerPoint or a graphics program and are able to identify the events that need to be graphed. In Figure 11–2, students have graphed the events of *Jumanji* by Chris Van Allsburg according to how exciting or boring the events are.

Literary Report Cards and Literary Passports: This activity allows children to "grade" characters in a book based on specified criteria such as creativity, honesty, courage, and intelligence. The teacher would model a "report card" based on a character that is familiar to them from a story read in class. Children love to grade characters, especially if the report card is structured to look like the one that the school uses. The ability to review the actions of a chosen character and develop a list of qualities that can be judged involves a great deal of inferential and higher order thinking skills. Children in grades 1 and 2 are capable of doing this activity with guidance from the teacher. If a student volunteers a negative attribute of the character such as "liar," the teacher should encourage the class to think of the antonym of this word, such as, "If someone does not lie and cheat, we would say they are very _____ (honest)," and then convert that attribute to an adverb ("honesty"). If the children use adjectives, adverbs, and verbs in their own report card, these words are acceptable. Figure 11–3 presents an example of a literary report card on Samantha from the book *Sam, Bang and Moonshine* by Evaline Ness, which is about a little girl "who had the reckless habit of lying" and gets into trouble because of it. Literary Passports are similar to report cards, but in this activity, students pick a character and then fill out a passport describing themselves. They can even draw a picture of themselves or find an image on the Internet or in a magazine that they can place on the passport. Figure 11–4 presents an example of a Literary Passport filled in for the book *Knuffle Bunny* by Mo Willems. This book combines cartoon drawings with photographs of Brooklyn, New York, and tells the story about what happens when Daddy does the wash with Trixie and loses Knuffle Bunny at the Laundromat.

Literary Posters: Literary posters are a creative way for children to develop many different skills and focus on the key elements of a story. The poster should not be "open-ended," but rather have a specific objective based on an aspect of the story. For example, a "Missing Person" poster would focus on the physical attributes of a character that is missing and help the children remember that character's habits, personality traits, likes and dislikes. This type of poster fits perfectly with *Sylvester and the Magic Pebble* by William Steig, or for older children, *A Wrinkle in Time* by Madeline L'Engle. If the book does not have a missing person, there might be a villain in the story, or a hero. "Wanted" posters modeled after police reports that describe what a villain might look like are fun for students to make. Other ideas might be a "Hero" poster, which would describe the hero in the book, or a "Garage Sale" poster, where students would list the contents of a home, store, or school that might be for sale with the selected price next to it. Figure 11–5 shows an example of a literary poster for the book *Auction!* by Tres Seymour and illustrated by Cat Bowman Smith. This is the story of a family who goes to an auction where "nobody could outbid Aunt Lou and Miss Logsdon when they got going." The poster depicts the items that were up for bid at the auction. This poster was done in PowerPoint and used clip art of the items listed in the book; Word could have been used just as easily.

Literary Letters and Journals: The literary letter is a simple activity, in which the student composes a letter to a character from a familiar story. It is also fun to have the children exchange letters and then adopt the role of the character and reply to the letter. This can be done via e-mail, where students respond to each other and print out their messages to show the teacher. In a literary journal, the writer adopts the personality of the character and writes a day in the life of that character. Children may want to write a few entries tracing the major events in the story or novel.

FIGURE 11-2

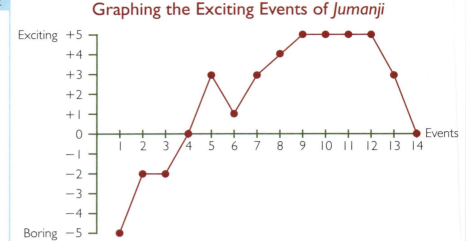

Graphing the Exciting Events of *Jumanji*

Events in Plot

1. Judy and Peter are left alone after their parents go out to the opera, and they are bored.

2. They go to the park and find a game called "Jumanji: A Jungle Adventure Game."

3. They start playing the game and learn that the first player to reach Jumanji and yell its name aloud is the winner.

4. Peter goes first and lands on a square that says "Lion attacks, move back two spaces."

5. A lion roars and follows Peter up the stairs into a bedroom.

6. Judy goes next and lands on a square that says "Monkeys steal food, miss one turn."

7. They find a dozen monkeys tearing the kitchen apart.

8. Peter goes next and lands on a square that says "Monsoon season begins, lose one turn." Rain begins to fall in buckets in the living room.

9. After being bitten by a tsetse fly and catching sleeping sickness, Peter wakes up to hearing a herd of rhinos stampeding through the living room.

10. Peter lands on a space that says, "Python sneaks into camp, go back one space" and finds an eight-foot python over the fireplace.

11. Judy lands on a space that says, "Volcano erupts, go back three spaces," and the living room starts to shake while lava flows out of the fireplace.

12. Judy rolls a twelve and yells "Jumanji" loudly as she lands on the last space.

13. Everything went back to normal: no monkeys, no volcano, no lion, no rhinos, no python. Peter and Judy run across the street to the park and drop the game under a tree.

14. Mother and father come home and find Judy and Peter fast asleep.

FIGURE 11-3

Harbor School
Report Card

Name: Samantha	A = Outstanding	D = Improvement
Grade: 3	B = Good	Needed
Teacher: Ms. Kirbstoan	C = Satisfactory	F = Failure

Subject	Grade	Comments
Creativity	A	Samantha is very creative.
Honesty	D	Samantha needs to work on this as sometimes she lies.
Courage		
Happiness		
Smartness		
Friendship		

Based on the book *Sam, Bangs and Moonshine* by Evaline Ness.

(Adapted from Johnson, T., & Louis, D. (1987). *Literacy through literature.* Portsmouth, NH: Heinemann.)

It is helpful when the teacher lists the major events of the story and then has the children respond to these events in their letters or journal entries. Figure 11–6 presents an example of a literary letter composed for the book *The Man Who Walked between the Towers* by Mordicai Gerstein. This is the story of Philippe Petit, a young French aerialist who spent almost an hour walking, dancing, and performing tricks between the two towers of the World Trade Center in 1974. The literary letter is from the New York City Police Chief who is charging him with a crime.

Story Maps and Visual Tools: A story map is an excellent way for children to organize, classify, and structure information from a text. These maps can be used as a prereading, during-reading, or postreading activity. They can help students reinforce important concepts by visually representing them, thereby facilitating short-term memory. Visual tools also promote long-term comprehension of conceptual information because the information is organized graphically and structured in such a way that it is much easier for children to remember and subsequently recall. Visual tools and story maps are excellent ways to have children respond to literature because children usually find them fun and helpful in organizing the material. The teacher can begin to introduce them by creating visual tools using PowerPoint or Inspiration that the children will use with a book they are reading. Eventually, the children might be able to create their own visual tools to help them comprehend and remember the story. Figure 11–7 presents an example of a story map for the book *Mirette on the High Wire* by Emily Arnold McCully, which is about another young aerialist who lives in France. This story map outline requires the student to fill in the setting, characters, problem, and solution. Figure 11–8 is a story pyramid that can be used as a story map, as well. In this visual tool, students start with one word to describe the character at the top of the pyramid, and then increase the responses by one word each as they work down the pyramid. This pyramid in Figure 11–8 has been filled in for *Pinduli* by Janell Cannon. This is a story about a striped hyena, Pinduli, who lives in the East African savanna with his mother. Pinduli meets a pack of wild dogs who laugh at her ears, a lion who criticizes her coat, and a zebra who says that her stripes are unpleasant. Pinduli tries to change herself and, in doing so, tricks the animals into believing she is a spirit. This is a beautifully illustrated book that contains a whole section describing different types of hyenas. Chapter 10 discusses other visual tools and includes many examples that can be used in the classroom.

FIGURE 11-4

Literary Passport:
Trixie

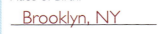

Age:	18 mo
Height:	2' 6"
Weight:	55 lbs
Gender:	Female
Marital Status:	Single

Place of Birth:

Brooklyn, NY

Home Address:

101 Park Place

Work/Occupation:

Baby

Personality	1 High	2 Med	3 Low
Courageous	✓		
Creative	✓		
Curious	✓		
Happy	✓ only with knuffle bunny		
Lonely			✓
Jealous			✓
Obedient			✓
Strong	✓		

What do you love to do?

Play with Knuffle Bunny

What do you hate to do?

Not have Knuffle Bunny

What are your hopes and/or dreams?

To be home with mommy, daddy and knuffle bunny

What are your biggest fears or problems?

To leave knuffle bunny behind

Personal Comments:

Aggle Flaggle Klabble!

Charting Activities: Charts allow children to visually see how concepts relate to each other and how information from books can be organized. Charts are useful tools for every grade level starting in kindergarten, when the teacher can draw a chart on an easel to display visual pictures and simple words. In the first and second grades, the teacher can identify the headings or criteria of what information will be presented down the columns and across the rows. In upper primary grades,

FIGURE 11-5

children can be asked to create their own charts using Word or Excel and identify how they wish to display their information. Charts are useful for comparing information or tracing the sequence of events through a week or the seasons. The chart below organizes the sequence of events from *The Very Hungry Caterpillar* by Eric Carle.

Day of Week	What the Caterpillar Ate	How Big He Was
Sunday		
Monday		
Tuesday		
Wednesday		
Thursday		
Friday		
Saturday		

FIGURE 11-6

Office of the Police Chief
City Hall
New York City, NY
July 15, 1974

Philippe Petit
Paris, France

Dear Mr. Petit:

You have been charged with a crime for walking on a tightrope between the two towers of the World Trade Center last month. You spent almost an hour walking, dancing, and performing tricks a quarter of mile in the sky, which was very danger-ous and foolish. I know you are a very experienced tight rope walker, but here in New York City it is a crime to put up a cable between two buildings and walk across. You are trespassing and causing much disruption in the daily lives of those who work and live in the area! The buildings are not even finished yet, and therefore it was most unwise to do this in a construction zone!! Although it was quite exciting to see you up there, you have caused the City of New York a lot of expense. I had to call up forty police officers, twenty for each side of the cable, who needed to arrest you when you were through. They must be paid overtime for the two hours they watched you walk, dance, run, and kneel on the cable. They even watched you lie down on it! You will be charged with a crime and brought to court for this foolishness.

Sincerely,

Captain John H. Smith

New York City Police Chief

The following chart can be used to compare *Lon Po Po: A Red Riding Hood Story from China* adapted by Ed Young to a traditional Little Red Riding Hood folktale.

	Lon Po Po	Little Red Riding Hood
Main Character(s)	Two sisters	Little Red Riding Hood
Setting	Their own home	Grandmother's house
What Happens to the Wolf	He is killed by the sisters	He is killed by the hunter
Personality of the Main Characters	Sisters are very resourceful/brave	Little Red is very silly for going off on her own

Literary Passports: Literary passports are an excellent way to introduce geography into a literacy lesson. Blank passport forms can be handed out to each member of the class, and each student must then identify a story character to enter information on the form. The students must make up plausible responses when the story does not provide explicit information and this should be brought to the students' attention. As an extension of this activity, the students will choose a partner; one child takes on the role of the interviewer and is given a blank passport form to fill in, while the other child takes on the role of the character from a book they just read. Partners are then

FIGURE 11-7

Name: _____

Book Title: <u>Mirette on the High Wire</u>

Author: <u>Emily Arnold McCully</u>

Genre: <u>Historical Fiction</u>

Setting (Where? When?)	Characters (Who?)
The widow Gateau's boardinghouse on English Street in Paris one hundred years ago.	Mirette, the widow Gateau's daughter; Mousier Bellini, a high wire performer; and an agent from London.
Problem	Solution
Bellini is world famous for his daring feats, but he is afraid to perform anymore.	Mirette begs Mousier Bellini to teach her how to wire walk, and he agrees. She becomes very good. An agent arranges for Bellini to perform in front of a crowd, but his fear stops him in the middle of the wire between two tall buildings. Mirette takes a risk and rushes out onto the wire to help him cross. The agent sees a wonderful future with his new high-wire act of Bellini and Mirette.

FIGURE 11-8

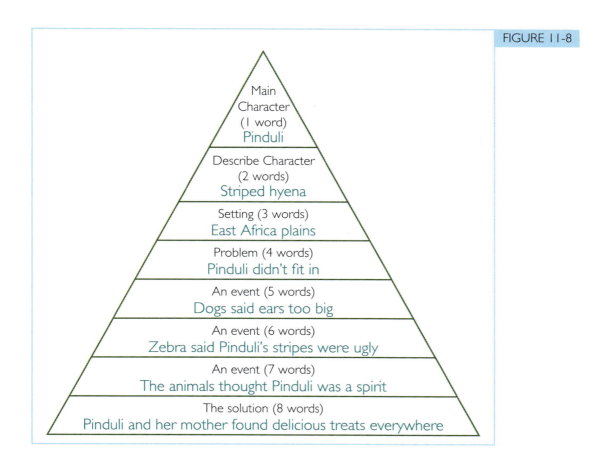

Main Character (1 word)
Pinduli

Describe Character (2 words)
Striped hyena

Setting (3 words)
East Africa plains

Problem (4 words)
Pinduli didn't fit in

An event (5 words)
Dogs said ears too big

An event (6 words)
Zebra said Pinduli's stripes were ugly

An event (7 words)
The animals thought Pinduli was a spirit

The solution (8 words)
Pinduli and her mother found delicious treats everywhere

reassigned and the roles reversed. The students should look up on a map where the fictional character is from (if it is from a real place) and give some background information on that location.

Literature Circles

A **literature circle** is a wonderful way for students to respond to books that they have read. Literature circles allow children who have read the same book or genre—or who have similar interests—to come together in a circle to discuss what they have read. This is an excellent way to get children to share experiences with books and talk about their own personal experience with a book. Studies of different student populations have shown that all children, when given the opportunity, guidance, and support, will benefit from participating in meaningful conversations about texts they are reading and from discussing their own personal experiences with them (Langer, 1995; Kong & Fitch, 2002). It has also been found that implementing literature circles, or book clubs, as they are commonly called, will help engage culturally and linguistically diverse learners in reading, writing, and talking about books (Kong & Fitch, 2002). A classroom learning community will develop where all children are given a chance to express their ideas openly and use discussion, writing, and free expression to develop language skills.

Literature circles consist of small heterogeneous groups of students who choose to read and discuss texts. Working in smaller groups allows students to collaborate in a more intimate manner and supports struggling readers who may feel uncomfortable expressing themselves in front of a large group. Groups can read the same text, read texts with a common theme, or read books of the same genre.

If students are reading the same book, the teacher can provide a prompt or question for the students to respond to as they read and discuss the book. For example, the teacher can ask about the setting of the book and provide passages describing the setting. The teacher also can ask about the main character and ask students to watch how the main character develops and matures over the course of the book and again provide passages showing how the character changes. Students' responses to this prompt act as a springboard for later group interaction. Student responses can be recorded in a journal, or just simply discussed at each literature circle meeting (Strickland, 1994).

If each student is reading a different book, more general prompts can be used to facilitate discussion. For example, if all students are reading fiction, they can be asked to describe their favorite character and then provide passages from the text to illustrate what the character is like. If students are reading nonfiction, they can be grouped according to topic (for example, books about animals, books about sport figures) and then asked to respond to questions such as, "How did this book help you learn about your topic (sports, animals)? Share passages with the group that you especially liked." If they are all reading different books, students can be asked to keep track of three facts that they have learned and can share with the group. Other prompts can ask students to compare and contrast different books, authors, illustrators, as well as to reflect on how their personal experiences helped them relate to the book (Strickland, 1994).

Literature circles help students move beyond the literal level of interpreting a book and move students to deeper meanings. As students listen to their classmates talk about their interpretations, they gain deeper understandings and develop higher order thinking. Such discussions help them interpret the book through the context of real-world experiences and different perspectives. This type of exploration is discussed further in the following section.

Interpreting Literature

In her book *Envisioning Literature*, Judith Langer (1995) claims that literacy fosters personal empowerment that results when people use their literacy skills to think and rethink their understandings of texts, themselves, and the world. She claims that using literature in the curriculum can potentially empower all students to interpret their own world differently and reflect on their own values. She claims that an understanding that a reader has about what is being read, written, discussed, or tested is an **envisionment**, and that all envisionments are subject to change at any time. After students read a text, they all have their own initial impressions that are subject to change in response to their own further reflection and others' ideas. The process of interpretation is primarily a social one that involves discussing and sharing envisionments that texts generate. These interpretations will change over time, influenced by discourse, exploration, and discovery.

What this means for the teacher is that the literary experience for all students from preK through high school should involve exploring possibilities (Langer, 1995) and trying out new experiences and ideas. After reading a book and initiating a response from students, teachers need to remain open and foster inquiry concerning the interpretation of the book. In a response-based classroom, each student is considered unique, with a complex social identity and personal interests, concerns, and perspectives. It is taken for granted that each person's diverse background is influenced by different social groups, values, and customs that will influence the envisionment that person creates. To negate or refute students' envisionments is to rob them of their personal identity, to diminish their cultural background, and to essentially make them invisible.

Teachers must be accepting of all interpretations and understand that each person will interpret literature differently, and that each interpretation is as valid and meaningful as the one the teacher brings to the conversation. Too often teachers squelch critical thinking, personal inquiry, and self-empowerment by assuming that there is one interpretation that is better or more correct than others; that is, the teacher knows what the author meant and will "teach" the class this knowledge. This prevents the class from becoming a dynamic community of learners who are actively exploring the process of finding meaning in the texts and sharing concerns, insights, and personal secrets concerning a literary experience. The goal is to help students become part of a discussion that is authentic, vibrant, and explores possibilities. This type of discussion will encourage students to become involved, to feel accepted, and to become self-empowered by literature. As the interpretation grows and changes over time, the class will start to share an envisionment and learn to accept and appreciate those opinions that differ from the rest.

Readers Theatre Workshop

Readers Theatre Workshop is an interpretive reading activity in which students read a written script to bring characters and plot to life. Unlike conventional theater, Readers Theatre does not use sets, costumes, props, or a stage, and the readers do not memorize lines. Rather, the goal is to have the students read the script aloud expressively, so that the audience can understand the text's action and character development. The protocol of Readers Theater is that the readers usually sit on stools or chairs in front of the classroom and as one reader is looking up at the audience voicing lines, the other readers are looking down. This enhances the presentation as the audience can focus on the one who is reading the script. Each reader takes the role of a character or, if necessary, takes on two roles. The narrator provides the background material, descriptions of setting, and transitions from scene to scene (Martinez, Roser, & Strecker, 1998/1999).

Readers Theatre Workshop can be implemented by either providing the scripts to the children or having the children take the book and develop a script themselves. Different websites are available that provide prescripted versions of books that the teacher can use. This is probably the easiest way to get started with Readers Theatre; after reading a book together as a class, provide a group with the script, give them time to practice reading their lines, and have them perform it to the class. Familiar stories with known characters and settings are an excellent way to introduce children to Readers Theatre. Once the class becomes familiar with the conventions of Readers Theatre, it is then recommended that older students try to script a book themselves. Usually a group will work together to develop a script, following the conventions of scripting that the teacher will model. It is important to choose texts for Readers Theatre that are within the readers' independent or instructional level of reading. It is also important to choose texts that are easily adapted to scripting. Stories that have a lot of dialogue, straightforward plots, and humorous events are usually excellent books to start with.

Additional teacher resources can be found on the *Literacy for Children in an Information Age* premium website for this chapter (**http://www.cengage.com/login**).

Readers Theatre Workshop promotes reading fluency in the classroom (Martinez, Roser, & Strecker, 1998/1999). This activity provides readers with effective reading models, whether it be the teacher reading the story aloud or peers reading the script aloud. These models can guide students in reading expressively, with appropriate pacing and phrasing. This helps students obtain deeper meanings of the story.

In addition, Readers Theatre gives students multiple opportunities for repeated reading of the same text, which has been shown to improve fluency (Dowhower, 1987; Reutzel & Hollingsworth, 1993). Young children love to read text over and over again, and Readers Theatre is especially motivating because the students will perform in front of the class. This is especially helpful for slower readers because it gives them a chance to practice rereading text until they feel comfortable with it before going in front of the class. They also get a chance to read with the support of a group so they are not reading alone to the whole class. This builds confidence and pride in reading, unlike round-robin reading in which one child reads to the whole class, which can cause frustration and embarrassment on the part of the reader.

Readers Theatre Workshop helps students understand characters and actually "get inside the characters' head." By becoming a character in a story and reading the lines of that character, students gain a deeper understanding and appreciation of the story. Students must project how the character would say that line and interpret the character's motives. The process of scripting forces students to discuss the story line and identify what is important and what is irrelevant to the main plot. They must sift through the text and determine significant events that tie the story line together so that their performance makes sense.

Many sites on the Internet provide a variety of resources for implementing Readers Theatre Workshop into the classroom. An excellent one is Aaron Shepard's Home Page (http://www.aaronshep.com). This website includes tips, scripts that can be used immediately, and practice sheets for the class to start their own scripting. This site allows teachers to begin implementing Readers Theatre immediately in the classroom.

Readers Theatre offers teachers an opportunity to incorporate repeated readings into their curriculum in a motivating and appealing activity. There is nothing more powerful than preparing a performance for an audience. This incentive is a wonderful way to get children to practice reading out loud and to respond to a story read in class. Children approach this activity with such energy and enthusiasm that it does not seem like they are "doing work." Teachers see an increase in confidence, an increase in fluency, an increase in the number of books read by individual children, and an increase in motivation to read after using Readers Theatre on a continuous basis.

Preparing for and performing a Readers Theatre Workshop encourages fluency, as well as a deeper understanding of character and plot.

Courtesy of Guilherme Cunha

A Visit to Ms. Duff's Classroom: Readers Theatre Workshop

Ms. Duff's fourth grade class is sitting in a circle on the floor expectantly waiting to receive their role in the upcoming Readers Theatre Workshop activity. They have gathered together in a large circle with Ms. Duff sitting at one end. She hands each student a folder that contains a script and proceeds to assign the various roles to each student in the class. Before they begin, Ms. Duff discusses the topic of fluency and what it is like to read fluently. She emphasizes how it is important to reread text to increase fluency and how it is fine to read the script again and again to "get it right." She stresses that Readers Theatre does not use any costumes or props, and that the readers do not have to memorize lines. The goal is to have the students read the script fluently, so that the audience can enjoy the story being told.

After this overview of what is expected, Ms. Duff signals that it is time to begin. The first "character" in the script reads his lines out loud and successive students follow, reading their lines, as well. At various times, Ms. Duff provides feedback to students who do not read their lines fluently. She has them reread the script and keeps assuring them that this is fine and that they are doing a good job. After the students have completed reading the script, Ms. Duff discusses the story with them and helps them achieve a deeper meaning of the plot. She relates the story to the students' own lives and then asks the students to take the script home and reread it over

the weekend so they can "perform" it again in class next week.

Readers Theatre Workshop can be implemented using the whole-class approach described above in Ms. Duff's classroom. Another approach is to implement Readers Theatre in small groups. The members will discuss the different roles in the script and decide who will take each part. Once the roles have been assigned, the small group practices reading the roles many times, rereading parts over and over again. When the students feel they are ready to "perform" their script to the class or after a designated period of time, the teacher will have each group come to the front of the classroom and read the script, sitting on stools or chairs. At that time, each member displays fluent reading, even struggling readers, as they had many opportunities to practice in the classroom and at home

before the actual performance. Familiar books with known characters and settings are an excellent way to begin. In addition, books with humor, action, and dialogue are excellent stories to have the students turn into Readers Theatre scripts themselves. In reviewing Ms. Duff's lesson, some of the strategies she used were:

- Activating prior knowledge by reviewing what Readers Theatre Workshop is and discussing what fluent reading is.
- Emphasizing fluency through a fun activity.
- Modeling expressive, fluent reading.
- Engaging all the students in reading for meaning.
- Summarizing the lesson by discussing the story and emphasizing the need for fluency through repeated readings.

Questions:

1. How does Readers Theatre Workshop promote fluency in the classroom?
2. What books in the classroom or school library would become good scripts for Readers Theatre Workshop?
3. How can Ms. Duff incorporate technology into her lesson?

Go to http://www.cengage.com/login to register your access code for the premium website for Literacy for Children in an Information Age, where you can watch an in-depth video exploration of Ms. Duff's classroom to see how she used these valuable strategies.

A response-based curriculum provides numerous opportunities for children to respond to all kinds of books, both fiction and nonfiction. Teachers and children value what each has to say about a book and accept differences of opinion and interpretation. Diversity is valued, and children's responses are viewed as an important process in the development of understanding of text. Peer comments become a significant part in shaping an individual's interpretation of reading and responding.

Organizing a Literature-Based Reading Program

Key Components of a Literature-Based Program

One of the key questions a teacher needs to ask when trying to move toward a literature-based reading program is, "How do I organize my classroom?" Integrating literature into the reading curriculum may translate into moving away from published basal reading programs and adapting literature as the primary source of reading material in the classroom, or using literature as a supplement to the regular series. It also may mean that a different approach to teaching reading—not the traditional one advocated by published reading programs—needs to be instituted. One of the key things to consider in moving to a new approach based on quality children's literature is variety and balance: variety in the type of books and materials the teacher chooses, and balance in the type of activities the teacher engages the students in (Strickland, 1994). Part of using literature in the classroom is collecting a variety of books and resources for the children to read: fiction, nonfiction, picture books, biographies, magazines, newspapers, audiotapes, videotapes, software programs, Internet sites, textbooks, and children's own writing should all be collected and stored in a class library. Once the books are collected, the teacher needs to engage children in literacy activities that balance their needs and skill levels with motivating and fun lessons.

Strickland (1994) lists four key components of a balanced literature-based reading program: (1) teacher-assisted and independent activities; (2) flexible grouping; (3) responses to literature; and (4) informal assessment.

Teacher-Assisted and Independent Activities – With teacher-assisted and independent activities the teacher engages a variety of literacy lessons that combine teacher-directed instruction, teacher assistance, and independent work on the part of the children. These activities include:

- *Teacher-assisted reading and writing:* This includes shared reading (see discussions in Chapters 3 and 4) and shared writing activities (see discussion in Chapter 8) where the students work with the teacher's support to complete literacy activities that they are still unable to accomplish independently. During shared reading, the teacher reads aloud to the students who will participate at certain points. After repeated readings, the students read along with the teacher and participate in activities before, during, and after the reading. In shared writing, the teacher helps the students write a class story or poem at an easel. The teacher solicits help from the students on the content and reinforces specific skills during this process.

- *Strategy lessons:* During strategy lessons, the teacher conducts a mini-lesson on a skill that the class needs to learn. For example, a strategy lesson can be on punctuation, or for older students, on more abstract concepts, such as characterization or using similes and metaphors in writing. These strategy lessons are usually teacher-directed, in which the teacher will introduce or reinforce a specific skill. These can be done for the total class or for a small group.

- *Independent reading and writing:* Independent reading and writing forms the basis of a literature-based reading program, where children are given plenty of time for independent silent reading and independent writing on selected topics. There should be a great deal of choice in the books the children choose to read and the type of writing assignments the children complete. For example, children can choose from three different writing assignments about a book they read: they can craft a short personal response to the book, create a newspaper article about an incident in the book, or illustrate a book jacket describing the book for new readers.

◆ ***Rereading:*** Students should have opportunities to reread sections of books that they are involved with. They can do this through choral reading in the class, partner reading with a buddy, reading along with the teacher, or reading along with an audiotape or videotape. Readers Theatre Workshop, as described earlier, is an excellent way to motivate children to reread passages as they practice for their performance in front of the class.

Flexible Grouping – A literature-based reading program uses many different ways to group students and is flexible in using these groups every day. Teachers create variations by moving students in and out of groups fluidly, thereby avoiding the pitfall of "ability groups," which tend to stigmatize certain children into ability levels. Teachers should also use various groupings throughout the day, going from whole-class to individualized to small-group instruction.

◆ *Whole-group instruction* allows the teacher to work with the whole class, usually to introduce a topic, give a strategy lesson, or do shared reading and writing. This type of grouping is an important part of the classroom routine because it ensures that all students share a common experience and relate to each other as a total class. Other types of groupings usually emerge from whole-group instruction to continue and reinforce the lesson.

◆ *Small-group instruction* allows the teacher and the students to work closely together in a shared, cooperative manner. There are two basic configurations when planning for groups: heterogeneous, where students of different ability levels and interests are grouped together; and homogeneous, where students of similar ability levels and interests are grouped together. It is important that either type of group is flexible and fluid, and that children are not assigned to one group for a long period of time, but are placed in a variety of groupings based on many different criteria, such as interests, ability, skill need, and personal preferences. There are many different ways in which small-group instruction can be organized in a literature-based reading class.

◆ *The literature-response group* enables a small number of students to share ideas and responses about a book they just read. These groups may be teacher or student-led, and they are an excellent way to support reading comprehension. These groups are heterogeneous and usually change with each new book or topic.

◆ *Research groups* are formed when a small group of students work together on a specific topic for a short period, lasting only a few weeks. Usually, the teacher closely monitors the group to ensure compatibility of the members and on-task behaviors. These groups are usually organized into heterogeneous groupings of children.

◆ *Interest groups* are formed when certain children share an interest in a certain topic, genre, author, or hobby. The children work together for the short term on literacy activities that grow out of their interests. For example, an interest group could be formed around the fantasy genre, where students discuss their favorite books, share their favorite wizard characters, research different authors who write fantasy, and perhaps write a letter to an author.

◆ *Cooperative groups* are formed to allow students to work together to accomplish a specific objective or goal. They could work together in pairs or in groups to respond to literature, conduct research, solve a problem, and work on various assigned tasks. These groups are heterogeneous in their makeup.

◆ *Strategy groups* allow the teacher to group children together who need help in a certain topic, skill, or strategy. Often, the teacher will notice certain children who need reinforcement on a skill or need to be retaught a topic. This group is usually organized homogeneously for that specific lesson. Each subsequent strategy group can be composed of different children who exhibit a need for further reinforcement.

◆ *Individualized instruction* is when the teacher works one-to-one with the student, usually in the form of a conference. All children should have one-to-one instruction at some time during the week because it allows teachers to monitor progress of individual students and it provides personalized attention to the student. During this instruction, children can receive more intensive reinforcement of skills, read aloud to the teacher, receive feedback on a writing assignment, or receive a quick mini-lesson on a specific strategy. During the individualized instruction, the teacher should focus on one objective: provide feedback on the child's writing; help the child with a specific reading skill; perform a miscue analysis; or just conference with the child, asking questions about recent books read and reading interests. The teacher should record his or her impressions of the instruction in a notebook and keep track of these progress reports.

Responses to Literature – It is important that children respond to the text that they are reading. The response does not have to be a formal "book report" or written response, but can be a more informal class discussion, fun activity, or literature circle discussion. A lack in the variety of ways in which we ask children to respond can lead to boredom and a dislike of reading. Some teachers, after reading a selection aloud or asking older children to read a selection silently, merely ask the students to do a think-pair-share— that is, think about a particular question and share their ideas with the person sitting next to them. This type of informal response involves the whole class, helps students look for deeper meanings in the readings, and is a motivating way to increase reading comprehension. All the methods described above are excellent ways to have children respond to literature.

Informal Assessment – When using a literature-based approach, assessment is a critical factor and teachers should use a variety of approaches for collecting data on student progress. Running records (Clay, 2000), in which teachers have a student read aloud a brief selection from a text and conduct a miscue analysis, recording the child's miscues, strengths, and weaknesses on an entry form is a recommended strategy to monitor on-going student progress in reading. A simple checklist used in one-to-one conferences or individualized instruction should also be used to document a child's progress in a variety of areas, including writing, comprehension strategies, phonic skills, and fluency. Tape recordings of the child's reading and written documentation provide excellent assessment data for a student over time. Writing rubrics that specify exactly what is expected in writing samples should be used, and these rubrics should correspond to writing checklists that students are given to follow and use as they assess their own writing. Conferencing is also an excellent way for teachers to keep continuous track of student progress, and each conference should be recorded in a notebook. Student portfolios that contain selections of student work, running records, writing samples, and tapes and discs of student work should be kept for each student. Many schools are heading toward electronic portfolios; that is, the collection of data is stored electronically and contains samples of word processing documents, multimedia presentations, and other literacy artifacts that represent student progress.

Readers' Workshop

Readers' Workshop is a strategy that Nancie Atwell (1987) introduced as an alternative to the traditional skills-based reading lesson and has been adapted as part of a balanced approach to literacy. Its main focus is to foster a love of reading within students by having them read books that they choose themselves, and then respond to books through writing in their journals, conferences with teachers, and sharing thoughts and ideas within small groups. Students learn to take more responsibility for their learning by being able to choose from a multitude of different types of texts (stories, informational books, biographies, poetry, magazines, brochures), thereby taking ownership of the reading and responding that occurs.

According to Atwell (1987), there are five basic principles of Readers' Workshop:

1. *Time:* Students need time to both look through books and also read independently. As the year goes on, the teacher can gradually increase the amount of independent reading time.

2. *Choice:* Students must have the opportunity to choose the books they want to read. As the year progresses, the students will begin to choose books that appeal to them and also challenge them.

3. *Response:* Students need to respond to the literature they are reading. This can be done though response journals, class discussions, literature circles, or projects.

4. *Community:* Students need to feel that they are part of a classroom community. Each student is both a learner and a teacher.

5. *Structure:* It is important that Readers' Workshop is a highly structured activity. Students need to understand the value of silent reading and the importance of sharing and listening during discussions.

Like the Writers' Workshop (see discussion in Chapter 8), the Readers' Workshop is broken up into four main parts:

Introduction—Read Aloud/Language Experience Story (10 minutes): The teacher starts the Readers' Workshop with background information and motivational comments to get them ready for their workshop. Usually, this would follow with a read-aloud, in which the teacher calls the students over to the reading corner and reads the students a short story, poem, or text that the class has written together. The teacher could also have the class work on a language experience story, in which the whole class participates in creating a story or retelling an event—such as a field trip or a visit from a class guest—with the teacher writing down their responses on a large easel. This text then becomes the focus of the Readers' Workshop.

Mini-lesson (10–12 minutes): Mini-lessons are short, focused lessons about workshop procedures, specific reading strategies, or literary skills. They should be meaningful to the students and concentrate on one strategy, skill, or process that addresses the students' needs. Mini-lessons can be for an individual student, for a small group of students, or for the entire class. The mini-lesson could focus on the following topics:

◆ Rules of Readers' Workshop
◆ How to choose a book
◆ How to conference with the teacher
◆ Giving a book talk
◆ The difference between fiction and nonfiction books
◆ Literary elements of fiction
◆ How to connect reading material to your life
◆ Unlocking unknown words
◆ Making predictions
◆ Self-monitoring strategies
◆ Reading at different speeds
◆ How to share your book with others
◆ Foreshadowing
◆ Similes and metaphors
◆ How to participate in a literature circle
◆ Describing characters

Independent Reading (20–25 minutes): The students select their own reading material, and then try a strategy that they were taught during the mini-lesson or work on a strategy that they selected as one of their goals. After they read the material for a set period of time, the students respond to what they have read. They can respond in a multitude of ways, from writing in their journal, to discussing the material with a partner, to creating a book report, to conducting further research into an area covered in the material. It is at this time that the teacher can work with small groups of students in guided reading groups while the rest of the class is reading independently. Teacher conferences take place at this time, with individual students or with groups of students. During conferencing, the teacher meets with individual students at a designated area or at their desks and reinforces, reteaches, and assesses reading strategies. To assess reading achievement, the teacher conducts a running record on each child. In addition, the teacher makes structured observations and takes anecdotal records of each child's progress. This allows the teacher to continuously assess each child and ensure that instruction is meeting the needs of every child in the class. Guided reading sessions also take place during this time.

Student Sharing (10–15 minutes): During student sharing, the students share what they have read with a partner, small group, or the whole class. Students can join in a literature circle to share their ideas and discuss their interpretations. They can talk about a strategy they tried during independent reading, their feelings about the material, or recommend a book. Sharing time is brief and provides the opportunity for all students to become involved with a community of learners. You can see an example of a teacher implementing Readers' Workshop in the TeachSource Video Case, "A Visit to Mr. Bryan's Classroom."

Assessment of Readers' Workshop is a critical component of the process. This is done through the following collection of data:

◆ Teacher's observations of the students using a checklist (see Figure 11–9 for an example of a Readers' Workshop Reading Observation Checklist)

◆ Running records taken during conferences (see Chapter 9) for a description of this assessment technique, in which the teacher asks the student to read a passage out loud, then performs a miscue analysis of the child's reading)

◆ Anecdotal records

FIGURE 11-9

Readers' Workshop Reading Observation Checklist

Name: _____

Date: _____

_____ 1. Pays attention while mini-lessons are taught

_____ 2. Asks questions and participates in question/answer session

_____ 3. Establishes eye contact

_____ 4. Involved in group discussions

_____ 5. Follows directions

_____ 6. Settles down quickly and reads

_____ 7. Reads silently; does not whisper or disrupt others

_____ 8. Discusses book with peers

_____ Total score

FIGURE 11-10

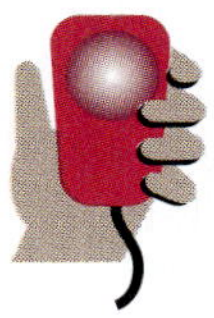

Readers' Workshop Self-Evaluation

Name: _____

Date: _____

What is my goal for today's class?

What did I actually accomplish today?

How did I do today? Was I successful?

What can I do better next time to achieve my goals?

Here is a list of two goals I would like to accomplish for the next Readers' Workshop class:

◆ Rating the students' reading logs according to a rubric
◆ Students' self-assessment of their own reading (see Figure 11–10 for an example of a Readers' Workshop Self-Evaluation Form)

An example of a sample lesson of a Reading Workshop is provided in Figure 11–11.

Using Literature With Diverse Students

Students with learning or reading disabilities generally demonstrate difficulties in the area of fluency, a major problem being their ability to read sight words, decode words, and read phrases and sentences automatically and rapidly (Chard, Vaughn, & Tyler, 2002). An important variable affecting fluency of students with LD is the type of text they are reading, and it is recommended that the difficulty of the text should be controlled. Students with LD should advance progressively through more difficult texts based on their performance, and they should be provided with consistent feedback on the words missed. It is also recommended that rereading the same text many times will improve the fluency for students with LD (Chard, Vaughn, & Tyler, 2002).

Although highly motivating, text found in literature such as storybooks and chapter books is not controlled for word choice or sentence structure. In addition, there is usually more text per page than other types of controlled texts. Therefore, in a balanced literacy classroom, literature should be used for read-alouds by the teacher or another expressive model to motivate students with LDs and to provide a rich literacy experience to share with others. If screened carefully for level of difficulty, literature can also be used as a text to improve fluency through practice reading and rereading after a teacher has read it aloud first. However, teachers need to be careful that deliberate attention is given to adjusting the difficulty level of texts as students develop their reading proficiency. If a text is too difficult, students with LD will experience

Example of a Readers' Workshop Lesson

Introduction (whole class) 10:00–10:10

- The teacher introduces the Readers' Workshop and reminds the class of the rules of Readers' Workshop.
- She asks the class, *Have you ever seen a frog? What does a frog look like? Where does it live?*
- The teacher calls the class over to the Reading Corner where they sit on a rug and she sits at a chair next to an easel.
- She takes out the book *Frog and Toad Are Friends* by Arnold Lobel.
- She does a quick picture-walk of the book asking the students what they think the story will be about.
- She does a Read-Aloud of the book.
- She asks one or two children what the book was about.

Mini-lesson (whole class) 10:10–10:25

- The teacher does a review of what word families are.
- She lists at least 4 words from the _og word family: *frog, hog, jog, log*.
- She asks the students to find the _og words on the Word Wall.
- They look at the cover of the book *Frog and Toad Are Friends* and she asks if they can find the _og word family on the cover.
- She asks if the children can elicit more words for that family.
- She asks the students to look at the word *toad* and see if they can list more words in the _oad word family.
- They review the book and some print concepts: where to find title, author, page number, and so on.

Independent Reading (students are working independently or self-grouped by book) 10:25–10:50

- The students choose something to read from the class library. They can reread *Frog and Toad Are Friends* if they like. She allows the students to work independently, with a buddy, or in small groups.
- Students are instructed to write down any words they find that are in a word family listed on the word wall, or any other word family they recognize. They are also to write down any word they cannot identify.

Conferencing

- The teacher confers with different students. She reviews strategies they used during reading—identifying word families, using picture clues, identifying sight words, using phonics to identify unknown words—and conducts a running record with a few students. She jots down anecdotal records while conferencing.
- She supports students having difficulty sounding out words—helping them identify initial consonants, final consonants, long or short vowels.

Responding

- Students share thoughts regarding characters, plot, sequence of events, if story is fantasy or real, and if they can relate the story to a personal experience.

Sharing (whole class) 10:50–11:00

- Choose a few students to share their reading with whole class.
- Referring back to *Frog and Toad Are Friends*, conduct teacher-guided discussion: *Did you like the story? Why? Was this something that could happen to you? Who were the main characters? Were they like you? What was this story about? What was the main idea? Was the story funny, happy, sad? Would you recommend this book to a friend? Why?*

Note: On some days, the teacher works with guided reading groups while the other students read independently. She will rotate a guided reading group so that each group gets a chance to work with her within a week.

FIGURE 11-11

great frustration, which will impede fluency; if a student is reading a text fluently, a slightly more difficult text should be assigned. For independent reading, the student should be familiar with 90 to 95 percent of the words. For guided reading sessions, text should be chosen that is at the student's instructional level, and the teacher should focus on increasing the rate and accuracy of reading. Opportunities to practice reading and rereading familiar text are recommended for students with LDs to enhance their reading fluency.

ELLs who have reached an oral language threshold that enables them to handle the vocabulary should also be working with graded readers with controlled text to ensure that the text difficulty keeps pace with vocabulary development. The child

Independent Reading and Guided Reading (demonstrated here), as well as Read-Aloud/ Shared Reading and Mini-lesson, are stages of Readers' Workshop.

should know 90 to 95 percent of the vocabulary in the text before it is used for instructional purposes. Authentic literature should supplement instruction through read-alouds, shared reading, and independent reading to ensure ELLs are exposed to text that reflects natural speech. Repeated readings of text are also highly recommended (Lenters, 2004).

Although studies of the effects of literature-based instruction on ELLs are few, educators support using authentic literature with ELLs, especially literature with content that is culturally familiar to them and helps bridge comprehension gaps (Anderson & Roit; 1996; Au, 2001; Collins, 2005; Gambrell, Morrow, & Pennington, 2002; Lenters, 2004). Krashen and Terrell (1983) theorize that students who are learning a second language acquire language naturally in small pieces that the student can understand without resorting to translation. They differentiate between language learning, which occurs as a result of formal study, and acquisition, which is the result of interaction and communication with others. Krashen and Terrell (1983) posit that acquisition is what teachers should be striving toward, and that a supportive classroom environment is most effective. Thus, the classroom should strive to facilitate many different types of activities and student-centered interactions, which a literature-based instructional program facilitates. In addition, Krashen and Terrell claim that an "affective filter" may interfere with this natural process. Multicultural literature, particularly by authors whose cultural backgrounds are similar to the students, will motivate the students to acquire language and become part of the classroom community.

Au (2001), who worked extensively with Native Hawaiians, believes that it is important for students of all backgrounds to read and respond to multicultural literature, but she believes that it is especially important for students of diverse backgrounds. When diverse students read only "mainstream literature" about the dominant cultures, they are unlikely to understand or appreciate their own self-worth and are unwilling to write or communicate about their personal experiences. Such texts can serve as an example of how students can write and explore their own cultural identities in pieces they compose during a writing workshop. The composing and sharing of these writings offer what Au calls a new form of culturally relevant literacy. Using multicultural literature that motivates diverse learners is one way to begin a transition toward **culturally responsive instruction**. About 45 percent of the questions on the National Assessment of Educational Progress standardized reading test, which is given nationally to assess children in the United States, required students to provide a personal response and take a critical stance. If students of diverse backgrounds are to compete with their mainstream peers, their instruction must ask them to respond critically to text and apply higher order thinking skills. Teachers must be sensitive to the needs of all students in the class and build on the strengths that students bring from their home cultures; they must make connections to students' home cultures and families (Au, 2001).

Children's literature can bring content-area studies to life and help students see the connection between the content they are studying and their own personal lives. It can also bring humor and fun into a content area many children deem boring or unexciting. Children can explore content through the eyes of other children and understand the significance of time, place, and events through personal stories. By identifying with main characters, children can be transported to a time and place they may not have any previous experience with and learn about the events that shaped history or impacted humankind. A perfect example of this is Lois Lowry's *Number the Stars,* a compelling story of two young girls, one of whom is Jewish, in Denmark during World War II. It tells the story of the sacrifices one family made for their Jewish friends by hiding the daughter in their home and helping the family escape the Nazis. This book is an excellent introduction to the Holocaust for children in the fourth, fifth, or sixth grade. It is a heartwarming tale that can emotionally affect its readers and introduce them to the horrors that occurred during that period. Through this story a seemingly difficult subject can be raised and discussed, and the students can relate to the personal story of the two girls.

Bringing literature into the content areas can begin with the teacher reading aloud from a related book for as little as 10 minutes a day. This can be highly motivating for all grade levels up to high school, especially if the book is chosen carefully and is a compelling story. However, this is just a beginning and teachers can expand read-alouds into a more integrated approach.

Using literature in content-area studies enriches the experiences children have with the discipline and helps them make connections to their own personal life.

STRATEGIES FOR TEACHING DIVERSE LEARNERS

Using Literature to Promote Literacy

1. Use literature to supplement reading instruction through read-alouds, shared reading, and independent reading to ensure that diverse learners are exposed to motivating text.

2. Use authentic literature that contains complex plots, rich character development, and quality use of language. The teacher should model expressive reading and fluency.

3. Incorporate literature that contains themes and values diverse learners can relate to.

4. Choose multicultural books whose content is culturally familiar to English language learners. Try to choose books by authors whose cultural backgrounds are similar to the students. This will motivate them to express themselves in similar ways.

5. Encourage students' families to engage in meaningful reading activities at home and read literature in their first language with their children.

6. If at all possible, acquire first-language books to match the English-language books in the classroom.

7. Find a bilingual volunteer to translate the story and make first-language translation tapes. If at all possible, have the parents or siblings translate the stories, and then have the student illustrate the book for placement alongside the English version in the classroom library.

8. Encourage English language learners of the same language to discuss the books they have read in literature circles or during Readers' Workshop. This will support comprehension and address gaps they may have in understanding the text.

9. Put authentic literature on audiotape for students with learning disabilities and English language learners. This is an excellent project for other students in the class or school.

10. Provide support for struggling readers in guided reading sessions. Be sure that they have read the text and have comprehended it before they participate in literature circle.

11. Provide a wide range of books, genres, topics, and themes in the classroom from which struggling readers can choose. Carefully consider:

   - The difficulty of the text, which should be kept relatively simple

   - The number of words on the page, which should be kept to a minimum

   - The number of high-frequency words (*at, like, me, in*), which should be used often, while the number of low-frequency words (*hyena, gyrated*) should be kept to a minimum

   - Vocabulary usage, which should be controlled and previously introduced and practiced

Literature can be used to supplement the textbook, although in many classrooms, teachers are starting to move away from predominant use of content-area textbooks and toward literature as the key focus of the curriculum. Stories provide a meaningful context to study different content areas and they are a powerful tool for learning. Students gain a greater insight into the world around them and the stories that are a part of the literary tradition. Chapter 12 will discuss using literature in the content areas in more depth.

STRATEGY BOX

Using Literature in the Classroom

Mrs. Santos incorporates a literature-based curriculum in her class that emphasizes responding to text. In the introductory scenario, she used many different approaches to promote comprehension and fluency of text in her classroom. She used the following strategies to promote literacy:

1. She used read-alouds to model expressive, fluent reading of text.

2. She used quality literature in the class to motivate students and to provide models of rich language, excellent character development, complex plots, and multicultural themes.

3. She had children reread passages from books over again a number of times to increase fluency.

4. She exposed children to a variety of genres and had many different types of books available in the classroom.

5. She provided a large variety of multicultural literature for children to read, especially by authors who come from a similar cultural background as the diverse learners in the classroom.

6. She used technology to support students' comprehension and literacy development of literature.

7. She used a response-based curriculum, ensuring that students responded to text in many different ways throughout the day.

8. She used literature circles to have students respond to books that have a common theme, a common topic, or a common author.

9. Students participated in Readers Theatre Workshop, in which they read a script of a book to the class. This promoted fluency and comprehension through repeated readings while students practiced the script.

10. She used Readers' Workshop to organize a literature-based curriculum that allowed students the freedom to select and read books of their own choice.

11. She had students read books that were on their appropriate level, and she monitored them to ensure they could successfully comprehend the texts.

12. Struggling readers were provided support and guidance during guided reading sessions and during conferences.

13. She assessed students using running records, anecdotal records, and structured observations.

Final Thoughts

There are many reasons to use children's literature in the classroom: It is highly motivating for children; it promotes achievement in all subjects, including reading; it contributes to language growth and development; it helps students become better writers; and it has great emotional appeal to readers. In our increasingly diverse classrooms, our students need to understand and appreciate cultural differences. Literature can show us how we are connected to one another, and it can help all of us appreciate and celebrate our differences. Multicultural literature can help diverse learners feel connected to the mainstream culture and help them feel motivated to read and be a part of the classroom community.

At this time when many adults and adolescents seem to be reading fewer books, classroom teachers need to explore the richness and variety of quality literature that is constantly being published. The IRA and the ALA are wonderful resources for finding out about quality books being published each year. It is worthwhile for teachers to stay current with these associations, with electronic databases, and with annual awards given to children's and adolescent literature so that they can select and provide a wide array of books for students to read.

EXPLORATION   Application of Concepts

Activities

1. *Have a show-and-tell session in your class.* Bring in three examples of Caldecott Medal or Caldecott Honor books with a multicultural theme and three examples of Newbery Medal books. Get into a large circle and share the books that each candidate has brought in. If you have not read the Newbery book, give a brief summary of it from the book jacket.

2. *Prepare a Readers Theatre Workshop presentation to the class.* Working in a group, develop your own script for a presentation or go to Aaron Shepard's Home Page (http://www.aaronshep.com) and find a script to use. In your group, practice using the prescribed conventions, in which you sit on a stool, use no props, and whoever is reading will look up while the other performers look down.

3. *Model a read-aloud to the class.* Choose a picture book and prepare a mini-lesson to have candidates respond to the text after the reading.

4. *Visit the ALA website (http://www.ala.org/alsc) and read about the Caldecott and Newbery awards, as well as the Coretta Scott King Award.* Print out a copy of all books that have won these medals. Choose one book from each award to read and order the book using an online library book service.

5. Visit the *Literacy for Children in an Information Age* premium website for this chapter (http://www.cengage.com/login). Choose three authors and visit their web pages. Present to a small group which author's web page you like best and explain why.

HOME–SCHOOL CONNECTION Reading Quality Literature At Home

It is important that parents and guardians promote literacy at home by reading to their children frequently and providing them with a variety of material to read, including quality children's literature, children's magazines, catalogs of children's toys and clothes, menus, and comic books. The following recommendations are important considerations for parents' early literacy involvement:

1. Parents and guardians should take their children to the library as often as possible. Public libraries have wonderful children's programs available on Saturdays and during summer vacation. Librarians read books to children, show movies, and offer arts and craft projects. Teachers should encourage parents to bring their children to the library to participate in these programs.

2. Many schools have programs that reward children for the number of books that they read. Teachers can institute such a program in their classroom and encourage parents to read the books with their children at home.

3. Teachers should encourage parents to go to the school book fair, if one is offered. This is a wonderful opportunity for parents and guardians to visit the school and look at quality literature together.

4. Teachers should work with the school's parent–teacher association (PTA) to create opportunities for parents and guardians to become involved in reading quality literature to their children. Special programs can be offered where authors come to talk to the students.

5. Consider having a lending library in the classroom for children to take books home. Use multicultural literature that is motivating and reassuring to children and their families, ensuring that their culture and language is respected and valued.

6. Have the class develop a literary newspaper where the children write summaries of the books that they read. These newspapers can be sent home and shared with parents and guardians.

7. During parent–teacher conferences, teachers can encourage the parents and guardians to read quality literature to their children. If the parents or guardians do not speak English, encourage them to read books to their children in their native language.

12 INFORMATIONAL TEXT TO IMPROVE CONTENT-AREA COMPREHENSION

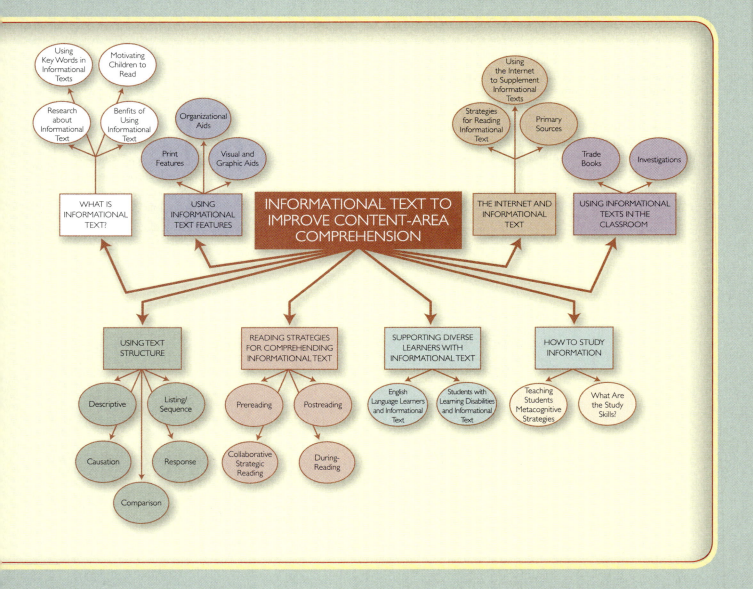

International Reading Association Professional Standards Addressed in this Chapter:

IRA STANDARD 1: FOUNDATIONAL KNOWLEDGE

Candidates have knowledge of the foundations of reading and writing processes and instruction. Candidates:

1.1 Demonstrate knowledge of psychological, sociological, and linguistic foundations of reading and writing processes and instruction.

1.2 Demonstrate knowledge of reading research and histories of reading.

1.3 Demonstrate knowledge of language development and reading acquisition and the variations related to cultural and linguistic diversity.

1.4 Demonstrate knowledge of the major components of reading (phonemic awareness, word identification and phonics, vocabulary and background knowledge, fluency, comprehension strategies, and motivation) and how they are integrated in fluent reading.

IRA STANDARD 2: INSTRUCTIONAL STRATEGIES AND CURRICULUM MATERIAL

Candidates use a wide range of instructional practices, approaches, methods, and curriculum materials to support reading and writing instruction. Candidates:

2.1 Use instructional grouping options (individual, small-group, whole-class, and computer-based) as appropriate for accomplishing given purposes.

2.2 Use a wide range of instructional practices, approaches, and methods, including technology-based practices, for learners at differing stages of development and from differing cultural and linguistic backgrounds.

2.3 Use a wide range of curriculum materials in effective reading instruction for learners at different stages of reading and writing development and from different cultural and linguistic backgrounds.

IRA STANDARD 4: CREATING A LITERATE ENVIRONMENT

Candidates create a literate environment that fosters reading and writing by integrating foundational knowledge, use of instructional practices, approaches and methods, curriculum materials, and the appropriate use of assessments. Candidates:

4.1 Use students' interests, reading abilities, and backgrounds as foundations for the reading and writing program.

4.2 Use a large supply of books, technology-based information, and nonprint materials representing multiple levels, broad interests, and cultural and linguistic backgrounds.

4.3 Model reading and writing enthusiastically as valued lifelong activities.

4.4 Motivate learners to be lifelong readers.

Key Terms

informational text
keywords
informational content question
text features
table of contents
index
glossary
text structure
descriptive text structure
listing text structure
causation (cause/effect) text structure

Focus Questions

1. What is informational text and why has it become an important genre for elementary-level students?

2. What are the important text features of informational texts, and why must they be understood by children to read these texts successfully?

response (problem/
   solution) text structure
comparison text structure
efferent stance
aesthetic stance
previewing
skimming
scanning
scaffolding reading
   experiences
thinkmarks
pause and reflect
comprehension monitoring
click or clunk
collaborative strategic
   reading
Investigations
poster
double-page spread

3. What are the different text structures and how do they help students improve their comprehension of content information?

4. What prereading, during-reading, and postreading strategies should students be taught to increase their comprehension of informational text?

5. What strategies can be used to support English language learners when reading informational text? To support students with learning disabilities when reading informational text?

6. How has the Internet impacted the way children read today? What strategies should be used to increase comprehension when children read material on the Internet?

7. How can trade books be used in the classroom and what benefit do they contribute to the literacy curriculum?

8. What is an investigation? Explain the difference between an investigation as a product and as a process.

Welcome to Mrs. Rodriguez's Second Grade Class: Working with Informational Text

Stretch Photography/Jupiter Images

Mrs. Rodriguez, a second grade teacher, first included informational texts during a summer workshop program with the purpose of improving her struggling readers' reading and writing abilities in the content areas. This group of children, many of whom were English language learners (ELLs), seemed to have a great deal of difficulty reading typical picture books that she and most of her colleagues commonly used to teach second graders how to read. Mrs. Rodriguez read these narratives out loud to the whole group, and later engaged students in shared reading activities. She also followed up her shared reading activities by meeting with small groups of children to improve their specific literacy skills, using guided reading and writing instruction.

Nevertheless, her struggling readers continued to struggle, and whatever success they had achieved appeared to dissipate over the summer vacation. Mrs. Rodriguez decided that some intervention was needed to correct this problem, particularly to help her least successful readers become higher achievers.

With help from her reading coach and two other grade level teachers, Ms. Chen and Ms. Wilson, Mrs. Rodriguez set out to determine whether using informational texts could make a difference for the children. She began by introducing the children to informational texts that contained key topics and new subject matter. This new approach had an immediate positive response from this diverse group of difficult-to-motivate children. Mrs. Rodriguez and her team of teachers were encouraged by this genuine response: Changing from narrative to informational books seemed to interest this group of children and actually motivated and excited them about reading for the first time.

Mrs. Rodriguez introduced informational texts and informational big books in the same manner that she used picture books, that is, by reading them aloud through shared reading and through small guided group instruction. Some of these topics included the hatching of baby chicks, the power and strength of a tiny Japanese beetle, how baby birds learn how to fly, and how baby turtles flee to the sea to avoid being eaten by big birds and other creatures. Mrs. Rodriguez and her two team teachers made plans together; they created mini-lessons on science and social studies with the purpose of helping the children increase their knowledge of content by reading informational texts. The children also engaged in science experiments and were asked to write their personal autobiographies.

They learned how to write about their own lives by paralleling the texts they were reading, which included texts about the childhoods of presidents, scientists, heroes, and explorers. It soon became quite evident that this diverse group of reluctant readers was eager to read more than ever before, and the ELL children found that reading about information was easier to understand compared with narratives that used more abstract descriptions about setting, plot, character, and theme. The children's newfound excitement for learning and their curiosity to learn more about these real-life topics eventually led to their interest in researching new information on the Internet. With their teachers' guidance, the children were able to take virtual field trips using the Internet, and they were able to pursue their interests by extending their information gathering. Visual literacy skills were also developed as Mrs. Rodriguez introduced her guided reading groups to charts, maps, photographs, captions, and lists, which they could later use to create their own graphic reports and posters.

A balanced reading program should not only be about *learning to read* using phonics and quality literature, it should also include a balance of different kinds of texts and genres with the instructional purpose of *reading to learn*. This above scenario shows how informational text can motivate children to read and help them make connections between their own lives and what they are reading. In addition, informational text contributes to content-area knowledge and expands students' knowledge base about important subject areas that they will learn about in their future years in school. This chapter describes how informational text can contribute to content-area comprehension.

What Is Informational Text?

Informational text (often called expository text) is text that enables readers to learn about the natural and social world because it is written with the purpose of presenting facts, concepts, and various forms of content. This content can be read or listened to by readers, particularly young readers who have until recently been brought up on a diet of reading narrative or fictional texts (Duke, 2003; Mooney, 2001). The term *informational* *text* is also preferred by most educators because it is more descriptive than **nonfictional text,** a term often used in the past that signifies contrast. Hoyt (2002), for instance, is emphatic that the term *nonfictional* no longer be used because it is not accurate in defining *informational texts.* In her words, "All that tells us is that this *isn't* fiction. The terms 'informational texts' or 'info texts' give us a much clearer picture of what these texts are and remind us clearly that we are reading to learn information, reading to pursue our own questions and interests" (p. 3).

Informational text comes in a variety of formats, including newspapers, magazines, how-to books, field guides, lists, and directions (Frey & Fisher, 2007). Many students have an insatiable appetite for reading information on repairing and building things, including cars, gadgets, toys, and a myriad of objects in our everyday world. In fact, informational text provides today's readers with a worldview of subjects, topics, and content that adds to their developing knowledge. At the same time, millions of dollars are spent in this country on informational materials to know more about everyday life and the lives and experiences of others living in our midst or around the globe. In fact, informational text is the most commonly read material by adults. Reportedly, approximately 85 percent of material read by most people is nonfiction (Duke, 2003). Informational texts are also very amorphous in that they come in a number of formats, such as menus, directions, advertisements, dictionaries, encyclopedias, hypertext, and computer software.

It is probably a safe prediction that because we are living in the throes of the information age, reading for information will not only continue to grow but should increase rapidly in the future. Therefore, it is necessary that our students learn how to master reading and understanding informational text in all forms, electronically and otherwise, just to survive. There is a growing interest in introducing more and more informational texts at the primary level, with some educators recommending that school literacy programs switch from the picture book–dominant curriculum to one that includes a preponderance of informational texts.

This shift in emphasis to informational text is also important if older children are to develop their ability to read content with greater understanding. Research states that a major crisis in reading is occurring at the upper elementary and middle school grades, in that these children are failing to read for meaning (Duke, 2003; National Institute of Child Health and Human Development [NICHD], 2000). Therefore, these older students are exhibiting great difficulty in reading successfully about specific subjects such as science, history, and mathematics. On the other hand, specific strategies for reading informational texts and for writing informational materials are necessary to promote higher order communication skills, a prerequisite for success in an informational, technology-based society. According to Hoyt, Mooney, and Parkes (2003), "The reading of informational texts is not so much about gathering information as it is about selecting and using information" (p. ix). Mrs. Rodriguez and her team members soon discovered this point of view to be quite true, particularly when their students realized how much they were learning as they began presenting their research findings, and needed to figure out what information to use after they had gathered it.

A balanced literacy program includes an emphasis on informational books and reading to learn.

Courtesy of Guilherme Cunha

Research About Informational Text

Nell K. Duke (2003) reports that there are several important advantages to including informational text in teaching of elementary school–age children. For one, her research shows that young children gravitate to informational text because they are usually curious to learn about interesting topics that they can relate to or that are fun and exciting, such as bugs, snakes, dogs, cats, penguins (and all the other things that interest them!). Therefore, given the opportunity, children not only enjoy reading informational texts but they can retell information and discuss the main ideas recalled from their readings.

The *Report of the National Reading Panel* (NICHD, 2000) claims that there is a precipitous drop at the fourth grade level nationwide in standardized test scores, which is an indication that difficult textbooks and informational text are introduced too suddenly, without transition or instruction, leaving students brought up on a steady diet of fiction at a great disadvantage. For this reason, Duke (2003) proposes that informational texts be introduced earlier in the primary grades to offset this serious problem. Furthermore, studies show that informational texts, specific subject matter textbooks, content-area vocabulary, and high-stakes testing occur more frequently once children enter fourth grade and beyond. In fact, adults read more than 75 percent more nonfiction than fictional texts. Another striking statistic reported by Duke (2003) is that 96 percent of the materials found on the Internet are in the form of informational text, and the likelihood of that increasing is, indeed, far greater in the future.

Another study reports that first grade children exposed to a combination of texts—one-third informational, one-third narrative, and one-third poetry or other genres—tend to write and read for comprehension better than those who were not exposed. The study indicates that children with low literacy skills benefited from using combined texts, which seemed to help "level the playing field" (Duke, 2003).

Although there are strong indications that introducing elementary children to informational text has many advantages, it is still too early to know how much is enough or perhaps too much. It is evident that there are positive studies showing that a balance of texts for children in the classroom is essential; that is, combining informational text, narrative text, and poetry or other genres such as biography is highly motivating to students when given the opportunity to select their favorite texts. Also, there is some evidence that ELLs, children with learning disabilities, and struggling readers are learning with less apparent difficulty when able to select informational texts to read over narrative texts. Similarly, these children appear to have less difficulty when given the choice to write using expository writing over creative writing.

Benefits of Using Informational Texts

Learning to read for information is a powerful tool that builds self-esteem, as well as knowledge. Informational text promotes student achievement in content areas such as science, social studies, and mathematics, while also supporting oral language and vocabulary development. Vocabulary is more readily developed and enriched when students encounter content-specific words that refer to specific concepts associated with each specific discipline (Nagy, 1988; Blachowicz & Fisher, 2004). Through the development of specific comprehension skills, read-alongs, repeated readings, writing, and grammar, children develop lifelong skills that will serve them throughout their schooling and in later years (Hoyt, 2002). Children need to be taught that they can use their prior knowledge and experiences as they learn about content information, which can improve their reading speed and accuracy, as well as their listening comprehension.

In addition, it is quite beneficial to teach children how to write informational and narrative text, such as stories. Interactive writing, for instance, helps children link writing to reading content and related informational skills. As children are reading diverse types of text, such as menus, grocery lists, recipes, directions, and notes, they should also be learning how to write this type of text. A good idea is to teach reading and writing as complementary processes. When a reading strategy is taught, children should also learn how to apply it in their writing. In this way, they become both effective readers and writers.

Teachers' VOICES   Informational Texts in the Classroom

I find that having access to a wide variety of informational texts in our school's book room has helped me improve my teaching in the content areas. Our district has science and social studies textbooks for the third and fourth grades. However, my students with learning disabilities are reading below grade level and the textbooks are too difficult for them to use. I am able to pull many different leveled informational texts on the same subject for my students. Having access to leveled informational texts allows my class to study and research the same topics in social studies and science, but on their independent and instructional reading levels. I like to use guided reading to teach comprehension, genre, and content literacy; for example:

• I use quality informational nonfiction books that students are interested in, on topics such as sports,

religion, animals, history, cooking, geography, and people, among others.

• I like to use informational trade books because they are quality, authentic literature, while traditional textbooks are not.

• Exposing children to informational text teaches them strategies they can use to read, comprehend, and write informatively.

• Literacy skills such as gathering information, summarizing, synthesizing, and making connections to prior knowledge and experiences are all involved in reading informational texts.

—*Stephanie Lawlor, Special Education Teacher*

Most children are highly motivated to read nonfiction, particularly when they are eager to acquire information about a topic that piques their curiosity, such as dinosaurs or animals. Children are also avid supporters of saving favorite animals from extinction: themes of "Save Our Planet," "Save Our Endangered Species," and "Save Our Lakes, Ponds, and Rivers from Pollution and Toxic Waste" are just some of the ecological unit projects that teachers can use to benefit their students (Frey & Fisher, 2007).

Using Key Words in Informational Texts

All children, including ELLs, children with learning disabilities, and struggling readers can benefit by developing informational vocabulary by focusing on **keywords.** When young children locate keywords that are essential to reading main ideas in informational texts and use them to retell, summarize, or synthesize what they recall from their research investigations, it is likely that they will learn and remember these new vocabulary words with greater ease. First, the teacher should model how to focus on keywords, by showing children that keywords are usually highlighted, set in bold type, or are italicized for the reader to notice because they are important words to know. Second, the teacher should teach children how to locate keywords by phrasing them as an **informational content question:** for example, Where do penguins live? The children are taught how to research these questions by looking up keywords, which in this case are *penguins* and *live*. To research these keywords and to

Teachers should teach children how to develop informational content questions.

learn more about penguins, the children look up *penguins live* in the table of contents or the index, enabling them to locate where they can read about penguins so that they can answer the content question. Children should also learn how to use keywords to write expository sentences. If the children are very young, they may not yet have developed a facility with writing, but they can learn how to use keywords to help them answer content questions with little difficulty. For instance, the children's research helps them to discover that penguins live in very cold climates and that they live in the South Pole, which is located in the region below South America. Hence, using keywords, the children are able to write, "Penguins live in cold climates in the South Pole." Eventually, young children will develop background information and, through their use of keywords, they will soon be able to string many more sentences together and begin writing expository paragraphs that have a beginning and an end, and that are quite intelligible to read.

Another feature of using keywords is that children retain words that they research and write in sentences that are essential to the content information that they have just learned. Children should be given a number of opportunities to explore researching information by answering essential questions that contain keywords. This process will help them develop a facility for investigating information by answering research questions. It will also help them develop their expository or informational writing, improve their content-area vocabulary, and build their concept information in a variety of subject areas. In fact, young children will increase their literacy ability overall, including their higher order thinking skills achievement (Cowen, 2003a).

Motivating Children to Read

Children are motivated to read through self-selection of topics and different types of informational texts that enable them to learn about many new topics in a variety of ways. They soon learn how informational texts come in a variety of forms that are accessible to them. They also can add to their knowledge about a subject by reading magazines, informational picture books, informational big books, newspapers, TV guides, recipes, or biographies. They can learn about volcanoes, tsunamis, earthquakes, and rainforests by reading descriptions and facts, as well as being treated to illustrations, photographs, and even real-life examples of informational text found on the Internet or in multimedia presentations (Coiro & Dobler, 2007).

Reading biographies about famous historical figures—including American presidents or other historical figures, such as Martin Luther King and Rosa Parks—can be exciting to children. Reading about famous scientists such as Benjamin Franklin, George Washington Carver, or Madame Curie can also provide new knowledge that children will enjoy learning by reading trade books, biographies, or other kinds of informational books. Children enjoy learning about how to use information and how to follow written directions to build things, such as a tree house, dog house, or bird house.

Teachers can create classroom libraries by taking field trips to the town library or by visiting the school library and signing out several favorite informational books on a theme or topic of choice. Magazines that adults read to acquire the latest information are now also available in modified text written for young readers, including *Time Magazine for Kids, World News Report for Kids, National Geographic Kids Magazine;* other children's classic news magazines include *Highlights, Weekly Reader,* and *Read Magazine.* These newly modified magazines and classics are highly motivating, enjoyable informational texts. They are extremely useful in helping them to build their knowledge about favorite topics, including world news and current events.

Teachers' VOICES   Motivating Students with Informational Texts

When teaching genre and content literacy through the exploration of fiction and nonfiction texts, teachers must understand and model the value of knowing various texts. Providing a foundation of varied texts helps engage students' interests in all types of reading including fantasy, realistic, informational, and biographical texts. With newfound knowledge about various texts, students are better able to exercise their knowledge in identifying literary elements, including characters, theme, and perspective. With the understanding of each element, students can transfer their knowledge by creating written or oral responses based on features of the text they have read, whether they are describing graphics or identifying characters or a setting by looking at the table of contents. Also, it is important to keep in mind that nonfiction should not be thought of as a simple text book, but rather a piece of literature that can be found in the sports section of a newspaper, a bible, a zoo pamphlet, a cookbook, or even a teen magazine. Exposing students to these different forms of texts engages their interest and also teaches them to use different strategies to gather information to fully comprehend and respond.

—*Kimberly Scheffler, Sixth Grade Teacher*

Using Informational Text Features

When writing informational text, authors use specific **text features** that help readers locate information quickly. For example, the *table of contents* and the *index* are two text features that are essential to readers who are reading for information or researching specific topics. The value of text features is that they help students locate and understand the texts they are using by scaffolding or making information easier and faster to find. Text features make information more accessible, and therefore help the reader comprehend the purpose, organization, and major concepts of the text. Consequently, informational text features enable the reader to search for new details and new ideas with greater ease and satisfaction. In fact, the text features that follow will explain how they can help students skim and scan text without having to read it in a specific order; instead, by going to the table of contents, the reader can look up the main idea of a certain topic to research and can turn to that chapter or section in the book to review it (Frey & Fisher, 2007). Such skills are also important as students use technology, exploring the Internet and using a hypertext approach as they search in a nonlinear way for specific information. The following *print features, graphic aids,* and *organizational aids* are some of the major features that teachers must help children learn about so they can apply them skillfully as they read informational text. Figure 12–1 presents some widely used informational text features and shows how readers should be using them to help comprehend text.

Informational Text Features

Readers should be able to identify and use the following informational text features when reading expository text:

Feature	Purpose	Readers Should Use It to:
BOLD PRINT	To highlight a key term or phrase	Remember key ideas
COLORED PRINT	To differentiate a separate thought, idea, process	Identify that a new, important idea is being introduced
ITALICS	To highlight a key term or phrase or for emphasis	Remember key ideas
TITLES	To identify the name of the text to be read	Predict what the text will be about
HEADINGS	To signify a new section with different content is coming up	Turn the heading into a question and read to answer the question
LABELS	To explain a graphic, picture, or photograph	Understand what the graphic, picture, or photograph is about and how it relates to the content being read
CAPTIONS	To explain a graphic, picture, photograph, or cartoon	Understand what the graphic, picture, or photograph is about and how it relates to the content being read
BULLETS	To highlight important information in an easy-to-read format	Quickly identify the list of important information being presented
FACT BOXES	To highlight important facts presented in the text	Identify and remember important facts
DIAGRAMS	To present visually important processes and components of the topic being studied	Understand visually the process being explained and/or identify the various components of the topic
MAGNIFICATIONS	To present a close-up visual image of a topic so that it can be more easily viewed	Understand the process or topic by seeing it visually presented in large scale
PHOTOGRAPHS	To present the content visually through realistic images	Visually understand and remember the image, which will help in comprehension and retention
CROSS-SECTION/ CUTAWAY	To visually present important processes and components of the topic being studied and which may not be understood unless the object is "opened up"	Understand visually the process being explained and/or identify the various components of the topic
TABLES	To present information in an easy-to-read and understand format	Identify the important information and synthesize it into a more comprehensive understanding of the topic
GRAPHS	To present quantitative information in an easy-to-read format	Identify important quantitative information and synthesize it into a comprehensive understanding of the topic based upon numeric data

FIGURE 12-1

continued

Informational Text Features—cont'd

Feature	Purpose	Readers Should Use It to:
TIMELINES	To present information in an easy-to-read sequential format	Identify the important sequential facts and synthesize them into a comprehensive sequential understanding of the topic
MAPS	To present geographical information in graphical format	Identify individual geographic regions and obtain a more general understanding of how geography affects the topic
TABLE OF CONTENTS	To present topics being covered at the beginning of the text	Identify important information that will be covered and make predictions to aid in the upcoming reading of text
INTRODUCTION	To introduce the important topics, ideas, processes to be covered in the upcoming text	Read it carefully as an advance organizer and highlight important topics that will be covered
INDEX	To provide a comprehensive listing of all topics, ideas, authors, and subjects that were covered in the text	Access important topics, ideas, authors, and subjects quickly for review and reinforcement
GLOSSARY	To help define key terms, often providing pronunciation	Define key terms that were presented in the text and to use this list of key terms to study from

FIGURE 12-1

Print Features

Some of the print features, included in a variety of trade books, informational books, magazines, and newspapers, that aid children in their quest for information include such unique visual support as:

- ◆ Bold print
- ◆ Colored print
- ◆ Special font types and sizes
- ◆ Italics
- ◆ Computer type print
- ◆ Old-fashioned typewriter print
- ◆ Cursive writing and artistic graphic artist print

Bold print is used to highlight keywords, key phrases, and key ideas that are important. Although not used as frequently, *colored print* highlights or focuses the reader's attention on important information in the text. The use of special font types or sizes also can be visually stimulating and memorable. *Italic print* can also be used as a more subtle reminder to students that variety in print is captivating. Some typewriter print and computer print can be very stark and can be used to create a special effect that relates to the information the author intends to emphasize. Cursive writing and other types of artistic print are sometimes used to convey special meanings, such as in documents and illustrations. In some informational text, writers use a special text for captions just to create a certain effect.

Teachers should point out these examples and call their students' attention to the variations in print features that are used chiefly in informational texts, but that are found in some narrative texts as well. In so doing, children can be encouraged to use these and other types of print features when they become more confident in writing their own nonfictional pieces.

Other important print features in informational texts are titles and subtitles, which are usually in bold, large print in newspapers and magazines. A title, such as the one on the cover of the February 2004 edition of *Time for Kids*, **THE POND IS OUR HOME,** is like a main idea statement. Although not as big an idea as a title, the subtitle is used to describe or provide more information or to increase interest by raising some questions for the purpose of reading about this particular text. For example, if children are asked, "Who lives in a pond?" the teacher can show them how to use keywords to write a subtitle using this information; for example, **Creatures Who Live in a Pond.** Students should be taught that the subheading can usually be turned into a question that needs to be answered during the reading of that section. Titles, headings, and subtitles or subheadings are usually written in bold print for emphasis. Titles and headings are generally printed in larger, capital letters for emphasis and to raise the reader's awareness by calling attention to the visual importance of these print features.

Reading and writing informational text should be taught reciprocally, because children learn to read better when they study how the author coveys information, and in turn, the child can use the written word as a model for writing about the information that is being studied. The more background knowledge children have with a variety of informational texts, the more they will learn about and make use of the myriad of possibilities of print features to be found in informational texts. In turn, with this reading background knowledge, the students can apply what they know about print in selecting, creating, and using these features in writing their own informational texts.

Visual and Graphic Aids

It is quite evident by reading the daily newspaper or a favorite magazine how important visual and graphic aids are to support the information. Visuals aids such as photographs, illustrations, charts, diagrams, maps, tables, timelines, graphs, or captions and labels are used to connect and expand the actual text. Other visual and graphic aids that are widely used in informational texts include bullets, fact boxes, side bars, and magnifications or close-ups to clarify an important point and to further assist the reader in making fast but necessary connections to facilitate reading and meaning acquisition (Frey & Fisher, 2007).

In Figure 12–2, a second grade student has drawn a ladybug as a diagram with labels that show the ladybug's wings, eyes, mouth, antenna, and legs. This diagram demonstrates that the student knows the body parts of a ladybug and new content words such as *antenna*. The diagram is an important text feature that teaches students how to read and write informational text by giving them tools to construct meaning.

Children need to learn how to use maps to locate geographic places throughout the world, especially in this global, technological society. The nature of informational text is to make world news and ideas accessible to children and adults; therefore, learning how to read maps is important for children because they need to use maps to locate places around the world. Children should also learn to draw or trace maps that illustrate areas of the world that need our help, such as preventing pollution or protecting rainforests.

Bar graphs, *line graphs*, and *circle graphs* are also used to aid readers to connect with text by clarifying information through the use of visual comparison and contrast images. Comparison and contrast is an extremely useful strategy in aiding student comprehension, and the graph is an excellent tool for helping children improve their knowledge and their growing understanding of new information. For instance, the student-made bar graph in Figure 12–3, created using Excel, shows the comparison and contrast of the height of different mammoths, demonstrating to students how huge these elephant-like mammals were when they lived more than 1 million years ago.

Other useful visual aids that are used to help readers compare and contrast information rapidly are tables and timelines. Tables give examples of information by condensing, highlighting, and showing similarities and differences among ideas, data, and other information mentioned in the text. Timelines, in contrast, show important dates and events in chronological order, also highlighting key patterns and historical milestones that are under investigation by students.

FIGURE 12-2   **A Second Grade Diagram: Ladybug's Body**

Organizational Aids (Table of Contents, Index, Glossary)

Once children begin to identify patterns, they start to understand about the organization of content, and they learn that information is generally more predictable and accessible. As a result, they begin to read, think, and learn like researchers. According to most experts, the **table of contents** is, by far, the most helpful text feature and the ultimate organizational aid (Hoyt, Mooney, & Parkes, 2003). The table of contents reveals the author's plan for reading a book; that is, the reader can determine the layout of the book's sequence by reading the table of contents before reading the introduction or the first chapter. The reader learns what the main topics and subtopics of the book are, which helps predict what the book will be about and help the reader become more interactive and purposeful. In effect, the reader will be able to read and check whether the predictions were correctly made. Also, if students are using a specific text to locate specific information related to an investigation or inquiry they are researching, the table of contents will enlighten them as to whether this text will satisfy their purposes.

The **index,** found at the end of the book, is a more detailed overview of the table of contents in that it helps the reader identify more information about the subject matter or the topics. Subject matter, topics, and authors are listed alphabetically in the index to aid the reader in scanning and locating information rapidly. The index helps the reader review, relocate, and find additional information or information that he or she overlooked during the initial reading, skimming, or scanning of the text. In other words, the index helps readers become more thorough in organizing and planning their own studies and investigations. In short, both the table of contents and the index enable the

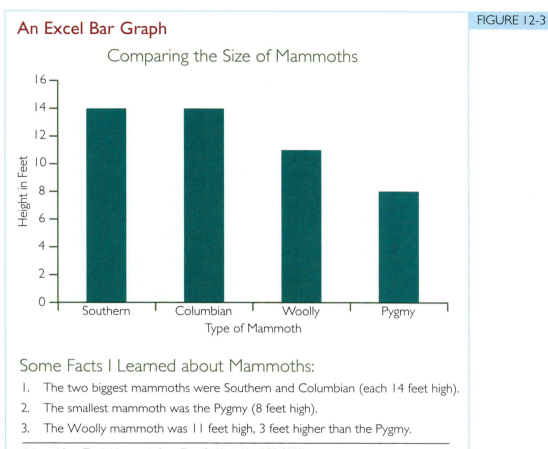

An Excel Bar Graph

FIGURE 12-3

Comparing the Size of Mammoths

Some Facts I Learned about Mammoths:

1. The two biggest mammoths were Southern and Columbian (each 14 feet high).

2. The smallest mammoth was the Pygmy (8 feet high).

3. The Woolly mammoth was 11 feet high, 3 feet higher than the Pygmy.

Adapted from That's Mammoth, from *Time for Kinds* (April 20, 2003).

reader to search for the organizational plan of the text(s) under study and to do so in the most efficient and rapid way.

The **glossary** serves as a specialized dictionary that contains only the keywords identified throughout the book; it may also provide a pronunciation key for sounding out new or difficult-to-pronounce words. The glossary is a helpful list of content vocabulary words that students can turn to and learn in the context of the text. Once students learn that this quick view for learning new words is at their fingertips, they are often willing to access these pages at the back of the book.

Finally, it is important to emphasize all of the text features presented in this section, because children tend to apply these features mostly when the teacher reinforces them during guided reading and scaffolded reading experiences. However, Hoyt (2002) reports studies showing that students fail to apply these strategies when they are reading independently. Therefore, the more activities and opportunities children have that reinforce the benefits of using text features in school, the more likely they are to apply these strategies when reading for meaning. These skills should become second nature to students while reading at school; otherwise, they will fail to apply what they have learned about text features on their own. Unfortunately, Hoyt (2002) reports that based on follow-up questionnaires, this is especially true with more reluctant and less successful readers who need to use these features more than others do.

Using Text Structure

Students process informational (or expository) text in a different way than they do narrative text or stories and, therefore, require different comprehension strategies for reading and different organizational skills for writing. As mentioned earlier, the focus of our primary grades is on reading narrative texts and writing stories; yet, as the student advances into upper primary and middle school grades, the focus shifts dramatically to informational text. Little instruction is given to students on expository reading strategies, and by the time they are reading textbook after textbook, teaching reading is no longer a part of the language arts program. Therefore, students rarely receive any substantive instruction in strategic reading of informational text, but are just expected to know how to "study" or read for meaning.

It is important that teachers give direct instruction on how to read informational text. Time should be spent on how textbooks are organized, how information is presented in a textbook, and how strategies can be used to help understand the information presented in the textbook. Teachers should have their students read frequently from newspapers, magazine articles, and informational books, which will help them learn expository style of writing. One approach is by teaching the different types of **text structure** found in informational text.

When analyzing informational text, there are different patterns or text structures that the reader can expect to find. How the information is organized depends on the type and purpose of the information to be presented. The reader must learn two basic things about expository structure: (1) the only purpose for the particular structure is to present the content or information in a clear manner; and (2) by knowing the different structures, the reader can begin to anticipate the type of information that will be presented or that should follow, based on the structure itself. It is important to keep in mind that not only should readers learn to *identify* each of the following five patterns in their reading, but they should also learn how to *write* using each text structure.

Descriptive Text Structure

Descriptive text structure presents information about a particular topic with no overall structure and basically just describes the information in general terms. It does not provide readers with any clue words to aid in comprehension; therefore, readers must use the basic strategies they have already learned to note details and to select the important information from the passage. Although this is one of the more difficult text structures for readers to identify important points in the text, it is the most frequently used structure in textbooks.

The following extract is an example from a fourth grade science textbook, *Science* (Houghton Mifflin Company, 2007):

> The skeletal system, or skeleton, is the system that gives the body shape and support, protects the organs inside the body, and works with the muscles to move the body. The skeleton is well designed for these three jobs because it is made of bone, a very hard tissue. The adult human skeleton has 206 bones. (p. A52)

As you can see, there are no clue words in this paragraph and the writing does not try to form relationships between concepts. The paragraph is merely describing something, in this case, what the skeletal system is.

A visual map of this paragraph would help the student see the important concepts being brought out and help delineate the relationships among them. A simple web using Inspiration software is helpful here (at right).

Can you see how this visual tool helps bring to life a rather bland description of a skeleton? This type of tool can help students—especially those with special needs, such as ELLs, children with disabilities, and struggling readers. It helps them instantly pull out of the text the important points being made.

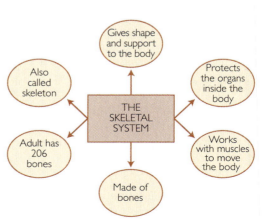

Listing Text Structure/Sequencing

Listing text structure presents a number of ideas or descriptions in a related group, listing the points one after another. The clue words that this type of text structure uses to denote the related points are: *first, second, next, before, after, initially, not long after,* and *finally.* The reader must be able to infer the relationship between the listed points and the overall topic. In this text structure, the listed points are related through sequence, the initial one coming first and subsequent points coming later.

The following extract is an example from a fourth grade science textbook, *Science* (Houghton Mifflin Company, 2007):

> The process in which some organisms change form in different stages of their life cycles is known as metamorphosis. Many insects change form four times, which is called complete metamorphosis.
>
> The egg, the first stage, hatches into a wormlike form called a larva. The larva eats and grows larger. The mealworm is the larva stage of a darkling beetle.
>
> Eventually the larva forms a hard casing around itself. This stage is the pupa. The adult insect emerges from the pupa. The insect looks very different at each stage. (p. A71)

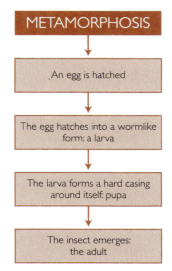

In this example, although the actual clue words *first* or *finally* do not appear, this textbook has many charts and graphs to list points in sequence. The textbook separates its listing text structure into "boxes" to clearly delineate the sequence of events or ideas. In this example, the process is explained using a listing text structure.

The visual tool to the right shows how the listing text structure can be visually presented to help children understand and remember the main points.

This type of visual tool is excellent to use with a listing text structure. Again, note how much easier it is for a student to organize and remember the concepts being presented.

Causation (Cause/Effect) Text Structure

Causation (cause/effect) text structure presents ideas grouped in a sequence so that a causal relationship is either stated or implied. It is frequently used in science, social studies, and math textbooks. The author often uses such clue words as *therefore, consequently, because, as a result of, since,* or *the reasons for.* With this type of text structure the student can instantly recognize the relationship of two concepts to each other: one concept (the cause) effected the second (the effect). This type of text structure helps students comprehend information and the relationship of events to each other. Unfortunately, it is not used frequently by authors of textbooks.

The following extract is an example from a fourth grade social studies textbook, *Social Studies; States and Regions* (Houghton Mifflin, 2008):

> The Civil War had ended slavery, but African Americans did not receive equal treatment. Most of them had no money, land, or education. As a result, they had trouble starting farms or businesses. They often had to eat, shop, and go to school in places separate from whites. African Americans were also denied the same civil rights that others had. Some states prevented African Americans from voting.
>
> Dr. Martin Luther King, Jr. helped organize a bus boycott. Soon boycotts and protests were taking place all over the South. These protests inspired other groups. Women, American Indians, Latinos, and others began to demand their civil rights. (p. 152)

In this paragraph, the clue word *as a result* should signify to the reader that a causation or cause/effect text structure was used. In this example, unequal treatment of African Americans after the Civil War caused them to have difficulty setting up businesses and farms. This caused civil unrest, which led to boycotts and protests. Eventually the boycotts and protests also caused many different groups to gain equal rights.

The organizer below shows this cause/effect relationship in an easy and visual way that students can understand quickly.

Response (Problem/Solution) Text Structure

Response (problem/solution) text structure presents a problem, question, or remark followed by a solution, answer, or reply. It is often used in math, science, and social studies. The author may use clue words such as *the problem is, the question is, one reason for the problem, a solution,* or *one answer is.* On identifying a problem, the reader should anticipate that a solution to the problem will follow. This type of text structure helps students comprehend the information as it points out how two events are related—through a problem and a solution to that problem. Again, this structure is not used frequently in textbooks.

The following extract is an example about the problems of using Earth's resources wisely from the fourth grade textbook, *Science* (Houghton Mifflin, 2007). The problem and solution is presented in a lesson entitled *How Can Resources Be Conserved?* and covers five or six pages.

> Main Idea: There are things people can do to protect Earth's natural resources and the environment. Problem and Solution: How can conservation laws help protect the environment? What are some ways to conserve natural resources? (pp. C60–C63)

The above example has one main problem presented in the lesson: how can we conserve the Earth's resources? It presents two main solutions: conservation laws that require companies and communites to control pollution, and the three R's of conservation—reduce, reuse, recycle. A visual tool below shows how this can be represented visually and clearly helps the reader grasp the problem and its solutions, which may not be easy to comprehend while reading so many pages of text.

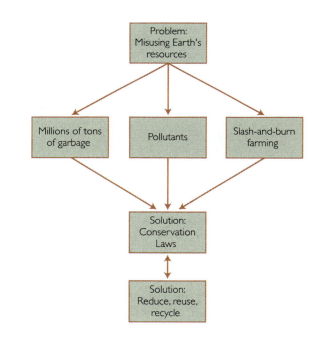

Comparison Text Structure

Comparison text structure requires the reader to note the similarities and differences between two or more objects or ideas. This type of structure is found in social studies and science texts. The author uses clue words such as *like, unlike, resemble, different from, same as, alike,* or *similar to.* The reader must be able to recognize objects or ideas being compared and the points of similarity or difference between them. This type of text structure helps students see the differences between concepts and allows them to note the relationship of different concepts to the main idea.

The following extract is an example from a fourth grade science textbook, *Science* (Houghton Mifflin, 2007). It takes two pages to describe three kinds of rocks and uses graphic tables to help the students see the difference in them.

> Three basic kinds of rock make up Earth's crust. Each kind forms in a different way and has different characteristics. (p. C8)

In the above paragraph, you can note the clue word *different,* which signifies to the reader that a comparison text structure is to follow that will compare different things. In this example, three different types of rocks, igneous, sedimentary, and metamorphic, are compared.

The visual tool below shows how three different concepts can be compared visually, also helping the student compare them across the same criteria (how they are formed, specific characteristics of each type of rock, and examples of each). This helps readers comprehend the material by classifying the information into distinct criteria.

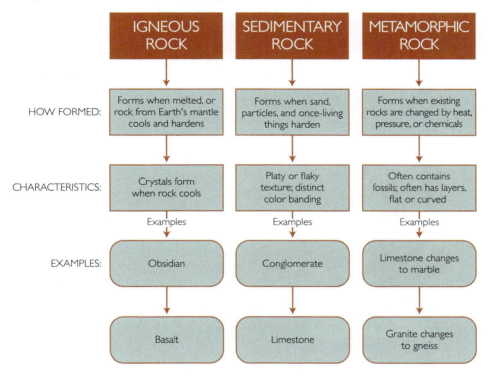

Each one of the text structures mentioned above is frequently used in textbooks, and students can be taught how to identify each structure. Identification of text structures increases comprehension. In addition, as each text structure is taught, children should learn how to use each one in their writing. Teachers should encourage students to use visual tools to map out the concepts that they are reading about, and teachers should be using visual tools in their instruction to help clarify confusing topics, as well as the overwhelming volume of concepts and ideas that are presented in textbooks and informational text.

Reading Strategies for Comprehending Informational Text

In a balanced literacy classroom, teachers need to teach readers specific strategies that will help them comprehend informational text. Learning to read and remember content information may be new and somewhat unfamiliar to young children; therefore, the teacher should read informational text for enjoyment during shared reading, in addition to picture books or narrative text. Teachers should model comprehension strategies through think-alouds, that is, by verbally articulating how adults read and think about informational text while they are reading. For example, "How does this heading help me understand what I am going to read next?" or "I am going to read these captions under the picture so that I can learn more information about this text."

Teachers should include the following five steps when teaching comprehension strategies as recommended by research (Duke & Pearson, 2002):

1. Start with an explicit description of the strategy and when and how it should be used.
2. Model the strategy in action, and then have students model the strategy.
3. Have students actively use the strategy in collaborative settings.
4. Give guided practice using the strategy with gradual release of responsibility.
5. Provide independent use of the strategy with constant feedback to the student and needed support as evidenced by monitoring of the strategy.

TEACHSOURCE VIDEO CASE

A Visit to Ms. Hernandez's First Grade Classroom: A Three-Step Process for Previewing

As we enter Ms. Hernandez's classroom, we see a literacy rich environment that includes colorful posters, pictures, and artwork depicting narrative as well as nonfiction books in the various content areas, including science and social studies. Posters and charts displaying animals, endangered species, and sea world creatures are colorful and inviting to the children. Ms. Hernandez is aware that primary level children need to be exposed to a variety of genres, especially informational text, which has often been neglected in the early grades.

Ms. Hernandez begins the lesson by inviting her first grade students to sit on the floor of the meeting area in front of the easel pad. Ms. Hernandez sits in a chair so that she is eye-level with the children as she explains that today they will learn how to use pictures from a book to ask questions. The informational text that Ms. Hernandez has chosen for this lesson is *Busy as a Bee* by Melvin

Berger. She uses this trade book in a unique way, engaging and motivating the children by previewing pictures from the book, modeling how to use a questioning strategy. She explains to the children how pictures can give us a lot of information about a topic. She explains that closely examining a picture can make us wonder and start to ask questions; when we ask questions, we begin to think more deeply about what we are reading.

Then Ms. Hernandez demonstrates by showing the students the first picture in *Busy as a Bee*,

making sure the text is covered so that children only see the pictures. Ms. Hernandez covers the text in advance, focusing the students' attention on each picture. Then, Ms. Hernandez asks the students what they notice and reminds them to look closely at the details. As questions arise, she writes them on sticky notes and attaches them to a chart that she has prepared in advance. Ms. Hernandez continues modeling this process with the other pictures in the text, leading the discussion and generating questions during this preview, which in turn activates the students' prior knowledge.

Ms. Hernandez then begins distributing the pictures she has copied from the book, giving one to each pair of students. She begins this insect study by asking the children, "Which body parts do you think help this insect eat?" The children respond to this and other content area questions, prompting one student to ask a very astute question, "Why is the pollen bag near the legs of the bee?"

Now that the children are highly motivated to learn more about bees, she puts this "generating-questions strategy" into practice, explaining to the children that they are now going to have a "knee-to-knee conference," and she pairs them so that they can begin asking their questions about the pictures to each other. When Ms. Hernandez gives the signal, the children leave the meeting area by pairs and quickly become very engaged in generating questions about their own pictures. Once the children generate and ask their questions, Ms. Hernandez gives each pair sticky notes and instructs them to write down their questions and to attach them to the pictures.

After a few minutes, Ms. Hernandez calls the students back to the meeting area with their sticky notes and pictures. She invites a few volunteers to share their questions with the class, instructing them to attach some questions to the class chart. The first two students' questions are: "Why does a bee have a stinger?" and "Why is the Queen Bee the largest bee?" These two questions

are excellent examples of how students can generate questions to help them gain a deeper understanding of the text and topic they are reading.

At the end of the lesson, Ms. Hernandez hangs the chart on the wall with all of the sticky notes attached. She will leave it up as a reference for future lessons with this text so that the students can refer back to their questions and to the chart to confirm their ideas, add new information or correct any misconceptions.

In reviewing Ms. Hernandez's lesson, she used the following strategies:

- Modeling for the students how to predict what the book will be about by doing a "picture walk"
- Helping students generate their own questions about the text based upon clues from the pictures
- Using a graphic organizer to present the students' questions about the book in a visual and highly organized way
- Directly and explicitly teaching an important reading comprehension strategy
- Providing guided practice and independent practice for the children on applying the strategy

- Providing collaborative learning among pairs of children to reinforce the strategy
- Sharing the pen with individual students by writing down their questions, a process used in interactive writing with young children
- Allowing the children to share with the class their own generated questions, as well as the new information they are learning about the content

Questions:

1. What would be a good follow-up lesson about bees to help create a home–school connection?
2. How could Ms. Hernandez integrate technology into this lesson?
3. Why is it so important that children learn how to read informational text in the primary grades?

Go to http://www.cengage.com/login to register your access code for the premium website for *Literacy for Children in an Information Age,* where you can watch an in-depth video exploration of Ms. Hernandez's classroom to see how she uses these valuable strategies.

Teachers can help children by posing questions that scaffold (or support) young readers' understanding of informational texts, and this can be done in guided reading groups. Also, it is suggested that questions can be designed by teachers to guide students' reading of informational texts before, during, and after reading. These questions can help children learn about setting a purpose for reading, reading about content, and reading about format. The teacher can also ask questions that will help children internalize how to use specific reading strategies that they can use to help them understand and remember content.

In scaffolding children's reading, teachers take on a more active role at first, but as they use scaffolding strategies to help children become more successful at reading informational texts, they start to hand over more of the responsibility to the student for learning from these texts. Although scaffolding reading is widely used in teaching children how to read narrative texts, it can also be used in teaching children about informational text (Graves & Graves, 2003). It is important to realize that the style of reading an informational text is quite different from reading fiction. Consequently, different reading strategies are required for comprehending informational texts.

Prereading Informational Text

The prereading stage is perhaps one of the most important stages in reading informational text. Too many readers will just pick up a textbook and begin reading, quickly losing interest and comprehension as they progress. The prereading stage involves carefully previewing the text and looking over what the text will be about, generating predictions and prequestions that need to be answered during the process of reading for meaning. The prereading stage should involve tapping into prior knowledge and building up background knowledge about the content of the text so that personal connections can be made.

Teachers should model how to preview an informational text as part of the prereading stage to help students *read to learn*. Teaching elementary-age children how to read for meaning requires that they also must learn how to study, how to remember facts and related information, and how to reflect on content-area information. Therefore, learning how to read informational texts requires a different purpose and disposition for reading compared to reading a narrative text.

When reading nonfiction, the reader's purpose is to carry away new knowledge or new information. However, when reading fiction, the reader's purpose is to experience pleasure and to live vicariously through the fictional lives and adventures of the characters. To carry away information effectively, an **efferent stance** (or approach) to reading is required, meaning that students learn how to read, analyze, and reflect on information. To do so demands that they learn how to use a different set of comprehension skills, which are quite different from simply reading for a personal, **aesthetic response** (Rosenblatt, 1978). These efferent comprehension skills that children must develop long before they reach middle school grades are apparently lacking today, because it is widely reported that the majority of students are having difficulty reading content information for meaning once they reach fourth grade and beyond (Adams; 1990; Hoyt, 2002).

One of the most important prereading strategies is **previewing** the text. A teacher should start with modeling how students can become better readers, and then set up small groups for guided reading sessions to demonstrate previewing a text as part of a prereading scaffolding session (Graves & Graves, 2003). In this way, the teacher will motivate students by explaining to them that before they actually read for information, they need to begin by previewing the text, which they can do quite quickly.

It is important to introduce key steps to young readers using a model that they can refer to for previewing informational texts. In this way, the students can follow along as the teacher begins modeling how to preview a text before it is read for the first time. As part of the previewing model, students need to learn how to **skim** (to read text rapidly for a specific purpose but without reflection) and to **scan** material (to search for a given word, date, phrase, or term, also without reflection).

The following steps for previewing and reading an informational text should be visibly accessible as a reference for all students, whether they are working individually, in guided reading/writing groups, or as a whole class. Therefore, these directions should be printed permanently on flip charts, wall charts, and graphic organizers.

Step 1: Previewing and Prequestioning
In the previewing and prequestioning stage, the students learn how to prepare for reading informational text by previewing it. The teacher should model how to do this first, and then have the students practice what they just learned. First, the teacher should have students choose an informational text and preview the following elements:

- Title of the book
- Author(s) names
- Other information on the cover
- Cover design (thinking about how it relates to the title)

- Back cover
- Information on the back cover
- Back cover design (thinking about how it relates to the title)
- Inside page for publisher, date of publication, and place of publication
- Table of contents (predicting the information this book will feature)
- First chapter or first pages of the book
- The pictures and read their captions
- Charts, diagrams, maps, and caption labels
- Chapter title
- Heading(s)
- Subtitles
- Keywords
- Questions at the front and back of the chapter

The teacher should have the children fill out the graphic organizer after they complete the preview of the text to answer key questions that indicate how much they learned about the book and the chapter (Figure 12–4). The purpose is to impress on the children how much they learned just by previewing the text without actually having read it. The teacher should also have the students write down key questions they have about the text and keep these questions close to them for reference while they are reading for meaning in step 3.

Step 2: Skimming and Scanning

During a subsequent meeting, the teacher provides feedback to the children by reviewing their responses recorded on the graphic organizer. In most cases, the teacher should provide positive feedback to the students about how much they have learned. The teacher begins by teaching the students how to skim or read through a chapter quickly without taking time for reflection as a first reading impression. The teacher demonstrates how this can be done by reading out loud at a fast pace. The teacher announces to the class that skimming is much faster and more effective when reading silently. Then the teacher uses a timer to see how fast the students can read one page silently; they are instructed to read as fast as they can and to signal when they have finished. This timing can be used to determine an average pace for most of the children. After all of the children complete this task, the teacher reminds them that they are only skimming each page, and that they will have a chance to return to read it more slowly for understanding and retention the next time around.

This same process can be done to teach scanning. The teacher gives the students a set keyword from the text and times the students to see how long it will take them to find this word. As the students become more adept at finding the keyword, the teacher can introduce phrases and increase the number of keywords that the students should locate quickly.

The use of small guided reading groups is essential in making this skimming and scanning approach work well because the teacher can group the children according to their initial timed reading into three different groups: faster, moderate, or slower paced readers. These groups should vary as the children learn how to adapt their speed and accuracy of reading to the content. As in step 1, the teacher can provide a few general questions related to the content they have just read or ask the children to retell what they remembered as a form of assessing their progress and determining interventions that might be required.

Step 3: Reading for Meaning

In the final stage, reading for meaning, the children are given an opportunity to read the entire chapter at a normal pace, while the teacher reminds them that they should refer to their prequestions that they had written down. The teacher should also mention that there will be comprehension questions about the content after reading for meaning.

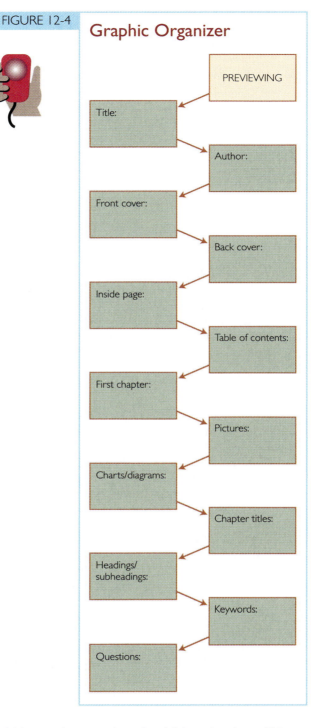

FIGURE 12-4

Graphic Organizer

PREVIEWING

Title:

Author:

Front cover:

Back cover:

Inside page:

Table of contents:

First chapter:

Pictures:

Charts/diagrams:

Chapter titles:

Headings/ subheadings:

Keywords:

Questions:

The purpose of this stage is to convince the children that they will become better readers because of the prereading strategies that they have learned and have been using. The teacher should remind the students that because they have skimmed the text before reading, now they will be familiar with it and understand it better. Questions should be designed to help students comprehend the text and develop higher order thinking skills.

During-Reading of Informational Text

Scaffolding reading experiences for children during the reading process allow children to learn and use strategies for acquiring information and improving comprehension during the reading session. During-reading scaffolding provides students with a coaching mechanism, not unlike what they might experience from their tennis or soccer coach. A coach provides support for an athlete to perform better during the actual play; similarly, a guided strategy supports the reader during the reading task. The following specific during-reading scaffolding activities will help students read informational texts with greater understanding:

◆ *Graphic organizers:* Graphic organizers help children identify and focus on important, relevant information and details while reading. Students find it helpful to fill out a graphic organizer while they are reading, especially when text is difficult or lengthy. Graphic organizers can be customized to reflect the teacher's specific objectives for the students who are reading an assignment with informational text.

◆ *Thinkmarks:* Student can complete a "**thinkmark**" during reading. A thinkmark is a bookmark with blank spaces or lines that students can keep right in the book they are reading. The children can easily write down any questions they have, make quick comments, or take notes about things they do not understand as they are reading. This is helpful with informational text because the student does not have to wait until they have completed reading a section and remember what they wanted to write down.

◆ *Highlighting key concepts:* During reading, students can highlight key concepts and key vocabulary words that they find in their informational texts. Students are also directed to highlight vocabulary words that they do not understand, so that they can revisit them at a later time.

◆ *Making connections (text-to-text/text-to-self/text-to-world):* During their reading, children are given a sheet of reusable dots. At various points during their reading, they can put different colors on the text depending on what they are thinking as they are reading. For example, students follow a chart displaying suggestions such as:

> *Green dot—I want to share this interesting information in discussion circles.*
>
> *Blue dot—This is a new key/challenging vocabulary word.*
>
> *Red dot—I do not understand this part. I need clarification.*
>
> *Yellow dot—I have a connection to make that is either:*
>
> 1. A connection to another text (text-to-text)
> 2. A connection to something I can personally relate to in my own life (text-to-self)
> 3. A connection to something I know about in the outer world (text-to-world)

An after-reading activity might be to share what students were thinking in a class discussion or in cooperative groups. Other lessons can then be developed from the dot activity.

◆ *Creating captions:* Students are given a picture, illustration, or visual aid based on the information they are reading. As the students reflect on what they are reading, they are required to create a caption for the picture or visual aid based on the information they are reading. This activity is evidence that the students comprehend what they are reading. The activity can be completed during independent reading or as part of a small-group guided reading activity.

◆ *Pause and reflect:* During reading, children are taught how to **pause and reflect** on what was just read. They can record their summary on a graphic organizer or in a notebook, or they can verbally retell what they remember from their reading. The children reflect on what was just read by comparing their new knowledge based on their prior knowledge or earlier prediction.

◆ *Scavenger hunt:* Informational texts like tradebooks and magazines, or different websites on the Internet can be used to complete a scavenger hunt. A list of questions that the students must answer is presented in the form of a graphic organizer.

The teacher can: (1) set up questions with blanks and give students answer choices to fill in the blanks; or (2) write the question and have the students answer the research item as part of the scavenger hunt.

- **Question generation:** Research supports that generating questions during reading is a highly effective strategy (NICHD, 2000). In this strategy, readers learn how to generate their own questions, and then answer them during reading. An excellent strategy with informational text is to have the students turn each heading into a question, and then have them read the section with the purpose of answering the question. For example, if a student is reading a textbook and a heading is "The First Settlers," the student forms questions such as: "Who were the first settlers?" "Where did the first settlers come from?" "Why did they come here?" The student then reads the section and answers the questions. Some readers do not know how to generate questions; therefore, it is important that they be given instruction on how to do so.

- **Comprehension monitoring:** **Comprehension monitoring** is a strategy in which readers learn how to regulate and monitor how well they understand what they are reading. This is especially true of informational text, which does not have a plot or structure to carry the student along. Many times students can be reading a textbook and thinking of something else, not monitoring or thinking about whether they understood what they just read. Students need to constantly self-monitor while they read, and if they find they do not understand something, they need to stop, go back, and review the text again.

- **Click or clunk? (Wright, 2006):** In the **click or clunk** strategy, students periodically check their understanding of sentences, paragraphs, and pages of text as they read. The teacher instructs students that during any reading assignment they should:

  Say "Click!" if they understand the sentence.

  Say "Clunk!" and refer to the strategy sheet, My Reading Checklist (Figure 12–5), to correct problems.

  - If the teacher finds that students start to distract each other as they call out these comprehension signals, once the students consistently use the technique effectively, they can start whispering the signal or use unobtrusive nonverbal signals (for example, lightly tapping the desk once for "click" and twice for "clunk") that still allows the teacher to monitor readers' use of this strategy.

  - It is also effective if students use a checklist in conjunction with click or clunk to apply simple strategies to monitor comprehension reading problems (see Figure 12–5). While reading, if students do not understand the text at the end of the sentence, paragraph, or page, they should refer to the strategy checklist to correct the problems.

Postreading Informational Text

Postreading of informational texts is an important component in the literacy program because it allows children to reflect, share, and ultimately derive deeper understanding and retain more information through the reinforcement and extension of what was read. Postreading of informational texts is an opportunity for children to reflect on their reading and to discuss the content they understood with a buddy or within a collaborative group after they have finished reading. Most children have participated in postreading discussions of narrative text and, therefore, probably feel comfortable in participating in such transactional discussions after reading informational text. The teacher should model the transactional or interactive process because, at first, children may not know exactly how to discuss content- or subject-specific information without more direct instruction. The teacher should also model how to use background knowledge to begin

FIGURE 12-5

My Reading Checklist

1. Check for sentence understanding: "Did I understand what I read in this *sentence?*"

_____ I had a problem with a **key word** in the sentence.

- I should try to infer the meaning from the context of surrounding words and passages.
- I should look for clues as to what the word means (pictures, synonyms, homonyms, clue words).
- I should look the word up in a glossary or dictionary.
- I should ask someone like my teacher or guardian for help.

_____ I had a problem understanding the whole sentence.

- I should try reading the sentences before and after the sentence.
- I should read the sentence again.
- I should try reading the whole passage out loud to myself.
- I should ask someone like my teacher or guardian for help.

2. Check for paragraph understanding: "Did I understand what I read in this *paragraph?*"

_____ I had a problem understanding the paragraph or passages I just read.

- I should look at the **heading** to see if that tells me what the main idea is.
- I should turn the heading into a question and see if I can answer the question.
- I should read the first sentence of the paragraph to see if I can figure out what the **main idea** is.
- I should reread the paragraph or passages and try to answer my question(s).
- I should ask someone like my teacher or guardian for help.

3. Check for page understanding: "Did I understand what I read on this *page?* Do I remember what I read?"

_____ I had a problem understanding and/or remembering the page(s) I just read.

- I should review the introduction, vocabulary words, and summary, if available.
- I should look at the **heading** of each section and turn each into a question.
- I should review the pictures, graphs, tables, and photographs.
- I should reread the page(s) trying to answer my question(s).
- I should use a graphic organizer to help me organize the key points visually.
- I should use sticky-notes to mark important points in the book.
- I should write down the important points in a notebook.
- I should summarize the important points in my head and/or in writing.

Adapted from Wright, J. (2006). "Click or Clunk?" A student comprehension self-check. Retrieved February 13, 2006 from http://www.interventioncentral.org/htmdocs/interventions/rdngcompr/clickclunk1.php.

a discussion on a topic the children are currently investigating or are familiar with, such as the Save our Pond project.

Recommended postreading strategies that research claims students need to learn include (NICHD, 2000):

◆ ***Forming questions about information students just read about.*** Students should learn how to generate questions about what they just read and then answer them, referring back to the text if necessary. Teachers should create questions that help students identify the main idea and reflect on the author's point of view and perspective. It is important that teachers and students form questions that promote higher order thinking and not just relate back to facts that were just read. This is an essential process enabling children to improve their comprehension skills. It is important that students receive the necessary feedback from the teacher to continuously monitor progress and improve comprehension.

◆ *Using graphic and semantic organizers to aid word and text understanding.* Students can either generate their own graphic organizers after they read informational text or fill out a teacher-made organizer designed to support understanding and retention of the information.

◆ *Summarizing text.* Readers need to summarize what they just read. Many struggling readers tend to include every detail in the story, failing to identify the important ideas and main topics being covered. It is important that teachers give direct instruction in how to identify the big ideas and main points of the text. This not only helps readers summarize, it will help them improve their overall reading comprehension and memory, and help them learn how to study. Learning how to study and to acquire study skills to improve reading, writing, and understanding of content is explained in detail later in this chapter.

Other postreading activities that teachers should use to reinforce the recommended comprehension strategies include:

◆ *Literature circles* to reinforce the content in an enjoyable and comfortable environment

◆ *Discussion groups* with the whole class and in small cooperative learning groups

◆ *Role-playing,* in which students can enact certain sequences of events from history, science, or mathematics

◆ *Dramatic presentations* of certain parts of the informational text, such as the signing of the Declaration of Independence

◆ *Creative writing* activities, such as writing a letter to a historical figure or famous scientist or mathematician

◆ *Projects* that involve research and investigation, including hands-on and creative approaches to the content just read

It is valuable to use this postreading experience as an opportunity for the children to explore their understanding of the content they just learned rather than have the teacher evaluate or test their reading knowledge by giving them a multiple-choice or essay examination. However, it is widely known that a large number of administrators, supervisors, teachers, and parents believe that children should be given a postreading examination just to prepare them for future high-stakes testing that they will experience eventually. However, when testing is used to help children cope with statewide or districtwide standardized testing, students should also receive scaffolding to help them learn about test-taking skills that include learning how to read and analyze testing directions, how to narrow down multiple-choice questions, and how to make informed guesses, all of which will help them improve their test scores.

Teachers' VOICES   Struggling Readers often Prefer Nonfiction

Children need multiple exposures to information and time to apply it before they have truly mastered it. As a special education teacher, I often beat myself up trying to come up with new ideas that will help my students achieve certain benchmarks. Then suddenly, I will have a student who seems to have made connections between different topics and lessons we have covered and exhibit solid knowledge of the subject matter. I find this to be especially true when my class is studying science and social studies. I am often amazed when I see a student who cannot remember the steps needed to unpack his book bag suddenly explain the metamorphosis of a butterfly! I think that nonfiction gives students the opportunity to hold on to information that often eludes them in fiction.

—*Zaneta Shannon, Special Education Teacher*

Collaborative Strategic Reading

The National Reading Panel's research (NICHD, 2000) has concluded that the most effective way to teach comprehension strategies, as described earlier, is in multistrategy instruction, where a combination of these comprehension strategies are used. It is quite effective when teachers and readers interact over text and try to understand it using all of the strategies together.

Collaborative strategic reading can be a powerful way to help children learn the strategies to effectively comprehend informational text (Duke & Bennett-Armistead, 2003). It is similar to cooperative learning in that it is done in small, collaborative groups and follows these specific steps:

◆ Students work in small, cooperative groups.
◆ Students apply four comprehension strategies:
  1. Preview (students think about what they already know, predict what the passage might be about, and preview the text)
  2. Use "click or clunk" (students monitor comprehension and use fix-up strategies as needed)
  3. Get the "gist" (students restate the most important idea of the text)
  4. Wrap up (students summarize and ask questions about the text to each other)
◆ Students have specific roles in their group: the leader, the click or clunk expert (the student who monitors how well the group understands the text), the gist expert (the student who determines whether the group identified the main idea of the text), the announcer, and the encourager.
◆ Cue cards may be used to support the students in their small, cooperative groups; for example:
  1. A clunk card that says: "Reread the sentences before and after the clunk and look carefully for cues."
  2. A student leader cue card says: "Did everyone understand what we read? If you did not, write your clunks in your learning log."
◆ Students complete learning logs before and after reading and review the steps they followed: prereading (preview, predict, background knowledge), during-reading (clunks they had), and postreading (what they learned from their reading, any questions they may have).

Supporting Diverse Learners with Informational Text

English Language Learners and Informational Text

Supporting ELLs is an important consideration when using informational text because diverse learners need to be exposed to both content and language experiences that build their knowledge of specific vocabulary words from the subject matter they are studying. ELLs need to be engaged in nonthreatening, hands-on experiences, where they are participating in small, cooperative groups enabling them to feel that they can speak freely. In a nurturing environment, they have more opportunities to respond to other children and are given more opportunities to clarify meanings pertaining to oral language, reading, and writing. In such environments, ELLs learn with less stress as a result of encountering fewer abstract language problems.

Research also suggests (Lee, 2005) that ELLs learn more readily from direct instruction with content-specific vocabulary. Some students may need more explicit guidance in articulating their linguistic and cultural experiences with content-related knowledge and practices. They need to learn subject-specific vocabulary based on their own cultural and linguistic experiences. Teachers should be sensitive to students' needs and provide the appropriate balance between teacher-directed and student-initiated activities.

Hands-on, inquiry-based instruction provides opportunities for ELLs to develop content understanding, engage in motivating activities, and construct shared meanings more readily than traditional textbook-based instruction (Lee, 2005). Hands-on activities are less dependent on formal mastery of the English language, thus reducing the linguistic demands on the students. Collaborative, small-group work also provides structured opportunities for developing English proficiency within the context of learning content. Lastly, inquiry-based instruction provides the scaffolding needed for ELLs to learn the processes of content-specific inquiry, such as learning how to hypothesize, experiment, collect data, and communicate results.

The use of graphic organizers can greatly benefit ELLs when reading informational text, such as textbooks. Informational text ususally contains unfamiliar technical vocabulary and is organized in a different structure than narrative text. This consequently requires students to perform more complex cognitive tasks to comprehend the material (Kim, Vaughn, Wanzek, & Wei, 2004; Lapp, Flood, & Ranck-Buhr, 1995). Graphic organizers such as semantic organizers, visual tools, and structured outline maps are associated with improved reading comprehension overall.

Students with Learning Disabilities and Informational Text

Students with learning disabilities can benefit from many of the same strategies used with ELLs, as can most children. Like ELLs, direct instruction about text structure, and how to use that knowledge strategically, is an effective way to improve comprehension of informational text. Exposing students to a wide variety of texts is important, but is not sufficient to promote comprehension. Explicit instruction is valuable, especially when teaching specific strategies. For example, an important strategy for children with learning disabilities is identifying the main idea of a passage. Teachers should provide

STRATEGIES FOR TEACHING DIVERSE LEARNERS

Informational Text for Content Understanding

1. Provide direct instruction with content-specific vocabulary words. Provide different strategies to help students remember the words.

2. Provide direct instruction about text structure and how to use that knowledge strategically. For example, teach students about cause/effect text structure and what the keywords are to identify this type of structure (therefore, consequently, because, as a result of). Model how to identify this type of text structure, showing how this information helps the reader anticipate that if a cause is introduced, an effect will follow. Then provide practice for the students to identify this type of structure, using clearly structured examples. Keep providing practice until the students can do this independently.

3. Relate content-specific vocabulary to the students' cultural and linguistic backgrounds so they can relate to the words through their own personal experiences.

4. Provide hands-on, inquiry-based instruction with teacher and peer support.

5. Use small-group, collaborative work.

6. Balance teacher-directed instruction with student-initiated activities based on students' needs.

7. Expose students to a wide variety of texts, and teach comprehension strategies through direct instruction.

9. Use graphic organizers to support the comprehension and retention of informational text for diverse learners.

10. Teach diverse learners study strategies to help remember and comprehend informational text such as textbooks.

11. Provide struggling readers with reading material that is on their level. If they cannot read the textbook, provide them with alternative informational texts on their reading level.

12. Provide audiotapes of informational books for diverse readers.

13. Be patient, sensitive, and culturally responsive; provide practice, feedback, and support on a continuous basis.

clear examples of a passage where the main idea is easily located. They need to consistently model the strategy being taught (identifying the main idea); they need to point out the sequence of tasks to accomplish this skill; and then they need to provide extensive practice and feedback where they slowly remove support to allow the student to work independently in finding the main idea (Williams, 2003).

Students with learning disabilities also benefit from hands-on activities to develop content understanding, as well as teacher support for inquiry learning. Strategies for effective content-area instruction include learning and memory strategies to help students remember academic content and strategies for studying from the text. When students are engaged in interesting activities in which they can actively manipulate concrete materials and apply higher level thinking, they will be more likely to succeed (Scruggs & Mastropieri, 2003).

Graphic organizers are also recommended for students with learning disabilities as well as ELLs. As mentioned above, informational text may contain unfamiliar technical vocabulary and is organized in a different structure than narrative text, which requires students to perform different cognitive tasks to comprehend the material (Kim, Vaughn, Wanzek, & Wei, 2004; Lapp, Flood, & Ranck-Buhr, 1995). Students with learning disabilities, who may already have difficulties reading and comprehending narrative text, can be especially challenged when interpreting specific content in informational text. Students with learning disabilities can benefit from the use of semantic webs, compare/constrast charts, and structured outline maps. These tools are associated with improved reading comprehension by helping readers identify and remember key concepts being presented.

How to Study Information Effectively and Independently

How to study to read information across the various content areas is an important skill that, until recently, has been grossly neglected, especially in teaching primary- and intermediate-level students. Not only have nonfiction and content materials been left out of the curriculum and instructional programs for most elementary-age children, but teaching younger children how to study and use information efficiently and effectively has also been neglected. Middle and high school students often recall that they were left to their own devices to learn how to study textbooks, learn concept vocabulary, locate information, and write research reports. Most students even complain that they were rarely given opportunities to learn how to prepare and study for weekly tests and long-term examinations. With the recent burgeoning growth in information and the fact that students will need to be information literate to succeed in their future endeavors, we need to provide an environment where students can develop study skills that will enable them to gather, locate, organize, plan, and use literacy skills and strategies to solve problems and to make important decisions that will be necessary to survive in this rapidly growing technological society (Moore, Moore, Cunningham, & Cunningham, 2006).

Teaching Students Metacognitive Strategies

Older students are found to be weak or poor in metacognitive strategies—that is, knowing how to learn about learning. Research shows that students lack knowledge in how to study and also lack the skills and strategies for becoming independent learners (Searfoss, Readence, & Mallette, 2001). Consequently, these researchers recommend that because of the lack of systematic teaching of study skills in early grades, it is important to teach students to become more independent learners by helping them develop greater knowledge in understanding information.

Students need to learn how to ask key questions that will improve their metacognitive capabilities. Hence, we need to teach our students how to raise questions that will enable them to get the gist of meaning or to summarize information. This can be done by the teacher modeling the process in a think-aloud, such as: "Do I know what this information is about? Can I retell what I've just read? What is the problem here? And, can I figure out what are some solutions?" We need to help children learn how to predict and verify what they are reading by asking questions such as: "What can I predict the results will be?" "What types of information will I need to know?" "How can I be sure that I am on the right track?" Finally, to solve problems, other questions that the student can be taught to ask are: "If I am not sure what the meaning of the text is, should I guess, ignore, or read on to find some clues?" "Should I reread parts of the text to find the missing information?"

It is important that classroom teachers start teaching children how to study as early as the primary grades and to continue teaching study skills through secondary school. This will help children develop the metacognitive strategies that are important for developing independent learning strategies and for developing independent, lifelong study skills.

What Are the Study Skills?

Searfoss, Readence, and Mallette (2001) recommend that the systematic teaching of at least five study skills strands are taught as early as kindergarten and emphasized through grade 12:

- ◆ Strand 1—Time Management
- ◆ Strand 2—Organizing and Retaining Information
- ◆ Strand 3—Locating Information
- ◆ Strand 4—Test Taking
- ◆ Strand 5—Writing

Each of these skills strands is described below.

Strand 1—Time Management

- ◆ *Purpose setting:* Searfoss et al. (2001) stress the importance of teaching children to know the purpose of each lesson so that they know what they will be asked to learn, and thus can plan ahead and know what is expected of them from the beginning to the end.
- ◆ *Modeling how to create a daily schedule:* Teachers can help students by modeling how to create a daily schedule to set goals for each day's learning. By planning each day with the students, teachers create schedule models by placing the daily work in a visible place— on a chalk board, wall chart, or easel—basically helping children to know what their responsibilities are for learning on a daily basis, which can be checked as they go along.
- ◆ *Modeling long-term, weekly, and monthly planning:* In a similar fashion to creating a daily schedule, weekly and monthly schedules that show what and when tasks and projects are due can be introduced gradually. Establishing performance-based rubrics can help children set goals; they know what quality levels and teacher expectations are. Due dates can also be incorporated into a time management plan. Searfoss et al. (2001) recommend that classroom teachers model how children can establish good work habits in school by using what new things they learn each day to practice as homework. Homework is useful in establishing good study habits and it teaches children how to plan and study independently. Teachers can help children set meaningful goals by asking them two key questions at the end of each school day:

  1. What important new information did you learn today?
  2. What more do you need to know to complete your homework tonight?

- ◆ *Using an assignment notebook to establish good study habits:* It is important to establish a foundation that helps children create a routine for developing good study and homework habits. Requiring children to keep an assignment notebook, student-made or store-bought, should be introduced to help young and older children develop a more long-term time-management plan once they have a clearer understanding of how to keep a daily study schedule. An assignment notebook can also contain a weekly and a monthly calendar to help students record assignment due dates and check them off when they have been completed. Keeping an assignment notebook helps students plan and manage their time better, enabling them to visibly track due dates and specific times for completing daily and long-term assignments.

Strand 2—Organizing and Retaining Information

Fundamental to all the organizational strategies listed below is that they are preview approaches, which can help clarify the student's thoughts before he or she reads the text. Previewing as a strategy has been found to improve children's comprehension, including those of lower achieving ability (Richardson et al., 2006). Specific preview/study strategies help children sense how information and texts are organized, which enable them to comprehend and retain information (Searfoss et al., 2001, p. 259). The first two strategies, DR-TA and SQ3R, are covered in more detail in Chapter 7.

DR-TA—Directed Reading and Thinking Activity – Through the DR-TA (Stauffer, 1969), students can learn how to predict reading a given text and how to make notes about what is actually learned by using three techniques:

1. Previewing text to predict what will be learned (writing down predictions)
2. Reading text and taking notes; writing about accuracy of predictions and adding important new ideas
3. Reviewing text and writing a summary about what he or she has learned

SQ3R—Survey, Question, Read, Retell, Review – In the SQ3R strategy (Robinson, 1946), the student is taught how to preview the text, ask questions about the text, and answer questions after reviewing the text. The student is taught the following skills:

1. **S**urvey: Preview the text before actually reading.
2. Ask **Q**uestions: Student generates questions about the text before actually reading the selection. The student then writes down the questions, which can be reviewed after reading the text.
3. **R**ead: Student reads to answer questions and to add other information.
4. **R**etell: Student retells what was learned by writing a summary.
5. **R**eview: Student reviews what was learned by discussing with a classmate the new information just learned, or by answering questions in step 2.

PREP System – PREP (Schmelzer, Christen, & Browning, 1980) stands for:

Preview the selection: Students first preview the title, pictures, graphs, and charts. They read the first and last paragraphs or the summary if one is provided. They use headings and subheadings to glean major ideas to be found. Then they can predict what the selection is about.

Read the selection: Next, the students read the selection while taking notes on a graphic organizer (provided by the teacher) for recording, reviewing, and retaining information.

Examine the selection by asking and answering questions about what was read using keywords known in reporting as the "five W's": who, what, when, where, why, and sometimes how.

Prompts should be used by students to help them remember what they read, such as mnemonics, acronyms, or recitation that requires them to ask, "What was worth remembering from this reading selection?"

Guided Lecture Procedure: Getting Young Children Ready for Note Taking – Searfoss et al. (2001) indicate that, in the primary grades, children can begin learning about taking notes as the teacher models by creating class stories on a chart and asking them to answer questions about the text read to them. First, they can work collaboratively with a small group, then later, they can work alone—prompted by the teacher—to retell or to write down brief notes about what they remembered when they listened to the new information.

are different and alike. They could begin by comparing the basic visual look and specific visual details, and then they could move on to discussing ways the content is similar and different. A helpful tool is a simple chart such as the one below that lists the features that should be compared.

	Visual Layout of Website	Graphics on Website	Explanation of Content	Source/ Author of Website
Website #1				
Website #2				
Website #3				

This exercise not only allows the students to practice the specific skill of comparing and contrasting, but it also allows them to become more critical readers and consumers of information. As they make comparisons and take notes, students will evaluate the quality and reliability of different source materials. Young children up through middle school will be able to do this exercise. It is recommended that the teacher choose the websites for children younger than fifth grade to visit.

3. Because the Internet provides information in blocks of text and can present a vast amount of information in one site, it is often difficult for students to see the relationships between many of the concepts being discussed. An important skill for students is to identify how the various pieces of information provided fit together. At one specific site, the teacher can provide a graphic organizer for the children to map out the cause/effect relationships within the text. Posing a "why" question helps students identify the cause of a specific event; then it is easier to find the effect. A good cause/effect graphic organizer is shown here:

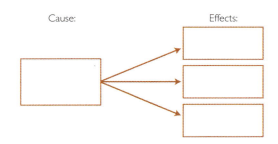

The Internet is quickly replacing books and paper text as the most widely read medium today. Consequently, we need to incorporate strategies that will help our students make sense of what they read and be excellent consumers of information. As more and more people turn to the Internet as their source of information, it is important that critical analysis of content be taught and that students learn to evaluate material so they can determine what is high- and low-quality information. Often, these skills become a matter of critical importance in the real world.

Primary Sources

Informational text provides a wealth of information on many varied topics that students read about, usually through the interpretation of an author who has written about a specific subject. Examples include reading about the Declaration of Independence, learning about life 100 years ago, and reliving a period of history. The Internet is a vast resource that will bring these experiences closer to readers by allowing them to access what is known as primary sources, or the original documents. Children can go to the Library of Congress and view actual documents on the computer screen; they can access a database of stored photographs from the New York Public Library on what life was like 100 years ago; they can see pictures of Chief Sitting Bull, the Sioux chief who defeated General Custer.

Courtesy of Guilherme Cunha

Graphic organizers help children record pertinent information from books and the Internet.

As explained in Chapter 2, a primary source is an original record created at the time that a historical event took place. Primary sources may include letters; manuscripts; diaries; journals; newspapers; speeches; interviews; memoirs; documents produced by government agencies, such as Congress or the Office of the President; photographs; audio recordings; moving pictures or video recordings; research data; and objects or artifacts, such as works of art or ancient roads, buildings, tools, and weapons. These sources help students interpret the past and they add concrete examples that bring historical periods to life so that children can more easily relate to them. Primary sources are excellent supplements in the classroom to support informational texts, especially when reading historical information about any subject area. Many primary sources are available in the humanities, science, social studies, and mathematics.

The following websites provide access to primary sources that can be used to supplement and enrich informational text. More resources are found in Chapter 2 on the Literacy for Children in an Information Age premium website (http://www.cengage.com/login).

Mr Lincoln's Virtual Library

http://memory.loc.gov/ammem/alhtml/alhome.html

Mr. Lincoln's Virtual Library highlights two collections at the Library of Congress that illuminate the life of Abraham Lincoln. It contains approximately 20,000 items, including correspondence and papers accumulated primarily during Lincoln's presidency.

EuroDocs

http://eudocs.lib.byu.edu/index.php/Main_Page

EuroDocs provides access to Western European primary historical documents.

Making of America

http://quod.lib.umich.edu/m/moagrp/

Making of America provides access to nineteenth century books and magazines.

The United States National Library of Medicine

http://www.nlm.nih.gov/hmd/ihm/

The National Library of Medicine has portraits, pictures of institutions, and graphic art illustrating the social and historical aspects of medicine.

Using the Internet to Supplement Informational Texts

Many websites are available on the Internet that can supplement the informational texts that students are reading in the classroom. Every subject area has hundreds of different sites that students can access to find out more about a specific subject. Teachers need to be careful in evaluating websites before students access them, to see whether the pages are appropriate and whether the text is written at an appropriate reading level. In addition, teachers should teach students how to evaluate websites to ensure that the information is meeting their needs. Too often a student will visit a website and not be able to read or comprehend the material, become frustrated, and decide not to search any further for additional information. Figure 12–6 provides some tips on evaluating websites.

Teachers can use the Internet for field trips (see Chapter 2 for a detailed discussion). On these field trips, students can visit a site that they just read about and learn more details about the topic of interest. This type of virtual "visit" helps the student relate to the topic in a much more personal way, making connections that might not otherwise occur.

Some sites provide a wide variety of materials that teachers can use to enrich and supplement what students are reading. Some of these sites are listed below:

Cyberschoolbus

http://www.un.org/Pubs/CyberSchoolBus/index.shtml

The Cyberschoolbus site is sponsored by the United Nations and contains a wealth of information on a variety of topics, such as information on world peace, different countries around the world, different ambassador's views, and human rights issues.

Public Broadcasting Service (PBS)

http://www.pbs.org/teachers/

PBS provides a wealth of resources for teachers and students. There are a number of topics that children and adolescents will find interesting.

Edutopia

http://www.edutopia.org

Edutopia is sponsored by the George Lucas Educational Foundation and offers an array of interesting topics for students and teachers, especially concerning digital content and how it affects education.

Scientific American

http://www.sciam.com

The Scientific American site is hosted by *Scientific American* magazine and contains many interesting topics related to science, technology, and social issues.

Center for Innovation in Engineering and Science Education (CIESE)

http://www.k12science.org/currichome.html

Evaluating Websites

Follow these steps to evaluate whether the website you are visiting is one you can rely on for valid information.

1) Check who is responsible for the website:

Many URLs (Uniform Resource Locator or website address) include the name and type of organization sponsoring the webpage. The 3-letter domain codes provide hints on the type of organization. Common domain codes are:

Domain	Sample Address
.edu = educational institution	http://docsouth.unc**.edu**
.gov = US government site	http://memory.loc**.gov**
.org = organization or association	http://www.theaha**.org**
.com = commercial site	http://www.historychannel**.com**
.museum = museum	http://nc.history**.museum**
.net = personal or other site	http://www.californiahistory**.net**

For the most part, those sites ending in .edu, .gov, and .museum can be assumed to contain scholarly information that will be based on research.

2) Check who is responsible for the website. Check for an Author.

Look for the name of the author or organization responsible for the page. Look for the following information:

- Credentials – Who is the author or organization and what sort of qualifications do they have?
- Contact address – Is an e-mail or some other contact information given?
- "About" link – Is there an "about," "background," or "philosophy" link that provides author or organizational information?

3) Check to see if there a clear purpose or reason for this site.

Websites can be created for a variety of purposes: to disseminate information, provide access to collections, support teaching, sell products, persuade, and many other reasons. Discovering the purpose can help determine the reliability of the site and the information it provides.

Some pages explicitly state their purpose, others do not. To find information about the purpose:

- Check for an "about" link – These links often provide some information about the purpose of the site.
- Find the home page for the site – Sometimes the home page includes the "about" link or other clues on the purpose of the organization sponsoring the site.
- Look for an agenda – Are documents slanted in some way to persuade you? If the purpose of the website is to persuade, you should examine the material very closely before accepting it as fact.

4) Check to see if the content is clearly explained, organized, and accessible.

Good web design not only makes an electronic resource easier to use, it is also one indication that the content is being maintained by a trustworthy source. Although standards of what constitutes "good web design" vary widely, clarity, simplicity, and easily understandable navigational links are some of the obvious signs. Some considerations are:

- Pages that are legible with clear explanations
- Obvious navigational links that provide access to other pages and obvious links on every webpage to the home page
- Clear instructions about special software requirements

Adapted from the Instruction & Research Services Committee of the Reference and User Service Association History Section in the American Library Association. Retrieved February 11, 2006, from http://www.lib.washington.edu/subject/History/RUSA.

FIGURE 12-6

CIESE's site is hosted by the Stevens Institute of Technology; CIESE sponsors and designs interdisciplinary projects that teachers throughout the world can use to enhance their curriculum through the use of the Internet. Their collaborative projects use real-time data available from the Internet, and students communicate with peers and experts around the world.

Discovery Channel

http://dsc.discovery.com/

The Discovery Channel offers a wealth of resources for teachers to incorporate into their curriculum and supplement informational text.

Using Informational Texts in the Classroom

Trade Books

Informational texts can be formidable, especially when they are published as subject matter textbooks such as science, social studies, or mathematics. Less intimidating, and more inviting, however, is the informational trade book. The trade book appeals to children of all ages in that the text and format are informal and engaging. The use of trade books across the curriculum is an excellent way to include informational text in the various content areas. Trade books are usually more highly motivating and are easier for most at-risk children to read and understand.

Trade books are those books that are published for the general public, rather than specifically for the classroom, and include novels, biographies, or informational texts. Trade books contain specific information and topics that allow children to learn about specific content areas in an in-depth way. Because the material is usually focused on a single topic or subject, it is often less fragmented to read and understand. Also, the students are less apt to become confused by having to sort out and organize a great deal of information. Trade books can also be used as an excellent transition into informational text in that they are written in a more reader-friendly style, and the author's tone and written language is almost story-like in presentation. Therefore, children who are accustomed to reading a great deal of narrative literature are better able to make the transition to learning information using this format in contrast with a textbook, which is far more complex and difficult to comprehend. Textbooks present information about content in chapter format, containing many more names, places, dates, and complex issues. To some degree, one might be able to conclude that trade books are more child-centered than most textbooks tend to be. Trade books are written with the child's interests in learning about new information in mind, and they deliver a more personalized approach that creates individualized quality. To make content more accessible, upper elementary grade and middle school teachers often try to find a balance for their own classroom libraries, so that children can research subject matter across the curriculum using a variety of trade books and other informational sources instead of relying on one or two genres.

Children should be given the opportunity to choose their own topics to study and to select appropriate trade books to learn about the topics they have chosen to research. Usually children will select a specific topic or a specific content area to research for their classroom project. As children conduct their inquiries, they should be given the opportunity to select from a number of materials and alternative texts to read and to locate information. Teachers can create a balanced classroom library of their own over time by increasing their classroom budget for book purchases. They can take class field trips to the community library so children may visit their school library more frequently and select trade books related to their projects. Children can also share their projects and trade books with the whole group, which often motivates their classmates to read these interesting informational books. Teachers should also make trade books available for independent reading time or in place of allowing children to read narrative books exclusively during this free reading period. Children benefit when they select from a variety of genres and informational texts, including trade books for research activities.

Investigations to Improve Reading, Writing, and Thinking

Investigations have become increasingly popular in classrooms across the country as a means of having students conduct research using informational text. The approach emphasizes the importance of helping young children learn how to read, write, and think about content information, and then present the information in a visual way using graphics, photos, and pictures. An investigation is a brief study rather than an in-depth research project, culminating in a **poster** or **double-page spread** that the children present to the class. The main purpose of the investigation is to teach children how to synthesize and present information in a "snapshot" visual representation based on the specific topics they have researched. Investigations help elementary through middle school students develop their ability to communicate knowledge in a nonthreatening and unique way.

Linda Hoyt (2002), who is often credited for popularizing what has become known as the *investigation approach*, indicates that the idea originated in the Australian school system. In fact, Hoyt first discovered the approach being used by a Beaverton, Oregon, classroom teacher, Patty Jo Foley, who had used investigations in the classroom. For too long, children have been denied the opportunity to research informational topics of their individual choice. Therefore, the investigation approach helps children explore their varied interests by collecting, thinking, and writing about new knowledge using the craft of informational writing. It is the craft of writing about information that older children and even college-level students refer to as writing about research (Hoyt, Mooney, & Parkes, 2003). Higher order thinking skills develop best when children can reflect on their own reading at their own pace, particularly when they are highly motivated about learning new information that they are inquiring about for their own personal knowledge and enjoyment (Moore, Moore, Cunningham, & Cunningham, 2006).

What Is an Investigation? – An *investigation* is both a process and a product. As a process, the investigation is the way children go about searching out information that interests them. The investigation is a research approach designed particularly for young researchers who are less apt to spend a great deal of time or to go into great depth learning about a given subject area or content field. Yet, the investigation is an excellent opportunity to help children experience what research is about on an introductory level. In this twenty-first century, it is critical that we teach children how to inquire about information using the Internet. Therefore, an investigation is a child's planned inquiry into a specific topic, or content area, but it is a brief study rather than an in-depth research examination. Through the aid of their teacher's verbal think-aloud modeling efforts, and through their introduction in learning about content information, young children can learn how to investigate and conduct research just like their older counterparts do. In the process, they learn about special features found in informational texts and about new content information and ideas through their own inquiries into personal interests, subject-specific areas, and project investigations.

As a product, an investigation is a unique format in which children must present their information on a regular-sized poster or double-spread sheet of paper (two loose-leaf papers put together). It introduces children to visual presentations in which informational text is formatted in small blocks, as graphics are carefully chosen to support the topic, and key ideas are highlighted. Therefore, the investigation serves as evidence of a "brief exploration" in which the child has comprehended new information gleaned from inquiry and reflection. Students must carefully design a planned layout that combines short descriptions, key ideas, keywords, essential questions, and essential components pertaining to the specific topic (Hoyt, 2002).

Planning an Investigation as a Vehicle for Informational Writing – The best approach to teaching children how to write an investigation is for the teacher to model the process by conducting a think-aloud, that is, verbalizing the process out loud as it is being modeled to the class. In this way, the teacher can act as a facilitator by creating a sample investigation as a vehicle for informational writing. Most children by now have already learned how writing as a process works; therefore, an investigation is really an extension of that process involving prewriting, drafting, revising, editing, and postwriting. Students present the investigation to others in the final stage, which only comes when the students and teacher believe that it is ready to be viewed by others (Calkins, 1986). The teacher must impress on the students that the investigation is a special format that uses informational text features that are somewhat unique to this style of writing, and that it contains features that narrative texts generally do not have. Figure 12–7 presents steps that students should follow in planning an investigation.

FIGURE 12-7

Steps in Planning an Investigation

The following steps should be followed by the students in planning a successful Investigation:

1. Choose a specific topic – one that is not too complicated.
2. Use a double-page layout, or small poster format for student presentations
    a. Place in 3-hole notebook as a record
3. Create a pre-text plan on the poster or pages that includes:
    a. Text Blocks (spaces for important text on the research/content)
    b. Titles
    c. Subtitles
    d. Headings
    e. Actual informational text that will be included
4. Create a pre-visual plan that includes:
    a. Graphic Blocks (spaces for visuals)
    b. Illustrations
    c. Diagrams
    d. Maps
    e. Charts
5. Use informational text features that include:
    a. Captions
    b. Titles and Headings
    c. Subtitles
    d. Bold words
    e. Italicized/ Highlighted words
6. Select topic and title for Investigation.
7. Research topic by reading informational texts
    a. Trade books
    b. Textbooks (scan for information)
    c. Magazines and newspapers
    d. Internet resources
8. Share research with peers and teacher.
9. Draft written information:
    a. Use sticky notes for new text
    b. Place sticky notes in text blocks
    c. Review short and long texts with peers
10. Rewrite for publishing/presenting:
    a. Review revised text information and visuals with teacher.
11. Replace all sticky notes with permanent text and visuals.
12. Create a colorful border using symbols related to topic for research.
13. Cite sources of informational text as references.

Examples of Investigations – The following vignettes were written by classroom teachers who have been using investigations in their classrooms. The investigation has helped their students conduct research, read informational texts, and develop a deeper understanding of content-area reading. The author of the first vignette, Jessica Kelly, is a fourth grade classroom teacher who uses the explorer project investigation to teach social studies. The author of the second vignette, Robyn Greenwald, is a sixth grade teacher who uses the investigation in science during a unit on the changing earth.

Explorer Project Investigation in a Fourth Grade Classroom

As a fourth grade teacher, I am always searching for interesting projects that allow my students to show their understanding of a content area in a unique way. I felt that an investigation would enable my students to demonstrate their knowledge, while allowing room for differentiation within the project. One area that many teachers struggle to make interesting to students is social studies. Therefore, I decided to focus my students' investigation on social studies, and the culminating project for our unit would be on exploration.

Once I decided on my focus area, I needed to come up with an exciting overview that would explain all of the important elements of the project while grabbing the students' interest. I decided to compose a letter from the editors of Scholastic Books "hiring" each student to create a double-page spread for their new books, Scholastic's Great Explorers. *The letter explained the directions and expectations to the students in an interesting and unique way. On receiving this letter, the students were instantly excited to begin this new project.*

After reviewing the letter and the expectations with the students, I showed them examples of double-page spreads. Next, the students were allowed to choose an explorer on whom they would focus their research. Once all students were clear on the directions and expectations and had chosen their explorer, their research began. At this point, I stepped back from a "teaching role" to that of a facilitator or coach. I simply helped the students with their research, answered questions, and offered advice. It was really wonderful to see the students take on the responsibility of researching and creating this double-page spread. All around the classroom, students were using technology, books, magazines, and encyclopedias to create their pages. I realized that I had created a great project when I heard the students talking about their explorers and their projects outside of the classroom. One student even brought the project up to a presenter during our class trip to Waterloo Village—a historical recreation of a revolutionary town in northern New Jersey.

From the start of the project, the students were aware of the directions and the expectations. Because I wanted the students to use a variety of resources, they were expected to use at least three books and two websites. As a teacher, I was happy to find that most of the students went above and beyond this expectation, trying to find out as much information as they could about the explorer each had chosen. In addition, the students had to include at least three pictures and one drawn diagram on their poster. Students had to include a written caption for each picture. Again, most of the kids exceeded these expectations. Overall, I was impressed with the students' desire to create a unique and creative poster that was visually stimulating. Even students who typically struggle to meet expectations succeeded. To guide the students, I developed a set of guidelines for them to follow as shown here:

INVESTIGATION POSTER REQUIREMENTS

1. *You must use at least **two** websites and **three** books to find your information.*

2. *You must create a rough copy and have it checked by Mrs. Kelly.*

3. *You must include the following on your final copy:*
   ◆ *A themed border*
   ◆ *At least three real pictures (from the Internet) with captions*
     a. *Your explorer*
     b. *A flag of his/her country*
     c. *Your choice*
   ◆ *At least one drawn diagram with labels*
   ◆ *At least one quote (something your explorer said or might have said)*
   ◆ *At least one paragraph of detailed information*
   ◆ *At least five important key vocabulary words with definitions (they should be bold or highlighted so they stand out)*
   ◆ *At least two websites to see pictures or to learn about your explorer*
   ◆ *A map of your explorer's route*
   ◆ *I assessed my students using a rubric that measured student performance in four critical areas:*
   ◆ *Quality of information*
   ◆ *Quality of resources*
   ◆ *Quality of the investigation poster*
   ◆ *Quality of oral presentation*

As mentioned earlier, most students far exceeded the expectations that I had and scored very well on the rubric. There were two major moments when I realized this was a wonderful project. One occurred when I realized that the students were speaking about their projects outside of the classroom. The second occurred when other fourth grade teachers began stopping by my classroom to get a look at the project they had been hearing about through the student grapevine. This all culminated when I was commended by my principal for my outstanding unit project.

Obviously, my students learned a great deal about their chosen explorer, but I feel they also learned a great deal more. By the end of this unit, students were able to use a variety of materials, texts, and the Internet to research a topic; to synthesize their research into at least one paragraph; and to find appropriate pictures to illustrate their findings and conclusions of their research. In addition, the students were able to share their knowledge with their peers and explain the purpose behind the layout of their investigation posters. Although my students learned a great deal from this investigation approach, I also learned that taking the time to create and plan for a project that included reading a combination of varied texts in the content areas and by holding high expectations for students to conduct research, I enabled them to succeed. This project also enabled the students to present their ideas creatively and effectively by meeting and going beyond my highest expectations. I discovered that students can learn so much more when they are given tools that enable them to read and interpret materials and texts from a variety of rich informational sources.

—*Jessica Kelly, Fourth Grade Teacher*

Our Changing Earth Investigation in a Sixth Grade Classroom

The final project that my students were to complete was an investigation poster that could be related to any topic that we had covered in our science unit. The students were allowed to choose from disastrous tsunamis, terrifying earthquakes, famous active/extinct/dormant volcanoes, famous mountains, scientists in the field (for example, volcanologists), or any other topic related to this unit. The students had a variety of topics from which to choose, and they were instructed to research a topic that piqued their interest during the course of the unit. From this, they were instructed to investigate and conduct further research about it that they had not obtained as prior knowledge. The students were asked to follow a particular rubric, which enabled them to focus on the essential elements of the investigation. The criteria allowed for successful results and expanded learning of their topic through nonfiction texts and outside informational books to which every child had access. This project was chosen to meet the diverse needs of the students, including ELLs and students with learning disabilities.

My students were aware of the following criteria by which their investigation poster would be evaluated. First, the students had to choose their topic and complete an investigation "planning sheet" (Hoyt, 2002). This planning sheet contains the following criteria:

- *Topic*
- *Title*
- *Sample of border to be used*
- *Keys/maps/diagrams to be included*
- *Three main ideas to research*
- *General layout of poster (including text blocks)*

My students were also required to include "culture" as one of their main ideas to display how "our changing Earth" can affect people all around the world in many different countries. They were given the option to include more than three main ideas if they wished; however, they had to include the information as a summary in their own words. The planning sheet motivated the students to learn about their topic and gave them a cohesive guideline to follow.

Regarding sources, the students were required to have at least three different sources from Internet sites, outside nonfiction informational texts, newspapers, and magazine articles. They were also required to write down these sources on a separate piece of paper when they handed in their projects. When the students found information associated with their topic, they wrote down their information on index cards on one side, with the source written on the other side, so they could trace back to where they located their information. This proved to be successful and truly enabled students to organize and present their findings in a neat and orderly manner.

This science investigation poster proved to be successful among the heterogeneous groupings of students within my classes. It allowed the children to work at a level that best suited them, and it enabled me to evaluate them based on what each child's individual "best" work was. They were also able to work at their own pace (within their own zone of proximal development) and include the material that they felt best suited their needs as far as finding key facts pertaining to their individual topics. The information- and knowledge-driven student could incorporate a high level of information, charts, graphs, definitions, computer graphics, and anything that allowed them to flourish within this setting. The child who is more artistic could incorporate his or her information together with elaborate drawings, pictures, or interesting facts. The ELL students were able to pick a topic that occurred in their hometown (for example, tsunami, earthquake in Turkey, Mt. Pinatubo in the Philippines) and incorporate information that is close to their hearts. Students with learning disabilities were able to complete the written component of the research with little difficulty, incorporating elaborate texts and fonts to jazz up their informational findings.

Finally, the students had to present their final science investigation posters to the class. Overall, the general consensus from the students was that this project proved to be extremely successful, and they were able to focus on researching a particular topic of interest to them to learn more in-depth information about it as a final project relating to the our changing Earth science unit. As each student presented a poster, the remaining students took notes and provided feedback to the presenter. The feedback consisted of positive comments that included constructive criticism, which was well received.

—*Robyn Greenwald, Sixth Grade Teacher*

STRATEGY BOX

Using Informational Text in the Classroom

In the introductory scenario, Mrs. Rodriguez was able to successfully work with her second grade class to increase students' achievement in reading and writing by incorporating informational texts into her curriculum. Informational text helped motivate her students to want to read and expanded their knowledge about important subject areas that they will learn about in their future years in school. Mrs. Rodriguez used the following strategies to promote literacy:

1. She enrolled in a summer workshop program with the purpose of improving her struggling readers' reading and writing abilities in the content areas. She wanted to continue improving her literacy instruction in the classroom to promote student achievement, so she pursued professional development in literacy.

2. She collaborated with the reading coaches and other grade level teachers to revise the literacy curriculum to fit the needs of her students.

3. She chose informational books that excited her students and to which they could relate.

4. Through read-alouds, shared reading, and small guided reading groups, she engaged her students in reading informational text that the students enjoyed.

5. She incorporated hands-on science, social studies, and mathematics activities that supplemented the informational texts she was reading that week.

6. She used writing to help the students relate the informational texts to their own lives. She had the students write autobiographies and stories paralleling the topics the class was reading about.

7. During mini-lessons, she taught the students specific comprehension strategies to help them understand informational text, such as recognizing text structure, identifying the main idea, summarizing, and using text features such as the table of contents and glossary.

8. She incorporated the use of the Internet into her lessons when students were researching topics they were excited about, and she had them take virtual field trips to provide more concrete experiences for them.

9. She developed their visual literacy skills through the use of charts, maps, diagrams, and tables.

10. She monitored her students' progress continuously and systematically by collecting data and anecdotal records on her students' achievements.

EXPLORATION   Application of Concepts

Activities

1. Select a short informational text. In a small group, build the background information related to the key topic of the text. Write down different activities that you could introduce in the classroom to help develop, build, and activate prior knowledge about this informational text.

2. Use the same short informational text to develop prereading, during-reading, and postreading activities to help support comprehending informational text. Present this to the class.

3. Prepare a lesson to teach a specific comprehension strategy that will show candidates how to understand and remember information from the text. Present this to the class.

4. Go through a social studies, science, or math textbook. Pick out examples of each type of text structure: descriptive, listing, causation, response, and comparison. Write each passage out and then, if possible, using Inspiration software, develop a graphic organizer for that passage depicting the type of text structure used. Be sure to underline all clue words for each type of structure you have chosen.

5. Find a long descriptive passage in a textbook. Develop a graphic organizer to help students pick out important points. If necessary, rewrite that descriptive passage into a listing, causation, response, or comparison passage.

6. Explore websites on informational text that are listed in this chapter and found on the *Literacy for Children in an Information Age* premium website for this chapter (http://www.cengage.com/login). Evaluate these sites using the form provided in Figure 1–4 in Chapter 1. Compile a "webliography" of good sites that promote comprehending informational texts.

7. Prepare a lesson on teaching an investigation. Establish a rubric for creating an investigation that uses a double-page spread, a border, text blocks, a diagram, a map, photographs, illustrations, and other visuals that show evidence that the candidate has internalized and comprehended the content investigated.

Final Thoughts

This chapter introduces the concept of informational text as one of the most recently discussed topics in elementary classroom literacy. It covers the importance of shifting from an almost exclusive use of narrative texts in elementary classrooms to incorporating informational texts to prepare children for reading in the various content areas, including social studies, science, and mathematics.

A balanced reading program uses a combination of texts and media, including many different genres, authors, and text-based materials. By using different types of books, text, and media, children are exposed to a richness of print and text that serve as models for writing prose and poetry, and that help students to develop new literacies as they read about information from a combination of rich text styles and formats.

HOME–SCHOOL CONNECTION   Tips to Help Children Improve Reading of Informational Text

Parents and guardians can help their children improve comprehension of informational text by following the eight tips listed below:

1. Ask their child's teacher what content is being taught in school. What can be done to help at home? Does their child struggle with comprehending information?

2. Ask the child's teacher for some advice in selecting informational trade books that parallel the textbooks being read in class.

3. Make recreational reading at home enjoyable by letting the child choose books on topics of interest, such as sports, animals, jokes, comic books, and hobbies.

4. Find accessible books for children with reading problems or learning disabilities by consulting with the teacher and specialists at the school.

5. Ask the child to describe the best part of the book and tell what it was about; ask questions that make the child elaborate upon the information he or she learned in reading.

6. Read information books, newspapers, magazines, recipes, or electronic information themselves, because studies show that children often read more for information when their parents and guardians do.

7. Build a home library that each family member will enjoy, and take advantage of public library book sales or neighbors who are giving away children's favorite books and magazines.

8. Check out literacy games in vocabulary, trivia facts, and rhyming and computer reading games by searching on "reading games" on the Internet.

(Adapted from Frey, N. and Fisher, D. (2007). *Reading for information in elementary school: Content literacy strategies to build comprehension.* Upper Saddle River, NJ: Pearson Education, Inc.)

13 DEVELOPING EFFECTIVE UNITS OF STUDY IN LITERACY

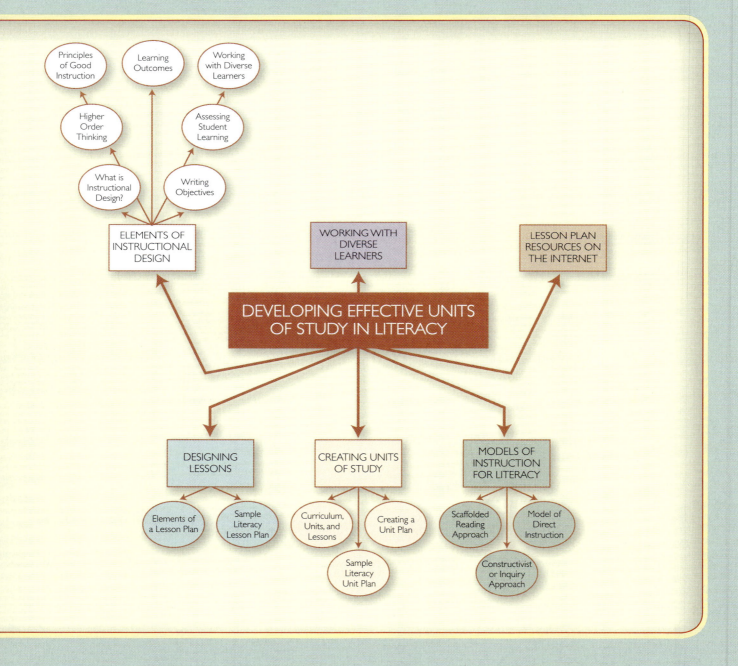

International Reading Association Professional Standards Addressed in this Chapter:

IRA STANDARD 2:   INSTRUCTIONAL STRATEGIES AND CURRICULUM MATERIALS

Candidates use a wide range of instructional practices, approaches, methods, and curriculum materials to support reading and writing instruction. Candidates:

2.1 Use instructional grouping options (individual, small-group, whole-class, and computer-based) as appropriate for accomplishing given purposes.

2.2. Use a wide range of instructional practices, approaches, and methods, including technology-based practices, for learners at differing stages of development and from differing cultural and linguistic backgrounds.

2.3. Use a wide range of curriculum materials in effective reading instruction for learners at different stages of reading and writing development and from different cultural and linguistic backgrounds.

IRA STANDARD 3:   ASSESSMENT, DIAGNOSIS, AND EVALUATION

Candidates use a variety of assessment tools and practices to plan and evaluate effective reading instruction. Candidates:

3.3 Use assessment information to plan, evaluate, and revise effective instruction that meets the needs of all students, including those at different developmental stages and those from different cultural and linguistic backgrounds.

IRA STANDARD 4:   CREATING A LITERATE ENVIRONMENT

Candidates create a literate environment that fosters reading and writing by integrating foundational knowledge, use of instructional practices, approaches and methods, curriculum materials, and the appropriate use of assessments. Candidates:

4.1 Use students' interests, reading abilities, and backgrounds as foundations for the reading and writing program.

4.2 Use a large supply of books, technology-based information, and nonprint materials representing multiple levels, broad interests, and cultural and linguistic backgrounds.

4.3 Model reading and writing enthusiastically as valued lifelong activities.

4.4 Motivate learners to be lifelong readers.

Key Terms

instructional design

target audience

prerequisite skills

learning outcomes

objective

Bloom's Taxonomy

principles of good instructional design

anticipatory set

co-teaching

curriculum

unit

lesson

topic of study

unit evaluation plan

direct teaching

Focus Questions

1.   What is instructional design and why is it important for beginning teachers to learn about it?

2.   When designing lesson plans, what strategies can a teacher use to accommodate the needs of diverse learners?

3.   What are the basic elements of a lesson plan? What principles of instruction should every lesson plan contain?

Focus Questions *(continued)*

4. What is the difference between curriculum, units, and lessons? What are the components of a unit plan?

5. What are different models of literacy instruction that a teacher can use in the classroom?

6. What sites on the internet provide teachers with resources for lesson planning?

Welcome to Ms. Walker's First Grade Classroom: Designing and Implementing Effective Literacy Lessons Based on Learning Theory

Courtesy of Bob Ebbesen/Alamy

Ms. Walker quietly asks for the students' attention and tells them that today they will be learning about a new kind of family—a word family. She brainstorms with the class for a few minutes to define what a word family is and how words in the same family all end with the same letters. She gives examples of the word family–*at* and writes them on the board. She then invites the students to the class's carpeted reading area and tells them that they are going to read a funny poem. She asks them to pay attention to the words in the poem

and determine whether they can identify any word families. She then introduces the poem "Hot Dog" by Shel Silverstein by asking the students if they have any pets. She initiates a short discussion on pets with some of the students sharing stories about their pets. She then reads the following excerpt from the poem, which is written on a large easel:

> HOT DOG
> I have a hot dog for a pet,
> The only kind my folks would let
> Me get.
> He does smell sort of bad
> And yet,
> He absolutely never gets
> The sofa wet.

Ms. Walker reads the excerpt of the poem aloud modeling expressive and fluent reading, and then discusses the meaning of the poem and why it might be funny. She has the students discuss what type of pet the author is talking about. She points out some of the words that are not phonetically controlled and might give the children trouble: *folks, absolutely,* and *sofa.* She then has the class read parts of the poem together a few times, again helping with the difficult words. She asks the students if they recognize any words that rhyme and belong to the same word family. She circles the words as the students say them, placing emphasis on the ending sound. She does a "think aloud" by taking each circled word and saying, "What sound does this word end with? What letters make up this sound?" and then writes the word under a list that is labeled "-*et*." She then models how to write all words from that family under the list and asks the students to read the words with her.

Ms. Walker then tells the students that they are going to identify more word families from the book *Green Eggs and Ham* by Dr. Seuss and group them together into the same word family. She also tells them that she would like them to practice reading these words to their partners and at home to their parents or guardians. Using one page that is written on the easel she models how to place words in the -*ouse* family all under the same column. She tells them they will do the same thing with other word families such as -*am*.

Ms. Walker pairs any English language learner with a buddy who can provide support and groups the students into groups of two and three. She hands them a blank organizer for them to record their word families, restating once more the ideas presented during the modeling. She roams the room, providing assistance while the students work, giving sufficient time and support for those who need it, and working individually with struggling readers. She then calls the class back to order and goes over the word families the groups have found. She tells them that they are going to continue this activity for a few more minutes, but working at their own desks to complete the activity independently. Ms. Walker continues

to roam the room providing individual support and feedback, asking students to read the words from their list, and encouraging them to read the words at home to a parent, guardian or older sibling. After another 10 minutes, she collects both the group papers and the individual papers to assess whether the students could identify words that belong to the same word family.

The above scenario describes a lesson that is focused on clearly identified objectives: The students identify words that belong to the same word family, group the words, and then read them. Ms. Walker clearly announces to the students what they will be learning today (word families) and what she expects them to do (identify the words, group them, and read them). Her "activities" are focused on achieving her objective, and she collects assessment data from each student at the end of the lesson to determine who has attained the objective and who needs more help. She also uses learning theory by selecting a poem the students will like and find funny; by modeling expressive reading; by having the class reread the poem, which promotes fluency; by modeling how to do the required task; by providing guided practice in groups; and by allowing each student to practice the task independently. This scenario shows a well-designed lesson that the teacher carefully thought about and spent time planning.

This chapter examines the role of instructional design and learning theory in developing and implementing effective units of study in literacy. It examines what a unit plan is and how it should be closely aligned to national and state standards.

Elements of Instructional Design

What Is Instructional Design?

Instructional design is based on theories of how people learn, and uses systematic procedures to ensure that the instruction is of high quality. The goal of instructional designers is to make learning easier, quicker, and more enjoyable. An instructional designer's job is to help every student learn, enjoy what he or she is learning, and be successful (Berger, 1996; Reigeluth, 1983).

The key to improving instruction is to know what methods of instruction to use and when they should be used. Too often, beginning teachers think that designing units of instruction for classes is a process that is done "on the fly" or is activity-based. In actuality, it is a much more complex and systematic process involving different tools. Much as a designer works creatively, trying out different ideas and revising plans many times before actually implementing the design, so must instructional designers work creatively and carefully in planning instruction. Architects would never start building a house without first going through a careful, long process of designing and revising the blueprints. A teacher must approach design of instruction in the same way using lesson plans to guide implementation.

When designing instruction, the teacher must know about the learner, the content, the goals of instruction, the learning environment, the teacher's own preferences, and the resources available. The teacher must consider who the learner or **target audience** is when designing instruction: the grade level, the developmental level of the learner, the background knowledge that the learner possesses, previous knowledge of the content area, and the motivational levels of the learner. When considering the content, the teacher must have a sufficient knowledge base to feel comfortable in teaching it. The teacher should consider what **prerequisite skills** are needed for the learner to master the instruction. Does the student have sufficient background, skills, and content knowledge to even start instruction in this unit? This requires enough knowledge of the content to either preteach requisite skills or design instruction at the appropriate level.

Learning Outcomes

The teacher must have carefully articulated **learning outcomes** to effectively design instruction. Learning outcomes are statements that specify what learners will know or be able to do as a result of a learning activity. Learning outcomes are usually expressed as broad-based statements about the desired outcomes of the instruction that can be measured. Creating learning outcomes means that the teacher starts by identifying the desired results at the end of instruction, and then working "backwards" to design instruction. This is different than the traditional approach, which is to define what topics need to be covered first and then working "forward."

When designing learning outcomes, the teacher should consider what important topics, concepts, strategies, and skills lie at the heart of the instruction. This includes asking the following questions (Wiggins & McTighe (2005):

◆ What are the big ideas and understandings about this lesson that I want to focus on?

◆ What is the enduring value of this instruction beyond the classroom?

◆ What elements comprise the heart of the discipline?

◆ What are the abstract or often misunderstood ideas that are required to understand this lesson?

◆ What aspects of this instruction will engage students in the learning process?

An example of an outcome is: "At the end of this unit, the student will know how to apply comprehension strategies involving inference to facilitate comprehension of text." This outcome is specific enough so that the teacher knows to focus on the comprehension strategy of inference, but broad enough so that specific steps for how to do this still need to be specified. The outcome should guide the development of the instruction, and be the end result that the teacher will ultimately assess. It should focus on the essential understandings that students will need to broaden their experiences in the area of literacy. The above stated outcome focuses on the key comprehension strategy of inferencing, which is an essential aspect of reading for understanding.

The teacher needs to consider the learning environment when designing instruction: where the unit will take place, how much time can be allocated, what limitations the environment will impose, and how the environment will contribute or detract from instruction. For example, if a teacher wants to design a unit that involves cooperative grouping of instruction and he teaches in a small classroom, he may not be able to set up the class as he desires, and he may have to alter some of his plans. Or, another teacher may try to implement a hands-on project in a classroom that has no walls and is in an "open-environment" school (similar to some schools that were built in the 1970s). This type of learning might become noisy and distract other classrooms unless strict guidelines are developed before the class begins. A teacher always needs to know what resources are available that will impact on the eventual implementation of the unit. If the teacher wanted to implement a problem-based learning unit that required use of computers for research and exploration of topics, but had only two computers available, the unit would have to be modified to adapt to the lack of technological resources or adapted so that the two computers could be used in creative ways throughout the unit of instruction.

Writing Objectives

Once a teacher has specified who the target audience is, researched the content to be taught, articulated the learning outcome of the instruction, considered the environment, and taken into account the available resources, he or she must now concentrate on writing objectives for the upcoming instruction. An **objective** is the building block on which the foundation of the instruction will rest. Another analogy is to relate objectives to a road map. A person taking a trip does not just get into a car and drive in a direction he thinks will lead him to his destination; he carefully maps out a route to follow. In the same manner, objectives become the road map for a teacher. Objectives point toward the specific direction that instruction should follow and map out a set route on how the teacher can get there. Too often, beginning teachers do not see the value in setting objectives and choose to forge ahead without knowing the route they will take.

Planning is a critical component of designing effective literacy lessons for children.

Examples of literacy objectives that relate to the learning outcome include:

> **Outcome:** At the end of this unit, the student will apply comprehension strategies involving inference to facilitate comprehension of text.

1. Given five inference questions to which he or she must write answers, the student will be able to infer meaning—with 100 percent accuracy—from passages in which the answers are not explicitly stated but implied.

2. Given five passages that contain inferred meaning, the student will be able to identify the clue words that help him/her determine what the implied meaning of the question is.

3. Given three inference questions to write, the student will be able to read a passage and create questions that require answers involving inference.

As noted above, each objective is written as a formal statement that includes several components. First, a statement that begins with "Given . . ." describes the conditions of learning under which the student must perform the skill. The first objective states that the student must write answers to questions ("Given five inference questions to which he or she must write answers . . ."); the second objective states that the student must read passages to identify clue words ("Given five passages that contain inferred meaning . . ."); and the third objective

David Ottenstein Photography

states that the student must write three questions ("Given three inference questions to write . . ."). The second component is the skill or strategy that the student is to achieve and that the teacher must assess. In the first objective, the skill is "to infer meaning from passages"; in the second objective, the skill is "to identify the clue words"; and in the third objective, the skill is "to read a passage and create [three] questions." Third, sometimes the criterion is included that specifies the level of achievement that is expected of the student. For example, the student must answer all five inference questions correctly for 100 percent accuracy to demonstrate achievement.

The criterion is based on the teacher considering several factors. First, how important is this skill for the student to be literate? You do not want a criterion lower than 100 percent for the objective: "Given letters of the alphabet to identify, the student will name every letter of the alphabet." Second, how important is the objective for the student to be able to achieve at a high level for the rest of the unit? If the objective is required knowledge, or skills needed for the rest of the unit, then the criterion should be set at 95 or 100 percent. Third, how important is the objective for the student to succeed within the subject area or vocation? You would not want the criterion to be any lower than 100 percent for the following objective: "Given an airplane to land, the pilot will analyze data on weather conditions and landing surface."

For many objectives, the criterion may not be appropriate and may be difficult to specify. In the third objective above ("the student will be able to read a passage and create [three] questions that require answers involving inference"), it is difficult to specify an exact criterion for creating inference questions. It is easier to specify a criterion for skill-based objectives than it is for more conceptual, higher order thinking objectives, and usually the criterion is not required when writing objectives. However, when writing objectives, teachers should be thinking about assessment criteria and what level of student performance on the objective demonstrates proficiency.

In addition to these three components, objectives often include the words "the student will be able to . . ." This is a convention that is usually followed when writing formal objectives. It is also noted that the objective refers to one student ("the *student* will be able to . . ."), and not the whole class or a group of students. This is to emphasize that the teacher must focus on each individual student and ensure that each achieves the objective.

Objectives are a critical component of lesson planning because they point the teacher in a specified direction. Objectives help focus the instruction on an attainable, measurable, and observable strategy, skill, or process. They are the foundation on which the teacher can now develop the rest of the lesson, and they specify how to assess each student in the class.

Assessing Student Learning in Instructional Units

Once objectives have been written, the teacher can focus on how to evaluate the student in the lesson or unit. If written correctly, each objective basically tells the teacher how to evaluate the student. For example, in the first objective above, the teacher will collect the student's written answers to five inference questions. In the second objective, the teacher will collect the clue words that helped the student determine what the implied meaning of the question was. In the third objective, the teacher will collect the three inference questions that the student created.

For each objective, some form of data must be collected. It is not enough to say that the objective will be evaluated by observation. Observation is a valid form of assessment, but only when accompanied by an observational checklist or observational journal that the teacher keeps and uses continuously to collect data on student performance. Beginning teachers have a difficult time conceptualizing this concept because they view lessons as activities, not objectives in which data must be collected and analyzed to assess student performance. The data do not have to be complex or difficult to collect. It can be homework assignments, written answers to questions, essays, paragraphs, journals, hands-on projects, written spelling words, or a paragraph where all clue words are circled. It can also be a miscue analysis, a running record, an observational checklist, or a written comment about the student's reading progress. The important point is that data must be collected for each objective to hold each teacher accountable and to show progress and growth over time. In this way, the teacher is implementing outcomes-based assessment as data is collected and analyzed for the learning outcome to ensure each student is achieving.

Higher Order Thinking

When looking at creating objectives, there are different levels of learning from which students can be operating. In 1956, Benjamin Bloom wrote *Taxonomy of Educational Objectives; The Classification of Educational Goals. Handbook I: Cognitive Domain.* The taxonomy was created to help teachers create units of instruction and to help assess these curricular programs through the specified objectives. Bloom wrote that there are three sources for writing educational objectives. One source for formulation of objectives is the information available about the students. What is their background knowledge, needs, and interests? Another source for objectives is available from investigations of problems and conditions of contemporary life. What are the problems that students might encounter in "real life," and what activities are they expected to perform? A third source of objectives comes from the subject matter. What types of learning should students be engaged in when studying this field? How might someone in the "real world" think about the subject or perform tasks associated with the subject? Bloom also stated that formulation of objectives must be tied to learning theory and how children learn best. When developing objectives for lessons, teachers must consider how to sequence the objectives so that children learn the processes, skills, and content in the most effective way possible and find the instruction enjoyable, challenging, and motivating.

Bloom's Taxonomy contains six major classes based on the hierarchical order of learning (Figure 13–1):

1. Knowledge
2. Comprehension
3. Application
4. Analysis
5. Synthesis
6. Evaluation

This hierarchy starts at the most basic level of learning, the knowledge level, which is memorization and recall of material. According to Bloom (1956), the most common educational objective in U.S. education is the acquisition of knowledge or information. Frequently, knowledge is the primary, if not sole, educational objective in a curriculum. Often, the only outcome teachers require is that the student gives evidence that he or she remembers the content, either by recalling or recognizing some idea, fact, or bit of information that was part of the unit of study. It is important to teach knowledge as a basis of all subject areas and to increase students' knowledge base about a particular topic. However, few educators would be satisfied with stopping at this level of instruction. Rather, teachers should be interested in what students can do with this knowledge, so that they can apply it to different situations and problems. We expect our students to be able to apply appropriate strategies and techniques to solving new problems and to use analysis to understand the new situation. We expect students to derive solutions to problems and to evaluate the appropriateness of the solution and revise their solution accordingly. This type of learning requires development of intellectual abilities and skills that promote higher order thinking. In solving problems that require intellectual skills, the student is expected to organize or reorganize a problem, to identify what material is appropriate, to remember such material, and to make use of it in the problem situation (Bloom, 1956). This goes far beyond just the knowledge level and requires teachers to design instruction that moves the student further along in Bloom's Taxonomy to the application, analysis, synthesis, and evaluation levels of learning.

Bloom's Taxonomy

Level	Description	Verbs for Writing Objectives
I. KNOWLEDGE	Knowledge of: a. Specifics b. Ways of means of dealing with specifics c. The Universals and abstractions in a field	KNOW: tell, list, cite, choose, arrange, find, group, label, select, match, locate, name, offer, omit, pick, quote, repeat, reset, say, show, sort, spell, touch, write, underline, point to, tally, transfer, recite, identify, hold, check.
II. COMPREHENSION	Comprehension by: a. Translation b. Interpretation c. Extrapolation	TRANSLATE: change, reword, construe, render, convert, expand, transform, alter, vary, retell, qualify, moderate, restate. INTERPRET: Infer, define, explain, construe, spell out, outline, annotate, expound, account for. EXTRAPOLATE: project, propose, advance, contemplate, submit, offer, calculate, scheme, contrive.
III. APPLICATION	Applying: abstract forms in: a. General Ideas b. Rules/Procedures c. Generalized Methods	APPLY: relate, utilize, solve, adopt, employ, use, avail, capitalize on, consume, exploit, profit by, mobilize, operate, ply, handle, manipulate, exert, exercise, try, devote, wield, put in action, put to use, make use of, take up.
IV. ANALYSIS	Analysis of: a. Elements b. Relationships c. Organizational Principles	ANALYZE: break down, uncover, look into, dissect, examine, take apart, divide, simplify, reason, include, deduce, syllogize, check, audit, inspect, section, canvass, scrutinize, sift, assay, test for, survey, search, study, screen.
V. SYNTHESIS	Synthesis by: a. Communicating b. Developing a plan c. Proposing a set of operation d. Developing a set of abstract relations	SYNTHESIS: create, combine, build, compile, make, structure, reorder, reorganize, develop, produce, compose, construct, blend, yield, breed, cause, effect, generate, evolve, mature, make up, form, constitute, originate, conceive, formulate.
VI. EVALUATION	Evaluating by: a. Internal standards b. External criteria	EVALUATING: judge, decide, rate, appraise, assay, rank, weight, accept, reject, determine, assess, reject, determine, criticize.

FIGURE 13-1

In using Bloom's Taxonomy, teachers should ensure that their objectives move the student up on the hierarchy of levels. The teacher should design units of instruction that start with requiring knowledge and then progressively require higher levels of learning from the student so that intellectual abilities and skills are taught as well. Literacy circles are an excellent example of instruction that promotes higher level thinking from students. As groups discuss texts that they have read, they learn to analyze different components of the book, they learn how to synthesize others' perspectives into a larger vision of what the book is about, and they learn how to evaluate the author's message and theme.

Bloom's Taxonomy can be used for more than just writing educational objectives. It can be used to assure that the evaluation of the student is aligned with the objective; that is, that the student's performance demonstrates the appropriate level of learning. Bloom (1956) states that assessment must be closely aligned to the objective; in fact, if the teacher is designing a unit that requires analysis and synthesis, then the student must be assessed at this level as well. In addition, Bloom's Taxonomy can be used to assess instruction and evaluation. A teacher can use the taxonomy to assess previous units of instruction that were taught to determine what level of learning was required from the student. The teacher can also assess items on tests—teacher-made tests, commercial tests, or standardized tests—to determine the level of learning that the test is requiring from the student. Lastly, the teacher can use the taxonomy to assess the type of questions that are being asked in the classroom during discussion and instruction. Is the teacher asking students for only recall and memorization answers, or is the teacher asking the student to analyze and synthesize material? Bloom's Taxonomy is a helpful tool that classroom teachers should be using while designing and assessing instruction.

Principles of Good Instruction

When designing instruction it is important that the teacher is knowledgeable about learning theory and understands basic principles of effective instruction. Many theorists have written about the principles of instructional design and the need to use systematic application of these principles in instruction to enhance learning (Ausubel, 1963; Bruner, 1966; Gagne, 1977; Gagne, Wager, Golas, & Keller, 2005; Reigeluth, 1983). The following principles should be used when designing and implementing lesson plans and units of study:

◆ *Activate prior knowledge.* One of the most important principles in learning theory is that the learner's prior knowledge must be activated before any meaningful learning can take place. David Ausubel (1963), a pioneer in studying learning theory, points out that two things are necessary for understanding to occur: (1) the content must be potentially meaningful, and (2) the learner must relate it in a meaningful way to his or her prior knowledge. If the learner has no background knowledge of the information that he or she is about to read, there is a good chance that the text will not be fully comprehended or retained. It is similar to reading a book on nuclear physics without having any prior knowledge or experience with the topic. Therefore, the teacher must spend a sufficient amount of time before a reading or writing assignment building up students' background knowledge and activating any prior knowledge the students may have regarding the topic to be covered.

◆ *Determine extent of prior knowledge.* It is advisable to assess how much students already know about the content to be taught. This can be done through several activities: use a K-W-L chart (see Figure 10–9), in which students enter what they Know in the K column, what they Want to learn in the W column, and what they Learned after reading about the topic in the L column; use a "quick write" at the beginning of the lesson, in which the teacher asks the students to write for five minutes on a topic they will be reading about to see what the students already know; and use preassessments that allow the teacher to quickly assess students' prior knowledge of the topic.

◆ *Preteach concepts.* Often, the lesson plan being developed is based on knowledge of a specific concept that the students must understand to fully comprehend the reading or writing assignment. Such concepts as *compassion, responsibility,* or *democracy* may need to be pretaught to ensure full understanding. The difference between preteaching vocabulary words and concepts is based on teaching the learner the conceptual meaning underlying a word, as opposed to applying a label to a word already known (Graves & Graves, 1994). An effective technique to preteach concepts is through brainstorming webs: the teacher writes the new concept in the middle of the web and discusses all of its various attributes with the class by "webbing out" from the circle. It is also important that the students can relate this new concept to their own lives.

◆ *Provide scaffolding.* The learner needs to be supported by the teacher as new skills and strategies are being taught. The teacher should provide support and guidance as new tasks are introduced, and then systematically remove this support as the learner continues to practice and master the task. Eventually, the scaffolding should be removed so that the learner is performing independently and achieving without any support. When this occurs, it is time to move on to a slightly more difficult task that again will require scaffolding and support.

◆ ***Provide constant feedback during instruction.*** The learner will need continuous feedback during instruction to ensure that he or she is on the right track. The teacher needs to ensure that when a new strategy or skill is introduced, the learner is receiving positive and corrective feedback to ensure mastery and full comprehension.

◆ ***Reinforce and maintain learning.*** Mastery of a new task needs much practice while it is being learned. Students need to practice new tasks under many different circumstances, with teacher support, with minimal teacher support, and independently. It is important that the teacher constantly reinforce the new learning after it is achieved so that students can maintain it as they move onward through the curriculum.

◆ ***Provide hands-on application.*** Learning theory tells us that students learn a subject better when it is taught in-depth. Hands-on applications allow the student to explore the topic further and to see the relationships between concepts. It provides the student with concrete activities to reinforce the learning and makes the topic less abstract. Students find hands-on projects motivating and enjoy applying what they have learned to a real-life situation.

◆ ***Differentiate instruction.*** In differentiated classrooms, teachers provide specific ways for each individual to learn as much as possible and as quickly as possible, individualizing according to student need. Teachers modify instruction so that each learner is provided with opportunities that address individual learning styles and learning preferences. This is especially important in today's increasingly diverse classrooms. (See Chapter 10 for a more detailed discussion of differentiated instruction.)

◆ ***Summarize and provide review.*** The teacher should always have a summary of the lesson. This summary should bring closure to the lesson and provide a review of the major concepts that were covered in the lesson. As in the introduction, the summary should relate the topic to the students' lives and make connections to concrete examples of how this lesson directly applies to each student. The summary is the last thing about the lesson that the student will remember, so the teacher should ensure that the student leaves the lesson remembering the important points.

These **principles of good instructional design** should be incorporated systematically in all lessons. Beginning teachers need to know that—just like a novel or a movie—lessons have a definite beginning, middle, and end, in which certain instructional features should be applied to make the lesson interesting, effective, and valuable. The beginning of the lesson, often called the **anticipatory set,** is where the teacher must "provide a hook" or catch the students' attention. The teacher should motivate the students with an interesting story, picture, discussion, or activity that the students will enjoy. The teacher should also activate prior knowledge, review previously taught concepts, and relate the upcoming instruction to the students' lives. The middle of the lesson is when the instruction takes place; here, the teacher must hold the students' attention. The different models of instruction (discussed later in this chapter) can be implemented during the middle of the lesson. The end of the lesson is when the teacher should summarize what the lesson was about, review the concepts and strategies that have been taught, and relate the lesson to the students' lives, stressing why this lesson is important. Children need to see the relevance and importance of what they are learning to their own lives. By using these principles, teachers can better ensure that understanding will occur and that children are responding positively to instruction.

Working with Diverse Learners

When designing instruction, it is important that the teacher takes into account the importance of accommodating diverse learners in lesson plans. Diverse learners include students with learning disabilities, English language learners, and struggling readers and writers, all of whom have different learning styles and varying needs.

Students with learning disabilities will have an Individualized Educational Plan (IEP) that will need to be addressed (see Figure 4–9). This includes specific instructional goals and special services that need to be provided by the school. Depending on the school district, **co-teaching** may be required, whereby a special education teacher and the regular teacher teach lessons together on an ongoing basis, providing extra support for all students, not just those with learning disabilities.

Co-teaching is an integral part of an inclusive classroom and is usually implemented with one teacher who is a general educator and one who is a special educator or specialist. Team-teaching generally refers to two general education teachers' combining classes and sharing instruction. In an elementary school, this might occur when two fourth grade teachers decide to teach their two classes (on a unit) together for a period of time.

In co-teaching, the general educator is usually primarily responsible for the content of the instruction, while the special educator is responsible for facilitating the learning process. Various combinations of students and group sizes are used and both teachers work with all the students. Co-teachers are firmly committed to "our" students, not "yours" and "mine."

In co-teaching, one of the most important aspects of working together is planning and developing lesson plans. Both the classroom teacher and the special education teacher need to discuss the following questions:

◆ What do we need to share so that we can effectively teach the class together?

◆ What content needs to be addressed, and how can we accommodate all students to learn the content? What methods should we use? What is the best way to deliver the content so all students will comprehend what is being taught?

◆ What will the classroom teacher do and what will the special educator do during the lesson?

◆ How will activities take place? What is the responsibility of both teachers?

◆ When, where, and how long will the lesson be?

◆ What additional resources and materials are needed to accommodate all students at all different levels?

It is helpful for the two teachers to develop a lesson plan that carefully outlines the roles and responsibilities of each teacher, the lesson objectives, the content to be taught, the instructional methodology to be used, and the assessment strategies used.

When designing lessons for diverse learners it is important to consider the following points:

◆ *Differentiation of instruction:* It is important that lesson plans provide different approaches that students can use to learn the content and different texts that students can read based on their reading level. Struggling readers and writers should be in a group of about three students (no more than four), and they should receive individualized instruction.

◆ *Intense instruction:* Diverse learners need more time to learn content, to read material, and to retain information. Teachers must be responsive to all students' unique needs, actions, and behavior. If necessary, the teacher must slow down, repeat, speed up or change pace, find an alternative explanation, or stop. Struggling readers should receive specialized reading instruction at least four (preferably five) days a week (Shaywitz, 2003).

◆ *Sufficient duration:* Diverse learners need an extended period to learn the content, much longer than other students in the class. A frequent error is to stop intensive instruction too soon. In addition, struggling readers need to have the instruction maintained and reinforced constantly or they will forget it and likely progress backward.

◆ *Direct instruction:* It is highly recommended that diverse learners receive direct instruction in reading, writing, spelling, and vocabulary development. Although many student learning occurs incidentally through everyday activities, struggling readers need direct instruction to reinforce literacy skills. The Model of Direct Instruction (presented later in this chapter) should be used for diverse learners.

◆ *Cooperative learning:* Diverse learners benefit from collaborating in groups, as their peers provide support and reduce the linguistic and cognitive load of diverse learners. This should supplement the direct instruction that they receive in guided reading groups and in mini-lessons.

◆ *Hands-on projects:* Diverse learners do well with hands-on projects and alternative ways to demonstrate proficiency of a task. It allows them to use different learning styles and build on their strengths.

◆ *Alternative ways to assess:* Diverse learners may know the content but be unable to express their knowledge because of linguistic difficulties. It is helpful to offer alternatives to the traditional means of testing (reading, writing, and answering multiple-choice questions) to assess content.

◆ *Accommodations:* Diverse learners may need additional accommodations in the classroom to support instruction and assessment. Such accommodations may be providing text on tape, recording tests using podcasts, using software to facilitate writing (text-to-speech, word prediction), allowing extra time for tests, and providing extra support with tutoring and buddy-support.

All of these factors should be taken into consideration when designing instruction for diverse learners. Lesson plans should accommodate all students' needs.

STRATEGIES FOR TEACHING DIVERSE LEARNERS

Developing Effective Units of Study in Literacy

1. Work closely with the specialists in the school and district to plan lessons that accommodate diverse learners' needs. Work with the English as a second language (ESL) specialist for accommodations for English language learners in the classroom. Be sure to consult with the special education specialist to address Individualized Educational Plan requirements for students with learning disabilities.

2. Plan alternative ways to accommodate diverse learners when developing lesson plans. Diverse learners may need extra time, different ways to present the content, different texts to read, assistive technology to support their learning, and testing accommodations.

3. Stimulate critical thinking and promote higher order thinking skills in the lesson. Encourage students to question the text, their peers, and their interpretation of material.

4. When developing lesson plans that focus on skills and strategies, ensure that direct instruction is incorporated into the procedure. Diverse learners benefit from direct instruction of skills such as phonics instruction, vocabulary development, and reading comprehension strategies.

5. Ensure that your lesson plans accommodate multiple intelligences and different learning styles. Plan for multiple ways in which students can demonstrate their knowledge and complete assignments.

6. When designing lessons, find out if additional resources are available. Software products that support reading and writing are very beneficial. In addition, supplemental textbooks written on the appropriate reading level might be required.

7. Use cooperative learning as part of the lesson plan procedure to provide guided practice and support of skills once the skill has been modeled by the teacher and thoroughly explained.

8. Provide hands-on projects that allow students to demonstrate their learning in various modalities other than just writing assignments.

9. Plan for projects to which diverse learners can relate. Use multicultural literature, allow students to read books written from authors who come from a similar cultural background, incorporate themes and topics with which students are familiar, and develop authentic activities that students can use in the world around them.

10. If possible, plan lessons to co-teach with the special education teacher. Work with the special education specialist so that you both know exactly what your responsibilities are and how the lesson will be structured so that all students' needs are met.

Designing Lessons

Elements of a Lesson Plan

Lesson plans are the basic instructional format that teachers must begin to work with. Although many schools do not usually require teachers to hand in formal lesson plans for every class and for every period, it is important that beginning teachers learn how to design and develop formal lesson plans. This will help the new teacher conceptualize the different components of a lesson plan and to plan accordingly. The formal lesson plan will be the road map that guides the teacher to designing and implementing effective instruction within the classroom.

The different components of a lesson plan are:

◆ *Objective:* All lessons must start with the specification of an educational objective that is based on Bloom's Taxonomy.

◆ *Standards:* The lesson plan should specify the state and/or professional standards that are being addressed by the objective.

◆ *Vocabulary:* The lesson plan should specify what key vocabulary words the lesson is revolving around. There should be no more than 10 vocabulary words per lesson for primary grade instruction. The vocabulary word(s) should focus on the key concept the lesson revolves around and help the teacher keep that concept in mind. For instance, if the lesson objective is, "Given five inference questions to answer, the student will be able to infer meaning from passages in which the answers are not explicitly stated but implied with 100 percent accuracy" the vocabulary word would be *inference.* Depending on the age of the students, other vocabulary words would be *implicit* and *explicit.* By focusing on the key concept, the teacher is ensuring that instruction will target the concept of *inference* and teach students *how to infer.*

◆ *Materials:* The lesson plan should specify what materials are necessary to conduct the lesson plan. The teacher needs to account for the resources available and make adaptations accordingly.

◆ *Procedure:* This is the heart of the lesson plan, and this is where the teacher will develop the step-by-step procedure used to teach the objective. The teacher must use learning theory to design a systematic and effective procedure for teaching the objective. The procedure must be closely aligned with the objective so that if the objective specifies that the student will "infer meaning from passages," the teacher must instruct students *how to infer meaning.* It is not enough to talk about what inference means or to demonstrate inference strategies: students must be engaged in learning how to actually infer meaning from passages. The procedure should also be knowledgeable of and incorporate different instructional strategies into the procedure. The different instructional strategies are discussed later in this chapter. The important point is that the objective guides what will be taught in the procedure.

◆ *Evaluation:* The teacher will develop the method of assessing the student on the educational objective. Data must be collected here, and often teachers use checklists, rubrics, and writing samples as their means of assessment. Miscue analyses, running records, and anecdotal records are often excellent sources of data to document oral reading progress of students.

◆ *Follow-up:* This is an optional but helpful component of lesson plans that allows the teacher to specify how the lesson will be reinforced and followed up after it is taught. Often, teachers use homework assignments or extracurricular activities as follow-ups to their lesson.

Sample Literacy Lesson Plan

The following example is a lesson plan for beginning readers (late kindergarten to first grade) that uses all the components listed earlier. In this lesson, the book *The Relatives Came* by Cynthia Rylant (1985) was read to the class the day before for pleasure and meaning. This book tells the story of what happens when many different relatives suddenly descend upon a family for a visit. After the first reading, the class discussed the theme of the book, the author's humorous style of writing, and the different narrative components of the book (character, setting, plot, problem, and resolution). On this second day, the teacher is now rereading the book and providing skill instruction in identifying consonant digraphs. On subsequent days, the teacher will have the students do repeated readings of the book with a partner to increase fluency.

This award-winning book does not have controlled vocabulary. This book could be substituted for a basal series reading book or one with controlled vocabulary used in guided reading sessions, which would benefit students with learning disabilities and English language learners who may need a more controlled text to read.

LESSON PLAN

First Grade Literacy

Objective:
1. Given passages to read from the book *The Relatives Came* by Cynthia Rylant (1985), the student will identify words that include the initial consonant digraphs *sh*, *th*, *ch*, *wh*, and will pronounce each word correctly.
2. Given five sentences to write, the student will use words with digraphs in meaningful sentences related to the story.

Standards Addressed:
California Content Standards English-Language Arts, Grade 1: 1.0 Word Analysis, Fluency, and Systematic Vocabulary Development: Students understand the basic features of reading. They select letter patterns and know how to translate them into spoken language by using phonics, syllabication, and word parts. They apply this knowledge to achieve fluent oral and silent reading.

Vocabulary:
Digraph, meaningful sentences

Materials:
1. 20 copies of the book *The Relative Came* by Cynthia Rylant (1985)
2. A flash card to each consonant digraph: *sh*, *th*, *ch*, *wh*
3. A graphic organizer with four column headings: *sh*, *th*, *ch*, *wh*
4. Lined sheets of paper for the class

Procedure:
1. Begin the lesson by reciting a silly poem, such as *Little Charlie Chipmunk* by Helen Cowles LeCron, which repeats a sound *(ch)* over and over again ("He chattered after breakfast and he chattered after tea").

   Ask the class if they know what sound is constantly repeated at the beginning of the words throughout the poem. Elicit from them the *ch* phoneme and ask them to pronounce words with that sound in it. Now ask them to make that sound in isolation, and elicit from them whether that sound is one phoneme or two. When the class decides that it is one phoneme, show them that it actually has two letters to represent that sound. Tell them there are other words that have sounds like that: *th*, *sh*, and *wh*. Write on the board these digraphs, and under each heading write one word that has the consonant digraph sound in it. Have the class fill in the chart until each digraph has at least five words under it. Read these words aloud to the children and have the students repeat these words chorally (together).

2. Now tell the class to gather in the reading corner and to get ready to read a book. Take out a copy of *The Relatives Came* by Cynthia Rylant (1985). Have an easel ready next to your chair. You will have divided the first sheet on the easel into four columns, and labeled each with one diagraph: *sh*, *th*, *ch*, and *wh*. First, read the story to the class again and have them take mental note of all digraphs they hear in the story. When the story is finished, discuss how it relates to the students' own lives and visits they have had from relatives. Review with the students the author's theme and the different narrative components that they learned the day before. Now model for them how to identify words that have initial digraphs in them. Turn to page 1 of the book and write all words that have a consonant digraph in them under the correct column. Do a think aloud as you go along, demonstrating how you isolate a sound to determine whether it is the correct one. Read those words out loud, and then have the students read those words out loud. When you have finished with page 1, demonstrate how to write a meaningful sentence using one word, again doing a think aloud and making sure that the students understand how it should relate to their own experiences with visiting relatives.

3. As a class, turn to page 2. Ask the students to help you find words that have initial consonant digraphs. Call on students and write their responses under the appropriate column on the easel. Now ask students to pronounce these words. As a class, read the words together. As a class, write down a sentence using at least one of the words.

4. Pair students before they leave the reading corner and give them the graphic organizer. Ask them to turn to pages 3, 4, and 5 of *The Relatives Came* and to write down in the appropriate column of the organizer all the words they find with that sound in it. Have them practice reading those words to each other. Also ask them to create one sentence with at least one of the words they found on each page. Walk around the room to observe and answer any questions. Give help where needed.

   Give the students time to complete this task. When they have finished, discuss some of the words the students found and write them on the easel to continue the list. Ask students to share some of their sentences. Write these on the board as well. As a class, read the new words together.

5. Now ask the students to independently find words that have initial consonant digraphs in them for pages 6 through 10. Ask them to create five sentences using at least one word found on each page. Ask them to continue doing this for homework and to practice reading these words to a family member at home.

6. The next day, have the students write five of these words on flash cards. The teacher will monitor which words the children choose to ensure that they are at the correct level for each child. Collect the worksheets and sentences from each student. Have them practice reading their words to a partner using the flash cards.

7. Summarize the lesson by reviewing what they have just learned. Go over the initial consonant digraphs that the class has just learned. As a class, try to compose a silly poem repeating one of the digraphs throughout the poem.

8. Have the students use the computer to investigate the author Cynthia Rylant (http://www.kidsreads.com/authors/au-rylant-cynthia.asp). Cynthia Rylant grew up in West Virginia in the Appalachian Mountains. The students should find West Virginia on the map and look at some books, pictures, or websites on the Appalachian Mountains.

Evaluation:

Students will hand in their page listing the initial consonant digraphs *sh, th, ch, wh* and the sentences they've completed independently. In addition, each student will be asked to come to the teacher's table and to read the five words on the flash cards. The teacher will record how many of these words the child read correctly. This will be done when the class is involved in independent seat work.

Follow-Up:

Have the class go home and record all the items they see at home that contain an initial consonant digraph. Have the students categorize the words into the correct column on their paper.

Accommodation for Diverse Students:

Struggling readers will spend more time with the teacher practicing the digraphs. They will be given support and guidance in writing down the digraphs. The book *The Relatives Came* will be put on tape so that they can listen to the story, and additional words beginning with the consonant digraphs will also be put on tape.

This lesson demonstrates how all the components of a lesson plan are aligned. The objectives must be focused and specific enough to teach within a time frame. The procedure must teach the behaviors, skills, and content that the objectives specify, and the evaluation plan must collect from each student data on each of the objectives. It is best if the evaluation is not based on group work but is collected from work done independently by each student. In this way, the teacher can be assured that the evaluation measures how the individual student is achieving and performing. In essence, the objectives, procedure, and evaluation must all be aligned to have a valid lesson plan.

If you review the above lesson, you will note that it includes certain elements of good instructional design. The beginning of the lesson, a silly poem, motivated the students and activated prior knowledge of consonant digraphs. During the middle of the lesson, the teacher provided scaffolding by first modeling the task and then supporting the students as they attempted to do the task. Students practiced in groups and independently before assessment occurred. The teacher provided a summary to the lesson, in which she reviewed what occurred and had the students try to apply this new skill to creating their own silly poem.

Creating Units of Study

Curriculum, Units, and Lessons

Beginning teachers often become confused with the terms *lesson, unit,* and *curriculum.* They do not understand how each fits into the daily routine of a classroom and what guidelines they must follow within their districts to teach literacy. An instructional designer looks at instruction as a whole—a continuous sequence of learning outcomes and objectives that are laid out to teach content, processes, and skills. How this instruction is "chunked" will determine the size and terminology that is applied to the instruction. The largest unit of instruction is the **curriculum,** which usually refers to the sequence of topics and objectives laid out for particular subject matter that spans the course of a year. The curriculum could also represent a sequence of topics that spans many years (the social studies or science curriculum in a middle school) or one semester (the curriculum of an introduction to literacy course). A curriculum is often represented in scope and sequence charts, which specify the topics to be studied, and in a matrix, which indicates the topics suggested for each grade level. The next level down in "chunking" instruction is called the **unit,** which usually represents a limited number of goals or outcomes and contains a sequence of objectives that covers a shorter period of time. Units often are called modules, especially within distance learning classes (where this type of instructional organization is becoming quite common). The unit will be taught within a set amount of time and focuses on one broad area within a subject area. Within schools, the unit is often composed of a **lesson.** A lesson contains specific objectives and is usually taught within a 45-minute to one-hour time frame. It is recommended that there be one educational objective per lesson so that the lesson is tightly focused and its objective can be achieved (Gagne, 1977).

Creating a Unit Plan

It is often much easier for a beginning teacher to create a unit plan than a lesson plan. The unit plan encompasses many different lessons and, therefore, usually has a set beginning and end; a unit allows the teacher to place the skills, processes, and content to be taught within a logical sequence and see how the instruction can develop over time. Often, lessons are single entities that are taken out of context of what came before and what will come after; therefore, lessons can be difficult for beginning teachers to design because they have no knowledge of what is to follow or what may have previously occurred. Although units are longer and more complex to design, they are usually easier to conceptualize and plan. There is ample time to develop the instruction and establish the processes and skills required to achieve the objective. Unit plans are usually the best place to teach beginning teachers the process of instructional design.

The process of designing a unit of study in literacy involves the following components:

◆ Choosing a topic
◆ Specifying the target audience
◆ Identifying the prerequisite skills needed before the unit begins
◆ Designing the learning outcomes
◆ Writing the educational objectives
◆ Planning the unit evaluation plan
◆ Developing the individual lesson plans

Each component is an important part of the process, and they all work together to create effective instruction.

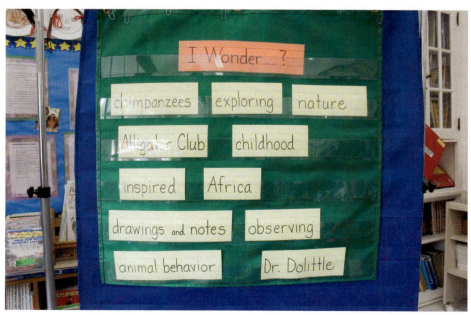

Courtesy of Guilherme Cunha

Teachers often use visual tools to introduce new units.

The first step in designing units is to choose a **topic of study.** The topic of study will usually come from the required sequence of topics to be covered in a particular subject area and the state content standards. However, the topic can also be one that the teacher has an interest in teaching or that students have chosen and will find motivating. The topic could be how to infer meaning of words from context clues in a passage, or it could be the onsets and rimes of particular word families. The topic could be how to write a paragraph with a clear topic sentence and supporting details, or it could be how to use adjectives in sentences. The topics chosen for unit plans will be a logical progression of material that has been covered in literacy throughout the year in a specific grade level. Once the topic is chosen, the teacher must choose the *target audience,* or for whom the unit will be designed. The more specific the target audience is, the more focused the instruction can be on meeting the students' needs. For example, if the target audience is third graders, then the teacher knows the approximate level toward which to gear the instruction. If the audience is second language learners in third grade who have intermediate competency with the English language, then the teacher can be even more specific in designing instruction.

Once the target audience is specified, the teacher will need to think of the prerequisite skills that the students will need before they start this unit. The *prerequisite skills* are those skills, processes, and background knowledge that the student will need to succeed in the unit. For example, if a teacher designs a unit on how to infer meaning from text, the student must be able to comprehend literal details from the text, because inference skills rely heavily on what is implied. Students must already have competency in comprehending stated details before going on to implicit details. Specifying the prerequisite skills is an important step that the teacher must think about so that there is a progression and sequence leading up to the unit of study. This step is an iterative process and will change depending on each of the following steps involved in designing a unit of study. As in the process of design, as one element changes, so must all the others.

The next step is for the teacher to think about the topic and the target audience. What topic will you be focusing on? Who is the unit targeting? The teacher should specify the grade and even the population within the class, if it is targeted for a specific group of students, like ELLs or struggling readers.

The next step is to create learning outcomes for the entire unit plan. Usually a good starting point is to think of what outcomes or end results you want to achieve. Is the unit designed to teach third graders about comprehension strategies? Is the unit designed to teach second language learners how to use clues from the text to obtain meaning? The learning outcome should be broad-based, but not so broad that the outcomes are not achievable within a specified period of time. The outcomes should be observable and measurable and clearly articulate what the students will accomplish at the end of the unit.

Once the learning outcomes have been initially written down, it is time for the teacher to work on developing the educational objectives that will address the learning outcomes. This could mean that the teacher will develop several educational objectives, depending on how broad the outcomes are and how much time is allocated to the unit. The objectives will need to be sequenced according to a hierarchy that the teacher chooses—from simple to complex, from beginning to end, from an introduction to a conclusion. The sequence of the objectives is important because it lays out the order of instruction that will occur and how the outcomes will be met. The sequence should be logical and transparent in that it makes sense as a reasonable way to teach the unit.

Each objective that is developed will eventually become a lesson plan, with perhaps two objectives becoming one lesson. Each objective should be correlated to state content standards. The objectives need to be specific, but not so specific that the lesson can be taught within five minutes. If that occurs, it is time to think in broader terms and to become more general. By the same token, the objectives should not be so broad that it would take weeks to teach the lesson. If that is the case, then that objective needs to be "chunked" into more specific tasks or objectives. It takes time and practice working with objectives so that they focus on the correct level of instruction to accommodate a well-designed lesson plan.

Once the objectives have been specified, it is time to think about developing a **unit evaluation plan.** The unit itself will need to be evaluated; that is, every student who completes the unit will need to be assessed on whether he or she achieved the learning outcomes and educational objectives that the unit includes. This is can be done through a portfolio, where work from each lesson is collected and documented to show achievement. It can also be done via a rubric, which would assess final competencies or educational objectives that the student must achieve on completion of the unit.

The last component of designing a unit plan is working on the individual lesson plans within the unit. As mentioned earlier, the objectives for each lesson should be specified as one of the first steps. The teacher must then take each objective and follow a systematic procedure to ensure that the lesson plan incorporates principles of instructional design, is valid, and meets the needs of the students. The teacher must put all these components together into an effective unit plan.

Sample Literacy Unit Plan

The following unit plan starts out with a specification of the target audience, the prerequisite skills, the learning outcomes, the standards addressed, the objectives, and the evaluation plan. This unit plan has four lesson plans that match the four objectives listed in the unit plan. Teachers may elect to develop more objectives for a lesson. Because the standards are addressed in the overall unit plan, they are not listed in each individual lesson below. However, teachers may want to specify exactly which standards each lesson is addressing.

UNIT PLAN

Target Audience:
Fifth grade students of mixed ability levels

Prerequisite Skills:
1. Students are able to read at grade level.
2. Students have worked with Venn diagrams and can identify similarities and differences.
3. Students can analyze a story by its setting, characters, problem, resolution, and theme.

Learning Outcome:
The student will learn about an author's perspective and how there can be more than one perspective in a story. The student will read two different versions of *The Three Little Pigs* and learn how to carefully consider the perspective being taken before making a judgment about something or someone.

Standards Addressed:
New York English Language Arts Reading Standard 3: Identify different perspectives, such as social, cultural, ethnic, and historical, on an issue presented in one or more than one text.

Objectives:
1. Given a graphic organizer with two columns with headings labeled "Main Characters" and "Important Events," the student will identify the main characters and the important events that took place in the traditional story of *The Three Little Pigs*.
2. Given a Compare/Contrast Thinking Process Map to complete, the student will compare and contrast the traditional story of *The Three Little Pigs* with *The True Story of the Three Little Pigs* by John Scieszka (1989).

3. Given a graphic organizer to complete, the student will analyze both sides of the opposing characters' views, decide who is guilty by giving evidence, and debate the topics.

4. Given a story to write, the student will choose a fairy tale and write an opposing character's view on the story, identifying the different characters and events that took place through his or her viewpoint.

Evaluation:

The student will be evaluated on a rubric provided for each lesson and a portfolio that the student must keep on each lesson's assignment. A unit evaluation matrix will also be kept to track individual progress in the unit.

LESSON PLAN 1

Objective:

Given a graphic organizer with two columns labeled "Main Characters" and "Important Events," the student will identify the main characters and the important events that took place in the traditional story of *The Three Little Pigs*.

Standards Addressed:

New York English Language Arts Reading Standard 2: Identify literary elements, such as setting, plot, and character, of different genres

Vocabulary:

Main characters, important events, summarize

Materials:

1. One big book of *Little Red Riding Hood* (there are many versions, but the one by Trina Shart Hyman is for slightly older students)

2. Easel with a marker

3. Copies of *The Three Little Pigs* (there are many versions on the market, but one that is current and humorous is by Steven Kellogg)

4. Crafts and materials from the art center

Procedure:

1. The students will gather around the big easel and sit comfortably on their carpet rugs waiting to begin. Start by asking the students what their favorite movie or cartoon is. After getting a few responses, choose one and ask the class who the main characters were in that movie. Write their responses, and then ask them what a main character is. Write their answers on the easel, and then ask them what they think an *important event* is. Discuss what the important events were in the movie. Write down all examples they give. Prompt the class to distinguish between *events* and *important events*. Then try to derive a class definition of the two vocabulary words: *main characters* and *important events*. Write these clearly on the easel.

2. Next, read aloud to the students a brief version of *Little Red Riding Hood* (or another familiar short story). Make two columns on the easel: "Main Characters" and "Important Events." First, go back through the book and model to the students how to pick out the characters that are important and play a significant role in the story. Do a think aloud when identifying the two main characters: Little Red Riding Hood and the wolf. Then ask the class if they

think the hunter is a main character; have them explain why or not. Write these characters under the heading "Main Characters."

3. Model for the students how to determine whether an event is important, and thus affects the story, by doing a "think aloud." Show them how you might think an event is important, but after thinking about it you cross if off your list because you feel it is not as significant as other events might be. Write at least two important events on the easel under the heading "Important Events." Have the students come up with other important events so that there is a sequence of events that tell the story. Then have the class determine which events were the most important and which events can be eliminated.

4. Now review the definition of what a main character is and what important events are. Go to the easel and review the main characters and important events of *Little Red Riding Hood*. Then ask if there are any questions about what the students have learned and answer any questions.

5. Tell the students that they will now be doing a similar task on a story they already know, *The Three Little Pigs*. Tell them that today they will analyze this traditional version of the story, but that tomorrow they will read a different version of this same story and compare the two, so they should pay attention to details.

6. Send the students back to their desks and give each of them a copy of *The Three Little Pigs*. Have them do a pair-share, reading this book aloud to each other.

7. When they complete the book, put them into groups of three to four students. Have them discuss what the main characters and important events are from the story they just read. Have the students list the main characters and events under the headings "Main Characters" and "Important Events." Walk around and give guidance and support where needed.

8. The students will then split up from their groups and go back to their desks to work independently. Give the students a graphic organizer with the same headings on it, "Main Characters" and "Important Events." Tell the students that they are to identify the main characters and important events from *The Three Little Pigs*. The teacher will work with any diverse learners who need extra support and guidance.

9. Collect the graphic organizers when the students have completed them. Then ask the students what the main characters and the important events in the story were. Write these down for future reference. Discuss their responses and focus on why events might be important and why some events are not considered important.

10. Tell them what they have just learned how to do by identifying important events in the correct sequence is to *summarize*. Give the definition of summarize and tell them that a summary is a short, concise retelling of the important events of a story. They all might have heard this word before and thought that they knew what it meant, but now they actually know how to summarize important events in a story. Review the lesson and point out that they will continue using these strategies in tomorrow's lesson. Tell them that when they go home tonight and watch television or read a book, they are to make note of the main characters and important events.

Evaluation:

The graphic organizer will be handed in and the student will get a plus (great), check (satisfactory), or a minus (needs improvement). The student will be assessed on the completeness and correctness of all main characters and events.

This instructional unit shows how a unit plan focuses on one theme, topic, author, or book. The four objectives of the unit plan become the individual objectives in each lesson plan. Each lesson plan needs to be evaluated, and the unit, as a whole, should also be evaluated using a matrix, portfolio, or rubric. Each lesson must build on the instructional components taught in the previous lesson, and concepts and skills must be reviewed and reinforced from one day to the next. Each lesson needs an anticipatory set, or beginning; a middle where the actual objective is being taught; and an end where the teacher summarizes, makes connections to the students' lives and to other subject areas, and pulls the total lesson together for the students.

Teachers' VOICES   "From Seed to Plant": A Unit For Primary Grades

A science unit that I use in my first/second grade classroom is "From Seed to Plant." I developed this unit to show students the process that occurs as a seed develops into a plant. Within this unit, students study varieties of seeds and plants and their uses. The children plant many seeds in the classroom and in an outside garden, make observations about plant growth, determine the needs of plants, and take field trips to a local greenhouse and to the New York Botanical Gardens.

At the beginning of the unit, the class studies varieties of seeds. Students examine seeds and try to determine the plants that will grow from these seeds. The unit progresses to the growth of a plant, and the class learns the parts of a plant by examining real plants and by making diagrams of plants. Eventually, the unit moves into specific plants and flowers that grow from seeds. The students examine different varieties of plants and determine several uses of plants. The children always love the lessons about the plants we eat!

This unit touches on many different academic areas, but I enjoy teaching it because it helps students become aware of the environment they are in and brings the cyclical aspect of nature to their attention. Throughout this unit, the students are observing and assessing the growth process from seed to plant, and they are engaged in daily hands-on activities. By the end of the unit, they are applying their knowledge to new situations and activities at the Botanical Gardens. At the Gardens, the children are given field notebooks to record specific data, and they are asked to find specific varieties of plants and seeds in the conservatory. At the end of the unit, I expect that the students will be able to name the various parts of a plant, to describe the transformation from seed to plant, to describe the various needs and uses of plants, and to gain a better understanding of the world around them.

—*Zaneta Shannon, Special Education Teacher*

Models of Instruction for Literacy

When designing instruction, a beginning teacher not only needs to know the different components of a unit plan and how a lesson plan is formatted, but how to design instruction that will be aligned with the objective. The educational objective is the road map that the teacher will follow when planning the lesson. The teacher also needs to think about how to get there; that is, what type of instruction is best suited to teach this objective. This falls under the domain of the "procedure" when designing the lesson— What is the best instructional model to use in the procedure for this objective? Teachers can make many different choices at this time when planning out the procedure. A frequently used model is to stand in front of the room and do **direct teaching,** or lecture the class about the content and then have a question-and-answer session or a discussion about the topic afterward. Direct instruction is a valuable tool that all teachers use, but it is not the only choice available. A teacher needs to know many different **models of instruction** that can be applied during the course of the day and use those that are specifically suited to the educational objectives being taught. The instructional models listed below are based on research in the field of literacy and are seen in the practices of the best teachers in literacy classrooms throughout the country. By using these practices, teachers will become more effective literacy teachers, thus helping improve children's reading and writing skills.

Scaffolded Reading Approach

The concept of scaffolding is at the center of the Scaffolded Reading Approach: the teacher provides a temporary supportive structure that enables the student to successfully complete a task that he or she would not be able to complete without this guidance and help (Graves & Graves, 1994). This approach is a gradual process in which the teacher starts out assuming most of the responsibility of the reading task and slowly removes the support provided until the student can accomplish the task with some help from the teacher. In the final stage, the student will be able to do the task independently with little or no support from the teacher. This process is recursive throughout students' schooling, in that once students achieve independence in a task, they should go on to a more difficult task that requires more support and scaffolding from the teacher. The teacher will start to remove the scaffolding and support provided and again the students will strive for independence. This type of scaffolding can be seen in the balanced classroom, where the teacher starts out reading a book aloud to a class (the teacher assumes total responsibility for reading), then has the class do shared reading (he or she assumes partial responsibility for reading), progressing to pair-share reading and guided reading (he or she removes even more support) to having the student read the book independently (all support is removed). The teacher would then move on to a bit more difficult book and follow the same progression.

A Scaffolded Reading Approach is a model in which the teacher provides prereading, during-reading, and postreading activities designed to assist a particular group of students in successfully reading, understanding, and enjoying text (Graves & Graves, 1994). It is a flexible model in that it provides a framework within which to operate and allows the teacher to choose strategies that are best suited for the group of students reading a particular text who have specific needs.

Prereading Activities

Prereading activities are those strategies and activities that prepare students to read the text. Some of these strategies are initiated by the teacher and others are done by the student. Prereading activities that the *teacher* should initiate include:

◆ *Motivating activities* are those activities that the teacher provides that will interest students to read the upcoming selection. These activities should incite enthusiasm and create a motivation for the students to find out more. Such activities usually involve hands-on experiences, drama, and active student participation.

◆ *Relating the reading to students' lives* is when the teacher shows how the upcoming text relates directly to experiences the students have had. An example of this is illustrated in the earlier lesson plan on *The Relatives Came* by Cynthia Rylant (1985). The teacher could hold a discussion about funny times the students have had when relatives came for a visit.

Good scaffolding results in successful, independent reading.

Courtesy of Guilherme Cunha

The teacher could ask the students to write about one visit, talk about this experience in a class discussion, or illustrate a visit. The important point is that the children see a direct connection between the upcoming text that is to be read and their own personal experiences.

- *Activating background knowledge* is when the teacher provides prompts and activities that will help the children use prior knowledge they may have on the passage to be read and use that prior knowledge while reading the passage. One way a teacher may activate prior knowledge before the text is read is through brainstorming sessions on the topic; the teacher asks the class to think of and discuss everything they know about a particular topic related to the upcoming reading and records the responses on an easel.

- Through *building knowledge about the topic,* the teacher provides the students with pertinent information about the topic of the reading. Often, students may not know anything at all about the topic on which they are about to read. It is important that the teacher provide background information so that the students can grasp and understand the material and place it within the context of previous information they learned. The teacher can build knowledge by showing the students a film or video on the topic, by taking them on a field trip, by showing them pictures of the topic, by showing them maps and graphs that relate to the topic, by providing informational books on the topic, and by bringing in guest speakers. All these activities are important prereading steps before the text is read.

- *Preteaching vocabulary and concepts* is when the teacher goes over important vocabulary words and concepts that will help the students comprehend the material. This can be done in a manner that is motivating to the students, such as playing Word Bingo or using flash cards to play games such as Old Maid and Concentration. Working with crossword puzzles and word games is another way to preteach vocabulary.

- *Prequestioning:* The teacher guides the students in asking questions about the upcoming reading assignment. Students should eventually be asking their own questions before they begin reading; as a precursor to this, the teacher can guide the students in helping them formulate their own questions.

- *Predicting:* The teacher guides the students in formulating predictions about the upcoming reading. Prediction is one of the most important strategies that students must engage in before they begin reading, and as a prereading strategy, the teacher can design activities that teach the students how to predict and verify whether the predictions were on target.

By designing lessons that have these prereading strategies, a teacher is ensuring that the student is provided with the necessary scaffolding needed to comprehend the material. The teacher is building support into the lesson by ensuring that appropriate prereading strategies will be provided to help the student read the material more effectively and with greater understanding.

During-Reading Activities

During-reading activities are those strategies that the student is engaged in while reading material. These activities help the student interact with the text and obtain information from the reading. If you recall, reading is an interactive process involving the reader, the author of the material, and the text. During-reading activities engage the student in strategies that would clarify meanings of the text the student is reading and help clarify the author's intent.

Some during-reading strategies that the *reader* should apply during the reading process are:

- **Predicting:** The reader must pause while reading the text and think about what will happen next. At this time, the reader asks questions concerning the text, formulates conclusions as to what has occurred to date, and posits hypotheses as to what will happen next. During this process, the reader needs to go back to initial predictions and either confirm or refute them, and then make new predictions based on this assessment. Comprehension is an ongoing during-reading process that is based on continuously revising predictions as new and pertinent information is gathered and then positing new hypotheses as to what will happen next.

◆ *Self-questioning:* The reader pauses, thinks a bit about what has been read, answers questions initially posed, and then asks more questions. This strategy is similar to prediction because it is a continuous process of asking questions, thinking about the answers, and asking new questions as the text continues. After reading, the reader must consider whether the questions have been answered. Immature readers usually want all questions answered on completion of the text; however, more mature readers often prefer to have some questions left unanswered and enjoy books that make them question further.

◆ *Self-monitoring:* The reader actively thinks about text information and controls his or her reading behavior. Monitoring strategies allow the reader to sort through complex material effectively, tracking whether full comprehension is occurring. If it is not, monitoring strategies direct the reader to go back a paragraph, a section, or even to the beginning to start over. An effective reader does this all the time, but poorer readers do not do any self-regulation of their reading habits and do not stop to consider whether they have obtained full meaning of the text.

◆ *Searching for clues:* The reader actively searches for clues throughout the text to unlock meaning. The clues could be in the pictures (picture clues), in the surrounding textual passage (semantic clues), in the grammar or structure of the sentence (syntactical clues), or in the phonic patterns recognized in a particular word (graphophonic clues). This is an active process that must occur during reading to help the reader unlock meaning.

◆ *Inferring meaning:* The reader uses the context of the sentence or passage to unlock the meaning of a word, phrase, or sentence. This strategy allows the reader to identify clues in the passage and hypothesize what an unknown word is without stopping during the reading process, and thereby interfering with fluency and losing meaning.

◆ *Making connections:* Readers make a connection with what they are reading to their own lives (text-to-self), to other texts they have read (text-to-text), and to the outside world (text-to-world). Students can use sticky notes to mark locations in the book where they have made such connections while they are reading, and then after they read they can fill in a graphic organizer or discuss their connections with the class.

Postreading Activities

Postreading activities encourage students to do something with the material they have just read, thereby thinking critically about their readings (Graves & Graves, 1994). Postreading strategies ask students to respond to what has been read, and that response can take a variety of forms. During this response, the students must apply, analyze, synthesize, evaluate, and elaborate the information and ideas from the text and connect that information to their own lives. The response should require the students to use higher order thinking skills on Bloom's Taxonomy.

Some postreading activities that the *teacher* should engage students in are:

◆ *Discussion:* The class or a small group discusses the readings and elaborates on many of the text's features to support comprehension.

◆ *Writing:* The reader responds to the text through a written response. This could be in a journal, as a creative writing piece, as a letter, or as a formal book report.

◆ *Drama:* The reader responds to the text through acting out roles of characters from the text. Children often find this a fun and motivating way to respond to the text, and it further helps them understand the more subtle points of the reading. Readers Theatre Workshop is an excellent way for children to respond to text without having to memorize lines as they read a prepared script.

◆ *Hands-on projects:* Hands-on projects are fun and motivating ways for children to respond to text as a postreading activity. This could involve arts and crafts projects, computer projects such as PowerPoint presentations or developing a picture, and collaborative research projects.

Some postreading strategies that the *reader* should apply after completing a text are:

- ◆ ***Drawing conclusions:*** The reader synthesizes the information from the text into a conclusion. Teachers can teach this strategy by purposely choosing books that have significant conclusions to be drawn. The teacher can help students learn this strategy through "think alouds" whereby the teacher models the process, through class discussion, and through guided questions.
- ◆ ***Summarizing:*** The reader identifies the important points in a text and condenses them into a few sentences. Teachers need to work on this strategy throughout the primary years, not only as a postreading strategy but as an ongoing process during reading.
- ◆ ***Making connections:*** The reader can discuss any connections (text-to-text, text-to-self, and text-to-world) made during reading by going back and looking at the student's notes that designate where the connection in the text was made and discussing this with the class. The student can also write about these connections as a postreading strategy by filling in a graphic organizer.

The Scaffolded Reading Approach model gives flexible guidelines to a teacher for developing a coherent lesson plan based on three phases of the lesson: what occurs before the reading takes place (prereading), what takes place while the reading is occurring (during-reading), and what happens once the reading is completed to reinforce and develop deeper comprehension (postreading).

Example: Scaffolded Reading Approach Lesson Plan

The following lesson plan is based on the book *Sophie* by Mem Fox (1994), the story of a little girl who loves her grandpa and her grandpa loves Sophie. The lesson is designed for a kindergarten or first grade classroom.

Objective:
Given a prediction strategies organizer, the student will predict what the book is about after taking a picture walk through part of the book.

Standards Addressed:
Massachusetts General Standard 8: Students will identify the basic facts and main ideas in a text and use them as the basis for interpretation. (8.1 Make predictions using prior knowledge, pictures, and text)

Vocabulary:
Predict

Materials:
1. A copy of the book *Sophie* by Mem Fox (1994)
2. A box wrapped as a gift
3. Copies of the Prediction Strategies Organizer

Procedure:
Before Reading
1. With the students in their seats, begin by asking if they have ever watched a show or a movie and halfway through figured out how it would end. Discuss their answers. Further elaborate by asking if anyone thought that Nemo in *Finding Nemo* would end up finding his father. Discuss why they thought this and what clues they gathered to guess this ending.

2. Explain that what they were doing is something called "predicting," and write the word "Predict" on the board. Ask students to share their ideas about what this word means, where they might have heard this word before (the weatherman?), and how they might use the word in their own lives. Activate prior knowledge they may have of this word and construct a web on the board of their responses around the word *predict*.

3. Give another example of prediction by showing the class a box that is wrapped as a gift with a big bow on it. Explain to the students that you can predict or guess what would be in the box using clues, such as the size of the box, its weight, and what it feels and sounds like when you shake it a bit. Show the students how you would predict what is in the box. Write a list of words on the board under the label "Clues." Now, under a column labeled "Prediction," write the students' predictions as to what might be in the box. Now open the box and see what is inside. Discuss their responses and why they were accurate or off target.

4. Tell the students that, much like the wrapped box, they can predict what a book might be about by searching for clues in the pictures, in the title, or even in the author's name if they are familiar with other books that he or she has written. Now ask the students to go quietly to the reading corner so the class can read a book together.

5. When they are sitting quietly in the reading corner and you are in your chair, introduce the book *Sophie* by Mem Fox (1994). Explain to the students that you would like them to predict what this book is about using clues found on the cover and in a brief picture walk of the first few pages. Pass out the Prediction Strategies Organizer and point out that this organizer is written on the easel next to you. Go over the two columns, "Clues" and "Predictions," and explain this is exactly what you wrote on the board when the class made their predictions about the wrapped box. Explain that, as a class, you will do this organizer together today, but from then on students will use this organizer to help them make predictions before they read a new book.

6. Ask the students if they have read any books by Mem Fox before. Remind them of the book by her you read a short while ago. Now take the class through a picture walk of the cover, title page, and first few pages of the book and have them write down all the clues they find that they think will tell them what this book is about. Write the clues down under the column "Clues." After all the clues are gathered, have the class come up with a few predictions that they think the book will be about. Write these down under the column "Predictions." Before beginning the actual reading, discuss what it is like to have grandparents: "Does anyone have a grandpa? Can you describe him to us?" Let a few children share their experiences.

During Reading

7. Now read the book aloud to the class expressively and fluently. While you are reading, pause at certain times and model how to ask questions about what might occur next. Do a think aloud at one point about whether you understand what is happening (self-monitoring). Show how you can go back to find meaning by rereading.

After Reading

8. Discuss the book with the class. Relate the book to the students' lives and allow a few students to discuss similar experiences they may have had with their grandparents.

9. Now go back to the original predictions and discuss whether they were accurate and why that might be so. If one prediction is a bit off, discuss why. Explain that there is no "right" or "wrong" prediction, but rather that accurate predictions are based on examining important clues, which can help in understanding the book.

10. Have the children go back to their seats and draw a picture of a grandparent or a relative or friend. Have them write one sentence using invented spelling to explain their drawing.

11. Have the students go to Mem Fox's web page (http://www.memfox.com) to learn more about Mem Fox. Have them explore other books written by Mem Fox. As a class, compose a message to Mem Fox that you can enter in her "Guestbook" page. Have students choose another book by Mem Fox to read. If there are too many choices, vote on the two books the class would like to read next during shared literacy.

Evaluation:

A record will be made of the students' predictions from what is written on the easel. The teacher will write down observations of students' ability to predict accurately. The drawings that the students complete will be handed in.

In examining this lesson, you can see that it is divided into three sections: before, during, and after reading. In each section, the teacher designs activities that support strategies that will help readers comprehend the text. In the prereading phase, the teacher was activating prior knowledge of the word *prediction*, relating the word to students' own lives, motivating an interest in the strategy through the use of a wrapped present in a box, preteaching the concept "prediction," and giving direct instruction in this important prereading strategy. The teacher also activated prior knowledge about the topic of the story—Sophie's relationship with her grandpa— and had students relate this to their own experiences. If you notice, the prereading phase is the longest of the three phases, which is quite different from how many beginning teachers conceptualize a reading lesson. They tend to think that once the class is called to the reading center, reading the book and following up on it afterward is the predominant part of the lesson. In a good reading lesson, much time is taken before the book is read to develop the prereading activities so children will better comprehend the text.

In the during-reading phase, the teacher read aloud and modeled expressive, fluent reading to the class. The teacher modeled how to do self-questioning by pausing at key points to pose questions. The teacher also modeled how to self-monitor reading both key during-reading strategies readers must use to effectively comprehend text while reading.

In the postreading phase, the teacher discussed the book with the class and had the students again relate the book's theme to their own lives. The students then went back to their original predictions to either confirm or refute them. Lastly, the students did an arts and crafts project to reinforce the author's theme and help the students relate it to their own previous experiences, and they visited Mem Fox's web page.

All three phases are an integral part of the reading process, in which the teacher must provide a level of scaffolding for the readers to fully comprehend the material. As students become more adept at these strategies, the amount of support can be reduced slowly so that students are independently using these strategies.

Teachers' VOICES   Scaffolding to Support Diverse Student Learning

I feel that scaffolding should be used in daily lessons in all classrooms for all children including struggling readers, writers, students with learning disabilities (LD), and English language learners (ELLs). No two children in a classroom are at the exact same level in each skill being taught; therefore, teachers must know how to scaffold the instruction and activity for each student to learn at his or her individual level of proximal development. This is also where differentiated instruction can come into play. Furthermore, it is imperative, especially for the struggling readers, writers, students with LD, and ELLs, that students not to reach their frustration level or become discouraged. Our job is not merely to teach content and skills. I believe that a huge part of our job is to build self-esteem, repair egos, and inspire and motivate our students. Scaffolding allows us to do this. It helps students who need additional support in the form of graphic organizers, visual tools, selecting appropriate level texts, and in other ways. I have had to truly think about how my lessons and activities can be scaffolded so that I reach each student in my diverse classroom.

—*Heather Bruno, Seventh Grade Teacher*

Model of Direct Instruction

Direct instruction involves having the teacher directly teach the skills, strategies, and knowledge to the class through a teacher-directed approach. Usually, the teacher stands in front of the class and directs the students to listen and follow along as the lesson proceeds, with students raising their hands if they have questions or interaction. This is a much more traditional approach to teaching that often includes "lectures" but can also include teacher demonstrations, teacher-directed discussion, and question-and-answer periods. Direct instruction should be used to:

- Introduce lessons
- Preteach concepts and vocabulary
- Demonstrate and model how skills and strategies should be used
- Reinforce concepts and main points of a lesson
- Summarize key points of a lesson and bring closure

The **Model of Direct Instruction** is a teacher-directed model that ensures that students receive the scaffolding they need while learning new skills and strategies. It is based on the teacher applying the following five steps:

1. *The teacher introduces the skill or strategy.* In this step, the teacher introduces what the skill will be about, talks about why it is important in the reading process, and relates it to the students' prior knowledge about reading. An example of this would be when the teacher introduces the concept of word families and talks about how word families share the same phonetic pattern or rime and how changing the beginning letter or onset makes this into a new word with the same phonetic pattern (*goat, boat,* and *coat* are all part of the same word family).

2. *The teacher models the skill or strategy.* At this time, the teacher models how to apply the skill or strategy. This can be done through actually demonstrating how the strategy is applied in the reading process or through think alouds, whereby the teacher verbally explains how the strategy would work while reading a passage. An example of the teacher modeling the skill of applying new onsets to rimes would be a teacher showing students on an easel or board how to change a rime into a new word by applying new onsets (the rime *oat* can become a different word by placing a *c* for *coat,* a *b* for *boat,* or a *g* for *goat* onto the rime).

3. *The teacher provides guided practice for the students.* At this step, the teacher will provide the students with a practice exercise that replicates the skill that the teacher just modeled. The students will practice the skill with the teacher providing guidance, help, and support. The students will receive feedback on their performance and will be given the chance to continue practicing under the guidance of the teacher, if necessary. For example, the teacher could divide the class into groups, give each group one word family, and ask them to apply different initial letters and see how many words they could generate within that word family. Each student would be asked to read each word generated to the group and then to the teacher.

4. *The teacher provides independent practice for the students.* The students would now be provided with the opportunity of trying out the strategy or skill on their own. The teacher would remove the support provided in the previous step to ensure that students can do the skill/strategy independently. For example, students might be given a familiar word family for homework and be asked to generate as many new words for the word family as possible. The students would be required to read each word to the teacher the next day.

5. *The teacher evaluates the student on the skill or strategy.* The student will be "formally" assessed on the skill or strategy. For example, after the student practices the skill twice, once with a group providing support and feedback and another time independently, the teacher may choose to evaluate the student on this skill and give a formal "grade." Usually in the classroom, informal assessment occurs with step 4, when the student does the skill independently, often as homework or as an in-class assignment. The teacher may elect to formally assess the student after independent practice by administering a running record, test, or quiz.

In this instructional model, the teacher assures that the skill or strategy is being taught properly, and that the students are receiving the necessary scaffolding to support their application of the skill: first, with the teacher modeling how the strategy is applied, and then by providing the necessary practice for the student to apply the skill or strategy in both guided and independent contexts. Only after the student has seen the skill demonstrated, and practiced it twice in different situations, does the teacher evaluate the student on the skill. This is quite different from the situation in which the skill is introduced and the student immediately practices it independently, a scenario often seen in classrooms. The Model of Direct Instruction is an excellent model for beginning teachers to practice and become familiar with as part of lesson planning and implementation in a balanced literacy classroom where there is a balance of authentic reading and writing with purposeful word study, including phonemic awareness, phonics, and vocabulary development.

Direct instruction is effective for teaching students skills, strategies, and concepts.

Courtesy of Guilherme Cunha

Notably, the Model of Direct Instruction can become embedded within a lesson using a different instructional approach, such as the scaffolded reading approach model discussed earlier. The Model of Direct Instruction can be a short part of a total lesson, focusing on the prereading introduction of a reading strategy or part of the postreading phase where a skill is reinforced. In fact, teachers should be using many different instructional approaches throughout the day, making instruction interesting and flexible, while also attending to the different learning styles of the students in the class.

Example: Model of Direct Instruction Lesson Plan

The following lesson plan is based on the book *Auction!* by Tres Seymour (2005), the story of a family who goes to an auction and how one little girl learns to bid for an item she really wants. The lesson is designed for a second or third grade classroom. It can either be implemented using an easel or a computer that has Inspiration software loaded on it and displayed on a projector.

Objective:

Given a Venn diagram to fill in, the student will compare and contrast a trip to a flea market or store that he went on with his family and the trip to the auction that took place in the book.

Standards Addressed:

Arizona Comprehending Literary Text: PO 1. Compare (and contrast) literary elements across stories, including plots, settings, and characters.

Vocabulary:

Compare, contrast, Venn diagram

Materials:

1. A copy of the book *Auction!* by Tres Seymour (2005)
2. Copies of the Venn diagram, enough for students to fill in twice, *or*
3. A Venn diagram template from the Inspiration software program projected from a computer onto a screen

Procedure:

1. Ask the students if they have a favorite baseball (or basketball, hockey, etc.) team. Ask them to describe characteristics of that team that they like. Now ask them to describe a team that competes against their favorite team. Ask them to describe this other team. Explain to the students that what they just did was to compare and contrast these two teams. Write the two words, "Compare" and "Contrast" on an easel or type them onto the computer so they are displayed in large letters. Brainstorm with the class what each word means and write the definitions under each word.

2. *Skill Introduction:* Next to the words "Compare" and "Contrast," draw on the board or using Inspiration create a Venn diagram and explain that this is a tool that will help them compare and contrast. Label one side of the diagram "tennis ball" and other side "soccer ball." Show the students a tennis ball and a soccer ball and ask them what these items are. Walk around the room with the balls and have the students carefully inspect the balls. Ask the students how these two balls are alike. Prompt them with criteria such as size, shape, colors, and how they are used. Write their responses in the intersection between the two circles. Now ask the students how these two balls are different. Write their responses in the two outer circles, one stating the differences for the tennis ball and the other stating the differences for the soccer ball. Again, be sure to organize the responses by criteria such as size, shape, sport, and color.

3. Explain to the students that what they just did was to compare and contrast two balls. Go over the definitions of these words again. Discuss the Venn diagram and how it is used and point out how the labels are important to help organize the students' thoughts.

4. *Modeling:* Draw another Venn diagram on the board or use Inspiration to show the template of a Venn diagram. Explain that you can also compare events as well

as objects. Tell a brief story to the class about how a friend celebrated a birthday party this past weekend. Now doing a think aloud, model how to use the Venn diagram to compare and contrast how you celebrate your birthday with how your friend celebrated his birthday. Show how you will start out by labeling the different sections of the circles: the midpoint will be "The Same," the left circle will be "My Birthday," and the right circle will be "My Friend's Birthday." Point out how you like to start with the events that are similar and write these in the midpoint labeled "The Same." Explain out loud how you use certain criteria to organize your thoughts, such as *time the party happened*, *the order of events*, *who attended*, and *the type of cake you like*. Then go on to the differences and explain how you will write these in two separate circles, one labeled "My Birthday" and the other labeled "My Friend's Birthday." Talk about how you organize your thoughts using the same criteria as before, and write down these differences. When you are through, continue thinking aloud about whether the Venn diagram looks complete and how you self-check to make sure that it says what you want it to say. Now discuss this process with the class to see whether they understand. Answer their questions.

5. *Guided Practice:* Place the students in groups of two. Pass out a Venn diagram worksheet to each student (or have them work from an Inspiration template that is provided with the program) and ask the students to compare and contrast their birthday parties with your friend's party. Have each student work on an individual worksheet receiving help, support, and feedback from their partner. Walk around the room to help set up the Venn diagram and answer any questions. When the students have finished, discuss their responses and collect their worksheets (or check their screens). Have a few students come up and write their responses on the easel or show their work to the class.

6. Now tell the students you are going to read *Auction!* They should help you read certain sections together. Tell them that when you are finished they will be comparing and contrasting a trip to a flea market or store with the trip to an auction that takes place in the book. They should keep this in mind and note details they can use as they read along.

7. *Independent Practice:* After reading *Auction!* again, pass out another Venn diagram to each student. Ask the students to complete them independently and hand them in for homework if they cannot finish them in class. Remind them to label the circles first, point out where to write the similarities and differences, and tell them to organize their thoughts carefully before writing.

8. Summarize the lesson by reviewing the process of comparing and contrasting and discussing how a Venn diagram is a helpful tool in this process. Tell them that knowing how to compare and contrast will help them in their literacy skills of both reading and writing. Ask the students what they might compare and contrast in their own daily lives and have them volunteer examples of this. Have the students go onto the computer and using a kids search engine such as Ask Jeeves for Kids (http://www.ajkids.com/) or KidsClick! (http://www.kidsclick.org/), have them do a search using the term "auction." Have the students come in with examples of what can be sold at different auctions and what they might want to buy at one.

Evaluation:

The Venn diagram that was handed in for homework will be collected and used to assess whether the student is able to compare and contrast a visit to a flea market or store with a trip to an auction in the book. If needed, reteaching will occur for those students who do not achieve this objective.

Follow-Up:

The students will draw a poster of items they saw at a flea market or store with approximate cost of each item.

In examining the above lesson, you can see that it follows a systematic, step-by-step approach to teaching the strategy of comparing and contrasting. All the steps of the Model of Direct Instruction are followed precisely. An important part of the lesson is that the teacher models the strategy by doing a think aloud. In this way, the students can see how the strategy is applied and actually listen to the teacher going through the thought process that an expert goes through while completing the task. This is an invaluable aid in teaching children effective literacy strategies. In addition, the lesson takes the students through a sequence of steps that goes from comparing and contrasting concrete examples (two types of balls) to more abstract examples of events (giving a birthday party). The modeling is done on a similar or parallel type of task; that is, the students will be asked to compare events in a book with events in their own lives. Modeling two concrete examples such as types of balls would not have been enough for many students to make the "jump" from the more concrete to the more abstract without the scaffolding provided by the teacher's modeling lesson. Second language learners and children with learning disabilities benefit from a careful and systematic sequence of instruction, where every step in the learning process is covered and where the teacher models the strategy or skill in as close a form to the required task as possible. This scaffolding provides the necessary background for them to go on and try the task in a guided situation without the fear of immediate failure.

Notably, in the above lesson, there is a clear opening that activates prior knowledge about the upcoming task and relates the lesson to the students' own lives. The opening should be motivating, interesting, and tap into students' background knowledge. Brainstorming is an excellent way to determine how much a class knows about a particular concept. By writing the key concept in a circle and then webbing outward with students' responses, the class and teacher build a web of what is known about a topic or concept. Students love to see their own ideas being written down; therefore, the brainstorming activity is highly motivating for students while activating prior knowledge.

In looking at the above lesson, there is also a clear closing that summarizes key points and again relates the lesson to the students' lives. It is important for students to constantly see how the lesson is meaningful to them and how it is closely connected to other subjects and daily routines. Students need to see relevance in what they learn and see how they can apply literacy skills to everyday life. The teacher should always try to make connections—to other subjects, to students' lives, and to other concepts learned in previous lessons.

All these components—a clear opening, following a systematic model of instruction, and a concise closure to the lesson—combine together to make a coherent and valid lesson plan. The Model of Direct Instruction is an excellent model for teaching skills, strategies, and processes. It provides the scaffolding needed for students who are just learning about the skill, helping them to achieve independence and mastery as the underlying support of the teacher is slowly removed.

Constructivist or Inquiry Approach to Literacy Instruction

The **constructivist approach** claims that each learner must actively construct meaning for himself or herself—that learning is based on the individual's background knowledge, experiences, and previous conceptualizations. Many renowned educational theorists have been strong advocates for constructivism in education and have written about the need for the learner to construct his or her own meaning, and not just to memorize the "right" answers and recite someone else's answer (Bruner, 1960, 1966; Jonassen, 1991; Piaget, 1970; vonGlaserfeld, 1989; Vygotsky, 1962). In the classroom, the constructivist approach usually means encouraging students to use active techniques such as experiments, real-world problem solving, and research-based inquiry projects: these help students create their own knowledge base and then to reflect on and talk about what they are doing and how their knowledge is growing. Teachers make sure they understand the students' preexisting conceptions, and guide the activity to address them and then build on them. The constructivist teacher provides the structure needed so that students can explore a problem by formulating and testing ideas, drawing conclusions and inferences, and then communicating and sharing this knowledge in a collaborative environment. Constructivism transforms the classroom into a noisy, busy place where active learning occurs. The teacher becomes a facilitator and guide, helping children confront misconceptions and deal with ambiguities.

Although this approach can appear to be nonstructured and ill-defined, constructivism involves developing structured activities to guide the learners in the direction that the teacher wants them to pursue. This approach can be much more work for the teacher, especially in the planning stages, where careful inquiry-based activities must be designed and carefully planned out, where resources for student research must be located, and where student materials to guide them through the process must be developed.

Assessment is a vital component in this approach because learners are often working on their own, at their own pace, and on different tasks. It is important that the teacher carefully assess each student's progress and provide the necessary support where needed. Being that students often work in groups for prolonged periods to solve designated problem or answer specified question, cooperative groups need to be carefully monitored to ensure that members are relating to each other in a positive manner, and that each member is participating equally in the total workload and not sitting back passively or being too ambitious. Although the group can receive a grade on their work, each student should be responsible for handing in individual work as well, so that the teacher can monitor how each student is progressing.

Students with learning disabilities can perform well in this environment because it allows them the opportunity to "learn through their strength" by providing many different learning styles to present material. Students with learning disabilities can focus on learning new material through the modality that suits them best, and they receive support from their group. The teacher needs to ensure that students with learning disabilities have the structure and support needed to succeed and are not feeling lost and confused during the process.

A constructivist approach can also benefit English language learners by providing them with the opportunity to interact with others in their group in a positive way and to use language in the classroom in a more informal, less threatening environment. This approach allows them to conduct research using the Internet and to learn material that is not exclusively from a textbook written in a language they may not fully comprehend. In the constructivist approach, a textbook becomes one of many resources available, and the student can explore different ways to increase knowledge—through videos, books, software programs, pictures, field trips, guest lecturers, and the Internet. This allows the ELL to explore material through other avenues than just reading and writing a second language. As with all children, second language learners need structure and support through the process so they understand what is expected of them and are clear as to what they need to produce.

The constructivist approach works well in the literacy classroom when the teacher wants to pursue a research project, and it allows the students to apply literacy skills and strategies to an authentic task. This approach is an excellent way to explore nonfiction topics in more depth and to build interdisciplinary connections while reinforcing higher order thinking. WebQuests (see the discussion in Chapter 2) are an example of applying a constructivist approach to an Internet-based project

The constructivist approach is quite different from teacher-directed instruction (see the description earlier in the Model of Direct Instruction section). If they were placed along a continuum, the Model of Direct Instruction would be at one end and constructivism would be at the other end. The Model of Direct Instruction is teacher-directed and is used to teach skills and strategies in a structured setting. The teacher does most of the talking and the interaction is teacher-student-teacher. The constructivist approach is student-centered and is used to foster inquiry and exploration of a topic, question, or problem. The interaction is not controlled by the teacher, but rather centers on students discussing and exploring ideas with the teacher helping out when needed and guiding the learning process. Both models are important to use in a literacy classroom and should be used frequently throughout the curriculum.

Example: The Constructivist Approach

The following lesson plan is based on the book *Aunt Harriet's Underground Railroad in the Sky* by Faith Ringgold (1991). This book is an excellent example of a fiction book that is based on historical facts. It focuses on the life of Harriet Tubman and the Underground Railroad, which helped bring more than 3,000 slaves to freedom. This lesson is designed for a fourth grade classroom.

Objectives:

1. Given a poster to create, each student in a group will answer the question, "If you were a conductor on the Underground Railroad and needed to safely bring a slave to freedom in Canada, what would be the best route and the best methods to use?"

2. Given a cause/effect visual tool to construct and a paragraph to write, the student will analyze the causes of the Underground Railroad and the effects it had on the future of the United States.

Standards Addressed:

Ohio Academic Content Standards: Apply effective reading comprehension strategies, including summarizing and making predictions, and comparisons using information in text, between text and across subject areas.

Vocabulary:

Underground Railroad

Materials:

1. A copy of the book *Aunt Harriet's Underground Railroad in the Sky* by Faith Ringgold (1991)

2. Copies of the Study Guide Visual Tool that will direct students to explore resources and search for information

Procedure:

1. Ask the students what they know about a railroad. Write their responses on the board underneath the word. Now ask the students if they ever heard of the Underground Railroad. Write their responses on the board again under the words "Underground Railroad." Give them some clues about the literal and figurative meanings of the word "underground" (for example, something not allowed in society, something that is hidden and forbidden).

2. Now show the students the cover of the book *Aunt Harriet's Underground Railroad in the Sky* by Faith Ringgold (1991). Have them try to predict what the book is about, even though the cover might not give them a good idea about what the Underground Railroad was. Have them pose questions from the cover and title. Ask them who they think Aunt Harriet might be.

3. Read the book to the class, showing the students the colorful pictures.

4. Discuss what the Underground Railroad really was, and discuss why the main characters "fly" in this book. Have the students discuss what "flying" might mean symbolically; that is, as an expression of freedom and the ability to get around easily and not be "enslaved." Discuss briefly who "Aunt Harriet" was and give some facts about Harriet Tubman's life (they are included on the last two pages of the book).

5. Now tell the students that they will participate in a project in which they must work cooperatively to try and solve a problem. Tell them that they will be conductors on the Underground Railroad in 1860 and that they must help

a group of slaves escape to Canada so they can reach freedom. Their task is to find out what would be the best route from Alabama to where they live to Canada, and to describe the best methods to use to bring these slaves to safety. They will create a poster that has a map of the route they will use, a list of facts about the Underground Railroad, and a description of the different methods they used to bring the escaped slaves to the North. They will work in groups using the Internet, books, videos, and maps to solve their problem.

6. Hand them copies of a study guide, which will give them a step-by-step approach to this project and have a list of resources they can use to do research. This guide will list Internet sites that have been carefully screened by the teacher to ensure that they are appropriate, contain the information needed, and are on the correct reading level. The teacher will also hand out a rubric for the poster so that all students know exactly what is expected of them to attain a high grade.

7. The teacher will work with each group as they conduct their research. The teacher will carefully monitor what sites the students are using on the Internet and ensure that a variety of resources are being used in addition to the Internet.

8. The teacher will oversee the groups as they construct their poster to make sure all the appropriate information is contained on the poster and that they are following the criteria stated on the rubric.

9. When the posters are completed, each group will have 10 minutes to present their poster and explain their methods and northern route as a conductor. After each presentation, the teacher will hang the poster on the wall.

10. When all groups have finished presenting, the teacher will debrief the class. They will discuss what the Underground Railroad was, why it was important, and what it was like to be an escaped slave at that time. The students will infer what it was like to be a conductor and what the implications of the Underground Railroad were on the population in Canada. The teacher will write some of the class's conclusions and generalizations on the board.

11. The teacher will summarize the lesson by reviewing what they learned about *Aunt Harriet's Underground Railroad in the Sky*. The teacher will give each student a chance to name one important thing he or she learned in this lesson before calling on another student to list one thing learned. This list will be written on an easel.

12. For homework, each student will construct a cause/effect visual tool about the causes of the Underground Railroad and its effect on the United States; each student will then write a paragraph based on the visual tool. They will also go to Faith Ringgold's website (http://www.faithringgold.com/) and find out about her history and the other books that she has written.

Evaluation:

The poster will be evaluated using a rubric. The group will be given a grade. Each student will hand in the paragraph for homework to assess knowledge about the Underground Railroad.

In examining this lesson, you can see that although it is constructivist in approach, it is still very structured. The topic is introduced in a structured opening, background knowledge is activated, and the concept is related to the students' everyday life (every child should relate to what a railroad is). The students are asked to solve a problem by posing as a conductor of the Underground Railroad and taking a slave to the North. They are given specific steps to follow in the study guide, specific resources to research, and a rubric that states the criteria they must meet for a grade. Once the structure is established and they are clear on what they need to accomplish, the students are allowed to work independently, building their own knowledge base about the topic. The teacher functions as a facilitator and a mentor, giving feedback, guiding them through the process, and being available to help when needed. The teacher's job is to explore the topic with the students and enjoy the learning process taking place, ensuring that each student feels comfortable in the process.

Importantly, after the presentations, the teacher debriefs the class. This is an important part of a constructivist approach where the teacher confirms conclusions, addresses misconceptions about a topic, and reinforces main ideas brought out about the topic being researched. The teacher must show how this activity relates directly to the student's own life by making connections to the outside world. The debriefing is a mandatory part of the inquiry process involved in a constructivist classroom. It is here that the major concepts are emphasized and reinforced and connections are made.

The classroom described above is a noisy, active environment where students are engaged in learning new material. The teacher is not directly teaching the students as in the Model of Direct Instruction and the teacher–student interaction is not a one-way interaction; that is, it is from the teacher to the student and back again to the teacher. This is a child-centered environment whereby student interacts with student, with the teacher intervening occasionally.

Courtesy of Vicki Cohen

Children construct their own meaning through collaboration.

Lesson Plan Resources on the Internet

The Internet is an excellent source for finding lesson plans that have already been developed, ideas to develop lesson plans, and resources to help a teacher develop a lesson plan. Many of the sites listed below are repositories of lesson plans developed by teachers for many different grade levels. A beginning teacher can modify these lessons to suit the needs of a specific class and tailor the lesson to the district curriculum. An important point to remember is that the lesson plans found at the sites listed below have not been evaluated on quality, validity, or implementation factors. Therefore, if a teacher chooses any lesson plan online or from any other source, care must be taken to ensure that it is appropriate for their students' needs and has incorporated principles of instructional design.

Thinkfinity

http://www.thinkfinity.org/

This site sponsored by Verizon allows teachers to search for lessons from its consortium partners. The site offers lesson plans, interactive activities and other online resources. Thinkfinity.org also provides a wealth of educational and literacy resources for students, parents and after-school programs.

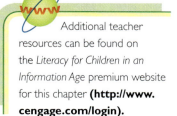
Additional teacher resources can be found on the *Literacy for Children in an Information Age* premium website for this chapter (**http://www. cengage.com/login**).

Blue Web'n

http://www.kn.pacbell.com/wired/bluewebn

This site, sponsored by AT&T, is a great site for teachers to join; every week the authors send links and a summary of the best new educational sites that they have found. The websites listed on this site have been evaluated according to quality and many of them are outstanding. This is an excellent site for teachers to visit first as they begin to develop lesson plans.

Teachers.Net

http://www.teachers.net

This site is sorted by grade level and subject matter. It offers many sample lesson plans and resources.

TeachersFirst

http://www.teachersfirst.com

Sign up to receive weekly postings of lesson plans, literature connections, and many helpful websites to use with your class.

A to Z Teacher Stuff

http://atozteacherstuff.com

This is a great site where teachers can find many different resources, including lesson plans.

Kathy Schrock's Guide for Educators

http://school.discoveryeducation.com/schrockguide/index.html

Kathy Schrock's Guide for Educators is a wonderful resource that all teachers can tap into. It provides links to a wide variety of sites that offer lesson plans in many different subjects and grade levels.

Lessonplanz

http://lessonplanz.com

This site offers many different lesson plans for teachers of literacy.

ERIC Clearinghouse on Reading, English & Communication

http://reading.indiana.edu

This site offers many different links to sites for lesson plans for teachers of literacy K–12.

The Lesson Plans Page

http://www.lessonplanspage.com

This site has more than 2,500 free lessons organized by subject.

   The above sites are excellent resources for beginning teachers to investigate and explore as a means of developing lesson plans and building up a repertoire of resources to use during the year. Although predeveloped lesson plans might be available to help the teacher, it is still important that teachers develop their own instructional units and know the appropriate procedures and principles to apply in doing so.

STRATEGY BOX

Developing Effective Units of Study in Literacy

The following strategies will help teachers develop effective units of instruction in literacy:

1. Always start the lessons by considering the learners in the classroom: their developmental levels, their background knowledge of what you plan to teach, their previous knowledge of the content area, their literacy levels, their motivational levels, and their special needs.

2. When designing instruction, take into account the content, the learning outcomes, the learning environment, your own preferences, and the available resources.

3. Write objectives that help focus the instruction on attainable and observable strategies, skills, or processes that meet state and professional standards in literacy.

4. Align the objectives with state standards and make sure that all objectives address state and national standards. Revise the objectives accordingly.

5. Ensure that your objectives and lessons are promoting higher level thinking.

6. Devise an assessment plan in which you collect evidence that students are progressing and achieving in literacy.

7. Make sure that your objectives, assessment, and procedure are all aligned so that you have a valid lesson plan.

8. Be sure to accommodate diverse learners such as English language learners and students with disabilities in the lesson plan.

9. Incorporate different models of instruction in the procedure of the lesson plan based on the needs of the students, the objectives of the lesson, and the available resources.

10. Be sure to use the Model of Direct Instruction when introducing a skill or strategy during a mini-lesson, guided reading session, or shared literacy experience.

11. Incorporate the use of technology into the lesson to motivate students and provide students with opportunities to learn new literacies.

Final Thoughts

It is important that teachers incorporate learning theory and principles of instructional design into their lesson plans. Lesson plans are the building blocks for effective instruction and, therefore, must be interesting, motivating, promote student achievement, and accommodate every learner in the class. This takes careful planning, thoughtful reflection, and self-examination to ensure that lessons are meeting the needs of all children. Good lesson planning comes with years of practice and refinement, and it is often helpful to receive feedback from mentors and supervisors to improve the design and implementation of lessons. However, it is important that teachers learn about the essential elements of effective lessons and incorporate them into their lessons. Development and effective implementation of quality lesson plans is an iterative process that promotes achievement for all children and helps our students develop into productive and contributing world citizens.

EXPLORATION   Application of Concepts

Activities

1. Develop learning outcomes and objectives for a literacy lesson for a specific grade level. In a group, design three different lessons using the same objective(s), which use the scaffolded reading approach, the model of direct instruction, and the constructivist approach. Discuss how each lesson has the same outcomes and objectives but is very different in the way that it is taught.

2. For each lesson above, design accommodations that would have to be made for ELLs, and for students with learning disabilities.

3. Observe a teacher during a literacy lesson. Take notes on which model of instruction is being used

in the class. Discuss which instructional model could have been used.

4. Develop a literacy lesson to teach a reading strategy to a specific grade level, such as teaching a phonic skill to first graders or teaching how to summarize informational text to fourth graders. In a group, critique the lesson plan to ensure it incorporates learning theory and instructional design elements.

5. Look up a lesson on a website listed in this chapter (or the companion website). Critique the lesson and redesign it so that it uses one of the instructional models presented in this chapter.

HOME–SCHOOL CONNECTION   Including Students, Parents, and Guardians in the Lesson Planning Process

Teachers often take great pride in communicating with the families of their students through a carefully planned newsletter about units and lessons that are being implemented. Each month, they report what students have achieved in each subject, what objectives they are working on that month, classroom current events, and upcoming unit projects. Yet each month, questions from students, such as "*What else are we going to learn in science?*" let one teacher know that her students were not reading her home–school connection communications; in fact, some newsletters were not making it out of book bags and into parents' and guardians' hands. To encourage communication with students and families, this teacher began assigning the newsletter as reading homework once a month. Students had to read the newsletter to a family member;

the teacher even gave a brief quiz the following day. Students who answered questions about the newsletter correctly won a small prize from a prize box.

By April, the teacher took the reading of the newsletter a step further and designed a series of expository writing lessons in which students planned, wrote, and formatted the newsletter themselves. By the end of the writing unit, students not only had a sense of pride in publishing a class newsletter, they understood how the writing process and expository writing can be used in real life. Furthermore, their parents and guardians were thrilled to see the fruit of their labor and felt involved in the lesson planning process.

(Adapted from Katie O'Brien, Fourth Grade Teacher)

14 MANAGING AND ORGANIZING A LITERACY PROGRAM

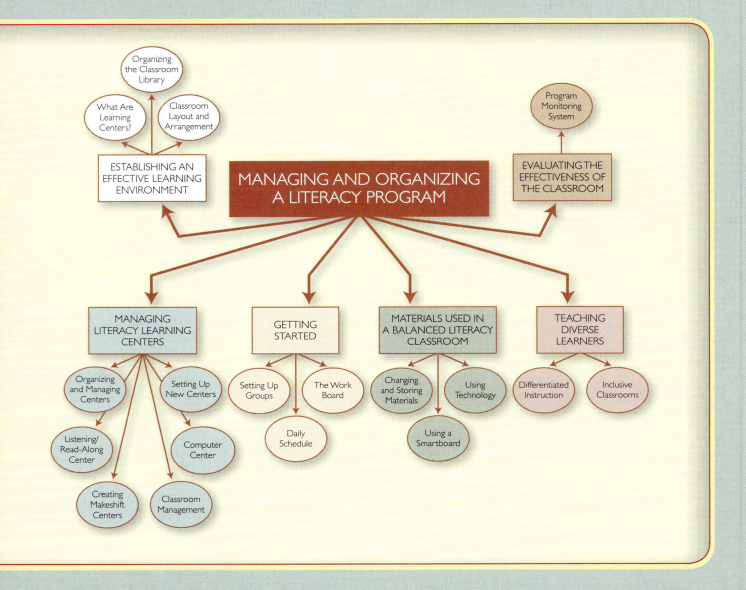

International Reading Association Professional Standards Addressed in this Chapter:

IRA STANDARD 2:   INSTRUCTIONAL STRATEGIES AND CURRICULUM MATERIALS

Candidates use a wide range of instructional practices, approaches, methods, and curriculum materials to support reading and writing instruction. Candidates:

2.1 Use instructional grouping options (individual, small-group, whole-class, and computer-based) as appropriate for accomplishing given purposes.

2.2 Use a wide range of instructional practices, approaches, and methods, including technology-based practices, for learners at differing stages of development and from differing cultural and linguistic backgrounds.

2.3 Use a wide range of curriculum materials in effective reading instruction for learners at different stages of reading and writing development and from different cultural and linguistic backgrounds.

IRA STANDARD 4:   CREATING A LITERATE ENVIRONMENT

Candidates create a literate environment that fosters reading and writing by integrating foundational knowledge, use of instructional practices, approaches and methods, curriculum materials, and the appropriate use of assessments. Candidates:

4.1 Use students' interests, reading abilities, and backgrounds as foundations for the reading and writing program.

4.2 Use a large supply of books, technology-based information, and nonprint materials representing multiple levels, broad interests, and cultural and linguistic backgrounds.

4.3 Model reading and writing enthusiastically as valued lifelong activities.

4.4 Motivate learners to be lifelong readers.

Key Terms

learning centers
classroom library
workshop environments
community meeting place
open-ended centers
listening center
read-along center
computer center
makeshift centers
nonconfrontational discipline
conflict resolution
whisper voice
work board
icons
rotation system
inclusion
program monitoring system

Focus Questions

1. Why is it so important to establish an effective learning environment? What factors are important to consider when establishing an effective literacy learning environment?

2. How should literacy learning centers be set up and managed?

3. Describe two centers that can be used in a balanced literacy classroom. How should they be organized?

4. How do you get started in setting up literacy learning centers? What does a teacher need to do to get children started in learning centers?

5. What materials are needed for the establishment of learning centers? What technological resources and materials can be used in learning centers to motivate students?

6. How can a balanced literacy classroom be managed and organized to accommodate diverse learners such as students with learning disabilities and English language learners?

7. How does a teacher evaluate the effectiveness of literacy learning centers and the learning environment?

Welcome to Mr. Roth's Fourth Grade Classroom: Managing and Organizing an Effective Literacy Program

Courtesy of image100/Jupiter Images

Mr. Roth teaches fourth grade in an inner-city school that is located in a low-socioeconomic section of a large city. The student population in his class is 75 percent African American and 25 percent Latino, and reading scores are generally below average. He has 32 students in his class, and the room is crowded; he has many concerns about classroom management, program implementation, raising test scores, and meeting the goals and objectives of the reading program. Mr. Roth was encouraged by the district reading coordinator to set up guided reading sessions, but after several attempts, he was frustrated. He received help from a local university: two professors observed his class and consulted with him—with their help, he set up a system that works for him. He has established portable learning centers and a daily schedule that allow him enough time to give intensive instruction to a group of students in a guided reading session while the other students worked at the centers. He works collaboratively with the special education teachers and the teacher of English language learners to plan the learning activities at the centers.

Working slowly over a six-week time span, Mr. Roth has introduced the children to the centers and helps them work independently. He works with them on establishing clear rules that are consistently and strictly enforced. He takes different groups of students to each center to demonstrate the activities they need to complete; he shows them how to retrieve their activity, share the resources in the crate, and put their completed assignment in the basket on the teacher's desk. The students watch and take notes while the teacher demonstrates a guided reading session with a small group of students, debriefing the class afterward to ensure that they have understood what was going on, emphasizing the importance of "quiet work" during the session. He also stresses that students must be responsible and accountable for the work they are assigned.

Each station that Mr. Roth has set up has a different focus. Center 1 focuses on word recognition, vocabulary development, and literal comprehension of text. Center 2 focuses on reading comprehension, writing, and responding to literature. Center 3 focuses on critical thinking and analysis of literature, encouraging students to synthesize and evaluate what they read. Center 4 is a research station where students are given informational text to read, and are then asked to conduct research on the Internet, finding information they needed to apply to complete activities.

Once Mr. Roth has established the routine and procedure of this literacy program, he finds that the learning centers in conjunction with the guided reading sessions are effective and that students' reading scores are improving. He then introduces a shared literacy experience in the first 30 minutes of a 90-minute literacy block, with a read-aloud and shared reading each day. After the shared reading each day, students get into their groups and rotate to a different learning center while he works with a guided reading group. He finds that students with diverse needs participate actively in their groups and are supported by their peers. English language learners are actively using English while connecting to culturally relevant texts and activities at the centers. On Fridays, Mr. Roth has different groups present their work to the class, which increases their self-esteem and confidence in speaking to audiences. Mr. Roth is proud of his students and feels a great sense of accomplishment in setting up a reading program that provides authentic literacy experiences to the children in his class. Perhaps most important, everyone in the class has fun, feels part of a community of learners, and is engaged in rich literacy activities that promote achievement (based on Guastello & Lenz, 2005).

In the following sections, you will learn how to create a balanced reading program like the one described above. As you read this chapter, try to note those strategies that help a teacher manage and organize an effective literacy classroom.

Establishing an Effective Learning Environment

It is important that teachers establish a well-organized, predictable classroom environment during the first days and weeks of the school year so that they can meet the various needs of all students. In fact, an effective, balanced reading program requires the teacher to provide a continuous, observation-diagnostic-intervention approach to literacy. Readers thrive in an environment where they are given ample opportunities to read, write, listen, use language in a variety of ways, and explore visual literacy. It is essential that teachers establish environments where literacy is not only taught but is also used in everyday activities that actively engage the students; children then learn that literacy is valued for both learning new information in the classroom and for recreation and pleasure (Paratore & McCormack, 2005).

Students' behaviors and interactions are directly influenced by the classroom environment that the teacher establishes, and classroom design is a critical factor in the success of instruction (Loughlin & Martin, 1987; Morrow, 2002). Classroom design is an important factor in fostering learning; how the classroom is set up can facilitate certain types of learning. Rooms divided into smaller spaces help increase verbal interaction between children and encourage children to focus on one activity. Developing one small area into a "room" focused on a theme or discipline helps increase children's use and enjoyment of this area. For example, a dramatic play area with story props, costumes, set designs, picture prompts, and scripts will ensure increased use of this area and also improve literacy achievement.

Dynamic Graphics/Jupiterimages

An effective balanced classroom is organized by learning centers.

The physical environment will also influence how the teacher behaves and plans for instruction. In a traditional room, with rows of seats and furniture, a teacher is more apt to teach with traditional lectures and teacher-directed activities. When the room is set up with quality work areas designed to foster specific literacy activities, the teacher invites students to work more collaboratively, encourages a more open and child-centered approach to instruction, and fosters more student choice in selecting activities. The teacher will find that classroom management is easier because children will be more engaged in learning activities and, therefore, less apt to become restless or bored, and act out.

A classroom that is designed to promote literacy is organized into **learning centers** that provide students with an abundant supply of materials for reading, writing, speaking, and developing visual literacy. The learning centers should provide real-life experiences to make literacy meaningful and functional for all children, so that they see a clear purpose for becoming literate. The learning centers should be spread out throughout the classroom and contain a rich supply of materials to support literacy development across the curriculum.

What Are Learning Centers?

A learning center is an excellent way to accommodate the various needs of students. Learning centers are designated areas of the classroom where students must accomplish meaningful tasks specified by objectives. Each learning center should be designed so that the tasks revolve around a specific theme, skill, or discipline. Although the number and type of learning centers varies from classroom to classroom, four centers that are typically found in a balanced literacy class are: (1) an independent or shared reading center, where children can read or reread text; (2) an independent writing center, where children can continue writing on a topic that was assigned or begin writing to a prompt that is located at the center; (3) a word study center, where children can practice identifying words that support reading and writing; and (4) a comprehension and language center, where students can read along to recorded books, engage in language activities, and develop language skills through structured tasks (Paratore & McCormack, 2005).

Tasks should focus on meaningful literacy objectives and not just include busy work to keep children quiet and on task. Learning centers should maximize children's opportunities to engage in the meaningful language experiences that they are engaged in. The activities should be structured and require the use of skills and strategies that have already been taught so that the children can work independently. The children should be able to complete the tasks within the specified time period, usually 15 minutes.

An essential criterion of a learning center is that the activities must advance children's reading or writing performance. Therefore, learning centers must first be performance-based. The tasks should demonstrate that children are developing as readers and writers. Second, learning centers must be accessible to all students. The tasks must reinforce skills and processes already taught in the classroom so that students are capable of working independently. The tasks must also be accessible to all children, including those with special needs and English language learners. The purpose of learning centers is to facilitate independent learning; therefore, the activities should have supporting resources such as recorded texts or alternate forms of the same activity to accommodate all children. Third, learning centers must be connected to a lesson that was previously taught in the classroom (Paratore & McCormack, 2005).

Establishing literacy learning centers is essential to enable children to work responsibly, independently, and in small groups, thereby freeing up the teacher to teach guided reading effectively (Fountas & Pinnell, 1996). Implementing learning centers also enables the teacher to provide one-on-one instruction to individual struggling readers, including English language learners and other special needs students. One of the most important goals of a balanced literacy program is to create a classroom environment that is seamless, so that children can move about the room freely and responsibly for the following purposes:

◆ Selecting their own books and materials

◆ Working independently and working with peers

◆ Balancing self-selected learning activities

◆ Engaging in self-sustained, silent reading

◆ Engaging in independent reading

◆ Engaging in inquiry projects with collaborative groups

◆ Reading around the print-rich room

◆ Engaging in reading circles

◆ Engaging in writing workshops

Many different types of literacy learning centers can be set up in the classroom. Figure 14–1 outlines a few of the different centers a teacher can arrange in the classroom

Different Types of Literacy Learning Centers

FIGURE 14-1

Frequently Used Literacy Learning Centers:

- ABC's and Make Words (Word Play Center)
- Independent Reading Center
- Listening/Read-Along Center
- Computer Center
- Writing Center
- Poetry Center
- Word Meaning Games
- Puppet Players' Stage
- Dramatic Play Center

Content-Area Centers:

- Focus Centers:
    - Mammals
    - Reptiles
    - Fish
    - Insects

- Subject Centers:
    - Science
    - Social Studies
    - Health and Wellness
    - Math Problems
- Art Center
- Technology Centers:
    - Computers
    - CD-ROM
    - Electronic Books
    - TV Cameras
    - Video Cam Recorder (VCR)
    - DVD Player

to facilitate independent learning that is engaging and meaningful to promote literacy achievement.

Classroom Layout and Arrangement

In designing the classroom, it is important that the teacher divide the classroom into different areas that contain materials pertinent to particular themes, activities, or content areas appropriate to the grade level, such as social studies, science, math, art, music, dramatic play, block play, and language arts. The materials should be manipulative, activity-based, and carefully designed so children can work independently on the activities.

In addition, the classroom needs to be arranged so that the teacher can meet quietly and privately with an individual child or small group of children. There should be a corner of the classroom for the teacher's desk or for a small table and chairs, where private conferences can take place.

The classroom should also be organized with specific functions in mind. For example, there should be designated areas for class meetings, whole-group instruction, small-group work, independent reading, and shared reading. Shelves, rugs, and furniture can be used to mark off the different areas and what their purpose will be.

The teacher should carefully use wall space for well-designed displays that enhance student learning and highlight student-generated work. The wall space can be used to post rules of the classroom, posters that specify steps of a specific procedure, such as how to write a well-composed essay, and charts and pictures that go along with a theme. Word walls should be posted in well-lit areas of the classroom where children can easily refer to them during literacy activities. In essence, it is important that the wall space be carefully used to help build literacy skills and promote a classroom where student learning is valued and displayed.

Figure 14–2 shows a floor plan that can be used for preschool through first grade classrooms, and Figure 14–3 shows a plan for second through fifth grade classrooms. With older children, it may be more difficult to implement learning centers; however, they can be used to house materials that supplement and enrich content areas being taught in the classroom. A box or shelf can serve as a learning center, and the actual activities can be done in other parts of the classroom (Morrow, 2002).

Organizing the Classroom Library

It is important that the teacher set up a designated area in the room for a **classroom library.** Classroom libraries enable children to learn strategies for selecting books and for sampling books from many different content areas and genres and also to read and reread books independently or with peers. A classroom library also allows the teacher to provide many different types of texts for children to read and to use authentic literature as part of literacy instruction.

Two important factors that teachers need to consider in setting up a classroom library are the organization of the space and the selection of books and materials. In organizing the space, the following suggestions may be helpful (Paratore & McCormack, 2005):

- Choose an area that is away from noisy and active areas so that children can read in a quiet environment. Make sure the area is well lit and has comfortable seating for at least five children. If possible, provide soft cushions, rugs, and chairs that will encourage reading for pleasure.
- Make the classroom library an important and valued area in the classroom. Focus attention on it, set up rules on the first day of class, and encourage children to use it every day. In this way, the teacher will teach children that the library is a valued part of literacy.
- Accumulate as many books as you can (a good rule of thumb is 8 to 10 books per child in your class). Try to bring new materials into the library on a regular basis so

Classroom Floor Plan for Pre-K Through First Grade

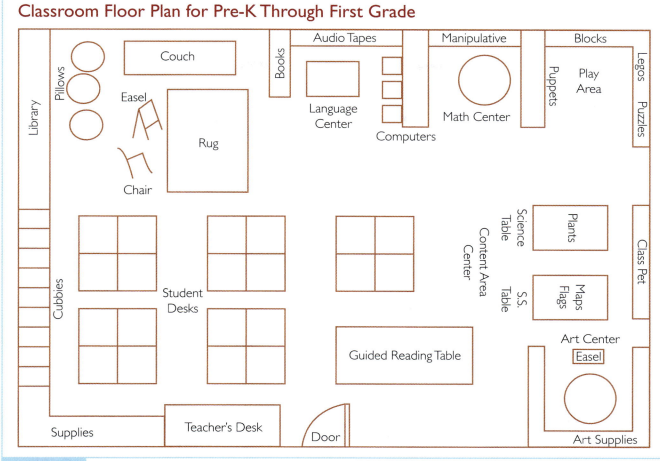

FIGURE 14-2

that the library always has something novel and interesting for children to explore. Many teachers use books from the school or local library to supplement their classroom library. It is also helpful to let parents know that if they are cleaning out their houses, to please donate any books that might be appropriate.

◆ Organize the books by category or genre, using color coding and labels to help children know where they can find a particular book. It is also helpful to keep all books together that relate to one theme that the class is researching.

◆ Level the books by reading difficulty: divide the books in each category into separate reading levels using color coding or lettering. In this way, the teacher can be assured that the children are choosing and reading books that are on their appropriate level. It is recommended that at least a minimum of three levels are established: easy, medium, and hard, with the levels depending on the grade of the classroom and abilities of the students.

In selecting books for the library, it is important that the teacher consider rich, high-quality literature as the primary criteria. Fisher, Flood, and Lapp (2003) suggest that teachers use the following four criteria to choose books: (1) high literary quality, (2) interesting and engaging aesthetic qualities, (3) concepts and ideas that are of high interest to students, and (4) content that leads children to new and unique discoveries. In addition to these criteria, the teacher should consider the abilities and interests of the students and provide a wide range of books from different content areas and different genres. It is also important that the teacher choose a wide variety of multicultural books, because this may be a primary way that many children are introduced to

Classroom Floor Plan for Second Through Fifth Grade

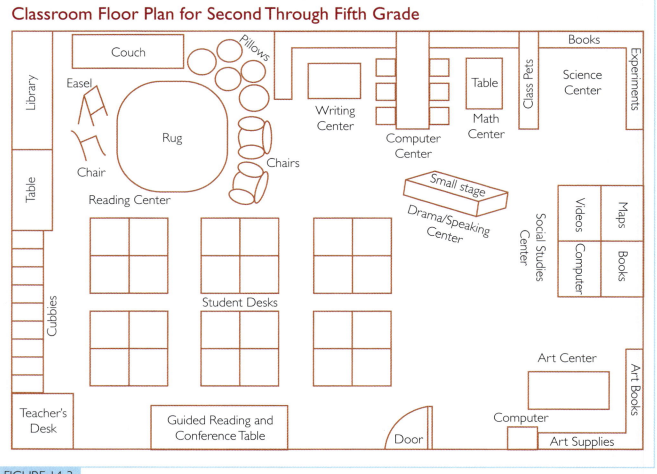

FIGURE 14-3

different cultures. Children also like to read about their own culture and feel that their cultural traditions are valued. There should be enough books for both girls and boys, because often boys like to read about different themes and content than girls.

Teachers should read the books that are chosen for the library carefully to ensure that they are appropriate. A wide range of expository books on different content areas should be included, as well as books that emphasize positive values and develop deeper awareness about the world and global community. The teacher should evaluate each book carefully to ensure that the text and illustrations do not perpetuate any stereotypes. Often, a teacher might be unaware that a book could cause a child to become upset, so the teacher needs to use sensitivity and insight into cultural traditions before selecting a particular book. For example, many children's books portray Columbus as a hero who had no faults and present his explorations as a great benefit to all. This might offend some children who have learned that, in fact, Columbus and his crew slaughtered many native inhabitants and brought widespread disease to this population. The best suggestion is to be open-minded and sensitive in choosing books that represent a fair and accurate portrayal of events.

Teachers should also choose many different resources in addition to books for inclusion in the classroom library. Magazines are an excellent and motivating addition, and there are many different excellent children's magazines available today. Menus, brochures about local places of interest, maps, and charts are all excellent additions to the library. In addition, many children enjoy having "books" they have created, laminated and placed in the library for other children to read and enjoy.

Managing Literacy Learning Centers

Learning centers are seamless educational settings that enable children to participate in a variety of collaborative **workshop environments.** A workshop environment is one in which children engage as active participants in learning to read by reading and learning to write by writing (Fountas & Pinnell, 1996). Workshops also enable children to engage in collaborative dialogues and cooperative inquiry projects, which further their development in thinking and oral expression. For children to succeed in such a highly social workshop environment, they need to know what to do, what is expected of them, and how to function responsibly when working collaboratively with peers or when working independently without the immediate physical presence of the teacher, who might be guiding another child or group of children.

The physical aspects of a balanced literacy classroom include the arrangement of furniture, and student cubbies or assembled egg crates for organizing folders, books, and supplies. Other physical considerations should include library bookcases or shelving for stocking instructional materials and technological resources as part of the educational plan based on constructivist and schema theory. The physical environment must provide a safe and inviting place for learning and student inquiry to occur and where all of the resources are accessible to children with little or no required immediate assistance from the classroom teacher. All of these arrangements must be considered in advance and are provided as part of the overall organizational plan to promote independent learners, who researchers write are the most successful learners (Fountas & Pinnell, 1996). Guidelines, therefore, must be arranged in advance to create several types of interesting literacy centers and content-area learning centers as well. Such plans should include:

◆ Organizing and managing centers
◆ Monitoring student behavior in centers
◆ Monitoring learning effectiveness in centers
◆ Assessing student individual needs
◆ Determining cooperative learning effectiveness
◆ Evaluating student achievement in literacy learning centers

Organizing and Managing Literacy Learning Centers

The organization and management of centers in a balanced literacy program should be viewed as central to the effectiveness of a balanced reading classroom. Learning centers are invaluable because they free up the teacher to assess and instruct children in guided reading groups while also providing intervention to struggling readers, English language learners, and individuals with special needs.

Whenever a new center is introduced, it is important to provide children with an orientation and a walk-through demonstration so that each child knows the answers to the following questions:

◆ What is the purpose of each center?
◆ What kinds of activities and what types of materials are available?
◆ How do students use the materials and keep records?
◆ How should students behave in the center?
◆ How should students work collaboratively in a cooperative group?
◆ How do various roles, assigned to each cooperative group, function?
◆ How should students negotiate traffic patterns in and around the center?
◆ What are the rules for working in each center?

It is important that the organizational and management plan allows students to help make the rules that govern the classroom; in this way the students themselves have ownership and self-regulate their own behaviors, as well as help regulate other students' behaviors (Curwin & Mendler, 1988; Kohn, 1996).

Whole-Class Instruction

Fountas and Pinnell (1996) recommend using whole-group instruction during the first days of the guided reading program—particularly for first graders—to provide them with an organized orientation to the classroom. Children must learn that there is a set routine to follow and that the teacher is an in-charge, confident leader. Once this concept is understood, the teacher may introduce some small-group work and independent reading. Shortly thereafter, the classroom is organized more for collaborative group work and for creating greater independence, because one of the important goals of a balanced literacy program is to have students become self-managed learners. Therefore, once the whole group has been given an orientation to the purposes of the learning center and how to use its instructional materials, during the ensuing days, the children will be introduced to other centers and shown how to use classroom space for more collaborative, small-group, and independent literacy activities (Fountas & Pinnell, 1996).

In most balanced literacy classrooms, a large group area, or **community meeting place,** is provided that is generally divided by a large area rug to comfortably accommodate a whole group. Most primary classrooms start the day by having a large group meeting, which is usually followed by the teacher conducting a read-aloud or shared reading activity to the whole group. The teacher usually addresses the whole group whenever a new learning center is introduced. Whole-group instruction can be used for the following purposes:

- ◆ Introducing a new skill or strategy
- ◆ Reinforcing new skills, strategies, or content
- ◆ Conducting daily morning routine such as going over the calendar and weather
- ◆ Participating in a read-aloud
- ◆ Participating in shared reading
- ◆ Participating in shared and interactive writing
- ◆ Introducing new equipment or materials
- ◆ Orienting the class before a field trip or debriefing after a field trip
- ◆ Reviewing major news events and community issues
- ◆ Conducting show-and-tell and sharing of personal accomplishments
- ◆ Addressing classroom rules and classroom management problems

In a balanced literacy program, every child is a unique learner and, therefore, requires a unique or differentiated academic program. This means that the teacher needs to use many different types of groupings for children, as well as whole-group instruction. It is best to keep whole-group instruction to a minimum during the school day and to use small-group instruction, which is catered to individual student needs, whenever possible.

Setting Up New Centers

Regardless of the size of the classroom or the size of the center, new centers must be introduced one at a time. It is also recommended that a new center be introduced only after the previous one is clearly understood and is functioning efficiently and without problems. An orientation must include an effective demonstration so that students know exactly what the purpose of each new center is and what the teacher's expectations are. Some centers will have specific tasks to complete; other centers will be more open-ended, requiring long-term activities such as observing the decomposition of wet leaves in a bottle or observing and tracking the rate of growth of plants from seedlings.

Other **open-ended centers** might include a writing workshop, where children, using the writing process, create their own texts, stories, or books. The process of writing a book might take several days or weeks. Each center must be carefully organized and managed by the teacher.

The following suggestions should prove helpful to teachers setting up a new center:

◆ Demonstrate and practice routines, do a walk-through with the children.

◆ Organize the layout of the center so that it is not congested and materials are accessible.

◆ Place student folders and work packets in a specific location.

◆ Label all of the routines, procedures, and materials simply and clearly.

◆ Demonstrate how each specific task is to be completed.

◆ Show children how to mark and correct answers, or how to collaborate with peers to get input and advice to make corrections or to make revisions.

◆ Demonstrate how students must return materials and supplies when finished.

◆ Maintain a daily, adequate supply of materials, markers, and supplies.

◆ Develop rules for behavior for each center with the students, who must also agree to follow the rules and help others abide by the rules as well.

◆ Reinforce the rules of the center. Students must learn that they cannot call out whenever they need help, but rather must be taught to seek advice from peers or to consult other resources that are in the center or in the classroom itself (this is essential or else the teacher will not be able to effectively attend to guided reading groups).

Depending on the size of the classroom, a teacher can create a permanent learning center, or a temporary one that can be taken down easily to make room for other activities. In large classrooms, it is advisable to set up designated centers that can be left up for some duration. Permanent centers are more efficient for the teacher to manage, but many teachers do not have large classrooms and must set up makeshift or temporary centers. If enough space is available in one or more corners of the room, a limited number of literacy centers should be established that are permanent, such as a listening/read-along center or a computer center. In this way, cumbersome equipment and paraphernalia need not be set up and pulled down several times during a short time span. It is nearly impossible to create a temporary multimedia or computer center: computer carts or laptop computers can always be used as an alternative to accommodate small areas, but this will be a more expensive alternative that school districts are often reluctant to incur.

Introducing students to centers is not a onetime activity, but this kind of orientation must occur each and every time a new center is opened. Even though children seem to be well-behaved and have internalized all of the routines delineated in the previous introduction to a center, this process must be reemphasized at the opening of each new center, because there is a tendency for children to forget or not carry over one set of rules to a different environment. Any child entering the program after the school year has begun must also be given the same orientation that was given to the whole class, to ensure that all students are made privy to the same rules, directions, routines, and teacher expectations. This approach should create a more level playing field for all new students entering the classroom and should develop consistency in positive student behavior.

The teacher must constantly model using a soft voice to emphasize the importance of students using the whisper voice, to follow rules, and act responsibly in each new center. Routines are important to children; when they are consistently enforced and monitored, children feel confident that the classroom is well managed and that their teacher is truly in charge (Marzano, Marzano, & Pickering, 2003; Willis, 1996). These routines should also be ongoing and consistently built into several centers so that children know how to work independently, can locate materials easily, and can follow simple directions to perform the tasks for reviewing or learning skills or concepts. Therefore, each new center must be well organized, clearly labeled, and well stocked with materials that children can work without teacher assistance. All centers should be organized so that children engage in activities for different purposes and do so successfully.

Different materials and equipment are found in each new center; therefore, a new set of rules and procedures must be introduced so that children know what is required of them, and can engage in activities purposefully. They must be informed at the outset how the rules and routines in the new center either remain the same or are different. Children must also be taught how to use their time meaningfully; for example, children need to know how many books they will have time to read, how many recorded texts they will have to listen to, or how much time they should spend on completing tasks while working in a given center. Learning how to judge their own use of time, as well as the quantity and the quality of their academic work, is an important learning trait to foster at this young age that will help forge their character and learning styles for the rest of their lives. Making sure that each center's unique learning environment is consistent with the philosophy of the balanced literacy classroom is necessary for providing consistency in learning. A major responsibility of the classroom teacher is to know whether all of her students' literacy skills are improving and that all aspects of the active centers are assessed to be producing effective and meaningful learning opportunities.

Listening/Read-Along Center

One of the most widely used and important centers in the elementary room is the **listening center.** The listening center is where children can sit and listen to books on tape, podcasts, music, poetry, and other textual material that the teacher has recorded for listening. The National Reading Panel (2000) reports that repeated reading, as a reading strategy, together with teacher feedback is extremely beneficial and has produced educationally significant results. Furthermore, it is reported that this strategy is effectively used in improving student reading comprehension and vocabulary development. With this research in mind, it is beneficial to combine the listening center with the **read-along center** because to achieve the benefits of the repeated reading strategy, students must be actively engaged in simultaneously listening to text and reading along with the reader. In the process of reading along, the student must be actively reading and listening simultaneously to the recorded text, and this should be done repeatedly. For example, a student might be required to listen to a particular section or to read a particular paragraph several times before being asked to read these identical passages aloud, without any miscues, to a teacher or to a peer. Often, the student's reading speed and accuracy are recorded and charted to determine how effective the repeated reading approach is in helping the student improve fluency, comprehension, and overall reading speed, which is converted into words per minute. In other words, the read-along or the repeated reading approach requires that the student pay close attention to both the aural and the written word, while exerting a high degree of on-task behavior.

The listening/read-along center suggests that the following equipment and materials are accessible:

- iPods with headphones (it is advisable that children bring in their own and keep them in their cubbies)
- Tape recorder (if the teacher chooses to use this instead of, or in addition to, the iPods)
- CD player with accompanying CDs of music and other recordings
- E-book reader, such as the Kindle, which reads the text out loud to the reader, and accompanying e-books
- Multiple headphone jack (where two to three children can read along or listen)
- Long table or flat surface so that students can read along and/or write while listening
- Electrical outlet nearby (essential)

◆ Books with matching audiotapes (commercial or teacher-made) or podcasts

◆ Words per minute chart and stopwatch or clock with minute hand for students to record words per minute for each book/tape

◆ Comprehension questions to record answers

◆ Student record book or student folder for repeated readings

◆ A sign indicating what the student should do after listening to the tape, CD, or podcast

◆ Storage boxes for leveled books and matching tapes or podcasts, each labeled accordingly

Teachers must monitor student engagement in listening comprehension. Students must be on task when listening and should not be seen just lying back listlessly; rather, they must be actively engaged in listening and thinking about the spoken text. Listening comprehension must then be checked as part of the activity to ensure that the student is not only hearing the words that are spoken, but that he or she also listens attentively with understanding. The listening/read-along center should be carefully designed and monitored to ensure that students do increase fluency and literacy achievement.

Computer Center

Most teachers will tell you that the most popular center—the one that seems to excite children the most—is the **computer center.** Most school districts have recognized the important benefit of introducing computers to elementary school students, and as a result, at the very least two to five computers should be available for setting up a computer center in most classrooms. Children appear to learn readily from the computer because of the immediate feedback that it provides. Computer software is becoming more sophisticated, in that it is visually colorful, graphically designed, and can provide a variety of texts to meet the appropriate levels of the children's reading abilities without frustrating them.

The computer performs much like a personal tutor does: it can help children improve skills in writing, grammar, vocabulary, and reading comprehension. Computers can also be helpful in reading with the different electronic talking books (also known as Living Books) available, which provide digitized speech and read the story out loud to the student just as the teacher would. Computer software can also be used interactively: children can replay a story and use it for repeated readings. They can also use hypertext to search for specific words, phrases, or sentences. The computer can be used to test a student's comprehension, word automaticity, or reading fluency; it can also be used to record the student's rate of reading and show how much progress the student has made in both fluency and accuracy over the long term. Software can be used by children, which can inform them of a book's readability level; therefore, teachers no longer have to make subtle recommendations to children about which books to choose (or not choose) because they may be too difficult to read. Some teachers use the computer center to reinforce skills students are learning in the school's computer lab, which is often better equipped with instructional programs for teaching phonemic awareness and phonics word attack skills, vocabulary skill development, or specific comprehension strategies. It is also helpful to have e-books available which the students can use on the computer (if an e-book reader is not available).

In a balanced approach to literacy instruction, children benefit from listening to recorded activities, as well as collaborating with peers to complete the activities.

Courtesy of Guilherme Cunha

In setting up the computer center, it is important that the teacher provide specific information and directions for the safe use of the equipment so that children do not damage it unintentionally. A set of rules and procedures must be posted prominently in the center and should include DOs and DON'Ts so that children do not mistreat the equipment. Some useful rules are: "Don't bang on the keyboard"; "If there is a problem, wait until someone can help you"; and "Follow directions carefully."

Some of the following suggestions for setting up a computer center may serve as a helpful checklist (Wait, 1992). The following items are needed:

- Two or more computers, each with a power strip; electrical outlet
- Computer tables to hold computers and provide space for children to write or to accommodate reference books
- Student earphones to accommodate electronic talking books Speech-to-text software
- Two student chairs for each computer
- Software, CD-ROMs
- Printer
- Student microphones to record audio
- Tablets that can be purchased to facilitate drawing on the computer

Creating Makeshift Centers in Small Rooms

When teachers are assigned to very small rooms, they must create **makeshift centers** to accommodate this lack of space by storing books and equipment on shelves or by placing materials and supplies in baskets, egg crates, or in empty boxes nearby. Teachers assigned to this kind of setting will need to teach children how to create their own centers every day by finding the materials under a given icon; instead of working in a specially designed work space, they will have to bring the center materials to their own desks to work. In many schools throughout the country, this lack of classroom space is often a realistic setting for most teachers. This makeshift center is not convenient; nevertheless, teachers assigned to smaller rooms just have to become more creative. Another idea is to place necessary materials and supplies on one or more moveable carts, which can be rolled into place once it is time for center activity, so that children have a place from which to gather their work materials and supplies.

Materials and supplies needed for makeshift centers are basically the same that teachers use in any center; for example:

- Children's literature books
- Big books
- Leveled books
- Sentence strips
- Manipulatives
- Magnetic boards and alphabet letters
- Chart paper and easels
- Student folders
- Name charts and word charts
- Pointers
- Scissors
- Electronic dictionaries, thesauruses
- CD players and CD-ROMs
- iPods and/or tape recorders with headsets

Teachers must also think about the various materials that are needed when working with children at their desks or in the centers. It is important to differentiate instruction, and the teacher should be prepared to have materials that are on each individual's level of reading and writing.

Classroom Management Using Centers

It is essential that the teacher set up a carefully structured environment that follows a set routine and maintains strict control over the class. The balanced literacy environment is created to promote children's freedom of movement and freedom to talk to peers in low tones for brief periods. In this relaxed environment, children need to learn that the rules of the classroom will be followed at all times. It is important that at the beginning of the year the teacher develop the rules of the classroom with the students' input and feedback, and then post them clearly on the wall. It will be necessary to remind students of the rules, especially at the beginning of the year, and the teacher must be consistent and firm in enforcing the rules, always keeping in mind that all children must be respected and shown that they are cared for.

The children must also learn that talking should be purposeful, and that idle conversations or clowning are not acceptable or responsible behavior. Occasionally, when children abuse this freedom, they must be called to task; however, they must be talked to privately and out of hearing range from peers to be reminded that they are abusing their freedom and that they are breaking the rules set by the student group. In addition, it is important that teachers use nonconfrontational tones and nonthreatening body language when disciplining students; otherwise, these students might feel that the teacher does not like them and respond by acting out.

Teachers should use **nonconfrontational discipline** when there is a problem with a child or between children. Teachers must always make it clear when speaking to a child about his or her poor behavior, that it is, indeed, the behavior or the specific act that she disapproves of, and not the child. If this problem should reoccur, however, a variety of behavioral interventions can be initiated to help resolve the conflict: one being to discuss this problem at the next daily, large-group community meeting. Without mentioning who has broken the rules, the teacher asks a student leader to lead a discussion about the issue of student freedom and responsibility. The student leader asks the group to find a reasonable solution for when children break the rules and to make recommendations that will help students learn from breaking the rules.

When there is a conflict with students over class rules or a conflict between two students, the teacher should use **conflict resolution** strategies to try to resolve it. The teacher should first model how to dialogue and problem solve; sometimes, an example from one of the children's stories is used as a way to broach solving a conflict. Children should suggest ways for monitoring classroom behavior to ensure that everyone is abiding by the rules that are set up by the group. They should also be empowered to set penalties for students who break the class rules. If this alternative still does not work, the teacher might be forced to assign the uncooperative student to work in another center or to complete a different, noncollaborative task, such as listening to a read-along activity independently. This student may not be allowed to work in social or collaborative settings until the teacher witnesses that the rules are being followed and the student is beginning to work cooperatively with others. However, many students prefer working independently, and they should be allowed to do so without feeling penalized.

Empowering peers to help resolve conflicts is a more democratic, collaborative approach to disciplining children with dignity. This peer group decision-making approach to discipline seems to be a more sensitive approach in contrast with most corrective student behavioral interventions (Curwin & Mendler, 1988; Kohn, 1996). Many experts believe that children must learn to commit and not to comply to following the rules out of fear; otherwise, their good behavior will be short-lived and unresolved. Having students establish classroom rules in a cooperative and collaborative fashion helps build commitment, which is important for building self-determination, good behavior, and good learning habits (Willis, 1996).

In addition to classroom rules, the teacher needs to create an engaging, interesting learning environment where children are happy and engaged in learning. Classroom management is less tedious when children are treated with respect and when the activities are both fun and rewarding.

It is important that students are required to use a **whisper voice** during all collaborative learning activities, particularly when working in centers. In this way, both freedom of movement and freedom of student talk can occur without interfering with the conduct of academic learning, much like the free, quiet interaction expected in most quiet libraries. Once children grow accustomed to using their collective whisper voice, it soon becomes second nature to them, and the result is immediately perceptible and important: it helps create a quiet, positive classroom atmosphere, conducive to real studying and learning. Others entering the whisper voice classroom will have to be reminded about speaking in their whisper voices, because the students will invariably become distracted, and in no time will be off task (Cowen, 1979).

Getting Started

An important step in getting started on learning centers is to carefully plan and organize the daily routine. This means that the teacher needs to carefully think about how many centers should be set up, on what centers to focus on, how many children are in the class, and how to divide the class into groups. Optimally, there should be enough centers set up so that each group can visit at least one center each day of the week, rotating on a daily basis. It would be expected that each group would spend approximately a half-hour to an hour at each center. Younger children might spend fifteen minutes to a half-hour at each center.

Setting Up Groups

It is best to create four to five small, diverse, heterogeneous work groups to work at centers. Depending on the size of the classroom and the number of children assigned to the class, the teacher should try to create cooperative groups that rarely exceed five students. A great deal of research regarding cooperative learning indicates that children learn the most in triads, pairs, and groups of four to five (Johnson & Johnson, 1989/1990). Once the number exceeds five, there is a tendency for children to lose focus; indeed, more off-task behavior often results, and discipline problems tend to increase.

Before placing students into small groups, the teacher must consider a number of management issues by raising several important questions, including the following (Fountas & Pinnell, 1996):

- Are all children included in work groups?
- Are the children grouped so that they can work well together?
- Are the groups diverse with regard to sex, race, culture, and language backgrounds?
- Are the groups heterogeneous in their ability to read, write, and communicate?
- Are the groups heterogeneous for special needs?

After groups are set up, the teacher must introduce one center to each group. Teachers often start by showing children how to use the **work board**. The students are told to look at the top of the work board to find their names listed and to check which group and which center they are assigned to each day. Some teachers assign a color or a symbol that signifies each group. Children may then look to see what color or symbol is placed next to their names or next to a center. **Icons** are then used to introduce children to the two to three activities to which they will also be assigned.

Once the groups are set up and introduced to the various centers, the teacher needs to develop a **rotation system** for the groups. This rotation system will help the teacher determine which groups go to which center on any given day and ensure that all groups have gone to a different center each day of the week. Many children love one specific center and would choose that center every day if they had a choice. The rotation system ensures that all children rotate through the different centers in a systematic way. The work board helps the teacher to organize this system.

The Work Board

The work board is designed to guide students through the various classroom centers by letting them know which center they will work in on a given day and what kinds of activities they will work with and in what order. Therefore, the work board is important in creating a rotation system for classroom centers, as well as for helping the teacher set up her guided reading groups. Simple icons from clip art can be used to set up the work board. The icons should be posted on the wall close to the work board. (See Figure 14–4

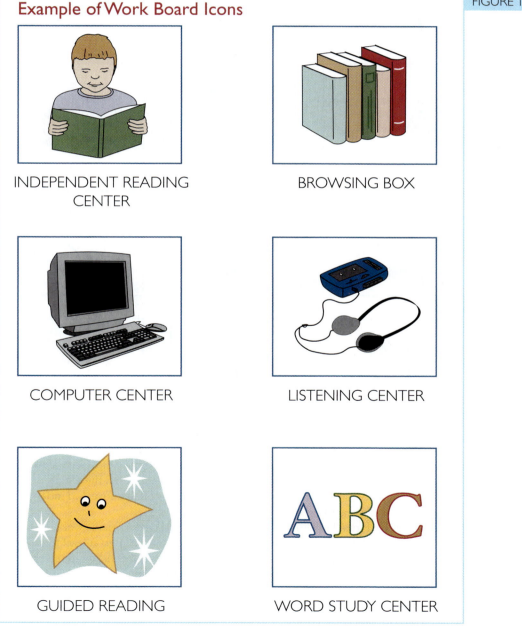

FIGURE 14-4

Example of Work Board Icons

INDEPENDENT READING CENTER

BROWSING BOX

COMPUTER CENTER

LISTENING CENTER

GUIDED READING

WORD STUDY CENTER

FIGURE 14-5

A Typical Work Board

Group A	Group B	Group C
Kyla Jake	Gerry Jamal	Frank Sarah
Michael	Shakita	Miguel
John	Christie	Sam
Kathy	Tyron	Melissa

for examples of work board icons and Figure 14–5 for a sample of the work board.) It is a good idea for the teacher to begin as early as possible to teach the children how to use the work board, so they can begin to engage in their collaborative and independent activities as soon as each center is open for use.

Fountas and Pinnell (1996) recommend that the first time students work in a center, they should start with only two activities and eventually build up to at least three activities each day over a four-day period. Based on the number of children in the class, the teacher usually selects three to four groups of children, making sure that each group can work cooperatively. Teachers must carefully monitor children's behavior during these first days and be particularly vigilant in observing how well students work together in groups. At the first sign of difficulty, intervention is necessary, and if the teacher assesses the groupings to be problematic, the groups might need to be rearranged.

The groups should be diverse and heterogeneous in ability. It is also recommended that all of the activities include some amount of reading, writing, listening, speaking, and visual literacy. To provide for flexibility and to ensure that the center contains ample materials, it is important not to assign two groups to one center at the same time. By the third week, students should be working independently with little or no direct intervention by the teacher. The teacher needs to carefully teach all routines and develop the students' understanding of the various icons and the use of the work board to ensure that students are ready to work independently.

First, the teacher monitors how well the children understand the various routines and can use the work board without confusion. Next, the teacher monitors each child's ability to work independently, collaboratively, and responsibly in the center. Finally, the teacher observes whether the children are able to self-regulate their behavior, so that they can engage in a variety of literacy activities in each of the established learning centers, while behaving responsibly and with an academic purpose in mind. The first days of establishing guidelines and routines for each new literacy learning center will affect the classroom atmosphere for the year; therefore, the teacher must be a confident leader and show the class who is in charge. Once this message has been established, the management of the centers should go smoothly.

Teachers use a variety of materials in making the work board, such as those used in creating magnetic boards, chalkboards, or corkboards. Other work boards are made from cardboard, oak tag, felt, and oilcloth products. Teachers who use pocket charts, name cards, and less durable materials, such as cardboard and oak tag, often laminate these products so that they can last throughout the school year. Icons and student names are usually basic designs printed on large index cards, oak tag, or file folders. The materials used to display icons and student names are kept simple so that changes can be made by hand or by computer whenever students enter or leave the program or if other adjustments are needed. Tape can be used on the back of these cards, making it easy for the teacher to rotate the icons and to rotate the children's names.

Basically, the work board should be created so that it is simple and easy to read. It should be designed to show which centers children are assigned to on given days while listing the activities in which they will be engaged. As mentioned earlier, some teachers assign groups by colors, such as the blue group, the yellow group, and so on. Sometimes, the icon will show only that the child will be engaged in the ABC center; however, once in the ABC center, another set of directions can be used to list a variety of activities from which the children can choose. One teacher refers to the routines that she provides as the KISS routine, which is short for Keep It Short and Simple.

Daily Schedule

To implement a balanced literacy program, the teacher needs to carefully plan out a daily schedule to accommodate all the curricular mandates that need to be covered in one day. The daily schedule will include a morning routine that usually involves reviewing class administrative tasks such as attendance, discussing the objectives for the day, and discussing the calendar. Usually, literacy activities take place first thing in the morning and encompass a two-hour block of time, often combining many different language activities such as spelling, word study, writing, and reading. Guided reading block usually lasts approximately one hour each day.

While the teacher is working with students in a guided reading session, groups of children are working at learning centers. The teacher should be located at a desk in the classroom so that every child is within range of vision and can easily be observed during the session. Often, the best place for a teacher to sit during guided reading is at a small desk at the back of the room, facing outward to the class, while the children sit facing the teacher with their backs to the centers. The teacher must manage the students effectively from afar while working with a guided reading group or working individually with a student. This is where the idea developed that teachers "have eyes in the back of their heads."

Teachers' VOICES   Alphabet Centers

I use alphabet centers in my first grade class in the following way:

The ABC's of Me

This is an alphabet center where the children take a file folder, paper, and pencil and write the alphabet on the sheet and something they like beginning with each letter.

It Is as Simple as ABC

The children take a file folder, paper, and pencil and form as many words as possible with the letters in the plastic bags. They then write the words on the paper.

Write the Words

The children take five cards from the plastic bag, a sheet of paper, and a pencil. They then think of a word that begins with each letter and write the word on paper.

—*Rachel Manzo, First Grade Teacher*

The following daily schedule is a sample of a 90-minute block spent on guided reading and literacy learning centers within a balanced literacy classroom. In this schedule, the guided reading group session lasts one-half hour and the teacher can see three groups in one day; but if the teacher feels that a longer session is needed, 45-minute blocks can be used instead.

	Group A	Group B	Group C	Group D
9:30–10:00	Guided Reading	Listening/Read-Along Center	Computer Center	Dramatic Play Center
10:00–10:30	Listening/Read-Along	Guided Reading	Dramatic Play Center	Computer Center
10:30–11:00	Computer Center	Dramatic Play Center	Guided Reading	Listening/Read-Along Center

In the model described in the Introduction scenario, the literacy session encompasses a 90-minute time block. The entire class takes part in a shared literacy experience for 30 minutes, in which the teacher does a read-aloud for the first 10 minutes, then the students engage in shared reading for the next 20 minutes, which includes discussion of the book. After this activity, four previously assigned groups engage in different activities. The teacher can work with one group in a guided reading session, while the other three groups rotate to different learning centers. The students at the centers work independently; the teacher works in the guided reading session. Once the guided reading session is complete, the teacher gives the group a brief activity: They can reread the story, read another story, or respond to a question that the teacher posed in the session. The teacher then moves among the different centers, monitoring the progress of students, providing support, answering questions, and collecting assessment data or works with another guided reading group. In this way, the teacher interacts with all students on a daily basis and provides assistance at the different centers.

Materials Used in a Balanced Literacy Classroom

Wait (1992) believes that the success of the learning center environment is largely dependent on several major components: (1) how well the teacher provides the students with an adequate supply of materials; (2) how well the teacher introduces the students to the centers while providing a clearly defined set of directions and routines for using materials effortlessly; (3) how well these materials are made readily accessible and easy to use by the children; and (4) how well the teacher has provided a variety of ability levels, genres, topics, and high-interest texts to keep children highly motivated and engaged. It does not make any sense, for instance, to set up a listening/read-along center using recorded books that provide little motivation regarding the various children's gender, culture, or ability levels. If this is the case, children will simply be bored and will resist learning, or even worse, they may engage in off-task behavior.

To provide a variety of leveled books, teachers often form planning and sharing teams so that they can rotate books on given days or weeks, which motivates children to search for new books in their various browsing boxes. Working with the school librarian and with the community librarian is another way of assuring that a good source of books is available, including a variety of genres such as biographies, sports, trade books, combined-text trade books, and books for thematic units. Once again, teachers who work in teams can rotate these resources throughout the school year. Sharing electronic materials, podcasts, software, CD-ROMs, and electronic talking books (Living Books) is an also important way of rotating costly materials and equipment.

Changing and Storing Materials

Literacy learning centers must provide many kinds of materials, manipulatives, games, multimedia packages, and books to keep children highly motivated and to keep them engaged in meaningful activities each week. Therefore, keeping track of when it is time to rotate books, materials, checksheets, student book lists, forms, and other supplies is absolutely essential. These materials and supplies must be inventoried on a regular basis by teachers, teacher aides, or students serving as monitors to inform the classroom teacher when they need to be changed or restored. Other ways of determining the rotation of materials, books, and supplies is to review student book lists, checklists, and "Time-to-Replace-Me" forms (placed at the bottom of each supply pile). In addition, preservice teachers often ask the following basic and important questions:

◆ Does the district supply all of the materials and books for the centers?

◆ Are there enough bookcases and storage areas for all of the materials?

◆ How can the teacher find alternatives to supply and store these materials and supplies?

◆ How does the teacher keep up with these centers on a week-to-week basis?

These are naturally thoughtful and realistic concerns or questions that need to be raised. But several words of advice must be given to preservice and first year teachers:

◆ Don't panic! Remember, classrooms cannot be transformed overnight.

◆ Meet with other grade-level teachers to brainstorm ideas for finding additional materials and storage containers.

◆ Seek out those teachers willing to give away materials and storage containers that they have collected over time.

◆ Many of the materials and storage containers that teachers use are available just for the asking and are usually free of cost.

Most districts provide teachers with paste, glue, scissors, file folders, art paper, and construction paper. Other materials that most districts provide include children's books, newspapers, magazines, and content-area textbooks. Principals often receive a small budget for purchasing supplementary items, including texts, materials, pet food, supplies, and petty cash classroom supplies. Some new funds are generally provided as well to stock new teachers' classrooms; therefore, it is important to ask what materials are available and what new materials or books, if any, can be purchased.

In addition, teachers are innovative and considered to be the official pack rats of the trade: they are well known by the proprietors of local businesses and shopping stores in the community, who gladly offer free boxes, crates, barrels, paper supplies, and other materials, whenever possible, to help them stock their meager classrooms. Teachers are often on the lookout for cast off containers of all kinds for storing center materials and for creating their own storage containers. Their hunt for materials often includes frequent trips to the deli, candy store, and the supermarket. These are great places to help find materials for learning centers; store personnel are usually willing to give away boxes and other throwaway items.

Materials that teachers can collect for centers include:

◆ Board games (teacher- and student-made)
◆ Cereal boxes, shoe boxes, and shopping market boxes for storing crayons, markers, puzzles, commercial games, student answer forms, and answer keys
◆ Egg crates for storing student folders, student portfolios, and library books
◆ Reclosable plastic bags for storing alphabet letters, magnetic letters or numbers, and game pieces
◆ Container cylinders for storing art supplies
◆ Coffee cans
◆ Large soda cups
◆ Oatmeal boxes
◆ Large boxes
◆ Plastic bags
◆ Brown envelopes
◆ Reading center furniture and rugs
◆ Used furniture (Salvation Army, parent contributions)
◆ Electronics such as computers, software, CD-ROMs, iPods, videos (many of which may be donated by corporations, community stores, organizations, and parents)

Teachers' VOICES   Phonics Center

My phonics center is just another fun way to have children practice writing words by manipulating letters. With a pen, I write letters on magnetic-ringed chips. I make individual bags for each child and number the bags. The children can pull out the letters they want to use from the bag and keep the rest safely inside the bag. Before children start this activity in the phonics center, I model the proper way to make the words on the overhead, sweeping away some letters with my "wand" (a teacher's pointer) to make new words or to find smaller words or rimes within the big word. They use their magnetic chips to make words by combining letters, and then the students sweep away some letters with the magnetic wand. They love using the wands!

The children can work in the phonics center with partners or alone. They can also record the words they have made on paper. It works best if you have them put the letters on white paper instead of on the wooden desks because the white paper makes the letters stand out better.

—*Melissa Begley, First Grade Teacher*

Using Technology in Learning Centers

Technology can be incorporated into each learning center and can provide an additional resource that students can use while working independently. Many classrooms have only a limited number of computers, and if there is only one computer in the classroom, it is recommended that a computer center be set up with many different types of applications that children can explore and share. If the classroom has more than one computer, it is recommended that they be distributed so that each center has at least one computer to enhance and enrich learning. If enough resources are available, a technology center can be set up that allows students to explore literacy through different technological tools. Determination of centers and how they are organized depends on available resources and how the teacher wants to distribute them throughout the classroom. Many teachers choose to set up a computer center with four or five computers instead of distributing them in the different centers, as described earlier.

Examples of how technology can be incorporated into the different learning centers are as follows:

◆ *Listening/Read-Along Center:* This center would benefit from books on tape or CDs for children to listen and read along with. Many libraries provide these resources for patrons to take out, and this activity is quite beneficial to struggling readers. In addition, electronic talking books are an excellent resource for this center because they provide embedded speech and interactive features on the screen. Many children's books have been converted to electronic talking books, in which digitized speech reads the selection aloud and different objects on the screen may be clicked on to provide interactive activities. In addition, there are many sites on the Internet that provide e-books for children to read, such as Story Place (http://www.storyplace.org), which provides stories for preschool and elementary school children with digitized speech in both English and Spanish. It is also helpful to have children record stories on either CD-ROMs or tape recorders for other children to use. English language learners can also record stories in their native language for other children to listen to.

◆ *Word Study Center:* It would be helpful if this center had a computer with software to reinforce basic skills in word recognition, phonic skills, and vocabulary development. Many software programs on the market provide basic drill and practice of these skills, which is motivating and beneficial to children, especially struggling readers. Many of these programs are in gamelike format or use funny and enjoyable characters to present the materials. Such programs as Reader Rabbit, Word Munchers (both from The Learning Company) and the Jump Start series (Knowledge Adventure) provide motivating ways to reinforce word study.

◆ *Reading Comprehension Center:* In this center, many school districts use computer managed programs which provide progress-monitoring assessment tools for reading, such as Accelerated Reader (Renaissance Learning). After children read a certain book, they log on to the computer and take an assessment test, which is then recorded into a database so that the teacher can track each student's progress. Many different software programs promote reading comprehension that students would find motivating. The teacher needs to ensure that the programs promote critical thinking and analysis and meet the goals of the reading program. In addition, using the computer to write is an excellent way for children to respond to text. Many programs are available that allow children to create their own pictures and write the text underneath their creations, such as KidPix (The Learning Company), and Storybook Weaver (The Learning Company). Inspiration and Kidspiration (Inspiration) are also wonderful programs that help children respond to text; with these software packages, they can create their own visual tools and story maps.

◆ *Inquiry Center:* This center calls for a computer that is hooked up to the Internet. Children learn to do structured searches using search engines, find material, evaluate whether the source or location is valid, critically evaluate the material for its relevance to the topic being researched, and apply information to solve the problem or answer the question. They could use electronic databases and online library catalogs to access primary source material and explore topics.

◆ *Writing Center:* At least one computer is also necessary at this center. Children enjoy typing their work using a word processor, which gives them clean and professional-looking material. It also allows for easy revision and for incorporation of electronic images into the work. Also, for students with learning disabilities and English language learners, it is helpful to have assistive technology such as "talking word processors," which provides text-to-speech capability, and word prediction software, which helps students figure out what word should be used and helps with its spelling. (Assistive technology is described in more detail in Chapter 2.) There are also many different software programs that provide writing prompts and help with writing, such as The Amazing Writing Machine (Broderbund) and Imagination Express (Edmark).

♦ *Arts and Crafts Center:* Computers are wonderful additions at this center, together with digital cameras and digital video. Many programs are available that allow students to create cards, photo albums, animations, newsletters, pictures, and artwork. Digital artwork has become the standard platform in the professional world, and there are many different ways in which children can explore digital applications in art. Such programs as Scrapbook (Nova Development US), Printshop (Broderbund) and KidPix (The Learning Company), Hyperstudio (Roger Wagner), and Photoshop Elements (Adobe) for older children are all wonderful additions to an art center. Tablets can be purchased that allow students to draw right on the computer, replacing the use of the mouse. These tablets are becoming quite popular and are excellent assistive devices for students with learning disabilities who might find it easier to navigate using a penlike device instead of a mouse.

♦ *Virtual Field Trip Center:* If there are enough computers in the classroom, teachers can set up a center where students can take virtual field trips based on the subject, theme, and topics being studied in class. There are many different sites that students can visit, including the White House, a pyramid, the Louvre, a rainforest, the Kremlin, and an ancient Roman Villa. (Chapter 2 describes virtual field trips in more detail.)

♦ *Content-Area Centers:* Much quality software and interesting Internet sites are available for children to explore different content areas. In science, there are sites that provide Internet projects where different classes across the country and world can collaborate and share real-time data on such things as earthquake activity, weather data, and volcanic activity (Center for Innovation in Engineering and Science Education located at http://www.k12science.org/currichome.html). Students can now do virtual dissections of frogs (see http://www.digitalfrog.com or http://www.froguts.com for products schools can purchase). They can navigate a complete three-dimensional musculoskeletal system to learn about bones in Bodywise by the Tool Factory (http://www.toolfactory.com). In social studies, students can access primary sources and investigate historical events. The Lewis & Clark Rediscovery Project (http://www.lcrediscovery.org) is a consortium of school districts located along the Lewis and Clark Trail that have compiled stories, maps, and graphics that provide glimpses of life along the historic and present-day Lewis & Clark Trail. Technology brings subject matter alive for many students, helping them to see concrete examples and applications of the subject.

♦ *Technology Center:* If there are enough resources, the teacher may wish to set up a technology center, as distinct from a computer center. The technology center will include such items as computers (either desktops or laptops), iPods, digital cameras, digital video cameras, software to edit video and photos, tablets to help students draw using a penlike device, SmartBoards where teachers and students can make presentations, handheld devices (personal digital assistants [PDAs]), where students can explore their application in education, digital projectors for displaying presentations off the computer, scanners for scanning images and text into the computer, and assistive technology that can support English language learners and students with learning disabilities. The technology center should have access to the Internet and be a center where groups or the whole class can meet to enrich all instruction throughout the day. It should also have a wide variety of software programs to support literacy development across the curriculum.

Using a SmartBoard in the Classroom

A typical SmartBoard system consists of a touch-sensitive white board connected to a projector and computer. The teacher can then run any computer application such as CD-ROMs, DVDs, the Internet, and other educational software, which will appear on

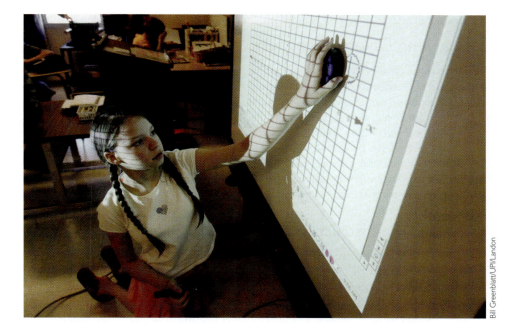

Technology centers can include smart boards, computers, and digital cameras.

Bill Greenblatt/UPI/Landon

the screen and allow the teacher to interact with those applications using a finger instead of a mouse. SmartBoards are becoming increasingly common in K–12 classrooms, where teachers have integrated this new technology across a variety of curriculum areas including English, mathematics, science, and social studies. It is a flexible teaching and learning tool that can be used in small-group instruction, whole-class instruction, teacher-directed learning activities, and student-directed learning activities. Both teachers and students can use the SmartBoard for presentations. There are many different manufacturers of SmartBoards and each comes with its own unique software that is used for interactive lessons.

There are several ways to use the SmartBoard in the classroom. One of the easiest is to use it with any of the interactive websites that have been discussed in this book and that are found on this book's website. Using the SmartBoard is just like using a web page on the computer, but it is displayed on the SmartBoard, together with the ability to manipulate the screen using your finger or other device.

Another way to use the SmartBoard is with any of the educational software that is loaded on a computer. For instance, a teacher can use a multimedia writing program such as Storybook Weaver (The Learning Company) on a computer and display it on the SmartBoard. The teacher and students can then compose a story together, and the teacher can allow students to come up and choose the background and pictures. The teacher can also teach basic word processing and other skills using Microsoft Office, which is displayed on the SmartBoard.

Another way to use the SmartBoard is to use the templates that come with the SmartBoard's accompanying software or to download templates from different websites. Templates are lessons that are saved in a particular format for manipulation using the computer and SmartBoard. Most templates require either the Smart Notebook software (this should be included with the SmartBoard), Kidspiration software (a version of Inspiration that is designed for preschool children), Inspiration software, Kid-Pix, or Microsoft PowerPoint. A good resource for SmartBoard templates can be found at The Teacher's Guide (http://www.theteachersguide.com/SmartBoards.htm) or the manufacturer's website.

Many districts have had successful experiences using SmartBoards, and if a district can afford the cost, there are many different brands and resources that can be found on the Internet by doing a search using Google. Teachers are experimenting with use of this technology, and it is an exciting development to watch.

Teaching Diverse Learners

Children must develop a sense of independence, be self-initiated learners, and display responsible behavior to perform well in literacy learning centers. Diverse learners excel in an environment that is student friendly, personalized, engaging, and interactive. English language learners and children with disabilities respond favorably to learning centers, which gives them the confidence to participate without fear of intimidation. Learning centers also provide a sheltered environment, or one that supports learners through peer collaboration and student-centered learning and, therefore, is more nurturing and supportive. Often, diverse learners feel free to express themselves verbally and in writing during learning center activities.

Differentiated Instruction

A great benefit of a balanced literacy program that uses guided reading and learning centers is that it provides differentiated instruction for all students (see Chapter 10 for a more detailed discussion). With differentiated instruction, teachers provide specific ways for each individual to learn as much as possible and as quickly as possible, individualizing according to student needs (Tomlinson, 1999). Diverse learners require individual attention, particularly if they are English language learners learning a new language or are students with learning disabilities in need of specific skill development. Research experts indicate that whenever possible, one-on-one intervention works best in helping diverse, struggling, and at-risk learners compared with having them learn in whole-group instruction settings (Clay, 1993; Fountas & Pinnell, 2000; Cowen, 2003a).

Teachers' VOICES   Differentiating Instruction Using Cooperative Care

I have my English language learners work together with other students in cooperative groups. This allows them to form their own meaningful conclusions and questions, which will promote comprehension and application of skills. In the end, when teaching native English speakers and English language learners, our lessons need to be formulated and based on the needs of both groups of students; therefore, a differentiated approach is needed by allowing a diverse group of students to respond and to participate based on their diverse linguistic needs. We need to make our students feel part of the learning community and the learning process. We must not only keep their attention,

we need to make learning more interactive. With this said, an immense amount of time is needed when planning; however, planning is only 50 percent of the job being fulfilled. Our planning needs to be differentiated so that instruction can be implemented effectively in the classroom. We are only fooling ourselves if we continue to drive our language arts/literacy curriculum toward the native English speaker and think that the English language learner is going to benefit, too!

—*James De Fillipps, Sixth Grade Teacher*

Literacy learning centers promote a social environment, which makes it easier for teachers to get to know their students more intimately because of the small-group and individualized settings. Teachers can use this more personalized role to stimulate student motivation and learning. This setting enables teachers to motivate children to participate in academic areas more fully and uninhibitedly. At the same time, this personalized, sheltered environment enables children to feel confident in sharing personal learning problems, as well as their accomplishments, with both teachers and classmates. A reciprocal process develops as a result, in that children begin to feel more confident and more secure, and they begin taking greater risks in learning to read. As a result, their reading improves, and shortly thereafter, it becomes quite evident that these diverse learners' self-concepts also improve (Cowen, 1979).

Children of diverse backgrounds prefer learning independently, particularly when they are empowered to:

◆ Select their own books

◆ Choose their own activities

◆ Balance the content they choose to learn

◆ Decide how much time to study

◆ Self-evaluate their completed work

This independence is also important in making diverse learners feel valued as capable individuals who can contribute both socially and academically as part of this new family-like community of learners. This interdisciplinary approach empowers children of diverse backgrounds to grow politically, environmentally, socially, culturally, and economically.

Inclusive Classrooms

In organizing and managing a literacy program, teachers will have many different types of learners in their classroom. In 1997, with the passage of the Individuals with Disabilities Education Act Amendment (IDEA), renewed in 2004, districts are required to provide a free appropriate public education (FAPE) to children with disabilities in the least restrictive environment (LRE). The general goal is to allow children with disabilities to be educated with their peers in the regular classroom to the extent possible (U.S. Government, 2005). **Inclusion** calls for teachers to form collaborative partnerships with the specialists in their schools for planning and delivering instruction and for monitoring academic progress and student behavior. As described in Chapter 13, the best inclusive arrangements are when special and regular classroom teachers work closely together to co-teach the class and their roles become so intertwined that it is difficult to ascertain who is serving the special populations.

Inclusion therefore means that the teacher must meet the needs of all children within the regular classroom, rather than removing the child from the class to receive supplemental services. This means that the regular teacher needs to accommodate all learners in the following ways:

◆ Collaborating or co-teaching with the special educators to help all children within the same classroom

◆ Assigning paraprofessionals or instructional assistants on a full-time basis to help an individual student who has severe needs

◆ Reducing class size in regular classrooms that include students with disabilities

◆ Adapting or modifying the curriculum, instruction, assignments, testing, or grading practices

◆ Providing flexible groupings of students to promote cooperative learning or peer tutoring opportunities (Meese, 2001)

Some controversy exists over the effectiveness of pull-out programs versus inclusion. Some teachers and parents believe that traditional service-delivery pull-out programs greatly benefit students with disabilities. In special pull-out programs, the students receive intense individualized instruction and usually have special adaptations made to promote successful intervention. Yet, many educators and parents feel that students with disabilities have a basic right to education in the regular classroom, and that many students with learning disabilities thrive and succeed in the regular classroom. When students are part of the regular classroom routine, they do not miss key elements

Courtesy of Bill Lisenby

Collaboratively planning literacy instruction with specialist teachers promotes inclusion and inclusive practices.

of the curriculum when they are pulled out for special instruction and they are not stigmatized by leaving at certain points in the day.

English language learners are also part of the inclusive classroom and need to be accommodated within the regular classroom environment. Classroom teachers need to maximize the inclusion of diverse cultures in the classroom through the use of multicultural literature, culturally sensitive instruction, testing accommodations, planning with the English language learner specialist, and cooperation and collaboration with parents and guardians. Teachers need to affirm the students' native language code while assisting the student to articulate and write in Standard English (Brown, 2002).

Learning centers can benefit an inclusive classroom in that it allows special needs students the opportunity to receive individualized instruction while participating in a group that is supporting the learner. Learning centers allow children to participate in decision making and engage in active learning while also encouraging language interaction, social communication, and responsibility for completion of tasks. Researchers (Genisio & Drecktrah, 1999) have found that center learning provides special needs children with a sense of empowerment, choice, and excitement in daily learning activities.

STRATEGIES FOR TEACHING DIVERSE STUDENTS

Managing and Organizing a Literacy Program

The following four variables are highly correlated to success in the inclusive classroom for diverse learners, including students with learning disabilities and English language learners:

1. **Classroom management and discipline**
   - Using efficient transitions between activities
   - Limiting negative responses and feedback to students
   - Maximizing engagement with all students
   - Using time efficiently

2. **Feedback during instruction**
   - Providing positive feedback consistently
   - Avoiding criticism
   - Establishing a good, positive relationship with students

3. **Instructional appropriateness**
   - Assigning tasks at the appropriate level
   - Allowing students to maintain high rates of correct responses
   - Varying instructional delivery techniques
   - Using multisensory learning

   - Rephrasing questions and providing cues when necessary to encourage independent engagement by all students
   - Accommodating different learning styles and intelligences
   - Making sure that the student is working in the zone of proximal development
   - Using alternative assessment tools when needed
   - Co-teaching with the specialists
   - Promoting critical thinking and inquiry
   - Expecting academic excellence for all

4. **Supportive environment**
   - Using supportive interventions
   - Responding supportively to problems
   - Encouraging students to support and cooperate with each other
   - Using punishment infrequently, if at all
   - Establishing parent–teacher communication and partnering
   - Working collaboratively with specialists in the school and district

Evaluating the Effectiveness of the Classroom

The use of reading and writing workshops for literacy improvement has been a part of most balanced reading approaches since the early major reading research studies were recorded in the early 1960s (Pressley, 2002; Cowen, 2003a). Determining the effectiveness of the various approaches has always been debated with such questions as: "Which reading approach is better than another?" What we do know, however, is that there is no one reading approach that is the best (Cowen, 2003a). Thirty years of research has informed the reading profession that a balance of instruction in phonemic awareness and phonics in tandem with meaningful literature, vocabulary, and specific comprehension are essential ingredients for producing successful literacy achievement (Pressley, 2002). The reading profession has also known for at least as long a period of time that observing children working independently and with their peers is an important process that helps the teacher assess how each child in his or her program is progressing—socially, academically, and linguistically.

Program Monitoring System

It is important in evaluating the effectiveness of the literacy environment that a **program monitoring system** be put into place. This means that the teacher is continuously monitoring the literacy program to ensure that an optimal and effective literacy environment and curriculum has been implemented, and that all children are achieving and improving. An important component of the program monitoring system is the use of observation.

In the early 1900s, Maria Montessori was instrumental in using the observational method in her Children's Houses, which will remain one of her major contributions to early childhood education. Although her observations were somewhat restricted to social learning behavior in relation to children's use of their own didactic materials (Montessori, 1964), Montessori's approach to continuous observation informed her timely interventions in working with specific children. The close monitoring of individual and small-group center activities is synonymous with Montessori's pedagogical approach; this monitoring of student learning through careful observation is an antecedent to continuous assessment of collaborative learning in centers. As Marie Clay attests (Clay, 1993), the classroom teacher is in a more unique position today to record natural and meaningful observations in helping children make consistent and necessary progress. Consequently, as reading teachers become more involved in diagnostic-driven instruction, they will continue to use student observation to create organized, systematic, and routine systems to monitor children's daily literacy encounters. Using careful observation, the teacher can monitor each student's literacy activities, and thereby plan systematic interventions in a more thoughtful and informed manner.

Another important component of a program monitoring system is providing positive feedback to children on their progress and achievement. According to Shirleen S. Wait (1992), when children are working diligently and meeting teacher expectations, they also need positive feedback that encourages them to continue progressing in this positive manner. Other ways of checking student progress include:

- Instituting student packets for organizing, recording, and self-checking their own work
- Reviewing student activities, in the form of work packets, on a daily or weekly basis
- Observing students on a continuous basis and recording anecdotal information
- Conferring with students on a weekly basis to review portfolios and work packets
- Publishing, recording, and sharing student products with other children, parents, teachers, and administrators
- Reviewing student portfolios monthly and/or every marking period (sharing progress with students over time)

- Sharing observation charts including students' use of time, time on task, and time off task
- Sharing with students the overall quantity and quality of work completed in each of the various centers
- Engaging students in self-evaluations based on an accumulation of data and information shared with each student

It is important that teachers share their observations with students and discuss their progress. Information on such things as use of time, quantity of work, and quality of work completed is a powerful learning experience on which each student can reflect. Sharing observational data with students and parents is an important process in which students become engaged in self-assessment; unfortunately, it is rarely used in the classroom.

As part of the program monitoring system, teachers need to monitor each learning center on a weekly basis. The classroom teacher must guard against her students not being challenged. She must be sure that all materials are educationally sound, and that children do not resort to filling in meaningless drill sheets or workbook pages in any of the centers. Therefore, it is important to monitor each center closely, maintaining only the highest literacy standards, learning objectives, and instructional materials. Some important questions that teachers can use to evaluate how well centers are meeting student needs are as follows:

- Are leveled books integrated into the centers so that each child is reading at his or her appropriate reading level?
- Are the work board and class rules monitored daily so that children know exactly what the routines are and what the teacher's expectations are for the various activities in each center?
- Are all of the centers well stocked with supplies and appropriate-level materials for each student's independent use?
- Are the children well trained to return materials and books to their proper places after they are finished with them?
- Are the centers carefully monitored to see that all of the children are actively engaged and are on task most of the time?
- Are the children's activities and programs monitored daily to ensure that each child's performance level is being met and challenged?
- What assessment tools are in place to ensure that each child's literacy achievement is being accurately assessed and accounted for in each center?
- When centers are not being used effectively, what procedures are in place to improve or discontinue them?

Another important component of the program monitoring system is collecting and analyzing data that the teacher collects from guided reading sessions and learning centers. During guided reading, teachers should be administering running records and collecting information on fluency such as rate of words read per minute and number of questions answered correctly on comprehension. In addition, data on vocabulary development and word identification should be gathered for each child. These data should be recorded each time the teacher meets with a group during guided reading. Anecdotal notes should be recorded as well to help the teacher track each student's level of progress.

Data should be collected from each learning center each time a group works at a center. The activities can be collected and assessed using a rubric. Scripts, group projects, artwork, and writing samples should all be collected, assessed on a rubric, and monitored carefully. This will help a teacher determine whether a group is working effectively together or having difficulty staying on task. It will help a teacher assess group dynamics and will help a teacher to rearrange groups, if necessary. Observational notes should be recorded as the teacher observes the different groups in learning centers.

Program Monitoring System

Type of Monitoring	Purpose	Data Collected	Action Taken
OBSERVATION	To ascertain whether all children are on task and behaving appropriately Ensure that all children are achieving	Anecdotal notes Observation checklist	Feedback to students, parents, other professionals, if needed
FEEDBACK TO STUDENTS	To allow children to become aware of their level of performance and self-regulate their behavior to improve	Anecdotal notes Record of student conferences	Conference with students Conference with parents
MONITORING OF THE ENVIRONMENT	To ensure that the learning centers and classroom environment is safe, secure, and child-centered promoting achievement	Checklist for each center Checklist for classroom Feedback from students Feedback from other teachers Feedback from parents	Revising the learning centers for more effective management Changing groupings of children Rearranging of the classroom Discussion and revision (if necessary) of class rules
ACHIEVEMENT DATA FROM STUDENTS	To ensure that all children are achieving and progressing in literacy	Running records Fluency rates Rubrics assessing group projects Anecdotal notes Comprehension scores/tests	Provide instruction in specific areas that data reveals need improving Provide child with readings on correct level Seek professional guidance, if necessary

FIGURE 14-6

As mentioned earlier, a teacher must monitor all activity from afar, and even if he or she is absorbed in working with a guided reading group, the teacher should also be keeping careful notes on the other groups working in centers.

A program monitoring system allows teachers to determine whether all children are learning and achieving. The monitoring system should include: (1) observation of all children in the class; (2) continuous feedback provided to students about their level of achievement; (3) weekly monitoring of learning centers to ensure that children are on task, learning, and using the materials appropriately; and (4) careful analysis of data collected from guided reading sessions and learning centers to determine individual progress. Figure 14–6 summarizes a program monitoring system in a balanced literacy classroom (Cowen, 1979).

Final Thoughts

The carefully managed, organized, balanced literacy classroom creates a beautifully orchestrated approach to student learning. Creating successful learning environments is important to the full development of a successful literacy program because researchers indicate that good classroom managers produce positive results and prevent most management and behavioral problems from occurring. Effective classroom management enables students to know what the teacher's expectations are for learning, what activities should be completed, and how to complete activities successfully. More importantly, because good classroom managers create a classroom that has many exciting activities, books, and materials to investigate, the children come to school eager to learn, eager to participate, and are highly motivated to engage in a variety of literacy learning tasks that will help them make a great deal of progress. This joy of learning that occurs in a sheltered, nurturing environment often produces students who continue to pursue literacy as a lifelong interest.

STRATEGY BOX

Managing and Organizing a Balanced Literacy Program

Mr. Roth set up a well-managed and well-organized balanced literacy classroom that meets his students' needs with the help of school specialists and professors from a local university. His students' reading scores are improving, and he and his students share a sense of pride and community engagement in pursuing enjoyable and motivating literacy activities. Mr. Roth used the following strategies to manage and organize his literacy program:

1. He developed centers that promote literacy and focused on advancing his students' reading and writing performance.

2. He ensured that his centers were performance-based, meaningful, and connected to what was being learned in his classroom.

3. He developed engaging and motivating activities that promote achievement.

4. He organized his classroom with specific functions in mind so that the centers would work best in the space provided.

5. He developed a classroom environment that was conducive to a collaborative workshop approach.

6. New centers were introduced only after the previous center was clearly understood and functioning efficiently. Students knew exactly what the purpose of each new center was and what the teacher's expectations were before they started working at it.

7. He established a highly structured environment that followed a set routine, and he maintained strict control over the class.

8. He created four to five small, diverse, heterogeneous groups to work at centers together.

9. He developed a rotation system for the groups, and the students knew what their schedule was. Students knew that they would work with him in a guided reading session at least once a week.

10. He planned out a daily schedule to accommodate all the curricular mandates that need to be covered in one day.

11. He provided differentiated instruction for all students.

12. All special needs students received individualized instruction while participating in a group that was supportive.

EXPLORATION   Application of Concepts

Activities

1. Observe several different classrooms in which literacy is being taught. Make a diagram of the room that shows the organization of the classroom environment, including the arrangement of the furniture, the accessibility of books, materials, and whether the teacher has provided learning centers. If so, describe the centers and how children use them.

2. Describe one teacher's use of technology in the classroom by explaining the various kinds of electronic instructional tools available and how they are used by the teacher to improve literacy instruction, as well as to manage, organize, and evaluate children's learning.

3. Describe how the teacher's classroom management and physical arrangement of the environment help in controlling student behavior.

4. From your observations of several classrooms, explain what you believe makes the difference between positive and negative classroom behavior. In other words, have you seen a classroom that was "out of control"? If so, explain why.

5. Interview a principal and one or more supervisors, and ask whether classroom management is a greater challenge to teachers today. If so, what are the major causes?

HOME–SCHOOL CONNECTION   Volunteering Helps Teachers Out

Parents and guardians often ask how they can become more connected to their child's classroom. One way is by volunteering to assist the teacher during specific activities and routines throughout the school year, which helps with the organization and management of the classroom. Research shows that children whose parents or guardians volunteer at school have a better attitude and higher academic achievement. Teachers who have assistance and help do a better job in managing the classroom. Parents and guardians who participate in the classroom are better prepared to support their child's schoolwork. Volunteer work can greatly affect the success of children in the classroom.

What kind of activities can parents and guardians do in the classroom? Below is a list of possible ways they can get involved:

1. Assist during daily work time when the students are involved in a variety of activities in their classroom: give guidance to students at learning centers, work with a reading group, or help students conduct daily jobs

2. Read aloud to a group of children while the teacher works with another group

3. Provide assistance for individual students to meet specific needs, such as taking a group of students to work on a specific skill or to practice fluent reading

4. Accompany the class on field trips

5. Share cultural traditions and/or ethnic background with food and celebrations

6. Compile and organize classroom work and projects

7. Help students with writing and editing during a writing workshop

8. Give short presentations about a profession or specific interest

9. Listen to students practicing oral reading

10. Work with students at the computer or technology center or provide technical assistance to the teacher

11. Help plan special days in the classroom, such as a class presentation to the school

It is helpful at the beginning of the year—for example during the open house/parent night—if the teacher passes out a form that asks for volunteers to help in the classroom. It is important to ask parents and guardians what kind of things they would like to do, and to find out convenient times for them to volunteer. This information is helpful before making a schedule for family helpers. Teachers particularly like to have volunteers during learning center time: this provides extra support for managing the classroom activities and monitoring student behavior. By volunteering, parents and guardians develop a more trusting relationship with the teachers and school, completing the home–school connection.

REFERENCES

Adams, M. J. (1990). *Beginning to read: Thinking and learning about print.* Cambridge, MA: MIT Press.

Airasian, P. W. (1997). *Classroom assessment: Concepts and applications.* New York: McGraw Hill.

Allen, R. (2001). Cultivating kindergarten: The reach for academic heights raises challenges. *Curriculum update* (pp. 1–8). Alexandria, VA: Association for Supervision and Curriculum Development.

Allington, R. L. (2005). The other five "pillars" of effective reading instruction. *Reading Today, 22*(6), 3.

Allington, R. L., & Walmsley, S. A. (2007). *No quick fix, the RTI edition: Rethinking literacy programs in America's elementary schools.* Newark, DE: International Reading Association.

American Library Association (ALA). (2005). Information literacy competency standards for higher education. Retrieved July 3, 2006, from http://www.ala.org/ala/acrl/acrlstandards/informationliteracy competency.htm

American Library Association (ALA) and Association for Educational Communications and Technology (AECT). (1998). The nine information literacy standards for student learning. Retrieved March 10, 2005, from http://www.ala.org

Anderson, K. (2003). Developing independent writers. *Language minority teacher induction program.* Retrieved April 19, 2003, from http://gse.gmu.edu/research/lmtip/arp/vol1.htm

Anderson, L. F. (1990). A rationale for global education. In K. A. Tye (Ed.), *Global education; from thought to action.* Alexandria, VA: Association for Curriculum and Development.

Anderson, R. C. (1977). The notion of schemata and the educational enterprise. In R. C. Anderson, R. J. Spiro, & W. E. Montague (Eds.), *Schooling and the acquisition of knowledge* (pp. 415–431). Hillsdale, NJ: Lawrence Erlbaum.

Anderson, V., & Roit, M. (1996). Linking reading comprehension instruction to language development for language-minority students. *The Elementary School Journal, 96,* 295–309.

Angelillo, J. (2005). *Writing to the prompt.* Portsmouth, NH: Heinemann.

Antunez, B. (2004). Reading and English language learners. Retrieved November 3, 2004, from http://www.readingrockets.org/article.php?ID=404

Armbruster, B. B., Lehr, F., & Osborn, J. (2001). *Put reading first: The research building blocks for teaching children to read.* Washington, DC: National Institute for Literacy.

Asp, E. (2000). Assessment in education: Where have we been? Where are we headed? In R. S. Brandt (Ed.), *Education in a new era.* Alexandria, VA: Association for Supervision and Curriculum Development.

Atwell, N. (1987). *In the middle: Writing, reading, and learning with adolescents.* Portsmouth, NH: Heinemann.

Atwell, N. (1998). *In the middle; new understandings about writing, reading, and learning.* Portsmouth, NH: Heinemann.

Au, K. H. (2001, July/August). Culturally responsive instruction as a dimension of new literacies. *Reading Online, 5.* Retrieved February. 15, 2006, from http://readingonline.org

August, D., Carlo, M., Dressler, C., & Snow, C. (2005). The critical role of vocabulary development for English language learners. *Learning Disabilities Research & Practice, 20*(1), 50–57.

August, D., & Shanahan, T. (Eds.). (2006). *Developing literacy in second-language learners: A report of the National Literacy Panel on language-minority children and youth.* Mahwah, NJ: Lawrence Erlbaum Associates.

Ausubel, D. (1963). *The psychology of meaningful verbal learning.* New York: Grune & Stratton.

Baidders, W., Bethel, L. J., Fu, V., & Peck, D. (2000). *Houghton Mifflin science discovery works.* Boston, MA: Houghton Mifflin.

Barnitz, J. G. (1998). Discourse diversity: Principles for authentic talk and literacy instruction. In M. F. Opitz (Ed.), *Literacy instruction for culturally and linguistically diverse students* (pp. 64–70). Newark, DE: International Reading Association.

Bear, D. R., Invernizzi, M., Templeton, S., & Johnston, F. (2000). *Words their way: Word study for phonics, vocabulary, and spelling instruction.* Upper Saddle River, NJ: Merrill/Prentice Hall.

Bear, D. R., Templeton, S., Helm, L. A., & Baren, T. (2003). Orthographic development and learning to read in different languages. In G. G. Garcia (Ed.), *English learners: Reaching the highest level of English literacy* (pp. 71–95). Newark, DE: International Reading Association.

Beck, I., Perfetti, C., & McKeown, M. (1982). The effects of long-term vocabulary instruction on lexical access and reading comprehension. *Journal of Educational Psychology, 74,* 506–521.

Bednarz, S., Clinton, C., Hartoonian, M., Hernandez, A., Marshall, P. L., & Nickell, P. (2000). *Share Our World.* Boston, MA: Houghton Mifflin.

Berger, C. (1996). Definitions of instructional design. Retrieved February 2006, from http://www.umich.edu/~ed626/define.html

Berliner, D. (2006). Our impoverished view of educational reform. *Teachers College Record, 108*(6), 949–995, Retrieved January 15, 2009, from http://www.tcrecord.org

Berne, J. I., & Blachowicz, C. L. Z. (2008/2009, December/January). What reading teachers say about vocabulary instruction: Voices from the classroom. *The Reading Teacher, 62*(4), 314–323.

Bieger, E. M. (1996). Promoting multicultural education through a literature-based approach. *The Reading Teacher, 49*(4), 308–312.

Birsh, J. R. (1999). *Multisensory teaching of basic language skills.* Baltimore, MD: Paul H. Brookes Publishing.

Bishop, R. S. (1993). Multicultural literature for children; making informed choices. In V. J. Harris (Ed.), *Teaching multicultural literature in grades k–8* (pp. 37–53). Norwood, MA: Christopher-Gordon Publishers.

Blachowicz, C. (1986). Making connections: Alternatives to the vocabulary notebook. *Journal of Reading, 29*(7), 643–649.

Blachowicz, C., & Fisher, P. J. (2002). *Teaching vocabulary in all classrooms* (2nd ed.). Upper Saddle River, NJ: Pearson Education.

Blachowicz, C. L. Z., & Fisher, P. J. (2004). Keep the "fun" in fundamental: Encouraging word awareness and incidental word learning in the classroom through word play. In J. F. Baumann & E. J. Kame'enui (Eds.), *Vocabulary instruction: Research to practice* (pp. 218–237). New York: Guilford.

Block, C. C., & Mangieri, J. N. (2002). Recreational reading: Twenty years later. *The Reading Teacher, 55*(6), 572–585.

Bloom, B. S. (1956). *Taxonomy of educational objectives; the classification of educational goals. Handbook I: Cognitive domain.* New York: Longman.

Bollino, J. (2005). "I'm a writer now!" The who, where, and when of an ELL newspaper. *The Quarterly 2005: National Writing Project.* Retrieved June 4, 2006, from http://www.writingproject.org

Bolton, F., & Snowball, D. (1993). *Ideas for spelling.* Portsmouth, NH: Heinemann.

Bond, G. I., & Dykstra, R. (1967). The cooperative research program in first-grade instruction. *Reading Research Quarterly, 2,* 5–142.

Boyle, O. F., & Peregoy, S. F. (1998). Literacy scaffolds: Strategies for first- and second-language readers and writers. In M. F. Opitz (Ed.), *Literacy instruction for culturally and linguistically diverse students* (pp. 150–157). Newark, DE: International Reading Association.

Bratcher, S. (1994). *Evaluating children's writing: A handbook of communication choices for classroom teachers.* New York: St. Martin's Press.

Bravo, M. A., Hiebert, E. H., & Pearson, P. D. (2005). Tapping the linguistic resources of Spanish/English bilinguals: The role of cognates in science. Retrieved October 18, 2005, from http://seedsofscience.org/ PDFs/Cognates.pdf

Brooks, W., & McNair, J. (Spring 2009). "But this story of mine is not unique": A review of research on African American children's literature. *Review of Educational Research, 79*(1), 125–162.

Brown, E. L. (2002). Mrs. Boyd's fifth-grade inclusive classroom: A study of multicultural teaching strategies. *Urban Education, 37*(1), 126–141.

Brown, K. J. (2000). What kind of text-for whom and when? Textual scaffolding for beginning readers. *The Reading Teacher, 53*(4), 292–306.

Bruner, J. (1960). *The process of education.* New York: Random House.

Bruner, J. (1966). *Toward a theory of instruction.* Cambridge, MA: Harvard University Press.

Buehl, D. (2001). *Classroom strategies for interactive learning.* Newark, DE: International Reading Association.

Bukovec, J. A. (1979). *An activity monitoring system.* Trenton, NJ: Department of Education.

Bukovec, J. A. (1982). Improving reading skills through auricular reading techniques. *The Reading Instruction Journal, 25*(2, 3), 32–37.

Calkins, L. M. (1986). *The art of teaching writing.* Portsmouth, NH: Heinemann.

Campbell, E. (2007). Tied up in knots; Spatial reasoning for visual literacy using 3-D dynamic modeling software. *Proceedings of the Visual and Computational Teaching and Learning Conference, Charleston, South Carolina.* Retrieved January 31, 2009, from http://www.cofc.edu/~thinking/

Carlo, M., August, D., McLaughlin, B., Snow, C., Dressler, C., Lippman, D. N., et al. (2004). Closing the gap: Addressing the vocabulary needs of English-language learners in bilingual and mainstream classrooms. *Reading Research Quarterly, 39*(2), 188–215.

Carnine, D. W., Silbert, J., Kame'enui, E. J., & Tarver, S. G. (2004). *Direct instruction reading* (4th ed.). Upper Saddle River, NJ: Pearson Education.

Carr, E., & Wixson, K. K. (1986). Guidelines for evaluating vocabulary instruction. *Journal of Reading, 29*(7), 588–595.

Cassidy, J., & Cassidy, D. (2005/2006, December/January). What's hot, what's not for 2006. *Reading Today, 23*(3), 1.

Cassidy, J., Garret, S. D., & Barrera, E. S. (2006). What's hot in adolescent literacy 1997–2006. *Journal of Adolescent & Adult Literacy, 50*(1), 30–36.

Caverly, D. C., Mandeville, T. F., & Nicholson, S. A. (1995). Plan: A study-reading strategy for informational text. *Journal of Adolescent & Adult Literacy, 39*(5), 190–199.

Center for Research on Education Diversity & Excellence (CREDE). (2002). *Research evidence; five standards for effective pedagogy and student outcomes.* Santa Cruz, CA: University of California.

Chall, J., Radwin, E., French, V., & Hall, C. (1979). Blacks in the world of children's books. *The Reading Teacher, 32*(5), 527–533.

Chall, J. S. (1967). *Learning to read: The great debate.* New York: McGraw-Hill.

Chard, D. J., Vaughn, S., & Tyler, B.-J. (2002). A synthesis of research on effective interventions for building reading fluency with elementary students with learning disabilities. *Journal of Learning Disabilities, 35*(5), 386.

Christen, W. L., Searfoss, L. W., & Bean, T. W. (1984). *Improving communication through writing and reading.* Dubuque, IA: Kendall/Hunt.

Clay, M. (1966). *Emerging reading behavior.* Unpublished doctoral dissertation, University of Aukland, New Zealand.

Clay, M. (1979). *The early detection of reading difficulties* (2nd ed.). Portsmouth, NH: Heinemann.

Clay, M. (1991). *Becoming literate; the construction of inner control.* Portsmouth, NH: Heinemann.

Clay, M. (1993a). *An observation survey of early literacy achievement.* Portsmouth, NH: Heinemann.

Clay, M. (1993b). *Reading recovery: A guidebook for teachers in training.* Portsmouth, NH: Heinemann.

Clay, M. (2000). *Running records for classroom teachers.* Portsmouth, NH: Heinemann.

Clements, D. H. (1994). The uniqueness of the computer as a learning tool: Insights from research and practice. In J. L. Wright & D. D. Shade (Eds.), *Young children: Active learners in a technological age* (pp. 31–50). Washington DC: NAEYC.

Cohen, V. (2003). Assessing distance learning instruction. *Journal of Computing in Higher Education, 14*(2), 98–120.

Cohen, V. (2005). *Electronic-portfolios as cognitive tools in a teacher education program.* Paper presented at the 3rd International Conference on Multimedia and ICT's in Education, Cáceres Spain.

Coiro, J. (2004). Reading comprehension on the Internet: Expanding our understanding of reading comprehension to encompass new literacies. *Reading Online.* Retrieved February 15, 2006, from http://readingonline.org

Coiro, J., & Dobler, E. (April/May/June 2007). Exploring the online reading comprehension strategies used by sixth-grade skilled readers to search for and locate information on the Internet. *Reading Research Quarterly, 42*(2), 214–250.

Coiro, J., Knobel, M., Lankshear, C., & Leu, D. J. (2008a). Preface. In J. Coiro, M. Knobel, C. Lankshear, & D. J. Leu

(Eds.), *Handbook of research on new literacies.* Mahwah, NJ: Lawrence Erlbaum.

Coiro, J., Knobel, M., Lankshear, C., & Leu, D. J. (2008b). Central issues in new literacies and new literacies research. In J. Coiro, M. Knobel, C. Lankshear, & D. J. Leu (Eds.), *The handbook of research in new literacies* (pp. 17–63). Mahwah, NJ: Lawrence Erlbaum.

Cole, A. D. (1998). Beginner-oriented texts in literature-based classrooms: The segue for a few struggling readers. *The Reading Teacher, 51*(6), 488–500.

Collins, M. F. (2005). ESL preschoolers' English vocabulary acquisition from storybook reading. *Reading Research Quarterly, 40*(4), 406–408.

Coltrane, B. (2002). *English language learners and high-stakes tests: An overview of the issues.* Washington, DC: Center for Applied Linguistics.

Combs, M. (1996). Emerging readers and writers. In L. Dixon-Kraus (Ed.), *Vygotsky in the classroom: Mediated literacy instruction and assessment* (pp. 25–41). White Plains, NY: Longman.

Computerworld. (2005). Survey: U.S. residents addicted to e-mail. Retrieved February 19, 2006, from http:// www.computerworld.com/softwaretopics/software/groupware/story/0,10801,102131,00.html

Cooper, J. D., & Kiger, N. D. (2005). *Literacy assessment: Helping teachers plan instruction.* Boston: Houghton Mifflin Company.

Cooter, R. B. (1990). *The teacher's guide to reading tests.* Scottsdale, AZ: Gorsuch Publishers.

Corporation for Public Broadcasting. (2002). Connected to the future; a report on children's Internet use from the Corporation for Public Broadcasting. Retrieved November 10, 2004, from http://www.cpb.org

Cowen, J. E. (1979). *Human reading strategies that work; the communications workshop.* Trenton, NJ: Department of Education.

Cowen, J. E. (2003a). *A balanced approach to beginning reading instruction: A synthesis of six major U.S. research studies.* Newark, DE: International Reading Association.

Cowen, J. E. (2003b). Graphic organizers and visual tools. In N. B. Smith (Ed.), *Be a better reader; teacher's edition* (8th ed.). Parsippany, NJ: Pearson Education.

Cullinan, B. E. (1992). Leading with literature. In B. E. Cullinan (Ed.),

Invitation to read: More children's literature in the reading program (pp. x–xxii). Newark, DE: International Reading Association.

Cunningham, P. (2000). *Phonics they use; words for reading and writing* (3rd ed.). New York: Longman.

Cunningham, P. (2002). What we know about how to teach phonics. In A. Farstrup & S. J. Samuels (Eds.), *What research has to say about reading instruction.* Newark, DE: International Reading Association.

Cunningham, P. M., & Cunningham, J. W. (2002). What we know about how to teach phonics. In A. E. Farstrup & S. J. Samuels (Eds.), *What research has to say about reading instruction* (pp. 87–109). Newark, DE: International Research Association.

Cunningham, P. M., & Hall, D. P. (1998). *The four blocks: A balanced framework for literacy in primary classrooms in teaching every child every day. Learning in diverse schools and classrooms.* Cambridge, MA: Brookline Books.

Curwin, R. L., & Mendler, A. N. (1988). *Discipline with dignity.* Alexandria, VA: Association for Supervision and Curriculum Development.

Davidson, J., Elcock, J., & Moyes, P. (1996). A preliminary study of the effect of computer-assisted practice on reading attainment. *Journal of Research in Reading, 19*(2), 102–110.

Dede, C. (2004). Making educational technology work: State policies in the north central region. NCREL Policy Issue 15. Retrieved October 15, 2004, from http://www.ncrel.org/policy/pubs/html/pivol15/intro.htm

Delpit, L. (1988). The silenced dialogue: Power and pedagogy in educating other people's children. *Harvard Educational Review, 58*, 280–298.

DiCerbo, P. A. (2000). Lessons from research: What is the length of time it takes limited English proficient students to acquire English and succeed in an all-English classroom? Washington, DC: National Clearinghouse for Bilingual Education, Center for the Study of Language & Education.

Dillon, J. T. (1988). *Questioning and teaching: A manual of practice.* New York: Teachers College Press.

Dixon-Krauss, L. (1996a). Spontaneous and scientific concepts in content-area instruction. In L. Dixon-Krauss (Ed.), *Vygotsky in the classroom: Mediated literacy instruction and assessment.* White Plains, NY: Longman Publishers.

Dixon-Krauss, L. (1996b). Vygotsky's sociohistorical perspective on learning and its application to western literacy instruction. In L. Dixon-Krauss (Ed.), *Vygotsky in the classroom; mediated literacy instruction and assessment* (pp. 7–24). White Plains, NY: Longman.

Dodge, B. (1997). Some thoughts about webquests. Retrieved June 22, 2004, from http://edweb.sdsu.edu/courses/edtec596/about_webquests.html

Dolly, M. R. (1998). Integrating ESL reading and writing through authentic discourse. In M. F. Opitz (Ed.), *Literacy instruction for culturally and linguistically diverse students* (pp. 161–167). Newark, DE: International Reading Association.

Dowhower, S. L. (1987). Effect of repeated reading on second grade transitional readers' fluency and comprehension. *Reading Research Quarterly, 22*, 389–406.

Doyle, M. A. (1998). Using writing to develop reading. In M. F. Opitz (Ed.), *Literacy instruction for culturally and linguistically diverse students* (pp. 146–149). Newark, DE: International Reading Association.

Duke, N. K. (2003). Informational text? The research says, "yes!" In L. Hoyt, M. Mooney, & B. Parkes (Eds.), *Exploring informational texts: From theory to practice* (pp. 2–7). Portsmouth, NH: Heinemann.

Duke, N. K. (2004). *Informational text and young readers: Findings from research.* Poster session presented at the annual conference of the International Reading Association, Reno, NV.

Duke, N. K., & Bennett-Armistead, V. S. (2003). *Reading and writing informational text in the primary grades: Research-based practices.* New York: Scholastic.

Duke, N. K., & Pearson, P. D. (2002). Effective practices for developing reading comprehension. In A. E. Farstrup & S. J. Samuels (Eds.), *What research has to say about reading instruction* (pp. 205–242). Newark, DE: International Reading Association.

Dukes, C. (2005). Best practices for integrating technology into English language instruction. *SouthEast Initiatives Regional Technology in Education Consortium News Wire, 7*(1), 3–6.

Durkin, D. (1993). *Teaching them to read* (6th ed.). Boston: Allyn & Bacon.

Dutro, S., & Moran, C. (2003). Rethinking English language instruction: An architectural approach. In G. G. Garcia (Ed.), *English learners: Reaching the highest level of English literacy* (pp. 227–258). Newark, DE: International Reading Association.

Eagleton, M.B. (2002, July/August). Making text come to life on the computer: Toward an understanding of hypermedia literacy. *Reading Online, 6*(1). Available: http://www.readingonline.org/articles/art_index.asp?HREF=eagleton2/index.html

The Education Alliance at Brown University. (2006). Teaching diverse learners: Ongoing assessment of language, literacy, and content learning. Retrieved June 3, 2006, from http://www.alliance.brown.edu/tdl/assessment/perfassess.shtml

Educational Testing Service. (2002). Digital transformation: A framework for ICT literacy, a report of the International Information and Communication Technologies (ICT) Literacy Panel. Retrieved October 16, 2004, from http://www.ets.org/research/ictliteracy/index.html

Ehri, L., Nunes, S., Willows, D., Schuster, B., Yaghoub-Zadeh, Z., & Shanahan, T. (2001). Phonemic awareness instruction helps children learn to read: Evidence from the national reading panel's meta-analysis. *Reading Research Quarterly, 36*, 250–287.

Eisner, E. W. (1997). Cognition and representation; a way to pursue the American dream? *Kappan, 78*(5), 348–353.

Feuerstein, R., Rand, Y., Hoffman, M. B., & Miller, R. (1980). *Instrumental enrichment.* Baltimore, MD: University Park Press.

Fisher, D., Flood, J., & Lapp, D. (2003). Material matters: Using children's literature to charm readers (or why Harry Potter and the Princess Diaries matter). In L. M. Morrow, L. B. Gambrell, & M. Pressley (Eds.), *Best practices in literacy instruction* (pp. 167–186). New York: Guilford Press.

Fisher, D., Flood, J., Lapp, D., & Frey, N. (2004). Interactive read-alouds: Is there a common set of implementation practices? *The Reading Teacher, 58*(1), 9–17.

Fitzgerald, J. (1999). What is this thing called balance? *The Reading Teacher, 53*(2), 100–107.

Flavell, J. H. (1977). *Cognitive development.* Englewood Cliffs, NJ: Prentice-Hall.

Flippo, R. F. (2003). *Assessing readers: Qualitative diagnosis and instruction.* Portsmouth, NH: Heinemann.

Foorman, B. R., Francis, D. J., Fletcher, J. M., Schatschneider, C., & Mehta, P.

(1998). The role of instruction in learning to read: Preventing reading failure in at-risk children. *Journal of Educational Psychology, 90*, 37–55.

Forgrave, K. E. (2002). Assistive technology: Empowering students with learning disabilities. *The Clearing House, 75*(3), 122–129.

Fountas, I. C., & Pinnell, G. S. (1996). *Guided reading; good first teaching for all children.* Portsmouth, NH: Heinemann.

Frey, N., & Fisher, D. (2007). *Reading for information in elementary schools:Content literacy strategies to build comprehension,* Upper Saddle River, NJ: Pearson Education, Inc.

Fry, E. (2002). Readability versus leveling. *The Reading Teacher, 56*(3), 286–291.

Fry, E., & Kress, J. (2006). *The reading teacher's book of lists* (5th ed.). San Francisco: Jossey-Bass.

Fuchs, D., Fuchs, L. S., & Vaughn, S. (Eds.). (2008). *Response to intervention: A framework for reading educators.* Newark, DE: International Reading Association.

Fuchs, D., Stecker, P. M., & Fuchs, L. S. (2008). Tier 3: Why special education must be the most intensive tier in a standards-driven, no child left behind world. In D. Fuchs, L. S. Fuchs, & S. Vaughn (Eds.), (pp. 71–104).

Gagne, R. M. (1977). *The conditions of learning.* New York: Holt, Rinehart and Winston.

Gagne, R. M., Wager, W. W., Golas, K. C., & Keller, J. M. (2005). *Principles of instructional design* (5th ed.). Belmont, CA: Wadsworth/Thomson Learning.

Galda, L., Cullinan, B. E., & Sipe, L. (2010). *Literature and the child* (7th ed.). Belmont, CA: Cengage/Wadsworth.

Gambrell, L. B., Morrow, L. M., & Pennington, C. (2002). Early childhood and elementary literature-based instruction: Current perspectives and special issues. *Reading Online, 5*(6). Retrieved January 3, 2006, from http://readingonline.org

Gambrell, L. B., Pfeiffer, W., & Wilson, R. (1985). The effects of retelling upon reading comprehension and recall of text information. *Journal of Educational Research, 78*, 16–220.

Gardner, H. (1993). *Multiple intelligences: The theory in practice.* New York: Basic Books.

Gardner, H. (1999). *Intelligence reframed: Multiple intelligences for the 21st century,* New York: Basic Books.

Gargiulo, R. M. (2006). *Special education in contemporary society.* Belmont, CA: Thomson Higher Education.

Gee, J. P. (2001). A sociocultural perspective on early literacy development. In S. B. Neuman, & D. K. Dickinson (Eds.), *Handbook of early literacy research* (pp. 30–42). New York: The Guilford Press.

Genisio, M., & Drecktrah, M. (1999). Emergent literacy in an early childhood classroom: Center learning to support the child with special needs. *Early Childhood Education Journal, 26*(4), 225–231.

Gentry, R. J., & Gillet, J. W. (1993). *Teaching kids to spell.* Portsmouth, NH: Heinemann.

Gersten, R., & Geva, E. (2003). Teaching reading to early language learners. *Educational Leadership, 60*(7), 44–49.

Girard, K. (2005). Lost in translation: Reaching out to English-language learners. *Edutopia, 1*(8), 36–38.

Glazer, M. G., & Burke, E. M. (1994). *An integrated approach to early literacy.* Boston: Allyn & Bacon.

Glazer, S. M., & Brown, C. S. (1993). *Portfolios and beyond: Collaborative assessment in reading and writing.* Norwood, MA: Chistopher-Gordon.

Gleason, J. (2001). *The development of language.* Boston: Allyn & Bacon.

Goldberg, A., Russell, M., & Cook, A. (2003). The effects of computers on student writing: A meta-analysis of studies from 1992–2002. *The Journal of Technology, Learning and Assessment, 2*(1), 1–52.

Good, T., & Brophy, J. (2000). *Looking in classrooms* (8th ed.). New York: Addison Wesley Longman.

Goodman, K. (1986). *What's whole about whole language?* Portsmouth, NH: Heinemann.

Goodman, K. (1996). *On reading.* Portsmouth, NH: Heinemann.

Graham, S., & Harris, K. R. (2003). Students with learning disabilities and the process of writing: A meta-analysis of SRSD studies. In H. L. Swanson, K. R. Harris, & S. Graham (Eds.), *Handbook of learning disabilities* (pp. 323–344). New York: The Guilford Press.

Graves, D. (1994). *A fresher look at writing.* Portsmouth, NH: Heinemann.

Graves, M., & Graves, B. (1994). *Scaffolding reading experiences.* Norwood, MA: Christopher-Gordon Publishers.

Graves, M. F., & Graves, B. B. (2003). *Scaffolded reading experiences: Designs for student success.* Norwood, MA: Christopher-Gordon Publishers.

Graves, M. F., & Watts-Taffe, S. M. (2002). The place of word consciousness in a research-based vocabulary program. In A. E. Farstrup & S. J. Samuels (Eds.), *What research has to say about reading instruction* (pp. 140–165). Newark, DE: International Reading Association.

Greeno, J., & Hall, R. (1997). Practicing representation; learning with and about representational forms. *Kappan, 78*(5), 361–367.

Grigsby, A. (2001). Let's chat: Chat rooms in the elementary school. *Educational Technology and Society, 4*(3), 85–86.

Guastello, E. F., & Lenz, C. (2005). Student accountability: Guided reading kidstations. *The Reading Teacher, 59*(2), 144–156.

Gunn, B. K., Simmons, D. C., & Kame'enui, E. J. (2004). Emergent literacy: Synthesis of the research. Retrieved November 7, 2004, from http://idea.uoregon.edu/~ncite/documents/techrep/tech19.html

Hagood, M. C. (2003). New media and online literacies: No age left behind. *Reading Research Quarterly, 38*(3), 387–391.

Hakuta, K., Butler, Y. G., & Witt, D. (2000). *How long does it take English learners to attain proficiency?* Santa Barbara, CA: The University of California Linguistic Minority Research Institute.

Halliday, M. A. (1975). *Learning how to mean.* London: Edward Arnold.

Hansen, J. (2001). *When writers read.* Portsmouth, NH: Heinemann.

Hansen, J. (2004). *"Tell me a story"; developmentally appropriate retelling strategies.* Newark, DE: International Reading Association.

Hargett, G. R. (1998). Assessment in ESL & bilingual education. Retrieved January 8, 2006, from http://nwrac.org/pub/hot/assessment.html#5

Hart, B., & Risley, T. R. (1995). *Meaningful differences in the everyday experience of young American children.* Baltimore, MD: P.H. Brookes.

Haywood, H. C., Brooks, P., & Burns, S. (1992). *Bright start; cognitive curriculum for young children.* Watertown, MA: Charlesbridge Publishing.

Heinze, J. (2005, November/December). Electronic learning: Supporting English language learners. *Scholastic Instructor.* Retrieved February 15, 2006, from http://teacher.scholastic.com/products/instructor/Nov04_El.htm

Hernandez, A. (2003). Making content instruction accessible for English language learners. In G. G. Garcia (Ed.), *English learners: Reaching the highest level of English literacy* (pp. 125–149). Newark, DE: International Reading Association.

Hibbert, K., & Iannacci, L. (2005). From dissemination to discernment: The commodification of literacy instruction and the fostering of "good teacher consumerism." *The Reading Teacher, 58*(8), 716–727.

Hiebert, E. H. (1988). The role of literacy experiences in early childhood programs. *The Elementary School Journal, 89*(2), 161–171.

Hiebert, E. H. (1999). Text matters in learning to read. *The Reading Teacher, 52*(6), 522–566.

Hiebert, E. H., Pearson, P. D., Taylor, B. M., Richardson, V., & Paris, S. G. (1998). *Every child a reader: Applying reading research to the classroom: Center for the Improvement of Early Reading Achievement.* Ann Arbor, MI: University of Michigan School of Education.

Holdaway, D. (1979). *The foundation of literacy.* Portsmouth, NH: Heinemann.

Holum, A., & Gahala, J. (2003). Critical issue: Using technology to enhance literacy instruction. Retrieved June 22, 2004, from http://www.ncrel.org/sdrs/areas/issues/content/cntareas/reading/li300.htm

Hoyt, L. (2002). *Make it real: Strategies for success with informational texts.* Portsmouth, NH: Heinemann.

Hoyt, L., Mooney, M., & Parkes, B. (2003). *Exploring informational texts: From theory to practice.* Portsmouth, NH: Heinemann.

Hurley, S. R., & Tinajero, J. V. (2001). *Literacy and assessment of second language learners.* Boston: Allyn & Bacon.

Hyerle, D. (1996). *Visual tools for constructing knowledge.* Alexandria, VA: American Society for Curriculum Development.

Institute for Education Reform. (1996). *Building a powerful reading program: From research to practice.* Sacramento, CA: California State University.

International Reading Association. (2001a). *Integrating literacy and technology in the curriculum: A position statement.* Retrieved July 31, 2004, from http://www.reading.org/positions/technology.html

International Reading Association. (2001b). *Second-language literacy instruction: A position statement of the International Reading Association.* Newark, DE: International Reading Association.

International Reading Association. (2004). *Standards for reading professionals, Revised 2003.* Newark, DE: International Reading Association.

International Reading Association and National Association for the Education of Young Children. (1998). Learning to read and write: Developmentally appropriate practices for young children. *The Reading Teacher, 52*(2), 193–216.

International Society for Technology in Education. (2000). *National educational technology standards for students: Connecting curriculum and technology.* Washington, DC: International Society for Technology in Education.

International Society for Technology in Education. (2003). *National educational technology standards for teachers: Resources for assessment.* Washington, DC: International Society for Technology in Education.

Jenkins, J. R., Vadasy, P. F., Peyton, J. A., & Sanders, E. A. (2003). Decodable text—where to find it. *The Reading Teacher, 57*(2), 185–189.

Jesness, J. (2004). *Teaching English language learners k–2: A quick-start guide for the new teacher.* Thousand Oaks, CA: Corwin Press.

Johns, J. (2005). *Basic reading inventory.* Dubuque, IA: Kendall/Hunt Publishing Company.

Johnson, D. D. (2001). *Vocabulary in the elementary and middle school.* Needham Heights, MA: Allyn & Bacon.

Johnson, D. W., & Johnson, R. T. (1989/1990). Social skills for successful group work. *Educational Leadership, 47*(4), 29–33.

Jonassen, D. (1991, September). Evaluating constructivist learning. *Educational Technology, 36*(9), 28–33.

Jones, J. (2003). *Early literacy assessment systems: Essential elements.* Princeton, NJ: Educational Testing Service.

Jones, S., & Fox, S. (2009). Generations online in 2009. Pew Internet Project Data Memo. Retrieved March 13, 2009, from http://www.pewinternet.org/Reports/2009/Generations-Online-in-2009.aspx

Kame'enui, E., Carnine, D., & Freschi, R. (1982). Effects of text construction and instructional procedures for teaching word meanings on comprehension and recall. *Reading Research Quarterly, 17*(3), 367–388.

Kim, A.-H., Vaughn, S., Wanzek, J., & Wei, S. (2004). Graphic organizers and their effects on students with LD: A synthesis of research. *Journal of Learning Disabilities, 37*(2), 105–118.

Kohn, A. (1996). *Beyond discipline: From compliance to community*. Alexandria, VA: Association for Supervision and Curriculum Development.

Kong, A., & Fitch, E. (2002/2003). Using book clubs to engage culturally and linguistically diverse learners in reading, writing, and talking about books. *The Reading Teacher, 56*, 352–362.

Koren, S. (1999). Vocabulary instruction through hypertext: Are there advantages over conventional methods of teaching? *Teaching English as a Second or Foreign Language 4*, p. A-2.

Krashen, S. D., & Terrell, T. D. (1983). *The natural approach; language acquisition in the classroom*. Englewood Cliffs, NJ: Alemany.

Kristof, N. (1996, December 1). Big wolves aren't so bad in japan. *The New York Times*, Sect. 4, pp. 1, 10.

Kuiper, E., Volman, M., & Terwel, J. (2005). The web as an information resource in K–12 education: Strategies for supporting students in searching and processing information. *Review of Educational Research, 75*(3), 285–317.

Labbo, L., & Sprague, L. (2002). Connecting a computer center to themes, literature, and kindergartners' literacy needs. *Reading Online*: International Reading Association.

Ladson-Billings, G. (1994). *The dreamkeepers: Successful teaching of African-American children*. San Francisco, CA: Jossey-Bass.

Laframboise, K. L. (2000). Said webs: Remedy for tired words. *The Reading Teacher, 54*(7), 540–542.

Langer, J. A. (1995). *Envisioning literature; literary understanding and literature instruction*. New York: Teachers College Press.

Langer, J. A. (2000). Excellence in English in middle and high school: How teachers' professional lives support student achievement. *American Educational Research Journal, 37*(2), 397–439.

Langer, L. (2001). Beating the odds: Teaching middle and high school students to read and write well. *American Educational Research Journal, 38*(4), 837–880.

Lapp, D., Flood, J., & Ranck-Buhr, W. (1995). Using multiple text formats to explore scientific phenomena in middle school classrooms. *Reading and Writing Quarterly: Overcoming Learning Difficulties, 11*, 173–186.

Larrick, N. (1965). What has happened to the all white world of children's books. *Saturday Review, 40*(6), 63–85.

LD Online Newsletter. (2006). What is the individualized educational program? *LD Online Newsletter*. Retrieved February 15, 2006, from http://www.ldonline.org

Lee, O. (2005). Science education with English language learners: Synthesis and research agenda. *Review of Educational Research, 75*(4), 491–530.

Lefever-Davis, S., & Pearman, C. (2005). Early readers and electronic texts: CD-ROM storybook features that influence reading behaviors. *The Reading Teacher, 58*(5), 446–454.

Lehr, F., Osborn, J., & Hiebert, E. H. (2004). *A focus on vocabulary*. Honolulu, HI: The Regional Educational Laboratory at Pacific Resources for Education and Learning.

Lenhart, A., Arafeh, S., Smith, A., & Macgill, A. R. (2008a). Writing, technology and teens. Pew Internet & American Life Project. Retrieved January 18, 2009, from http://www.pewinternet.org

Lenhart, A., Arafeh, S., Smith, A., & Macgill, A. R. (2008b). Teens and social media. Pew Internet & American Life Project. Retrieved January 18, 2009, from http://www.pewinternet.org

Lenhart, A., Madden, M., Macgill, A. R., & Smith, A. (2007). The use of social media gains a greater foothold in teen life as they embrace the conversational nature of interactive online media. Pew Internet & American Life Project. Retrieved March 13, 2009, from http://www.pewinternet.org/topic

Lenters, K. (2004). No half measures: Reading instruction for young second language learners. *The Reading Teacher, 58*(4), 328–336.

Lerner, J. (2003). *Learning disabilities; theories, diagnosis, and teaching strategies*. Boston: Houghton Mifflin Company.

Lesaux, N. (2003). Reading instruction and literacy in English language learners and other at-risk children. *Harvard Graduate School of Education News*. Retrieved November 3, 2004, from http://www.gse.harvard.edu/news/features/lesaux12012003.html

Leu, D. (2001). Internet project: Preparing students for new literacies in a global village. *The Reading Teacher, 54*(6), 568–572.

Leu, D. (2002). The new literacies: Research on reading instruction with the internet. In A. Farstrup & S. J. Samuels (Eds.), *What research has to say about reading instruction* (pp. 310–336). Newark, DE: International Reading Association.

Leu, D. J., Jr., Kinzer, C. K., Coiro, J., & Cammack, D. W. (2004). Toward a theory of new literacies emerging from the Internet and other information and communication technologies. In R. B. Ruddell & N. Unrau (Eds.), *Theoretical models and processes of reading* (5th ed.). (pp. 1570–1613). Newark, DE: International Reading Association. Available: http://www.readingonline.org/newliteracies/lit_index.asp?HREF=leu/

Leu, D. J., O'Byrne, I., Zawilinski, L., McVerry, J.G., & Everett-Cacopardo, H. (May 2009). Expanding the new literacies conversation. *Educational Researcher, 38*(4), 264–269.

Lewis, C., & Fabos, B. (2005). Instant messaging, literacies, and social identities. *Reading Research Quarterly, 40*(4), 470–501.

Linn, R. L., & Miller, M. D. (2005). *Measurement and assessment in teaching*. Upper Saddle River: Pearson Prentice Hall.

Lipson, M. Y., & Wixon, K. K. (2008, August/September). Reading in a diverse world: World Congress offers idea, reflections on literacy world wide. *Reading Today, 26*(1), 1, 7.

Loughlin, C. E., & Martin, M. D. (1987). *Supporting literacy; developing effective learning environments*. New York: Teachers College Press.

Lyon, G. R. (1994). *Research in learning disabilities at the NICHD*. Technical document. Bethesda, MD: National Institute of Child Health and Human Development, National Institutes of Health.

Mann, V. A. (2003). Language processes: Keys to reading disability. In H. L. Swanson, K. R. Harris, & S. Graham (Eds.), *Handbook of learning disabilities* (pp. 213–228). New York: The Guilford Press.

Mantero, M. (2002). Evaluating classroom communication: In support of emergent and authentic frameworks in second language assessment. *Practical Assessment, Research & Evaluation, 8*(8). Retrieved September 15, 2006, from http://PAREonline.net

Martinez, M., Roser, N. L., & Strecker, S. (1998/1999, December/January). "I never thought I could be a star": A Readers Theatre ticket to fluency. *The Reading Teacher, 52*(4), 326–334.

Marzano, R. J., Marzano, J. S., & Pickering, D. J. (2003). *Classroom management that works: Research-based strategies for every teacher*. Alexandria,

VA: Association for Supervision and Curriculum Development.

Marzano, R. J., Pickering, D. J., & Pollock, J. E. (2001). *Classroom instruction that works: Research-based strategies for increasing student achievement*. Alexandria, VA: Association for Supervision and Curriculum Development.

Mastropieri, M. A., & Scruggs, T. E. (1998). LD online: Enhancing school success with mnemonic strategies. Retrieved May 21, 2006, from http://www.ldonline.org/article/5912

McCarrier, A., Pinnell, S. G., & Fountas, I. C. (2000). *Interactive writing: How language and literacy come together, K-2*. Portsmouth, NH: Heinemann.

McMahon, S. (1996). Book club: The influence of Vygotskian perspective on a literature-based reading program. In L. Dixon-Krauss (Ed.), *Vygotsky in the classroom: Mediated literacy instruction and assessment*. White Plains, NY: Longman Publishers.

Meese, R. L. (2001). *Teaching learners with mild disabilities; integrating research and practice* (2nd ed.). Belmont, CA: Wadsworth/Thompson Learning.

Mercer, C. D., & Mercer, A. R. (2005). *Teaching students with learning problems* (7th ed.). Upper Saddle River, NJ: Pearson Education.

Mesmer, E. M., & Mesmer, H. A. E. (2008/2009, December/January). Response to intervention: What teachers of reading need to know. *The Reading Teacher, 62*(4), 280–290.

Micklos, J. (1996). Multiculturalism and children's literature. *Reading Today, 13*(3), 1–8.

Moats, L. C., & Farrell, M. L. (2005). Multisensory structured language education. In J. R. Birsh (Ed.), *Multisensory teaching of basic language skills* (pp. 23–41). Baltimore, MD: Paul H. Brookes Publishing.

Mokhtari, K., Kymes, A., & Edwards, P. (2008/2009). Assessing the new literacies of online reading comprehension: An informative interview with W. Ian O'Bryrne, Lisa Zawilinski, J. Greg McVerry, and Donald J. Leu at the University of Connecticut. *The Reading Teacher, 62*(4), 354–357.

Montessori, M. (1964). *The Montessori method*. New York: Harper and Row Publications.

Mooney, E. M. (2001). Traveling in depth. In L. Hoyt, M. Mooney, & B. Parkes (Eds.), *Exploring informational texts: From theory to practice*. Portsmouth, NH: Heinemann.

Moore, D., Moore, S. A., Cunningham, P. M., & Cunningham, J. W. (2006). *Developing reading and writing in the content areas K-12* (5th ed.). Boston, MA: Pearson Education, Inc.

Morrow, L. M. (2002). *The literacy center; contexts for reading and writing*. Portland, ME: Stenhouse Publishers.

Morrow, L. M., & Gambrell, L. B. (2000). Literature-based reading instruction. In M. L. Kamil, P. B. Mosenthal, P. D. Pearson, & R. Barr (Eds.), *Handbook of reading research* (Vol. 3, pp. 563–586). Mahwah, NJ: Lawrence Erlbaum Associates.

Moustafa, M. (1998). Reconceptualizing phonics instruction. In C. Weaver (Ed.), *Reconsidering a balanced approach to reading* (pp. 135–157). Urbana, IL: National Council of Teachers of English.

Moustafa, M., & Maldonado-Colon, E. (1998). Whole-to-parts phonics instruction: Building on what children know to help them know more. *The Reading Teacher, 52*(5), 448–456.

Nagy, W. E. (1988). *Teaching vocabulary to improve reading comprehension*. Newark, DE: International Reading Association.

National Association for the Education of Young Children (NAEYC). (1996). *Technology and young children—Ages 3 through 8*. Retrieved February 18, 2009, from http://www.naeyc.org/about/positions/pdf/PSTECH98.pdf

National Association for the Education of Young Children (NAEYC) and National Association of Early Childhood Specialists in State Departments of Education (NAECS/SDE). (2004). Where we stand on curriculum, assessment, and program evaluation. Retrieved March 17, 2009, from http://www.naeyc.org/about/positions/pdf/StandlCurrAss.pdf

National Association for the Education of Young Children (NAEYC) and the National Association of Early Childhood Specialists in State Departments of Education (NAECS/SDE). (2003). *Early childhood curriculum, assessment, and program evaluation: Building an effective, accountable system in programs for children birth through age 8*. Washington, DC.

National Center for Education Statistics. (2003). Status and trends in the education of Hispanics. Retrieved October 30, 2004, from http://nces.ed.gov/pubs2003/2003008.pdf

National Center for Education Statistics. (2004). The condition of education, 2004. Retrieved April 15, 2006, from http://nces.ed.gov/programs/coe

National Council of Teachers of English. (1996). Standards for English Language Arts. Retrieved October 16, 2004, from http://www.ncte.org/about/over/standards/110846.htm

National Early Literacy Panel. (2008). *Developing early literacy: Report of the National Early Literacy Panel*. Washington, DC: National Institute for Literacy.

National Educational Technology Plan. (2004). PDAs for assessment and data-driven decision-making. Retrieved February 15, 2005, from http://www.ed.gov/about/offices/list/os/technology/plan/2004/site/edlite-stories.html

National Endowment for the Arts. (2004). *Reading at risk: A survey of literary reading in America*. Washington, DC: National Endowment for the Arts.

National Institute of Child Health and Human Development (NICHD). (2000). *Report of the National Reading Panel. Teaching children to read: Reports of the subgroups*. Washington, DC: NICHD.

National Reading Panel. (2000). *Teaching children to read: An evidence-based assessment of the scientific research literature on reading and its implications for reading instruction*. Washington, DC: National Reading Panel.

National Writing Project. (1999). Profiles of the National Writing Project; improving writing and learning in the nation's school. Retrieved April 1, 2003, from http://www.writingproject.org/downloads/profiles.pdf

Norton, T., & Land, B. (2004). *Literacy strategies: Resources for beginning teachers*. Upper Saddle River, NJ: Pearson Education.

Oblinger, D. (2003). Boomers, gen-xers, and millennials: Understanding the "new students." *Educause Review*. Retrieved October 29, 2004, from http://www.educause.edu/ir/library/pdf/erm0342.pdf

Ogle, D. M. (1986). KWL: A teaching model that develops active reading of expository text. *Reading Teacher, 39*(6), 564–570.

Ogle, L., Sen, A., Pahlke, E., Jocelyn, L., Kastberg, D., Roey, S., & Williams, T. (2003). *International comparisons in fourth-grade reading literacy: Findings from the Progress in International Reading Literacy Study (PIRLS) of 2001. U.S. Department of Education, National Center for Educational Statistics*. Washington, DC: U.S. Government Printing Office.

Opitz, M. F., & Zbaracki, M. D. (2004). *Listen hear! Twenty-five effective listening comprehension strategies*. Portsmouth, NH: Heinemann.

Ortega, A., & Ramirez, J. (May 2002). Parent literacy workshops: One school's parent program integrated with the school day, *The Reading Teacher*, (55)8, 726–729.

Paiget, J. (1970). *The science of education and the psychology of the child*. New York: Grossman.

Palincsar, A. S., & Brown, A. (1984). Reciprocal teaching of comprehension-fostering and comprehension-monitoring activities. *Cognition and Instruction, 1*, 117–175.

Paratore, J., & McCormack, R. (2005). *Teaching literacy in second grade*. New York: The Guilford Press.

Paris, S. G. (2003). *What K–3 teachers need to know about assessing children's reading*. Naperville, IL: Learning Point Associates. Retrieved February 15, 2005, from http://www.learningpt.org

Partnership for 21st Century Skills. (2004). Learning for the 21st century; a report and mile guide for 21st century skills. Retrieved October 16, 2004, from http://www.21stcenturyskills.org

Pinnell, G. S., & Fountas, I. C. (1998). *Word matters; teaching phonics and spelling in the reading/writing classroom*. Portsmouth, NH: Heinemann.

Pinnell, G. S., & Jagger, A. M. (2003). Oral language: Speaking and listening in elementary classrooms. In J. Flood, D. Lapp, J. Squire, & J. Jensen (Eds.), *Handbook of research on teaching the English language arts* (2nd ed.). (pp. 881–913). Mahwah, NJ: Erlbaum.

Pressley, M. (1998). *Reading instruction that works: The case for balanced teaching*. New York: The Guilford Press.

Pressley, M. (2000). What should comprehension instruction be the instruction of? In M. Kamil, P. Mosenthal, P. D. Pearson, & R. Barr (Eds.), *Handbook of reading research* (Vol. 3, pp. 545–562). Hillsdale, NJ: Erlbaum.

Pressley, M. (2002). *Reading instruction that works: The case for balanced teaching* (2nd ed.). New York: Guilford Press.

Quenneville, J. (2001, Summer). Tech tools for students with learning disabilities: Infusion into inclusive classrooms. *Preventing School Failure, 45*(4), 167–170.

Quiroga, T., Lemos-Britton, Z., Mostafapour, E., Abbott, R. D., & Berninger, V. W. (2002). Phonological awareness and beginning reading in Spanish-speaking ESL first graders. *Journal of School Psychology, 40*(1), 85.

The Radicati Group. (2008). Wireless email market, 2008–2012. Retrieved March 13, 2009, from http://www.radicati.com/?p=1419

Rainie, L. (2009). Teens and social media. Pew Internet & American Life Project. Retrieved January 18, 2009, from http://www.pewinternet.org

Raphael, T., & Au, K. (2005). QAR: Enhancing comprehension and test taking across the grades and content areas. *The Reading Teacher, 59*(3), 206–221.

Raphael, T. E. (1982). Question-answering strategies for children. *The Reading Teacher, 36*, 186–191.

Raphael, T. E. (1986). Teaching question/answer relationships, revisited. *The Reading Teacher, 39*, 516–522.

Rasinski, T. V. (2003). *The fluent reader: Oral reading strategies for building word recognition, fluency and comprehension*. New York: Scholastic.

Rasinski, T., & Padak, N. D. (2001). *From phonics to fluency: Effective teaching of decoding and reading fluency in the elementary school*. New York, NY: Addison-Wesley Educational Publishers Inc.

Reigeluth, C. (1983). *Instructional-design theories and models* (Vol. 1). Mawah, NJ: Lawrence Erlbaum Associates.

Reinking, D. (1997). Me and my hypertext; a multiple digression and analysis of technology and literacy (sic). *The Reading Teacher, 50*(8), 626–642.

Reinking, D., & Rickman, S. S. (1990). The effects of computer-mediated texts on the vocabulary learning and comprehension of intermediate-grade readers. *Journal of Reading Behavior, 22*, 395–411.

Reutzel, D. R., & Hollingsworth, P. M. (1993). Effects of fluency training on second graders' reading comprehension. *Journal of Educational Research, 86*, 325–331.

Reutzel, D. R., & Mitchell, J. (2005). High-stakes accountability themed issue: How did we get here from there? *The Reading Teacher, 58*(7), 606–608.

Richardson, J. S., Morgan, R. F., & Fleener, C. (2006). *Reading to learn in the content areas* (6th ed.). Belmont, CA: Thomson-Wadsworth.

Richardson, W. (2006). The educator's guide to the read/write web. *Educational Leadership, 63*(4), 24–27.

Rideout, V., Roberts, D. F., & Foehr, U. G. (2005). *Generation M: Media in the lives of 8–18 year olds*. Menlo Park, CA: The Henry J. Kaiser Family Foundation.

Rivera, C., Stansfield, C., Scialdone, L., & Sharkey, M. (2000). *An analysis of state policies for the inclusion and accommodations of English language learners in state assessment programs during 1998–1999*. Arlington, VA: George Washington University, Center for Equity and Excellence in Education.

Robinson, F. (1946). *Effective study*. New York: Harper Brothers.

Rog, L. J. (2001). *Early literacy instruction in kindergarten*. Newark, DE: International Reading Association.

Rosenblatt, L. M. (1978). *The reader, the text, the poem: The transactional theory of the literary work*. Carbandale, IL: Southern University Press.

Rosenshine, B. V., & Meister, C. (1994). Reciprocal teaching: A review of research. *Review of Educational Research, 64*(4), 479–530.

Routman, R. (1988). *Transitions: From literature to literacy*. Portsmouth, NH: Heinemann.

Routman, R. (1994). *Invitations: Changing as teachers and learners K-12*. Portsmouth, NH: Heinemann.

RTI Action Network (2009). What is RTI? Retrieved March 29, 2009, from http://www.rtinetwork.org/Learn/What/ar/WhatIsRTI

Rumelhart, D. E. (1981). Schemata: The building blocks of cognition. In J. T. Guthrie (Ed.), *Comprehension and teaching: Research reviews* (pp. 3–26). Newark, DE: International Reading Association.

Rupley, W. H., Logan, J. W., & Nichols, W. D. (1998/1999). Vocabulary instruction in a balanced reading program. *The Reading Teacher, 52*(4), 336–346.

Salomon, G. (1997). Of mind and media; how culture's symbolic forms affect learning and thinking. *Kappan, 78*(5), 375–380.

Samuels, S. J. (1979). The method of repeated readings. *The Reading Teacher, 32*, 403–408.

Saskatchewan Education. (2002). *English Language Arts: a curriculum guide for the elementary level*. Saskatchewan, Canada: Government of Saskatchewan.

Saunders, W. M., & Goldenberg, C. (1999). *The effects of instructional conversations and literature logs on the story comprehension and thematic understanding of English proficient and limited English proficient students*. Santa Cruz, CA: Center for Research on Education,

Diversity & Excellence, University of California, Santa Cruz.

Schmar-Dobler, E. (2004). Reading on the internet: The link between literacy and technology. *Reading Online*. Retrieved February 10, 2006, from http://readingonline.org

Schmelzer, R., Christen, W., & Browning, W. (1980). *Reading and study skills book one*. Thackerville, OK: Twin Oaks Publishing.

Schwartz, R. M., & Raphael, T. E. (1985, November). Concept of definition: A key to improving students' vocabulary. *The Reading Teacher, 39*, 198–205.

Scoter, J. V., Ellis, D., & Railsback, J. (2001). *Technology in early childhood education. Finding the balance*. Northwest Regional Educational Laboratory. Retrieved February 18, 2009, from http://www.nwrel.org/request/june01/child.html

Scruggs, T. E., & Mastropieri, M. A. (2003). Science and social studies. In H. L. Swanson, K. R. Harris, & S. Graham (Eds.), *Handbook of learning disabilities* (pp. 364–379). New York: Guilford Press.

Searfross, L. W., Readence, J. E., & Mallette, M. H. (2001). *Helping children learn to read: Creating a classroom literacy environment* (4th ed.). Boston: Allyn & Bacon.

Selznick, B. (2007). *The Invention of Hugo Cabret*. New York: Scholastic Press.

Tanaka, S. (2008). *Amelia Earhart: The legend of the lost aviator*. Illustrated by David Craig. New York: Abrams Books for Young Readers.

Seng, S. (1998, November). *Enhanced learning: Computers and early childhood education*. Paper presented at the Educational Research Association Conference, Singapore. (ERIC Document Reproduction Service No. ED 431 524)

Shaywitz, S. (2003). *Overcoming dyslexia: A new and complete science-based program for reading problems at any level*. New York: Alfred A. Knopf.

Shepard, L., Kagan, S. L., & Wirtz, E. (1998). *Principles and recommendations for early childhood assessments*. Washington, DC: National Education Goals Panel.

Silver, H., Strong, R., & Perini, M. J. (2000). *So each may learn: Integrating learning styles and multiple intelligences*. Alexandria, VA: Association for Supervision and Curriculum Development.

Simmons, D. C., Fuchs, D., & Fuchs, L. S. (1991). Instructional and curricular requisites of mainstreamed students with learning disabilities. *Journal of Learning Disabilities, 24*, 354–360.

Sinatra, R., Beaudry, J. S., Stahl-Gemake, J., & Guastello, E. F. (1998). Combining visual literacy, text understanding, and writing for culturally diverse students. In M. F. Opitz (Ed.), *Literacy instruction for culturally and linguistically diverse students* (pp. 173–179). Newark, DE: International Reading Association.

Sipe, L. R. (2001). Invention, convention, and intervention: Invented spelling and the teacher's role. *The Reading Teacher, 55*(3), 264–273.

Slavin, R. E., & Cheung, A. (2003). *Effective reading programs for English language learners; a best-evidence synthesis* (No. 66). Baltimore, MD: John Hopkins University.

Sloan, W. M. (2009, January). Creating global classrooms. *ASCD Education Update, 51*(1), 4–7.

Smith, A. F., & Czarra, F. R. (2003). Teaching in a global context. *ASCD Infobrief* (Vol. 32). Alexandria, VA: Association for Supervision and Curriculum Development.

Smith, F. (1973). *Psycholinguistics and reading*. New York: Holt, Rinehart & Winston.

Smith, F. (1985). *Reading without nonsense* (2nd ed.). New York: Teachers College Press.

Smith, J. L., & Johnson, H. (1994). Models for implementing literature in content studies. *The Reading Teacher, 48*(3), 198–208.

Snow, C. E. (2002). *Reading for understanding: Toward an R & D program in reading comprehension*. Santa Monica, CA: RAND Corp.

Snow, C. E., Burns, S., & Griffin, P. (Eds.). (1998). *Preventing reading difficulties in young children*. Washington, DC: National Academy Press.

Soifer, L. (1999). Development of oral language and its relationship to literacy. In J. R. Birsh (Ed.), *Multisensory teaching of basic language skills* (pp. 19–56). Baltimore, MD: Paul H. Brookes Publishing.

Southwest Educational Development Laboratory (SEDL). (2005). The cognitive foundations of learning to read: A framework. Retrieved March 12, 2005, from http://www.sedl.org/reading

Spear-Swerling, L. (April 2006). LD online: Vocabulary assessment and instruction. Retrieved May 14, 2006, from http://www.ldonline.org/spearswerling/8089

Spiegel, D. L. (1999). The perspective of the balanced approach. In S. M. Blair-

Larson & K. A. Williams (Eds.), *The balanced reading program; helping all students achieve success* (pp. 8–23). Newark, DE: International Reading Association.

Stahl, S. A. (1986). Three principles of effective vocabulary instruction. *Journal of Reading, 29*(7), 662–668.

Stallings, J. (1980). Allocated academic learning time revisited, or beyond time on task. *Educational Researcher, 8*(11), 11–16.

Stauffer, R. G. (1969). *Directing the reading-thinking process*. New York: Harper & Row.

Stein, D., & Beed, P. L. (2004). Bridging the gap between fiction and nonfiction in the literature circle setting. *The Reading Teacher, 57*(6), 510–518.

Strickland, D. (1998a). Principles of instruction. In M. F. Opitz (Ed.), *Literacy instruction for culturally and linguistically diverse students* (pp. 50–52). Newark, DE: International Reading Association.

Strickland, D. (1998b). *Teaching phonics today; a primer for educators*. Newark, DE: International Reading Association.

Strickland, D. (1998c). What is basic in beginning reading? Finding common ground. *Educational Leadership, 55*(6), 6–10.

Strickland, D. S. (1994). Organizing a literature-based reading program. In B. E. Cullinan (Ed.), *Invitation to read: More children's literature in the reading program* (pp. 110–121). Newark, DE: International Reading Association.

Strickland, D. S. (2002). The importance of effective early intervention. In A. Farstrup & S. J. Samuels (Eds.), *What research has to say about reading instruction* (pp. 69–86). Newark: DE: International Reading Association.

Stuart, M. (2004). Getting ready for reading: A follow-up study of inner city second language learners at the end of key stage 1. *British Journal of Educational Psychology, 74*(1), 15.

Tabors, P. O., & Snow, C. E. (2001). Young bilingual children and early literacy development. In S. B. Neuman & D. K. Dickinson (Eds.), *Handbook of early literacy research* (pp. 159–178). New York: Guilford Press.

Taxol, J. (1993). The politics of children's literature; reflections on multiculturalism and Christopher Columbus. In V. J. Harris (Ed.), *Teaching multicultural literature in grades k-8* (pp. 1–36). Norwood, MA: Christopher-Gordon Publishers.

Tennyson, R. D., & Cocchiarella, M. J. (1986). An empirically based instructional design theory for teaching concepts. *Review of Educational Research*, 56(1), 40–71.

Tharp, R., Estrada, P., Dalton, S., & Yamauchi, L. (2000). *Teaching transformed: Achieving excellence, fairness, inclusion and harmony.* Boulder, CO: Westview Press.

Thomas, D. (1961, Winter). Poetic manifesto, *Texas Quarterly, 4,* 226.

Tierney, R. J., Readence, J. E., & Dishner, E. K. (1995). *Reading strategies and practices* (3rd ed.). Boston: Allyn & Bacon.

Tomlinson, C. (1999). *The differentiated classroom.* Alexandria, VA: Association for Supervision and Curriculum Development.

Tomlinson, C. A., & McTighe, J. (2006). *Integrating differentiated instruction and understanding by design.* Alexandria, VA: Association for Supervision and Curriculum Development.

Tompkins, G. E. (2000). *Teaching writing; balancing process and product.* Upper Saddle River, NJ: Prentice-Hall.

Topping, K. (1997). Electronic literacy in school and home: A look into the future. *Reading Online.* Retrieved August 7, 2009, from http://www.readingonline.org/international/inter_index.asp?HREF=future/index.html

Trachtenburg, P. (1990). Using children's literature to enhance phonics instruction. *The Reading Teacher, 43,* 648–654.

Tucker, P. D., & Stronge, J. H. (2005). *Linking teacher evaluation and student learning.* Alexandria, VA: Association of Supervision and Curriculum Development.

Turbill, J. (2002). Getting kindergarteners started with technology: The story of one school. *Reading Online.*

Tye, B. B. (1990). Global education; from thought to action. In K. A. Tye (Ed.), *Schooling in America today: Potential for global studies.* Alexandria, VA: Association of Supervision and Curriculum Development.

United States Census Bureau News (2008, August 14). An Older and More Diverse Nation by Midcentury. Retrieved March 21, 2009, from http://www.census.gov/Press-Release/www/releases/archives/population/012496.html

United States Department of Education. (1994). Improving America's Schools Act of 1994. H.R. 6, 103rd Congress. Washington, DC: United States Government.

United States Department of Education. (1977). *1977 code of federal regulations.* Washington, DC: Author.

United States Department of Education. (2006). *Assistance to states for the education of children with disabilities and preschool grants for children with disabilities; final rule.* Eric.ed.gov/ERICDocs/data/ericdocs2sql/content_storage_01/0000019b/801b/e9/95.pdf

United States Government. (2005). Individuals with Disabilities Education Improvement Act of 2004. P.L. 108-446, 108th Congress.

Vail, P. L. (1991). *Common ground; whole language and phonics working together.* Rosemont, NJ: Modern Learning Press.

Valdez Pierce, L. (2002). Performance-based assessment: Promoting achievement for English language learners. *ERIC/CLL News Bulletin, 26*(1), 1–3.

Vardell, S. M., Hadaway, N. L., & Young, T. A. (2006). Matching books and readers: Selecting literature for English learners. *The Reading Teacher, 59*(8), 734–741.

Vaughn, S., Mathes, P. G., Linan-Thompson, S., & Francis, D. J. (2005). Teaching English language learners at risk for reading disabilities to read: Putting research into practice. *Learning Disabilities Research and Practice, 20*(1), 58.

Vellutino, F. R., & Fletcher, J. M. (2005). *Developmental dyslexia.* In J. S. C. Hulme (Ed.), *The science of reading: A handbook* (pp. 362–378). Malden, MA: Blackwell.

Vellutino, F. R., Sipay, E. R., Small, S. G., Pratt, A., Chen, R., & Denckla, M. B. (1996). Cognitive profiles of difficult-to-remediate and readily remediated poor readers; Early intervention as a vehicle for distinguishing between cognitive and Experimental deficits as basic causes of specific read disability. *Journal of Educational Psychology, 88*(4), 601–638.

von Glasersfeld, E. (1989). Cognition, construction of knowledge, and teaching. *Synthese, 80,* 121–140.

Vygotsky, L. S. (1962). *Thought and language.* Cambridge, MA: MIT Press.

Vygotsky, L. S. (1978). *Mind in society; the development of higher psychological processes.* Cambridge, MA: Harvard University Press.

Wait, S. S. (1992). *Reading learning centers for the primary grades.* West Nyack, NY:

The Center for Applied Research in Education.

Weaver, C. (Ed.). (1994). *Understanding whole language: From principles to practice* (2nd ed.). Portsmouth, NH: Heinemann.

Weaver, C. (1996). On the nature of whole language instruction. In C. Weaver, L. Gillmeister-Krause, & G. Vento-Zogby (Eds.), *Creating support for effective literacy education.* Portsmouth, NH: Heinemann.

Weaver, C. (Ed.). (1998). *Reconsidering a balanced approach to reading.* Urbana, IL: National Council of Teachers of English.

Weir, B. (1989). A research base for pre-kindergarten literacy programs. *The Reading Teacher, 42*(7), 456–460.

Wenglinsky, H. (2004). Facts or critical thinking skills? What NAEP results say. *Educational Leadership, 62*(1), 32–35.

West, J., Denton, K., & Geronimo-Hausken, E. (2000). *America's kindergartners.* Washington, DC: National Center for Education Statistics.

Whitehurst, G. J., & Lonigan, C. J. (2001). Emergent literacy: Development from prereaders to readers. In S. B. Neuman & D. K. Dickinson (Eds.), *Handbook of early literacy research* (pp. 11–29). New York: Guilford Press.

Wiggins, G. P., & McTighe, J. (2005). *Understanding by design.* (2nd ed.). Alexandria VA: ASCD.

Williams, J. P. (2003). Teaching text structure to improve reading comprehension. In H. L. Swanson, K. R. Harris, & S. Graham (Eds.), *Handbook of learning disabilities* (pp. 293–305). New York: Guilford Press.

Willis, S. (1996). Managing today's classroom: Finding alternatives to control and compliance. *Education Update, 38*(6), 3–7.

Wright, J. (2006). "Click or Clunk?" a student comprehension self-check. Retrieved February 13, 2006, from http://www.interventioncentral.org/htmdocs/interventions/rdngcompr/clickclunk1.php

Wylie, R. E., & Durrell, D. D. (1970). Teaching vowels through phonograms. *Elementary English, 47,* 787–791.

Yopp, H. K. (1992). Developing phonemic awareness in young children. *The Reading Teacher, 45*(9), 696–703.

Yopp, H. K., & Yopp, R. H. (2000). Supporting phonemic awareness development in the classroom. *The Reading Teacher, 54*(2), 130–143.

SOFTWARE PROGRAMS

Please note that many of the software programs listed here are still being sold, but not by the
   original company. They may be found online at such sites as Amazon.com

Accelerated Grammar & Spelling. Renaissance Learning: http://www.renlearn.com

Accelerated Reader. Renaissance Learning: http://renlearn.com

Accelerated Writer. Renaissance Learning: http://renlearn.com

The Amazing Writing Machine. Broderbund, http://www.broderbund.com

Carmen Sandiego Word Detective. The Learning Company

CAST UDL Editions. CAST: http://www.cast.org/products

Clicker. Crick Software: http://www.cricksoft.com

Clicker Writer. Crick Software: http://www.cricksoft.com

Co-Writer. Don Johnston: http://www.donjohnston.com

Creative Writer 2. Microsoft.

Destination Reading. Houghton Mifflin Harcourt Learning Technology: http://www.hmlt.
   hmco.com/DR.php

Dragon Naturally Speaking Professional 10. Dyslexic.com: http://dyslexic.com

Imagination Express Series. Riverdeep: http://www.riverdeep.netInspiration

Inspiration Software, Portland, OR: http://www.inspiration.com/

Jump Start series. Knowledge Adventure: http://www.knowledgeadventure.com

Just Grandma and Me. Broderbund Software, Novato, CA

KidPix 4: The Learning Company

Kidspiration. Inspiration Software, Portland, OR: http://www.inspiration.com/

KidsWorks Deluxe. English Software: http://www.educationmax.com

Kurtzweil 3000. Kurtzweil Educational Systems: http://www.kurzweiledu.com/

Living Books. Kids Click: http://www.kidsclick.com/living_books.htm

Penfriend. Crick Software: http://www.cricksoft.com

Philips. http://www.speech.philips.com/index.php?id=715

Plurals–No Problem!; The Punctuation Marks; and Antonyms, Synonyms and Homonyms.
   Thomas S. Klise Company: http://www.klise.com/learn/grammar/plurals.htm

PowerPoint. Microsoft: http://www.microsoft.com

The Print Shop. Broderbund: http://www.broderbund.com

Reader Rabbit. Broderbund: http://www.broderbund.com

Reading for Meaning. Tom Snyder Productions: http://www.tomsnyder.com

Roger Wagner's HyperStudio 5. The Software MacKiev Company: Mackiev.com

Storybook Weaver Deluxe. Riverdeep: http://www.riverdeep.net

Texthelp. Texthelp Systems: http://www.texthelp.com

Ultimate Writing & Creativity Center. The Learning Company.

Wiggleworks. Scholastic: http://scholastic.com

Wordbar. Crick Software: http://cricksoft.com

Word Munchers. The Learning Company, Minneapolis, MN

Word Munchers for the 21st Century (PCI Education): http://www.pcieducation.com/

Write On! Plus the Writer's Resource Library. Humanities Software/Sunburst: http://store.
   sunburst.com

Write: Out Loud. Don Johnston: http://www.donjohnston.com

The Writer's Resource Library. Broderbund: http://www.broderbund.com

Aardema, Verna. *Why Mosquitoes Buzz in People's Ears*. New York: Dial Press, 1975.

Alexander, Lloyd. *The Book of Three (The Prydain Chronicles)*. New York: Holt, 1964.

Armstrong, William Howard. *Sounder*. New York: Perennial Library, 1969.

Berger, Melvin. *Busy as a Bee*. Marlborough, MA: Newbridge Educational Publishing, 1995.

Blume, Judy. *Superfudge*. New York: Dutton, 1980.

Tales of a Fourth-Grade Nothing. New York: Dutton, 1972.

Bolden, Tonya. *George Washington Carver*. New York: Abrams Books for Young Readers, 2008.

Bray, Rosemary. *Martin Luther King*. New York: Greenwillow Books, 1995.

Briggs Martin, Jacqueline. *Snowflake Bentley*. Boston: Houghton Mifflin, 1998.

Brown, Jeff. *Flat Stanley*. New York: HarperCollins, 1996.

Bryan, Ashley. *Let it Shine: Three Favorite Spirituals*. Atheneum Books for Young Readers, 2007.

Bunting, Eve. *Smoky Night*. Illustrated by David Diaz. San Diego: Harcourt Brace, 1994.

Burleigh, Robert. *Seurat and La Grande Jatte: Connecting the Dots*. New York: Abrams Books for Young Readers, 2005.

Cannon, Janell. *Pinduli*. Orlando, FL: Harcourt, 2004.

Carle, Eric. *The Very Hungry Caterpillar*. New York: Philomel Books, 1987.

The Very Busy Spider. New York: Philomel Books, 1989.

Have You Seen My Cat? New York: F. Watts, 1973.

Casey, Amy John. *Can You Find It? (Celebration Press Ready Readers)*. Modern Curriculum Press, 1997.

Chambers, Veronica. *Amistad Rising: A Story of Freedom*. San Diego: Harcourt, 1998.

Cleary, Beverly. *The Mouse and the Motorcycle*. New York: Morrow/Avon, 1965.

Ramona and Her Father. New York: Morrow/Avon, 1977.

Ramona and Her Mother. New York: Morrow/Avon, 1979.

Ramona Quimby, Age 8. New York: Morrow/Avon, 1981.

Strider. New York: Morrow/Avon, 1991.

Ramona's World. New York: Morrow/Avon, 1998.

Cole, Brock. *The Giant's Toe*. New York: Farrar, Straus & Giroux, 1986.

Cole, Joanna. *Anna Banana: 101 Jump Rope Rhymes*. Illustrated by Alan Tiegreen. New York: Morrow Junior Books, 1989.

The Magic School Bus: Inside the Human Body. Illustrated by Bruce Degen. New York: Scholastic, 1990.

The Magic School Bus Lost in the Solar System. Illustrated by Bruce Degen. New York: Scholastic, 1992.

The Magic School Bus on the Ocean Floor. Illustrated by Bruce Degen. New York: Scholastic, 1994.

The Magic School Bus in the Time of Dinosaurs. Illustrated by Bruce Degen. New York: Scholastic, 1995.

The Magic School Bus and the Electric Field Trip. Illustrated by Bruce Degen. New York: Scholastic, 1999.

Colier, James, and Colier, Christopher. *My Brother Sam Is Dead*. New York: Macmillan, 1974.

Cooper, Susan. *Over Sea, Under Stone*. San Diego: Harcourt, 1966.

Greenwitch. New York: McElderry, 1973.

The Dark Is Rising. Illustrated by Alan E. Cober. New York: Atheneum, 1973.

The Grey King. New York: McElderry, 1974.

Silver on the Tree. New York: McElderry, 1977.

Cowley, Joy. *Frightened*. New York: The Wright Group/McGraw-Hill, 2004.

Curtis, Christopher Paul. *Bud, Not Buddy*. New York: Delacorte, 1999.

D'Aulaire, Ingri. *Christopher Columbus*. New York: Doubleday, 1955.

Norse Gods and Giants. New York: Doubleday, 1986.

dePaola, Tomie. *26 Fairmount Avenue*. New York: Putnam, 1999.

Here We All Are. New York: Putnam, 2000.

On My Way. New York: Putnam, 2001.

What a Year. New York: Putnam, 2002.

Dowell, Ruth. *Move Over, Mother Goose!* Illustrated by Concetta C. Scott.

Mt. Rainier, MD: Gryphon House, 1987.

Falconer, Ian. *Olivia*. Atheneum/Anne Schwartz Book, 2000.

Fleischman, Paul. *I Am Phoenix: Poems for Two Voices*. New York: HarperCollins, 1986.

Joyful Noise: Poems for Two Voices. New York: HarperCollins, 1988.

Florian, D. *Insectlopedia: Poems and Paintings*. New York: Harcourt Brace & Company, 1998.

Forbes, Esther. *Johnny Tremain*. Illustrated by Lynd Ward. New York: Dell, 1969.

Fox, Mem. *Sophie*. Illustrated by Aminah Brenda Lynn Robinson. Orlando, FL: Harcourt Brace & Company, 1994.

Freedman, Russell. *Lincoln: A Photobiography*. New York: Clarion, 1989.

The Wright Brothers: How They Invented the Airplane. New York: Holiday House, 1991.

Eleanor Roosevelt: A Life of Discovery. New York: Clarion, 1993.

The Voice That Challenged a Nation: Marian Anderson and the Struggle for Equal Rights. New York: Clarion, 2004.

Gerstein, Mordicai. *The Man Who Walked between the Towers*. Brookfield, CT: Roaring Brook Press, 2003.

Giblin, James Cross. *Secrets of the Sphinx*. New York : Scholastic Press, 2004.

Griffith, Patricia. *The Snow Game*. Chicago, Ill.: Open Court Pub. Co., 1995.

Hall, Donald. *Ox-Cart Man*. Illustrated by Barbara Cooney. New York: Viking, 1979.

Helen Cowles, LeCron. *Little Charlie Chipmunk*. In M.H. Arbuthnot, Ed. *The Arbuthnot Anthology of Children's Literature*. Glenview, IL: Scott, Foresman & Co., 1971.

Hodges, Margaret. *St. George and the Dragon*. Illustrated by Trina Schart Hyman. Boston: Little Brown, 1990.

Hyman, Trina Schart. *Little Red Riding Hood*. New York: Holiday House, 1982.

Jacobson, Jennifer. *All about Bats*. Modern Curriculum Press, 1996.

Jeffrey, Laura S. *Dogs: How to Choose and Care for a Dog*. New York: Enslow Publishing/Random House, 2005.

Juster, Norton. *The Hello, Goodbye Window.* New York : Michael di Capua Books/ Hyperion Books for Children, 2005

Keats, Ezra Jack. *The Snowy Day.* New York: Viking, 1962.

> *Whistle for Willie.* New York: Viking, 1964.

Keller, Holly. *Ten Sleepy Sheep.* New York: Greenwillow Books, 1983.

Kellogg, Steven. *The Three Little Pigs.* New York: HarperTrophy, 2002.

King, Virginia. *Breakfast.* New York: McGraw Hill Education, 1993.

Konigsburg, Elaine L. *The View from Saturday.* New York: Atheneum, 1996.

L'Engle, Madeline. *A Wrinkle in Time.* New York: Farrar, Straus & Giroux, 1962.

> *The Arm of the Starfish.* New York: Farrar, Straus & Giroux, 1965.

> *A Wind in the Door.* New York: Farrar, Straus & Giroux, 1973.

> *A Swiftly Tilting Planet.* New York: Farrar, Straus & Giroux, 1978.

Lewis, C. S. *The Chronicles of Narnia: The Lion, the Witch and the Wardrobe.* Illustrated by Pauline Baynes. New York: HarperCollins, 1994.

Lobel, Arnold. *Frog and Toad Are Friends.* New York: HarperCollins, 1970.

Lowry, Lois. *Number the Stars.* Boston: Houghton Mifflin, 1989.

> *The Giver.* Boston: Houghton Mifflin, 1993.

> *Gathering Blue.* Boston: Houghton Mifflin, 2000.

Madonna. *The English Roses.* New York: Callaway Books, 2003.

Markle, Sandra. *Crocodiles.* Minneapolis, MN: Carolrhoda Books/Lerner Publishing Group, 2005.

Jr. Martin, Bill. *The Bill Martin Jr Big Book of Poetry.* New York: Simon & Schuster Books for Young Readers, 2008.

McCully, Emily Arnold. *Mirette on the High Wire.* New York: G.P. Putnam's Sons, 1992.

McDermott, Gerald. *Anansi the Spider: A Tale from the Ashanti.* New York: Holt, Rinehart and Winston, 1972.

Muth, Jon. *Zen Shorts.* Scholastic Press, 2005.

Ness, Evaline. *Sam, Bangs and Moonshine.* New York: Henry Holt and Company, 1966.

Norton, Mary. *The Borrowers.* Illustrated by Beth Krush and Joe Krush. San Diego: Harcourt, 1953.

Patent, Dorothy Hinshaw. *When the Wolves Returned: Restoring Nature's Balance in Yellowstone.* Illustrated by Dan and Cassie Hartman. New York: Walker Books for Young Readers, 2008.

Pierce, Tamora. *Alanna the First Adventure.* New York: Atheneum, 1983.

Prelutsky, Jack. *The Mean Old Mean Hyena.* Illustrated by Arnold Lobel. New York: Greenwillow Books, 1978.

> *Read-Aloud Rhymes for the Very Young.* Illustrated by Marc Brown. New York: Knopf, 1986.

> *For Laughing Aloud: Poems to Tickle Your Funnybone.* Illustrated by Marjorie Priceman. New York: Knopf, 1991.

Pullman, Philip. *The Golden Compass.* New York: Alfred A. Knopf, 1996.

> *The Subtle Knife.* New York: Random House, 1997.

> *The Amber Spyglass.* New York. Knopf, 2000.

Rey, H. A. *Curious George.* Boston: Houghton Mifflin Company, 1941.

Ringgold, Faith. *Tar Beach.* New York: Crown, 1991.

> *Aunt Harriet's Underground Railroad in the Sky.* New York: Crown, 1993.

Rowling, J. K. *Harry Potter and the Goblet of Fire.* Illus.Mary Grandpre. New York: Scholastic, 2000.

Rylant, C. *The relatives came.* New York: Bradbury, 1985.

Sachar, Louis. *Holes.* New York: Farrar, Straus & Giroux, 1998.

Scieszka, Jon. *The True Story of the Three Little Pigs.* Illustrated by Lane Smith. New York: Viking Juvenile, 1989.

> *Science Verse.* Illustrated by Lane Smith. New York: Penguin Group, 2004.

Seeger, Laura Vaccaro. *First the Egg,* Roaring Brook Press, 2007.

Selznick, Brian. *The Invention of Hugo Cabret.* New York: Scholastic Press, 2007.

Sendak, Maurice. *Where the Wild Things Are.* New York: HarperCollins, 1963.

> *Outside Over There.* Illustrated by Janeyee Young. New York: HarperCollins, 1981.

Dr. Seuss. *The Cat in the Hat.* New York: Random House, 1957.

> *Green Eggs and Ham.* New York: Random House, 1960.

> *Fox in Socks.* New York: Random House, 1965.

Seymour, Trey. *Auction!* Illustrated by Cat Bowman Smith. Cambridge, MA: Candlewick Press, 2005.

Shefelbine, John. *Fun with Zip and Zap.* New York: Scholastic, 1998.

Silverstein, Shel. *Where the Sidewalk Ends.* New York: HarperCollins, 1974.

> *A Light in the Attic.* New York: HarperCollins, 1981.

> *Falling Up.* New York: HarperCollins, 1996.

Slobodkina, Esphyr. *Caps for Sale.* Glenville: IL: Scott, Foresman, 1940.

Speare, Elizabeth George. *The Witch of Blackbird Pond.* Boston: Houghton, 1958.

> *The Sign of the Beaver.* Boston: Houghton, 1983.

St. George, Judith. *So You Want To Be President?* Illustrated by David Small. New York: Philomel, 2000.

Steig, William. *Sylvester and the Magic Pebble.* New York: Simon & Schuster, 1969.

> *Doctor DeSoto.* New York: Farrar, Straus and Giroux, 1982.

Steptoe, John. *Mufaro's Daughters: An African Tale.* New York: Lothrop, Lee & Shepard, 1987.

Stevenson, James. *Could Be Worse!* New York: Greenwillow Books, 1987.

Taback, Simms. *Joseph Had a Little Overcoat.* New York: Viking, 1999.

Taylor, Mildred. *Roll of Thunder, Hear My Cry.* New York: Dial, 1976.

Tolkien, J. R. R. *Lord of the Rings.* Boston: Houghton, 1967.

Udry, Janice. *Thump and Plunk.* New York: HarperCollins, 1981.

White, E. B. *Charlotte's Web.* New York: HarperCollins, 1952.

Williams, Vera. *Music, Music for Everyone.* HarperCollins, 1988.

Willems, Mo. *Knuffle Bunny.* New York: Hyperion Books, 2004.

Wisniewski, David. *Golem.* New York: Clarion, 1996.

Woodson, Jacqueline. *The Other Side.* New York: Putnam's, 2001.

The Wright Group. *Marti and the Mango.* New York: McGraw-Hill, 2004.

Young, Ed. *Lon Po Po: A Red Riding Hood Story from China.* New York: Philomel, 1989.

Zelinsky, Paul O. *Rapunzel.* New York: Dutton, 1997.

NAME INDEX

SUBJECT INDEX